Silent Summer: The State of Wildlife in Britain and Ireland

Over the past 20 years dramatic declines have taken place in UK insect populations. Eventually, such declines must have knock-on effects for other animals, especially for high-profile groups such as birds and mammals.

This authoritative, yet accessible, account details the current state of the wildlife in Britain and Ireland and offers an insight into the outlook for the future. Written by a team of the country's leading experts, it appraises the changes that have occurred in a wide range of wildlife species and their habitats and outlines urgent priorities for conservation. It includes chapters on each of the vertebrate and major invertebrate groups, with the insects covered in particular depth. Also considered are the factors that drive environmental change and the contribution at local and government level to national and international wildlife conservation.

This book is essential reading for anyone who is interested in, and concerned about, UK wildlife.

NORMAN MACLEAN is Emeritus Professor of Genetics at Southampton University and has a strong interest in wildlife, conservation and river management. He has helped to run student field courses for more than 20 years and has authored and edited more than a dozen textbooks and reference books in genetics and cell biology. He is an Elected Fellow of the Linnaean Society and of the Institute of Biology.

Silent Summer: The State of Wildlife in Britain and Ireland

Edited by

NORMAN MACLEAN
University of Southampton

CAMBRIDGE
UNIVERSITY PRESS

CAMBRIDGE UNIVERSITY PRESS
Cambridge, New York, Melbourne, Madrid, Cape Town, Singapore,
São Paulo, Delhi, Dubai, Tokyo

Cambridge University Press
The Edinburgh Building, Cambridge CB2 8RU, UK

Published in the United States of America by Cambridge University Press, New York

www.cambridge.org
Information on this title: www.cambridge.org/9780521519663

© Cambridge University Press 2010

First published 2010

Printed in the United Kingdom at the University Press, Cambridge

A catalogue record for this publication is available from the British Library

Library of Congress Cataloguing in Publication data
Silent summer: the state of wildlife in Britain and Ireland / [edited by] Norman Maclean.
p.   cm.
Includes bibliographical references and index.
ISBN 978-0-521-51966-3 – ISBN 978-0-521-73248-2 (pbk.)
1. Animal populations–Great Britain.   2. Animal populations–Ireland.
3. Plant populations–Great Britain.   4. Plant populations–Ireland.   5. Endangered
species–Great Britain.   6. Endangered species–Ireland.   7. Nature conservation–Great
Britain.   8. Nature conservation–Ireland.   9. Nature–Effect of human beings on–Great
Britain.   10. Nature–Effect of human beings on–Ireland.   I. Maclean,
Norman, 1932–   II. Title.
QL255.S55 2010
333.95′4160941–dc22   2010012372

ISBN 978-0-521-51966-3 Hardback

Contents

Contributors

N.J. AEBISCHER
Game and Wildlife Conservation Trust, Fordingbridge, Hampshire, UK

JOHN BAXTER
Scottish Natural Heritage, Edinburgh, UK

CYRIL BENNETT
Salisbury, Wiltshire, UK

STEVE BROOKS
Department of Entomology, Natural History Museum, London, UK

M.T. BURROWS
Scottish Association for Marine Science, Argyll, UK

RICHARD CHADD
Environment Agency, UK

ANDY CLEMENTS
British Trust for Ornithology, Thetford, Norfolk, UK

KELVIN F. CONRAD
Peterborough, Ontario, Canada

JOHN F. CRAIG
Dumfries, UK

KARL L. EVANS
Department of Animal and Plant Sciences, University of Sheffield, Sheffield, UK

BRIAN EVERSHAM
Wildlife Trust for Bedfordshire, Cambridgeshire, Northamptonshire and Peterborough, UK

J.A. EWALD
Game and Wildlife Conservation Trust, Fordingbridge, Hampshire, UK

RICHARD FOX
Butterfly Conservation, East Lulworth, Dorset, UK

KEVIN J. GASTON
Department of Animal and Plant Sciences, University of Sheffield, Sheffield, UK

WARREN GILCHRIST
Fleet, Hampshire, UK

CHRIS P. GLEED-OWEN
CGO Ecology, Bournemouth, UK

R. M. GOODHEAD
School of Biosciences, University of Exeter, Exeter, UK

DAVE GOULSON
School of Biological and Environmental Sciences, University of Stirling, Stirling, UK

TIM HALLIDAY
Department of Life Sciences, The Open University, Milton Keynes, UK

RICHARD HARRINGTON
Department of Plant and Invertebrate Ecology, Rothamsted Research, Harpenden, Herts, UK

S.J. HAWKINS
School of Ocean Sciences, Bangor University, Anglesey, UK

KAREN A. HAYSOM
Bat Conservation Trust, London, UK

MICHAEL HUGHES
Environmental Change Research Centre, University College London, London, UK

GARETH JONES
School of Biological Sciences, University of Bristol, Bristol, UK

IAN J. KILLEEN
Biodiversity and Systematic Biology, National Museum Wales, Cardiff, UK

PETER KIRBY
Peterborough, Cambridgeshire, UK

ANDREW LACK
School of Life Sciences, Oxford Brookes University, Oxford, UK

N. LEADER-WILLIAMS
Durrell Institute of Conservation and Ecology, University of Kent, Canterbury, UK

CHRISTOPHER LEVER
Winkfield, Berkshire, UK

NORMAN MACLEAN
School of Biological Sciences, University of Southampton, Southampton, UK

PETER S. MAITLAND
Fish Conservation Centre, Haddington, UK

JUDITH MARSHALL
Natural History Museum, London, UK

DAN MERRETT
Bat Conservation Trust, London, UK

N. MIESZKOWSKA
Marine Biological Association of the UK, Plymouth, UK

PETER MILL
School of Biological Sciences, University of Leeds, Leeds, UK

P.S. MOSCHELLA
CIESM, The Mediterranean Science Commission, Monaco

KEN NORRIS
Centre for Agri-Environmental Research, University of Reading, Reading, UK

ADRIAN PARR
Bury St Edmunds, Suffolk, UK

MARK S. PARSONS
Butterfly Conservation, East Lulworth, Dorset, UK

MIKE PIENKOWSKI
UK Overseas Territories Conservation Forum, Peterborough, UK

C.D. PRESTON
Centre for Ecology and Hydrology, Monks Wood, UK

PAUL A. RACEY
School of Biological Sciences, University of Aberdeen, Aberdeen, UK

ROBERT A. ROBINSON
British Trust for Ornithology, Thetford, Norfolk, UK

A.M. ROSSER
Durrell Institute of Conservation and Ecology, University of Kent, Canterbury, UK

D.B. ROY
Centre for Ecology and Hydrology, Monks Wood, UK

CARL SAYER
Environmental Change Research Centre, University College London, London, UK

ROBIN SHARP
Chair Emeritus of the IUCN/SSC European Sustainable Use Specialist Group

CHRIS R. SHORTALL
Department of Plant and Invertebrate Ecology, Rothamsted Research, Harpenden, Herts, UK

N.W. SOTHERTON
Game and Wildlife Conservation Trust, Fordingbridge, Hampshire, UK

T.H. SPARKS
Institute of Zoology, Poznan University of Life Sciences, Poland

ALAN J.A. STEWART
Department of Biology and Environmental Science, University of Sussex, Brighton, UK

ALAN STUBBS
Buglife – The Invertebrate Conservation Trust, Peterborough, UK

H.E. SUGDEN
School of Ocean Sciences, Bangor University, Anglesey, UK

J.A. THOMAS
Department of Zoology, University of Oxford, Oxford, UK

R.C. THOMPSON
School of Biological Sciences, University of Plymouth, Plymouth, UK

CHARLES R. TYLER
School of Biosciences, University of Exeter, Exeter, UK

MARTIN S. WARREN
Butterfly Conservation, East Lulworth, Dorset, UK

IAN P. WOIWOD
Department of Plant and Invertebrate Ecology, Rothamsted Research, Harpenden, Herts, UK

D.W. YALDEN
School of Life Sciences, University of Manchester, Manchester, UK

Foreword

How do you know which way to go if you do not know where you are? And how can you plan for the future if you do not know the state of the present? If we are concerned about the environmental future of Britain and Ireland, then we must know as much as possible about its present condition.

Happily, this country has never been short of expert naturalists – people who have a particular affection for bumblebees and bats, who take pleasure in noting the dates of the changes that take place each year in the woodlands and hedgerows, on mountainsides and heathlands, who chart the arrival of returning migrants in spring or the arrival of first-time immigrants. This book contains the reports of over 40 of the most dedicated of such experts, professional scientists who devote their lives to studying their chosen subjects.

Their accounts, needless to say, report change. That is hardly surprising. The natural world, everywhere, is changing and has always done so. It changed when human beings settled these islands in the wake of the retreating glaciers 13 000 years ago. They were themselves the instruments of change. Over the centuries, they cleared forests, cultivated the earth and introduced new species of animals and plants. They even modified existing species and turned them into something quite new. But the pace of change began to accelerate dramatically three or four centuries ago when men devised machinery that suddenly gave them huge power, and even the illusion that they were able to – and had a right to – mould the natural world in whatever way they wished to suit their own particular purpose.

This country was at the forefront of those developments, and indeed devised some of the most important and influential of them during that industrial revolution. But now the changes they initiated have come to a climax. The increasing size of the human population has driven us to claim so much of the natural world that there is no longer any corner of our landscape that is not affected by our presence.

So now change must take a new direction. Now it must enable us not only to accommodate the still increasing number of people for whom these islands are home, but it must also have a proper concern for the needs and welfare of the natural world beyond ourselves. To do that, to plan with detail and confidence, it is essential that we know where we are. That is why this book is so important. It gives us a bench-mark. It not only records our present position, but it will enable us in the coming years to discern the direction in which we are going and the progress we have made in the journey.

It is invaluable now – and in the years to come, it will be irreplaceable.

David Attenborough

Preface

This book is designed to appeal to people with a general interest in wildlife and concern for its future, and also to provide an authoritative reference for students of biology, conservation, ecology and environmental science on what has happened to wildlife in Britain and Ireland over the last 50 years. We also discuss how wildlife conservation is planned and managed in Britain and Ireland in the twenty-first century, and Britain's role in managing wildlife conservation overseas.

There is widespread unease about wildlife decline, its reality, severity and longevity. Here my co-authors and I have tried to give an accurate appraisal of the changes that have occurred in a wide range of wildlife species and their habitats, to outline what are urgent priorities now, and to provide some insights into what is likely to happen in the future. There are chapters on each of the vertebrate groups and all of the major invertebrate groups. Insects are covered in more detail than other animal taxonomic groups, partly because they are more numerous, and partly because they underpin many food chains, serving as important food items for other insects, spiders and all the vertebrate classes. At a glance it will be clear that the fauna is covered in more detail than the flora, and that some invertebrate groups, and non-flowering plant groups such as bryophytes, are omitted, simply to keep the volume within reasonable limits.

The geographical scope of the book is, as the title indicates, Britain and Ireland. This includes the Channel Islands, Isle of Man, and Orkney and Shetland, but different chapters cover slightly different areas, depending on the area from which the data have been gleaned. There is also a chapter on wildlife and conservation in the British Overseas Territories, including such far-flung places as St Helena, which represent an often neglected area of our national responsibility. Finally, since Britain and Ireland make a significant financial, intellectual and political contribution to wildlife conservation worldwide, and also since what is happening by way of conservation overseas can have profound effects on our own wildlife through migration or accidental introduction, a chapter is included on conservation in this wider context.

As well as documenting the state of abundance or scarcity of the fauna and flora, the book also discusses the reasons for changes in animal and plant populations, including such drivers as water pollution (with a specialist chapter on endocrine disrupters), urbanisation, intensive agriculture and climate change. We also emphasise the relationship between wildlife conservation and field sports, and the roll of introduced vertebrates and flowering plants on our wildlife. There is also a chapter on how nature conservation is managed and organised in Britain and Ireland.

Acknowledgements

First and foremost I should acknowledge the input of all the co-authors whom I persuaded to write chapters for this book. Without exception they are amongst a small group of authorities in their fields, and sometimes they are the most celebrated of these; they have given of their time, energy and expertise most generously. Since almost all the chapters were peer reviewed by other chapter authors and then reviewed independently, there was a lot of improvement and revision for all, so I am most grateful to all the authors for their patience and determination to turn in a final quality chapter.

I agreed with the publishers from an early stage that we should find an independent person with overall expertise to read and criticise all the chapters, and Professor Colin Galbraith of Scottish Natural Heritage has fulfilled this role outstandingly well, giving of his time and expertise unstintingly. Without him the quality of the book would have been much reduced.

Both the co-authors and Colin Galbraith have been driven to do what they did primarily by concern for wildlife conservation, and I salute their devotion to this cause.

I am also delighted to acknowledge my great indebtedness to Enid Scappaticci, who has given of her free time and secretarial skills to help this project at every stage and to Annie Cardew who made the comprehensive index.

To Dominic Lewis of CUP whom I talked into taking on this publishing project, and to Lynette Talbot, Jo Tyszka and Caroline Brown who have steered it expertly through the final organisational stages of publishing, I am also greatly indebted.

To Sir David Attenborough who, in his still busy life, found time to write a foreword, I extend my considerable gratitude. Surely no one has changed the way people think of the planet and its wildlife more than this man.

Also thanks to my wife Jean, who continues to tolerate and encourage my obsessions with science and the natural world.

Abbreviations

ABP	Associated British Ports
ACAP	Agreement on Conservation of Albatrosses and Petrels
AES	agri-environmental schemes
APE	alkylphenol polyethoxylate
ARCT	Amphibian and Reptile Conservation Trust
BAP	biodiversity action plan
BAT	British Antarctic Territory
BAS	British Antarctic Survey
BASC	British Association for Shooting and Conservation
BCT	Bat Conservation Trust
BES	British Ecological Society
BGCI	Botanic Gardens Conservation International
BI	Birdlife International
BIAZA	British and Irish Association of Zoos and Aquaria
BIOT	British Indian Ocean Territory
BMS	Butterfly Monitoring Scheme
BMWP	Biological Monitoring Working Party
BRC	Biological Records Centre
BSBI	Botanical Society of the British Isles
BTO	British Trust for Ornithology
BVI	British Virgin Islands
BWARS	Bees, Wasps and Ants Recording Society
BWI	Bird Watch Ireland
CAP	Common Agricultural Policy
CBD	Convention on Biological Diversity
CCW	Countryside Council for Wales
CEH	Centre for Ecology and Hydrology
CFCs	chlorofluorocarbons, used in refrigeration and listed as greenhouse gases as contributors to global warming

CI	Conservation International
CITES	Convention on International Trade in Endangered Species of Wild Fauna and Flora
CMS	Convention on Migratory Species
CPRE	Campaign to Protect Rural England
DCS	Deer Commission for Scotland
DDE	dichlorodiphenyldichloroethylene, the breakdown product of DDT left in soils and materials exposed to DDT
DDT	dichlorodiphenyltrichloroethane, a persistent insecticide
DEFRA	Department for Environment, Food and Rural Affairs
DfID	Department for International Development
DICE	Durrell Institute of Conservation and Ecology
DNA barcodes	codes which resemble price barcodes, but which are made up of DNA sequences which are unique to individuals and can be used to distinguish them
DNA	deoxyribonucleic acid, the molecular carrier of genetic information
DWPT	Durrell Wildlife Preservation Trust
EA	Environment Agency
EC	European Commission
EDC	endocrine-disrupting chemical
EEZ	Exclusive Economic Zone
EIA	Environmental Impact Assessment
EIFAC	European Inland Fisheries Advisory Commission
EN	English Nature (now Natural England)
EPS	European Protected Species
ES	Environmental Stewardship
EU	European Union
FAO	Food and Agriculture Organisation
FBI	Farmland Birds Index
FCO	Foreign and Commonwealth Office
FFI	Fauna and Flora International
FMD	Foot and Mouth Disease
FPS	the former Fauna Preservation Society, now Fauna and Flora International (FFI)
GBC	Game Bag Census
GCT	the former Game Conservancy Trust, now the Game and Wildlife Conservation Trust
GDP	gross domestic product

GrASP	Great Ape Survival Project
GSPC	Global Strategy for Plant Conservation
GWCT	Game and Wildlife Conservation Trust (formerly GCT)
HCT	the former Herpetological Conservation Trust (now Amphibian and Reptile Conservation Trust, ARCT)
HDC	hormone-disrupting chemical
HSE	Health and Safety Executive
IASRB	International Atlantic Salmon Research Board
ICES	International Council for the Exploration of the Sea
IGY	international geophysical year
IIED	International Institute of Environment and Development
IUCN	International Union for Conservation of Nature and Natural Resources (World Conservation Union)
JNCC	Joint Nature Conservation Committee
MAFF	the former Ministry of Agriculture, Fisheries and Food, currently part of DEFRA
MEA	multilateral environmental agreements
MS	Mammal Society
MSB	Millennium Seed Bank
NARRS	National Amphibian and Reptile Recording Scheme
NASCO	North Atlantic Salmon Conservation Organization
NBMP	National Bat Monitoring Programme
NCC	the former Nature Conservancy Council, now split into separate bodies for England, Scotland and Wales, as well as the INCC
NE	Natural England
NGC	National Gamebag Census run by GWCT
NGO	non-government organisation
NHM	Natural History Museum (London)
NIEA	Northern Ireland Environment Agency
OECD	Organisation for Economic Co-operation and Development
OTEP	Overseas Territories Environmental Programme
PACEC	Public and Corporate Economic Consultants
PCB	polychlorinated biphenyl, an organic pollutant used in manufacturing
PCP	pentachlorophenol, an organic insecticide
PFR	pike fry rhabdovirus
POP	persistent organic pollutant
RBGE	Royal Botanic Gardens Edinburgh
RBGK	Royal Botanic Gardens Kew

RIS	Rothamsted Insect Survey
ROV	remotely operated vehicles
RS	Royal Society of London
RSPB	Royal Society for the Protection of Birds
SAC	special area of conservation (plural is SACs)
SNCO	Statutory Nature Conservation Organisation
SNH	Scottish Natural Heritage
SOC	Scottish Ornithologists' Club
SPA	special protection area
SSSI	site of special scientific interest
SWA	Southern Water Authority
TBT	tri butyl tin, an anti-fouling compound used on hulls of boats and ships
TCI	Turks and Caicos Islands
TRAFFIC International	Trade Records Analysis of Flora and Fauna in Commerce, an international network that monitors wildlife trade around the world
TRIM	Trends in Indices for Monitoring
UKBAP	United Kingdom Biodiversity Action Plan
UKOT	United Kingdom Overseas Territories
UKOTCF	United Kingdom Overseas Territories Conservation Forum
UNEP	United Nations Environment Programme
UNESCO	United Nations Educational, Scientific, and Cultural Organisation
UV	ultraviolet
VTG	vitellogenin, female egg yolk protein
WAGBI	Wildfowlers Association of Great Britain and Ireland
WCA	Wildlife and Countryside Act
WCMC	World Conservation Monitoring Centre
WHS	World Heritage Site
WT	Woodland Trust
WWF	World Wildlife Fund. First established as such in 1961, and changed to World Wide Fund for Nature in 1986 and known simply by original initials since 2001
WWT	Wildfowl and Wetlands Trust
WWTW	waste water treatment works
ZSL	Zoological Society of London

1

Introduction

Norman Maclean

The sending of vehicles and people into space from the 1960s onwards culminated in the eventual landing on the Moon's surface by Neil Armstrong and Buzz Aldrin on board Apollo 11 in July 1969. This did much more than mark our break outside the Earth's atmosphere and signify our serious entry into space. We all shared in a profound alteration in our perceptions by looking back at planet Earth from space, seeing for the first time our Earth home from an objective distance. This new view of Earth has brought many important adjustments to our mind-set. We saw our Earth as a largely blue planet, unique in the solar system for its abundant water and marked excess of water coverage over bare land masses. It also stood out as a green planet, certainly unique in the solar system for its abundance of plant life, as well as possessing a hugely diverse community of animals that depended on these plants. To this day we remain uncertain whether any other object in space has evolved a living biodiversity. We may indeed be unique in the Universe.

The 1960s also hold for us all a striking coincidence, for in 1962 Rachel Carson published her dramatic and prophetic book *Silent Spring*, warning us of the possible catastrophic effects of the widespread contamination of our world ecosystems by human-engineered pollutants.

Rachel Carson was born in May 1907 on a small farm in Pennsylvania, USA. She became a nature writer and marine biologist with the US Bureau of Fisheries. Her 1962 book *Silent Spring* emphasised the environmental damage resulting from the widespread use of DDT and other pesticides. Her book proved to be the springboard for the environmental movement and the creation of the US Environmental Protection Agency. Not all her observations and predictions proved to be well founded, and she was clearly wrong to suppose that DDT was a carcinogen. However, she was much more right than wrong, as my generation has lived to discover. She was posthumously honoured in 1980 by the award of the Presidential Medal of Freedom.

At this time I was a post-graduate student in the Zoology Department of Edinburgh University and, like most of my fellow students, my knowledge and views of ecology

Silent Summer: The State of Wildlife in Britain and Ireland, ed. Norman Maclean. Published by Cambridge University Press. © Cambridge University Press 2010.

were hugely influenced by these two emotive events – the view of planet Earth from space, and the views of Rachel Carson on the environmental damage being inflicted on our planet by human activities. So, from the 1960s onwards, those of us in the biological sciences have superimposed the Rachel Carson view of Earth on the Apollo view of Earth. The planet may be gloriously blue, but a closer look reveals that its fresh and salt water are no longer healthy, and its amazing greenery is also fast disappearing as we reduce the rainforest and industrialise the Earth's surface.

This book is an attempt to update our view of our own country's wildlife. It is almost half a century since Armstrong and Carson so greatly altered our viewpoint and gave us for the first time a new awareness of our responsibility for planet Earth management. How has our environment fared and have Rachel Carson's remarkable prophecies proved to be correct? In this multi-author book, we endeavour to present, in as unbiased and accurate a fashion as possible, a view of the comparative health or sickness of the wildlife with which we share Britain and Ireland, and also to try to predict future change and understand the drivers of such change, both in the past and in the future.

Neil Armstrong's view of Earth from space was insufficiently detailed to reveal any signs of sickness on our planet. That requires a more detailed view of our planet's ecology, using close examination with binoculars and microscopes and careful cataloguing over extended time periods. That is what this book provides for Britain and Ireland, and UK overseas territories. The broad conclusion is that indeed all is not well; many species have declined in range and/or numbers, although there are also success stories, species which have responded to conservation activities. The human imprint on our environment is now very severe and increasing, although positive conservation can halt, even reverse, some of the worst effects. Even given the wonderful evolutionary resilience of ecosystems, we have to consider seriously the possibility that we are in the middle of another great extinction which yet may come to rival those of the Permian, 250 million years ago, which led to the demise of some 96% of all extant species (Fortey 1999; Benton *et al.* 2003), or the extinction of the dinosaurs some 65 million years ago. This latter extinction is now believed to have resulted from a huge meteorite crashing into what is now the Yucatan peninsula of Mexico at an estimated speed of 30 km s^{-1} (Alvarez 1997). What is unique about the planet's present malaise is that it is almost entirely the result of the activities of one species, ourselves, at the expense of most of the others. The present world population of 6.7 billion (a billion is a thousand million) is expected to rise to 9 billion by 2050, while the present UK population of just over 60 million may well rise to 80 million by 2050. Although factors such as climate change and pollution will place ever increasing difficulties in the way of effective wildlife conservation in the UK, it is the inexorable rise in human population that poses the most serious threat. A further 10 million people in the UK by 2030 will place huge demands on land for further housing, and more roads will be needed to link the new housing complexes with existing conurbations. In the face of such expected population increases it is hard to be optimistic about the future of Britain's wildlife. The anticipated world human population increases are, if anything, even more worrying.

Of what particular value is a current appraisal of the state of Britain and Ireland's wildlife in the greater scheme of things? There seem to be several points to consider. One is that the UK is a developed and prosperous economy, but one that accepts that the state of our wildlife is a barometer of our priorities, political, social and economic. True, the UK is a small landmass in world terms, but that concentrates the global forces which threaten biodiversity and ecology worldwide, including polluted seas, overfishing and climate change. Small land masses such as the UK serve as relatively isolated crucibles in which change can be monitored in great detail and fine scale.

The UK is also a nation with a long history of serious interest in the natural world, both at home and abroad. This interest continues to be expressed in the context of our involvement with conservation and how it can be best managed. We are the inheritors of a significant legacy from figures such as Gilbert White and Charles Darwin; our continuing national fascination with the natural world is underlined by the astonishing success of numerous television series involving David Attenborough and his collaborators. Thus a national appraisal should serve as an indication of what is happening in a relatively 'best practice' situation, where conservation is taken very seriously and monitoring of wildlife changes is a popular national interest.

It also seems to me that concern for our own back yard is fundamental and telling. If all is not well here, we should be deeply worried about the wider context. If we, as a wealthy, developed and environmentally concerned nation do not seem to be spending enough of our GDP on our natural environment, what hope is there for less fortunate countries with much bigger problems of poverty, poor productivity and poor infrastructure? Furthermore, what hope is there of our persuading the rest of the world to help pay for the preservation of the remaining rainforest, to relieve poverty in order to reduce the consumption of bushmeat species (wild animals caught and killed and sold for food in markets), or to encourage reduction of carbon emissions, if we ourselves have serious problems of wildlife declines, habitat destruction and polluted waterways?

There is an important temporal aspect to much of this preamble. In the first place people under 50 or so may know little or nothing of the Rachel Carson story and her impact on environmental ecology. These latter generations of people have perhaps also never known the wildlife abundance that preceded the more recent declines. I am old enough to remember stubble fields teeming with mixed flocks of finches, buntings and sparrows in winter. These same stubble fields also resounded at sunset to the creaking calls of numerous Grey Partridges. Even more impressive were the insect numbers everywhere. The common insects were then truly abundant. Every field teemed with Meadow Brown and Small Tortoiseshell Butterflies, every garden with Small and Large White Butterflies. Hatches of mayflies on rivers were incredibly dense. There is a striking memory of pulling into petrol stations, and invariably having to clear one's windscreen of all the dead flies that had accumulated on it. Indeed for a time almost every car was equipped with a plastic accessory fitted to the front crown of the bonnet. This was an insect deflector, designed to reduce the splattering of one's windscreen with dead insects that was at that time commonplace. So Rachel Carson was not wrong about the dramatic insect declines that would follow from the widespread use of pesticides. If insects are so evidently less abundant, the fish, birds, amphibians, reptiles and mammals that prey upon them are also likely to be scarcer. Does the evidence bear this out?

Another memory is of gamekeepers' gibbets, strung with the remains of weasels, stoats, crows, moles, magpies and raptors. Top predators such as Peregrines, Sparrow Hawks and others also suffered very severely from the pesticides of which Rachel Carson had warned. Fortunately many of these have recovered well, testifying to the benefits of effective conservation, although some are still only slowly recovering from the declines which were inflicted in years gone by.

The book is designed to appeal to two distinct groups of readers. One is people with a general interest in wildlife and concern for its welfare. The other is more particular, namely undergraduate students in the Biological Sciences, particularly courses in ecology, conservation and environmental science. The volume is structured so that we first take the reader through a consideration of the factors affecting wildlife populations. These include general developments such as the spread of towns and industrial sites and the road systems which link them, and the frequent destruction of habitat that has accompanied these developments. However, some developments may help to counteract these problems. Society is gradually becoming more eco-aware, and the spread of organic farming and the highlighting of green issues is certainly to be welcomed. International concern about energy use, carbon production, pesticide use and climate change will surely bear some fruit, even if some of the efforts seem to be too little too late.

We also consider other important factors such as the introduction of non-native animals including, for example, Mink, Canada Geese and Mitten Crabs, to name just three, and their effects on native species; also the effects of plant introductions such as the Wild Rhododendron and Japanese Knotweed. In addition we consider the effects of water pollution, climate change and agricultural intensification.

Then follows in Part II consideration of how wildlife conservation is now managed, both in the UK and elsewhere, and how the not inconsiderable costs are met.

Part III makes up the bulk of the book and contains case histories of the various animal and plant groups, and how species within these groups have fared over the last 50 years and how they are likely to fare in future.

It is important to realise some general principles that affect wildlife numbers and species. The first is that wildlife has probably always been in a dynamic state, adapting to profound changes in climate such as ice ages, and, in the last few thousand years, to the increasing impact of human activity. It is important to stress that human activity is not always a negative in terms of wildlife. Mammals such as Harvest Mice and Brown Hares have no doubt prospered as a result of agricultural practice, at least until the recent intensification of agriculture in the last 40 years. Birds such as Corn Buntings, Yellow Buntings and House Sparrows also thrived on a cereal-rich agriculture which involved winter stack yards, winter stubble with ample spilled grain and crops with plentiful numbers of weeds to provide additional seed. Only with the more recent improvements in farming efficiency have these once abundant birds begun to show symptoms of widespread decline.

Another point to stress is that wildlife prosperity or decline can be measured in many different ways. One is simply to chart species within defined areas in terms of presence or absence at particular times. Another more difficult parameter to consider is the actual abundance of individual species at different time periods. This is tricky, not only because counting individual numbers of a species can be difficult, but more because in past times when a particular species such as the Meadow Brown Butterfly was widespread and very abundant, people did not bother to count them. Now, when they are much less common, we have no hard data to use for the previous abundances since there then seemed little point in counting an already abundant species. Thus observations of what biologists call biomass are difficult and rarely available. We have sought to include them in the book whenever possible, but it has not always proved possible.

We have also sought to give the Part III chapters a common structure, so that the reader can become familiar with where to find particular information.

The numerous insect chapters deserve comment. There are many more insect species in the wildlife of Britain and Ireland than all of the animal vertebrate groups *in toto*. Also insects form the food for many of the vertebrates listed, and so declines in insect numbers are a frequent cause of decline for some of the vertebrate species. As Rachel Carson predicted, there have indeed been dramatic declines in many British insects, especially moths and riverflies, and this has been an important factor in the declines charted for many species of insectivorous vertebrates such as bats.

Since UK territory includes the UK Overseas Territories, we include a chapter on these. We also include a chapter on British involvement in conservation in the rest of the world. Also, as many species overseas have experienced sharp declines, UK zoos have come to take on a major responsibility as curators of examples of species now rare in the world. This has allowed UK zoos to become heavily involved in reintroduction programmes of species such as Tamarin Monkeys and Scimatar Horned Oryx, and has given increasing recognition to the role of zoos as wildlife centres where breeding stocks of species may persist even if they become extinct in the wild.

References

Alvarez, W. (2008). *T. Rex and the Crater of Doom*, Princeton, Princeton University Press.

Benton, M.J. and Twitchett, R.J. (2003). How to kill (almost) all life: the end-Permian extinction event. *Trends in Ecology and Evolution*, **18**, 358–365.

Fortey, R. (1999). *A Natural History of the First Four Billion Years of Life on Earth*, New York, Vintage.

PART I

Factors driving changes in wildlife

2

Climate change

T.H. Sparks, C.D. Preston and D.B. Roy

Summary

The climate of the British Isles is changing rapidly and is predicted to continue doing so during the twenty-first century. During the course of the twentieth century, temperature rose by approximately 1 °C. The consequences of this have been seen in the abundance, distribution and phenology (life-cycle timing) of some of the British wildlife. Most changes are consistent with a warming Britain; growth of populations of warmth-loving species, northwards expansion of many species and advanced spring phenology. Changes in phenology, in particular, demonstrate the most consistent changes in wildlife as a consequence of a warming climate. In this chapter we present examples of these changes and discuss possible implications for the future.

Introduction

The Central England Temperature Series summarises the temperature of central England from 1659 onwards. It has been shown to be highly correlated with temperatures from individual stations across the UK, except northern and western extremities. As such it can be considered to be broadly representative of the temperatures of the British Isles. Figure 2.1 shows annual mean temperatures averaged in decadal blocks 1660–9, 1670–9 etc. The final point represents the mean of the eight years 2000–7. With the exception of a warm decade in the 1730s there appears to have been a steady rise in temperature which has accelerated in the last two decades. Indeed, 2006 was the warmest year in the 1659–2007 period and nine of the ten warmest years in the series have occurred since 1989.

Silent Summer: The State of Wildlife in Britain and Ireland, ed. Norman Maclean. Published by Cambridge University Press. © Cambridge University Press 2010.

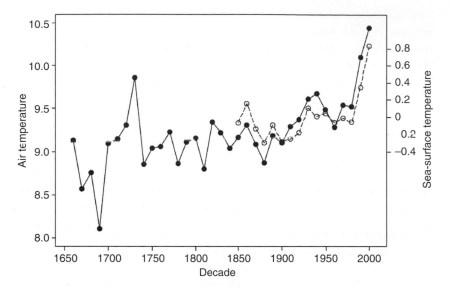

Figure 2.1 Decadal mean Central England Temperatures (°C) 1660–2007 (solid line and symbols) and sea-surface temperatures around the British Isles (°C, anomalies from 1961–90 average) 1850–2007 (dotted line, open symbols). N.B. the final points do not cover a full decade.

Despite the decade-to-decade variability in temperature, there can be little doubt that the climate of the British Isles is warming. Figure 2.1 also shows trends in sea-surface temperatures around the British Isles since 1850 (10°W–5°E, 50°N–60°N; data source Hadley Centre) and the correlation with the Central England Temperature is very high ($r = 0.90$, $P < 0.001$). There is no composite temperature record for the fresh waters of the UK, but these will be rising at a similar scale, for example the long-term record at Lake Windermere has seen an increase of *c.* 1 °C, mainly in the last two decades. Data from other sources (sediments, tree rings, ice cores) suggest that global temperatures are now warmer than at any time in the past 1000 years, probably for longer. Whilst there were warmer spells in Britain before the Holocene, these have not occurred in the era dominated by *Homo sapiens* or in an environment characterised by man-modified landscapes.

In its most recent report, the Intergovernmental Panel on Climate Change conclude that, 'Most of the observed increase in global average temperatures since the mid-twentieth century is very likely due to the observed increase in anthropogenic GHG [greenhouse gas] concentrations'. The rise in temperature shown in Figure 2.1 of *c.* 1 °C over the last century is relatively modest compared to that expected in the twenty-first century when temperature increases of 2–4 °C are predicted. Other features of a changing climate in the twenty-first century are likely to include sea-level rise and changes in the regional and seasonal distribution of precipitation.

For thousands of years British wildlife has been greatly affected by human activities, including, in recent decades, developments such as land-use intensification and nitrogen deposition. Can climate change be added to the list of factors affecting wildlife? What have been the temperature-related changes, if any, to the wildlife of the British Isles? If such changes can be detected in the twentieth century, will these be of value in prediction of changes under more rapidly increasing temperatures in the twenty-first century? In this chapter we examine the evidence for climate-driven changes in British wildlife. By necessity, these make use, and stress the importance, of long-term data sets. Monitoring wildlife has been, for many years, the poor relation of scientific research (if indeed considered as science at all). Now the value of such data is being recognised and the importance of distribution atlases, population monitoring and other observational studies is increasingly acknowledged. In this short chapter we cannot attempt a complete evaluation of temperature-related changes, but have selected examples we believe will demonstrate how influential even a modest temperature change has been on wildlife.

Changes

Temperature may affect wildlife in a number of different ways and in the following sections we focus on abundance, distribution and phenology (the timing of life-cycle events). We regret the imbalance in this chapter, with many more examples of phenology and far fewer on abundance effects, but this reflects the literature published to date. Other potential effects, such as on morphology or behaviour, are not considered here. It should be borne in mind that temperature changes may be direct, e.g. via physiological change, or indirect, e.g. through changes to prey, predators or habitats. Furthermore, other pressures, such as land-use change, may mask or accentuate temperature-related changes (e.g. Warren *et al.* 2001).

Abundance (population increases and decreases)

Most of the data available on population effects relate to animals, and examples are dominated by short-generation invertebrates (e.g. Warren *et al.* 2001; Beaugrand *et al.* 2002). However, changes to population size in plants (e.g. Sturm *et al.* 2001) and birds (e.g. Frederiksen *et al.* 2004) have also been demonstrated. In the latter case, declines in reproductive performance and population size have been reported for some seabirds in the North Sea. This appears linked to distributional and population shifts in elements of the birds' foodweb. Distributional and phenological shifts in marine plankton may be affecting elements higher in the foodweb, principally lipid-rich sand eels. This is adversely affecting certain seabirds and possibly also Harbour Porpoises, *Phocoena phocoena*, (Macleod *et al.* 2007) for whom sand eels are also a key component of the diet. These indirect effects of climate change may also be affected by human fishing pressure and it is difficult to assess the relative importance of each.

Data from the UK Butterfly Monitoring Scheme have been analysed to assess the influence of climate on the abundance of butterflies. In general terms, butterflies appear to benefit from warmer summers for both current and future generations, but effects on individual species vary considerably. In a study of general butterfly abundance, Dennis and Sparks (2007) suggested the general benefits of warmer summers, but the detrimental effects of wetter, milder winters. Since both of these may be a feature of future British climate it is difficult to predict the long-term changes in populations. Warren *et al.* (2001) considered that declines in butterflies associated with the loss of suitable habitats would have been far worse than they actually were had it not been for a warming climate.

There has been some evidence of differential change in UK butterflies. Mobile, generalist species such as the Small White, *Pieris rapae*, have been increasing by an average of 27%, while the more sedentary, habitat specialist species such as the Pearl-Bordered Fritillary, *Boloria euphrosyne*, declined by 30%, suggesting species capable of capitalising on warmer conditions have indeed done so.

Warmer temperatures have been associated with an increased number of southern species, e.g. Lepidoptera, such as the European Corn Borer, *Ostrinia nubilalis* (Sparks *et al.* 2007) and marine plankton. Both of these are consistent with known temperature responses of species, e.g. Sparks *et al.* (2005) for Lepidoptera.

Plant records of montane species outside Britain have shown the expected declines. In Britain, effects are difficult to study because of the small populations of many strictly montane species and the difficulty of ensuring that the rugged terrain in which they grow has been thoroughly searched.

There are only limited studies on the effects of temperature on plant populations in the UK. One of the few is a study of the Lizard Orchid, *Himantoglossum hircinum*, whose increase in both the number of populations and the number of flowering plants in each population has been attributed to rising temperature (Carey *et al.* 2002). Expectations are that warmth-loving, southern species will benefit most from a warming climate, while montane specialists will decline. The evidence for the latter has not yet been clearly demonstrated for Britain, but remains an expectation, given scientific studies elsewhere.

Distribution

Climate may dictate the distribution of species through physiological thresholds of temperature and water availability. Distribution may then be further constrained by the extent of suitable habitat, soils etc. Changes in the latitudinal or altitudinal ranges of plant and animal distributions have been described in response to previous changes in climate. Therefore we would anticipate that changes have already occurred in response to current climate warming.

However, range shifts may be episodic rather than gradual and may lag behind temperature increases. The dispersal ability of a species dictates its ability to exploit new climatically suitable areas, and even to avoid those becoming unsuitable. It may be easier to discern range shifts in relatively sedentary species than in migratory species with large interannual variation in movements. The ability of species to adapt to a changing climate *in situ* has hardly been explored. Can genetic adaptation occur sufficiently quickly to match a rapidly changing climate?

Latitudinal shifts

In their global assessment of range shifts, Parmesan and Yohe (2003) found that 80% of the 434 studied species had shifted in accordance with climate-change predictions. As a recent example, it has been reported that the distributions of both exploited and non-exploited North Sea fishes have responded markedly to recent increases in sea temperature, with nearly two-thirds of species shifting in mean latitude or depth, or both, over 25 years. For species with northerly or southerly range margins in the North Sea, half have shown boundary shifts with warming, and all but one shifted northward (Perry *et al.* 2005). It has also been found that fish species with shifting distributions have faster life cycles and smaller body sizes than non-shifting species, showing once more the expected differential response among species. There have also been widespread changes in the distribution of warm- and cold-water plankton in the North Sea.

Changes in vascular-plant distributions are difficult to assess, in part because plants are less well dispersed than winged insects or birds. Seeds tend to be spread around by human activity, and this makes it difficult to assess whether changes have been caused simply by these acts of dispersal, or whether it is only now that a species is able to take advantage of such opportunities and become established in new areas. Two plant atlases for the British Isles allow such changes to be assessed. The first (Perring and Walters 1962) was based on data for the period 1930–60; the repeat survey (Preston *et al.* 2002) took place in the years 1987–99. Because the field-work effort differed between the two atlases it is not advisable to make a direct comparison of distributions in the two atlases. Instead a relative-change index has been calculated for each species. Examination of these suggested that species associated with a northern distribution have declined relative to those with a southern or more general distribution. Although this result might initially seem to show the effects of a changing climate, a more detailed analysis (unpublished) suggests that it is largely the result of habitat modification. Northern species tend to occupy acidic, low-nutrient habitats which have been lost or highly modified in southern England. However, a more recent survey of tetrads (2 × 2 km grid squares) recorded by the BSBI (Botanical Society of the British Isles) in 1987–8 and 2003–4 revealed evidence for the effects of warmer climate in a number of habitats (Table 2.1).

There have been some marked changes in the distribution of some British butterflies. In particular, there have been range increases in the Speckled Wood, *Pararge aegeria*, and Essex Skipper, *Thymelicus lineola*, compatible with a warmer climate.

Table 2.1 *Examples of habitats in which the distribution of species appear to have been significantly affected by climate change. Based on a survey of sample tetrads in 1987–88 and 2003–4 reported by Braithwaite* et al. *(2006).*

Habitat	Examples of changes	Possible climate factor contributing to change
Broad-leaved woodland	Increase of Hart's-tongue Fern, *Phyllitis scolopendrium,* and Stinking Iris, *Iris foetidissima*	Warmer January temperatures
Boundary and linear features (e.g. roadsides)	Increase of annual species (e.g. Squirrel-tail Fescue, *Vulpia bromoides*) and some perennials (e.g. Alexanders, *Smyrnium olusatrum*)	Warmer January temperatures
Calcareous grassland	Increase of annual species (e.g. Field Madder, *Sherardia arvensis*) and species with south-ern distributions (e.g. Pyramidal Orchid, *Anacamptis pyramidalis*)	Warmer January temperatures
Built-up areas and gardens	Increase of species with southern distributions (e.g. Prickly Lettuce, *Lactuca serriola* and Wall Barley, *Hordeum murinum*)	Warmer July temperatures and/or reduced rainfall

Across Europe a polewards movement has been detected. Northwards movements in Odonata have been identified and extended to a much wider range of taxa (Hickling *et al.* 2006).

Northwards movements can be most easily detected in new arrivals of species, of which the Little Egret, *Egretta garzetta*, is a recent spectacular example, but for which there is also a growing list of species, particularly of invertebrates.

Altitudinal shifts

Changes in plant distributions on mountains have been noted elsewhere in Europe, but not in Britain. This may be a consequence of a more limited altitudinal range in Britain, the species-poor nature of many of our upland plant communities and the rar-ity of many Arctic-montane species.

Difficulties in detecting distributional changes

Reports on distributional change are heavily biased to those of range-edge expan-sion. For longer-lived species, range shifts resulting from population growth are likely to occur more rapidly than mortality/extinction in areas becoming less suitable. Furthermore it may be easier to detect a species in a new location (e.g. a single record is sufficient) compared to the extinction of a species in its current location (which may require repeated visits over several years to confirm absence). Hence reports of expan-sion may occur an order of magnitude more quickly than reports of contraction.

Climate-linked invasions, extinctions and new communities

Because of their novelty, invasion by non-native species may be the most easy to detect. However it may be difficult to separate the contributions of man-assisted dispersal and climate in such invasions.

The consequences of climate-driven distributional change at longer timescales could be the extinction of many species (Thomas *et al.* 2004). Consequently, novel plant communities may be formed in response to climate change. Species assemblages without a modern analogue are evident in the fossil record. These communities are believed to have resulted from differential migration rates during past climatic changes. Some of the examples of range shifts mentioned earlier involve community-level changes. There are also likely to be changes in the composition and structure of the new communities, e.g. since changes in distribution are often asymmetrical, with species invading faster from lower elevations or latitudes than resident species are receding upslope or poleward, there will likely be a (possibly transient) increase in species richness of the community in question.

Phenology

Recent reviews of evidence for biological impacts of climate change have been dominated by phenological examples (e.g. Rosenzweig *et al.* 2008). Britain has a long tradition of recording the beginning and end of the seasons, as determined by plant and animal activity, for example return of migrant birds, or leaf fall. From 1875–1947 and since 1998 there have been large-scale networks in the British Isles and the UK, respectively. There has also been a large number of individual recorders, foremost of whom must be the late Richard Fitter who recorded flowering dates of several hundred plant species between 1954 and 2000, while living at Chinnor in Oxfordshire. The history of plant phenology in Europe was recently summarised by Nekovar *et al.* (2008).

Most phenological data were not collected with the notion that they would make useful climate-change indicators, but rather they may have been collected for general Natural History interest, to evaluate the effect of environment on phenology, the impacts of climate on agriculture, or as a by-product of, for example, population monitoring. However, the sheer volume and duration of phenological data has made them useful for studying the effects of a changing climate on biological systems.

Figure 2.2 shows the strong relationship between first Oak (*Quercus robur*) leafing dates and temperature for a historic (Marsham) and a current (Combes) record. The relationships with temperature are both highly significant ($P < 0.001$) and suggest a 1 °C increase in temperature would be associated with a 7.5±0.4 or 8.5±0.9 day advance in leafing for the Marsham and Combes records, respectively. There is a hint of non-linearity in the relationship in Figure 2.2, i.e. the response to temperature appears steeper above 6 °C.

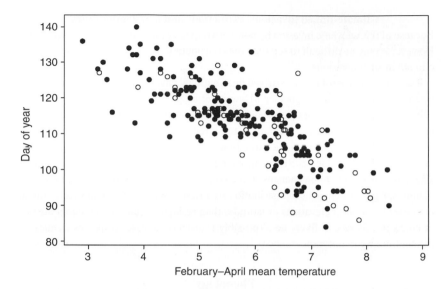

Figure 2.2 The relationship between first Oak-leafing dates and February–April mean Central England temperature from the Marsham family record 1746–1958 in Norfolk (solid circles) and the Jean Combes record 1950–2008 in Surrey (open circles).

Fitter and Fitter (2002) analysed the phenology of 385 plant species in Oxfordshire and concluded that the average first flowering date was 4.5 days earlier in the last decade of the twentieth century compared to 1954–89. Gange *et al.* (2007) investigated phenology of a large number of fungal species over a 50 year period in Wiltshire and showed major changes in the timing of fruiting.

In a study of data from the UK Butterfly Monitoring Scheme, Roy and Sparks (2000) examined the flight periods of 35 species/generation combinations. Of these, 26 species had a significantly earlier beginning of the flight period (e.g. Figure 2.3) and 25 had extended the length of their flight period. In nearly all cases, changes in phenology were associated with warmer temperatures. Strong correlations were present between first and mean records suggesting that changes in first dates also involved a shift in the whole flight period. There was no clear relationship between changing phenology and changing abundance. Similar reported advances in phenology include those for Odonata, North Sea plankton, bird migration and bird breeding. There has been some evidence of adaptation by migrating birds (Sparks and Tryjanowski 2007).

Our experience suggests that such temperature responses are the norm, particularly for species becoming active early in the year. A recent review of phenological change in Scotland showed how responsive species were to temperature, and indeed the extent of change in phenology that had already occurred.

Table 2.2 reveals changes in spring and autumn events, and in events associated with migration and breeding. Such changes have been widespread across the British

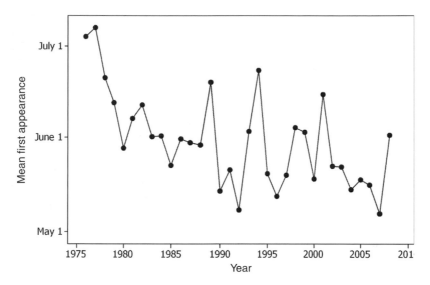

Figure 2.3 The change in first appearance of the Comma Butterfly, *Polygonia calbum,* in Britain 1976–2008.

Isles. It is also clear that there is a wide range of response to temperature. Species have responded by different amounts depending on localised warming (Menzel *et al.* 2006). The simplistic view that nature will just shift earlier en masse in spring is unlikely to be a reality. With differential change in phenology, questions arise as to where this may generate problems, for example synchrony in food chains, or changing the competitive balance in communities. There may also be changes in the relationships between species. Fitter and Fitter (2002) list a number of species where a reduced likelihood of hybridisation is likely to occur as plants change phenology at different rates, and others where hybridisation may become more common as phenologies tend to become more similar. Fitter and Fitter (2002) also suggested greater change in annual species than in perennial species, and in insect-pollinated species rather than wind-pollinated species.

Changed phenology may result in changed competition; early species may be able to gain a competitive advantage if they reproduce early. Furthermore the earliest breeding individuals may be the most productive; passing a disproportionately higher contribution of genes to successive generations. In some birds and invertebrates, additional broods may be possible, if the breeding season is extended.

There are, so far, few reported examples of synchrony problems with the relatively modest warming so far experienced, but they may be a feature of our natural world over the coming century, as predicted temperature increases continue. One example of possible disruption concerns the phenological plasticity of Oak trees and moth caterpillars relative to that of Great Tits, *Parus major.* Oak leafing can progress

Table 2.2 *A summary of some phenological trends and responses in Scotland adapted from Sparks* et al. *(2006). 'Trend' indicates the average change in phenology (negative values indicate earlier events) and 'Response' summarises how events respond to increasing temperature (again negative values earlier).*

Source/Taxa	Events	No. of series	Trend days/ decade	Response days/°C
Bird Nesting	First egg	25	–1.1	–2.4
Scottish Bird Report	Spring arrivals	3	–7.4	–5.3
Scottish Bird Report	Autumn departures	3	2.4	5.0
Deeside Bird Records	Spring bird arrivals	39	–4.1	–2.5
North Ronaldsay	Spring bird arrivals	82	–3.4	–3.0
North Ronaldsay	Autumn bird departures	82	–2.1	–1.1
Fair Isle	Spring bird arrivals	43	–1.3	–0.5
Moths	First appearance	22	–1.1	–6.3
Moths	Mean appearance	22	–0.9	–5.1
Aphids	First appearance	46	–4.7	–12.5
Butterflies	First appearance	30	–2.7	–5.4
Butterflies	Peak appearance	30	–3.5	–5.1
Fred Last	Plant flowering	208	–3.3	Not available
UKPN	Plants	14	–2.7	–7.5
UKPN	Birds	16	–1.8	–0.6
UKPN	Frogspawn	2	–1.0	–6.4
UKPN	Lawn cutting	4	–10.1	–4.6

rapidly in warm springs, the development time of caterpillars from egg to pupae can almost halve, but the incubation period of eggs is fixed. The bird has to anticipate the peak caterpillar crop for its chicks several weeks ahead. A suddenly warm spring may disrupt this planning and reduced chick weights and greater mortality are the consequence of phenological asynchrony. There is expected to be strong selection pressure for species to maintain their synchrony, particularly in tightly linked systems. Asynchrony may occur under rapid climate change, but may only be temporary.

Some species will undoubtedly benefit from phenological change. It is likely that the distributions of some species are limited by low temperatures and at range edges they are unable to successfully complete a life cycle. A relaxation of phenological bottlenecks may encourage some of the distributional expansions, both latitudinally and altitudinally, reported earlier in this chapter. We saw earlier that some phenological response may be non-linear. Differential change and non-linear change will

both contribute to making predictions of future phenology less simple, but it is important that phenological research shifts its balance from identifying climate impacts to
predictive modelling.

Conclusions

This chapter is biased towards phenology and this reflects the bias present in the published literature on the effects of a warming climate on wildlife. The detection of
changes in plant and animal populations, whether of abundance, distribution or phenology relies on the availability of long-term data. Such data were, until very recently,
scientifically unfashionable, but now their potential and value is recognised. Sources
of long-term data are being actively sought and investigated to determine if climate
signals can be seen within these records. Whilst much research funding is still short
term in nature, a number of new networks have recently emphasised the commitment
to long-term research. However, we are also still reliant on a few dedicated individuals running long-term research projects, often on a limited budget. Many recording
networks rely on volunteers and we hope that the opportunity to study the impacts of
climate change will make this an increasingly attractive and interesting area for study
by amateur naturalists.

A fairly recent phenomenon has been the use of long-term data for purposes for
which they were not originally intended. Examples would include the abstraction of
phenological data from schemes established to monitor populations (e.g. of butterflies
or migrant birds) or demography (e.g. nest record schemes). Distributional data can
also be extracted from population-monitoring schemes. Such exploitation of data sets
has to be commended and gives added value to the monitoring schemes.

Such studies can only examine the species and the aspects of species that have
been monitored. Thus we may be restricted in studies of synchrony within food webs
because we may not have data on all aspects of the web taken from the same locality.
New schemes plan to overcome these restrictions, but it will be some years before they
have sufficient useful data for investigation.

There are a number of priority areas for ongoing research. We still need to identify
and exploit existing data resources, and possibly need to think laterally about the 'data'
we exploit. Undoubtedly, greater use of photographic evidence will provide more evidence of habitat change and museum, herbarium and other historic records may tell
us more about recent distributional shifts. The consequences of extreme events (e.g.
storms, droughts, floods, sea surges, heatwaves) likely to become more frequent under
global climate change have so far received scant attention.

To date, research has focused on evidence of climate impacts. It is important
that this continues to identify where change is already happening and is used to
help alert conservationists, policy-makers and the general public to climate-related
change. However, there is a growing need to exploit this information to predict

likely future changes in population status and distribution and to identify species, communities and habitats that will both benefit and suffer as a consequence of climate warming.

References

Beaugrand, G., Reid, P.C., Ibañez, F., Lindley, J.A. and Edwards, M. (2002). Reorganization of North Atlantic marine copepod biodiversity and climate. *Science*, **296**, 1692–1694.

Braithwaite, M.E., Ellis, R.W. and Preston, C.D. (2006). *Change in the British Flora 1987–2004*, London, Botanical Society of the British Isles.

Carey, P.D., Farrell, L. and Stewart, N.F. (2002). The sudden increase in the abundance of *Himantoglossum hircinum* in England in the past decade and what has caused it. In Kindlmann, P., Willems, J.H. and Whigham, D.F., eds., *Trends and Fluctuations and Underlying Mechanisms In Terrestrial Orchid Populations*, Leiden, Backhuys, pp. 187–208.

Dennis, R.L.H. and Sparks, T.H. (2007). Climate signals are reflected in an 89 year series of British Lepidoptera records. *European Journal of Entomology*, **104**, 763–767.

Fitter, A.H. and Fitter, R.S.R. (2002). Rapid changes in the flowering time in British plants. *Science*, **296**, 1689–1691.

Frederiksen, M., Wanless, S., Harris, M.P., Rothery, P. and Wilson, L.J. (2004). The role of industrial fisheries and oceanographic change in the decline of North Sea black-legged kittiwakes. *Journal of Applied Ecology*, **41**, 1129–1139.

Gange, A.C., Gange, E.G., Sparks, T.H. and Boddy, L. (2007). Rapid and recent changes in fungal fruiting patterns. *Science*, **316**, 71.

Hickling, R., Roy, D.B., Hill, J.K. Fox, R. and Thomas, C.D. (2006). The distributions of a wide range of taxonomic groups are expanding polewards. *Global Change Biology*, **12**, 450–455

MacLeod, C.D., Pierce, G.J. and Santos, M.B. (2007). Starvation and sandeel consumption in harbour porpoises in the Scottish North Sea. *Biology Letters* **3**, 535–536.

Menzel, A., Sparks, T.H, Estrella, N. *et al.* (2006). European phenological response to climate change matches the warming pattern. *Global Change Biology*, **12**, 1969–1976.

Nekovar, J., Koch, E., Kubin, E. *et al.* (eds.) (2008). *The History and Current Status of Plant Phenology in Europe*, Brussels, COST.

Parmesan, C. and Yohe, G. (2003). A globally coherent fingerprint of climate change impacts across natural systems. *Nature*, **421**, 37–42.

Perring, F.H. and Walters, S.M. (eds.) (1962). *Atlas of the British Flora*, London, Botanical Society of the British Isles.

Perry, A.L., Low, P.J., Ellis, J.R. and Reynolds, J.D. (2005). Climate change and distribution shifts in marine fishes. *Science*, **308**, 1912–1915.

Preston, C.D., Pearman, D.A. and Dines, T.D. (eds.) (2002). *New Atlas of the British and Irish Flora*, Oxford, Oxford University Press.

Rosenzweig, C., Karoly, D., Vicarelli, M. *et al.* (2008). Attributing physical and biological impacts to anthropogenic climate change. *Nature*, **453**, 353–358.

Roy, D.B. and Sparks, T.H. (2000). Phenology of British butterflies and climate change. *Global Change Biology*, **6**, 407–416.

Sparks, T. and Tryjanowski, P. (2007). Patterns of spring arrival dates differ in two hirundines. *Climate Research*, **35**, 159–164.

Sparks, T.H., Collinson, N., Crick, H. *et al.* (2006). *Natural Heritage Trends of Scotland: Phenological Indicators of Climate Change*, Scottish Natural Heritage Commissioned Report No. 167 (ROAME No. F01NB01).

Sparks, T.H., Dennis, R.L.H., Croxton, P.J. and Cade, M. (2007). Increased migration of Lepidoptera linked to climate change. *European Journal of Entomology*, **104**, 139–143.

Sparks, T.H., Roy, D.B. and Dennis R.L.H. (2005). The influence of temperature on migration of Lepidoptera into Britain. *Global Change Biology*, **11**, 507–514.

Sturm, M., Racine, C. and Tape, K. (2001). Climate change: increasing shrub abundance in the arctic. *Nature*, **411**, 546–547.

Thomas, C.D., Cameron, A., Green, R.E. *et al.* (2004). Extinction risk from climate change. *Nature*, **427**, 145–148.

Warren, M.S., Hill, J.K., Thomas, J.A. *et al.* (2001). Rapid responses of British butterflies to opposing forces of climate and habitat change. *Nature*, **414**, 65–69.

3

Agriculture, woodland and semi-natural habitats

Ken Norris

Summary

The extensive forests and woodlands that predominated in the British Isles in pre-Neolithic times have been largely replaced by managed landscapes dominated by agriculture, together with some woodland and remnant areas of other semi-natural habitats such as bogs, heathlands, fens and marshes. Agricultural management intensified significantly since 1945, reducing the value of farmland to wildlife. In response, considerable public funds are currently being spent to encourage farmers to implement agri-environmental management, which is designed to reduce the impact of intensive farming on wildlife. There is a current debate about whether such schemes will work, and uncertainty about how agricultural land use might change in the future. Although much of the British Isles was formerly wooded, by 1900 only 5% of the land surface was woodland. Over the last 50 years, there has been a significant expansion in woodland area, but young- and old-growth habitats remain uncommon. Supporting woodland wildlife into the future will require new approaches that promote the development of diverse woodland habitats. Semi-natural habitats and their wildlife have become increasingly fragmented and isolated within landscapes dominated by agriculture, forestry and urban development. Their future depends on the success of current attempts to restore key habitats. Landscapes in the British Isles are becoming increasingly recognised for the multiple functions they perform, in addition to producing food and timber, which could have important implications for the way we view nature conservation in the future.

Introduction

Historically, the landscapes of the British Isles were very different from those we see today (Rackman 1986). The extensive forests and woodlands that predominated in

Silent Summer: The State of Wildlife in Britain and Ireland, ed. Norman Maclean. Published by Cambridge University Press. © Cambridge University Press 2010.

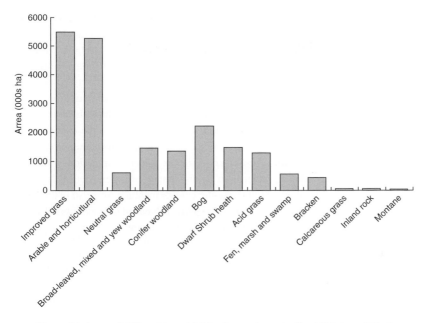

Figure 3.1 Areas of different terrestrial land cover types in Great Britain and Northern Ireland. Data are from the Countryside Survey 2000 (http://www.countrysidesurvey.org. uk/archiveCS2000/).

pre-Neolithic times have been largely replaced by managed landscapes dominated by agriculture, together with some woodland and remnant areas of other semi-natural habitats, such as bogs, heathlands, fens and marshes (Figure 3.1). Agricultural management witnessed a dramatic increase in intensification after 1945, driven by a desire for self-sufficiency in food production, and the influence of European agricultural policy after the UK joined the European Union (EU) in 1973. This intensification resulted in substantial increases in the yields of a range of land-based commodities, but also significant over-production problems in Europe. Policy reform within the EU is in the process of removing production-linked subsidies and encouraging farmers to improve their environmental stewardship through agri-environmental payments. However, serious questions are being asked about the effectiveness of these policies, and, ironically, we may be entering into a new period of intensification due to high commodity prices, food-security concerns and competition for land from non-food crops. Over the same post-war period, woodland area has increased, but the characteristics of woodland have also changed considerably, resulting in a lack of young- and old-growth habitats. Semi-natural habitats have continued to be lost and degraded, but recent projects are beginning to restore them.

These changes illustrate the dynamic nature of landscapes in the British Isles as land use and management responds to a range of social, economic, technological and environmental drivers of change. These changes have a long history. Against this dynamic background, assessing the health of wildlife populations and their habitats is difficult because the answer depends critically on the time period over which any assessment is made. Contemporary landscapes, dominated by managed habitats, are a poor surrogate for the forest and woodlands that pre-dated extensive agriculture. Even in recent history, particular species have expanded their range in response to the expansion of agriculture, only to then decline as production methods became more intensive.

Our assessment of the health of biodiversity in the wider countryside is heavily influenced by recent experience, rather than by any longer-term perspective. In many ways, this parallels the development of the wider environmental movement in the latter part of the twentieth century, which was itself heavily influenced by concerns about the environmental impacts of agriculture brought to public attention by influential texts such as Rachel Carson's *Silent Spring*, published in 1962. It also reflects the availability of long-term monitoring data on the population trends of a range of species, which only date back to the 1960s for birds, and much more recently for other animal and plant groups.

As a result, the current health of biodiversity in the wider countryside is assessed over a 40–50 year time window, from the 1960s onwards. Even though this only represents a small period of time when viewed against the 6500 years of agricultural land-use change in the British Isles, it is the primary driver of current conservation priorities and policies. To reflect these priorities, this chapter takes a modern perspective on the health of biodiversity in relation to agriculture, woodlands and other semi-natural habitats; although it also argues that developing a more flexible vision for conservation is likely to be needed as we consider future changes to landscapes and the multiple functions they perform.

Agriculture

Recent changes in land use and management

Post-war changes in agriculture in the British Isles reflected a drive for improved food security through self-sufficiency (Shrubb 2003). Agricultural landscapes were also heavily influenced over this time period by European agricultural policy, following the UK's entry into the EU in 1973. This brought UK agriculture under the Common Agricultural Policy (CAP), providing production-linked subsidies to farmers. These socio-economic conditions fuelled perhaps the most rapid period of intensification in the history of agriculture in the British Isles.

Arguably, the policies were successful in the sense that agricultural productivity increased substantially after the war. However, the policies also fundamentally altered the way land was used and managed (Vickery *et al.* 2001; Robinson and Sutherland 2002). The diversity of land uses within landscapes was substantially reduced, with a shift from mixed farming systems to increasingly specialised farms based predominantly on arable or pastoral production systems. This specialisation occurred over large scales such that much of eastern Britain is now arable farmland, whereas much of the west is pastoral farmland. At the same time, farm size increased and management became increasingly mechanised and dependent upon chemical inputs (fertilisers and pesticides). Non-farmed habitats, such as hedgerows, also disappeared, as field sizes were expanded to make more efficient use of available land and machinery.

Arable and pastoral production systems also changed. Hay meadows were replaced by intensively managed grasslands, which were cut mechanically several times per season, and which were also fertilised, re-seeded and drained to maximise silage (grass) production. Livestock numbers increased dramatically. Arable crops were sown in the autumn rather than spring, and root crops were increasingly replaced by oil seed rape.

Taken together, these changes mean that agricultural landscapes have changed over the last 50 years from landscapes dominated by numerous small, extensively managed farms with a diverse range of land uses, to landscapes dominated by a much smaller number of intensively managed, specialised farms. Landscapes have become more homogeneous (Benton *et al.* 2003).

The health of farmland biodiversity

How has farmland biodiversity changed over the post-war period in response to these changes in land use and management? The realisation that the post-war intensification of agriculture had potentially important implications for farmland biodiversity in general is relatively recent. In 1995, the British Trust for Ornithology (www.bto. org) published a paper reporting widespread declines and range contractions among lowland farmland birds in Britain (Fuller *et al.* 1995). Prior to this, although population declines and range contractions had been described for several individual farmland bird species with restricted geographical ranges (e.g. Cirl Bunting, *Emberiza cirlus*, Corncrake, *Crex crex*, Stone Curlew, *Burhinus oedicnemus*), no evaluation of the health of bird biodiversity in the wider countryside had been made. This work was very influential in setting the subsequent research and policy agenda for conservation in relation to agriculture, and bird population trends (or the health of farmland bird populations) have become an important part of agricultural sustainability in UK Government policy. The Farmland Birds Index (FBI) was first published in 1998 (Gregory *et al.* 2004). The FBI consists of the population trends of 19 farmland bird species, many of which have shown pronounced recent (since 1970) population declines. The UK Government is pledged to halt and reverse population declines as measured by the FBI by 2020, which is a key target for agricultural sustainability in the UK.

The fact that declines and range contractions among a suite of lowland farmland bird species could be described is a reflection of data availability. The atlas and long-term census data used for the 1995 paper were only available from 1970 onwards. Prior to this, data become increasingly sparse and anecdotal. Nevertheless, attempts have been made to reconstruct the historical ranges of some bird species over a longer period of time, and this reveals a very different picture of change (see Figure 3.2). It seems quite likely that a number of bird species may have benefited from the expansion of extensive agriculture in the British Isles, although historical data prior to the nineteenth century are sparse (Holloway 1995). This is because extensive agriculture was very good at providing their ecological requirements, particularly for nesting and feeding. It is perhaps not surprising that species like the Cirl Bunting subsequently declined in the face of agricultural intensification, because the associated changes in farming almost certainly reduced nesting and food resources. Interestingly, there has been little, if any, real debate between scientists, policy-makers or the public about the implications of a longer-term perspective on conservation priorities and policies. At present, the benchmark for assessing the current health of farmland biodiversity is the 1970s. Whether this is the right benchmark requires further debate, a debate that would benefit from further work on the historical ranges of animal and plant species in the British Isles.

Leaving aside the issue of the time period over which biodiversity health is assessed, the 1995 paper also stimulated new research to understand the causes of farmland bird population declines. This work made use of a range of approaches, but, in broad terms, research involved attempting to link agricultural land use or land-use change to population trends, or more detailed studies that aimed to understand the demographic mechanism (i.e. reduced fecundity or survival) responsible for the population decline. Studies on individual species included a blend of both approaches, and research conducted on the Corncrake (Figure 3.3) has become a classical example of applied conservation science leading to the development of management measures to promote population recovery (Green and Stowe 1993; Green *et al.* 1997).

In contrast to farmland birds, our understanding of the health of other components of farmland biodiversity is much less well developed. This largely reflects the scarcity of large-scale (national), long-term data. Nevertheless, comparable declines have been reported in a range of other animal and plant groups (Robinson and Sutherland 2002; Benton *et al.* 2003; Biesmeijer *et al.* 2006).

Agri-environmental management

It is now widely accepted that post-war agricultural intensification has resulted in widespread biodiversity declines in the British Isles. Having described population declines and range contractions, and developed an understanding of the underlying causes, efforts over the last decade have focused on developing and implementing land-management solutions to promote population recovery (Vickery *et al.* 2004).

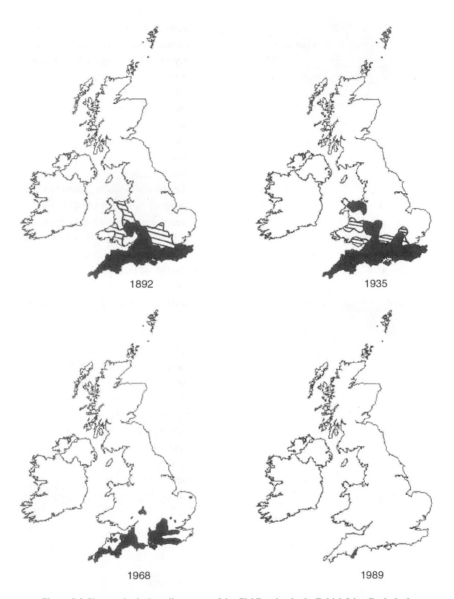

Figure 3.2 Changes in the breeding range of the Cirl Bunting in the British Isles. Dark shading indicates 'present', grey shading 'present, but very local'. The Cirl Bunting was first discovered in Britain in 1800, but probably arrived during the eighteenth century. Its range then expanded in the nineteenth century, only to contract in the twentieth century as agriculture became more intensive. (Redrawn from Evans (1997), *British Birds*, **90**, 267–282.)

(a)

(b)

Figure 3.3 The applied ecology of corncrakes. These birds nest in grass fields, where they become vulnerable to mowing operations (a) that destroy eggs (b) and chicks. Payments to farmers have led to more sympathetic mowing practices and corncrake populations are recovering as a result (see colour plate) (Photos: Glen Tyler, RSPB.)

Management to enhance the value of farmland for biodiversity is being delivered through agri-environmental schemes (AES). These schemes involve Government payments to farmers in return for the uptake of wildlife-friendly land-management options, such as the planting of new hedgerows, uncultivated field margins, or more sympathetic crop management. In England, the primary AES is the Environmental Stewardship (ES) Scheme, which consists of two levels of management – the Entry Level Scheme (ELS) that is designed to introduce basic agri-environmental management to the majority of farms, thereby benefiting biodiversity in general, and the Higher Level Scheme (HLS) that is designed to deliver more targeted management options to species or habitats of high conservation value. ES was introduced in 2005, during which 13 000 agreements covering 1.5 million hectares were established (Butler *et al.* 2007). ES costs about £320 million per annum to implement. Comparable schemes are also being implemented in Scotland, Wales and Northern Ireland.

AES are, however, controversial. There is currently an intense debate in Europe about whether they are effective. There is evidence that carefully designed and targeted measures for specific species of high conservation value can be effective in promoting population recovery (Peach *et al.* 2001), but evidence for general biodiversity benefits are equivocal (Kleijn and Sutherland 2003). The controversy essentially boils down to three main issues: are schemes designed properly, are farmers taking up the right options and is option uptake sufficient to deliver the required biodiversity benefits? For farmland birds in England the answers would be 'yes', 'no' and 'probably not, but we really don't know'. Analysis of the options available under ELS suggests that there are an appropriate range of options available to farmers to deal with most of the ecological problems caused by post-war intensification. However, farmers are not taking up the right blend of options, focusing on implementing hedgerow and margin management, instead of modifying the management of the productive parts of fields (Butler *et al.* 2007). Unless this changes, it is difficult to see how the Government commitment to halting and reversing the decline in farmland bird populations can be achieved, because many of the declining species depend on nest and food resources being available within fields rather than in field margins and hedgerows. Resolving this issue is complicated by the fact that we have little idea about the exact uptake of the management options we need in different landscapes to halt and reverse population declines. Research on the question of 'how much agri-environmental management is enough?' is urgently needed. Making a comparable assessment of AES for biodiversity groups other than farmland birds is severely hampered by rather vague scheme objectives for other groups, and a much poorer understanding of the links between land-use change and populations. Taken together, these issues mean that AES will remain controversial until we clarify the biodiversity objectives and develop an understanding of exactly what needs to be done to achieve these objectives.

The future

Much uncertainty surrounds how agricultural land use might change over the next 10, 20, 50 or 100 years. Recently, fallow land (set aside) has re-entered production, removing a potentially important wildlife habitat. High current commodity prices, concerns about food security and demand for land for the cultivation of renewable energy crops all suggest a renewed drive for higher yields and associated intensive management. Reform of agricultural policy within the EU will affect land-use decisions, as will climate change over the next 50–100 years. To design measures to protect farmland biodiversity within this dynamic environment we need a significant shift in our approach from a reactive one, in which we respond to changes after they have happened, to one in which we plan ahead in response to anticipated future changes. The scientific tools we need to support this forward-looking approach are beginning to emerge (Rounsevell *et al.* 2006), but more work is needed to integrate this work with biodiversity science (Norris 2008). We also need policy-makers and other users to engage with the emerging science in order to plan for a more sustainable future.

Woodland and other semi-natural habitats

Recent changes in habitat areas and management

Although much of the British Isles was formerly wooded, by 1900 only 5% of the land surface was woodland. Over the last 50 years, there has been a significant expansion in woodland area, in both broad-leaved woodland (Hopkins and Kirby 2007) and forestry plantations (Mason 2007). These gross changes in woodland area, however, mask a complex array of ecological changes over the same time period. Broad-leaved woodlands have seen a loss of ancient woodland, but an expansion of younger woodland through planting schemes. Woodland composition has also changed dramatically. In 1947, 21% of broad-leaved woodland was classified as coppice, 28% as scrub and 51% as high forest, whereas by 2002, 97% was classified as high forest (Hopkins and Kirby 2007). The composition and structure of broad-leaved woodlands have also been affected by a range of management changes (e.g. increased grazing pressure, game management) and other factors (e.g. pollution, climate change). Remaining woodlands tend to be fragmented and isolated within wider landscapes dominated by agriculture.

Immediately after the last war, woodland in the British Isles consisted of roughly similar proportions of broad-leaved and conifer woodland (Mason 2007). There then followed a significant expansion of conifer plantations, mainly in the uplands, but also in areas of formerly ancient broad-leaved woodland, so that conifers now represent about two-thirds of the woodland area. These high-forest conifer plantations, like the majority of broad-leaved woodland, have now entered a closed-canopy phase. Taken together, all these changes mean that woodlands in the British Isles today lack young-growth and old-growth habitats (Fuller *et al.* 2007).

Agricultural and forestry land use has had a major direct impact on wildlife in these habitats, but these activities have also profoundly affected the extent and quality of other semi-natural habitats in the British Isles, such as bogs, heaths, fens and marshes. These habitats have declined as land has been converted to agriculture and forestry, as well as to other uses such as urban and transport developments. Over the last two centuries such habitat loss has been significant. For example, only 5% of the 95 000 hectares of lowland raised bog estimated to be present in the 1800s now remains, and only one-sixth of lowland heathland in England is left. The remaining habitat has also been degraded by inappropriate management, such as land drainage, over- and under-grazing by livestock, nutrient enrichment (mainly through agriculture), and changes in burning and cutting regimes. Bog, heath, fen and marsh habitats now make up <20% of the area of terrestrial habitats in the British Isles (see Figure 3.1), and tend to be highly fragmented in the landscape. Nevertheless, the conservation value of these semi-natural habitats is widely recognised, plans have been developed through the UK Biodiversity Action Plan (UKBAP) to protect, manage and restore them (http://www.ukbap.org.uk), and there are ongoing restoration projects aimed at increasing their extent and quality (http://www.rspb.org.uk/reserves/guide/l/lakenheathfen/index.asp).

Biodiversity health

In comparison with farmland birds, concerns about the health of bird biodiversity in woodland are more recent. An index of population trends across a suite of woodland species, similar to the Farmland Birds Index (see above), showed a 20% decline over the last 25 years of the twentieth century, and a number of woodland species have been added to the lists of threatened species over the same time period. Recent large-scale surveys of predominantly broad-leaved woodland have shown a mixed picture of population trends across species (Hewson *et al.* 2007); with some long-distance migrants and woodland specialists showing significant (>25%) declines (Garden Warbler, *Sylvia borin*, Lesser Redpoll, *Carduelis cabaret*, Lesser Spotted Woodpecker, *Dendrocopos minor*, Spotted Flycatcher, *Muscicapa striata*, Tree Pipit, *Anthus trivialis*, Willow Tit, *Poecile montanus*, Willow Warbler, *Phylloscopus trochilus* and Wood Warbler, *P. sibilatrix*), whereas other species, such as the Great Spotted Woodpecker, *Dendrocopos major*, and the Great Tit, *Parus major*, showed significant (>25%) increases. The picture for some species is confused by contrasting trends from different surveys. Nevertheless, it is quite clear that some populations are declining significantly. Attempts to understand the causes of these declines are still in their infancy, but a number of causal factors have been proposed (Fuller *et al.* 2007).

For biodiversity groups other than birds, the overall picture is less clear, due to patchy data. For example, there are changes in the abundance of tree species consistent with observed changes in woodland management, such as apparent declines in coppiced species, such as Sweet Chestnut and Hazel, and a change from Oak/Beech woodland to Ash/Sycamore woodland that probably reflects, in part, the replacement of old-growth with new woodland (Hopkins and Kirby 2007). There is evidence that the loss of young-growth, open habitats in woodlands might be associated with a loss of plant diversity, and population declines in some butterflies (Asher *et al.* 2001). There is also evidence that young- and old-growth woodlands have more distinctive biodiversity than contemporary woodland (Warren and Key 1991).

It must be the case that biodiversity associated with semi-natural habitats in the British Isles has experienced significant range contractions and population declines as habitat has been lost, fragmented and degraded. Historical data on range and abundance are lacking for many taxa and only relatively recent for those that have been well studied (e.g. birds), making it difficult to quantify the actual extent of these past changes. We do know that many species associated with semi-natural habitats are now highly localised in their distribution, and tend to exist in relatively small, isolated populations. Well-known examples include the Marsh Fritillary Butterfly (*Eurodryas aurinia*), Natterjack Toad (*Bufo calamita*) and Bittern (*Botaurus stellaris*). Such populations are particularly vulnerable to extinction, so restoration projects that increase the extent and quality of suitable habitat are particularly important. While much still remains to be done, some populations are showing signs of stability and recovery due to conservation interventions (Buckley and Beebee 2004).

The future

There seems to be a general consensus that policy and management should aim to produce diverse woodlands consisting of a range of growth stages through the restoration, in particular, of young- and old-growth habitats (Fuller *et al.* 2007). Some progress is being made in this direction, although there are challenges to overcome, such as developing financial incentives for appropriate management and addressing over-grazing issues. There is current concern about declines in key tree species (e.g. oak decline; www.forestresearch.gov.uk/fr/INFD-7B3BLF), and uncertainty surrounds the potential future impact of climate change on biodiversity in woodland. There is now compelling evidence that the timing of important events such as tree bud burst is getting earlier in spring, and that this in turn affects insect and bird populations (Visser *et al.* 2006). Whether these phenological changes are detrimental to important populations remains to be seen, although there is evidence that some species can show remarkable flexibility in their response to climate change (Charmantier *et al.* 2008).

The fate of biodiversity associated with semi-natural habitats depends on ongoing attempts to restore these habitats. The success or failure of these attempts will be affected by technical difficulties associated with restoration, financial support for restoration work, and drivers of land-use change in the wider countryside such as agriculture. Uncertainties surround the future impact of particular factors, such as nutrient enrichment from airborne sources and climate change, because it is currently unclear what their impact might be and how they might be managed effectively.

Multi-functional landscapes

The main problem with discussing agriculture, woodlands, forestry or any other semi-natural habitat is that these terms encourage us to consider these land uses in isolation. Government policy, land-management practices and public attitudes also recognise these land-use divisions. It is arguably this rather 'isolationist' view of land use that has been so detrimental to the biodiversity of managed habitats over recent years because management has been targeted very much towards commodity production, such as food, animal feed and timber. Policy and management are increasingly recognising the multi-functional value of land uses and the landscapes within which various land uses are practised. This means recognising that agriculture and forestry practices have implications for biodiversity, natural resource management (e.g. flooding, water quality) and aesthetic value, as well as producing important commodities (Sutherland 2004; Kareiva *et al.* 2007; Norris 2008). Policies have been developed to address issues of multi-functionality. For example, the Environmental Stewardship (ES) scheme (see also above) is not just aimed at enhancing biodiversity on farmland through payments to farmers, but also aims to improve other environmental values.

Almost inevitably, this multi-functional view will generate land-use conflicts because of trade-offs between different objectives. We already know that intensive agriculture, which efficiently produces food and animal feed, has a detrimental impact on biodiversity and other environmental values. We know much less, however, about trade-offs between different environmental values, and this is an area in which further research is needed. Nevertheless, we need to increasingly think of our landscapes as multi-functional ecosystems that consist of a range of managed and semi-natural habitats and that produce a range of ecosystem services (e.g. food, animal feed, timber, biodiversity, flood protection, clean water, aesthetic values) that are important to our wellbeing. We will need to develop land-management strategies for a range of objectives, which could mean, ironically, that we need to spare land for wildlife conservation and resource protection by intensifying production on agriculture land (Green *et al.* 2005). This so-called ecosystems approach will have a profound effect on the research, management and policy agendas over the next decade and beyond.

Concluding remarks

Some conservationists have expressed concern that an ecosystems approach might compromise protection for individual species (Sutherland *et al.* 2008), and perhaps undermine the conservation targets and priorities that have been established. While such compromises are almost inevitable, an ecosystems approach forces us to acknowledge and address the multiple functions our landscapes perform, and to develop solutions to conflicts we identify. We need to increasingly look forward and ask how landscapes are likely to change in the future, what impact changes might have on a range of ecosystem services, including biodiversity, and how change might be managed to achieve specific outcomes. In so doing, it is sobering to recall that landscapes in the British Isles, and its wildlife, have experienced several millennia of change. Against this dynamic background it seems odd to develop rigid conservation priorities and targets based on changes over the last 40–50 years. Instead we need to develop a more flexible approach (in terms of science, policy and practice) that recognises the dynamic nature of landscapes dominated by managed habitats and the multiple functions these landscapes perform.

References

Asher, J., Warren, M., Fox, R. *et al.* (2001). *The Millenium Atlas of Butterflies in Britain and Ireland*, Oxford, Oxford University Press.

Benton, T.G., Vickery, J.A. and Wilson, J.D. (2003). Farmland biodiversity: is habitat heterogeneity the key? *Trends in Ecology and Evolution*, **18**, 182–188.

Biesmeijer, J.C., Roberts, S.P.M., Reemer, M. *et al.* (2006). Parallel declines in pollinators and insect-pollinated plants in Britain and the Netherlands. *Science*, **313**, 351–354.

Buckley, J. and Beebee, T.J.C. (2004). Monitoring the conservation status of an endangered amphibian: the natterjack toad *Bufo calamita* in Britain. *Animal Conservation*, **7**, 221–228.

Butler, S.J., Vickery, J.A. and Norris, K. (2007). Farmland biodiversity and the footprint of agriculture. *Science*, **315**, 381–384.

Charmantier, A., McCleery, R.H., Cole, L.R. *et al.* (2008). Adaptive phenotypic plasticity in response to climate change in a wild bird population. *Science*, **320**, 800–803.

Fuller, R.J., Gregory, R.D., Gibbons, D.W. *et al.* (1995). Population declines and range contractions among lowland farmland birds in Britain. *Conservation Biology*, **9**, 1425–1441.

Fuller, R.J., Smith, K.W., Grice, P.V., Currie, F.A. and Quine, C.P. (2007). Habitat change and woodland birds in Britain: implications for management and future research. *Ibis*, **149**, 261–268.

Green, R.E., Cornell, S.J., Scharlemann, J.P.W. and Balmford, A. (2005). Farming and the fate of wild nature. *Science*, **307**, 550–555.

Green, R.E. and Stowe, T.J. (1993). The decline of the Corncrake *Crex crex* in Britain and Ireland in relation to habitat change. *Journal of Applied Ecology*, **30**, 689–695.

Green, R.E., Tyler, G.A., Stowe, T.J. and Newton, A.V. (1997). A simulation model of the effect of mowing of agricultural grassland on the breeding success of the corncrake (*Crex crex*). *Journal of Zoology*, **243**, 81–115.

Gregory, R.D., Noble, D.G. and Custance, J. (2004). The state of play of farmland birds: population trends and conservation status of lowland farmland birds in the United Kingdom. *Ibis*, **146**, 1–13.

Hewson, C.M., Amar, A., Lindsell, J.A. *et al.* (2007). Recent changes in bird populations in British broadleaved woodland. *Ibis*, **149**, 14–28.

Holloway, S. (1995). *Historical Atlas of Breeding Birds in Britain and Ireland: 1875–1900*, London, T. and A. D. Poyser.

Hopkins, J.J. and Kirby, K.J. (2007). Ecological change in British broadleaved woodland since 1947. *Ibis*, **149**, 29–40.

Kareiva, P., Watts, S., McDonald, R. and Boucher, T. (2007). Domesticated nature: shaping landscapes and ecosystems for human welfare. *Science*, **316**, 1866–1869.

Kleijn, D. and Sutherland, W.J. (2003). How effective are European agri-environment schemes in conserving and promoting biodiversity? *Journal of Applied Ecology*, **40**, 947–969.

Mason, W.L. (2007). Changes in the management of British forests between 1945 and 2000 and possible future trends. *Ibis*, **149**, 41–52.

Norris, K. (2008). Agriculture and biodiversity: opportunity knocks. *Conservation Letters*, **1**, 2–11.

Peach, W.J., Lovett, L.J., Wotton, S.R. and Jeffs, C. (2001). Countryside stewardship delivers Cirl Buntings (*Emberiza cirlus*) in Devon, UK. *Biological Conservation*, **101**, 361–373.

Rackman, O. (1986). *The History of the British Countryside*, London, Dent.

Robinson, R.A. and Sutherland, W.J. (2002). Post-war changes in arable farming and biodiversity in Great Britain. *Journal of Applied Ecology*, **39**, 157–176.

Rounsevell, M.D.A., Reginster, I., Araujo, M.B. *et al.* (2006). A coherent set of future land use change scenarios for Europe. *Agriculture Ecosystems and Environment*, **114**, 57–68.

Shrubb, M. (2003). *Birds, Sythes and Combines*, Cambridge, Cambridge University Press.

Sutherland, W.J. (2004). A blueprint for the countryside. *Ibis*, **146**, 230–238.

Sutherland, W.J., Bailey, M.J., Bainbridge, I.P. *et al.* (2008). Future novel threats and opportunities facing UK biodiversity identified by horizon scanning. *Journal of Applied Ecology*, **45**, 821–833.

Vickery, J.A., Bradbury, R.B., Henderson, I.G., Eaton, M.A. and Grice, P.V. (2004). The role of agri-environment schemes and farm management practices in reversing the decline of farmland birds in England. *Biological Conservation*, **119**, 19–39.

Vickery, J.A., Tallowin, J.R., Feber, R.E. *et al.* (2001). The management of lowland neutral grasslands in Britain: effects of agricultural practices on birds and their food resources. *Journal of Applied Ecology*, **38**, 647–664.

Visser, M.E., Holleman, L.J.M. and Gienapp, P. (2006). Shifts in caterpillar biomass phenology due to climate change and its impact on the breeding biology of an insectivorous bird. *Oecologia*, **147**, 164–172.

Warren, M.S. and Key, R.S. (1991). Woodlands: past, present and potential for insects. In Collins N.M. and Thomas J.A., eds., *The Conservation of Insects and their Habitats*, London, Academic Press, pp. 155–211.

4

Vertebrate animal introductions

Christopher Lever

Summary

Invasive alien species are, after habitat loss, the principal factor in the decline or extinction of native organisms. The Wildlife and Countryside Act 1981 and the Wildlife (Northern Ireland) Order 1985 prohibit the future introduction and release into the wild of non-native species in Britain and Northern Ireland. Corresponding legislation in the Republic of Ireland is the Wildlife Act 1976 and the European Communities (Natural Habitats) Regulations 1997. The European Union Habitats and Species Directive requires member states to restore natural biodiversity, whenever practicable, by reintroducing formerly native species that have become extinct. Whereas, in times past, the practice of introducing exotics was acceptable, now the reintroduction of former native species is seen as the way forward.

Introduction

The impact of invasive alien species on native fauna and flora is, after habitat destruction, the most important factor in the decline or extinction of indigenous organisms. Arguably the most significant single factor affecting introduced species in Britain during the past half century has been the enactment of the Wildlife and Countryside Act 1981. Hitherto, those wishing to release exotic species into the wild had what amounted to virtually a free hand. Section 14 Part I of this Act lays down that:

> (1) Subject to the provisos of this Part, if any person releases or allows to escape into the wild any animal which (a) is of a kind which is not ordinarily resident in and is not a regular visitor to Great Britain in a wild state; or (b) is included in Part I Schedule 9, he shall be guilty of an offence.

Silent Summer: The State of Wildlife in Britain and Ireland, ed. Norman Maclean. Published by Cambridge University Press. © Cambridge University Press 2010.

Schedule 9 lists a total of 42 introduced alien or reintroduced formerly native species (10 mammals, 17 birds, 3 reptiles, 6 amphibians and 6 fish), some of which, after a lapse of nearly 30 years, have either died out naturally or, as in the case of the Coypu, *Myocastor coypus*, have been deliberately eradicated by man. On the other hand, since 1981, several new exotic species have escaped from captivity and have become naturalised in Britain.

The UK government has international obligations to address the problem of introduced species, principally under the provisions of the Convention on Biological Diversity (CBD), the Bern Convention on Conservation of European Wildlife and Habitats and the EU Habitats and Species Directive. In fulfilment of these obligations, *The Review of Non-Native Species Policy*, published by the Department for the Environment, Food and Rural Affairs (DEFRA) in 2003, makes a number of recommendations for controlling invasive species.

Because of the threat they pose to native organisms, the CBD considers that the eradication of alien species is the best management option for mitigating their impact on native biodiversity (Bremner and Park 2007). This is clearly so, but in Britain only two naturalisd mammals have so far been deliberately exterminated – the Muskrat, *Ondatra zibethicus* (1937), and the Coypu, *Myocastor coypus* (1987). A contentious attempt is currently under way to eliminate the Ruddy Duck, *Oxyura jamaicensis*, and a similar policy is under consideration for the Rose-ringed Parakeet, *Psittacula krameri*.

It is generally acknowledged that stakeholder support is fundamental to the success of any conservation project, and this is especially so when something as sensitive as the control or extermination of a species is contemplated – in particular if it is aesthetically attractive.

Not all introduced species, of course, have a negative impact on alien ecosystems. If, however, we wish to conserve the world's biodiversity, we must understand and admit that some naturalised species can, and do, cause ecological harm of one kind or another, and accept that sometimes unpalatable remedial measures have to be taken. Consequently, the control of invasive species has come to be recognised as not simply a scientific issue, but also a social and political one.

A factor that will have a major influence on the future of both alien and native species in Britain is a change in climate caused by global warming as a result of greenhouse-gas emissions resulting from the burning of fossil fuels. Although some introduced (and native) species will benefit from global warming, others will suffer. According to *The Climatic Atlas of European Birds* (2008) and the Intergovernmental Panel on Climate Change, for many species a rise in temperature of only 2 °C (very much less than may occur) will cause often devastating reductions in range, habitats and populations. Species that need a colder climate will be driven north from England to Scotland, while some of those already there will disappear.

The UK Climate Change Bill proposes a reduction in CO_2 emissions of at least 60% by 2050. This target is based on a report by the Royal Commission on Environmental

Pollution in 2000. Since then, developments in the science of climate change show that this target is far too low to avoid the most serious consequences. WWF-UK, the Tyndall Centre for Climate Change Research, the UN Human Development Report 2007/2008 and leading scientists have all made it clear that the government must accept the latest scientific advice that clearly indicates that Britain should aim to reduce its CO_2 emissions by at least 80% by 2050. In October 2008, the Climate Change Secretary, Ed Balls, announced that the government had accepted this advice and would incorporate in the Climate Change Bill an increased target of 80% for the reduction of greenhouse emissions by 2050 (see also Chapter 2).

Mammals

The Rabbit, *Oryctolagus cuniculus*, was introduced to England from southern Europe either by the Normans (reigned 1066–1154) (Lever 1977; Harris and Yalden 2008) or by the succeeding early Plantagenets (Sykes 2007).

The Rabbit was for many years, and in some places still is, the prime agricultural pest in Britain. Prior to the arrival of myxomatosis in 1953, Rabbits caused an estimated £40–50 million of damage annually. Intensive grazing by Rabbits can eradicate valuable grasses and clover, and result in the transformation of ling heathland to grassland, but can maintain large stretches of chalk downland, preventing reversion to scrub. One beneficial result of grazing by Rabbits, after they recovered from myxomatosis some 50 years ago, was the re-establishment of the Large Blue, *Maculinea arion*. This butterfly lays its eggs on Wild Thyme, *Thymus polytrichus*, and egg and larvae survival is best on closely grazed turf where the host ant, *Myrmica sabuleti*, on which the butterfly depends, is most abundant. The recovery of Rabbits restored this optimum habitat, and provided conditions suitable for the Large Blue's reintroduction since 1983. Rabbits also cause damage to a wide range of agricultural crops, including cereals, roots and pasture, and to horticulture and forestry; they eat the bark of young trees and can be a major cause of the failure of woodland generation.

Myxomatosis remains endemic throughout the UK, and when population densities of Rabbits build up it breaks out and reduces local communities. 'The Rabbit remains, or perhaps has recovered its position as, a major pest', Yalden (1999: 263) wrote, 'and could easily be further reduced by novel control techniques, including new diseases. Rabbit Haemorrhagic Disease...was reported in Britain in 1994'.

From an estimated pre-breeding population of around 100 million Rabbits, pre-myxomatosis, the number fell to about 1 million in 1959 and was only 20 million in 1986; a decade later it had recovered to only some 37.5 million, and the distribution pattern had changed considerably. Whereas before myxomatosis 94% of cultivatable land was infested by Rabbits, by 1970 the figure was only 20%. When predators are common there is evidence that, with the help of recurrences of albeit now less virulent strains of myxomatosis (to which some populations may be acquiring a degree of immunity), Rabbits can to some extent be controlled (Harris and Yalden 2008).

The future of the Rabbit in the UK is difficult to assess, but at least in the near future we are unlikely to see a return to pre-myxomatosis numbers or to the same extent of agricultural damage.

The earliest documented introduction of the Grey Squirrel, *Sciurus carolinensis*, from North America was in 1876, to Macclesfield in Cheshire. Following a series of later introductions the species rapidly became established in parts of southern England, and by 1970 was widespread in southern, central and parts of northern England, Wales and the southern uplands of Scotland. By the turn of the century the total British population was around 2.5 million.

As the Grey Squirrel has continued to advance, so has the range of the native Red Squirrel, *S. vulgaris*, contracted. In coniferous woodland (the Red Squirrel's favoured habitat) both species can exist sympatrically, whereas in the Grey Squirrel's preferred environment, deciduous forest, the alien is pre-eminent. The reasons for this remain uncertain, but may be connected with diet – the Grey Squirrel feeds largely on acorns and beech mast, whereas the latter prefers the cones of Scots Pine, *Pinus sylvestris*, and Larch, *Larix decidua/kaempferi*. A major factor in the Red Squirrel's decline in recent years has been the parapoxvirus which causes high mortality in Red Squirrels, and was introduced by Grey Squirrels, in which it is relatively harmless. There is a real potential for the rapid spread of the virus and a correspondingly rapid decline in the Red Squirrel population. The growth rate of young Red Squirrels is slightly lower in the presence of Grey Squirrels, and the former's recruitment of young into the population is thus reduced. Furthermore, the reproductive success of female Red Squirrels may be slightly lessened in summer in the presence of Grey Squirrels, and the larger Grey Squirrel steals the seed food caches of Red Squirrels in winter and spring (Gurnell and Mayle 2003). The Red Squirrel, however, remains widely distributed in many parts of Scotland, e.g. the Borders and Highlands, and it is important to continue to exclude Grey Squirrels from these and similar areas.

Other ecological and economic impacts caused by Grey Squirrels include damage to amenity and commercial woodland by bark stripping, by damaging some tree species more than others, altering the composition of the canopy, and by seed consumption preventing natural tree regeneration; this can also reduce the food resources of a variety of seed-eating woodland birds and such mammals as the threatened Hazel Dormouse, *Muscardinus avellanarius*. Grey (and Red) Squirrels also take the eggs and young of a variety of nesting birds, though the impact of this, other than locally, is uncertain. Damage by Grey Squirrels to arable and fruit crops, garden plants (in particular corms, bulbs and newly sown seed) can be a local problem.

The eradication of Grey Squirrels in Britain (except perhaps on offshore islands such as Anglesey) is no longer practicable, and in any case would incur much opposition. Control and containment can be achieved by trapping, by poisoning with Warfarin (so long as Red Squirrels are absent) and shooting. The development of an immunocontraceptive, currently under review, may be a long-term solution, and would be more acceptable on humanitarian grounds.

The future of the Red Squirrel may depend on the management of coniferous woodlands to encourage the native species and discourage the invasive. This, coupled with targeted control of Grey Squirrel immigration, may be the way forward (Gurnell and Mayle 2003). Of vital importance is the continued exclusion of Grey Squirrels from the last strongholds of the Red Squirrel, such as the Isle of Wight, Brownsea and Furzey Islands in Poole Harbour, Dorset, and the old Caledonian pine forests of the Scottish Highlands.

American Mink, *Mustela vison*, that had escaped from fur farms were first reported to be breeding in the wild on the River Teign, near Moretonhampstead in Devon, in 1956. From the late 1960s, the population increased explosively and became naturalised throughout most of southern Devon. By the 1970s, Mink occurred in nearly every English, and in most Scottish and Welsh, counties. Shortly thereafter, Mink became established on Lewis in the Outer Hebrides, an island previously free of terrestrial predators.

The Mink is a generalist carnivore, feeding mainly on small mammals and riverine birds (e.g. Coots, *Fulica atra*, and Moorhens, *Gallinula chloropus*) and fish. Among the Mink's prey is the Water Vole, *Arvicola terrestris*, and research has shown a strong correlation between the presence of Mink and an absence of Water Voles. The Water Vole has suffered the most rapid and serious decline of any British mammal in the twentieth century, and is now one of our most threatened species; human activities have contributed to the serious decline of the Water Vole, but predation by Mink has almost certainly been the principal factor (Harris and Yalden 2008).

Studies of seabirds on the west coast of Scotland in places infested by Mink have revealed startling declines in the populations of such colonially nesting species as Common Terns, *Sterna hirundo*, Black-headed Gulls, *Larus ridibunda*, and Common Gulls, *L. canus*.

It was at one time feared that the Mink would out-compete and prevent the re-establishment of the native Otter, *Lutra lutra*. In fact, the reverse seems to have been the case; Otters are almost exclusively piscivores, so there is only limited competition between the two species (Yalden 1999) and in recent years there has been a noticeable decrease in the Mink population where the two species overlap. In the early 1990s the pre-breeding population of Mink may have been in excess of 110000 – by the turn of the century it had fallen to around 40 000. Mink are, however, continuing to spread in East Anglia and North Yorkshire, and through the Hebridean islands. 'The machair and blackland habitats on the Uists and Benbecula', wrote Macdonald (2003: 48), 'are amongst the most important wader breeding grounds in Europe. Machair, a shell-enriched sand dune habitat, is itself one of the rarest habitats in Europe... The arrival of the carnivorous American mink has drastically altered the "predator-free" status of the islands and, many fear, threatens the future of ground-nesting birds ...'.

The survival in Britain of the Water Vole and that of waders on islands in western Scotland depends largely on the successful control of Mink. To achieve this, Scottish Natural Heritage was recently awarded a grant of £1.65 million by the EU to eradicate Mink in the Outer Hebrides. Early unpublished reports are encouraging. On the British mainland, if Otters continue to increase, Mink are likely to continue to decline. Aleutian Disease, caused by an uncontrollable parvovirus, has been identified in naturalised Mink populations in the UK; unfortunately, while it might help to reduce the Mink population, it also infects other species, including mustelids, such as Otters and Polecats, *Mustela putorius*. The latter seems to be spreading back into England from its stronghold in Wales, but Aleutian Disease, if it were to become widespread in Mink, could become a serious threat to these two recovering native species (Macdonald 2003).

Of the six species of deer presently living in the wild in Britain only two, the Red Deer, *Cervus elaphus*, and the Roe Deer, *Capreolus capreolus*, are natives.

A large form of Fallow Deer, *Dama dama clactoniana*, occurred in Britain during the Hoxonian period, some 250 000 years BP. The present form, *Dama dama*, was introduced to England by the Normans during the eleventh century, and is now widely distributed in parts of southern and central England. The 1990s population was *c.* 100 000.

The Sika Deer, *Cervus nippon*, was first introduced in 1860 to Powerscourt in Ireland, which subsequently became the source of translocations to the British mainland. In the last 30 years, as a result of additional habitat created by newly maturing conifer plantations, Sika have greatly extended their range in England, Ireland and especially Scotland (Harris and Yalden 2008). The English and Scottish population in the 1990s was *c.* 11 500, and is now perhaps 23 000, with a further 20 000–25 000 in Ireland.

The Chinese or Reeves's Muntjac, *Muntiacus reevesi*, was first introduced, to Woburn Park in Bedfordshire, in the early twentieth century. It was not until the 1930s and 1940s, however, when further introductions were made in Northamptonshire, Warwickshire, Oxfordshire and on the Norfolk/Suffolk border, that the species became well established, and during the past half century it has been steadily expanding its range westwards and south into Kent. The Muntjac's 1990s population was *c.* 40 000 and is now thought to be > 100 000.

The Chinese Water Deer, *Hydropotes inermis*, was also introduced to Woburn Park in the early twentieth century. Today it remains confined mainly to the wetlands of Cambridgeshire and Norfolk. Its population in the 1990s was *c.* 650, and is now believed to be around 1500. Unlike the other introduced deer, the Chinese Water Deer has proved to be a relatively harmless addition to the British fauna.

For much of the data on the impact of Fallow, Sika and Muntjac in Britain I am indebted to Mayle (2003).

Heavy grazing and browsing by deer causes a reduction in tall growing herbs and ferns (apart from Bracken, *Pteridium aquilinum*) and an increase in grasses and lower growing species.

The most biologically rich woodlands are usually small, ancient and semi-natural ones, many of which have been traditionally managed by coppicing. Large numbers of these woods are favoured by Fallow and Muntjac, and the regrowing coppice stools are vulnerable to browsing for up to the first five years. Deer browsing also affects shrub and ground flora, especially Bramble, *Rubus fruiticosus*. Several rare or nationally important species associated with coppiced woodland are susceptible to browsing by deer, such as the Early Purple Orchid, *Orchis mascula*, Greater Butterfly Orchid, *Platanthera chlorantha*, and Oxlip, *Primula elatior*, as well as some more common ones. In some localities, Sika Deer have caused serious damage in agriculture, commercial forestry and native woodlands.

The impact of deer on woodland flora can also affect other animals; browsing by deer on Honeysuckle, *Lonicera periclymenum*, for example, reduces the preferred low egg-laying sites of the White Admiral butterfly, *Limentis (Ladoga) camilla*.

Intensive grazing by Fallow Deer and Muntjac can result in a reduction in the species variety and numbers of associated small mammals, such as the Wood Mouse, *Apodemus sylvaticus*, and Bank Vole, *Myodes (Clethrionomys) glareolus*.

A reduction in the understorey of woodlands can also adversely affect those woodland birds that depend on it for breeding and foraging.

Defoliation by Muntjac of Bramble and other shrubs in winter can adversely affect both native Roe Deer and introduced Chinese Water Deer by reducing the amount of winter browse, and a high density of Muntjac may lead to the exclusion of the other two species.

Hybridisation between Sika and native Red Deer tends to occur most frequently where colonising stags attempt to infiltrate land already occupied by the other species. Most of these contacts have occurred in northern and western Scotland, and it seems probable that on the Kintyre Peninsula in Argyllshire complete genetic and phenotypic introgression is likely, as has already occurred in Co. Wicklow in Ireland. Sika Deer have a higher breeding rate and reach higher densities than Red Deer. To try to maintain the genetic integrity of Red Deer in Scotland, the Deer Commission for Scotland has recommended the rigorous control of Sika Deer wherever they occur, and it is illegal to introduce them to islands where Red Deer are found.

Birds

The naturalised bird that has undoubtedly caused the most ecological and economic harm in Britain is the Greater Canada Goose, *Branta canadensis*, a native of much of North America.

The earliest reference to the species in Britain was during the reign (1660–85) of Charles II, who had some in his collection in St James's Park in London.

As late as the 1940s, Greater Canada Geese occurred principally only in parks and lakes of large private estates in England. By the 1970s, however, partly as a result of translocations by man, the species had also become established on reservoirs, flooded gravelpits, rural meres, urban lakes in public parks, marshes and slowly flowing rivers.

Between 1989 and 2000, the British population of Greater Canada Geese increased by a staggering 166% (an average rate of 9.3% p.a.). The latest estimate is a total of around 90 000 individuals. The increase has occurred principally in places where the population density was low, especially in near-waterless lowland habitats. There seems no reason why both the numbers and distribution of Greater Canada Geese should not continue to expand until all suitable habitats have been occupied.

The ecological and economic impact of Greater Canada Geese has been summarised by Watola *et al.* (1996).

On agricultural land, the birds are recognised as a significant, if local, pest. They tend to remain on good feeding sites for a long period of time, which leads to cumulative damage to pastures and crops, especially those near water. Damage can also be caused by over-grazing such crops as cereals, oilseed rape and sugar-beet. Spring pasturage can also be adversely affected by trampling, grazing and fouling.

In urban and rural localities, parks, golf courses and other amenity areas can also be damaged by fouling, trampling and overgrazing. Footpaths may become slippery and dangerous to the public, and the birds' faeces may contain pathogens that pose a hazard to human health.

Greater Canada Geese also contribute to the eutrophication of those waters on which they occur, and the increase in nutrients caused by their droppings can promote the formation of algal blooms that produce toxins. The birds also eat the young shoots and submerged rhizomes of the Common Reed Mace, *Phragmites australis*, and willows, *Salix* spp., causing river-bank erosion.

Greater Canada Geese may compete with native waterfowl for food, and nesting and roosting sites. Anecdotal evidence suggests that, by sheer weight of numbers, they may drive away ducks and Mute Swans, *Cygnus olor*, and can compete for grazing with Eurasian Wigeon, *Anas penelope*. On the other hand, the geese give these and other species early warning of potential predators and, by uprooting submerged vegetation, make it available to dabbling ducks.

Where they occur near major airfields, their size, weight and tendency to congregate in large flocks make Greater Canada Geese a threat to air traffic.

The methods of controlling Greater Canada Geese include culling adults, reducing reproductive output and behaviour modification. The species is partially protected under the Wildlife and Countryside Act 1981, so that although during the shooting season Greater Canada Geese may be legitimately shot, control outside the shooting season can only be done legally under licence.

Short-term control is usually achieved by shooting the adults in the shooting season or rounding them up during the moult, when they are flightless, in early July. Shooting has the disadvantage of encouraging survivors to move elsewhere, thus spreading the population even more widely into urban areas where shooting is impossible, and of driving away non-target species. Culling during the moult, which is the most humane way of lowering the number of adults, and shooting both have the disadvantage of attracting public opposition.

In the absence of techniques for the chemical or immunological sterilisation of Greater Canada Geese (which are currently being researched), control of reproduction can be achieved either by shooting adults on the nest (an emotive solution likely to be unacceptable to the public) or by the substitution of real eggs with imitation ones. Alternatively, the eggs can be pricked, hard-boiled, or coated with liquid paraffin which kills the embryo, before returning them to the nest. This method has the advantage of being seemingly more acceptable to the general public.

Methods of influencing the birds' behaviour include relocation, scaring, exclusion, habitat modification and the use of chemical repellents.

Of these techniques, relocation tends to result in the formation of new sub-populations in hitherto uncolonised areas, or the return of the birds to the site of origin. Scaring by an auditory or visual contrivance is generally unsuccessful in the long term, since the birds quickly become used to the stimuli produced.

Among chemical repellents, methyl anthranilite is both non-toxic to man and biodegradable, and is known to repel geese, but is only effective in the short term.

All these current methods of reducing the population of Greater Canada Geese in Britain are likely to prove, at best, a short-term palliative measure rather than a long-term solution.

No other alien bird species has caused such controversy during the past 50 years as the Ruddy Duck, *Oxyura jamaicensis*, a native of North America, the West Indies and western South America.

Since the founder stock escaped from the then Wildfowl Trust at Slimbridge in Gloucestershire in 1952–53, the species has thrived and spread, and by the 1990s, when the population of over 3400 included some 570 breeding pairs, the birds had been recorded in most English counties as far north as Yorkshire, though the principal concentrations were in Cheshire, Greater Manchester, Yorkshire and the West Midlands (Lever 2009). In Scotland, by the early 1990s Ruddy Ducks had become regular breeders on Tayside in Perthshire and in Fife. In Wales, Anglesey became one of their main British strongholds; in Ireland, Ruddy Ducks are centred on Co. Wexford and in Ulster.

The impact of British Ruddy Ducks in Europe (especially Spain) is one of the most contentious issues among conservationists, polarising opinions of laymen and scientists alike.

Ruddy Ducks had not been recorded in Europe before the species became naturalised in Britain; by the early 1990s it had been reported in European countries as far east as the Ukraine. Soon after Ruddy Ducks first appeared in Spain in 1973, concern was expressed about the potential impact, through hybridisation, on the closely related and threatened native White-headed Duck, *Oxyura leucocephala*.

Since Ruddy Ducks, almost certainly mainly, if not exclusively, from Britain, began to appear in any numbers in Europe in the 1980s, controversy has raged about the need to 'control' (i.e. eradicate) the species in Britain in order to protect the population of White-headed Ducks in Spain, where the Ruddy Duck was first reported as breeding in 1991, when hybrids with White-headed were also recorded.

At a conference in March 1993 it was resolved to control the number and distribution of Ruddy Ducks in the Western Palearctic in order to safeguard the future of the White-headed Duck.

Walton (2001) has outlined the case for the prosecution.

Habitat destruction and over-shooting reduced the Spanish population of White-headed Ducks to only 22 individuals in the 1970s, but as a result of conservation measures it had recovered to several hundred breeding pairs by the turn of the century, and hybridisation with Ruddy Ducks from Britain has been identified as the principal threat to its survival.

Ruddy Ducks and White-headed Ducks only occur in the wild sympatrically as a result of intervention by man. Because of different mating strategies, in mixed populations the former will always dominate the latter; thus Ruddy Duck genes pass relatively quickly into the White-headed Duck population, with a consequent loss of genetic factors that make the latter a distinct species; such introgression can eventually result in the loss of the weaker species and the survival only of the dominant one. There seems no apparent reason why the above process should not occur in hybridising Ruddy Ducks and White-headed Ducks.

Gibson (2001) puts the case equally persuasively for the defence.

Although the Ruddy Duck and White-headed Duck are known to be capable of producing fertile hybrid offspring, there is no clear idea of the repercussions that this would cause in the wild. If both species share a common ancestor, and the White-headed Duck evolved millions of years ago and became especially adapted to the Eurasian environment, is it not more likely to survive as a species than either hybrids or pure Ruddy Ducks? It is possible that Ruddy Ducks would never establish a viable breeding population within the range of the White-headed Duck, and that Ruddy Ducks and their hybrid offspring would always be a minority of the 'super-species' population.

Perhaps an even more likely scenario is that after an initial period of colonisation by Ruddy Ducks, with some degree of hybridization, the position would stabilise and both species would survive intact allopatrically. Alternatively, if White-headed Ducks were to die out as a result of introgression, might not evolution result in the Ruddy Duck in Europe eventually becoming genetically distinct from Ruddy Ducks in North America? Evidence already exists, says Gibson, that European Ruddy Ducks have developed diagnostic DNA differences from their American ancestors, so that they may be already worthy of conservation in their own right.

The belief that, if unchecked, the Ruddy Duck would overwhelm the White-headed Duck is based on the prediction that Ruddy Duck genes will continue to flow into the White-headed Duck population; this theory is in turn based on the presumption that if uncontrolled, the British Ruddy Duck population will continue to increase. There is also reason to believe, says Gibson, that the British Ruddy Duck population may already be near its maximum sustainability level. (With plenty of apparently suitable habitat as yet uncolonised, this must be at least debatable.)

Thus, the sole justification for controlling Ruddy Ducks in Britain is as a precautionary measure to protect the White-headed Duck abroad. But is this a serious biodiversity problem? If the latter species were to become extinct, it would be extremely unfortunate, but equally the same could be said if the Ruddy Duck were to die out in Britain at the hands of man. Might it not be more practical and feasible for the Spanish (and, if necessary, other foreign authorities) to shoot immigrant Ruddy Ducks after their arrival? Most Ruddy Ducks disperse to Europe in winter, so there would be ample time for their removal before the breeding season. By shooting Ruddy Ducks in Britain, however, we would be losing an attractive and, to many people, a welcome addition to the British avifauna.

In 1998, the British government created the Ruddy Duck Task Force, which found that control was feasible and, by local trials, that shooting was the most effective method, and this policy is supported by the Royal Society for the Protection of Birds (RSPB). The policy of the RSPB Scotland on the Ruddy Duck includes the following statement:

> RSPB Scotland wishes to see the survival of *both* [their italics] the white-headed duck and the ruddy duck. To achieve this, there is an urgent need to reduce the UK population of ruddy ducks to a level at which birds are not spreading to continental Europe and threatening the white-headed duck.

Since, however, Ruddy Ducks from Britain began to appear on the continent from 1965, when the British population numbered only around 10 pairs, to reduce the British population 'to a level at which birds are not spreading to continental Europe' appears impossible. Only *eradication* of Ruddy Ducks in Britain will achieve this objective – something the RSPB and some other conservation organisations seem reluctant to acknowledge.

In 2005, a five-year project, costing in total £3.34 million and funded jointly by the Department for Environment, Food and Rural Affairs (DEFRA) and the European Commission, was announced to deal with the perceived threat posed to White-headed Ducks by Ruddy Ducks, whose then British population numbered around 4400. This eradication campaign, which is scheduled to last until August 2010, has resulted in a huge fall in the UK Ruddy Duck population.

Rose-ringed Parakeets, *Psittacula krameri*, natives of parts of the Sahel, Pakistan, India, Sri Lanka and southeastern China, first escaped or were released by aviculturists in the late 1960s. Perhaps surprisingly, the birds flourished and soon became established, especially in the southern suburbs of London. Between 1994 and 2006, the population increased by an extraordinary 302%, and by the latter year, the birds were said to be present in every London borough. The current annual rate of increase is around 30%. Estimates of the present population in southeast England vary from 6000 pairs to 30 000 individuals. One pandemonium (the apt collective term for parrots) that roosts in Hersham near Esher in Surrey is estimated to number some 7000 birds. Predictions of the population by the end of the decade vary from 50 000–100 000.

Rose-ringed Parakeets in Britain nest mainly in holes in trees made by woodpeckers (Picidae) or in the previous nest cavities of several other species, and because they are early breeders they compete advantageously with native birds for prime nesting sites.

In orchards, Rose-ringed Parakeets have caused damage to the buds and mature fruit of, especially, apples, pears and plums – they are wasteful feeders as they tend to spoil fruit by taking only one or two pecks before moving on. Two of the crops most seriously affected in India, Maize, *Zea mays*, and Sunflowers, *Helianthus annus*, are being increasingly grown in Britain.

Rose-ringed Parakeets also pose a potential human health risk through psittacosis – a contagious avian disease caused by chlamydiae and transmissible (especially by parrots) to man as a form of pneumonia.

In March 2007, DEFRA and the RSPB commissioned the Central Science Laboratory to assess the potential threat posed by Rose-ringed Parakeets in Britain.

The control of Rose-ringed Parakeets would inevitably be a bone of contention between those who value the presence of this attractive bird in their gardens, and conservationists and those whose livelihoods depend on the land. Whatever means of eradication were chosen, they would be likely to upset many stakeholders, and coupled

Figure 4.1 First introduced to Britain c. 1874, the Little Owl is the only naturalised vertebrate that is of practical benefit to man (see colour plate). (Jill Pakenham/BTO.)

with the potential danger to the public, might prove unacceptable. Severe winters, such as that of 1986, which eliminated the Merseyside and Manchester sub-populations, might cause a reduction in the countrywide population, but have not occurred since 1989.

The Little Owl, *Athene noctua*, a native of much of the Palaearctic, was first successfully introduced to England from continental Europe in about 1874. Between about 1900 and 1930 its spread was little short of explosive, and by the latter date it occurred in every county south of the Humber. Subsequently the rate of expansion slowed, and it was not until the 1950s that the Scottish border counties were reached.

The Little Owl is a true *rara avis* in that of all naturalised vertebrates in Britain it is the only one that is of practical benefit to man; the bulk of the species' diet consists of injurious insects and other invertebrates.

The main limiting factor in the spread of the Little Owl in Britain is its inability to withstand prolonged hard winters; relatively few pairs breed above 300 m, which explains the species' absence from the Cambrian Mountains of central Wales, the English Lake District of Cumbria, northern and western Wales, the northern Pennines, the North Yorkshire moors and upland regions of Devon and Cornwall. The Little Owl is one of the species likely to benefit from global warming; a relatively modest increase would enable it to colonise suitable habitats in many of the above regions, and also to spread further north than its present limit in Scotland (Lever, 2009).

Reptiles and amphibians

Most of the reptiles and amphibians currently naturalised in Britain – mainly in southern England – are at or near the northern limit of their natural range. A rise in temperature of only 2 °C as a result of global warming (it could in fact be very much more) would enable them to become more firmly established (Lever, 2009). Amphibians, especially, are sensitive to alterations in spring temperatures, since raised temperatures advance their breeding season. This can increase reproductive success, which may in turn raise population densities to a level at which it stimulates emigration and thus an expansion of range; indeed, this spread is already occurring in the case of three naturalised water frog species – the Marsh Frog, *Rana ridibunda*, the Edible Frog, *R.* kl. *esculenta*, and the Pool Frog, *R. lessonae*. On the other hand, early drying out of breeding pools, which affected Natterjack Toads, *Bufo calamita,* in the drought years of the early 1970s, could reduce populations.

An extremely serious threat to the survival of amphibians worldwide (including the UK) is the recent emergence of the pathogenic, virulent and highly transmissible fungus, *Batrachochytrium dendrobatidis*, which causes cutaneous chytridiomycosis, resulting in a high rate of mortality among infected individuals. It was first discovered in the UK in 2004 in an introduced population of American Bullfrogs, *Rana catesbeiana*, at Cowden on the Sussex/Kent border. It seems improbable that the infection will remain confined to southeast England, and it may well spread into native British amphibians over a wide geographical area. The fungus has already caused numerous amphibian fatalities worldwide, and were it to become widely disseminated and endemic in Britain, it could have a catastrophic effect on native amphibians (Cunningham *et al.* 2005). Research is currently under way in the UK into means of combating this devastating disease.

The most firmly established alien reptile species in Britain are the Wall Lizard, *Podarcis muralis*, the Western Green Lizard, *Lacerta bilineata*, and the Aesculapian Snake, *Zamensis longissimus*; the first of these occurs naturally on Jersey in the Channel Islands, as also does the Green Lizard, *Lacerta viridis*, which has been unsuccessfully released in southern England (see also Chapter 19).

Fish

One of the naturalised fish species that has spread most widely since its introduction, from Germany to Woburn Abbey in Bedfordshire in 1878, and the one that has arguably had the greatest impact, is the Zander or Pike-Perch, *Sander lucioperca*.

Subsequent introductions of the species were made in the twentieth century, one of the largest being in 1963 when 97 Zander from Woburn were placed in the Great Ouse Relief Channel in Norfolk. This resulted in the rapid colonisation of the fenland river systems of the Great Ouse, Nene and Welland. In 1976 it was found that Zander had been released in waters in the catchment areas of the Rivers Severn and Trent (notably in Coombe Abbey Lake, Coventry) and the Midlands canals. Despite the provision of the Wildlife and Countryside Act 1981 and the subsequent Import of Live Fish Act, Zander are continuing to be spread illegally by sport anglers in East Anglia, the west Midlands and southern England (Davies *et al.* 2004).

In the early 1970s it became apparent that there was a poor recruitment to cyprinid stocks in waters occupied by Zander compared with unoccupied waters, with a consequent imbalance in the predator/prey relationship. Control by electrofishing and chlorination and dechlorination of infested waters helps to prevent further natural expansion of the species' range. On the other hand, the Zander has become a popular and valuable sporting quarry.

The two most recent additions to the British icthyofauna are the Sunbleak, *Leucaspius delineatus*, of continental Europe and Russia and the Topmouth Gudgeon, *Pseudorasbora parva*, of eastern Asia. Both species first appeared in Britain in the mid-1980s, having been imported by an ornamental-fish farmer near Romsey in Hampshire.

Initial dispersal of Sunbleak is believed to have been via the River Test to Broadlands, from where they were spread by human agency to Stoneham Lakes in the Itchen Valley. In 1990, Sunbleak appeared in the Kings Sedgmoor Drain in Somerset, from where they soon spread and are now very common in drains, rivers and watercourses of the

Somerset Levels; they also occur in some adjacent stillwaters and in angling lakes near Sherborne in Dorset. Again, dispersal is likely to have been made by man.

Topmouth Gudgeon were first reported in the wild in Britain in 1996, the fish having dispersed naturally from a farm near Romsey to Tadburn Lake, a tributary of the River Test, and through human agency to an ornamental pond in High Wycombe in Buckinghamshire, and to other ponds in Staffordshire, Cumbria, Cheshire and Epping Forest, Essex and elsewhere.

The future dispersal of both species is likely to be anthropogenically, and Pinder and Gozlan (2003: 81) 'predict that the invasive capabilities [of *P. parva*] will result in Topmouth Gudgeon becoming widespread and very abundant throughout Britain'. Although both species provide food for predatory fishes, they also themselves prey on the eggs and larvae of large native and introduced (e.g. Zander) species and compete for food and refugia with smaller ones. In Europe, *P. parva* acts as a vector for such parasites as *Anguillicola crassus* and *Clinostomum complanatum* and as a carrier of Pike fry rhabdovirus (PFR).

Reintroductions

Article 22 of the EEC Council Directive 92/43/EEC (the 'Habitats' Directive') requires member states, whenever practicable, to seek to restore their biodiversity by the reintroduction of formerly native species that have died out. There is thus an important difference between the undesirable introduction of alien species and the desirable *re*introduction of formerly native species that have disappeared. Successful reintroductions of extinct native species include the Red Kite, *Milvus milvus* (deliberately released in England, Scotland and Ireland since 1989) and the White-tailed Eagle, *Haliaeetus albicilla*, (deliberately released in Scotland and Ireland since 1975); there is a proposal to release the latter also in parts of eastern England.

Of previous reintroductions, the Western Capercaillie, *Tetrao urogallus*, whose chick survival rate is poor in damp conditions, would be likely to die out if global warming with wetter summers were to continue. Within the next 50 years, Red Kites are likely to have become widespread again in many parts of Britain, including urban localities where, in medieval times, they were valuable scavengers. Similarly, the White-tailed Eagle should be restored to much of its former coastal Scottish and Irish habitats and also in parts of East Anglia.

Experimental reintroductions are currently being made with European Beavers, *Castor fiber*, in Knapdale in Argyll and with Great Bustards, *Otis tarda*, on Salisbury Plain in Wiltshire. Beavers have been successfully reintroduced to several European countries where, however, demographic conditions are very different from those in overcrowded Britain. Common Cranes, *Grus grus*, are due to be released on the Somerset Levels in autumn 2010, and there is a possibility of the reintroduction of the Burbot, *Lota lota*, to its former habitats in eastern England. Other proposed reintroductions,

Figure 4.2 The Red Kite has been widely and successfully reintroduced in England, Scotland and Ireland, and by 2050 is likely to be widely established (see colour plate). (Jill Pakenham/BTO.)

some perhaps more practical than others, involve the Grey Wolf, *Canis lupus*, the Lynx, *Lynx lynx*, the Brown Bear, *Ursus arctos*, and the Elk, *Alces alces*.

As Yalden (1999: 272) concludes, 'To restore something like the full magnificence of the European fauna to at least a small part of these islands would be an appropriate target for the next millenium.'

Acknowledgements

To Professor Norman Maclean, Professor Colin Galbraith and Dr Derek Yalden for their valuable comments.

References

Bremner, A. and Park, K. (2007). Public attitudes to the management of invasive non-native species in Scotland. *Biological Conservation,* **139**, 306–314.

Cunningham, A.A., Garner, T.W.J., Aguiler-Sanchez, V. *et al.* (2005). Emergence of amphibian chytridiomycosis in Britain. *Veterinary Record,* **157**, 386–387.

Davies, C., Shelley, J., Harding, P. *et al.* (2004). *Freshwater Fishes in Britain: The Species and Their Distribution*, Colchester, Essex, Harley Books.

Gibson, I. (2001). Controlling ruddy ducks – the case against. *Glasgow Naturalist,* **23** (Supplement), 99–102.

Gurnell, J. and Mayle, B. (2003). Ecological impacts of the alien Grey Squirrel (*Sciurus carolinensis*) in Britain. In Poland Bowen, C., ed., *Conference Proceedings of The Mammals Trust UK and Kent Mammal Group*, London, People's Trust for Endangered Species/Mammals Trust UK, 40–45.

Harris, S. and Yalden, D.W. (eds.) (2008). *Mammals of the British Isles: Handbook*, 4th edition, London, The Mammal Society.

Lever, C. (1977). *The Naturalized Animals of the British Isles*, London, Hutchinson.

Lever, C. (2009). *The Naturalized Animals of Britain and Ireland*, London, New Holland.

Macdonald, D. (2003). American mink and ethics of extinction. In Poland Bowen, C., ed., *Conference Proceedings of the Mammals Trust and Kent Mammal Group*, London, People's Trust for Endangered Species/Mammals Trust UK, 46–48.

Mayle, B. (2003). The impact of introduced deer on the natural environment. In Poland Bowen, C., ed., *Conference Proceedings of the Mammals Trust UK and Kent Mammal Group*, London, People's Trust for Endangered Species/Mammals Trust UK, 49–52.

Pinder, A.C. and Gozlan, R.E. (2003). Sunbleak and Topmouth Gudgeon – two new additions to Britain's freshwater fishes. *British Wildlife* (December), 77–83.

Sykes, N. (2007). *The Norman Conquest: A Zooarchaeological Perspective*, BAR International Series 1656, Oxford, Archeopress.

Walton, P. (2001). The ruddy duck and the white-headed duck population control in the UK. *Glasgow Naturalist,* **23** (Supplement), 91–98.

Watola, G., Allen, J.R. and Feare, C.J. (1996). Problems and management of naturalised introduced Canada Geese *Branta canadensis* in Britain. In Holmes, J.S. and Simons, J.R., eds., *The Introduction and Naturalisation of Birds*, London, The Stationery Office, 71–78.

Yalden, D. (1999). *The History of British Mammals*, London, T. and A.D. Poyser.

5

Plant introductions

Andrew Lack

Summary

Plant introductions to the British Isles can be divided into those introduced before 1500, the 'archaeophytes', numbering *c.* 150 species and considered in Chapter 35, and those introduced later, the 'neophytes'. The neophytes comprise a very large number in total, but with about 230 species having spread far from their original introduction site. Most neophytes have spread in the twentieth century. A remarkable number spread mainly or entirely by vegetative means. Neophytes occur throughout the British Isles, but are most common in disturbed sites and especially in south-east England. Certain neophytes have a particularly interesting historical distribution or exhibit taxonomic and ecological problems that have generated much research. Freshwater habitats contain several fast spreading and abundant neophytes that spread vegetatively.

Most neophytes are attractive insect-pollinated plants introduced initially for their ornamental qualities and, though they can become abundant in places, do not pose ecological problems. Examples are the Ivy-leaved Toadflax, some bellfowers and the Buddleia. They are broadly welcomed. A few have invaded sensitive habitats, but widespread 'problem' plants are very few in number: Japanese Knotweed, 'Wild' Rhododendron, New Zealand Pigmyweed, Himalayan Balsam and in a few places Hottentot Fig; maybe one or two others locally.

The widespread planting of trees, both native and non-native, and the spread of 'wild flower mixes' for roadside and meadow plantings has led to some mixing of native and non-native genetic material. Most of these have become inextricably mixed.

Introductions generate contradictory responses. Many people enjoy the colourful displays of plants that are considered pests by some conservationists.

Silent Summer: The State of Wildlife in Britain and Ireland, ed. Norman Maclean. Published by Cambridge University Press. © Cambridge University Press 2010.

Control measures can be prohibitively expensive and not worthwhile in ecological terms or, if biological control is attempted, may have unintended consequences. It is almost impossible to predict what the next invaders may be as the successful ones have widely differing characteristics. It is likely that several more species will invade, especially if our climate gets warmer.

Introduction

The British Isles have a native vascular flora of approximately 1300 species (excluding the asexual 'microspecies'), a fairly modest number by global standards. The number of plant species, hardy in our climate, that have been introduced into these islands exceeds that number by at least 20 times. The possibility of introductions establishing themselves in our flora is immense. Many have done so, with increasing frequency, ever since Neolithic agriculture first arrived in Britain some 6000 years ago. The distribution of about 1500 introduced species was recorded in the New Atlas by Preston, *et al.* (2002a), though many of these can be classed as casual and not establishing persistent populations. This encyclopaedic atlas is a treasure house of reference for all plant distribution and is referred to heavily here.

The early introductions, from Neolithic to *c.* 1500 AD, are known as 'archaeophytes' and constitute a small group of about 150 species. They are primarily agricultural weeds, herbs of culinary or medicinal use and a few trees. They are well integrated with the native flora and many, especially the agricultural weeds, have declined hugely since 1950. They will be considered in Chapter 35. The remainder, known as 'neophytes', have been introduced since 1500 and many have only established since 1900 or later. Most were introduced as garden ornamentals, with some others arriving accidentally as seeds. It is these that are considered in this chapter. In addition, a number of native trees and ornamental plants have been planted widely outside their native British range and some have established themselves, blurring the native and alien distributions.

Williamson and Fitter (1996) estimated that about 10% of neophytes to Britain had 'escaped' beyond their initial introduction site and about 10% of these had become established as self-sustaining populations. These introductions have not only added to the overall diversity of our flora, but they have also been the object of some fascinating ecological and taxonomical studies. They have provided some difficult problems for us, and have contributed to our culture in diverse ways.

The neophyte introduced plants have often been described in pejorative terms, especially 'alien', with its sinister overtones of green men, and 'invader' and 'invasive', playing on the fact that, as an island nation, we have resisted human invasion since 1066 – a 'successful introduction' becomes an 'alien invader'. Most neophytes were omitted from popular floras of the 1950s and 60s, and even from the standard British Flora of Clapham *et al.* (1952, 1962) and the Atlas (Perring and Walters 1962). The more recent standard flora of Stace (1991, 1997) and the New Atlas (Preston *et al.* 2002) gave them much greater weight, coinciding with the acknowledgement of the contribution of the great numbers of established immigrant people in the country.

In a chapter of this nature it is impossible to discuss all the neophyte plants, but I have chosen representative examples from the range that we have. I include the most interesting taxonomic and ecological studies and what are considered to be the most problematic of the plants in their invasive qualities. The great majority of neophytes have naturalised only to a limited extent, often surviving solely near gardens, or occur occasionally but do not persist, mainly in disturbed areas. Although these may tell a historically interesting story, they are mainly not considered here. Neophytes that have established persistent wild populations and have colonised much further than the range in which they were originally introduced number around 230 species.

Origins of the neophyte flora

Neophytes originate from temperate regions across the world. Many come from other parts of Europe, including some of our best known: Sycamore and Horse Chestnut, native to central Europe and 'Wild' Rhododendron, native to the Black Sea and Iberia. Others come from North America, such as the American Willowherb, most of our evening primroses and the Canadian Waterweed; South America, such as the Fuchsia; New Zealand, e.g. the Pigmyweed, or from China and Japan, such as the Buddleia and the notorious Japanese Knotweed. Those from warmer parts of the world are rarely persistent, but a few, such as the Hottentot Fig from South Africa, and one or two aquatics may do so in places. If the climate does warm, and especially if we have warmer winters, there is considerable potential for more plants from warm temperate zones to colonise and invade.

Characteristics of a successful neophyte

Neophytes come in so many different forms that it is hard to predict which species will thrive. We can make some general statements, although there are many exceptions. Firstly, there are most neophytes where people are most active, with more species colonising disturbed places with fertile soil than elsewhere. This means that roadsides, gardens, 'waste' land, derelict sites in towns and building sites are the places where they are most likely to be found (Williamson and Fitter 1996). There are more neophytes in south-east England than elsewhere. A habitat that appears particularly full of neophytes is fresh water, but this is probably due to the speed of spread rather than the overall number of species (Preston 2002). Our native freshwater flora is quite rich by European standards (Preston and Croft 1997). I will consider these in a separate section.

The success of an introduced plant cannot be accurately predicted by extrapolation from its characteristics in its native terrain. Having said that, it is generally true that plants that are abundant in their native land are likely to be the ones that thrive best outside it, as they are often the most adaptable. As for their biological characteristics, many successful neophytes are woody species with showy insect-pollinated flowers, though this may be simply because these are the ones most likely to be introduced as ornamentals. They are often tall and fast growing. Of the herbaceous plants, one of our notorious neophytes, the Himalayan Balsam, is said to be our tallest annual plant. Mode of dispersal or reproduction, which one might think as important in affecting colonisation, shows no particular correlation with spread. Indeed a most unexpected feature of a remarkable number of successful introductions is the fact that they are sterile and spread entirely by vegetative fragmentation or suckers. Will this make them vulnerable to attack by a herbivore or pathogen at some later date?

There still remains the question as to why certain plants spread so well and others do not. The widely recognised idea that an introduced plant thrives without the parasites or pathogens it encounters in its native land may be important for some species, though often not well tested (Keane and Crawley 2002). Other factors may be important, such as generalist herbivores preferring native plants. It is clear that the interaction between each species and its habitat is often subtle, and it is hard to predict what will make a successful introduction.

A number of neophytes have established from just a few plants introduced from a single wild population or even from a cultivated form. This means that they often have a narrower genetic base than they have in their native lands, especially if they then spread mainly or entirely by vegetative means. This, in itself, is not surprising, but it does lead to some looking different from the native populations.

Four contrasting introductions

To illustrate the variety of plants and our response to them, let us consider four introductions with very different stories, the first three associated with my native and home city of Oxford.

Oxford Ragwort, *Senecio squalidus*

The Oxford Ragwort was introduced from the flanks of Mount Etna, Sicily, to the Oxford Botanic Garden in the seventeenth century. First it established on the garden walls and a few other places, and remained restricted until the mid-nineteenth century. It then made its way to the new railway in the 1870s and from Oxford spread rapidly along the railway to London and thence across the country, colonising the disturbed places so closely associated with railways. It is still spreading in both range and habitat. It provides what is usually a welcome splash of yellow in disturbed soil such as railway ballast that resembles the disturbed soil of its native volcanic habitat.

But on Mount Etna itself we do not find the British form. Instead, there are two related species, the lowland *Senecio chrysanthemifolius* and the upland *S. aethnensis*. These two species are sometimes regarded as sub-species, but show many morphological differences. Where they overlap there are hybrid swarms of variable plants and it is from one of these that our plant is derived. It has then evidently stabilised, from a limited genetic base, as an independent entity, with no contact with the source population and acts as a good species spreading successfully in Britain (Abbott *et al.* 2000).

The spread of the Oxford Ragwort is well documented, but the story does not finish there, because this plant has hybridised with our native Groundsel, *Senecio vulgaris*, several times. By the end of the nineteenth century a form of Groundsel with ray florets had appeared. This has been shown to be derived from introgressive hybridisation (i.e. hybrids forming that then cross with one or both of the parent species) between these two species (Abbott *et al.* 1992). Then in the early twentieth century there appeared a polyploid derivative in north Wales and independently in Scotland, from two further different hybridisation events. This has been named the Welsh Groundsel, *Senecio cambrensis*. Other derivatives, such as the 'York' Groundsel, *Senecio eboracensis*, have appeared (Lowe and Abbott 2003), and, though this one may have disappeared again, others may well be found. Sterile hybrids with another neophyte, Sticky Groundsel, *Senecio viscosus*, have been found in London and elsewhere.

This species has generated much interest. There is little doubt that it will continue to do so, as it continues to spread, and we can expect further hybridisations and rapid evolution.

In this context it is worth mentioning two other genera that have hybrid derivatives of introductions in this country. One is the Cord Grass that is considered later. The other, the evening primroses, *Oenothera* species, have made themselves very much at home on sand dunes, especially in the west. The taxonomy of the evening primroses is complicated (Rostanski 1982) but one, probably of hybrid origin, has been named after Wales, *O. cambrica*.

Snakeshead Fritillary, *Fritillaria meleagris*

The Fritillary occupies a small number of wet meadows along the Thames and a few other southern and south-eastern rivers. Where it occurs it is usually abundant, such as in its classic locality in the grounds of Magdalen College, Oxford (Figure 5.1). Its habitat has few, if any, other neophytes. The Fritillary disappeared from many of its known sites during the early twentieth century, but since 1960 has increased again under protection. It can spread quickly in its favoured habitat (Pearman 2007).

Figure 5.1 Fritillaries in their classic locality, water meadows by the River Cherwell, Magdalen College, Oxford (see colour plate).

The Fritillary has been revered, especially in Oxford: e.g. it is the emblem of the Oxford Urban Wildlife Group; it was voted Oxfordshire's county flower in 2002; it is the name of the Ashmolean Natural History Society journal and of a magazine of Oxford's womens' colleges in the early twentieth century and it has been celebrated in poetry. Geoffrey Grigson said that everyone should walk in a Fritillary field before they died (Ridler 2005). It has been considered native, though one suspects that this was often a kind of wishful thinking. It was first recorded in the wild in 1736, but is exuberantly showy and grows in such easily accessible places that it is inconceivable that it was missed by all previous naturalists. The evidence is overwhelming that it is a neophyte (Pearman 2007). Despite its neophyte status, it is a symbol of a declining habitat, where it occurs, and has stimulated much conservation work on the habitat as a whole.

Birthwort, *Aristolochia clematitis*

This strange, evil-smelling herb may even class as a pre-1500 introduction, though known in the 'wild' only since 1685 (Preston *et al.* 2002). It is poisonous and, like most such plants, can induce abortion, or induce and assist in child-birth. It was used this way probably because of association with the uterus-like shape of the flower. It now has a fascinating relict distribution, growing almost entirely by a few old nunneries and monasteries, mainly in eastern England, including Godstow Nunnery in Oxford. As Blamey *et al.* (2003) drily point out, it is the 'source of a drug used to save peccant medieval nuns from their misbehaviour with peccant monks', though, in fact, the nuns were seen as the midwives for local people, and grew numerous medicinal plants. The Birthwort is very persistent, but has disappeared from several known haunts, and is slowly declining everywhere. It may die out completely without help, as it is no longer cultivated.

New Zealand Willowherb, *Epilobium brunnescens*

This modestly attractive creeping herb was first recorded in the wild in 1904 in Edinburgh. It was probably introduced by accident with other ornamentals from New Zealand. It immediately made itself at home here and spread with astonishing speed, aided by its tiny wind-blown seeds and ability to root at nodes. It is found in all sorts of places where you would not expect to find a neophyte,[1] favouring wet and open places in moorland and among mountain rocks at mid altitudes. It now occurs throughout Scotland, Wales and the hill districts of England and Ireland. It is especially abundant in places famed for their collection of rare native montane plants, like the lower slopes of Ben Lawers in Perthshire and Ben Bulben in Sligo. Around Ben Bulben it forms an almost monospecific stand in places (personal observation).

Despite its abundance and the fact that it grows in what appear to be sensitive places, I have never come across any author worried about it outcompeting native plants. It creeps along the ground and will never overtop any other plant, and perhaps serious competition with natives is unlikely; either that or any problems may go unnoticed. When seen in the wild it gives every appearance of being native, even to the extent of occasionally hybridising with native willowherbs (Kitchener and McKean 1998). Braithwaite *et al.* (2006) suggest that it now occupies nearly all of its favoured upland habitat.

Plants of fresh water

Our freshwater habitat has been invaded by a succession of introductions that have spread particularly fast, so it is worth considering this habitat separately. Most of these plants appear to be sterile in this country and have spread vegetatively. An early example is the Sweet Flag, *Acorus calamus*, with its delicious orangey, almost Cointreau-like scent, first recorded in the wild in 1668. It is now distributed widely, mainly in lowland England by artificial lakes and canals. All the British plants are triploid and sterile. Its distribution is probably stable, but it is similar to some other aquatics and is easily overlooked. Another early introduction, the Water Soldier, *Stratiotes aloides*, may

---

[1] New Zealand has suffered so seriously from introductions from Europe that there seems a pleasant sense of justice that at least one New Zealand plant has colonised these islands so effectively. The Pigmyweed, though, is another matter altogether – see section below.

be native in the Norfolk Broads, but it was first recorded in 1633 and even there only female plants are known. It is introduced elsewhere and may persist vegetatively in canals and lakes for some time. The Fringed Water Lily, *Nymphoides peltata*, is native in the Fens of East Anglia, but it is a popular ornamental, and it too has been widely naturalised and can cover shallow ponds with dense foliage. But these three have been far outshone by several other plants.

The Canadian Waterweed, *Elodea canadensis*, introduced by 1842, became one of our most common and familiar submerged aquatics after spreading throughout lowland Britain and Ireland. It favours still or slowly moving silty water, colonising and sometimes clogging lakes, canals and natural waterways. Its invasive qualities were noted early and by the 1860s it was given several Latin nicknames, such as '*Babingtonia pestifera*', after the Cambridge professor who was thought to have encouraged it. Though it spread so rapidly, it was noted even by 1860 that it had declined in some places where it had been first reported. It was still vigorously colonising other places. There seemed to be some sort of 'boom and bust' going on over a period of less than 10 years. The reason is unknown, but may be limitation of iron in the water (Preston 2002).

Much more recently, a close relative, Nuttall's Waterweed, *Elodea nuttallii*, again from North America, started spreading. This was first seen in Oxfordshire in 1966, grows more quickly than the Canadian Waterweed and is now commoner in much of England. Nuttall's Waterweed had reached southern Scotland and northern Ireland by 2002 (Preston *et al.* 2002b). There have been some noticeable local declines in the distribution of the Canadian Waterweed over this period. This may be direct replacement or part of the boom-and-bust cycle repeating itself. Either way, it is likely that these plants have replaced our native submerged plants in many places.

Two further submerged species, the Curly Waterweed, *Lagarosiphon major*, this time from South Africa, and the Parrot's Feather, *Myriophyllum aquaticum*, from South America, are commonly grown as aquarium or pond plants and have established themselves since 1944 and 1960, respectively. Both are confined to southern England and Wales. Though much less common at present than either of the others, it is possible, in a warming climate, that they too will spread.

The distribution and abundance of these four plants, along with the numerous native aquatics, will undoubtedly change, and probably radically, within the next 50 years. All four are dioecious and known only as females in this country;[2] all spread entirely by vegetative means.

Two tiny floating aquatics, both natives of North and South America, the Water Fern, *Azolla filiculoides*, and the Least Duckweed, *Lemna minuta*, have increased rapidly since 1980. Vigorous vegetative spread can lead to either or both covering still ponds and canals, mainly in southern England, although they can disappear as rapidly as they arrived. The Water Fern was first recorded in 1883, but remained local, mainly

---

[2] It is interesting to note that Nuttall's Waterweed has been introduced to Japan as well, and there all plants are male (Preston and Croft 1997).

near the sea, until the 1960s or later. It is unknown why it has spread so vigorously in recent years. Curiously, there is evidence that it occurred here in previous interglacials. The Least Duckweed was first recorded in 1977 and has spread explosively, reaching Ireland in 1993, and actually is likely to be under-recorded, as it is very similar to the native Common Duckweed, *Lemna minor.* Again the dynamics of these two common introductions and with our five native duckweed species will undoubtedly change over the next few decades.

Finally in this group we come to the New Zealand Pigmyweed, *Crassula helmsii*, seen as a particularly aggressive invader. This is native of Australia and New Zealand and was first seen in the wild in 1956, but has spread mainly since 1980. It continues to do so. It has now colonised the edges of ponds, canals and indeed almost any waterway down to a depth of 3 m or so, across England and locally in Wales. It usually forms dense pure stands, excluding all other plants. It is too early to say what effect it is having, or will have, on our native flora. It may well pose a serious threat to some rarities in local-ities where the marginal flora is rich, e.g. in the New Forest to the Hampshire Purslane, *Ludwigia palustris* or Slender Marsh Bedstraw, *Galium constrictum.* It is a plant that conservationists dread finding. It spreads so fast that most attempts to eradicate it seem to be futile. Containing it in a sensitive site is probably the best that can be achieved. More recently still, the Floating Pennywort, *Hydrocotyle ranunculoides*, from North America, may be doing something similar. First recorded as naturalised in 1991, it too appears to be spreading like wildfire. Monospecific carpets are now recorded in some sites

There are some further aquatics that have naturalised in a few places.

Widespread, but welcome

The Fuchsia, *Fuchsia magellanica*, was first recorded in the wild in 1857. A native of temperate South America, it appears to be mainly a cultivar raised in a Scottish nursery that has naturalised so extensively in hedgerows in western Britain, the Isle of Man and, especially, Ireland. It is sterile, and spreads by vegetative suckering. In its native land the hanging red flowers and copious nectar strongly indicate that it is pollinated by hummingbirds, but bumblebees visit it regularly in these islands, though to no avail for seed production. Despite its extensive colonisation of hedges, stream banks and rocks, it appears not to have displaced native plants to any great extent and it is much loved. It is probably still increasing slowly. The Isle of Man voted it as its 'county' flower in 2002.

The Buddleia or Butterfly Bush, *Buddleja davidii*, was introduced into Britain from China in the 1890s. It became popular in gardens immediately for its own ornamental qualities, and the fact that the flowers are extremely attractive to butterflies, espe-cially the colourful vanessids. It is easy to grow, grows quickly and, though usually short-lived, sets abundant seed that is dispersed by the wind. It had naturalised by the 1920s, though it was still local by 1960. Since then it has spread rapidly across lowland areas, mainly in towns and dry waste places, forming large populations on building sites and by railways, in particular. These are a most welcome ground cover and splash of colour on otherwise derelict sites, especially as there are nearly always butterflies feeding from them. Owen (1991) noted, too, that many herbivorous insects in Britain will eat the leaves. This is rather surprising as the *Buddleja* genus (recently placed in Scrophulariaceae, a widespread European family, but sometimes regarded as a separate family, Buddlejaceae) is not native to Europe. This fact further adds to its attraction as an addition to our flora.

There are many attractive introduced plants that have spread widely as weeds of gardens and waste places. Most of these are viewed favourably and they do not appear to be displacing native species. Purple Toadflax, *Linaria purpurea*, Yellow Corydalis, *Pseudofumaria lutea*, several bellflowers, *Campanula* spp., Red Valerian, *Centranthus ruber*, Slender Speedwell, *Veronica filiformis* (another that spreads almost entirely by vegetative means), some cranesbills, *Geranium* spp. and wood-sorrels, *Oxalis* spp. are good examples, and our most characteristic wall plant, the Ivy-leaved Toadflax, *Cymbalaria muralis*, also comes in this category. There are many others.

Some others have become associated with particular places, such as the Pearly Everlasting, *Anaphalis margaritacea*, on mine spoil in South Wales, the Goat's Rue, *Galega officinalis*, on roadsides in London and its surrounds (though spreading rapidly), the Maltese Cross, *Lychnis chalcedonica*, in Bristol, voted as its county flower in 2002, and the Monkey Flower, *Mimulus guttatus*, and its hybrids that have colonised damp ground and along rivers throughout, but has been adopted by Newcastle-upon-Tyne as its county flower.

Problem plants

Just a few introductions do pose problems, though, even for these, it is usually only in certain sensitive places that they may actually do any damage or out-compete native plants. New Zealand Pigmyweed and Floating Pennywort, both aquatics, are considered above. Here I will discuss others that have gained notoriety for their vigorous spread.

Japanese Knotweed, *Fallopia japonica*, and its relatives

This may, these days, be the most hated and feared of all our plants. It forms impenetrable thickets 3–4 m high or so and it has been said of it that it has the biodiversity value of concrete! (though in fact bees visit the flowers and the leaves are said to be good forage for cattle). By the 1930s it was known as 'Hancock's Curse' in Cornwall. This contrasts with attitudes when it was first introduced, winning a horticultural gold medal in Holland in 1847 and being described as 'splendid', 'graceful' and other such terms (Bailey and Conolly 2000).

As with so many introductions, our plant is sterile, and spreads purely by vegetative means. The entire British population is one male-sterile clone, introduced probably because it was more colourful than the fully hermaphrodite forms. But that vegetative spread is astonishingly vigorous and it was aptly described, even early on, as 'inextirpable'.

Spread has been particularly vigorous on waste ground by rivers, but it will occur almost anywhere. It can push its way through quite thick tarmac. In one of the places it grows most densely, around Swansea, it has been recorded covering 99 out of 40 000 ha (400 km^2) in many habitats, but especially on derelict sites near the docks (Bailey and Conolly 2000). It has colonised nature reserves and amenity sites where it is especially unwelcome. It has recently been reported from the London 2012 Olympic site. Many attempts have been made to eradicate it, and it became an offence to introduce it in 1981, along with the Giant Hogweed, *Heracleum mantegazzianum*.

On 4 May 2008, a *Sunday Telegraph* headline heralded a new attempt to control it with 'The insect army called up to fight Knotweed', and on 6 January 2009, the *Guardian* suggested 'New herbicide offers hope in battle against Japanese Knotweed' (note the language of war in both). The former was the introduction of a psyllid plant louse that feeds on its sap. Biological control can be effective, as for the prickly pear cactus, *Opuntia* sp. in Australia when the cactus moth was introduced, but equally often has gone wrong. Let us see what happens with this. The new herbicide, known as 'Tordon', is to be used at more than 120 sites across London to remove it from parts of the underground train network. It is claimed that it is undermining bridges and blocking sight lines. This herbicide is toxic to many plants.

The cost of removing it can be great – one estimate suggests that eradication from a 50 m^2 area by digging and dumping would cost around £160 000; spraying it would cost £4000, but might destroy much else and may need some follow-up. The Department for Environment, Food and Rural Affairs has estimated that the cost of complete eradication from Britain would come to a staggering £1.56 billion, based on 0.5% of the country being infested. Certainly much time and effort is spent surveying it and spraying or destroying patches, but one cannot help but wonder what is being damaged by it. If its roots penetrate buildings or recreation grounds, then removal is clearly warranted, though it is far from the only plant that can do this. In some places it is likely that it has a positive effect, stabilising banks that would be eroded if it is removed. Evidence of genuine ecological 'damage' or of native plants declining as a result of its spread is almost entirely lacking.

Fallopia japonica is the commonest species, but its larger, very striking, relative, *F. sachalinensis* can be just as persistent and the hybrid between them may be spreading too. Another relative, the Russian Vine or 'Mile-a-Minute Plant', *F. baldschuanica*, can also, as its name suggests, grow with phenomenal speed. But it does not spread vegetatively – growth is from a single root – and it does not appear to naturalise in the same way, though recorded from many parts of the country.

'Wild' Rhododendron, *Rhododendron ponticum*

Thickets of naturalised Rhododendron are a familiar sight in many parts of the country. They are always this species,[3] which was first introduced in 1763 from the isolated population in Iberia. It has spread vigorously since then, across heaths, rocky places and in woodland understorey. This time it is seed that is responsible for most of the spread, though it can sucker locally. Once a plant is established it does cast a deep shade allowing no other plants to grow and its leaves create an acidic litter. A bush can live for a century or more.

It strongly favours acid soils and a wet climate, and is commonest, and potentially most of a 'problem', in parts of south-west England, Wales, western Scotland and Ireland. It is one of the most characteristic plants of the Killarney oak woods and the hillsides of Snowdonia, especially where there is plenty of spoil from the slate mines. It does not spread much, if at all, in the drier parts of England or on basic soils.

The native Oak woods of south-west Ireland are not extensive and it is here that it has taken over as the most common understorey shrub. It has largely replaced the holly, *Ilex aquifolium*, though that is still common, and, perhaps in a few places, the much more restricted Strawberry Tree, *Arbutus unedo*. But there is no evidence that the Strawberry Tree has declined as a result of Rhododendron invasion – it declined in medieval times to its present distribution in Kerry, but is now stable. Interestingly, the Strawberry Tree is considered an invasive alien itself on part of the Great Orme in North Wales.

In some woodlands in western Scotland, Rhododendron has taken over in a similar way to the Irish woods. In their survey of Argyll and Bute, Edwards and Taylor (2008) estimated that Rhododendron covers 4654 ha, 85% of this in woodland, and that more than 15000 ha may potentially be invaded. The cost of eradicating it would be more than £9.3 million now. Even if eradication only happens on sites with some nature conservation designation (1252 ha), the costs would run to £3.2 million. Any delay and the costs may soar.

The Rhododendron, like the Knotweed, is considered a pest, but a careful look at its spread reveals that it will only establish on disturbed soils and the seedlings are vulnerable to competition (Cross 1975). It will not establish where there is continuous ground cover of vascular plants or mosses. This is why it has taken so successfully to the disturbed sites of abandoned slate mines in North Wales. But surely most people would welcome it on such unprepossessing habitat where it is not replacing any native plant; in June it can be a magnificent sight (Figure 5.2). Indeed the Rhododendron has many supporters throughout its naturalised range.

In a few places, mainly on lowland heathland, local clearance may well be essential to help particular rare animal species, such as the Ladybird Spider, *Eresus cinnaberinus*, in Dorset, or plants, such as the Tunbridge Filmy Fern, *Hymenophyllum tunbrigense*, in Kent.

---

[3] DNA evidence suggests that there has been a small amount of hybridisation with an American species, *R. catawbiense* and, possibly, *R. maximum*. Plants from eastern Scotland may be more cold-tolerant as a result (Milne and Abbott 2001).

Figure 5.2 'Wild' Rhododendron covering a hillside near Beddgelert, N. Wales (see colour plate).

When considering 'control', we must consider what will happen if the Rhododendron is removed. Thick ground cover is seen as valuable for nesting birds and, in places, Rhododendron is encouraged for this purpose. Many woods have lost much of their ground cover through intensive deer grazing (Chapter 35). Perhaps Holly will reappear or other dense shrubs, but not unless grazing is controlled. Will these provide a different environment from the Rhododendron? Or are they perceived as 'better' simply because they are native? Would we consider the Rhododendron differently if it had established itself after the last glaciation rather than being introduced? It did occur naturally in the previous interglacial, so this is a real possibility. This may be an unfair question, as its distribution in relation to all the other plants would then have stabilised much earlier, but it does seem fairly stable in many places now and it is undoubtedly here to stay.

Himalayan (Indian) Balsam, *Impatiens glandulifera*

This tall, handsome plant, with its 'orchid-lipped, loose-jointed, purplish, indolent flowers' (Stevenson 1982) is loved for its showiness and loathed in equal measure for its invasive qualities. The flowers actually come in many shades of purple, pink and white, and are much visited by bumblebees. Its spread has been explosive since first being introduced in 1839 from the Himalayan region, though mainly since 1960. Its distribution has undoubtedly been enhanced by balsam lovers throwing seeds in suitable

Figure 5.3 Himalayan Balsam growing as an almost pure stand, Boundary brook, Oxford (see colour plate).

places. It is abundant along river courses and other damp places through most of low-land Britain, often forming monospecific stands (Figure 5.3). It is still spreading and consolidating its distribution.

It has the classic invasive qualities of fast, tall growth, up to 3 m, and large leaves. Despite being an annual, growing from seed every year, it will out-compete almost all other vegetation ('even *Urtica dioica* [stinging nettles]' – Preston *et al.* 2002). It is claimed that, on dying down in the autumn, the exposed soil may be easily eroded. Nature reserve managers organise 'Balsam bashing' days on the assumption that it is out-competing native plants. There is no doubt that other plants would grow where it is growing, but, as far as I know, there is no evidence that any rarity has declined as a result of its spread. Bumblebees frequently favour it over other plants, and, with a gen-eral decline in populations of bumblebees, anything that may boost their populations must surely be welcome. There is no evidence that seed set is significantly reduced in any native species as a result of its presence. In the wet summer of 2008, I noticed many plants that had been nearly defoliated, but could not identify the organism(s) involved. The most likely was a combination of a chrysomelid beetle and molluscs. Maybe some herbivorous invertebrates are catching up with it.

Two other balsams were introduced earlier in the nineteenth century, the Orange Balsam, *Impatiens capensis*, from North America, that colonises river banks and the Small Balsam, *I. parviflora*, from Central Asia, that spreads in shady woodland. Both can become abundant locally, and continue to spread, though neither is as common or invasive as the Himalayan.

Giant Hogweed, *Heracleum mantegazzianum*

This species is in a somewhat different category, as it is not particularly common, but contact with it causes large blisters on the skin when exposed to sunlight. For this reason it is dangerous, especially to children, and planting of it became an offence in 1981. The blister usually disappears within a day or two, but a scar can persist for months.

It is a magnificent statuesque umbellifer, 3 m or so high with umbels bigger than dinner plates. Originally introduced from Turkey in 1893, it has been planted in large gardens and naturalised usually along water courses close by. It is never a nuisance ecologically and is really only a problem where human contact is likely. As with the Knotweed and Rhododendron, attempts have been made to eradicate it along particular river systems, and costs can escalate with continued treatment necessary.

Spanish Bluebell, *Hyacinthoides hispanicus*

English bluebells, *Hyacinthoides non-scripta*, raise stronger emotions than almost any other native plant. Bluebell woods hardly occur outside these islands and are a much-prized national treasure. The bluebell is our national flower and symbol of the Botanical Society of the British Isles. So when the larger Spanish bluebell, introduced as a garden plant in the seventeenth century, started spreading and was perceived to be hybridising with our bluebell, it was as if a national institution was under attack. As with so many introductions, it appears to have spread particularly in recent years. People have been asked to destroy Spanish bluebells in the interest of maintaining the integrity of 'our' plants. There is no doubt that both the Spanish version and the fully fertile hybrids have been spreading over the last century or so but, so far at least, are almost confined to gardens, hedgerows and roadsides. Occasionally they have reached the edge of bluebell woods and the hybrids can spread. Do these pose a genuine threat to our bluebells? Time will tell.

Common Cord Grass, *Spartina anglica*

The cord grass that is familiar around our coasts is a tetraploid derivative of hybridisation, arising in about 1890, between the rare native *Spartina maritima* and the American introduction *S. alterniflora*. It has proved to be stronger than either parent, and a vigorous colonist of salt marshes. It has been planted deliberately to stabilise mud and has colonised itself in many other places. It has been seen as an intruder on mud flats rich in bird life, but appears to have stabilised in recent years. It may be a stage in succession in salt marshes and gradually dies out in the presence of other plants.

Vulnerable places: the Lizard Peninsula

This, the most southerly point of mainland Britain, with its unusual geology and almost frost-free climate, is a small area of great botanical richness. It is also, for the same reason, prone to invasion by introductions. The most serious of these is the Hottentot Fig, *Carpobrotus* (*Mesembryanthemum*) *edulis* (note the derogatory name). This very striking, frost-sensitive plant from South Africa, spreads large mats on some of the richest of the Lizard's cliffs, mainly or entirely by vegetative means. Here control and in places eradication, seems the only option. It appears to be spreading and has been deliberately planted in other parts of the south-west to stabilise sand dunes and may be becoming a problem in the Channel Islands as well. This is one species that may well spread elsewhere if the climate warms.

Other plants that may pose a threat to the Lizard include the Japanese Rose, *Rosa rugosa*, that forms large thickets on the cliffs (and elsewhere in Britain), and two garlic species, the Three-cornered, *Allium triquetrum*, and the Rosy, *A. roseum*. All three of these are increasing.

Trees

Some of our common trees occur here only as introductions, such as Sycamore, *Acer pseudoplatanus*, Turkey Oak, *Quercu cerris*, Horse Chestnut, *Aesculus hippocastanum*,[4] and most conifers, but most of our genuine native trees have been planted outside their native range. Native and introduced distributions of many species have become inextricably blurred. Some species have particular value as historical indicator species, the Small-leaved Lime, *Tilia cordata*, being the prime example. This has led Rackham (1986) to lament: 'Part of the value of the native lime tree lies in the meaning embodied in its mysterious natural distribution; it is devalued by being made into a universal tree.'

Some trees have naturalised in the vicinity of plantings. Sycamore can sometimes be seen as a problem, though much admired in many places. As for threats from naturalised trees, this is most apparent on lowland heath, a threatened habitat that needs constant management anyway. This is often invaded by conifers, especially Scots Pine, *Pinus sylvestris*, and Spruce, *Picea* sp., but equally by native broad-leaved trees, especially the Birch, *Betula pendula*.

Genetic introduction

A final thought is about the fashion for introducing 'wild flower mixes' of seeds for meadows and roadsides. Most mixes in the last 10 years or so have local sources, but

---

[4] Horse chestnuts appear to be increasingly suffering from infestations of a leaf miner, *Cameraria ohridella*, first recorded in 2002, and several diseases, especially cankers, *Phytophthora* and *Pseudomonas* spp., perhaps aggravated by the miner. This may lead to serious declines. Mild winters may be one cause.

this was not true in the 1980s. Local gene pools have almost certainly been disrupted or added to without documentation. And one must question, even in current mixes, whether, for instance, seed from the Midlands is more 'local' to Kent than seed from northern France. Sometimes cultivars of some of the legumes, such as Sainfoin, *Onobrychis viciifolia*, or Birdsfoot Trefoil, *Lotus corniculatus*, have been used rather than the native forms. Field margin mixes have frequently included Phacelia, *Phacelia tanacetifolia*, from California, as it attracts so many insects, including hoverflies. Larvae of these can control aphids, so it is much liked by farmers. How disruptive these introductions have been and how the native flora has been affected we shall probably never know.

Conclusion

Some non-native plants are common and appear to have stabilised in distribution; others are spreading rapidly. They generate contradictory reactions among different people. There is no doubt that many are attractive plants greatly appreciated by the public, even those that are considered pests by conservationists such as Rhododendron and Himalayan Balsam. Among conservationists there is frequently an antagonistic reaction to non-native plants, though, as we have seen here, actual damage may be much more limited than one might initially assume. The 'damage' that they do is often seen as a result of them being non-native, effectively ignoring the fact that many native plants have similar properties. The question is whether they pose a real threat to any aspect of our native biodiversity. As far as I can see, a mere handful of plants may pose ecological problems, but essentially, even with these, problems are confined to small areas of particular value. Any control measures should be concentrated on these sites, as total eradication will be prohibitively expensive or impossible, and cannot be justified in ecological terms. And these plants have much interest, despite the heartache. One thing is for certain: that many of these are here to stay and we will have to get used to them.

If we are interested in future predictions, we must remember that only a minute proportion of the vast number of plants that have been introduced have proved to be seriously invasive. It is almost impossible to predict which species will be next. We can say with some degree of certainty that if the climate changes it will affect the alien flora just as it will affect the native flora. We are likely to see some new 'invaders'. Perhaps we will see some as 'successful introductions' enhancing our flora that may otherwise be diminishing. They can add not just colour and variety to our landscape, but can be most attractive to insects or birds too. It seems important to separate out what we have to see as xenophobia from the qualities that we may be wanting for our flora.

Acknowledgements

I am most grateful to Drs Chris Preston, Mike Pienkowski and Colin Galbraith for constructive comments on this chapter.

References

Abbott, R.J., Ashton, P.A. and Forbes, D.G. (1992). Introgressive origin of the radiate groundsel, Senecio vulgaris L. var. hibernicus Syme: Aat-3 evidence. *Heredity*, **68**, 425–435.

Abbott, R.J., James, J.K., Irwin, J.A. and Comes, H.P. (2000). Hybrid origin of the Oxford ragwort, *Senecio squalidus* L. *Watsonia*, **23**, 123–138.

Bailey, J.P. and Conolly, A.P. (2000). Prize-winners to pariahs – a history of Japanese Knotweed s.l. (Polygonaceae) in the British Isles. *Watsonia*, **23**, 93–110.

Blamey, M., Fitter, R. and Fitter, A. (2003). *Wild Flowers of Britain and Ireland*, London, A and C Black.

Braithwaite, M.E., Ellis, R.W. and Preston, C.D. (2006). *Change in the British Flora 1987–2004*, London, Botanical Society of the British Isles.

Clapham, A.R., Tutin, T.G. and Warburg, E.F. (1952, 2nd edn. 1962). *Flora of the British Isles*, Cambridge, Cambridge University Press.

Cross, J.R. (1975). Biological flora of the British Isles: *Rhododendron ponticum*. *Journal of Ecology*, **63**, 345–364.

Edwards, C. and Taylor, S.L. (2008). *A Survey and Strategic Appraisal of Rhododendron Invasion and Control in Woodland Areas in Argyll and Bute*, Midlothian, Forest Research.

Keane, R.M. and Crawley, M.J. (2002). Exotic plant invasions and the enemy release hypothesis. *Trends in Ecology and Evolution*, **17**, 164–170.

Kitchener, G.D. and McKean, D.R. (1998). Hybrids of *Epilobium brunnescens* (Cockayne) Raven and Engelhorn (Onagraceae) and their occurrence in the British Isles. *Watsonia*, **22**, 49–60.

Lowe, A.J. and Abbott, R.J. (2003). A new British species, *Senecio eboracensis* (Asteraceae), another hybrid derivative of *S. vulgaris* L. and *S. squalidus* L. *Watsonia*, **24**, 375–388.

Milne, R.I. and Abbott, R.J. (2001). Origin and evolution of invasive naturalised material of *Rhododendron ponticum* L. in the British Isles. *Molecular Ecology*, **9**, 541–556.

Owen, J. (1991). *The Ecology of a Garden*, Cambridge, Cambridge University Press.

Pearman, D.A. (2007). 'Far from any house' – assessing the status of doubtfully native species in the flora of the British Isles. *Watsonia*, **26**, 271–290.

Perring, F.H. and Walters, S.M. (1962). *Atlas of the British Flora*, London, T. Nelson and Sons.

Preston, C.D. (2002). 'Babingtonia pestifera' – the explosive spread of *Elodea canadensis* and its intellectual reverberations. *Nature in Cambridgeshire*, **44**, 40–49.

Preston, C.D. and Croft, J.M. (1997). *Aquatic Plants in Britain and Ireland*, Colchester, Harley Books.

Preston, C.D., Pearman, D.A. and Dines, T.D. (2002a). *New Atlas of the British and Irish Flora*, Oxford, Oxford University Press.

Preston, C.D., Telfer, M.G., Arnold, H.R. *et al.* (2002b). *The Changing Flora of the UK*, London, DEFRA.

Rackham, O. (1986). *The History of the Countryside*, London, J.M. Dent and Sons.

Ridler, A. (2005). *Snakeshead Fritillaries*, from http://www.poetryarchive.org.

Rostanski, K. (1982). The species of *Oenothera* L. in Britain. *Watsonia*, **14**, 1–34.

Stace, C.A. (1991, 2nd edn. 1997). *New Flora of the British Isles*, Cambridge, Cambridge University Press.

Stevenson, A. (1982). *Himalayan Balsam,* poem from collection *Minute by Glass Minute*, Oxford, Oxford University Press.

Williamson, M.H. and Fitter, A. (1996). The characters of successful invaders. *Biological Conservation*, **78**, 163–170.

6

Urbanisation and development

Kevin J. Gaston and *Karl L. Evans*

Summary

Over the last 50 years, the human population of the UK (Britain and Northern Ireland, excluding overseas territories) has both expanded and become substantially more urbanised. The consequences for wildlife have undoubtedly been complex, with the low priority that has been given to monitoring schemes in urban environments compounding the difficulty in drawing overall conclusions. Nonetheless, it is clear that substantial areas of natural and semi-natural habitats have been lost, and that the richness and abundance, particularly of more specialist and previously narrowly distributed species associated with these habitats, have declined. Conversely, some more generalist species have greatly benefited, as have others that could exploit some of the more novel environments occurring in urban areas. Moreover, urban areas have become more significant for wildlife over the past 50 years, in large part because they figure more prominently in landscapes, because of a marked increase in awareness of and conservation efforts for urban biodiversity, and because urban areas hold a substantial proportion of the national populations of some species that have experienced dramatic declines in the wider countryside.

Introduction

Over the last 50 years the human population of the UK has grown by more than 15% (Figure 6.1; from 52.8 million in 1961 to 60.6 million in 2006; National Statistics 2007a). The annual growth rate has been an order of magnitude higher in urban areas than in rural ones, such that over 90% of the population now lives in the former. The extent of urban areas has thus also markedly increased, together with their associated

Silent Summer: The State of Wildlife in Britain and Ireland, ed. Norman Maclean. Published by Cambridge University Press. © Cambridge University Press 2010.

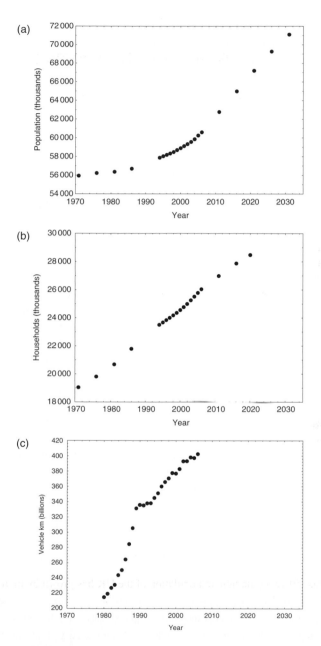

Figure 6.1 Estimated and future projected changes for the UK in (a) human population size, (b) number of households and (c) vehicle km. (From data in DfT (2007) and National Statistics (2007b).)

infrastructure, such as the length of roads. Indeed, the urbanisation of the UK has grown at a substantially faster pace over the last 50 years than has the human population, in part as a consequence of economic and social trends, including reduced employment in agricultural sectors, greater life expectancy, increased divorce rates and associated declines in mean household size.

What has been lost

Habitat

Urbanisation (broadly defined here to include towns and cities and other areas of development) has obviously led to significant erosion of the wider countryside. Estimates of the extent of urban or developed land can vary markedly, depending on the type and spatial resolution of the data and the precise land-use definitions employed (e.g. how infrastructure and settlement size are treated). However, one approach gives an estimate for 1998 of *c.* 10% of the total land surface of Great Britain (Haines-Young *et al.* 2000), and another for 2000 of *c.* 7% of the total land surface of the UK (Fuller *et al.* 2002). Concerns over the negative impacts of urbanisation and development on wildlife in the UK have repeatedly resulted in vigorous disputes over the siting of potential new developments. These have included contention over planned housing developments, motorways, railways, airports, port facilities, shopping centres, power stations, wind farms, reservoirs and recreational developments. The best-known examples are often those which went ahead despite opposition, sometimes after formal public enquiries took place at least partially on environmental grounds (e.g. Newbury bypass, Robin Hood airport, Cardiff Bay barrage, Teesdale reservoirs, Cairngorm ski developments). Such developments, and the expansion of urban areas more generally, have been particularly marked in the lowlands of southern England, both through the planned development of new urban centres, such as Milton Keynes, and less formalised suburban sprawl. For most taxa, lowland England has historically been one of the most species-rich areas of the UK, thus increasing the potential for urbanisation to have negative impacts on biodiversity. For example, large expanses of the lowland heathlands have been lost to development, and that which remains supports a number of nationally scarce and threatened species, but is adversely affected by urbanisation.

Even within existing urban areas, available evidence suggests that the extent of green space has also declined substantially over the last 50 years (Figure 6.2). This has resulted chiefly from a combination of the loss of brownfield sites (including some abandoned industrial areas of notable wildlife interest) and municipal green spaces (e.g. school playing fields) to development, and the increasing density of housing within new developments and within existing housing areas through infilling and backland development (Royal Commission on Environmental Pollution 2007). It has been further exacerbated by the extension of existing buildings, the paving over of front gardens to

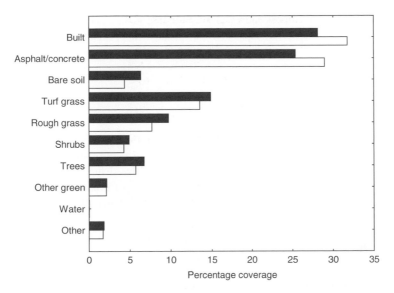

Figure 6.2 Percentage of area covered by different land-cover types in 1975 (filled bars) and 2000 (open bars) for sample sites in Merseyside. (From data in Pauleit *et al.* (2005).)

provide off-road parking, road-widening schemes and the general progressive erosion of smaller green spaces.

Associated with increased levels of urbanisation has been a wide variety of other changes in urban areas that have had impacts on wildlife. Structural changes include increased fragmentation of green space (some through declines in the average sizes of domestic gardens; Royal Commission on Environmental Pollution 2007), reduction of habitat connections to the wider countryside, changes in the age and structural composition of the building stock and channel engineering of water courses. Combined with management practices that often involve the simplification of urban green spaces (e.g. through tree surgery, removal of understorey vegetation), these changes have often led to net declines in habitat diversity. Other changes include increases in temperature (through urban heat-island effects), run-off, car traffic, noise pollution, light pollution, salting of roads in winter, quantities of topsoil and turf being moved around and in numbers of domestic cats. In addition to the direct local effects, urbanisation and its associated changes have influences over much larger areas, particularly through the demand for resources and the production of waste material (including pollutants). This said, urbanisation is a more efficient way of packing a given number of people into a landscape, such that per capita demands on resources are lower than would be the case if the same human population was distributed at lower density across a much larger area.

Determining how these various factors have interacted to influence urban wildlife is not straightforward as wildlife monitoring schemes in the UK have until very recently ignored urban areas almost entirely. Understanding of the changes that have taken place as a consequence of the expansion and development of urbanisation is thus rather poor and extremely fragmentary, and much must be inferred from indirect evidence or by extrapolation.

Species richness

Recent urbanisation has probably directly resulted in the extinction of very few species at the national level. Regionally or locally, the effects of urbanisation on species richness can be complex. However, unsurprisingly, native richness almost invariably declines steeply, at least from moderate to high levels of urban cover (Hardy and Dennis 1999; Tratalos *et al.* 2007). In some cases, although not all (see below), it simply declines across full rural–urban gradients, principally as a consequence of habitat loss, fragmentation and disturbance (Davis 1978, 1979; Sadler *et al.* 2006). Overall, species richness has almost certainly declined in previously established urban areas that have experienced significant increases in building density over the past 50 years. The influence of new developments on species richness will depend on their density, previous land use and the higher taxa being considered. However, given the density of most new housing developments in recent decades, it seems likely that species richness will generally have been depleted. For example, comparing the avifaunas of sample suburban 1 km × 1 km areas with adjacent rural ones suggests that urbanisation has, on average, resulted in the loss of four breeding bird species, with this figure rising to eight in East Anglia (Henderson *et al.* 2007).

Populations

Species differ markedly in their responses to urbanisation, with those that thrive in urban environments argued typically to be relatively generalist and more broadly distributed in other habitats. The long-term nationwide monitoring of urban biodiversity has been best for garden birds. The most dramatic losses have occurred in Starlings and House Sparrows, with the average number recorded per garden having declined by 77% and 64%, respectively, since 1979; other common urban birds also appear to have declined, such as the Blackbird (down by 39%) and Robin (37%; RSPB 2008). Other data confirm the general direction of some of these trends with the loss of large winter roosts of Starlings from many urban areas, and autumn counts of House Sparrows in some London parks have declined by an order of magnitude or more (Figure 6.3). A final avian example is the Swift, *Apus apus*, which predominantly breeds in urban areas and whose UK population has declined by 26% since 1994, when monitoring began (Baillie *et al.* 2007). The causes of these declines are not well understood.

Evidence is accruing that there have also been long-term, and often substantial, population declines in urban areas for species of other groups. These include large

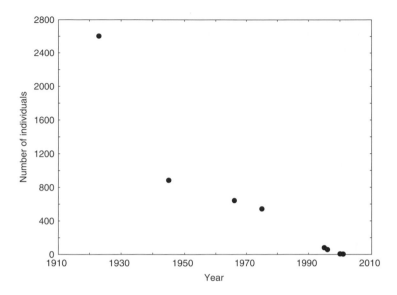

Figure 6.3 Changes in the numbers of House Sparrows in Kensington Gardens, London. (From data and sources in De Laet and Summers-Smith 2007.)

moths and bats (Guest *et al.* 2002; Fox *et al.* 2006). It seems probable that a wide variety of taxa have experienced such changes.

In some species that are sensitive to habitat fragmentation, such as amphibians, barriers to gene flow resulting from the structure of the urban environment can alter the genetic composition of populations. This can include the loss of genetic diversity, relatively high genetic differentiation between sites, genetic drift and inbreeding depression (e.g. Hitchings and Beebee 1997).

What has been gained

Habitat

In contrast to the dramatic expansion of urban areas, there are rather few counter examples of the creation of genuinely new major pieces of green space from previously developed land. The clearance, particularly of previously industrial sites and of areas of older social housing, sometimes resulted temporarily in such space, but this was often completely or in large part lost again to fresh development (e.g. Liverpool garden festival site); a growing proportion of land that is being developed for residential use has previously been developed (DEFRA 2006). Nonetheless, there have been some significant attempts dramatically to improve the quality of individual urban green spaces, with notable examples perhaps including, depending on how narrowly one defines urban areas, Barn Elms (London), Rainham Marshes (London), Sandwell Valley (Birmingham), Potteric Carr (Doncaster) and Old Moor (Barnsley), and numerous smaller-scale initiatives.

More generally, the quality of many urban areas has doubtless substantially improved for wildlife. Perhaps most obviously, the levels of some atmospheric pollutants have declined, although they may remain problematic and exceed target levels, particularly in inner city areas, as a consequence principally of vehicle emissions. Hard data are not available, but some consider that anecdotal evidence suggests levels of pesticide use in urban areas have declined (particularly recently and in domestic gardens). Levels of some pollutants have also fallen significantly in many urban rivers and streams, although, again, they may often still exceed those that are desirable (Royal Commission on Environmental Pollution 2007). In addition, growth and maturation of urban trees in many areas in recent decades will have increased the amount and quality of habitat they provide to other organisms.

Species richness

Across gradients from rural to low or moderate urbanisation, native species richness may sometimes increase, through some combination of intensive agricultural use in rural areas negatively influencing biodiversity, increased habitat heterogeneity in suburban areas promoting local species richness and/or increased human dispersal of propagules (especially of plants; Hodkinson and Thompson 1997, Robinson and Sutherland 2002; Tratalos *et al.* 2007). This complicates any simple prediction of the consequences of urbanisation for richness.

A small number of native species have apparently freshly colonised urban environments over the last 50 or so years. Such events have been best documented for birds, where it appears to be, at least in part, a consequence of broader expansions of population size or range. For example, prior to the 1980s the only confirmed reports of Peregrines, *Falco peregrinus*, nesting in urban environments related to very occasional breeding on Salisbury cathedral. However, following recovery from DDT poisoning and persecution, Peregrines have increased throughout the UK and the species now regularly nests in a number of towns; in the most recent national survey *c.* 4% of breeding individuals are found in towns and cities, along with an increasing number of non-breeding and wintering individuals (Crick *et al.* 2003). Similarly, although it had bred elsewhere, London developed as the centre of Britain's Black Redstart, *Phoenicurus ochruros*, population in the 1940s, often associated with derelict bomb sites and old docks, and a further marked expansion occurred from the late 1960s, although there have been subsequent losses in some areas, perhaps as suitable sites have declined with modern developments (Brown and Grice 2005). The Collared Dove, *Streptopelia decaocto*, first bred in Britain in the early 1950s as part of a natural range expansion from central Asia, and now occurs sufficiently disproportionately in urban areas to be one of just four bird species considered to be urban specialists (DEFRA 2003).

In addition to the effect on native species richness, across many taxonomic groups, the numbers of species in urban areas is increased by the presence of alien species. This is particularly the case for plants, for which the trend is so marked that total species richness tends to increase with levels of urbanisation, even in rather highly developed areas. Presence in the horticultural trade is closely associated with plant invasions, the probability of which increases with the length of time for which a species has been traded; historical net increases in urban plant species richness due to the establishment of exotic plant species thus seem highly likely. Over the last 50 years some urban areas have been colonised by exotic species in other taxonomic groups, including invertebrates (e.g. Harlequin Ladybird, *Harmonia axyridis*, which has spread rapidly since arrival in Britain in 2004; leaf-mining moths, *Phyllonorycter leucographella* and *Phyllonorycter platani,* which established in south-east England in the mid-1980s and early 1990s, respectively), birds (e.g. Ring-necked Parakeet, *Psittacula krameri*, which became established in London in the 1960s), and mammals (e.g. Grey Squirrel, *Sciurus carolinensis*, which has expanded its range in Scotland and Northern Ireland in recent decades). The subsequent elevation of urban species richness has, however, been less noticeable in these taxonomic groups than is the case for plants. Moreover, long-term impacts of some introductions on species richness may be negative due to hybridisation or competition with native species, or their predation.

Populations

The populations of some species have undergone notable net increases in urban areas, perhaps more so than in any other broad habitat type. These include species that have, or are suspected to have, benefited from improvements in the quality of freshwater habitats (e.g. Salmon, *Salmo salar*, and Otter, *Lutra lutra*), and in air quality (e.g. some ephiphytic lichens and bryophytes, some molluscs). Some appear to have responded to greater levels of either intentional (e.g. garden feeding of wild birds such as tits and finches) or unintentional anthropogenic resource provision (e.g. gulls and corvids exploiting landfill and other refuse), de-icing salt treatment of roads (e.g. Foxtail Barley, *Hordeum jubatum*, Danish Scurvygrass, *Cochlearia danica*) and reductions in persecution or poisoning (e.g. Sparrowhawk, *Accipiter nisus*, Otter). Others have become firmly established or more widespread and numerous following initial introduction from their native ranges (e.g. Butterfly-bush, *Buddleja davidii*, Purple Toadflax, *Linaria purpurea*), have increased in abundance in urban areas at least partly as a consequence of a more widespread population increase (e.g. Woodpigeon, *Columba palumbus*, Long-tailed Tit, *Aegithalos caudatus*, Goldfinch, *Carduelis carduelis*), or have altered their migration strategy and increasingly winter in developed areas (e.g. Blackcap, *Sylvia atricapilla*, Chiffchaff, *Phylloscopus collybita*).

Urbanised landscapes often create strong selection pressures that differ from those in more natural environments. This can lead to urban populations rapidly developing traits that are highly divergent from those expressed by rural counterparts and may thus promote increased intraspecific functional and genetic diversity. One classic example concerns the development of resistance to heavy-metal pollution in grasses, which has occurred at a number of industrial sites in Britain. Few other instances have as yet been documented for Britain, but they doubtless exist; elsewhere urban ruderal plants have been found to produce seeds with lower dispersal ability (Cheptou *et al.* 2008), and urban ant populations to have increased thermal tolerance (Angilletta *et al.* 2007).

What has become more important

Due to insufficient monitoring, it is unclear whether urban areas of the UK have overall become better or worse for wildlife over the past 50 years. On balance, it seems likely that habitat quality has been stable or has improved in many of the urban green areas that have persisted, making these better for wildlife (largely as a consequence of changes in pollutants), but that per unit urban area, the extent of areas that are suitable for much wildlife has diminished (largely as a consequence of increased building density). Equally, however, it also seems likely that urban areas have become more significant for wildlife over the past 50 years. In part, this is simply because the extent of these areas has increased, and thus they figure more prominently in landscapes. In part, it is because of a marked increase in awareness of, and conservation efforts for, urban biodiversity, including local initiatives for urban environmental planning and management (including local nature reserves), and wider interest in providing resources for urban wildlife (e.g. nest boxes, food for birds, ponds). In part, it also arises because urban areas hold a substantial proportion of the national population of a small number of species, i.e. those that appear to do reasonably well in suburban areas, but have experienced dramatic declines in the wider countryside, typically as a consequence of intensive agriculture. Potential examples include the Common Frog, *Rana temporaria*, Song Thrush, *Turdus philomelos*, and Hedgehog, *Erinaceus europaeus*. In some cases these high proportions may reflect increasing absolute numbers, but in others abundances are declining in urban areas (e.g. Song Thrush).

The future

The human population of the UK is projected to increase to 65 million in 2016, 70 million in 2028 and to reach 71 million by 2031 (National Statistics 2007b).

Substantial growth in urban areas and associated infrastructure is thus almost inevitable. Indeed, a number of major new developments are presently at the discussion, planning or implementation stage, with concerns in many cases being expressed as to the environmental consequences if they go ahead (e.g. Thames Gateway regeneration project, expansions of Heathrow, Lydd and Stansted airports, Severn barrage, M4 relief road, London array offshore windfarm). Rural areas immediately adjacent to existing suburban developments appear to be less intensively managed, and to contain more broad-leaved woodland, than rural areas further away from urban developments (Henderson *et al.* 2007). Future suburban sprawl may thus be particularly damaging to biodiversity. The increased building (and especially housing) density of many existing urban areas, particularly in the lowlands of England, is also likely to continue.

Without concerted efforts to improve the quantity and quality of suitable habitats in urban areas for wildlife, it is difficult to escape the conclusion that many species will undergo marked declines in coming years. Such changes may even go relatively unnoticed due to the lack of systematic monitoring in urban areas for most taxa, with birds now being a notable exception. Remarkably, however, there are currently no plans to include the existing urban bird index in the next suite of sustainability indicators when they are revised in 2010. This would be particularly ironic, given that substantial evidence is now available as to the importance of interactions with wildlife, and nature more generally, for human health and wellbeing, and for support for wildlife conservation, and the predominance of such interactions within urban areas.

Acknowledgements

We are grateful to J.E. Booth, Z.G. Davies, R.A. Fuller, C. Galbraith, S. Gaston, D. Knight, N. Maclean and R. Sharp for comments and discussion.

References

Angilletta, M.J., Wilson, R.S., Niehaus, A.C. *et al.* (2007). Urban physiology: city ants possess high heat tolerance. *PLoS One*, **2**, e258.

Baillie, S.R., Marchant, J.H., Crick, H.Q.P. *et al.* (2007). Breeding birds in the wider countryside: their conservation status 2007, BTO Research Report No. 487 (http://www.bto.org/birdtrends).

Brown, A. and Grice, P. (2005). *Birds in England*, London, Poyser.

Cheptou, P-O., Carrue, O., Rouifed, S. and Cantarel, A. (2008). Rapid evolution of seed dispersal in an urban environment in the weed *Crepis sancta. Proceedings of the National Academy of Sciences, USA*, **105**, 3796–3799.

Crick, H., Banks, A. and Coombes, R. (2003). Findings of the national Peregrine survey 2002. *BTO News*, **248**, 8–9.

Davis, B.N.K. (1978). Urbanisation and the diversity of insects. In Mound, L.A. and Waloff, N., eds., *Diversity of Insect Faunas*, Oxford, Blackwell Scientific, pp. 126–138.

Davis, B.N.K. (1979). The ground arthropods of London gardens. *London Naturalist*, **58**, 15–24.

DEFRA (2003) *Measuring Progress: Baseline Assessment*, London, DEFRA.

DEFRA (2006) *e-Digest of Environmental Statistics*, http:www.defra.gov.uk/environment/statistics/index.htm.

De Laet, J. and Summers-Smith, J.D. (2007). The status of the urban house sparrow *Passer domesticus* in north-western Europe: a review. *Journal of Ornithology*, **148** (Supplement 2), S275-S278.

DfT (2007). *Transport trends,* 2007 edn, London, Department for Transport.

Fox, R., Conrad, K.F., Parsons, M.S., Warren, M.S. and Woiwod, I.P. (2006). *The State of Britain's Larger Moths*, Newbury, Pisces Publications.

Fuller, R.M., Smith, G.M., Sanderson, J.M. *et al.* (2002). Countryside Survey 2000 Module 7. Land Cover Map 2000. Final Report CSLCM/Final. Centre for Ecology and Hydrology, Monks Wood.

Guest, P., Jones, K.E. and Tovey, J. (2002). Bats in Greater London: unique evidence of a decline over 15 years. *British Wildlife*, **14**, 1–5.

Haines-Young, R.H., Barr, C.J., Black, H.I.J. *et al.* (2000). *Accounting for Nature: Assessing Habitats in the UK Countryside*, London, Department of the Environment, Transport and the Regions.

Hardy, P.B. and Dennis, R.L.H. (1999). The impact of urban development on butterflies within a city region. *Biodiversity and Conservation*, **8**, 1261–1279.

Henderson, I., Chamberlain, D., Davis, S. and Noble, D. (2007). Changes in breeding bird populations due to housing development based on bird densities and assemblages along urban-rural gradients, BTO research report no. 464, Thetford, BTO.

Hitchings, S.P. and Beebee, T.J.C. (1997). Genetic substructuring as a result of barriers to gene flow in urban *Rana temporaria* (common frog) populations: implications for biodiversity conservation. *Heredity*, **79**, 117–127.

Hodkinson, D.J. and Thompson, K. (1997). Plant dispersal: the role of man. *Journal of Applied Ecology*, **34**, 1484–1496.

National Statistics (2007a). *Population Trends 130*, London, National Statistics.

National Statistics (2007b). News release: *UK population set to increase to 65 million over the next ten years*, London, National Statistics.

Pauleit, S., Ennos, R. and Golding, Y. (2005). Modeling the environmental impacts of urban land use and land cover change – a study in Merseyside, UK. *Landscape and Urban Planning*, **71**, 295–310.

Robinson, R.A. and Sutherland, W.J. (2002). Post-war changes in arable farming and biodiversity in Great Britain. *Journal of Applied Ecology*, **39**, 157–176.

Royal Commission on Environmental Pollution (2007). Twenty-sixth report: the urban environment. Available at http://www.rcep.org.uk.

RSPB (2008). Bird Garden BirdWatch. Available at http://www.rspb.org.uk/birdwatch/about.

Sadler, J.P., Small, E.C., Fiszpan, H., Telfer, M.G. and Niemelä, J. (2006). Investigating environmental variation and landscape characteristics of an urban-rural gradient using woodland carabid assemblages. *Journal of Biogeography*, **33**, 1126–1138.

Tratalos, J., Fuller, R.A., Evans, K.L. *et al.* (2007). Bird densities are associated with household densities. *Global Change Biology*, **13**, 1685–1695.

7

The Great Game: the interaction of field sports and conservation in Britain from the 1950s to 2008

Robin Sharp

Summary

Field sports have shaped and been shaped by the countryside over hundreds of years, reaching a peak around 1900. In spite of the decline of some species and the number of gamekeepers since WW II, game bags remain substantial, partly due to release of large numbers of reared pheasants and partridges. Habitat managed for shooting and hunting foxes is beneficial for other species of fauna and flora, but the interaction of Grouse, Hen Harriers and keepers remains unresolved. Numbers of wintering wildfowl have increased by *c.* 40%, partly due to collaboration between shooters and conservationists following post-WW II conflicts. Deer populations are large and expanding and require management strategies. Shooters are spending *c.* £2 billion annually, including £250 million on habitat conservation. A new European Charter on Hunting and Biodiversity provides a framework for enhanced co-operation between field sports and conservation interests.

Introduction

Over a long historical perspective, hunting, shooting and fishing have been deeply rooted in British culture as admired pursuits, while conservation is a relative newcomer. Superficially, field sports and conservation of wildlife appear to be in direct conflict and the story of the last 50 years is not without its record of clashes between the two interests. Yet it may come as a surprise to those whose understanding of wildlife conservation is shaped by beguiling television images of 'wild nature' that field sports, as practised over the last 50 years, have been almost universally good for the hunted species and the non-hunted, non-predators that thrive in the same habitat.

Britain may have very few endemic species, but is gloriously endowed with large and spectacular populations of wintering wildfowl and waders, and has continually

Silent Summer: The State of Wildlife in Britain and Ireland, ed. Norman Maclean. Published by Cambridge University Press. © Cambridge University Press 2010.

increasing and arguably over-abundant deer numbers. While there are management issues about some game birds, over-hunting, scarcely figures as a factor in recent decline. The finger points rather to intensive agriculture and forestry.

Game is wildlife which may be legally hunted, along with pest species. This chapter aims to assemble population trend information where available, examines some questions about the effect of game management on associated wildlife and presents the socio-economics of wildlife use and international agreements to secure sustainable outcomes. We shall look briefly at small game, wildfowl and deer. It is necessary to appreciate that there is no natural state of wildlife or game species in Britain to which we can revert as an ideal benchmark. Both game and the landscape have been managed over hundreds if not thousands of years.

Small game: the landscape management background

Small game is mostly birds, such as Pheasant, Partridge, Grouse, Snipe and Woodcock, and mammals such as Rabbits and Hares. Their status and current trends need to be understood against a broad historical background of countryside management and shooting practice over some 300 years.

When the 1671 Game Laws made shooting the prerogative of the 16 000 landowners, only one-third of the countryside was arable under the three-field rotational system. Slow flint-lock muzzle-loading guns were used to shoot birds on the ground, while retrieving dogs were introduced in the eighteenth century, and round shot allowed birds in flight to be targeted. Between 1750 and 1850, the Enclosure Acts transformed the landscape, hedging in arable land, adding turnips and clover to produce more winter fodder to increase stock and thus manure to add further to productivity (for this and many unattributed references in this section see Tapper 1992).

In the late nineteenth-century cheap grain from the American prairies caused impoverished traditional land-owners to sell out to rich industrialists, who were not dependent on agricultural income, but very keen to invest in game management. The combination of hedges providing nesting cover for Partridge and Pheasant, cereal crops offering good foraging and crop rotation provided a near perfect habitat for game birds and Hares alike. The replacement of muzzle-loading by breech-loading around 1860 led to the design of the sporting gun, using smokeless cartridges and ejectors, which is still in use today. However, it was not until the 1840s that the railways opened up Highland Grouse shooting as a commercial activity for impoverished Scottish landlords.

Against this background one more ingredient was needed to make the Edwardian era the high point of game shooting in Britain. This was the gamekeeper, who had essentially two functions: controlling predators and preventing poaching. Their numbers peaked at 20 056 in England, Wales and Scotland in 1911, when most of lowland Britain was covered with a network of well-keepered estates. By 1951 they had declined to 4391, when the national census ceased to record them separately. By extrapolation it has been deduced that there were some 2500 full-time keepers and a total of 3000, including part-timers, in 1990.

Traditionally, gamekeepers treated as vermin any bird or mammal which was known to take game birds or their eggs and chicks. This meant not only Foxes, Stoats, Crows and Magpies, but Buzzards, Kites, Eagles, Harriers, Pine Martens, Polecats and Wildcats as well. There can be no doubt about their success. The decline in the numbers of gamekeepers during the twentieth century and the increasing restrictions on species which could be killed and the methods of vermin control available to them correlate strongly with the recovery of these species over the same period, though positive human interventions played a part in some cases.

Along with the decline in gamekeeper numbers and their effectiveness in controlling predators, the twentieth century witnessed further significant changes in land management and economics. After WW II, nearly all game shooting was at a standstill. In the lowlands the 'Food from Our Own Resources' policy led to intensive production, with separation of arable and dairy farms. Larger tractors encouraged increased field size which led to the removal of 800 000 km of hedgerows by 1974, while increased crop spraying reduced flora and thus the insects that depended on it. In the uplands, sheep numbers increased under the incentive of payments per head, causing serious encroachment of heather moorland to the detriment of Grouse and other moorland birds.

As prosperity grew, those land-owners who wanted to maintain sport shooting for commercial or recreational reasons invested in and managed small woodlands, whilst restoring field margins and hedgerows, prompted by the scientific work of The Game Conservancy Trust and modest agri-environmental grants from the public purse. The large traditional shoots which might take place once or twice a season gave way to more frequent smaller shoots where shooters would pay for a day's sport. To provide the supply of birds needed for this level of activity in the face of less suitable habitat for breeding and increased protection for predators, the stocking of captive-reared Pheasants and Partridges, released from predator-resistant pens, has come to dominate the lowland small-game shooting scene. Around 80% of Pheasant, *Phasianus colchius*, and most Red-legged Partridges, *Alectoris rufa*, currently shot are from releasing programmes.

In the absence of full ecological monitoring for the main game species, estate game bag records from over 500 estates covering at peak 1.5 million hectares over the period 1961 to 1985 were analysed for trend information by The Game Conservancy Trust's National Game Bag Census (NGC), along with a smaller sample of estate bag data going back to 1900. The bag records show the number of birds shot for each day of shooting in a defined shoot area, thus allowing the number of birds killed per km^2 per area per year or bag density to be determined. From this, long-term trends and the geographical distribution by county have been derived. These are discussed below by groups of species.

Small game: trends in main species

Rabbits (*Oryctolagus cuniculus*) have suffered from a chequered history since their introduction around 1100 for food supply (see Chapter 4). They were enjoyed as 'off the ration' meat in the 1940s, as the present writer can attest from his boyhood experience of eating them in rural Lincolnshire. Following myxomatosis in 1954, few people wished to eat any of those remaining. Nevertheless, bag records since 1960 show a gradual rise and the taste for wild Rabbit is slowly returning. Shooting is mainly for control purposes.

The introduced Brown Hare (*Lepus europaeus*) is widespread in Europe. It has adapted to arable farming systems and does not need woodlands or hedges as long as there is ground cover to avoid predation of leverets. Brown Hares can be killed as agricultural pests, as well as game, and may be taken incidentally or in occasional organised shoots, as well as being a poacher's favourite. Although the bag trend since 1900 is down, there was a post-war upsurge until 1960, followed by a marked downward trend until 1980, after which near stability was maintained. Since the post-1960 decline was experienced on the Continent as well, simplification of arable systems may be a cause. However, changes in Fox numbers due to reduced keepering may also be involved, as Fox abundance seems to correlate with changes in Hare bags. By contrast, the Mountain Hare (*Lepus timidus*) is a native which thrives on managed heather moorland. Indigenous in the Scottish Highlands, it was also introduced to the Borders, North Wales and the Peak District. After a steep decline from 1930 to 1946 numbers recovered, fell again twice, but from 1980 began a significant recovery with around 1000 in the Peak District alone. More recently there has been a decline in areas across Scotland. For Hares see also Chapters 4 and 15.

Partridges and Pheasants have always been central to shooting sport in lowland Britain. The Grey Partridge (*Perdix perdix*) is specially favoured (see Chapter 18), but has also suffered the most serious decline among the major game species. The Red-legged Partridge was introduced for shooting in the eighteenth century and has thrived, especially in East Anglia. The chicks appear to be less dependent on insects than Grey Partridges and thus less affected by the use of herbicides (Green 1984), but numbers were probably held back by the increase in predation which accompanied the decrease in gamekeepers. After it was found that Redlegs were much easier to rear than Greys, the number released rose from around two per km^2 in 1960 to an average of 70 per km^2 from 1980 to 1990, thus leading to a substantial growth in bags and population numbers (Tapper 1992).

The Pheasant, which may have come in with the Normans, is now the most numerous gamebird in Britain. An estimated 15 million are shot annually, of which perhaps 80% are hand-reared (Tapper 1992; PACEC 2006). Because of the volume of releases, both population and bag numbers are on an upward trend, but there may be a slight decline in the wild population. The rearing method is to keep the chicks in brooder units and then release them into pens on the shoots, usually in

Figure 7.1 The Red Grouse affords the most prestigious and expensive shooting in Britain.
To thrive it depends on skillfully managed heather moorland (see colour plate). (Photograph
by Laurie Campbell.)

woodlands, after six or seven weeks. Winter feeding through hoppers keeps the
birds on the estates. The ecological effects of creating and maintaining woodland
for pheasant management are generally positive, provided the density is not too high
(Draycott *et al.* 2008).

The Red Grouse (*Lagopus lagopus scoticus*) still affords the most prestigious and
expensive shooting in Britain. While remaining entirely wild, it requires skilful management for its numbers to be maintained or restored. Moreover the external factors
which affect its success and cyclical patterns are still not fully understood. It is present
on heather moorland throughout Scotland, in parts of Wales, northern England, the
Peak District and the south-west. Figure 7.1 shows the bird resplendent in its essential
habitat.

The main management technique is to burn heather in strips at different times
to provide young shoots for eating and older heather as nesting cover close at hand.
Predation control is also important, with the consequences mentioned later in this
chapter. Perhaps surprisingly, the highest bags have always come from the northern
English moors, where trends from 1900 and 1960 are more or less stable. In Scotland
there has been substantial overall decline, masking a steep decline from 1930 to 1945,
a recovery up to 1970 followed by a serious decline until 1987, when a slight recovery
occurred. Game Conservancy Trust research found that the impact of predators in
Scotland was much more severe than had previously been thought (Hudson 1992). It is

highly likely that the cycles in Grouse bags are due to disease, especially the parasitic worm, strongylosis (Hudson and Dobson 1990).

For the Ptarmigan (*Lagopus mutus*), the still widely spread grouse species of Scottish alpine habitats and the Nordic countries, NGC data show negative trends in bags of −70% since 1961, with most of the decline occurring in the last 10 years (Aebischer and Harradine 2007). It is less shot now than before, but its estimated population size of over 10 000 breeding pairs, though cyclic, is considered stable. A BTO survey in 2006 testing the use of non-expert volunteers (i.e. climbers and hill-walkers) recorded the highest encounter rates in the Cairngorms and none at all in Skye and Mull, where previous Bird Atlas surveys found Ptarmigan presence (Calladine and Wernham 2007).

The spectacular Black Grouse (*Tetrao tetrix)* is unfortunately much less common in Britain and Continental Europe than it was. Its preferred habitat is birch and pine woodland with bushes and patches of open ground where it is a highly selective feeder on berries, shoots and trees. Increased grazing pressure by deer and sheep appears to be a causal factor. Its geographical spread is currently similar to that of the Red Grouse, but it was once present in every English county. Trend numbers from 1900 are severely down, but from a low point during the years 1963 to 1975 there was a slight recovery up to 1990. Since then the Black Grouse Biodiversity Action Plan target for numbers of males at leks in northern England has been reached ahead of the deadline. In 2008 the Forestry Commission announced a £830 000 plan running to 2012 for improving 50 sites important for Black Grouse in Scotland, where current breeding male numbers are estimated at 3500, after a decline of 29% over the last decade.

The even more splendid Capercaillie (*Tetrao urogallus*), a bird of northern coniferous forests with a specialised diet, now hangs on in Scotland, having already been made extinct once and then so successfully reintroduced in the ninteenth century that one can find a recipe for it in Mrs Beeton. Since 1960 numbers again fell dramatically with lack of old open pine forest, abundance of predators such as Foxes (*Vulpes vulpes*) and Crows (*Corvus corone*) and recoveries among Pine Marten (*Martes martes*) and Wildcat (*Felis sylvestris*) being the main factors. Intensive restoration measures are now in place under the Biodiversity Action Plan and appear to be working, with numbers increased from 1100 in 1994 to 2000 in 2004. Breeding success is generally low, with as few as 30% of hens rearing a brood. There are serious knowledge gaps about the precise nature of predation and the survival rates of adult birds.

Happily there is a better story to tell for two elusive, but much sought after lowland birds, the Woodcock (*Scolopax rusticola*) and the Common Snipe (*Gallinago gallinago*). Woodcock have extended their range to breed throughout Britain, except the south-west (Gibbons *et al.* 1993), but are very selective in choosing types of open woodland for males to perform their nocturnal circular flight displays, known as roding, and foraging ground rich in invertebrates. Spring shooting was common, but then thought to be damaging until research showed that Woodcock are not monogamous and that if a dominant male was removed by shooting, another would soon take its place (Hirons 1983). A special survey in 2003 estimated at least 78 000 breeding males in Britain (Hoodless *et al.* in press). There is also a significant inward migration of Woodcock from Sweden to East Anglia and the south-west in the winter, the high point being the first full moon in November. Bags are always small, but highly valued both because the bird is a challenging shot and the eating is excellent, if not for all tastes. From 1962 the bag trend is upwards, with hard winters producing bigger bags, 2009 proving to be no exception.

The Common Snipe breeds throughout most of Britain, but moves south from breeding to wintering areas, while there is also an inward winter migration from Scandinavia and Eastern Europe. Between 20 and 30 million Snipe are estimated to move through Europe from the east during the autumn. Nesting on wet open pasture in tussocks of grass, where the eggs are vulnerable to trampling by livestock and predation, Snipe have a low breeding success (Mason and Macdonald 1976) indicating possible replenishment by the inward migrants. Snipe shooting has to be specially organised, except on Grouse moors, where wet areas may occur. During the 30 years to 1990 bags showed little real change, but were well down on pre-war levels. The smaller Jack Snipe (*Lymnocryptes minimus*) is much less common and no longer a game species.

An overview of changes in game bags per km^2 of key species between the first and ninth decades of the twentieth century is given in Table 7.1.

A major factor in the declines appears to be the growth in the numbers of predators of small game such as Polecat, Mink, Fox, Magpie and Carrion and Hooded Crows, stemming partly from the greatly decreased number of gamekeepers and partly from

Table 7.1 *Game bags per km^2 as an index of long-term trends during the twentieth century*

	1900–10	1980–9
Pheasant	14.80	48.60
Grey Partridge	27.50	5.50
Red-legged Partridge	0.82	9.60
Woodcock	0.50	2.10
Common Snipe	0.45	0.14
Brown Hare	15.80	9.00
Rabbit	36.50	12.40
Lowland total	**96.37**	**87.34**
Red Grouse	58.59	26.23
Black Grouse	0.59	0.03
Capercaillie	0.23	0.06
Mountain Hare	2.03	1.08
Upland total	**61.44**	**27.40**

(*Source*: Tapper 1992)

increased opportunities for opportunistic predation from roadkill, landfill sites and urban waste. Against this trend has been the huge increase in the numbers of reared and released Pheasants and Red-legged Partridges. Overall, small game species are still relatively abundant where the habitat permits, with Grey Partridge, Black Grouse and Capercaillie being species of concern.

Some issues connected with small game

Red Grouse and Hen Harriers: with and without keepers

One of the most contentious issues relating to small game is the effect of Hen Harriers (*Circus cyaneus*) on breeding Red Grouse and the effect of gamekeepers on Hen Harriers. Before legal protection was afforded to Hen Harriers in 1961, they were one of the principal species which gamekeepers made it their business to remove from Grouse moors. Where Harriers are present on a Grouse moor and their numbers grow, the argument from the game management side is that they will destroy or badly damage the shooting interest, thus making it pointless to employ keepers to manage the moor and control predators generally. This has now been established scientifically (Thirgood *et al.* 2000), although still contested by Scottish Natural Heritage. Owners and managers of Grouse shoots believe that some control of Harriers should be allowed. However, Harriers are fully protected by law under the EC Birds Directive (EC 1979), which is fiercely upheld by bird protectionists, notably the RSPB, who argue that the species is endangered in the UK and draw attention to the inescapable fact that illegal killing still takes place, presumably in support of game interests.

Long-term studies to throw light on these issues have been continuing in phases at Langholm Moor, Scotland, since 1990, facilitated by the owner, the Duke of Buccleuch. From 1990, birds of prey were given full protection and there was active keepering to control other predators and carry out heather burning and parasite control. From 2000, due to the decline in Grouse numbers and the economic loss associated with it, keepering ceased. The findings so far are that the number of Harriers rose from two breeding females in 1992 to 20 in 1997 (Redpath and Thirgood 1997), perhaps assisted by an explosion in the vole population, and then declined to two by 2004, rising to four in 2006, while the pre-shooting density of Grouse was halved by 1998 and fell even lower after that before rising slightly. While Harrier numbers were rising, Meadow Pipit numbers were falling, along with the reduction in Grouse density, but numbers of Golden Plover, Curlew and Skylark were two to three times more abundant during the keepering period than afterwards. From 2001 numbers of Carrion Crows increased fourfold and numbers of Foxes significantly.

The strong inference is that general predator control by keepers is beneficial, not only to Grouse, but to other important species, while a complete absence of keepers is bad news for Harriers and other ground-nesting species, as well as Grouse (Baines *et al.* 2008). The precise role of the Harriers in determining the level at which Grouse moor management is no longer viable remains unclear, bearing in mind fluctuations in the Grouse population due to strongylosis and other variables affecting breeding success. Moreover, so long as no control of Harrier numbers is permitted, it will not be possible to see whether economic Grouse moor management and a reasonable number of Harriers can co-exist satisfactorily. This is currently being addressed by a new collaborative study at Langholm, chaired by Scottish Natural Heritage. A further complication is that while Grouse shooting contributed some £14.7 million and 940 jobs to the economy in Scotland in 2000, the majority of estates were still conducting the sport at a loss (Fraser of Allander 2001).

Fox hunting and habitat management: is there a benefit?

The law in England, Wales and Scotland now forbids the killing of a hunted Fox by hounds. However, contrary to the claims made before the legislation was enacted, organised riding to hounds in pursuit of Foxes continues on a large scale. A recent study showed that where Fox hunts were managing woodland within a hunt area by such practices as tree planting, coppicing, felling, and ride and perimeter management, vegetation cover was present in 86% of managed woodland compared with 64% in unmanaged. As a result, the managed area had an average of four more plant species than the unmanaged, and greater plant diversity, while butterfly species numbers averaged 2.2 in the managed compared with 0.3 for the unmanaged area (Ewald *et al.* 2006).

Do the practitioners of field sports contribute more than other private land-owners to conservation?

Three areas in central England, each falling within the area of a Fox hunt, were studied to see whether there were differences in new woodland and hedgerow planting between a random sample of hunting and non-hunting farmers. Those who hunted and shot had all planted new woodland, while nearly 70% of those who only shot, 60% of those who only hunted and 38% of those who did neither had done so. New hedgerow planting had been carried out by 100% of those who both hunted and belonged to an advisory group on hedgerow conservation, but only by less than 20% of those who did neither. Moreover, new planting apart, the hunters and shooters maintained more woodland and longer, more diverse hedgerows than the non-practitioners. This suggests that those who hunt and/or shoot provide significant conservation benefits, offering scope for policies to be devised to incentivise such practices (Oldfield *et al.* 2003). Broadly similar evidence was obtained from a questionnaire survey of shooting and non-shooting farms in Essex, where farms practising driven shooting constituted 10% of all holdings in the county.

Are there benefits for song birds from a range of game-management practices?

Intensive game management has been carried out on a farm at Loddington, Leicestershire, since 1993 to allow The Game and Wildlife Conservation Trust to make comparisons with neighbouring farms where such a regime is absent. This has comprised eliminating predators such as Magpies (*Pica pica*), Crows, Foxes and Stoats, reducing pest numbers (e.g. Woodpigeons (*Columba palumbus*), Rooks (*Corvus frugilegus*) and Rabbits), thinning and replanting woodland, widening field margins and replanting set-aside as 20 m wide strips using bird-seed options, as well as providing hopper feeding for pheasants. There were major increases in hedgerow residents (e.g. Wrens (Troglodytes troglodytes) from 47 to 141 pairs, Song Thrushes (*Turdus philomelos*) 14 to 56 pairs), resident seed-eating Finches (e.g. Chaffinches (*Fringilla coelebs*) 135 to 229 pairs, Greenfinches (*Carduelis chloris*) 15 to 62 pairs) and migratory Warblers and Flycatchers (e.g. Blackcaps (*Sylvia atricapillata*) 19 to 38 pairs, Willow Warblers (*Phylloscopus trochilus*) 28 to 47 pairs). In 2002, predator control was stopped and this was followed by reductions in numbers of most species in the first two groups (Tapper 2007).

Similar studies in Scotland have shown that game crops provide a summer habitat for song birds and butterflies, producing 80 times as many birds and 15 times as many butterflies as on nearby conventional crops (Parish and Sotherton 2004a). There is also ample evidence that game crops provide important food sources in winter for farmland passerines, Kale and Quinoa being especially important.

Effect of gamekeeping on birds of upland areas

The RSPB, in collaboration with The Game Conservancy Trust, surveyed birds on 232 sites managed and not managed for Grouse in Northern England and Scotland in 1995 and 1996. In this survey, bird distribution and abundance varied between sites according to whether they were managed for Grouse or not. Not surprisingly, more Red Grouse and fewer Crows were found on managed moors. Meadow Pipit (*Anthus pratensis*), Skylark (*Alauda arvensis*) and Whinchat (*Saxicola rubetra*) were between 1.5 and 3.9 times less abundant on Grouse moors, but Golden Plover (*Pluvialis apricaria*) and Lapwing (*Vanellus vanellus*) were five times, and Curlew (*Numenius arquata*) were twice as abundant on Grouse moors (Tharme *et al.* 2001). In the light of this, the Game Conservancy identified four 1200 ha sites in Redesdale, Northumberland, for an eight-year study from 2000 to 2008 to examine the effect of predator control for Grouse on breeding success and abundance of waders and other moorland birds. One site had predator control throughout the period, another had none, while of the other two one operated as a control for the first four years and the other for the second four. Breeding stocks of Red Grouse increased by around 400% after three years of predator control. In three of the sites, all the waders bred better where predators were controlled (Fletcher 2008). In another survey, the North Pennines area of Grouse moors was found to contain 700 pairs of Golden Plover and 3900 pairs of Curlew, the presence of which attracted Natura 2000 designation, as did the North York Moors Grouse moors for their high density of Merlin (*Falco columbarius*) (Tapper 2005).

Wildfowl and wildfowling: post-war conflict and consensus

Wildfowl in Britain have been shot as sport and for the pot for as long as the requisite guns have been available. Yet a seminal book, which captured the interface between the conservation and shooting of wild ducks and geese in Britain in the post WW II period, was justifiably entitled *A Wealth of Wildfowl* (Harrison 1973). The author revealed that, thanks to its estuaries, mudflats, marshes and wetlands, the British Isles hosted a large and diverse population of, mostly wintering, wildfowl, coming from a range of Arctic or near-Arctic regions. This remains the case today as a result of imaginative collaboration at that time between leading wildfowlers and conservationists.

Post-war Britain saw the emergence or transformation of many public institutions, which have since contributed to the richness of our cultural life. In the present context, one was the Wildfowlers' Association of Great Britain and Ireland (WAGBI). Founded in 1908 and effectively run for the next 40 years by Stanley Duncan, a wildfowler from Hull, the Association was revitalised in 1947 to meet the challenge of expected restrictive legislation, which for the first time would put the rules governing wildfowling onto a national rather than a local level. It was to counter the threats to wildfowl in Britain and throughout the European flyway that Sir Peter Scott, himself a former wildfowler, founded the then Severn Wildfowl Trust (now the Wildfowl and Wetlands Trust) at almost the same time. Combining the establishment of reserves open to the visiting public with a brief to assemble much-needed scientific information, the Trust immediately became the focal point for wildfowl conservation. Holding the ring was the official Nature Conservancy, conceived and then directed by the redoubtable Max Nicholson to pioneer science-based conservation policies throughout the kingdom.

While WAGBI members feared any national legislation, the then quite small RSPB believed that wildfowl numbers were in decline, while the heavyweight Wildfowl Inquiry Committee of the International Committee for Bird Preservation (British section) broke up in acrimony in 1954 owing to profound disagreements about the status of wildfowl, especially the Brent Goose (*Branta bernicla*). Peter Scott attempted to mediate in the *Shooting Times,* assuring wildfowlers that wildfowl were a natural resource which could and should be harvested, but that research into their population numbers was necessary for conservation purposes, while at the same time explaining to protectionists that rocket netting of large numbers of Pinkfeet (*Anser brachyrhynchus*) for scientific monitoring was not harmful. When Lady Tweedsmuir used disputed data to justify including a ban on Brent shooting in the Protection of Birds Bill, such policy-making without agreed on-the-record data was deeply upsetting to WAGBI.

Nevertheless, once the Bill was enacted, WAGBI undertook to uphold it and held a joint meeting with the Wildfowl Trust to restore better relations. Max Nicholson then held a series of tea parties at the Conservancy headquarters in Belgrave Square to weld together 'the finest team for wildfowl conservation that this country has ever seen'. Writing in WAGBI's *The New Wildfowler* (Sedgwick *et al.* 1961), he argued that wildfowl counts and related research were essential if the facts were to be established, that these must involve input from wildfowlers, that information about the development of reserves should be shared openly with wildfowlers to avoid rumours of dark conspiracies, that wildfowlers should accept the need for conservation of habitats and stocks, while protectionists should recognise the legitimacy of wildfowling properly conducted and finally that large-scale practical experiments were needed to show that management of reserves could co-exist successfully and amicably with wildfowling. These remain key principles for the sustainable use of wildlife.

Out of these efforts came an important legacy. The Conservancy's Wildfowl Conservation Committee became responsible for the establishment of a National System of Wildfowl Refuges, designed to increase the stock to the advantage of sportsmen and naturalists alike. The first refuge was on the Humber and soon came the spectacular achievement of Caerlaverock on the Solway where 1500 acres of grazed merse and 12 000 acres of foreshore, which hosted the Spitzbergen population of Barnacle Geese (*Branta leucopsis*), were declared a National Nature Reserve. At the same time, and in agreement with the local wildfowlers, controlled shooting was to be permitted in certain areas. In 1970 the Wildfowl Trust established a visitor centre, enabling the public to observe one of the outstanding wildlife spectacles in Britain. Very quickly a network of 21 National and 26 Regional Refuges was built up, using official designations to complement the reserves being set up by the Wildfowl Trust and the RSPB. Once all this was in place, habitat management was instituted with the objective of increasing wildfowl and other wildlife numbers, where feasible.

Wildfowl: long-term trends

The co-operation cemented through these joint efforts proved to be a spur to the strengthening of the wildfowl counts and the acceptance of their results by all sides. By any standards, these have been among the most rigorous and well-supported monitoring schemes in the story of conservation. Started by the Wildfowl Inquiry Committee and then transferred to the Wildfowl Trust in 1954, the National Wildfowl Counts have been carried out by volunteers monthly during the winter at synchronised times at specific important wetland, estuary and coastal sites, the number rising from 500 sites in 1951/2 to 2000 at the present day. Now named the Wetland Bird Survey (WeBS), they cover all wildfowl and wader species, as well as other wetland birds. Table 7.2 sets out long-term trends in the numbers of wild ducks and geese counted.

The count numbers are the highest monthly totals in the September/March period in 2006/07 from the *c.* 2000 sites where counting now takes place, for species where

Table 7.2 *WeBS long-term trends for England, Wales and Scotland: geese and ducks in 1966/7, with range of values 1966/7–2006/7, relative to an index of 100 in 2006/7*

Species	66/7[a] Index	Low Index	High Index	Count 06/07 (Index = 100)
Pink-footed Goose	33	28	132	203 167
Euro White-fronted Goose	671	100	2154	1341
Greenland White-front Goose	48[b]	48	143	14 996
Iceland Greylag	80	70	152	73 740
Re-established Greylag	8	6	100	27 746
Canada Goose	16	16	100	52 486
Svalbard Barnacle Goose	15	13	108	29 635
Dark-bellied Brent	19	16	143	88 738
Light-bellied Brent	10	1	228	3352
Shelduck	74	70	132	48 667
Wigeon	60	60	126	324 362
Gadwall	11	11	127	15 018
Teal	32	32	125	127 019
Mallard	173	100	182	121 545
Pintail	32	32	125	25 348
Shoveler	40	37	122	11 687
Pochard	155	100	185	25 160
Tufted Duck	58	58	110	53 511
Scaup	700	77	1054	3038
Eider	45	36	171	21 556
Goldeneye	95	78	166	12 171
Red-breasted Merganser	37	37	183	3425
Goosander	50	50	207	2643
Ruddy Duck	4[c]	4	240	2078
Total counted in 2006/07				1 292 429

Notes: [a] = unless otherwise noted; [b] = 82/83; [c] = 68/69.
(*Source*: Wetland Bird Survey (WeBS) administered by the BTO, JNCC, WWT and RSPB.)

over 1000 were counted and, with a few exceptions, where figures are not comparable or reliable. Because there will be some birds at smaller sites where there is no counting, a considerable number in the case of Mallard (*Anas platyrhynchos*), Teal (*Anas crecca*) and Tufted Ducks (*Aythya fuligula*), which are partly inland species, the figures represent minima, not estimates of the total wintering population. For years prior to the latest, indices are used, taking 100 to equate with the latest count, because the number of sites has increased substantially over the years, so that total counts would not accurately indicate trends. Thus if 100 is in the 'Low' column it means that the latest count produced the lowest total for that species since 1966/7 (except for b and c), while if 100 is in the 'High' column it means that the latest count was the highest. Taking Scaup as an example, the 1966/7 index figure means that the count then was equal to 7×3038 (21 266) while the lowest and highest counts in between were 77% and 1054% of 3038 respectively. If the last count is not the highest, it does not follow that the species is on a declining trend, either in the long or the short term, because winter numbers can fluctuate according to breeding and weather conditions. In particular, it should be noted that in a number of important cases the 2005/6 count figures were considerably higher than those for 2006/7 (Musgrove, *et al.* 2007).

Nevertheless, the table reveals some striking trends. Four species have shown overall long-term declines: European White-front (*Anser albifrons albifrons*), Mallard, Pochard (*Aythya farina*) and Scaup (*Aythya marila*). Two have been more-or-less stable, though with a slight overall increase, subject to rises and falls in the intervening years: Iceland Greylag (*Anser anser*) and Goldeneye (*Bucepaela clangula*). Eighteen have increased either in a straight line (re-established Greylag and Canada Goose (*Branta canadensis*)) or in a fluctuating mode. Many of the increases are spectacular (e.g. Pinkfoot × 3 or *c.* 140 000 birds, Dark-bellied Brent × 5 or *c.* 72 000 birds, Wigeon (*Anas penelope*) × 1.6 or *c.* 122 000 birds) especially when set against the declines in many inland species. Just taking these counts on their own and offsetting reductions against increases, there was a net gain of at least 500 000 wild ducks and geese in Britain in the winter of 2006/07, compared with the estimated position in 1966/67. Another indication of success is that about 2.2 million waterbirds of all kinds are estimated to be present in January in UK Special Protection Areas designated under the EC Birds Directive, about 40% of the total in the UK (Stroud, personal communication).

Explanations for this gratifying situation differ according to species. For example, Pinkfeet historically bred in small interior desert areas in Iceland and showed low productivity, but their numbers grew and breeding success improved as they moved to the agricultural lowlands. Greylag, which are more widely dispersed, also increased, but declined slightly after 1990. Both species are hunted in Iceland and Britain. Reduction of hunting pressure in Iceland is considered to be a factor in the recovery of Greenland White-front numbers, although strangely, in view of their relatively low numbers in the UK and a reported decline over the last decade, shooting of White-front is still permitted here. On the other hand, shooting of Barnacle and Brent Geese is banned under the 1981 Wildlife and Countryside Act, notwithstanding their current large and healthy populations. The British Association for Shooting and Conservation (BASC), the successor of WAGBI and celebrating its centenary in 2008 (Downing 2007), takes a leading role in encouraging responsible shooting. When in the 1980s it emerged that lead shot falling into wetland areas was being ingested by waterbirds, whether or not target species, and causing their long-term poisoning, BASC worked with the authorities (despite some unwilling members) to establish the precise scientific position and to move towards ultimate phasing out in 1999. Alternatives to lead shot now in use include steel and combinations of tungsten with other materials.

The role of the habitat in these population increases or recoveries does not seem to have been subject to quantitative analysis. On the one hand, there has been a substantial increase in wildfowl reserves in the wake of the National Wildfowl Refuge initiative of the 1960s and they have been adaptively managed for favourable conservation status. On the other hand, at least until the 1990s when reforms began and the worst perverse subsidies were withdrawn, conflicting pressures from agricultural policy to drain inland wetlands for production were negative for wildfowl. It may also be the case that there is now greater tolerance for wintering geese feeding on farmland. The balance of habitat effects remains obscure.

Deer

Wild deer are large mammals present in most areas of England, Wales and Scotland and yet their presence goes largely unnoticed by the general public, until they collide with traffic. Except for Red Deer (*Cervus elaphus*) they have not been a major focus for sport shooting, as they are on the Continent and in North America. However, interest in stalking lowland deer is thought to have taken off when servicemen returning from WW II brought back continental traditions. This was when the British Deer Society began life with most members being stalkers. The six wild species comprise two natives: Red Deer and Roe Deer (*Capreolus capreolus*), one naturalised: Fallow Deer (*Dama dama*) and three nineteenth- or early twentieth-century introductions: Sika (*Cervus nippon*), Muntjac (*Muntiacus reevesi*) and Chinese Water Deer (*Hydropotes inermis*). For more information on the history and distribution of these species over the British Isles see Chapter 15 and for the impact of the introduced species on native deer and vegetation see Chapter 4. There has been no systematic nationally funded effort to establish numbers, but one recent estimate is of interest, notwithstanding its admitted shortcomings (Table 7.3).

What has been monitored is the rate of spread to new areas of all six species over the years between 1972 and 2007. Table 7.4 summarises the information collected from observation surveys, based on 10 km squares, the most recent organised by the British Deer Society.

These increases in distribution across the country are noteworthy, even if some of the expansion may reflect greater survey effort. In spite of the lack of formal counting, it is virtually certain that numbers have grown substantially along with spread of populations. The JNCC Tracking Mammals Partnership's latest report (Battersbury 2005) provides somewhat higher estimates of population numbers than those given in Table 7.3, especially for Roe Deer. NGC bag records from 1961 show Red Deer increasing by 165% and Roe increasing by 520%, while Muntjac increased by 1400% from 1980. Range expansion and growing numbers are, in principle, welcome for recreational, economic and aesthetic reasons; for some negative aspects see Chapter 4.

The Deer Commission for Scotland (DCS), now merged with Scottish Natural Heritage, is a government agency which is dedicated to monitoring and managing deer

Table 7.3 *National abundance estimates of each species of deer*

	England	Scotland	Wales	Relative confidence in estimate
Red	$14\,000^b$	$301\,500^c$	250^b	Moderate
Roe	$90\,000^c$	$>200\,000^c$	3000^a	Very low
Fallow	$110\,000^b$	$17\,000^a$	$>1000^b$	Moderate-low
Sika	2600^b	$25\,000^b$	$>1^c$	Moderate
Muntjac	$86\,500^a$	0^c	6000^a	Low
Chinese Water Deer	1500^b	0^b	0^b	High

Superscript letters after each estimate represent whether it was considered to be: [a] over-estimated, [c] under-estimated or [b] probably close to the true population size, based on discussion with deer specialists and best professional judgement.
(*Source:* Ward and Young 2005.)

Table 7.4 *Range expansion of British deer populations 1972–2007*

	Chinese Water Deer	Fallow	Muntjac	Red	Sika	Roe
Number of 10 km squares at 1972	23	249	40	576	69	778
Number of 10 km squares at 2002	50	568	472	844	317	1567
Number of 10 km squares at 2007	136	1025	816	1200	451	2022
Annual rate of change 1972–2002	2.0%	1.8%	8.2%	0.3%	5.3%	2.3%
Annual rate of change 2003–7	22.2%	12.5%	11.6%	7.3%	7.3%	5.2%

(*Source:* Ward *et al.* 2008.)

populations north of the border. The Commission has pursued a vigorous programme of surveying and culling at regional level. However, in a recent report, the Chairman ventured the view that at national level, Red Deer densities were remaining stable, although the species was spreading into new areas. Just over 100 000 deer of all species were culled in Scotland in 2005/6 to protect the natural heritage, prevent damage to woodland or agriculture or for public safety (Anon 2006, 2007). In August 2008, *The Scotsman* reported the arrival in Scotland of Chinese traders to negotiate the purchase of deer 'pizzles' which are judged to improve athletes' stamina and to have anti-inflammatory and injury-healing properties.

In England and Wales there is no single body concerned with these matters, but in 1995 The Deer Initiative was formed to ensure 'the delivery of a sustainable, well-managed wild deer population in England and Wales'. Made up of a range of statu-tory, voluntary and private bodies, who have signed up to a Deer Accord, its main spon-sors are DEFRA and the Forestry Commission. It promotes regional Deer Management Groups and has published an Action Plan for the Sustainable Management of Wild Deer Populations in England (Anon 2004). However, there is no view at a national level as to whether there are too many deer in some areas for the good of biodiversity. In a linked effort, the National Deer Collisions Project claims that 'the toll of deer involved annually in traffic collisions in the UK is estimated to lie between 40 000 to 74,000'. Bearing in mind that 120 000 deer are estimated to be shot each year (see Table 7.5), this would mean that humans are responsible for up to 200 000 deaths annually in a total population of *c*. 860 000 deer (Table 7.3 summed). It should be noted that the Deer Initiative consider that a current offtake of *c*. 350 000 from a British deer popula-tion of 1.5 to 2 million is more probable (personal communication).

To improve deer management and to enhance the welfare of wild deer, the Regulatory Reform (Deer) (England and Wales) Order 2007 amended the Deer Act 1991. It extended the hind season for deer by four weeks; allowed smaller-calibre rifles to be used to shoot Chinese Water Deer and Muntjac; allowed the licensed taking of deer out of season and at night to protect natural heritage, preserve public health and safety, or prevent serious property damage. Nevertheless, in the light of the continual growth of deer numbers and their range expansion, there is a need for communication with the wider public, based on more systematic monitoring of deer populations and their local impacts in order to promote understanding, both of the benefits this can bring and the necessity of control measures.

Table 7.5 *Numbers of main quarry species shot in GB and NI 2004 (000s)*

Pheasant	15 000
Partridge	2600
Duck	970
Grouse	400
Woodcock/Snipe	250
Goose	47
Deer	120[a][b]
Pigeon	3600[a]
Rabbit	590[a]
Hare	47[a]

Notes: [a] These species are shot both for sport and various control purposes.
[b] The Deer Initiative suggests a much larger figure – see above.
(*Source*: PACEC 2006.)

Table 7.6 *Participants and gun days by type of shooting GB and NI 2004 (000s)*

	Participants	Gun days
Driven lowland game	330	1500
Walked-up lowland game	270	1800
Grouse (driven and walked-up)	47	59
Deer stalking	86	680
Coastal wildfowling	71	370
Inland wildfowling	94	400
Pest control (pigeon, rabbit)	330	5400
Total	480	10000

(*Source*: PACEC 2006.)

What is being shot and by whom?

In line with our longstanding traditions of *laissez faire* and libertarianism, there has been no requirement for British hunters to record annual game bags and submit them to a regulating authority. Game-bag censuses, such as those operated by GCT in relation to small game and by BASC for wildfowl, are purely voluntary and more useful for identifying trends than overall volumes. The best picture obtainable is from a survey of shooters in 2004 (PACEC 2006). This produced the information in Table 7.5. Respondents said that 99% of the birds shot were destined for the food chain, 44% being sold to dealers and the remainder consumed by the shooting provider or taken away by the guns to eat.

In addition, shooters surveyed said they shot 380 000 Corvids, 120 000 Foxes and 170 000 Squirrels, as well as Rats, Mink, Stoats, Weasels and feral cats.

The number of people taking part in shooting by the type of shooting and the number of days shooting they enjoyed ('gun days') are also instructive, bearing in mind that many shooters indulge in more than one kind of shooting – see Table 7.6.

The benefits to biodiversity conservation from shooting sport are very substantial. The survey found that shoot providers were operating over 15 million hectares, or two-thirds, of the rural landscape, but carrying out active shoot management over two million hectares. They were spending some £250 million annually in operational, staff and capital costs on such habitats as woodlands, moorlands, spinneys, stubble, cover crops, beetle banks, hedgerows, grass strips, conservation headlands, wetlands, glades and rides, flight ponds and river/stream banks. These, along with pest-control activities carried out by shooters and gamekeepers, were contributing not only to game conservation, but to the conservation of song birds, waders, butterflies, plants and flowers in the ways identified by the research projects mentioned earlier in this chapter, on a scale equivalent to that of the statutory conservation agencies, but over a much wider area of the countryside. Shooting-related conservation work occupied an estimated 2.6 million work days, equivalent to 12 000 full-time jobs, in 2004. The figure of £250 million does not include expenditure on management of land, which is only for hunting with hounds. If this total management effort were removed, the results would be seriously negative for conservation.

Turning to the purely economic aspects, PACEC estimated that shooters were spending £2 billion a year on goods and services, e.g. for equipment, travel and accommodation and to providers, while the gross value added to the UK economy was £1.6 billion. Support was provided for 31 000 direct jobs and 39 000 indirect, making 70 000 in all. The importance of these numbers for conservation is that they represent a powerful political and economic force for using land and water in ways that benefit biodiversity. To a very large extent, recreational shooters and hunters finance these activities out of their own pockets, a contribution which should be acknowledged by conservationists when funding for wildlife programmes from taxpayers is likely to be under extreme pressure for the foreseeable future. On the other hand, shooters and hunters, tending to be rugged individualists, seem reluctant to account to the wider world for what they are doing and to explain the benefits that flow from their activities.

Trends in wildlife users

If we look at the wider context of the numbers of people participating in wildlife-related activities, we find that the balance seems to be changing. In common with trends in the rest of Europe, shooter numbers are declining somewhat, bird-watching numbers are increasing, while the number of anglers has remained roughly constant for a decade (Kenward and Sharp 2008). However, with 6.6 million shooters, 24 million anglers and 6.2 million bird-watchers in the 27 EU member states, the numbers remain very significant. Shooter numbers are also edging down in the United States and Canada, according to the large quinquennial surveys carried out by governments there (Sharp and Wollscheid 2009). If this were to lead to declines in expenditure on land management for wildlife-related recreation there would be serious implications for conservation of species and habitats.

Policy context

Because land management for field sports is so significant for conservation of habitats, it is important to communicate both within the conservation world and to policy-makers and the public an understanding of wildlife use, including field sports, in Britain, which places it firmly within the context of a holistic vision of conservation. In recent years, this understanding has gathered around the concept of 'sustainable use' of wildlife. Pioneered in the 1980s by the International Union for the Conservation of Nature, the concept is best articulated in a Policy Statement adopted at its second World Conservation Congress in 2000. This asserts that 'the use of wild living resources, if sustainable, is an important conservation tool because the social and economic benefits derived from such use provide incentives for people to conserve them'. The Convention on Biological Diversity of 1992 made sustainable use one of its three objectives, along with conservation and equitable sharing of the benefits of genetic resources. In 2004, with significant inputs from IUCN's Sustainable Use Specialist Group, CBD adopted The Addis Ababa Principles and Guidelines for the Sustainable Use of Biodiversity (Convention on Biological Diversity 2004).

In all these contexts 'use' expressly includes non-consumptive use, such as wildlife watching. Although animal welfare concerns are often voiced in campaigns to end or restrict hunting of wild animals, it is noteworthy that in the Royal Society for the Prevention of Cruelty to Animals' (RSPCA) report *The Welfare State: Measuring Animal Welfare in the UK 2007*, none of the four topics selected for attention in the wildlife section relate to hunting or shooting sport in the UK. The ethical questions raised by hunting are much deeper and include whether wild or domestic animals should be killed for consumption or pleasure. These questions are discussed in a recent book which offers a global perspective on recreational hunting (Dickson 2009).

Within these policy formulations are two insights which have not always been clearly distinguished. The first is the objective that all use of wild resources should be sustainable, in the sense that in the medium to long term, the resource should not be depleted by exploitation, even if other factors such as habitat removal or pollution threaten its survival. The second insight is that use, if sustainable, is a positive conservation tool because of the incentives it provides and because it addresses the issue of what has been described as incentive-driven conservation in the 87.5% of the planet's land surface that lies outside areas where some degree of protection is given to wildlife (Hutton and Leader-Williams 2003). If this is understood, it follows that conservationists and users of wildlife resources, in the present case, practitioners of field sports in Britain, should have a strong and explicit agenda for collaboration.

One framework for such collaboration is the National Biodiversity Action Plan and its subsidiary plans and targets, expressly established to implement the UK's domestic commitments under the CBD. A second framework is the recent European Charter on Hunting and Biodiversity, adopted in 2007 by the Bern Convention of the Council of Europe (CoE 2007). Based on the CBD Addis principles, the Charter lays down principles and supporting guidelines which are applied to hunters and hunt providers, on the one hand, and to regulators and wildlife managers, on the other.

A third is the European Commission's Sustainable Hunting Initiative set up in 2001 to promote co-operation between organisations concerned with the conservation and sustainable use of wild birds under the provisions of the EC Birds Directive, notably BirdLife International and the Federation of Associations for Hunting and Conservation of the EU. The background to this is that in Malta, Cyprus, Italy and elsewhere, there remains a very strong tradition for shooting migrating song birds, Turtle Doves and raptors, some for food, and some simply for sport. The enforcement of local laws to limit this activity often seems to be lax and some of the shooting is illegal under European legislation, though in reporting to a conference on progress towards the 2010 Biodiversity Target in the European Parliament in February 2009, Environment Commissioner Stavros Dimas claimed success for the Commission's efforts in this area.

This chapter has shown that overwhelmingly the target species for field sports in Britain have fared well over the last half century. So have the associated species which benefit from game management, a practice that has helped to counteract the damaging effects of mainstream agricultural policy on biodiversity. More gamekeeping, game crops and skilful habitat management would undoubtedly achieve even more. The European Charter, appropriately adapted to our situation, could be the key to the necessary collaborative strategy.

Acknowledgements

Warm thanks are due to Nick Sotherton, Robert Kenward, David Stroud, Andy Musgrove, Alastair Ward, John Calladine and Nicholas Aebischer for their assistance.

References

Aebischer, N.J. and Harradine, J. (2007). Developing a tool for improving bag data of huntable birds and other bird species in the UK. A report to DEFRA and the Scottish Executive, Wrexham, Game Conservancy Trust, Fordinbridge and British Association for Shooting and Conservation.

Anon (2004). *Action Plan for the Sustainable Management of Wild Deer Populations in England*, Wrexham, The Deer Initiative.

Anon (2006 and 2007). *Annual reports 05/06 and 06/07*, Inverness, The Deer Commission for Scotland.

Baines, D., Redpath, S., Richardson, M. and Thirgood, S. (2008). The direct and indirect effects of predation by Hen Harriers *Cirus cyaneus* on trends in breeding birds on a Scottish grouse moor. *Ibis*, **150**, Supplement 1, 27–36 (10).

Battersbury, J. (2005). *UK Mammals: Species Status and Populations Trend*, Peterborough, JNCC/Tracking Mammals Partnership.

Calladine, J. and Wernham, C. (2007). *Extensive Monitoring of Arctic-Alpine Birds in Scotland: A Pilot Survey to Test the Potential for Using Volunteer Surveyors*, Stirling, British Trust for Ornithology Scotland.

CoE (2007). European Charter on Hunting and Biodiversity, Bern Convention document T-PVS (2007) 7 revised, Strasbourg, France, Council of Europe.

Convention on Biological Diversity (2004). Addis Ababa Principles and Guidelines for the Sustainable Use of Biodiversity (Decision VII/12), Montreal, Canada, Secretariat of the Convention on Biological Diversity. Available at http://www.biodiv.int.

Dickson, B. (2009). The ethics of recreational hunting. In Dickson, B., Hutton, J. and Adams, W., eds., *Recreational Hunting, Conservation and Rural Livelihoods*, Oxford, Wiley-Blackwell.

Downing, G. (2007). *A Sporting Century: The History of the British Association for Shooting and Conservation*, Shewsbury, UK, Quiller Press.

Draycott, R.A.H., Hoodless, A.N. and Sage, R.B. (2008). Effects of pheasant management on vegetation and birds in lowland woods. *Journal of Applied Ecology*, **45**, 334–341.

EC (1979). Council Directive 79/409/EEC on the Conservation of Wild Birds.

Ewald, J.A., Callegari, S.E., Kingdon, S.E. and Graham, N.A. (2006). Fox-hunting in England and Wales: its contribution to the management of woodland and other habitats. *Biodiversity and Conservation*, **15**, 4309–4334.

Fletcher, K. (2008). *Predation Control and Moorland Birds. Review of 2007*, Fordingbridge, Game and Wildlife Conservation Trust.

Fraser of Allander Institute (2001). *An Economic Study of Scottish Grouse Moors: An Update (2001)*. Fordingbridge, Game Conservancy Ltd, for the Game Conservancy Scottish Research Trust.

Gibbons, D.W., Reid, J.B. and Chapman, R.A. (1993). *The New Atlas of Breeding Birds in Great Britain and Ireland:1998–1991*, London, T. and A.D. Poyser.

Green, R.E. (1984). The feeding ecology and survival of partridge chicks on arable farmland in East Anglia. *Journal of Applied Ecology*, **21**, 817–830.

Harrison, J. (1973). *A Wealth of Wildfowl*, Ealing, Corgi Books.

Hirons, G. (1983). A five year study of the breeding behaviour and biology of woodcock in England – a first report. In Kalchreuter, H. ed., *Proceedings of the 2nd European Woodcock and Snipe Workshop*, Slimbridge, International Waterfowl Research Bureau.

Hoodless, A.N, Lang, D., Aebischer, N.J., Fuller, G. and Ewald, J.A. (in press). Densities and population estimates of breeding Eurasian Woodcock *Scolopax rusticola* in Britain in 2003, *British Birds*.

Hudson, J. (1992). *Grouse in Space and Time: The Population Biology of a Managed Gamebird*, Fordingbridge, The Game Conservancy.

Hudson, J. and Dobson, A.P. (1990). Red grouse population cycles and population dynamics of the caecal nematode *Trichostrongylus tenuis*. In Lance, A.N. and Lawton, J.H., eds., *Red Grouse Populations Processes*, London, British Ecological Society and Royal Society for the Protection of Birds.

Hutton, J.M. and Leader-Williams, N. (2003). Sustainable use and incentive-driven conservation: realigning human and conservation interests. Oryx, **37**, 215–226.

Kenward, R. and Sharp, R. (2008). Use nationally of wildlife resources across Europe (UNWIRE). In Manos, B. and Papathanasiou, J., eds., *GEMCONBIO: Governance and Ecosystem Management for Conservation of Biodiversity*, Thessaloniki, Greece, Aristotle University of Thessaloniki, pp. 82–86.

Mason, C.F. and Macdonald, S.M. (1976). Aspects of the breeding biology of the snipe. *Bird Study*, **23**, 33–38.

Musgrove, A.J., Collier, M.P., Banks, A.N. *et al.* (2007). *Waterbirds in the UK 2005/06: The Wetland Bird Survey*, Thetford, BTO/WWT/RSPB/JNCC.

Oldfield, T.E.E., Smith, R.J., Harrop, S.R. and Leader-Williams, N. (2003). Field sports and conservation in the United Kingdom. *Nature*, **423**, 29.

PACEC (2006). *The Economic and Environmental Impact of Sporting Shooting*, Cambridge, PACEC Consultants.

Parish, D.M.B and Sotherton, N.W. (2004a). Gamecrops as summer habitat for farmland songbirds in Scotland. *Agriculture, Ecosystems and Environment*, **104**, 429–438.

Parish, D.M.B and Sotherton, N.W (2004b). Gamecrops and threatened farmland songbirds in Scotland: a step towards halting population declines? *Bird Study*, **51**, 107–112.

Redpath, S.M. and Thirgood, S.J. (1997). *Birds of Prey and Red Grouse*, London, Stationery Office.

Sedgwick, N.M., Whitaker, P. and Harrison, J. (eds.) (1961). *The New Wildfowler*, London, Herbert Jenkins.

Sharp, R. and Wollscheid, K. (2009). An overview of recreational hunting in North America, Europe and Australia. In Dickson, B., Hutton, J. and Adams, W., eds., *Recreational Hunting, Conservation and Rural Livelihoods*, Oxford, Wiley-Blackwell.

Tapper, S. (1992). *Game Heritage*, Fordingbridge, The Game Conservancy Trust.

Tapper, S. (2005). *Nature's Gain: How Gamebird Management has Influenced Wildlife Conservation*, Fordingbridge, The Game Conservancy Trust.

Tapper, S. (2007). *Singing Fields: Why Gamekeeping Helps Birds in the Countryside*, Fordingbridge, Game and Wildlife Conservation Trust.

Tharme, A.P., Green, R.E., Baines, D., Bainbridge, I.P. and O'Brien, M. (2001). The effect of management for red grouse shooting on the population density of breeding birds on heather-dominated moorland. *Journal of Applied Ecology*, **38**, 439–457.

Thirgood, S.J., Redpath, S.M., Rothery, P. and Aebischer, N.J. (2000). Raptor predation and population limitation in red grouse. *Journal of Animal Ecology*, **69**, 504–516.

Trout, R.C., Tapper, S.C. and Harradine, J. (1986). Recent trends in rabbit populations in Britain. *Mammal Review*, **16**, 117–123.

Ward, A.I., Etherington, T. and Ewald, J. (2008). National deer ranges: five more years of change. *Deer*, **14**, 7.

Ward, A.I. and Young, R. (2005). National deer abundance estimates 2004, unpublished, Nympsfield, Central Science Laboratory.

8

Going fishing: recent trends in recreational angling

Robin Sharp and Norman Maclean

Summary

Angling is the most commonly practised field sport and has deep historical roots. In Britain the most important impact by far during the last half century has been the progressive environmental clean-up of rivers and lakes under the pressure of the EU Water Directives. Although comprehensive techniques for measuring changes in fish abundance over time are fairly recent, there is clear evidence from electric and acoustic surveys, as well as from limited long-term catch data, that coarse fish stocks are doing well in all regions and that any problems are site specific. Among game fish, wild Brown Trout are well distributed in faster-flowing rivers, but most fish caught are from stocking, while the Grayling is a popular alternative. Salmon and Sea Trout, the most sought after and economically valuable game fish, present the most complex picture. While rod-and-line catches by sport fishers have generally held up, there has been a massive long-term decline in commercial net and similar catches, indicating major problems for these intensively monitored migratory species in the marine environment. A case study reveals the apparently conflicting objectives of anglers and the Wildlife Trust on the River Itchen. The increasing concern of anglers over the impact of Cormorants on fish stocks is discussed. Freshwater angling is a valued recreation for up to 3.5 million people in England and Wales and contributes at least £2.5 billion to the economy annually. Seen as part of a wider environmental stewardship, sustainable angling has much to contribute to conservation of Britain's freshwater species and habitats.

Silent Summer: The State of Wildlife in Britain and Ireland, ed. Norman Maclean. Published by Cambridge University Press. © Cambridge University Press 2010.

Introduction

Angling is the most popular field sport by far. If not exactly classless, it is practised by people from right across the social spectrum, though most are male. At the outset of his classic description of the sport as a calm recreational experience, *The Compleat Angler or Contemplative Man's Recreation* of 1653, Izaak Walton wrote 'my discourse is like to prove suitable to my recreation, calm and quiet.' Somewhat less contemplative and more class conscious was Dame Juliana Berners, a hunting nun, who penned a treatise on *Fysshinge with an Angle* in 1496. The publisher expressed concern that it might fall into the hands of those who were not gentlemen, who through immoderation in angling might 'utterly destroye it'. Sustainability is not a new concern.

It is hard to imagine how such an apprehension arose when there must have been an abundance of fish in our lakes and rivers and vastly fewer anglers. However, even when considering the last half century we have to admit that estimating the size of fish stocks and trying to establish trends is a very uncertain science indeed. Happily, recent developments in measuring techniques are just beginning to give us a toe-hold on what is happening.

Prior to these developments, the only information was about catch numbers for sport fish and, in a few cases, catch per unit of effort in competitions for coarse fish. What was also clear was that fresh-water quality had deteriorated seriously as a result of industrial pollution in urban areas and, after the intensification of agriculture post-World War II, of chemical run-off in the countryside. Nevertheless it needed the shock of the European Union Water Quality Directives in the mid 1980s, culminating in the Water Framework Directive of 2000, to shatter our complacent vision of Britain as a green and clean, pleasant land and to stimulate a costly programme of fresh-water clean-up. Well-publicised heralds of progress have been the return of Salmon to the Thames, the Clyde and other urban rivers and the re-establishment of the fish-eating Otter in many watercourses from which it had previously disappeared.

It follows that the current status of the environment in which angling in Britain takes place is broadly favourable. The sport is thriving and, where trend information is available, fresh-water fish stocks are rising. The position is rather mixed, however, in respect of salmonids and eels which pass part of their life cycle in distant marine waters. In this chapter we shall consider trends in coarse fishing and game fishing, as well as some of the pressures on stocks, the conflicts which angling can engender (including a case study) together with the social and economic significance of the sport.

Coarse fishing

There are 17 species of coarse fish which are native or naturalised in England and Wales and regularly fished for (see Table 8.1). Coarse fish are those fished for sport which are not game fish such as Salmon and Trout.

Table 8.1 *Coarse fish native or naturalised in England and Wales and targeted by anglers*

Dace, *Leuciscus leuciscus*	Barbel, *Barbus barbus*
Chub, *Leuciscus cephalus*	Roach, *Rutilus rutilus*
Rudd, *Scardinius erythrophthalmus*	Carp, *Cyprinus carpio*
Crucian Carp, *Carassius carassius*	Orfe, *Leuciscus idus*
Goldfish, *Carassius auratus*	Gudgeon, *Gobio gobio*
Pike, *Esox lucius*	Perch, *Perca fluviatilis*
Common Bream, *Abramis brama*	Silver Bream, *Blicca bjoerkna*
Tench, *Tinca tinca*	Ruffe, *Gymnocephalus cernuus*
Bleak, *Alburnus alburnus*	Grangling, *Thymallus thymallus*

(*Source:* Environment Agency 2004.)

These species are found in much of England and Wales in rivers, canals, lakes, reservoirs and still waters such as ponds and artificially created fishing lakes. The only exceptions are the steeper fast-moving rivers of the uplands, where salmonid species hold sway. Pike, Roach and Perch have been present in Scotland since at least 1790. Crucian Carp, Grayling, Common Bream and Chub have been present since 1880, while Common Carp, Goldfish, Gudgeon, Rudd, Orfe and Dace have been recorded since 1970 and Ruffe appeared by 1990 (Davies *et al.* 2004). Barbel are now present in the River Clyde and a small population has existed there since at least 1997, but coarse fish species are, for the most part, not native to Scotland.

Most of Britain's fresh-water fishers spend the bulk of their time in coarse fishing, which means that the health of coarse fish stocks is of considerable social and economic importance. The abundance and distribution of these fish are also important water quality indicators, so that one of the main objectives of fish monitoring is to determine changes in water quality.

Measuring fish numbers is extremely difficult. The success of anglers in a fishing competition where effort is measured, will reveal relative abundance at a place and point in time, but such monitoring has been limited to a relatively small number of stretches of important rivers and is affected by a variety of variables apart from species abundance. The technique of electric fishing surveys has been developed to stun and extract the fish so as to distinguish individual species details. It can be used on small- to medium-sized rivers and canals. Acoustic surveys are effective in larger waters, covering long stretches of a river in a single day. They measure biomass, but cannot distinguish species. Taken together, these monitoring methods are beginning to provide a scientific approach to measuring trends in coarse-fish abundance and to identifying problems and their causes.

Thus, in 2002, the Environment Agency used electric surveys on 350 sites to provide data which to some degree could be compared with that collected in the early 1990s. They found that coarse fish were present in 98% of sites, a considerable improvement on the previous surveys. Classifying the sites from A to F, 13% of sites were in class A, with an average fish mass of 3.2 kg per 100 m². The Warwick Avon scored highest with 11 kg per 100 m². The River Lee had four class A sites in rural Hertfordshire, but fared much less well in its course through East London, where lack of vegetation cover was considered to make the fish especially vulnerable to Cormorants (*Phalacrocorax carbo*). One of the very few fishless rivers, the Wantsum in Kent, was found to be contaminated by saline intrusion. Rheophilic species, such as Dace, Chub and Barbel, were doing well in faster-flowing rivers, while limnophilics such as Roach and Gudgeon were faring well in quieter waters. The waters of the clay catchments in the south-east and East of England, including the Witham and the Nene, were favourable for both categories. The abundance of predators, such as Pike and Perch, was related in the classic fashion to abundance of prey. The most striking finding was that more than half of the 350 sites had 8 to 14 species present, with the Mole in Surrey and Lymm in Lincolnshire both recording the maximum species richness (Environment Agency 2004).

Acoustic surveys, also in 2002, covered 150 km of 20 rivers, but results from only 70 km were deemed reliable. These measured the number of fish per 1000 m³ for each 100 m of the stretch surveyed. The results ranged from 2.93 fish on one stretch of the Mersey to 190.83 on a section of the Ribble. There were surprising variations on non-tidal stretches of the Thames, with Dayes to Benson producing only 9.07 fish, but Iffley to Sandford recording 109.23.

A longer perspective is given from catch data from 10 large lowland rivers between 1976 and 2002 (see Figure 8.1). The aggregated data show a trend line of grams per hour fished rising fairly steadily from 60 at the beginning of the period to 160 at the end. The main factor seems likely to be an increase in fish stocks, but improved skills and a better choice of fishing spots may also have contributed.

This evidence conflicts with the view often aired by anglers that the quality of river fishing has deteriorated in recent years. An interesting case is that of angling on the Trent where improvements in water quality led to an increase in the numbers of Barbel, Chub and Bream, which are harder to catch than the previously more

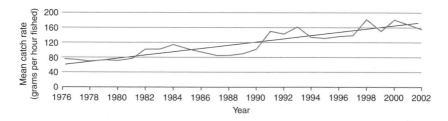

Figure 8.1 Mean catch rates from 10 principal coarse-fishery rivers. (*Source:* Environment Agency.)

Table 8.2 *Fish biomass in types of still water: max kg per hectare*

Natural	500
Improved	2 250
Intensive	14 280

(*Source:* Environment Agency 2004.)

numerous limnophilic species. The anglers who did not adapt their methods complained of smaller catches (Lyons *et al.* 2002). On the River Nidd in Yorkshire, a flow-gauging weir was installed in 1978 and match catch records showed an immediate fall in catches above the weir. After various unsuccessful attempts to improve fish passage upstream, the weir was removed in 1999, followed by a four fold increase in catch rates.

Most monitoring so far has been of moving waters, but still waters also deserve attention, not least because, according to a survey in 1994, more than 50% of anglers prefer them. Although there has been a massive loss of ponds due to agricultural policies over the last half century, there were estimated to be 250 000 still waters in Great Britain in 2000 (Countryside Survey 2000) and of these 30 000 in England and Wales are considered suitable for fishing. A sample survey of 260 still-water coarse fisheries categorised 3% as entirely natural, 77% as natural, but improved and 20% as intensive, with fish biomass on a rising scale (see Table 8.2).

Most of these still waters contained at least eight species, with Roach in the lead, closely followed by Carp, Bream, Perch and Tench. Natural waters were dominated by Bream, Roach, Pike, Perch and Rudd; improved had Carp, Roach, Bream and Crucian Carp; while intensive fisheries focused strongly on Carp. The overall angler catch rate of 1.722 kg per angler hour was well above the catch rates for rivers and canals, whether in Britain or the rest of Europe. In the opinion of the Environment Agency, well-managed still-water fisheries can withstand high angling pressure without affecting their performance, but badly managed ones produce a range of environmental problems culminating in fish dying.

Coarse fishing also takes place in Scotland, where it is regulated and monitored by the Scottish Government. It has greatly increased in popularity in recent years. There is a relative paucity of native species and as a result, many coarse species have been introduced to catchments where they never occurred previously, with consequent problems for the native ecosystems. The introduction of Ruffe to Loch Lomond is a well-documented example of this and there are now at least six coarse-fish species established there which are alien to the loch (Adams and Maitland 1998). Because of the international importance of Salmon fishing in Scotland, coarse fishing has attracted less monitoring than in England and Wales.

Fishing for Trout and Grayling

Trout (*Salmo trutta*) is the most widely available native game fish in the lowlands while Grayling (*Thymallus thymallus*), though not considered a game fish, belongs to the salmonid family. The non-native Rainbow Trout (*Oncorhyncus mykiss*) is also widely spread, but mostly by stocking: natural spawning occurs in only a small number of places. The native Trout is notable in so far as a proportion of Trout fry from eggs laid in the upper reaches of rivers turn into smolts and after one to three years migrate downstream to the sea and become Sea Trout, which are substantially larger than the fresh-water Brown Trout. Both variants are, however, of the same species.

There is plenty of information about the distribution of Brown Trout, but little knowledge of its abundance. Trout are found in some 48 000 km (70%) of river length in England and Wales, especially in Wales, where 98% of river length features Trout, the north and the south-west (Environment Agency 2002). Where Brown Trout are found above insurmountable barriers, as is the case for 25% of river length, and have not been subject to stocking, the fish are truly wild and much valued by anglers (Ministry of Agriculture, Fisheries and Food 2000; Simpson 2001). Trout are also found in natural still waters. Electric fishing surveys were carried out in 2002 and data from 173 salmonid river sites were classified by abundance and age size. Trout were present in all sites and in only 6% lacked all the age classes. Over 60% of sites were in category C or above on a scale of A to F. Catch returns for adult Brown Trout are not generally available. Issues affecting Trout populations are similar to those for Salmon and include acidification, siltation and low flows. A decline in fly life on chalk rivers has also been observed (Environment Agency 2004).

In Scotland, wild Brown and Sea Trout are major sport species of economic importance. Valuable data on abundance have been obtained for many rivers and burns and good catch statistics are available for some lochs (e.g. Lochs Lee and Leven).

The Grayling is more restricted in its natural distribution, though it has been introduced over a long period into rivers across England and Wales and in Scotland as far north as the River Tay. It currently favours chalk rivers such as the Test and Avon, while elsewhere is found in the Severn, Ribble, Trent, Ouse and Wharfe, as well as several rivers in Wales. Improved water quality has seen significant increases in catches, such as from 50 to 1200 per year in the Don after industrial pollution had been cleaned up. On the other hand, higher water temperatures in drought seasons are thought to be causes of decline in the Witham and other eastern/East Anglian rivers. A survey of Grayling catches via anglers' log-books revealed that Grayling were caught in 57 rivers in England, Wales and Scotland in 2001/02, when 4200 fish were caught in 671 visits, while the following year 89 rivers saw 8800 caught in 1415 visits. In that year the highest catch per unit of effort was on the Hampshire Avon.

Most trout anglers catch stocked fish, even though two-thirds would prefer to fish for wild trout. While stocking is extensive, the Wild Trout Trust is promoting the conservation and improvement of wild Trout fisheries. Grayling are almost universally caught and released. Interest in this fish has prompted the formation of the Grayling Society. Fly fishing is the most used angling method. Brown Trout and Grayling are also available in Scotland, the latter being attractive because it can be fished for outside any restricted seasons for game fish.

Salmon and Sea Trout in England and Wales

Wild Atlantic Salmon (*Salmo salar*) is the king of British game fish and fishing for Salmon is important both recreationally and economically. The Sea Trout, or, as some call it, Salmon Trout, rather lives in its shadow, while making extremely good eating. Both species are widely present in England, Wales and Scotland in fast-flowing rivers and are subject to special legislation, long-term monitoring and specific conservation efforts. However, separate regimes apply, as between England and Wales, on the one hand, and Scotland, on the other, and the relevant data are not regularly brought together. We will address the former first.

As in the case of Brown Trout, electric surveys of 173 rivers were carried out in 2002. They found that for Salmon fry, parr and smolts less than half the sites reached classes A to C relative to a 1990 baseline. Since, like Sea Trout, Salmon migrate to the sea after up to three years in the rivers where they hatched and then return after up to three years at sea, what happens in the marine environment is critical. Pollution, fishing of species on which Salmon feed or high sea fishing of Salmon themselves may be factors in the decline in catches of returning Salmon on the Severn, Wye and Dee that were well known for them. To protect what are called multi-sea winter fish from exploitation, netsmen cannot kill them before 1 June and rod anglers must return all salmon caught before 16 June. Rod rather than net catches are best for judging adult abundance and, in spite of concern about stocks, there has been no significant trend in England and Wales since 1956. The declared rod catch in 2002 was 15 231 compared with a previous five-year average of 14 925. Since 1974, improvements have been seen in the North-east on the Coquet, Tyne, Tees and Wear, while declines occurred on the Test, Itchen and Hampshire Avon. Net catches of Salmon were 38 279 in 2002, slightly above the previous five-year average of 37 009.

Sea Trout are found in 26% of all rivers in England and Wales, mostly in the north, south and south-west. Because fry and parr cannot be distinguished from Brown Trout and little is known about their survival at sea, rod catches and counters are the only indicators of relative abundance. Rod catch rates showed an upward trend over the nine years to 2002. At 49 796, the total for 2002 was a 20% increase on the five-year mean and 39% over the long-term average since 1978. Increases and declines for individual rivers largely matched changes in Salmon rod catches. Rivers in Wales accounted for more than 50% of the total. Net catches of Sea Trout were 36 997 in 2002, some 4% below the previous five-year average, with restrictions on net fisheries effort being the most likely explanatory factor. However, figures recently published for 2006 show rod catches at 24 269, 43% below the five-year mean of 42 338, and net catches of 25311, a decrease of 21% on the five-year mean (Environment Agency 2007).

Measures to address concerns about Salmon stocks include the promotion of catch and release, which had reached nearly 56% of fish caught in 2006 (59% for Sea Trout), protection of spring Salmon by restrictions on the dates for the opening of the fishing season, the closure of mixed-stock fisheries and other net fisheries closures. Specially teasing have been the problems of the chalk rivers of southern England, where long-term declines have been recorded from 1954 to 1992. One factor identified has been fine sediment run-off from agricultural land causing siltation and thus lack of oxygen reaching Salmon eggs. Recent slight upward trends may be a response to various strategies to address the situation.

Salmon and Sea Trout in Scotland

Salmon fishing in Scotland is internationally important. There are nearly 400 Salmon rivers, among the best, if not the best, in Europe, providing a long tradition of prestigious and economically valuable angling. However, as in England and Wales, the conservation status of the species must be seen in the context of commercial fishing by nets (the two types being classified as 'fixed engine' and 'net and coble') and of recreational fishing, mainly, though not exclusively, by rod and line. The latest available catch figures are shown in Table 8.3.

It should be noted that in 2007 fishing effort in both types of commercial net fishery was at its lowest since 1952, while numbers of rod catches showed an increase of 19% over the previous five-year average. There were increases in spring Salmon and grilse catches and no significant change in summer Salmon catches. (NB: Grilse are fish returning after their first year at sea.) However, for reasons unknown, grilse returning to Scottish rivers were significantly smaller than previously, but the number of fish is considered to have shown a distinct short-term increase.

Valuable data on the abundance of Salmon and Sea Trout are available for some Scottish rivers from fish counters, many of them associated with hydro-electric schemes.

Looking at the longer term, it is clear that there has been a major decline in the numbers of Salmon being caught by Scottish net fisheries over 50 years (from *c.* 500 000 in the 1960s to 25 000 in 2006), so that these catches are perhaps 5% of their past highest recorded levels. Effort has reduced to reflect both the availability of wild Salmon and a drop in demand due to competition from farmed Salmon. This decline in netting has acted as a buffer for rod catches because it has allowed the number of Salmon entering rivers to remain more or less stable, at least for the time being. Escapees from fish farms may interbreed with the wild population resulting in losses of genetic variability, including loss of naturally selected adaptations, thus leading to reduced fitness and

Table 8.3 *Salmon catch figures in Scotland 2006 by type of fishing*

Type	Retained	Caught and Released	Total
Fixed engine	18 800	nil	18 800
Net & coble	6 161	nil	6 161
Rod & line	38 430	47 471[a]	85 901
Total	63 391	47 471[a]	110 862

Note: [a] There is no information as to whether some fish may be
caught and released more than once.
(*Source:* Derived from Fisheries Research Services 2008.)

performance. These escapes, therefore, constitute a major threat to wild populations, although when one considers that some 400 000 farmed Salmon escaped from Scottish fish farms in 2000 it is perhaps surprising that no direct impacts appear to have been established (Anon 2006).

At the same time there is general agreement that factors in the marine environment, such as climate change and over-exploitation, must be responsible for the overall long-term problems of Salmon in our region. Thus the North Atlantic Salmon Conservation Organisation (NASCO) is active in monitoring national catch rates and encouraging safe-guarding measures, while currently sponsoring a major research project into the marine issues affecting Salmon via the International Atlantic Salmon Research Board (IASRB).

Sea Trout are also very significant in Scotland. In 2006, 10 063 Sea Trout were caught by rod and line and 8149 by net fisheries. Of the rod-and-line catch 51% was released. Overall trends are broadly similar to those for Salmon, but the current situation seems rather worse, not least in comparison with England and Wales. One distinctive feature is the contrast between the two coasts. Since 2003, rod catches of Sea Trout in Scotland have been among the lowest for the last 55 years, with the west coast faring worse than the east coast with a drop of 51% of the previous five-year average. Net fisheries on the east coast show no long-term trend (Fisheries Research Services 2008). Monitoring of lice on Sea Trout in June 1998–2000 by the Association of West Coast Fisheries Trusts found that at least 14–40% of Sea Trout in that region of Scotland were infected with potentially lethal infestations of lice (Butler 2002). Wild Salmon also suffer from this problem, which derives almost wholly from contact with farmed Salmon.

A case study from the River Itchen

The River Itchen in Hampshire is a classic English chalk stream designated as an SSSI, and typified by clear, clean alkali water and abundant riverine weed growth. It also provides a prime example of some degree of alienation and mistrust between anglers and wildlife conservation interests.

Rising from springs bubbling up from underground aquifers in the chalk, the Itchen water is of rather steady temperature year round and is little subject to flooding. The soils which surround the present river in its middle and lower reaches suggest that in pre-pastoral times of more than 2000 years ago, the river consisted substantially of braided streams flowing through marshland, with willow and alder thickets and islands. In Roman and post-Roman times, the river was narrowed and managed to allow cultivation of riverside fields, as well as to promote angling. From medieval times onwards, it was also managed to allow temporary flooding of neighbouring 'water meadows' in late winter and early spring. This was partly to allow fertilisation of the meadows by the winter silt particles suspended in the water, but more importantly to prevent frosting of the grass in the water meadows and thus bring forward by two or three weeks the early spring plant growth in the meadows. This was often referred to as an 'early bite' for the grazing sheep and cattle.

After this period, the water flows were regulated to avoid flooding of the fields and increase the flow in the main river and its subsidiary carriers. Such water meadows not only allowed stock animals to prosper, but also fostered a rich flora, together with breeding bird species such as Yellow Wagtail, *Motacilla flava*, Redshank, *Tringa totanus*, Common Snipe, *Gallinago gallinago*, and Lapwing, *Vanellus vanellus*. During spring and summer, the main flows were confined to the river. Riverside vegetation was trimmed to provide access and line casting by fishermen. The river weed growth of plant species such as Water Crowfoot (*Ranunculus* sp.) and Water Parsnip (*Berula erecta*) was cut by scythe about five times in the year to prevent flooding of riverside banks and fields, and prevent damming up of the water flow by the weed growth. Such a management regime favoured growth of fish such as Brown Trout, crustaceans such as the White-clawed Crayfish, *Austropotamobius pallipes*, and mammals such as Otters, *Lutra lutra*, and Water Voles, *Arvicola terrestris*. Such alkali chalk streams also harboured a very rich invertebrate life of *Gammarus pulex* (freshwater shrimps) and numerous species of riverflies (see Chapter 22) of the insect orders Ephemeroptera and Trichoptera (Mayflies and Caddisflies). This in turn guaranteed rapid growth of the resident Brown Trout.

Over the past 200 years, the river has come to be regarded as a prime Trout fly-fishing river of international repute. Indeed much of the early evolution of imitative Trout fly fishing with 'dry' flies (floating imitations of natural Ephemeroptera or Trichoptera species) fished upstream, and later of sunk 'wet' fly imitations of ephemeropteran nymphs also fished upstream, was worked out on this river. Over the last 100 years, the river has also been stocked with Trout reared in nearby Trout farms to enhance the resident population of Trout in the face of the increased angling pressure. (Traditionally Trout are caught and killed if above a length of 12 or 14 inches, and so angling can markedly reduce the resident Trout population.)

In recent years (since about 1995) the middle Itchen above Winchester has become the battleground for a serious disagreement about riverine management styles between the local Wildlife Trust and the angling interests. The Wildlife Trust was able to purchase the water meadow areas north of Winchester, together with the riparian rights, and sought to manage it primarily as a reserve for wildlife conservation. They declined to allow the local angling club to continue to rent much of the river for fishing, and imposed fairly stringent management conditions on the reduced parts of the Itchen carriers on which they agreed to allow fishing to continue. The areas under management by the Wildlife Trust were very 'lightly' managed, so riverside vegetation was minimally cut, as were the in-stream weeds, and much of the adjacent land was left to nature and was rapidly invaded by Phragmites Reeds *Phragmites australis*, Stinging Nettles *Urtica dioica*, and other invasive species. It is interesting to examine the sentiments on either side of this particular fence, since they illustrate well the misunderstandings which often arise.

On the one hand, the angling management argued for a continuation of river-bank trimming to allow access and line casting by fishermen, regular cutting of the in-stream waterweed, continuation of fishing and stocking, but otherwise minimal disturbance, with continued grazing and haymaking in adjacent fenced meadowland. The fishermen argued that they were sympathetic to wildlife. They considered that the rich fauna and flora of the river and adjacent water meadows was largely a direct result of the centuries of management imposed, and was in no way reduced by it.

Conversely, the Wildlife Trust administration and members tended to be unsympathetic to continued fishing and saw fishermen as alien to good conservation practice. They also advocated a policy of 'return to nature' rather than a continuation of the management policy that had been developed over some hundreds of years. They saw the priorities as encouraging Otters, Water Voles, White-clawed Crayfish and water-side birds and plants, and were reluctant to believe that the earlier abundances of both had been a result of the fairly strict management of the river and its verges. One of us (N.M.) undertook a survey of the fauna and flora in the areas of the river and adjacent fields which either remained under close management for fishing, or had been allowed to go 'back to nature' in the avowed interests of wildlife by the Wildlife Trust. Perhaps not surprisingly, the species richness and abundance in the managed area was significantly greater, even for species such as the Water Vole which was seen as a flagship conservation objective, as compared with the minimally managed 'reversion to nature' section under the complete control of the Wildlife Trust.

The dispute rumbles on currently, which is a pity, for the Itchen river offers a truly rich and diverse fauna and flora under traditional management, as recorded in Janet Marsh's delightful book on the Upper Itchen around Easton (Marsh 1984), and is also precious to Trout anglers because of its unique history and classic chalk-stream fishing. Here is a situation where mutual understanding by both conservationists and fishermen is desperately needed. The Itchen would never have become such a rich wildlife community were it not for the long history of management for Trout fishing, and it seems churlish to try to put the management style back to what would have obtained more than 2000 years ago, when braided streams amid marshland and Alder/Willow thickets must have been the norm.

Conflicts with cormorants

The depredations of cormorants on fish have attracted much attention in recent years as their numbers and distribution have expanded dramatically, to the annoyance of anglers and commercial-fishery managers right across Europe. Cormorants are general fish predators, consuming around 500 g of fish per day, with a preference for Roach, Perch, Rainbow or Brown Trout. Two sub-species of the Greater Cormorant are distinguished (though with difficulty in the field), *carbo*, which was traditionally coastal, and *sinensis*, which was and remains an inland bird.

In Britain, the most noticed phenomenon has been the growth of often large inland breeding colonies, which began with one at Abberton Reservoir in Essex in 1981 and had risen to 35 in 2005, when the total breeding population was estimated at 10 729 pairs of which 2184 were inland, perhaps 25% of the inland nesters being *sinensis* coming from the Continent (Newson *et al.* 2007). Linked with this expansion has been an increase in the number of winter roosts from 285 in 1996–8 to 359 in 2003, three-quarters being inland (Worden *et al.* 2004), which is considered consistent with a total UK population estimate of 24 900 individual birds and still growing.

On the Continent, the most remarkable phenomenon has been the spread of *sinsensis* nesting sites and numbers since 1965 (see the maps in Figure 8.2). At a European level, the latest estimates are that *sinensis* numbers grew by 35%, from 171 000 to 232 000 pairs, between 2000–2 and 2006 and that overall there are at least 1.2 million birds in the Western Palearctic region, which tend to move west and south in the winter (WICRG 2008). A primary reason for the growth in Cormorant numbers is that, whereas in the past they were severely controlled by fisheries interests, they have been protected in the ever expanding European Union since the passing of the Birds Directive in 1979 (EC 1979). The growth of stocked fisheries, especially, but not only in still waters, and the increase in eutrophication of waters are other identified factors. Studies at the European and UK levels have conceded that Cormorants damage individual fisheries to different extents, but are inconclusive as to whether they are limiting fish numbers overall or merely responding to the abundance of suitable prey (Carss 2003).

On many stocked trout fisheries, essentially every fish caught is scarred by previous Cormorant attack. The managers of such waters have tried to counter the Cormorant problem by culling (which is permitted in Britain under licence) or by stocking with large Trout which are too big for Cormorants to swallow. This in turn is a very expensive solution. In Bavaria 6000 Cormorants were culled, but soon replaced by birds from elsewhere, so the current scientific consensus is that nothing but a massive cull across Europe would make a permanent impact, which is considered unacceptable to the wider public. In England and Wales in 2004 DEFRA authorised a cull of 3000 birds for the following two years and 2000 a year thereafter, but the effects of this are not yet established. The provision of underwater refuges in stocked fisheries and more overhanging vegetation are other remedies which are being tried. The European REDCAFE project, now succeeded by INTERCAFE, used a multi-stakeholder

Cormorant (*Phalacrocorax carbo*) in Europe – Breeding Colonies

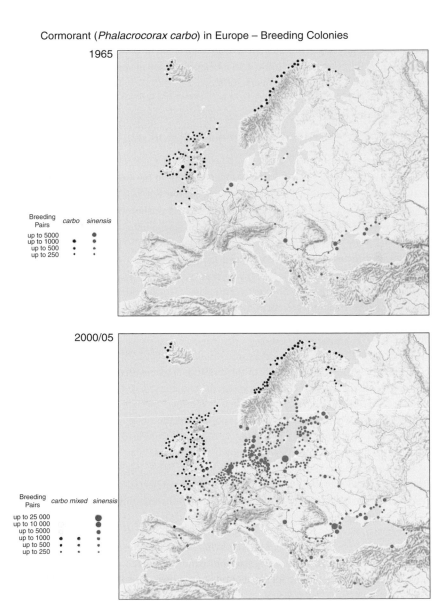

Figure 8.2 Maps of 1965 and 2005 cormorant distribution across Europe (see colour plate). (Maps compiled from multiple sources by Franz Kohl, Austria.)

approach and conflict-resolution techniques to promote greater scientific and operational understanding of what can be done, but with only limited success as far as anglers are concerned (Carss 2003). In late 2008, the European Parliament adopted the Kindermann report, calling for improved pan-European monitoring of Cormorant numbers and impacts and recommended that in view of the migratory nature of the species the Commission produce an overall management plan to regulate numbers, instead of, as hitherto, leaving individual member states to act or not according to their own judgments (European Parliament 2008).

Social and economic aspects of angling

A recent survey has revealed that 5.8 million people in England and Wales, or 13% of the population over 12, claimed to have been angling in the preceding two years and 4.2 million in the preceding year (Simpson and Mawle 2005). This figure includes sea angling, which, according to the survey, attracted 1.5 million participants in the previous two years, but is not otherwise discussed in this chapter. The figures for freshwater fishing are, respectively, 3.5 million and 2.6 million. These numbers had not changed significantly from those obtained in surveys in 1997 and 2001 and point to high rates of loss and recruitment. They contrast with the number of people buying rod licences annually, which has been between 1 and 1.2 million since the 1990s. The vast bulk of licences are annual licences for coarse fishing, though around 300 000 are for short terms and under 30 000 for Salmon and Sea Trout, which are showing a steady decline.

A poll of 2600 rod-licence holders in 2001 showed that 95% of anglers were male, contrasting with 75% in the survey of the public as a whole mentioned above, indicating that most women who fish do so rather infrequently and do not bother to obtain a licence. Moreover, men between 35 and 54 formed the largest group among rod-licence holders, whereas among the wider population the age group 15–24 had a higher than average representation. The median number of fishing trips was 15 and the mean 26. The types of fishing practised are shown in Table 8.4.

Most of the coarse fishers did not fish for game species, but most game fishers also fished for coarse fish. Only a third of coarse fishers preferred rivers to still waters, a trend which has been evident for some time, especially among younger anglers. Carp,

Table 8.4 *Types of fishing by rod-licence holders in England and Wales 2000/01*

Coarse fishing	86%
Brown or Rainbow Trout	24%
Salmon or Sea Trout	7%
Grayling	5%

(*Source:* based on Simpson 2001.
Note: Figures do not sum because some anglers practise more than one type.)

Roach, Tench and Bream were the preferred fish. A majority of Trout anglers preferred to fish on rivers, but, in practice, 78% fished on still waters. Of rod-licence holders, 18% had stayed away overnight on fishing trips, demonstrating one aspect of angling's contribution to local economies. In Wales, tourism interests are actively encouraging visitors to come for angling holidays via the Fishing Wales initiative. In Stoke, the SAFE (Stoke Angling for Everyone) project is promoting participation via school and community links and receiving local authority support, while in Durham, the Get Hooked on Fishing project is aiming to reduce youth offending.

Expenditure by coarse anglers in England and Wales on licences, tackle, travel, accommodation and other direct costs is estimated at around £2 billion annually, while that by Salmon and Trout anglers has been put at £545 million per year (Spurgeon *et al.* 2001). In Scotland, a study found that anglers were spending £113 million annually with Salmon and Sea Trout anglers accounting for 65% of the total. Of the total expenditure, £37 million was being spent by locals, £17 million by visitors from elsewhere in Scotland and £59 million by those from outside Scotland (Radford *et al.* 2004). All these figures demonstrate that wild living resources, when extracted sustainably, make a significant contribution to livelihoods, while being important components of healthy ecosystems, which enable a wide range of non-targeted species to flourish. The Bristol Avon at Limpley Stoke (see Figure 8.3) is a good example of a river that combines a rich conservation, recreational and economic resource.

Recent legislation in Scotland is aimed at improving fish welfare and protecting biodiversity and native fish populations. Thus it is now illegal to use gaffes or landing nets with knotted mesh, and live-baiting with vertebrates is completely banned. All stocking requires a licence and there is an assumption that there will be a complete ban on the introduction of any fish not already established in a catchment.

Angling as part of wider environmental stewardship

Over the last two decades there has been a growing understanding that environmental sustainability requires an integrated approach on the part of all who affect or are affected by a sphere of activity. Those who use wildlife commercially or recreationally need to understand and co-operate with those who want to conserve it for other reasons and with those whose activities might in the past have paid no attention to it, as well as vice versa. In the case of angling, this has led to a number of codes of conduct for specific national or local fisheries which have been worked out with other stakeholders in mind. In Scotland, the formation of the Freshwater Fisheries Forum and the development of a Strategic Framework for Scottish Freshwater Fisheries (Anon 2008) provides a promising initiative of this kind.

At the international level, the European Inland Fisheries Advisory Commission (EIFAC), chaired in 2008 by Phil Hickley of the Environment Agency, have produced a Code of Practice for Recreational Fisheries (EIFAC 2008). A key principle is that

Figure 8.3 The Bristol Avon at Limpley Stoke (see colour plate). (Photograph courtesy of the Environment Agency.)

'Relevant international, national and regional administrations, fishing rights holders and other parties and persons that own or are responsible for fisheries resources shall protect, promote and encourage access to recreational fisheries while ensuring exploitation is sustainable and that potentially conflicting societal demands are taken into account.' The Code is already being applied in Britain by the Association of Stillwater Game Fishery Managers. It is to be hoped that its enlightened approach is taken up and adapted as necessary by others engaged in the various sectors of angling. An important further step was the decision of the Bern Convention of the Council of Europe in November 2008 to set in hand the preparation of a European Charter for Angling and Biodiversity which would build upon the EIFAC Code and promote trust between anglers and conservationists.

Acknowledgements

Many thanks are due to Phil Hickley, Miran Aprahamian, Robert Kenward, Peter Maitland, Colin Bean and Stuart Newson for their kind assistance.

References

Adams, C.E. and Maitland, P.S. (1998). The Ruffe population of Loch Lomond, Scotland: its introduction, population expansion and interaction with native species. *Journal of Great Lakes Research,* **24**, 249–262.

Anon (2006). *Review and Synthesis of the Environmental Impacts of Aquaculture,* Edinburgh, Scottish Government.

Anon (2008). *A Strategic Framework for Scottish Freshwater Fisheries.* Available at only http://www.scotland.gov.uk/Publications/2008/06/26110733/0.

Butler, J.R.A. (2002). Wild salmonids and sea louse infestations on the west coast of Scotland: sources of infection and implications for the management of marine salmon farms. *Pest Management Science,* **58**, 595–608.

Carss, D.N. (ed.) (2003). Reducing the conflict between Cormorants and fisheries on a pan-European scale REDCAFE: Pan European Overview. Final Report to European Commission (August 2003). See also www.intercafeproject.net .

Countryside Survey 2000 (2000). *Accounting for Nature: Assessing Habitats in the UK Countryside,* London, Department of the Environment, Transport and Regions.

Davies, C.E., Shelley, J., Harding, P.T., McLean, I.F.G., Gardiner, R. and Pierson, G. (eds.) (2004). *Freshwater Fishes in Britain. The Species and Their Distribution,* Colchester, Harley Books.

EC (1979). Council Directive 79/409/EEC on the Conservation of Wild Birds.

EC (2000). Directive 2000/60/EC of the European Parliament and of the Council establishing a framework for the Community action in the field of water policy.

EIFAC (2008). EIFAC Code of Practice for Recreational Fisheries. EIFAC Occasional Paper. No 42. FAO, Rome, Italy.

Environment Agency (2002). Inventory of trout stocks and fisheries in England and Wales. Environment Agency R&D Project W2–062/TR. Bristol Environment Agency.

Environment Agency (2004). *Our Nation's Fisheries,* Bristol, Environment Agency.

Environment Agency (2007). *Fisheries Statistics Report 2006,* Bristol, Environment Agency.

European Parliament (2008). Draft report on the adoption of a European Cormorant Management Plan to minimise the increasing impact of cormorants on fish stocks, fishing and aquaculture. Brussels, Belgium, Committee on Fisheries of the European Parliament. 2008/2177(INI).

Fisheries Research Services (2008). *Scottish Salmon and Sea Trout Catches 2006,* Faskally, Perthshire, Fisheries Research Services, The Scottish Executive.

Lyons, J., Hickley, P. and Gledhill, S. (2002). An evaluation of recreational fisheries in England and Wales. In Pitcher, T.J and Hollingsworth, C.E., eds., *Recreational Fisheries :Ecological, Economic and Social Evaluation,* Oxford, Blackwell Science Ltd.

Marsh, J. (1984). *Janet Marsh`s Nature Diary,* London, Peerage Books.

Ministry of Agriculture, Fisheries and Food (2000). *Salmon and Freshwater Fisheries Review,* London, Ministry of Agriculture, Fisheries and Food.

Newson, S.E., Marchant, J.A., Elkins, J.R. and Sellers, R.M. (2007). The status of inland-breeding Greater Cormorants in England. *Britsh Birds,* **100***,* 289–299.

Radford, A., Riddington, G., Anderson, J. and Gibson, H. (2004). *The Economic Impact of Game and Coarse Angling in Scotland*, Edinburgh, The Scottish Executive.

Simpson, D. (2001). Survey of rod licence holders. Environment Agency R&D Project W2–057/TR, Bristol, Environment Agency.

Simpson, D. and Mawle, G.W. (2005). *Public Attitudes to Angling 2005,* Bristol, Environment Agency.

Spurgeon, J., Colurullo, G., Radford, A.F. and Tingley, D. (2001). Economic evaluation of inland fisheries. Environment Agency R&D Project W2–039/PR/1 (Module B). Bristol, Environment Agency.

WICRG (2008). *Cormorants in the Western Palearctic: distribution and numbers on a wider European scale.* Leaflet issued by IUCN/Wetlands International Cormorant Research Group. The Netherlands, Wetlands International.

Worden, J., Hall, C. and Cranswick, P. (2004). *Cormorant, Phalacrocorax carbo, in Great Britain: results of the January 2003 roost survey*, Slimbridge, Gloucestershire, Wildfowl and Wetland Trust.

9

Impacts of hormone-disrupting chemicals on wildlife

C.R. Tyler and R.M. Goodhead

Summary

Wildlife in Britain and Ireland has been shown to be adversely affected by exposure to chemicals that alter the balance of hormones in the body. Effects in wildlife are predominantly, but not exclusively, found in species living in and/ or closely associated with the aquatic environment. The best-known examples of this so-called phenomenon of endocrine disruption in British and Irish wildlife include eggshell thinning in birds of prey, imposex in marine snails, where male sex organs grow in females, and alteration of sexual development in fish, including intersex where both male and female sex tissues are contained within an individual that is normally single sexed. Some of these effects have resulted in population-level consequences and in marine snails they have even caused localised population extinctions. The causative chemicals of endocrine disruption in wildlife are wide ranging and they include natural and synthetic steroids, pesticides and a variety of industrial chemicals. Adding to the complexity of the problem, most wildlife populations are exposed to mixtures of these hormone-disrupting chemicals (HDCs) that can accumulate in their bodies and are additive in their effects in the body. Such exposures are well illustrated in seals and otters that have been shown to contain high body concentrations of organochlorines, polybrominated diphenyl ethers (PBDEs, used as flame retardants) and polychlorinated biphenyls (PCBs) in their fatty tissues, all of which disrupt how hormones work. Recently, laboratory studies have shown HDCs with oestrogenic (female-like) activity can affect brain development in birds (e.g. Starlings, *Sturnus vulgaris*) and features of behaviour in both birds and fish. These alterations could have far-reaching consequences for wildlife populations generally in Britain and Ireland, but as yet this has not been investigated.

Silent Summer: The State of Wildlife in Britain and Ireland, ed. Norman Maclean. Published by Cambridge University Press. © Cambridge University Press 2010.

Introduction

More than 200 000 man-made chemicals are discharged into the environment that are diverse both in their structure and the nature of their potentially harmful effects. They include heavy metals, organochlorine pesticides, plasticisers, wetting agents (surfactants) and pharmaceuticals. Effects of chemicals on wildlife have historically been focused on lethality that results from accidental chemical spills, most notably from oil along our coastlines and from pesticide poisonings. Sub-lethal, chronic effects of chemical exposures are less easily detected in animals, but chemically induced reductions in the ability to reproduce, altered patterns of development and effects on the body's defence system have all been documented in wildlife of Britain and Ireland. Some of these biological effects are attributed to exposure to hormone-disrupting chemicals.

Endocrine disruption in wildlife emerged as a recognised phenomenon in the early 1990s (Colborn and Clement 1992), but knowledge that chemicals can modify hormone systems was shown in laboratory studies with birds and mammals much earlier, in the 1930s (Cook *et al.* 1933). Some examples of chemical effects on wildlife in Britain and Ireland that were established some time ago, notably eggshell thinning in birds of prey and imposex induction in marine snails, have only recently been recognised as endocrine-disruption events, as an understanding of their effect pathways in the body have been established. In Britain and Ireland, endocrine disruption has now been reported in invertebrates, fish, birds and mammals, and in the worst-case scenarios has led to population crashes and even localised extinctions. This chapter aims to provide the reader with an insight into the phenomenon of endocrine disruption, focusing on some of the better-known case examples in British and Irish wildlife and, where known, identifying the chemicals causing these effects.

Hormone-disrupting chemicals

Most HDCs identified work by copying the natural hormones in the body. The most frequently reported hormone mimics affect processes controlled by sex steroids, specifically sexual development and reproduction. Oestrogenic (female-assigning) chemicals are the most commonly found in these studies and feminisation of exposed males has been reported in a wide range of wildlife species. The most comprehensively researched case is the intersex condition in fish living in English rivers, described later in this chapter. Chemicals that block the effects of oestrogens (anti-oestrogens) are also present in the environment and they produce symptoms similar to those caused by exposure to male sex hormones (androgens). Anti-oestrogenic chemicals entering the environment include pharmaceuticals used to treat breast cancer and osteoporosis. Chemicals that block the effects of male hormones are more common than anti-oestrogens and include pharmaceuticals developed as anti-cancer agents, various pesticides and their breakdown products. Anti-androgens create a similar overall effect to oestrogens and it has been suggested that some of the feminised responses seen in wildlife populations may result from chemicals blocking the workings of the androgen pathway, rather than as a consequence of exposure to (or possibly in addition to) environmental oestrogens. One of the best examples of hormonal disruption in wildlife of Britain and Ireland is an androgenic effect, namely imposex in marine snails, caused by exposure to the anti-fouling agent tributyl tin (TBT, discussed as a case example below). No androgenic responses have been reported in vertebrate wildlife in Britain and Ireland, but in the United States of America, masculinisation occurs in Fathead Minnows (*Pimephales promelas*), living in waters receiving effluent discharges from cattle production units that use the androgen 17β-trenbolone in feed to boost meat production.

Other chemicals discharged into the aquatic environment have a similar structure to thyroid hormones. Thyroid hormones are fundamental in the normal development and workings of the brain and sex organs, as well as for metamorphosis in amphibians and in growth and regulation of metabolic processes. Thyroid-mimicking chemicals therefore can potentially affect a very wide range of body processes. In the US, developmental effects in wildlife populations indicative of alterations in the thyroid system are reported widely, and they include malformation of limbs in birds and mammals, the production of small eggs and chicks in birds and impaired metamorphosis in amphibians (reviewed in Rolland 2000). Links between high body loads of thyroid-disrupting chemicals and a range of physiological disorders have been shown in some mammals in Britain and Ireland, and these are also detailed in the case examples below. Known thyroid-disrupting chemicals include many members of the polyhalogenated aromatic hydrocarbons (PHAHs), such as PCBs, dioxins, polyaromatic hydrocarbons (PAHs) and PBDEs.

The number of chemicals identified with hormone-active activity that are released into the British and Irish countryside has increased considerably as the realisation of their possible adverse effects on wildlife (and possibly humans too) has driven a programme of systematic screening. The list of HDCs now includes natural oestrogens, pharmaceutical oestrogens used in birth control and menopause treatments, various organochlorine pesticides, photosynthesis-inhibiting herbicides, PCBs, dioxins, PBDEs, bisphenols, alkylphenol polyethoxylates used as non-ionic surfactants in detergents, plastic and paint formulations, phthalates (the most abundant man-made chemicals in the environment), used in lubricating oils, insect repellents, cosmetics and to impart flexibility to plastics, and naturally occurring oestrogens produced by fungi (mycoestrogens) and plants (phytoestrogens). Furthermore, some HDCs have been shown to affect more than hormone systems, and they can even affect the functioning of the nervous and defence (immune) systems along with the body processes they control. Although the likelihood for biological harm has not been assessed fully, for most of these HDCs, amounts in ambient environments in Britain and Ireland (away from hotspots of chemical discharges) would suggest that for most they are insufficient to do so (see Goodhead and Tyler 2008). The exceptions to this are detailed in the following section. It should also be emphasised, however, that most studies on the effects of HDCs under laboratory conditions have not considered long-term exposures, encompassed full life cycles or considered mixture effects (see below). We have, therefore, probably not yet realised the full extent of endocrine disruption in wildlife in Britain and Ireland, or indeed globally.

Case studies

Few studies have been able to provide an unequivocal link between a specific HDC and a population-level impact for any wildlife species anywhere in the world. This, in part, is because of the complexity of the chemical environment to which most wild-life populations are exposed. Two exceptions to this are for organochlorine pesticides (most notably DDT and its metabolites), responsible for the decline of raptor populations and for TBT; inducing localised extinctions of some marine snails, both documented in Britain and Ireland. There are, however, other examples where very strong associations have been established between specific chemicals, or groups of chemicals, and endocrine-disrupting effects. In some cases these are at levels likely to impact on populations.

Organochlorine pesticides and eggshell thinning in birds of prey

Chemically induced disturbances of hormone systems that lead to altered patterns in reproduction were documented in bird populations in the 1960s. Declines in raptor populations were seen across the whole of Britain and were linked to a contamination of the countryside with pesticide residues (namely, DDT, aldrin and dieldrin and their metabolites). The Merlin (*Falco columbarius*) was particularly hard hit and from the 1960s onwards they included some of the most contaminated birds. Sparrowhawks (*Accipter nisus*) also suffered and there were significant declines from the period 1957–63, following the widespread use of these pesticides (Newton and Haas 1984). It was hypothesised at the time that exposure to organochlorine pesticides caused hatching failure, but it wasn't until Ratcliffes' landmark paper (1967) that the role of DDT in eggshell thinning was discovered, and its significance in the decline of some species of predatory birds firmly established. In Sparrowhawks across Britain, exposure to these pesticides caused the mean eggshell thickness to be reduced by 11–20%. Hatching failure resulted because the eggs produced with thinned shells were crushed by the adult birds when they were incubated (Peakall 1983). Failure to lay and increased embryo deaths were also shown to contribute to a reduced breeding success in Sparrowhawks contaminated with these organochlorine pesticides. Peregrine Falcon (*Falco peregrines*) populations suffered too and extensive surveys of British populations in 1961 and 1962 showed a precipitous decline, compared with pre-war levels, and again these were subsequently linked with increased body burdens of DDE. High body burdens of dieldrin in populations of Shags (*Phalacrocorax aristotelis*) on the Farne Islands were also shown to correlate with a lowered breeding success. Supporting the roles of these pesticides in the declines of raptor populations, subsequent restrictions on their use resulted in the recovery of Sparrowhawk, Merlin and Peregrine populations. In the case of Sparrowhawks, this occurred progressively from the less arable west of Britain, east across the country and for Peregrine Falcons from south to north. One study provided evidence that the banning of dieldrin from sheep dips in 1966 improved the breeding success of Golden Eagles (*Aquila chrysaetos*) in west Scotland. Despite many years of study into how *p,p'*-DDE causes eggshell thinning, there is still uncertainty. Arguably, the most popular theory is that it involves disturbances in the metabolism of the hormone prostaglandin, putting it firmly into the arena of endocrine disruption. Studies on HDCs in passerine birds are rare, but a series of studies on the eggs of the Dipper (*Cinclus cinclus,* Figure 9.1) in Wales has found PCBs, another group of organochlorine chemicals, are at levels amongst the highest in Europe, although an association with adverse reproductive effects has not been shown.

Other studies on birds in the USA have shown that DDT and some other HDCs can induce changes in nesting and courtship behaviours. In populations of Bald Eagles (*Haliaeetus leucocephalus*) and Laughing Gulls (*Larus atricilla*) these disruptions have been linked with decreases in the size of the populations. Organophosphate exposure to wild Starlings has also been correlated with decreased parental care. Thus, in the case of the decline in British raptors it seems plausible that sub-lethal behavioural effects could have contributed to their decline through similar effects on breeding behaviours. Further behavioural changes recorded in birds exposed to HDCs and other chemicals under laboratory conditions include a decreased sexual arousal, altered coordination, memory effects, alterations in response to maternal calls and fright stimuli, and effects in males on singing (in Starlings) and displaying (reviewed in Zala and Penn 2004). Alterations in normal singing and displaying have the potential to impact on the ability of wild birds to establish and maintain a breeding territory, and affect mate choice and thus in turn could affect the genetics of populations. This has not been investigated in any wild birds in Britain and Ireland, but studies of this nature are underway in the USA.

TBT and imposex in snails

The occurrence of imposex, which is where a penis and/or a vas deferens (a male-specific sex structure) develops in a female, was first reported in the Dog Whelk (*Nucella lapillus*) in the coastal regions of Plymouth, Millport (in Scotland) and Black Rock (in Sussex) in 1970. It was hypothesised that the anti-fouling agent TBT in paints applied to boats and in marinas was responsible. This was subsequently proven, and at some sites exposure was shown to have resulted in reproductive failure and

Figure 9.1 Dipper (*Cinclus cinclus*) eggs in Wales are amongst the most highly contaminated with polychlorinated biphenyls anywhere in Europe (see colour plate). (Photograph by Charles R. Tyler.)

population-level declines, especially along the south coast of England, including the Helford, Fal, Salcombe and Dart estuaries and in Plymouth Sound (Bryan *et al.* 1986). The imposex condition was later reported at locations spanning the entire coastline of Britain, from Shetland to Cornwall. Worldwide, imposex has now been shown to occur in over 150 species of marine snails. Laboratory studies subsequently established that tiny concentrations of TBT, as low as 1 ng l^{-1} in the water, induced imposex in Dog Whelks exposed as larvae or juveniles. Retrospectively, the widespread declines in mollusc populations, especially in the vicinity of harbours and in busy shipping lanes, around Britain and Ireland were not surprising, given that TBT in these areas reached levels exceeding 30 ng l^{-1} during peak use.

In 1987, the UK government limited the use of TBT-based anti-fouling paints to vessels over 25 m in length and in 1988 set an environmental quality target (EQT) at 2 ng l^{-1}. After this, concentrations of TBT in the water column declined; for example, in the dockyards and marinas of the Thames and Mersey estuaries a decade after the UK TBT legislation, levels in the sediments were an order of magnitude lower than those previously observed before the ban. In the Crouch Estuary (Essex), invertebrate species that were affected by TBT contamination were subsequently shown to recover and included the re-establishment of a native oyster population. Indeed, since 1987, Dog Whelk populations have shown recovery at all affected sites studied around Britain. Surveys conducted in 2002, however, showed that TBT concentrations close to shipping activity, for example in the Firth of Forth, were still at levels that would likely mean breeding difficulties for the resident snail populations. Whether or not genetic diversity has been impacted by TBT is not known, but given the extent of population losses, this seems likely.

In 2003, the International Maritime Organisation called for a global ban on the application of TBT-based paints and a complete ban on TBT on all European vessels was put into operation in January 2008. Interestingly, despite the known harmful effects of TBT, it is still used widely as an anti-bacterial agent in clothes, nappies and sanitary towels, providing further routes of entry into the environment (e.g. via landfills). Another organotin, triphenyl-tin (TPT), is widely used as a fungicide and to control algae in Britain and Ireland, and has been shown under laboratory conditions to induce sexual disruption in various species of snails at environmentally relevant concentrations. We may, therefore, not yet have realised the wider endocrine-disrupting impacts of the organotins on molluscs of Britain and Ireland.

There are no other proven examples of chemically induced endocrine disruption in wild invertebrate populations in Britain and Ireland, despite the fact that many chemicals discharged are known to be capable of disrupting insect hormone systems, notably juvenoid- and ecdysteroid-regulated processes that control development, growth and maturation. These chemicals include methoprene, used as an insecticide, bisphenol A, lindane and some phthalates. Equally, however, there has been extremely little research to investigate HDC effects in wild invertebrate populations.

Feminisation of fish

The story for the feminisation of fish in the UK originated from observations of intersex (the simultaneous presence of both male and female sex cells within a single gonad; see Figure 9.2) in a common freshwater fish, the Roach (*Rutilus rutilus*), living in wastewater treatment works (WWTW) settlement lagoons. Another finding independently established that effluents from WWTW were oestrogenic to fish, inducing the production of a female egg-yolk protein (vitellogenin, VTG) in males (Purdom *et al*. 1994). Some of the effluents surveyed were extremely oestrogenic, inducing up to one million-fold induction of VTG in caged fish for a three-week exposure and contaminating rivers with oestrogen for up to 5 km distances downstream of the effluent discharge. VTG induction is a biomarker of exposure to oestrogens, rather than necessarily a sign of an adverse health effect, but in young fish, the inappropriate production of VTG, even at low levels could have survivorship implications, as their energy budget is most critically balanced at this time in their lives. Furthermore, very high circulating levels of VTG can cause kidney failure.

Major surveys have since established a widespread occurrence of intersex in Roach populations living in UK rivers (44 out of the 51 study sites surveyed; Jobling *et al*. 2006), and in the most extreme cases, half the testis is comprised of ovary tissue. Importantly, the intersex condition in Roach has been shown to affect their ability to produce gametes. Small numbers of wild Roach cannot produce (release) any gametes

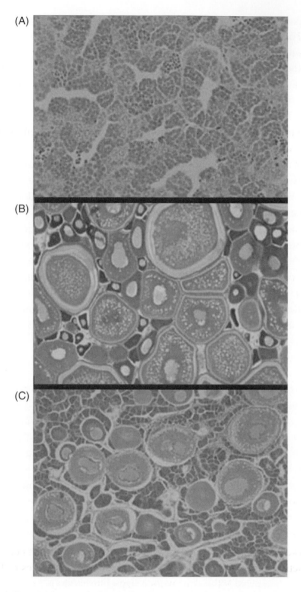

Figure 9.2 Gonadal intersex in Roach (*Rutilus rutilus*), characterised by the presence of developing eggs in the testis of 'male' fish. Panel A shows a section taken through a normal testis with the tiny sperm developing within lobules. Panel B shows a section through a normal ovary illustrating the huge developing eggs (compared with the sperm cells). Panel C shows an intersex gonad, where both male and female sex cells are present in the same gonad (see colour plate).

at all due to the presence of severely disrupted gonadal ducts. In other intersex Roach found, male gametes are produced that, although viable, are of poorer quality compared with normal males. Fertilisation and hatchability studies have shown that moderately and severely intersex Roach are compromised in their reproductive capacity and produce less offspring than Roach from uncontaminated sites, under laboratory conditions. Other biological effects recorded in wild Roach and attributed to HDCs in WWTW effluents include abnormal concentrations of blood sex-steroid hormones, altered spawning times and egg production rates in females, as well as reduced testis development in males. The level of oestrogenic impact seen in freshwater fish in English rivers appears to be greater than for elsewhere in Europe, and globally. Why this is the case is not known, but it may relate to the fact that often a considerable proportion of the flow of UK rivers can be made up of treated WWTW effluent; 10% WWTW effluent is a common level of contamination, and for some rivers it comprises more normally 50% of the flow. In extreme cases in England, and generally in the summer months, during periods of low rainfall, treated wastewater effluent can make up the entire flow of the river.

Sexual disruption as a consequence of exposure to HDCs also occurs in fish living in estuaries and coastal waters in Britain and Ireland. Studies on the Flounder (*Platichthys flesus*) from estuaries in the north of England have shown elevated levels of blood VTG and testicular abnormalities, and again these have been linked with exposure to WWTW effluents. Studies in 1999 found blood VTG concentrations in flounder from estuaries in the Tees, Mersey and Tyne up to a million-fold higher than in fish from reference sites. A more recent survey on the Flounder has shown a general decline of VTG levels in fish from estuaries where they were previously very high, including in the Tyne, Mersey and Clyde and this has been linked with improved treatment of the discharged effluents. Elevated blood VTG has also been shown in the Dab (*Limanda limanda*) and in the Cod (*Gadus morhua*) that live all of their lives offshore, indicating that endocrine disruption is occurring in fish in the open sea off British and Irish coasts.

The natural steroidal oestrogens, oestradiol-17β (E_2) and oestrone (E_1), together with ethinyloestradiol (EE_2, a component of the contraceptive pill) have been identified as making up the major oestrogen fraction of WWTW effluents in Britain. Horse oestrogens used in hormone-replacement therapy and alkylphenolic chemicals derived from the breakdown of industrial surfactants have also been shown to contribute to the oestrogenic activity of some WWTW effluents. Laboratory exposures of fish to these chemicals have shown that VTG synthesis, disruption to the development of the reproductive duct and oocytes in the testis, can all be induced, albeit for the latter effect, at concentrations generally higher than that found in effluents and receiving rivers (Tyler and Routledge 1998). EE_2 is present at considerably lower concentrations in the aquatic environment than the natural steroidal oestrogens, but it is exquisitely potent in fish, inducing VTG, intersex and causing reproductive failure in fish at environmentally relevant concentrations. In a study in Canada, a whole experimental lake was contaminated with 5–6 ng EE_2 L^{-1}, and over a seven-year period there was a complete population collapse of the resident Fathead Minnow fishery. In English rivers, a study on 43 sites (39 rivers), found the incidence and severity of intersex in Roach were both significantly correlated with the predicted concentrations of the E_1, E_2 and EE_2 present in the rivers at those sites. Oestrogenic chemicals alone may not be the only contributing factor in the feminisation of Roach in English rivers, however, as UK WWTW effluents are also anti-androgenic and this activity could contribute to the feminisation phenomenon. Other non-point (diffuse) sources of gender-bending HDCs into the aquatic environment have received less attention, but, in theory, significant amounts of steroidal oestrogens could enter our surface waters from run-off from livestock farming. High level usage of alkylphenolic chemicals in the extraction of oil on offshore oil rigs has also been suggested to contribute to the oestrogenic effects in fish living in their immediate vicinity in the open seas.

Under laboratory conditions, some steroidal oestrogens and some anti-androgens (e.g. fenitrothion – an organophosphorous pesticide) have been shown to disrupt both courtship and nesting behaviour in the Three-spined Stickleback, *Gasterosteus aculeatus*, a fish species found throughout both fresh and brackish waters of Britain and Ireland. In those studies, exposed males became less aggressive and showed reductions in the intensity of the zig-zag dance towards the females in the courtship displays, and had a reduced nesting activity. In the exposures to fenitrothion, there was also a reduced production of spiggin (a glue protein produced in the kidney and used to make the nest). These effects seemed to operate by causing reductions in the concentrations of the male sex androgen 11-ketotestosterone circulating in the blood. No studies of this nature have yet been applied to wild populations of fish in Britain and Ireland, but it illustrates that HDCs may potentially affect fish populations through disruptions in their normal patterns of behaviour.

Reproductive disruptions and immunosuppression in mammals

Endocrine disruption has been reported in a wide range of wild mammals on the North American continent. Examples include low sperm counts, poor sperm motility and high incidences of sperm malformations in the Florida Panther (*Felis concolor coryi*), reduced baculum size in Otters (*Lutra lutra,*), masculinisation of Black (*Ursus americanus*) and Grizzly (*Ursus arctos horribilis*) Bears, pseudohermaphroditism in Polar Bears (*Ursus maritimus*) and genital abnormalities in White-tailed Deer (*Odocoileus virginianius*). In Europe too, population-level declines in marine mammals (as a consequence of reproductive failure and immunosuppression) have also been linked with PCBs and DDT exposure. Assigning causality to these conditions is complicated by the fact that body burdens of many chemicals besides PCBs/DDT products in these animals are often high. Nevertheless, studies in the laboratory have shown that fish contaminated with mixtures of PCBs and organochlorine pesticides caused impairment of reproductive success when fed to seals and led to a reduced bacculum length in mink.

In Britain and Ireland, high body concentrations of various organochlorine HDCs such as PCBs and DDT, recorded at over 4000 µg kg^{-1}, have been associated with reductions in reproduction and suppressive effects to the immune system in Harbour Seals (*Phoca vitulina*) and Grey Seals (*Halichoerus grypus*). Furthermore, other studies support an association between a high PCB body burden and an increased susceptibility to disease in Grey Seals. This finding lends strong support to the suggestion that HDC exposure in seals may have contributed to the incidence of the *Phocine distemper* outbreak responsible for the decline in populations in 1988, especially around the Scottish coast. Further study into the endocrine-disrupting effects of other chemicals in seals in Britain has provided evidence for modulation of thyroid hormone levels by PBDEs, DDT and PCBs. These HDC contaminants are also passed on to pups in the milk due to mobilisation of these chemicals from the blubber during lactation; PBDE levels in pups from the Farne Islands have been recorded at 460 ng g^{-1} body tissue and are linked with higher circulating levels of certain thyroid hormones. Thyroid disturbances in seal pups are likely to result in wide-ranging alterations in their physiology and development, but there is no substantive evidence to support this expectation. In Harbour Porpoises (*Phocoena phocoena*), PBDEs have been found at concentrations up to 6900 µg kg^{-1} in animals off the coasts of Wales and England, although again the consequences of this have yet to be studied.

Chemicals with hormone-disrupting activity may also have contributed to the population-level declines of the Otter (*Lutra lutra*; Figure 9.3) in the 1950s–80s in Britain (Mason and Macdonald 1986). A variety of factors probably account for the demise of the Otter populations, but there is a general consensus that anthropogenic contamination has played a primary role. A wide variety of compounds have been detected in Otter tissues and spraint, including DDT and its breakdown products, PCBs, dieldrin and lindane, all established HDCs and reproductive toxicants. PCB levels measured in Otter spraint from the east of England found 44% were sufficiently high as to exert a negative effect on populations. High PCB levels in the Otter's food chain has also been hypothesised to account for the slow re-colonisation rates of lowlands from upland unpolluted reaches of rivers in Britain. Confounding data have also been published showing that in some areas (e.g. Shetland) high PCB levels in Otters had no apparent effect on a thriving population. It is the case, nevertheless, that as the levels of organochlorine pesticides and PCBs have become much reduced, Otter populations have made substantive recoveries in many regions of England and Wales.

In rodent models, HDCs have been shown to affect a wide range of behaviours, including motivation, general communication and learning abilities. Most of the effects reported for HDCs on behaviours are suppressive, but an exception to this is for exposure to the environmental oestrogen, bisphenol A, where an increased boldness has been reported in laboratory rats. Nothing is known on whether HDCs are affecting behaviours in mammalian wildlife in Britain and Ireland.

Figure 9.3 Chemicals with hormone-disrupting activity contributed to the declines in the Otter (*Lutra lutra*) populations in Britain in the 1950s–80s (see colour plate). (Photograph by Charles R Tyler.)

Chemical mixtures, sensitive life stages and species susceptibility

In the environment away from hot-spot discharges, most HDCs identified individually are unlikely to play a significant role in health disruptions in wildlife, given their relatively low hormonal potencies compared with endogenous hormones. As part of a mixture, however, they may contribute towards a disruptive effect, and most of the wildlife in Britain and Ireland is exposed continually to complex mixtures of HDCs. Controlled laboratory exposure studies that replicate environmentally relevant mixtures of HDCs are lacking, but simple environmental mixtures of alkylphenolic chemicals, pesticides and plasticisers have been shown to be additive in their oestrogenic effects (reviewed in Goodhead and Tyler 2008). Many HDCs also have the capacity to build up in the body to very high levels (e.g. in fish steroidal oestrogens and alkylphenolic chemicals have been shown to concentrate up to 40 000-fold). Given these facts, the mixture effects and exposure threats of HDCs to wildlife populations of Britain and Ireland have not been adequately addressed.

Potentially sensitive life periods for HDC effects in wildlife include embryo development, when up to 90% of the genome is transcribed. Early life too is a potentially highly sensitive phase for chemical effects, as this is when many key features of developmental programming occur, including sex assignment, and when various behaviours are defined. Indeed, many of the reproductive abnormalities seen in wildlife are believed to be manifested during embryogenesis and early development. Studies in laboratory rats have shown that extremely small differences in the concentrations of endogenous sex hormones surrounding developing embryos can have profound effects on subsequent sex-related behaviours, illustrating further the susceptibility of early life stages to HDCs that affect sex steroid hormone concentrations at this time. Development abnormalities seen in fish eating birds living in and around the Great Lakes, Canada are known to have resulted from exposure of the embryos to thyroid-disrupting chemicals deposited into the eggs during their formation in the female. Similarly, effects on limb formation in birds and mammals, and impaired metamorphosis in amphibians reported in the US occurred as a consequence to exposure to HDCs during early life. There is also very substantive evidence that the disruptions seen in gonad development in Roach in English rivers result from exposures to HDCs during early life. Exposure to oestrogen during early life in Roach has shown to affect the timing of sexual differentiation, accelerate the development of female sex characteristics and even sensitise females to oestrogen effects in later life.

Other life stages potentially susceptible to the effects of HDCs that mimic sex hormones include puberty and final maturation. Altered timing of puberty and/ or the timing of gamete production could affect any seasonal-breeding animal; timing of reproduction is critical, of course, for ensuring maximal survivorship of their offspring (i.e. where there is maximal food availability). Smolting, the event in some fish (e.g. salmonids) that prepares them for their transition between fresh and saltwater has also been shown to be sensitive to some HDCs. This process is associated with changes in a suite of hormones, including corticosteroids and prolactin, and it has been shown to be disrupted upon exposure to both alkylphenols and E_2. None of these potentially sensitive biological processes and life stages has been well studied in the environment. This section serves to illustrate that the timing of exposure to HDCs can be critical to the nature of the effect seen and in the magnitude of the effects produced. The fact that exposure to environmentally relevant concentrations of environmental oestrogens during early life can impact on the reproductive development (and reproductive capabilities) of fish in English rivers, however, indicates that special attention should be applied to the discharge of HDCs in fish spawning areas.

Most vertebrates are responsive to steroidal hormones and their mimics. The hormonal systems signalling these responses, and their controlling factors, are highly conserved. It would be easy to assume therefore, that an HDC effective in one verte-brate will be equally effective in another. Indeed, it is the case that rodent models are thought of as being sufficiently similar to humans to make them suitable for informing on the effects of HDCs for the protection of human health. This may not always be the case, however, as despite the many similarities in hormones and their receptors in vertebrates, there are some clear distinctions too. For example; sexual development is oestrogen dependent in birds, but not mammals, and thus bird reproductive develop-ment may have a greater sensitivity to oestrogen mimics compared with mammals. In mammals too, the developing foetus is protected from abnormal hormonal exposure by high maternal levels of α-fetoprotein and sex-steroid-binding globulin, but for egg-laying organisms there is no equivalent system. Fish and amphibian eggs are deposited into the aquatic environment and can therefore be exposed constantly to HDCs and other chemicals throughout embryo development, making them especially vulner-able, although the chorion (a surrounding membrane) offers some degree of protection against chemical uptake.

Examples of differences in the responses of wildlife organisms to HDCs include the differences in sensitivity to phthalates and bisphenols between molluscs, crustaceans and amphibians compared with fish. In invertebrates, biological effects are observed at exposures in the ng l^{-1} to low μg l^{-1} range, compared with high μg l^{-1} for most effects in fish (reviewed in Oehlmann *et al.* 2008). In addition, aquatic snails tend to concentrate pollutants in their bodies to a greater level than fish, possibly due to poorer capabilities for metabolic detoxification. Even between more closely related species, differences in responses to HDCs are sometimes apparent, possibly due to differences in metabolic capability. As an example, trout show a greater sensitivity to steroid oestrogens com-pared with Roach and Carp (*Cyprinus carpio*).

The effects of some HDCs appear to be specific to a particular organism or group of organisms. As an example, TBT is associated with imposex in over 150 species of prosobranch molluscs (snails), yet no or very little data exist on TBT inducing impo-sex on any other groups of invertebrates. Thus, both the nature and the severity of the biological effects of HDC can differ greatly between species, making it difficult to make any generalisations. Factors other than differences in animal physiology that can affect species susceptibility to HDCs include differences in their habitat and ecological niche. Considering the aquatic environment, organisms living in and or closely associated with the sediments are more likely to be exposed to high con-centrations of HDCs compared with animals living higher up in the water column, as most HDCs are hydrophobic in nature and build up in the sediments. Animals at higher levels in the food chain/web are also likely to be at greater risk from HDCs compared with animals at lower levels, as HDCs can build up to very high levels. This is not always necessarily true, however, as a study on the Pike (*Esox lucius*), a top predatory fish living in English rivers, did not find effects on sexual disruption to the level seen in the Roach (a primary food source) in the same rivers.

Some concluding thoughts

Rachel Carson, in her book *Silent Spring*, raised public consciousness on the wider implications to wildlife populations of exposure to man-made chemicals, most notably for pesticides. Endocrine disruption has served to heighten this awareness further and for some wildlife populations of Britain and Ireland, illustrated that even without overt toxicity some chemicals can nevertheless induce harm to individuals, or indeed whole populations, through more subtle ways that modify their hormone systems. Indeed, for two examples, organochlorine pesticides in birds of prey and TBT in marine molluscs, chemically induced endocrine disruption has led to population-level declines and even localised population extinctions. Extensive laboratory studies with HDCs and wildlife species indigenous to Britain and Ireland have provided convincing supporting evidence to indicate that population level effects of HDCs in other wildlife is possible and in some cases, likely (e.g. for some freshwater fish). Furthermore, in making our assessments on the potential hazards of HDCs to wildlife, laboratory work has shown that we need to be especially mindful of potentially sensitive life stages, delayed effects, differences in species sensitivity and mixture effects. HDCs can also affect behaviours, with potential impact on populations through altering breeding patterns and changing the normal genetic structure of populations, but almost nothing has been researched in this regard for wildlife in Britain and Ireland.

Historically, there has been a need to prove a population-level effect on wildlife before remedial action or the banning of a suspected causative chemical (as for the cases for TBT and DDT), and this has generally been when populations have crashed and even resulted in local extinctions. Even with this information, the process of banning a chemical from use has often taken many years, even decades, to implement. Providing a positive end to this chapter, in a few instances, information obtained from case studies on endocrine disruption in wildlife in England has led to the adoption of the precautionary principle, where even in the absence of population-level effects data, sufficient likelihood for harm to wildlife has been shown to support programmes to remediate for the adverse effects seen. Examples of this include the phasing out of some alkylphenolic chemicals from use in the textile industry shown to induce feminised responses in fish, and also include a programme to implement the most effective treatment process for the removal of steroidal oestrogens from WWTW effluents before their discharge into rivers. Both activities have been driven by the UK Environment Agency, working in partnership with the textile and water industries, respectively.

References

Bryan, G.W., Gibbs, P.E., Hummerstone, L.G. and Burt, G.R. (1986). The decline of the gastropod Nucella-Lapillus around southwest England: evidence for the effect of tributyltin from antifouling paints. *Journal of the Marine Biological Association of the United Kingdom*, **66**, 611–640.

Colborn, T. and Clement, C. (1992). *Chemically-Induced Alterations in Sexual and Functional Development: The Wildlife/Human Connection*, Princeton, Princeton Scientific Publishing Co.

Cook, J.W., Dodds, E.C. and Hewett, C.L. (1933). A synthetic oestrus-exciting compound. *Nature*, **131**, 56–57.

Goodhead, R.M. and Tyler, C.R. (2008). In C. H. Walker, ed., *Organic Pollutants*, London, Taylor & Francis Ltd, In Press.

Jobling, S., Williams, R., Johnson, A. *et al.* (2006). Predicted exposures to steroid estrogens in UK rivers correlate with widespread sexual disruption in wild fish populations. *Environmental Health Perspectives*, **114**, 32–39.

Mason, C.F. and Macdonald, S.M. (1986). *Otters: Ecology and Conservation*, Cambridge, Cambridge University Press.

Newton, I. and Haas, M.B. (1984). The return of the Sparrowhawk. *British Birds*, **77**, 47–70.

Oehlmann, J., Kloas, W., Kusk, O. *et al.* (2008). A critical analysis of the biological impacts of plasticizers on wildlife. *Philosophical Transactions of the Royal Society*, In Press.

Peakall, D.B., Lew, T.S., Springer, A.M. *et al.* (1983). Determination of the DDE and PCB contents of Peregrine Falcon eggs: a comparison of whole egg measurements and estimates derived from eggshell membranes. *Archives of Environmental Contamination and Toxicology*, **12**, 523–528.

Purdom, C.E., Hardiman, P.A., Bye, V.V.J. *et al.* (1994). Estrogenic effects of effluents from sewage treatment works. *Chemistry and Ecology*, **8**, 275–285.

Ratcliff, D. (1967). Decrease in eggshell weight in certain birds of prey. *Nature*, **215**, 208.

Rolland, R.M. (2000). A review of chemically-induced alterations in thyroid and vitamin A status from field studies of wildlife and fish. *Journal of Wildlife Diseases*, **36**, 615–635.

Tyler, C.R. and Routledge, E.J. (1998). Oestrogenic effects in fish in English rivers with evidence of their causation. *Pure and Applied Chemistry*, **70**, 1795–1804.

Zala, S.M. and Penn, D.J. (2004). Abnormal behaviours induced by chemical pollution: a review of the evidence and new challenges. *Animal Behaviour*, **68**, 649–664.

10

Water pollution: other aspects

Michael Hughes and Carl Sayer

Summary

The UK is home to a diverse array of aquatic organisms. However, it is also
densely populated and our fresh waters have been subjected to a barrage of
pollution over the last 150 years. The most widespread problem in the UK
is eutrophication. Increased nutrient supply to lakes and rivers has caused a
reduction in biodiversity, poorer water quality and a loss of amenity value to
society. Acid deposition of sulfur and nitrogen oxides from fossil-fuel burning
has altered the biological and chemical balance of many of our upland lakes
and rivers, with adverse impacts on acid-sensitive species. Some of these sites
are showing signs of recovery as levels of acid deposition have declined. An
equally pervasive problem, and certainly less well studied, is pollution from
persistent organic pollutants (POPs). Legislation and an increased awareness
of the potential hazards has helped to reduce pollution, nevertheless there are
few routine monitoring activities for POPs in our fresh waters and recent ad hoc
studies show that pollution is still occurring from sources within and outside
the UK. Pollution from heavy metals has occurred across the UK, and whilst
direct sources have been reduced, diffuse pollution from atmospheric deposition
is still a problem, especially where mercury is concerned. For many of these
pollution issues, lake sediment studies and biological and chemical monitoring
programmes have been invaluable in providing baseline data with which to
assess environmental change. However, we need to do more to study the effects
of pollution on the health of aquatic ecosystems and ensure that monitoring is
continued. We also need to develop a deeper understanding of how different
types of pollution interact and how their effects are being influenced by climate
change.

Silent Summer: The State of Wildlife in Britain and Ireland, ed. Norman Maclean. Published by Cambridge
University Press. © Cambridge University Press 2010.

Introduction

The United Kingdom is rich in freshwater resources, and lakes and rivers are an important part of our landscape. They supply us with water for drinking and irrigating crops and are places for outdoor pursuits such as angling and boating, but perhaps most importantly they are habitats for a diverse array of plants, mammals, fish, insects and other creatures.

Approximately 1% of Great Britain's land surface is covered by standing water (Hughes *et al.* 2004). With the exception of the Scottish lochs and Cumbrian lakes, many of the larger water bodies are reservoirs that were built or created from existing water bodies during the last 200 years to supply water to an ever-growing urban population. However, the majority are smaller water bodies formed since Britain emerged from the last ice age, 10 000 years ago. Some of these are natural in origin, but many have been created and include ornamental lakes, agricultural marl pits, flooded pits of extractive industries (clay, sand, gravel, peat), decoy ponds and farm ponds, to name a few. All standing waters contain sediment deposits – layers of biological remains and particulates from the atmosphere and washed in from the surrounding land – and those with minimal disturbance and undisturbed catchments act as environmental archives. Algae, aquatic plants, invertebrates and even fish leave remains in the sediment which can be identified to track changes in species assemblages over time. This approach, known as palaeolimnology, has proved extremely useful in studies of environmental change and can help to elucidate the influences on lake-catchment ecosystems of both climate and human activities over long time periods.

Rivers too exist in both natural and modified states in the UK and have long been used to supply energy and cooling water to industry and serve as drains for industrial and agricultural waste water. The UK has some 5000 km of major rivers, not to mention the many thousands of tributaries and headwater streams which start their lives in the higher, wetter reaches of the country. Rivers, although not generally useful as archives of environmental change due to their dynamic nature, act as barometers of health for the areas they pass though. The ecological quality of river systems is affected by changes in flow, water quality, channel geomorphology and habitat availability.

Pollution of lakes and rivers has occurred ever since humans started farming and carrying out industrial processes such as mining and smelting. However, it is only since the eighteenth century that these activities have had a significant effect on the state of our fresh waters. Today, they are subject to a number of pressures, including nutrient enrichment, acidification, chemical pollution, abstraction, climate change and invasive species.

This chapter attempts to summarise the major aspects of water pollution in the UK during the last 50 years and highlight the most pressing issues which exist now. Whilst an effort has been made to treat the UK as a whole, statistics are often reported separately for England and Wales, Scotland and Northern Ireland. Eire is not specifically mentioned here, although it has been subjected to many of the same types of pollution, especially eutrophication.

Specific groups of aquatic species are mentioned elsewhere in this book (e.g. dragonflies, otters, fish, riverflies and amphibians) and other aspects relating to water quality (such as climate change, agriculture and forestry practices, industrialisation) are covered in previous chapters. Here, with the exception of endocrine-disrupting chemicals (EDCs) which have been dealt with in detail in the preceding chapter, we focus on the causes and effects of the main sources of pollution affecting UK fresh waters. It should be noted that water pollution is a very wide topic and entire textbooks have been devoted to just single types of pollution. The reader looking for comprehensive accounts of water pollution should consult Mason (2002) or Smol (2008) for a palaeolimnological perspective.

Pollution

Pollution can be defined as the presence in, or introduction into, the environment (especially as a result of human activity) of harmful or poisonous substances.[1] Pollutants enter the freshwater system in a variety of ways. Pollution occurring in small amounts over a wide area is termed 'diffuse' and includes atmospheric deposition and agricultural run-off, whilst pollution occurring at a specific location is termed 'point source', such as effluent from a sewage treatment works or discharge of chemical waste from a factory. Point-source pollution incidents may have dramatic and visible effects (such as fish kills), but the effects of diffuse pollution are usually more widespread, although often harder to see and measure. This chapter will focus on eutrophication, acidification and various forms of chemical pollution, including POPs and heavy metals.

Eutrophication

The increase in supply of nutrients to an ecosystem, typically nitrogen and phosphorus compounds, is termed eutrophication. In freshwater systems, this results in an increase in primary productivity, decreased oxygen levels and a subsequent reduction in water quality. Excessive growth of phytoplankton and algae (often referred to as 'blooms') inevitably leads to increased turbidity of the water and eventual loss of biodiversity, as fewer species are adapted for survival in these conditions. Eutrophication has been brought about in the UK (and especially England) by diffuse pollution from agricultural run-off (fertiliser and animal wastes), aquaculture (such as cress beds and fish farms), sewage treatment works effluent and septic-tank overflows, all containing nitrates and phosphates, and atmospheric deposition of ammonia – a nitrogen compound.

---

[1] *Oxford English Dictionary* http://dictionary.oed.com.

Since the first forest clearances made by our Neolithic ancestors, nutrients have been transferred to the aquatic environment at an ever-accelerating rate. Bronze Age farming and large-scale forest removal, the agricultural and industrial revolutions, establishment of sewage systems from the Victorian era, various phases of agricultural intensification (e.g. post-1945 and 1980s) and the introduction of phosphorus-rich detergents since the 1950s have all contributed to the eutrophication legacy. Few, if any, of our lakes and rivers have survived the ravages of eutrophication. Even the remotest of mountain lakes and the largest of Scottish lochs show signs of nutrient enrichment in the form of changing plant communities (e.g. Bennion *et al.* 2004). However, it is in lowland lakes and rivers that eutrophication has been most pronounced.

Nowhere in the UK are the consequences of freshwater eutrophication better understood than in the Norfolk Broads. The Broads are a collection of around 50 flooded medieval peat workings in eastern England. Since the middle of the last century they have been transformed from clear water lakes, with abundant and species-rich communities of water plants, invertebrates and fish, to murky, plantless lakes where species diversity is much reduced. In the Broads, sewage effluent and agricultural fertilisers have been a major source of nutrients for at least a century and when local naturalist Ted Ellis was asked to write a second edition of his 1968 book, *The Broads*, he could not be moved to do so. He was so saddened at the ecological damage he had seen during his lifetime, a second edition, he said, would need to be a different book altogether. Since then there have been improvements. The Broads Authority[2] has long been pushing for reductions in nutrient loading and over the last three decades, several lake restoration projects have taken place. Firstly, efforts were made to turn off the supply of phosphorus by stripping it out at sewage works, or by isolating the Broads from nutrient inputs via dams and stream diversions. Furthermore, and often in addition to the above, in some parts of the system phosphorus release from sediments has been countered by sediment removal, an expensive operation, to say the least.

The Broads example is essential to the UK eutrophication story because so much has been learned. A comprehensive and well-funded monitoring programme does indeed show a clear post-1980s reduction in phosphorus concentrations (Kelly 2008), while annual plant surveys show favourable responses in lake biology. However, even after 25 years of hard work it is clear that actual biological recovery is a slow process and may not follow a straight path. For example, while a number of Broads have seen water plants return, in others, despite intensive restoration work, the waters remain green and plant-free, or if vegetation has returned, this has been temporary.

So why has restoration been so slow and patchy? Part of the problem lies in the store of phosphorus in river and lake sediments which is re-released back into the water during the summer months. Furthermore, while much has been done to counter phosphorus inputs from sewage treatment works, more diffuse agriculturally derived sources of

---

[2] The Broads Authority is the statutory body with overall responsibility for the Broads National Park.

phosphorus, and in particular nitrogen, have never really been tackled. Groundwaters in many parts of lowland Britain (especially England) are already polluted with nitrogen, and in areas of low rainfall the problem is exacerbated. Remedial treatment of groundwater is prohibitively expensive and so the only way to tackle this problem must be prevention of pollution in the first place. To this end, 55% of England has been designated as a Nitrate Vulnerable Zone (NVZ) under the EU Nitrates Directive.[3] Farmers operating in an NVZ must implement a set of 'measures' that specify best practice in use and storage of fertiliser and manure – the main sources of agricultural nitrogen. However, even if we stopped applying nitrogen to the land today, there will still be a legacy of groundwater pollution for hundreds of years to come. Since many rivers and streams, especially in the south-east of England, are groundwater fed, this should be a topic of interest to anyone concerned with aquatic ecosystems.

As if the nitrogen story wasn't bad enough, there is now evidence that atmospheric nitrogen may be a significant problem in some areas. This nitrogen is derived from agricultural activities and vehicle emissions and gets into the atmosphere in a gaseous form only to be dumped later in rain and snow. In lowland England, deposition of atmospheric nitrogen may not be a major problem, as concentrations in precipitation are modest compared to other agricultural sources. However, in naturally nutrient-poor upland regions it may be a very real environmental problem and, apart from its acidifying potential, we know little about its consequences, although detrimental changes to sensitive aquatic plant and macro-invertebrate communities are suspected (Curtis and Simpson 2007).

So what of the future? Clearly, eutrophication is with us for some time yet. While we know a lot about the extent and effects of eutrophication in a few well-studied regions and in key conservation sites, we know relatively little of the extent and consequences of eutrophication in many thousands of other water bodies. Further, while Environment Agency monitoring data for rivers[4] has been tracking nutrient trends, effects on in-river ecology are much more poorly understood, particularly with regard to interactions between eutrophication and low flow conditions. How will eutrophication interact with other stressors on aquatic systems, such as invasive species and climate change? For example, a major agent of eutrophication in the UK is the non-native Common Carp (*Cyprinus carpio*) which, through inappropriate stocking, is now widespread in the UK. Carp re-suspend lake sediments and this can cause nutrient release and disturbance to macrophyte root systems. At today's water temperatures in the UK, the carp is on the edge of being able to spawn successfully and so populations in most waters are only sustained by periodic stocking. However, with current trends in

---

[3] The EU Nitrates Directive 91/676/EEC was adopted in 1991 and has the objective of 'reducing water pollution caused or induced by nitrates from agricultural sources and preventing further such pollution'. As well as Nitrate Vulnerable Zones (NVZs), the directive has established a voluntary code of good agricultural practice.

[4] Environment Agency Indicators – Nutrients in Rivers http://www.environment-agency.gov.uk/research/library/data/58820.aspx.

water temperature warming set to continue, we may reach a point where these carp can reproduce, leading to an explosion of numbers and subsequent eutrophication.

Surface water acidification

Acidification of surface waters is associated with a decrease in pH (and rise in toxic forms of aluminium) caused by the introduction of acid, usually in the form of acid rain. Acid rain is caused by the burning of fossil fuels for energy production and transportation, and resultant release to the air of sulfur dioxide (SO_2) and oxides of nitrogen (NO_x). It has been the main cause of surface water acidification in the UK since the industrial revolution. There have always been natural sources of acidity (rainwater is naturally acidic and organic acids are leached from some soils), but the additional load from anthropogenic sources has exceeded the natural buffering capacity of some systems, which have thus become acidified.

The term 'acid rain' was first used more than 150 years ago in a paper describing the impact of coal combustion on air quality and rainwater chemistry over Manchester (Smith 1852). But it was not until the late 1950s that it was suggested that acid rain might affect the chemistry and biology of lakes and rivers in Scandinavia, and a further 20 years before any evidence was sought to confirm this in the UK. Initial investigations in the UK centred around the Salmon fisheries in Scotland and, together with lake sediment studies in Galloway (ironically funded by the Central Electricity Generating Board), provided the evidence needed to show that acidification of upland lakes and rivers had begun in the mid-1800s and had since caused major changes in aquatic biota. Technological improvements (such as flue-gas desulfurisation) and policy changes in the UK and Europe (e.g. UNECE Convention on Long-range Transboundary Air Pollution[5]) have helped to reduce the amounts of SO_2 and NO_x being released by the UK by significant amounts and some previously acidified systems are now showing signs of recovery.

Palaeolimnology, the study of lake sediments to reconstruct historical environmental conditions, was key to providing the evidence needed by policy-makers that acidification was real and widespread, and research was soon being funded by the Department of the Environment.[6] Battarbee *et al.* (1984) showed that acid-sensitive lakes in Galloway, Scotland had experienced changes in their diatom floras, indicative of acidification, from around 1840 and this helped to dispel the idea that recent afforestation was the cause of acidification. Diatoms are microscopic unicellular algae with silica cell walls that are preserved in lake sediments, and some species are highly

---

[5] The United Nations Economic Commission for Europe's Convention on Long-range Transboundary Air Pollution (UNECE CLRTAP) was set up in 1979 to develop policies and strategies to combat discharge of air pollution. The convention has been extended with eight protocols, including 'Control of Nitrogen Oxides' and 'Reduction of Sulphur Emissions'. See http://www.unece.org/env/lrtap for more information.

[6] The Department of the Environment (DoE) become the Department for Environment, Transport and Regions (DETR) in 1997 and today is known as the Department of Environment, Food and Rural Affairs, or DEFRA.

sensitive to changes in acidity. By mapping changes in diatom species assemblages throughout a sediment core and combining this with radiometric dating, it is possible to reconstruct the environmental history of a lake. The Galloway studies showed that lake water pH had dropped by as much as 1.5 units at some sites. As well as the observed changes in diatom flora, this drop in pH is enough to cause the decline of Salmon, Brown Trout and aquatic invertebrate populations.

Lakes and rivers most susceptible to acid rain are those with already acid soils (such as peaty podzols typical of heather moorlands) overlying geological formations that are particularly resistant to weathering (such as granites and sandstones) and thus have a restricted capacity to neutralise acidic pollutants (i.e. low acid-neutralising capacity). These surface waters are mostly found in upland regions and include Cumbria, the Pennines (both in England), Snowdonia (Wales), Galloway (Scotland) and Mourne (Northern Ireland). Afforestation in these regions is known to exacerbate acidification by scavenging polluted aerosols from the atmosphere. In some cases it is not the acidity itself which is harmful, but the fact that lower pH results in increased availability of some toxic elements, especially aluminium.

Acidified freshwater ecosystems typically exhibit reduced numbers of plant and macro-invertebrate species, and loss of fish (especially salmonids) with subsequent effects up the food chain. The decline of Atlantic Salmon (*Salmo salar*) and Brown Trout (*Salmo trutta*) has been strongly linked with acidification. Laboratory experiments have shown that hatching and growth of Salmon eggs is significantly reduced if exposed to low pH (< 5) for prolonged periods (Buckler *et al.* 1995), while *in situ* experiments at the River Bladnoch in Galloway confirm these findings with some heavily acidified streams showing survival rates as low as 0 to 5%.[7] Mayflies are also sensitive to acidic conditions and some have disappeared completely from acidified systems – resulting in a reduced food supply for organisms further up the food chain. On top of the direct effects of acidification, aluminium toxicity, which may be increased at low pH, adversely affects plant and algae growth, is toxic to fish and causes reduced survival in aquatic macro-invertebrates (Gensemer and Playle 1999).

Other notable UK species which have been affected by acidification are the Dipper (*Cinclus cinclus*) and Natterjack Toad (*Bufo calamita*). Enhanced stream-water acidity in dipper habitats has been shown to cause a decline in aquatic invertebrate biomass, particularly of larval Trichoptera (caddisflies) and Plecoptera (stoneflies), which in turn adversely affects Dipper breeding success (Logie 1995; Ormerod *et al.* 1985). Across Europe the presence of successful populations of Dippers is seen as an indicator of an unpolluted stream system. However, for Dippers, as well as other birds, there is much evidence that acidification also leads to thinner eggshells, which further impairs breeding success. Acidification impedes calcium uptake at the bottom of the

---

[7] 2006 figures from the Galloway Fisheries Trust, which is leading the Conservation of Atlantic Salmon in Scotland (CASS) project. See http://www.gallowayfisheriestrust.org and http://www.snh.org.uk/salmonLIFEproject/.

food chain and results in lower calcium levels in the eggshells, making them more susceptible to damage.

Acidification in the UK is monitored using networks of lake and river sites (e.g. UK Acid Waters Monitoring Network[8]) and recently some sites have started to show clear signs of chemical recovery, although biological recovery is less clear (Monteith *et al*. 2005). Early indicators of improvement include the reappearance of acid-sensitive diatoms and aquatic plants; increasing numbers of macro-invertebrate predators (caddisflies and stoneflies) and in some sites, the reappearance of juvenile Brown Trout. Continued monitoring will show whether or not pre-acidification species assemblages can be attained, but in the meantime sites in some regions remain unnaturally acidic and are still susceptible to episodic acidification, which can occur during periods of high flow.

Pesticides and other man-made chemicals

Today there are a vast array of synthetic compounds in existence and hundreds more are developed each year. It is widely considered that the most problematic of these for the environment are the so-called persistent organic pollutants or POPs. These are man-made organic chemicals which do not readily break down in the environment. Classes of POPs of environmental concern are organochlorines (OCs) (which include DDT), polychlorinated biphenyls (PCBs), polybrominated diphenyl ethers (PBDEs) and organotins. Sources of POPs in aquatic systems include pesticides, combustion processes (transport and incineration), electrical components, flame retardants and building materials. POPs can biomagnify in food webs, that is, they pass up the food chain in increasing concentrations, and the volatility of some means that they can be transported long distances and therefore pose a threat to ecosystems anywhere, no matter how far from the pollution source. Measuring POPs in aquatic systems is difficult due to the low levels present, but fish tissue is often used for analysis, as bioaccumulation means that POPs are present in higher and more easily measurable concentrations.

When Rachel Carson wrote Silent Spring, the use of pesticides to control agricultural pests was in its infancy. The main protagonist in her story was DDT (dichlorodiphenyl-trichloroethane), one of the first synthetic pesticides, which was used to combat typhus in World War II and as a general insecticide. It had also proved efficient at controlling malaria-carrying mosquitoes, although the insects soon showed resistance. DDT readily found its way into water courses and its widespread use and acute toxicity led to fish kills and fish-eating bird poisoning on an unprecedented scale. It was banned in the US in 1973, and subsequently worldwide under the Stockholm Convention. It took another

---

[8] The United Kingdom Acid Waters Monitoring Network (UKAWMN) was established in 1988 and comprises 21 freshwater sites across the UK. For each site data are gathered annually on fish, aquatic macrophyte, macro-invertebrate and diatom species occurrences. Water chemistry is measured monthly. See http://www.ukawmn.ucl.ac.uk for more information.

10 years before it was banned in the UK in 1984, but its persistence in the environment means that even today it can still occasionally be found in trace amounts in food such as meat and fish.[9]

When DDT was introduced, little was known about the effects it might have in the wider environment. Today in the UK there are approximately 300 chemical compounds approved for use as pesticides alone and, unlike DDT, they are thoroughly tested before being approved for use (Control of Pesticides Regulations 1986). However, this testing does not include what happens when these compounds are accidentally or unintentionally released into the environment. There are several routes for pesticides to enter the freshwater system. The most direct is via surface run-off to rivers and lakes adjacent to the treated area. A smaller percentage is leached into groundwater by rainfall or irrigation water. Pesticides, like other POPs, may also be volatilised and pass into the atmosphere where they may travel large distances before being deposited in rainfall back to the land and thus to the rivers and lakes.

Incidents where large amounts of pesticide are accidentally released occur mainly as a result of poorly stored agricultural chemicals. The UK's Health and Safety Executive (HSE) reported that for 2007–08 there were 94 incidents,[10] less than any year in the preceding decade. It should be noted that such reports focus on incidents affecting human health rather than the wider environment. This decline in serious incidents is largely down to increased awareness and improved handling procedures amongst farmers and contractors. Incidents, when they do occur, can have devastating, although not usually long-lasting, effects locally.

Diffuse pollution from pesticides could also be expected to have decreased, although this is harder to measure. Government statistics for England and Wales[11] indicate that the area of land sprayed with pesticides has steadily increased over the last decade (from 40 million hectares in 1990 to 58 million hectares in 2005), whilst the actual weight of pesticide applied has decreased (27 750 tonnes in 1990 to 23 600 tonnes in 2005). So, despite increasing areas being sprayed, there are improvements due to use of less-persistent chemicals and less-concentrated applications. Furthermore, improved farming practices (such as use of buffer zones between fields and water courses) mean that fewer pesticides are ending up in our fresh waters. Environment Agency statistics for England and Wales in the last decade suggest that there is no significant trend in the percentage of surface waters (rivers) containing pesticides $> 0.1 \ \mu g \ l^{-1}$,[12] which remains

---

[9] The UK Working Party of Pesticide Residues (WPPR) (now the Pesticide Residues Committee) conducted monitoring between 1977 and 2000 and regularly found residues of DDT in dairy products, meat, potatoes and fish. However, it is usually impossible to rule out illegal use of the pesticide as the source of contamination. Current monitoring suggests that DDT residues in UK produce are much reduced. See http://www.pesticides.gov.uk/prc_home.asp for more information.

[10] Health and Safety Executive Pesticide Incidents Report 2007–08 http://www.hse.gov.uk/fod/pir0708.pdf

[11] Environment Agency Pesticide Use in England and Wales http://www.environment-agency.gov.uk/research/library/data/34397.aspx

[12] 0.1 $\mu g \ l^{-1}$ is the EU drinking-water standard for a single pesticide, total pesticides not to exceed 0.5 $\mu g \ l^{-1}$ (Drinking Water Directive 98/83/EC). These figures are really a substitute for zero since member states are of the opinion that drinking water should contain no pesticides.

fairly constant at about 7% in England and 2% in Wales[13]. According to these figures, in England, the Thames and North-east areas have the highest amounts of pesticide pollution. In Scotland, SEPA carries out some monitoring of pesticides in surface water and groundwater. Their monitoring under the Water Framework Directive (see box) indicates that 22% of Scotland is as risk from agricultural pesticides.[14] The kinds of pesticides commonly found in UK fresh waters include synthetic compounds such as diuron, isoproturon, fenpropimorph, mancozeb, bentazone, atrazine and derivatives, flutriafol, carbendazim and simazine. Although many pesticides are currently being withdrawn from use following recent EU legislation,[15] the long-term effects of these and other POPs on aquatic biodiversity are only now starting to become apparent, as the preceding chapter on endocrine disruption shows.

So far we have concentrated on pesticides as the major source of POPs in aquatic systems, but there is growing evidence that other classes of compound may be significant. For example, polybrominated diphenyl ethers (PBDEs) are toxic flame retardants used to fire-proof consumer electronic plastics, furniture and mattresses. Recent monitoring in the UK (and elsewhere) has found these compounds in fish (including farmed Salmon), sea birds and birds of prey, but little is known about their effects on human health and they are not routinely monitored. Fish caught in mountain lakes in Scotland and northern Europe have been found to contain unusually high concentrations of PBDEs (Gallego *et al.* 2007). So how did these chemicals get into remote mountain lakes? The most plausible explanation is that they are released to the atmosphere during incineration or disposal, transported in the atmosphere and deposited in dust, rain and snow to remote areas. There is evidence too that PBDEs and other POPs may be further concentrated in mountain lakes by a process known as 'cold trapping', whereby volatile compounds are more easily stored in the colder water of high altitude lakes – the global distillation model. Some PBDEs are known to affect brain development in mammals, but it is not yet clear what the impact of these chemicals in our aquatic systems will be.

A final example of pollution from POPs worthy of mention is that of tributyltin (TBT). TBT is a persistent and highly toxic organotin compound typically used in anti-fouling paint and well known as a major pollutant in marine environments. Once released into the environment TBT usually degrades quickly, but in anaerobic sediments it can persist for decades. Despite being banned in the UK in 1987 the legacy of TBT lives on today. Apart from being implicated in mollusc imposex (see previous chapter) palaeolimnological studies in the Norfolk Broads (Sayer *et al.* 2006) have shown that pollution from TBT is also strongly implicated in the dramatic shift from

---

[13] Environment Agency Pesticides in Fresh Waters http://www.environment-agency.gov.uk/research/library/data/34239.aspx.

[14] State of Scotland's Environment 2006, Supplementary material http://www.sepa.org.uk/scotlands_Environment/data_and_reports/idoc.ashx?docid=e81a27d5-b0f7-48a5-81b8-b201419a7340&version=-1.

[15] European Parliament http://www.europarl.europa.eu/news/expert/infopress_page/066-45937-012-01-03-911-20090112IPR45936-12-01-2009-2009-false/default_en.htm.

clear-water macrophyte-rich lakes to turbid phytoplankton-dominated lakes during the 1960s and 1970s. The suspected mechanism for this is that TBT reduces numbers of grazing organisms (such as snails and zooplankton) which in turn leads to an increase in phytoplankton. This increase, in a finely balanced and sensitive system, causes a step-change in the ecosystem that cannot be easily reversed (the so-called *stable states* theory). However, unravelling the effects of TBT from eutrophication and other pollutants is difficult – all too often the case in lakes and rivers where several factors may be affecting change at once. The persistence of TBT in lake sediments, as with other chemical pollutants, is a major cause for concern – if the sediments become re-suspended (through storm events, dredging activities or biological disturbance for example), then the pollutant can once again become biologically available.

Heavy metals

Among the heavy metals, mercury (Hg), lead (Pb), cadmium (Cd) and nickel (Ni) are the major pollutants in our lakes and rivers. Heavy-metal pollution can affect biological systems in three ways – by acute toxicity (i.e. fatal dose) by disrupting the food chain and by affecting the 'health' of organisms (i.e. reduced growth and reproductive success). Heavy-metal pollution in lakes and rivers is often perceived to be rather localised (where industrial effluent or mine water enters a watercourse for example), but heavy metals can be transported large distances in the atmosphere and may be found in remote places far away from industry. For example, recent studies have found high levels of heavy-metal contamination in Arctic and Antarctic organisms and in remote lakes on the Tibetan Plateau (N. Rose, personal communication).

Mercury has long been known as a highly toxic pollutant and its effects in freshwater systems have been studied for more than 50 years. Natural sources exist, but it is human sources (such as fossil-fuel burning, metal-processing industries and incinerators) which are responsible for the majority of mercury found in our environment today. The problem with mercury is its propensity to volatilise into the atmosphere whereupon it is transported long distances and then deposited in rain as particulates. Once in the aquatic environment it is transformed by bacteria into the more toxic form of methyl mercury, which then biomagnifies in the food chain – the largest amounts are found at the top of the food chain in predatory fish and fish-eating birds and mammals.

Sediment studies of lakes across the UK show concentrations of mercury rising dramatically in the last 100 years (e.g. Yang and Rose 2003). However, looking at concentrations in sediment may be misleading as concentration is very sensitive to sediment properties such as organic matter content. Flux rates are a more reliable measure of pollution as they give an estimated value of pollutant per m^2 per year. UK lake sediments indicate a peak flux of mercury between 1950 and 1970 and a subsequent decline. This mirrors figures for mercury emissions, which have declined in the UK since the 1970s.

In the UK at least, heavy-metal pollution has been much reduced over the last few decades. Cadmium, lead, nickel and mercury are all identified as priority substances for emissions reductions under the EU Water Framework Directive (see box) and Environment Agency figures for the release of these metals to controlled waters do indeed indicate significant reductions.[16]

EU Water Framework Directive

The Water Framework Directive (2000/60/EC) came into force in December 2000 and establishes an integrated approach to the protection, improvement and sustainable use of Europe's rivers, lakes, estuaries, coastal waters and ground-water. The directive became law in 2003 and is co-ordinated in the UK by the Department of Environment for Northern Ireland, the Scottish Environmental Protection Agency and DEFRA (for England and Wales).

The directive is heralded as a holistic approach to water-quality management and seeks to enhance the status and prevent further deterioration of aquatic ecosystems, promote sustainable use of water and reduce pollution. It will also be used to help mitigate the effects of floods and droughts. All inland and coastal waters are required to reach at least *good status* by 2015. For surface waters this status has two components – ecological and chemical.

Key stages along the route to full implementation of the directive are the development of monitoring programmes, characterisation of water bodies and the development of *programmes of measures* which will be summarised for each river-basin district in a River Basin Management Plan (RBMP). There are 20 river-basin districts in the UK and Ireland.

More information can be found at http://www.euwfd.com and http://www.wfduk.org.

Once again, a legacy of pollution remains in lake and river sediments and diffuse sources continue to add to the burden. A study in England and Wales by Nicholson *et al.* (2003) found that the majority of heavy metals (up to 85% in some areas) found in agricultural soils were from atmospheric deposition and the remainder were from fertilisers (especially livestock manures and sewage sludge), agrochemicals and inorganic fertilisers. Of course, what goes on the land eventually ends up in rivers and lakes and palaeolimnological studies (e.g. Yang and Rose 2005) show clearly a pattern

---

[16] Environment Agency Pollution Inventory Data http://www.environment-agency.gov.uk/research/library/data/34205.aspx.

of increasing heavy-metal pollution throughout the last 150 years. Sites closest to industrial sources show the largest concentrations, but even in remote sites atmospheric deposition has left its mark. There is some suggestion that climate change might increase the bioavailability of heavy metals (by remobilisation in soils especially) and this would exacerbate their effects on aquatic biota.

Climate Change

Climate change has been mentioned elsewhere in this book, so here we will focus on the effects climate change has on the physical, chemical and biological characteristics of lakes and rivers. Current climate-change scenarios for the UK predict warmer, wetter winters and drier, hotter summers (Jenkins *et al.* 2007), and whilst some work has been carried out on the effect these changes will have on the water supply and aquaculture industry, there is less research on how biodiversity might be (or has already been) affected.

The main factors affecting biodiversity in rivers are flow (water quantity), water quality (including temperature) and habitat availability. When flow is reduced, any pollutant entering the system will be more concentrated. Temperature directly affects chemical dynamics and increased temperature generally leads to reduced oxygen capacity. We have seen that long, hot summers can lead to dangerous toxin-producing blue-green algae (cyanobacteria) blooms, which in some cases have caused the deaths of livestock and can cause illness in humans who come into contact with the algae. Climate warming combined with reduced throughput of lakes and slow-moving river sections, increased nutrients due to eutrophication and higher susceptibility to stratification will result in an increased occurrence of algal blooms. Recent years have already seen several severe blooms in Scottish lochs and park lakes. In winter, warming will reduce snow and lake ice cover in high-altitude regions, which will lead to changes in hydrological regimes that will have cascading effects downstream. Climate-change scenarios also predict an increase in intensity of rainfall. This may result in detrimental acidification episodes in upland streams and rivers and physical effects on habitats such as scouring and washing away of fish eggs.

In short, the effects of climate change can be expected to exacerbate the effects of other stressors of aquatic systems (e.g. acidification, chemical pollution and eutrophication) and may have already profoundly altered the hydrological regimes of many of our freshwater systems.

Recovery of the River Thames

Nowhere in the UK is there a better example of a recovering river system than the River Thames. Declared 'biologically dead' in the 1950s and formerly known as the 'Great Stink', the tidal Thames has recorded 122 species of fish in the last 25 years, as well as occasional sightings of dolphins, seals, porpoises and even whales. Improvements started in the 1960s with the decline in industry and associated effluent and improved sewage treatment practices. Salmon had already returned as early as 1974 and are now joined by a wide variety of freshwater, brackish and marine species, including the Sea Lamprey (*Petromyzon marinus*), which is nationally rare.

In 2008 it was reported that Short-snouted Seahorses (*Hippocampus hippocampus*) were now breeding in the Thames estuary. However, the Thames is at the northern edge of the Seahorse's range and so we cannot be sure whether this is a sign of climate warming or improving water quality.

Despite the improvements, however, there are still problems. During periods of heavy rainfall, there can be large inputs of sewage effluent from Combined Sewer Overflows (CSOs) at over 50 locations along the tidal Thames. The resultant reduction in dissolved oxygen levels is alleviated by the deployment of oxygenating boats which can help to return the river to normal levels within 24 hours. Whilst efforts are underway to improve the sewerage system further, the problem is exacerbated by intense periods of heavy rainfall, which are predicted to increase under UKCIP climate-change scenarios.

Acknowledgements

The authors would like to thank the following people who have helped with the preparation of this manuscript: Neil Rose, Rick Battarbee, Helen Bennion, Gavin Simpson and Martin Kernan (Environmental Change Research Centre, UCL) and Don Monteith (Centre for Ecology and Hydrology).

References

Battarbee, R.W., Thrush, B.A., Clymo, R.S. *et al.* (1984). Diatom analysis and the acidification of lakes. *Philosophical Transactions of the Royal Society of London. Series B,* **305**(1124), 451–477.

Bennion, H.B., Fluin, J. and Simpson, G.L. (2004). Assessing eutrophication and reference conditions for Scottish freshwater lochs using subfossil diatoms. *Journal of Applied Ecology,* **41**(1), 124–138.

Buckler, D.R., Cleveland, L., Little, E.E. and Brumbaugh, W.G. (1995). Survival, sublethal responses, and tissue residues of Atlantic salmon exposed to acidic pH and aluminium. *Aquatic Toxicology,* **31**, 203–216.

Curtis, C. and Simpson, G.L. (2007). *Freshwater Umbrella – The Effect of Nitrogen Deposition and Climate Change on Freshwaters in the UK.* Report to DEFRA under contract CPEA17. London. ENSIS Ltd.

Gallego, E., Grimalt, J.O., Bartons, M. and Lopez, J.F. (2007). Altitudinal gradients of PBDEs and PCBs in fish from European high mountain lakes. *Environmental Science Technology,* **41**(7), 2196–2202.

Gensemer, R.W. and Playle, R.C. (1999). The bioavailability and toxicity of aluminium in aquatic environments. *Critical Reviews in Environmental Science and Technology,* **29**(4), 315–450.

Hughes, M., Hornby, D., Bennion, H. *et al.* (2004). The development of a GIS-based inventory of standing waters in England, Wales and Scotland together with a risk-based prioritisation protocol. *Water, Air and Soil Pollution: Focus,* **4**(2–3), 73–84.

Jenkins, G.J., Perry, M.C., and Prior, M.J.O. (2007). *The Climate of the United Kingdom and Recent Trends*, Exeter, Met Office, Hadley Centre.

Kelly, A. (2008). *Lake Restoration Strategy for the Broads*, Norwich, Broads Authority.

Logie, J.W. (1995). Effects of stream acidity on non-breeding dippers *Cinclus cinclus* in the south-central highlands of Scotland. *Aquatic Conservation: Marine and Freshwater Ecosystems,* **5**(1), 25–35.

Mason, C.F. (2002). *Biology of Freshwater Pollution*, Harlow, Pearson Education Limited.

Monteith, D.T., Hildrew, A.G., Flower, R.J. *et al.* (2005). Biological responses to the chemical recovery of acidified fresh waters in the UK. *Environmental Pollution,* **137**(1), 83–101.

Nicholson, F.A., Smith, S.R., Alloway, B.J., Carlton-Smith, C. and Chambers, B.J. (2003). An inventory of heavy metals inputs to agricultural soils in England and Wales. *Science of the Total Environment,* **311**(1–3), 205–219.

Omerod, S.J., Boilstone, M.A. and Tyler, S.J. (1985). Factors influencing the abundance of breeding Dippers *Cinclus cinclus* in the catchment of the River Wye, mid-Wales. *Ibis,* **127**(3), 332–340.

Sayer, C.D., Hoare, D., Simpson, G.L. *et al.* (2006). TBT causes regime shift in shallow lakes. *Environmental Science and Technology,* **40**(17), 5269–5275.

Smith, R.A. (1852). On the air and rain of Manchester. *Memoirs and Proceedings of the Manchester Library and Philosophical Society,* **2**, 207–217.

Smol, J.P. (2008). *Pollution of Lakes and Rivers: A Paleoenvironmental Perspective*, Maldon, USA, Blackwell Publishing.

Yang, H. and Rose, N.L. (2003). Distribution of mercury in six lake sediments cores across the UK. *Science of the Total Environment,* **304**, 391–404.

Yang, H. and Rose, N. (2005). Trace element pollution records in some UK lake sediments, their history, influence factors and regional differences. *Environment International,* **31**, 63–75.

11

Twenty-five key questions in ecology

Norman Maclean

Summary

This chapter is slanted very much towards a section of our expected readership, namely students of ecology and environmental science. I should also acknowledge help from my co-authors over formulating this chapter, especially Rob Robinson, the author of our bird chapter (Chapter 17).

In 2005, a workshop was organised in the UK for which 654 people from government and research centres with a specific interest in ecology were invited to draw up a list of questions to which policy-makers in UK ecology most urgently needed answers. One thousand and three questions were initially generated and discussed by the workshop participants. At a further two-day workshop this list was refined, initially to 188 questions and then finally to 100 questions.

This final shortlisting was done by the 'policy' people, but not the 'academics' at the meeting. This was then published in the *Journal of Applied Ecology* in 2006 (see Sutherland *et al.* 2006). I have now further reduced the initial list of 100 to a list of 25. Of necessity, some significant questions are left out, but I have tried, wherever possible, to merge numbers of questions into one over-arching question. The questions are not placed in any rank order of importance, but are grouped roughly into topic areas.

A subsequent paper in the same journal (Sutherland *et al.* 2008) uses the technique of horizon scanning to identify new potential 'threats and opportunities facing UK biodiversity' and this is discussed later in this chapter. Bill Sutherland has already agreed to the presentation of his publications in this format.

Silent Summer: The State of Wildlife in Britain and Ireland, ed. Norman Maclean. Published by Cambridge University Press. © Cambridge University Press 2010.

Species population change and interactions

1. What criteria should be used to determine policy regarding invasive species, new and existing disease organisms, and accidental or intentional releases of non-native species?
2. How can we effectively monitor terrestrial and aquatic invertebrate biomass, particularly those which are key resources for other taxa, such as moths? Why have woodland birds and many butterfly and moth species declined so sharply?
3. What are the impacts of domestic and feral cats and dogs on wildlife?
4. How can we manage large herbivores (deer and domestic animals, such as sheep and cattle) sustainably?
5. How can we better understand the epidemiology of existing and emerging diseases such as bird flu within wildlife reservoirs to ensure protection of humans and livestock? What will be the impact on agriculture of the present disease problems of the Honeybee, *Apis mellifera*?

Human impacts on biodiversity

6. What are the environmental consequences of agricultural practices, ranging from the ultra-intensive to free range and how can we best manage the introduction of new technologies, such as GM plants in agriculture.
7. What are the impacts of recreational activities, including field sports and freshwater fishing, on wildlife, and how can the field sport/wildlife welfare equation be optimised?
8. Which are, or will become, the major environmental hazards amongst chemical pollutants of land and water, and how can they be best monitored, controlled and reduced?
9. What impact does plastic litter and refuse dumping have on wildlife both on land and in the adjoining sea?
10. What are the effects of light and noise pollution on wildlife and how can they be reduced?

Landscape management and conservation

11. Is it better to segregate or co-manage areas for food production and wildlife conservation?
12. How do we best create, or re-create, habitat for wildlife, for example saltmarsh, semi-natural grassland or re-stock forest clear-fells?

13. How can provision for wildlife be maximised in new and existing urban development, and how can the consequent habitat fragmentation be mitigated?
14. Is it better to extend existing patches of wildlife habitat or to create new separate patches?
15. How do we extend the reserve network to effectively conserve marine biodiversity?

Adapting to climate change and energy demand

16. What species are the best indicators of the impacts of climate change?
17. What is likely to be the relationship between climate change and future appearance and expansion or decline and extinction of particular species?
18. What are potential impacts of terrestrial and marine wind farms and tidal barriers?
19. What are the long-term biodiversity impacts of climate adaptation measures, such as floodplain restoration, biofuel cropping or carbon sequestration?
20. How effective will our reserve network be in the face of climate change, and how do we ensure a permeable landscape to allow biodiversity room to adapt through distributional shifts?

Integrating conservation and wider policy

21. What are the impacts of international ecological policies on UK species, particularly migrants, and how are they best implemented in a UK context?
22. How can wildlife be best conserved in a situation of national and international human population increase and desire for economic gain?
23. How can a value be placed on biodiversity so that its comparative worth as a contributor to human wellbeing can be determined?
24. What rights and privileges should be accorded to non-human species as sharers of the planet Earth's resources?
25. What is our vision for biodiversity within our landscape, managed, as it is, primarily for humans, and how do we measure progress towards a wider sharing of resource between humans and wildlife?

Expected impacts on biodiversity up to 2050

A subsequent meeting of government organisation representatives, charities, businesses and 12 academics was organised, and involved consultation with 452 individuals. The aim this time was to 'horizon scan', that is to identify topics and problems involving wildlife which have the potential to impact on biodiversity by 2050. The area covered was the UK excluding Overseas Territories.

A total of 25 issues were agreed in a final session as having highest relevance. This was published under Sutherland *et al.* (2008). I list here all 25, with some explanatory comment of my own.

1. *Nanotechnology*: This involves particles of less than 100 nm size, which are believed to have many novel characteristics of activity and potential biological properties. There is some evidence that such particles may bring benefits, such as binding pollutants, but may pose problems such as adversely affecting the function of some biological membranes (Maynard 2006).

2. *Invasive potential and ecosystem impacts of 'artificial life'*: 'Organisms' can now be engineered from synthetic nucleotide arrays, and also by mixing organic and non-organic materials through self-assembly. There is concern regarding intentional or accidental release into the environment of such artificial organisms or other robotic 'biomimetics'.

3. *Accidental consequences of new pathogens engineered by biotechnology*: Experimental viruses with contraceptive effects have been produced for use against Red Foxes, *Vulpes vulpes*, which are a non-native pest species in Australia (Hardy *et al.* 2006). Future control and regulation of newly engineered pathogenic viruses or bacteria will be difficult, and possible impacts on wildlife are envisaged.

4. *Direct impacts of novel pathogens*: This threat comes from the new emergence or transport of novel pathogens. Two mentioned are the emergence of Devil Facial Tumour Disease in Australian Tasmanian Devil, *Sarcophilus laniarius*, (as discussed by Hawkins *et al.* 2006). (This is actually a cell infection from biting within a population so in-bred that they have immune tolerance of one another's tissue – in this case a malignant cell line. It is not a microbial pathogen), and the threat from new fungal pathogens such as forms of phytophthera fungus proving troublesome in the context of plant disease in both the USA (Holdenrieder *et al.* 2004) and the UK. The recent spread of the amphibian chytrid fungus is also very important.

5. *Control of new pathogens may itself bring new threats to wildlife*: Increased use of habitat modification or insecticides to control new outbreaks of diseases such as malaria in the UK may prove themselves a threat. Reduction of wetlands to help prevent spread of diseases such as avian influenza could also happen.

6. *'Invasional meltdown' following climate change*: Some potentially invasive species could be encouraged to establish in the UK by retraction of ice and snow, and ocean temperature change. However, some new arrivals (say Little Egret, *Egretta garzetta*, Cattle Egret, *Bubulcus ibis*, and Eurasian Spoonbill, *Platalea leucorodia*) may be perceived as beneficial additions.

7. *Large-scale ecosystem restoration*: Recent habitat restoration programmes for recovery of species such as Corncrake, *Crex crex*, and Bittern, *Botaurus stellaris*, may be the precursors of much larger attempts at habitat restoration (see discussion in Sutherland 1994).

8. *Future encouragement for range change following climate change*: Much of our current fauna and flora is relatively non-dispersive and thus cannot easily spread to make use of new suitable habitat following climate change. Some butterflies, such as Adonis Blue, *Polyommatus bellargus*, and Silver Spotted Skipper, *Hesperia comma*, provide good examples. Future provision of corridors to give access to new suitable habitat may be necessary.

9. *Climate change may bring increased frequency of extreme weather events*: Increased numbers of storms may have serious impacts on our woodlands, but the full impacts of anticipated extreme weather events on wildlife community structure are very hard to predict. Certainly storm-driven vagrancy in birds and insects might lead to establishment of new species from distant land masses.

10. *Geo-engineering planet Earth*: Various schemes have been proposed whereby the planet's weather patterns might be altered following dramatic human intervention. These are hard to evaluate, and include injecting sulfur dioxide into the stratosphere, iron fertilisation of ocean plankton and laying reflective plastic shields over deserts (see discussion in Cicerone 2006). There could be benefits and there could be negative impacts for wildlife.

11. *Adopting an ecosystem approach*: Many of our current human activities, such as sport fishing and shooting, agriculture, aquaculture and forestry, involve interfaces between conservation interests and, for example, energy demands and food production. Funding for farming and forestry may well change from EU Common Agricultural Support Policies to emphasis on renewable energy and human health. Thus common practices, such as livestock grazing and controlled heather burning, may be phased out, with consequent problems for ecosystems.

12. *Increased risk of fire*: Climate change is likely to bring an increased frequency of serious fires in woodland and heathland. New means of predicting and managing fires are needed.

13. *Increased human demand for biomass and biofuel*: The present stated aim of the UK Government is that by 2020, one-fifth of total energy supply should come from renewable resources. Examples of such include biomass crops, such as willow and the grass *Miscanthus*, bioethanol extraction from beet, and biodiesel from oil seed rape. Such developments could put new demands on semi-natural habitat and increase uses of herbicides and pesticides. However, this is as much an opportunity as it is a threat to wildlife and the habitat that best fosters it.

14. *New pressures on agriculture for food production*: These pressures are likely to lead to agricultural changes as the problems of feeding a poor and an affluent world continue. Even small changes can have major effects. Thus as screw tops replace corks in much of the wine industry, so does the future prospects for Spanish cork oak forests, and the rich biodiversity which they contain, look gloomy.

15. *Acidification of oceans*: The pH of the world's oceans is reliably predicted to decrease by up to 0.5 pH units by 2100, due to increased atmospheric CO_2 (Haughan *et al.* 2006). This could pose particular problems for marine life which

depends on calcareous eco-skeletons such as many molluscs, crustaceans, corals and many planktonic faunal organisms.

16. *Reduction in cool marine habitats on continental shelves*: Shallow seas adjacent to land are warming more quickly than the land itself. This is having, and will increasingly have, profound effects on cold-water communities of birds and mammals which depend on in-shore fish stocks (see Harris *et al.* 2007).

17. *Increased demand for offshore power generation*: Major investment in coastal and off-shore power generation may well impact on marine and coastal biodiversity (Gill 2005). The biodiversity impacts of the construction maintenance and eventual decommissioning need to be urgently determined.

18. *Increased frequency of high energy coastal storms and tsunamis*: There is concern that marine construction and drilling may increase the frequency of tsunamis, and the UK coastal biodiversity is conspicuously vulnerable since it is increasingly squeezed between the sea and sea-wall defences. Much of the north Norfolk coast and the Norfolk Broads is at risk from salt water ingress following storms.

19. *Risk to coastal habitats from sea-bed rises*: Increases of 0.6 m in sea level in the current century have been predicted (Hansen 2007), and even this may be an underestimate. One mitigating defence would be the development of more shore and sub-tidal habitat.

20. *Changes in freshwater flows*: Both changes in urban water demand and climate change may pose future problems for flooding impact. Thus fresh water is increasingly channelled into rivers or conduits, often with poor summer flows coupled with an inability for these to operate effectively in times of winter flooding. Water abstraction may require extensive water redistribution. Also, flooding brings increased risks of water pollution and consequent effects on the ecology of freshwater biocommunities.

21. *Future changes in wildlife may be rapid and may render current legislation inadequate or obsolete*: The changes in species composition and distribution following changes in climate and land use may be rapid and cause current legislation devised to protect wildlife inappropriate.

22. *New technologies such as the internet and electronic sensors may empower more people*: The internet, the mobile phone, even personal DNA analyses based on specific DNA barcodes, are likely to make it easier for many more people to be better informed about the environment and to monitor air or water pollution themselves. This will in turn put more pressure on politicians and decision-makers.

23. *There are signs of a decline in interest in nature, especially amongst children and young adults*: It has been calculated that children spend only half the time outdoors compared to 20 years ago. If early encounters and memories of wildlife are not realised, there will surely be a reduced concern for wildlife protection. Encounters with the natural world also foster awareness and both physical and mental health (see discussions in Fuller 2007 and Pretty 2007).

24. *Monetary value will increasingly guide future decision-making about priorities and wildlife conservation*: Financial evaluations of biodiversity and green benefits are more likely in future. Decisions about conflicts of interest in land use and landscape planning will probably be made increasingly in terms of financial cost/benefit ratios (see Stern 2007 and Balmford *et al.* 2002).

25. *Fear of contracting disease from wildlife may increase and reduce sympathy for wildlife conservation*: Infections such as rabies or avian influenza can cause widespread panic and can rapidly tip the scales in favour of culling rather than conservation. Ways of reducing media exaggeration and calming human anxiety will certainly be important (see discussion by Peterson *et al.* 2006).

Comment

These lists of questions make daunting reading. Many of them are big questions, such as, for example, the effects of plastic litter and refuse dumping. Huge numbers of marine creatures like seals, whales and birds (see Figure 36.1 of an entangled gannet) become lethally entangled in plastic and some such as Leatherback Turtles, *Dermochelys coriacea*, eat plastic bags in mistake for jellyfish. Yet the plastic non-degradable bag has become a characteristic feature of our shopping culture worldwide. Refuse dumps have changed the behaviour of urban Foxes and many gull species, which now scavenge inland as frequently as on the sea.

A major conclusion that emerges in one's mind from reading through these questions and problems is a familiar one, namely that the main change in our environment is the *rate* of change, which in so many cases greatly exceeds the evolutionary adaptive powers of wild species. When factors such as climate change, human population increase and agricultural diversification into biofuels are compounded, it becomes clear that we live in a highly dynamic situation. The rates of potential adaptive evolution amongst bacteria and viruses can readily match and even outstrip changes occurring within say five years, but larger organisms with smallish populations and low breeding potential take longer. Adaptive behaviour, such as the exploitation of peanut feeders by Eurasian Siskins, *Carduelis spinus*, of niger seed by European Goldfinches, *Carduelis carduelis*, and of garbage dumps by Herring Gulls, *Larus argentatus*, can be quite rapid, that is within a few years, but speciation in vertebrates takes minimally thousands of years (as in the explosive speciation of fish in some African Great Lakes), and more frequently about one million years.

Although many of these questions are big, probably none are as big as a more familiar, but increasingly pressing problem, namely how can the world, and we in Britain and Ireland, control our population size? The expected population increase over the next 20 years is clearly not sustainable from many points of view, namely food production, water availability, energy consumption and survival of the wildlife with which we share the space.

References

Balmford, A., Bruner, A., Cooper, P. *et al.* (2002). Economic reasons for conserving wild nature. *Science*, **297**, 950–953.

Cicerone, R.J. (2006). Geoengineering: encouraging research and overseeing implementation. *Climate Change*, **77**, 221–226.

Fuller, R.A., Irvine, K.N., Devine-Wright, P. Warren, P.H. and Gaston, K.J. (2007). Psychological benefits of greenspace increase with biodiversity. *Biology Letters*, **3**, 390–394.

Gill, A.B. (2005). Offshore renewable energy: ecological implications of generating electricity in the coastal zone. *Journal of Applied Ecology*, **42**, 605–615.

Hansen, J.E. (2007). Scientific reticence and sea level rise. *Environmental Research Letters*, **2**, 024002.

Hardy, C.M., Hinds, L., Kerr, P. *et al.* (2006). Biological control of vertebrate pests using virally vectored immunocontraception. *Journal of Reproductive Immunology*, **71**, 102–111.

Harris, M.P., Beare, D., Toresen, R. *et al.* (2007). A major increase in snake pipefish (*Entelurus aequoreus*) in northern European seas since 2003: potential implications for seabird breeding success. *Marine Biology*, **151**, 973–983.

Haughan, P.M., Turley, C. and Portner, H.O. (2006). *Effects on the Marine Environment of Ocean Acidification Resulting from Elevated Levels of CO_2 in the atmosphere.* OSPAR Commission, http://hdl.handle.net/10013/epic.25159.

Hawkins, C.E., Baars, C., Hesterman, H. *et al.* (2006). Emerging disease and population decline of an island endemic, the Tasmanian devil *Sarcophilus harrisi*. *Biological Conservation*, **131**, 307–324.

Holdenrieder, O., Pautasso, M., Weisberg, P.J. and Lonsdale, D. (2004). Tree diseases and landscape processes: the challenge of landscape pathology. *Trends in Ecology and Evolution*, **19**, 446–452.

Maynard, A.D., Aitkin, R.J., Butz, T. *et al.* (2006). Safe handling of nanotechnology. *Nature*, **444**, 267–269.

Peterson, M.N., Mertig, A.G. and Liu, J. (2006). Effects of zoonotic disease attributes on public attitudes towards wildlife management. *Journal of Wildlife Management*, **70**, 1746–1753.

Pretty, J. (2007). Social capital and the collective management of resources. *Science*, **302**, 1912–1915.

Stern, N. (2007). *The Economics of Climate Change*, Cambridge, Cambridge University Press.

Sutherland, W.J. (1994). How to help the Corncrake. *Nature*, **372**, 223.

Sutherland, W.J., Armstrong-Brown, S., Armsworth, P.R. *et al.* (2006). The identification of 100 ecological questions of high policy relevance in the UK. *Journal of Applied Ecology*, **43**, 617–627.

Sutherland, W.J., Bailey, M.J., Bainbridge, I.P. *et al.* (2008). Future novel threats and opportunities facing UK biodiversity identified by horizon scanning. *Journal of Applied Ecology*, **45**, 821–833.

PART II

Conservation in action

PART II

Conservation in action

Introduction

12

Conservation in action in Britain and Ireland

Andy Clements
Dedicated to the memory of Sir Martin Doughty, 1949–2009

Summary

Nature conservation in the UK today is very different from that practised 50 years ago. A wide range of organisations contributes to looking after a healthy environment and it is vital that we make this work relevant and accessible to the general public. The financial resources for biodiversity conservation have grown enormously and devolved governments look after a broad environmental agenda. The evidence-based approach to understanding changes in our species populations and habitats, and how to address them, will be increasingly important in the context of climate change. The legislative basis for nature conservation is strong, and domestic law is underpinned by European Directives and international conventions. Key cases demonstrate the effectiveness of the legislation and the Public Inquiry at Dibden Bay is a good example of how the regulatory framework can secure protection. The organisation of statutory nature conservation and the contribution of the voluntary sector each have their own limitations and successes. Some issues as yet remain intractable, and for the future we look to an ecosystem services approach to bring together our efforts at protecting wildlife for its own sake and for the value it brings to society and humanity. As new marine legislation comes forward, how we protect our seas in future will be a key measure of our success.

Introduction

There are many accounts of the history of nature conservation in these islands, for example Adams 1996, and much written about the status of species and habitats and about biodiversity by which our view of the health of the environment is often measured. Despite

Silent Summer: The State of Wildlife in Britain and Ireland, ed. Norman Maclean. Published by Cambridge University Press. © Cambridge University Press 2010.

decades of effort and resources directed at the conservation of wildlife, the message is often one of doom and gloom, depicting the losses in extent and quality of habitats, the declines and extinctions of species and the damaging impacts of human activities on the wider environment. There are comparatively few contributions that deal with the ways in which a healthy environmental future is being secured, or ones that analyse the costs and benefits of such methods, and the successes that have already been achieved. Sceptics would say this dearth of literature reflects the reality of the situation, but is that really the case? There is much to applaud in the modern, evidence-based approach to nature conservation, with optimism in some quarters where there have been significant achievements, but of course there is much still to do (DEFRA 2006). A legislative approach has been the basis for habitat and species protection, and that platform has grown stronger domestically, and with the addition of European Directives and their implementation. The cast of actors on this stage is now more varied than ever, from global organisations bringing pressure to bear on national governments and setting an agenda of international treaties and plans, for example in the Millennium Ecosystem Assessment, 2005, down to very local communities taking action in their own backyard through the BBC's Breathing Places mass participation campaign. Membership of nature conservation organisations is growing, and the agenda gets broader. The RSPB boasts 'a million voices for nature', whilst the Wildlife Trust's partnership can call on 750 000 people to support its programmes and activities. Financial resources for the conservation of nature have grown beyond most people's expectations in the last two decades, both directly, in terms of grant-in-aid from government to nature conservation agencies, and indirectly, as a result of targeting funds from the agricultural sector through sensitive land management schemes such as Environmental Stewardship. Our knowledge base is growing all the time, and the National Biodiversity Network seeks to bring together all the available data – a colossal task, given, for example, the more than 100 million data records on birds alone held by the British Trust for Ornithology (BTO). Knowledge, and its use in decision-making, is the key to ensuring the best options for our environment in the future. It is worth remembering that each successive generation of nature conservationists finds a world degraded in wildlife terms compared to the previous one. Evidence provides a tool to help address this impoverishment of human experience, providing absolute and not just relative values for measuring conservation success. There also needs to be a collective view about what that success looks like. To what extent is nature conservation merely for self-interest and to what extent part of our moral duty to look after the planet? The emphasis on action to address climate change seems to suggest the latter, but we must remember that a cool planet without rich biodiversity would be a rather hollow result.

UK and European legislation

Our Common Law did not concern itself directly with the conservation of nature or the countryside, and so the impressive legal foundation we now have is wholly statutory.

Many have said, and we can all recognise, that nature conservation is now backed by a formidable raft of legislation that increasingly enables and underpins positive protection. The last 12 years have seen significant advances, with a general broadening of the provisions, most notably the Open Access provisions and further strengthening of the protection of Sites of Special Scientific Interest (SSSI) introduced by the Countryside and Rights of Way (CRoW) Act 2000. There is now a comprehensive duty on public bodies to conserve biodiversity enshrined in the Natural Environment and Rural Communities Act 2006, and this Act also set up Natural England. The wide and complex array of environmental legislation for England and Wales is very ably brought together and updated by Fry (2008). Similar provisions exist in Scotland through the Nature Conservation (Scotland) Act 2004, and in Northern Ireland through The Environment (Northern Ireland) Order 2002.

Present-day nature conservation law dates back to the National Parks and Access to the Countryside Act 1949, the first significant piece of legislation that set up the three elements of protection that we still have today: the designation and protection of sites, the establishment of a statutory advisor for wildlife matters and the protection of species. National Nature Reserves – land owned, often by the state, and managed principally for nature conservation, Local Nature Reserves – identified by Local Planning Authorities as places of nature conservation value for the local community, and SSSIs all have their origins in this Act. Two highly significant aspects of the approach to nature conservation emerged from this starting point. Firstly, the National Nature Reserves were set aside for nature and those studying the subject, thus presenting a somewhat unwelcoming attitude to the general public. Secondly the legislative requirement for SSSIs was simply that the Local Planning Authority was notified of their existence, so in many cases owners and users of the land remained unaware of this situation, and there were no distinct provisions to ensure protection. It is interesting that the most recent legislation already mentioned is still addressing the disadvantages of these early approaches.

It was not until the Wildlife and Countryside Act 1981 that more extensive provisions relating to SSSIs were enacted. Owners and occupiers were required to be notified of the importance of their sites, and the law further required the listing of activities which, if carried out on the SSSI land, were potentially damaging, and over which the owner/occupier of the SSSI was legally bound to consult the statutory nature-conservation body before carrying out any of the activities. However, the measures were perhaps not as successful as hoped, and were memorably described by Lord Mustill in 1992 in Southern Water Authority vs. Nature Conservancy Council as 'toothless', requiring only patience on the part of those wishing to carry out damaging operations. Not only that, but practitioners were becoming increasingly concerned that the protection afforded was negative, only stopping damage (in some cases) and not encouraging the positive management of wildlife sites. The CRoW Act addressed this point and led to strong focus from the millennium onwards on getting the one million or so hectares of SSSI land into a favourable condition for the species and habitats protected there.

Figure 12.1 Maintaining the biodiversity of our seas will be a test of new marine legislation (see colour plate). (Photograph by Paul Sterry/Nature Photographers Ltd.)

Landscape and wildlife conservation were joined through the statutory advisors in Scotland, Scottish Natural Heritage (SNH), and in Wales, the Countryside Council for Wales (CCW), at the time of the break-up of the Nature Conservancy Council in 1991. Under the visionary chairmanship of Sir Martin Doughty at English Nature, and latterly Natural England, landscape and wildlife protection came under the same roof here in 2006. It is tempting to think that the institutional arrangements for these statutory bodies are now settled, but of course with the creation of the Government's new Department for Energy and Climate Change and the gap still to be filled by effective marine nature conservation legislation (Figure 12.1), there will certainly be more change. The recent publication of the draft Marine Bill and announcement in February 2009 of a Marine Management Organisation raises the issue of fit with the existing institutional arrangements.

Part 1 of the Wildlife and Countryside Act 1981 deals with the protection of species. Protected species are listed in Schedules to the Act, which are updated every five years on the advice of the Joint Nature Conservation Committee, the Government advisor at the whole of the UK level. Strict licensing controls apply to developments affecting these species and to a range of activities, such as photography and bird ringing, this last activity licensed on behalf of the statutory advisor by the BTO.

The impact of the European Union on our wildlife law has been highly significant and positive. Both the Birds Directive 1979 and the Habitats and Species Directive in 1992 which spawned, respectively, Special Protection Areas for Birds (SPA) and Special Areas of Conservation (SAC), collectively known Europe-wide as Natura 2000, have had a tangible influence on nature-conservation successes, and examining a few examples here will illustrate the point. In a similar way, the Water Framework Directive should, by 2015, ensure better ecological status for our inland and coastal waters, and soon the Environmental Liability Directive should ensure the prevention and remediation of damage to the natural environment.

Although not enshrined so definitely in the law, international treaties and conventions, such as the Ramsar Convention on the Conservation of Wetlands of International Importance, have driven progress, focused our priorities and enabled programmes that build contributions from many sectors. Species conservation has benefited from the global intergovernmental approach adopted by The Convention on Migratory Species (The Bonn Convention) with its associated treaties on taxa such as cetaceans and birds occurring for part of their lifecycle in UK habitats.

Case studies

It is useful to look at progress through the experience of a few important case studies, demonstrating both strengths and weaknesses of our nature-conservation policies and practice. Past failures, well illustrated by the road-scheme protests in the 1980s and 1990s at Aston Rowant, Twyford Down and Newbury, have been, to some extent, replaced by more successful cases. Where site protection is contentious, often as a result of competing land uses, decisions can be evaluated at public inquiries where opposing evidence is tested. If there is no recourse to this approach available, then land-owners or other land-users may test the decisions of the statutory nature conservation advisor through the courts.

Over the last six years, in England and Wales a number of High Court cases are significant in understanding the context for effective site protection. In 2003, Aggregate Industries (UK) Ltd challenged the renotification of SSSIs within the Thames Basin Heaths Special Protection Area for heathland breeding birds on the Hampshire/Berkshire border. The renotification by English Nature included additional land owned by Aggregate Industries, and they challenged the decision to confirm the SSSI, on the grounds that the process was not compliant with Human Rights, and that English Nature's Council were effectively acting as 'judge and jury' in decisions both to notify and confirm the site. The outcome upheld the decision of the statutory nature-conservation advisor, but resulted in changes to the way its decisions were taken. From then on the initial decisions to notify sites were taken by the executive in private, whereas confirmation later was a decision of the non-executive Council, meeting and hearing objections, in public.

The protection of the Stone Curlew (*Burhinus oedicnemus*) in the Brecklands of East Anglia provided the arena for a tussle about the relative validities of domestic and European law. In Fisher vs. English Nature (2003), the land-owner challenged the need for SSSI protection, given the designation of an SPA for the Stone Curlew under the EU Birds Directive. His view was that the presence of an SSSI lowered the value of his land, and was not necessary, given the protection afforded by the European provisions. The birds use high-value agricultural land, as well as adjacent grass heaths, and English Nature had carefully drawn up special schemes with the agricultural estates to ensure that farming practices for high-value vegetables could continue and not damage the nesting success of the birds. The High Court (and then the Court of Appeal and the House of Lords) decided in favour of English Nature, who had maintained Government policy in ensuring that all SPAs also needed to be notified as SSSIs. This case resisted the attempt to drive a wedge between European and domestic law protecting important wildlife sites.

Trailer & Marina (Leven) Ltd vs. the Secretary of State for the Environment, Food and Rural Affairs and English Nature (2004) looked at site protection from the perspective of the human rights of land-owners and occupiers. The owners of the Leven Canal in Yorkshire, which had long been an SSSI, had argued that the stringent restrictions placed on their use of the canal by the no longer 'toothless' protection introduced by the CRoW Act were incompatible with Article 1 of the 1st Protocol of the European Convention on Human Rights, and that the continued SSSI notification was in fact appropriation of the land. The Court of Appeal supported the High Court judge's view that SSSI notification represented the lesser intrusion in human rights terms of control of use, which had no requirement for compensation, although in any event, management agreements were available which offered some financial compensation.

A High Court case in 2004, concerning a quarry at Halkyn Common in Wales, was the subject of a challenge by the Trustees of the Duke of Westminster to the Welsh Assembly Government's refusal to grant a licence for the translocation of Great Crested Newts (*Triturus cristatus*). This would have enabled the quarry to restart work under an existing planning permission. The decision of the judge to refuse permission for a licence was upheld by the Court of Appeal on the grounds that there were not imperative reasons of overriding public interest, but that the Countryside Council for Wales might consider issuing a licence on conservation grounds! They refused, and the application was dropped.

Determining a case about cockle fishing in the Waddenzee in 2004, the European Court of Justice determined that the decision-maker could only allow the activity to go ahead if there was certainty about the lack of any damaging effect to the special features of the protected site. This decision re-emphasised the fundamental precautionary principle embedded in nature-conservation legislation – a high bar for developers and decision-makers alike to clear. These cases together illustrate the breadth of the arguments and conflicts of interests between those seeking to use the legislation to protect wildlife and the places where it lives, and those affected by the legal protection of habitats and species.

Dibden Bay

A celebrated case that demonstrates well the implementation of the legislation protecting internationally recognised wildlife sites is Dibden Bay. Proposals from Associated British Ports (ABP) to construct a container terminal at Dibden Bay in Southampton Water were the subject of a major Public Inquiry in 2001–2, spanning more than a year. Dibden Bay, on the opposite side of the estuary from the port of Southampton itself, is part of the Solent and Southampton Water Special Protection Area for birds, and Special Area for Conservation, under the European Birds and Habitats Directives. English Nature's statutory advice on studying the proposals was that there would be damage to the features of importance in both the SPA and the SAC. The port company disagreed and challenged English Nature's advice, and this challenge drove the environmental topic at the Public Inquiry, the arguments being heard over more than a month.

English Nature importantly adopted a very clear position that it was not against the development per se. The advisor's objectives were to ensure all parties understood the importance of the protected sites, and heard evidence leading to the conclusion that the development would be damaging and crucially that the Directives were understood and their provisions properly implemented. English Nature's private view at the time was that the development might be able to go ahead with appropriate recognition of the damaging effects, and compensatory measures put in place to maintain the network of protected areas and the special habitat and species features.

At the end of the Public Inquiry the Inspector's report clearly recognised the evidence provided by the statutory advisor and gave the Secretary of State (SoS) guidance as to the decisions that could be made. A possibility was that the SoS could be minded to grant permission for the proposals to go ahead if appropriate compensation could be identified, agreed and implemented. However, on 20 April 2004 the SoS announced that ABP's application for permission to construct a container terminal at Dibden Bay was refused, on the grounds of unacceptable environmental impacts.

The conservation community saw this decision as a major victory and a demonstration of the power of the EU and domestic wildlife legislation, when properly weighed in decision-making about the effects of major infrastructure on the environment. The costs are sobering. The container terminal was a £650 million development. ABP are quoted as having spent in the region of £40 million getting the proposals to the end of the Public Inquiry, including a rumoured £3 million legal bill for the inquiry itself. English Nature's total staff, advisory and legal costs probably reached £1 million. On the day of the decision, ABP's share price lost an amount equivalent to their costs to date, making the whole venture an expensive £100 million mistake. English Nature remained of the view that the port's challenge of the statutory nature conservation advice was unnecessary and that the collective effort should have been applied in a positive way to enable the development to go ahead firmly within the terms of the Habitats and Birds Directives. They said so, when invited to the Board of ABP for a discussion afterwards, and indeed this port company has subsequently led the way in this positive approach, seeking and gaining permission for developments on the Humber Estuary, providing compensatory habitat and avoiding a public inquiry in the process.

These development cases at Dibden Bay and on the Humber illustrate well, on the one hand, the power of the legal conservation provisions when opposing a developer who does not appropriately recognise the importance of the environment, and on the other hand, their flexibility and practicality to enable collaboration towards an effective solution, when the developer does give environmental considerations appropriate weight. Interestingly, even the Humber outcome was challenged by a port competitor in Humber Sea Terminals vs. the Secretary of State for Transport (2005), on the basis that English Nature had effectively privatised the appropriate assessment of ABP's proposals on the Humber, by drawing together the stakeholders to agree a package of compensatory habitat. However, English Nature's approach was endorsed, as the Humber Sea Terminals' challenge failed.

Statutory nature conservation

At the beginning of the 1990s, the Nature Conservancy Council (NCC) had been the statutory advisor in England, Scotland and Wales for nearly a decade, following the Wildlife and Countryside Act 1981. However, the politics of the day can influence nature conservation directly and, following a report proposing to end tax incentives for planting trees on the Flow Country of north-west Scotland (unfortunately launched in London) the then Secretaries of State for the Environment and for Scotland – Nicholas Ridley and Malcolm Rifkind – engineered a break-up of the NCC into separate country agencies. The received wisdom at the time was that the NCC's chief scientist team had become too powerful and political in its use of scientific evidence to oppose Government policy.

The creation of English Nature, CCW and SNH was seen by some, at the time, as a negative and retrograde step. However, benefits of this approach have become clear. The broader progress more recently towards devolved governments for Scotland and Wales has meant that environmental issues at that national level were already well catered for institutionally, effectively giving the environment agenda in Scotland and Wales a head start. The new country agencies enabled the most appropriate institutional arrangements to be put in place in each case, with landscape coupled to biodiversity conservation in Wales and Scotland. The financial and staff resources for delivering nature conservation in three separate agencies have been dramatically increased over the decade following their creation in 1991. The last year of the NCC saw an annual budget of £42 million and staff numbers at 785, while by 2006 the three Great Britain agencies together spent around £220 million with a total staff of 2245, admittedly by then in Wales and Scotland covering a broader remit than solely nature conservation.

Some in the nature conservation community have continued to view these changes as negative, particularly scientists mourning the passing of a generation of top-quality ecological specialists, and the start of more corporate initiatives drawing funds away from the science of protecting biodiversity. Changes have continued to take place, most recently with the creation of Natural England in 2006, replacing English Nature with a much broader agency joining nature conservation with the Countryside Agency's landscape agenda and the Rural Development Service's delivery of Government's Environmental Stewardship. There is no doubt that the disruption associated with creating a single agency out of three existing bodies has been acute, and bureaucracy has grown accordingly. Real concerns have been apparent that the new body is focused on environmental issues, at the expense of biodiversity conservation, although the publication of the *State of the Natural Environment Report* by Natural England (2008) signals a welcome re-engagement with its biodiversity roots. The agenda has undoubtedly become broader, encompassing our engagement with the natural world, health, climate change, and energy and food security. A body of around 2300 staff and operating expenditure of around £240 million devoted to addressing these issues is potentially powerful, and we hope to see it match the high expectations generated by its ambitions.

Inevitably there are differences of approach in Scotland, Wales and England. For example, the notification of Sites of Special Scientific Interest in Scotland has been subject to review by area boards of Secretary of State appointed members, and this has had the potential to dilute the concept of a nationally important network of protected areas. The Scottish Advisory Committee on SSSIs is likely to be abolished under new legislation. In Wales, the agri-environment schemes have been delivered by CCW for some years, an initiative known as Tir Gofal, only to be taken back into the Welsh Assembly Government at the very time England devolved its scheme to the delivery body, perhaps damaging CCW's credibility with its hard-won constituency of farmers. Undoubtedly in the first decade of this century, English Nature, and subsequently Natural England, have led the way in the positive management of SSSIs. The contribution to the Government's Public Service Agreement (PSA) target to have 95% of England's SSSIs in favourable condition by 2010 has been impressive. From a starting point for the project in 2003 of around 58% meeting the target, to around 80% in 2008 means that more than 260 000 hectares of our best wildlife sites have been secured through positive management and the mitigation of damaging impacts (English Nature 2006). More impressive than the efforts of the statutory nature-conservation advisor alone is that action has been galvanised across a very broad front of other Government departments and agencies, local authorities, the voluntary sector, business and industry, the farming community and individuals. It is also clear to all involved what remains to be done to achieve the 2010 target, through policy initiatives, practical land-management solutions, legislative change and better regulation, and tightening of the conservation objectives for the SSSIs themselves. Despite devolved governments and separate country agencies, there is strong common purpose across the UK and a clear focus in all countries on positive partnerships with land managers. This is the key to delivering nature conservation through appropriate land management and, in due course, may well enable widespread partnerships on the management of carbon. Site monitoring programmes, once again enabled by these constituencies of site-based stakeholders, allow us, for the first time, to understand the national health of our most important places for wildlife.

Having separate country agencies has necessitated the formal co-ordination of certain UK Government responsibilities for nature conservation and, since 1991, this has been largely achieved through the Joint Nature Conservation Committee (JNCC). The English, Scottish and Welsh agencies contributed funds and staff to the JNCC support unit, which was established as a separate company limited by guarantee in 2005, and receives services such as common standards monitoring of habitats and species at a UK scale. JNCC also has an important marine programme and delivers the Government's nature conservation priorities for the UK Overseas Territories across the world.

In Ireland, the statutory advisor on nature conservation is the National Parks and Wildlife Service that is part of the Government's Department of the Environment, Heritage and Local Government. In July 2008 Northern Ireland created a new broad agency of Government, the Northern Ireland Environment Agency (NIEA) that covers the remit of three bodies in England, nature conservation, environmental protection and the architectural heritage.

Statutory nature conservation has not only been about the dedicated agencies. The Environment Agency, Forestry Commission, the Ministry of Defence (MoD), the Crown Estate, the Department for Environment, Food and Rural Affairs (DEFRA) itself and National Parks all make highly significant contributions. By way of example, the MoD owns and manages 85 000 ha of SSSIs, and regards this activity as second in importance only to delivering skilled and motivated armed forces through the use of its extensive training estate. Salisbury Plain is the largest extent of semi-natural calcareous grassland in north-west Europe, and is also a major part of that training estate. In the last decade, a significant joint project involving the MoD Defence Estate, English Nature, RSPB, Butterfly Conservation and the Wiltshire Wildlife Trust, and funded by the EU Life fund for the protection of Natura 2000, has delivered a substantial contribution to restoring this SSSI to favourable condition. Initiatives such as removing plantations, an extensive grazing cattle herd and scrub management with an armoured vehicle in an area of unexploded ordinance(!) have all improved the habitat for species such as the Marsh Fritillary Butterfly (*Euphydryas aurinia*), and for chalk grassland flora. Similarly, the Environment Agency has, over the last few years, contributed millions of pounds through the Asset Management Programme and the Review of Consents that together address the damaging effects on the environment of point-source and diffuse pollution, and water abstraction, all affecting our most important wildlife sites. They have their own workforce of nature conservation professionals working alongside those at Natural England and the CCW. The Forestry Commission has evolved from a timber grower to an agency with a multi-functional forest estate, primarily concerned with recreation in the countryside and with nature conservation, although recent initiatives on wood-fuel will mean a re-emphasis on commerce along-side habitat restoration. They too employ professional nature-conservation staff, and undertake joint research, for example, with the BTO on the effects of deer on our native woodland bird populations.

The National Parks of England, primarily established to ensure the conservation of our best landscapes, also deliver significant benefits to biodiversity and nature conservation. For example, in the Lake District, the Helvellyn massif now has extensive sheep grazing at levels which improve the upland grassland and heath habitats for wildlife. Over 100 000 ha of land, both within and outside the SSSI, are managed in partnership with Natural England and hill farmers to encourage sustainable farming practices and so support the working community.

The voluntary sector

Nature conservation in the UK is exceptionally well supported by a strong and broad array of voluntary organisations. Three major players are the National Trust, the RSPB and the Wildlife Trusts. Membership of these bodies is impressive, with the National Trust at 3.5 million, RSPB at over 1 million and the Wildlife Trusts around 750 000. This huge support base gives nature conservation a powerful political voice, and all three organisations make an effective contribution to the policy process. The National Trust's policy statement on the future of our coasts with respect to sea-level rise, and the RSPB's opposition to the Isle of Lewis wind farm in Scotland resulting in refusal of permission, are examples. Such engagement illustrates how the approach to nature conservation has evolved over the last few decades. We have moved away from blanket disapproval of development and blaming particular sectors for the ills we see in the environment, to a more mature recognition that all have a stake in our natural world, and that understanding each other's perspectives is an important element in partnerships that can find solutions. It does mean that powerful voluntary organisations are sometimes seen more alongside Government than in opposition to it, and some at the radical end of the movement see this as weak. However, such advocacy does require an ever-present reliance on evidence, and trusted sources of impartial scientific research and results, like the BTO, will have an increasingly important role in influencing decision-making for the environment.

In addition to the juggernauts of the voluntary sector, there are many small organisations with activities focused on particular taxonomic groups, or even single issues. Butterfly Conservation and the Botanical Society of the British Isles are long established, while BugLife and Amphibian and Reptile Conservation (ARC) probably represent a more recent focus on interesting a younger audience through an overtly modern approach. The whole sector is attempting to make wildlife, nature and the environment more relevant to people in their daily lives. This push for recognition and support refocuses the debate about whether nature conservation activity is important only for the value it brings to society, or for its own sake. Perhaps these two things are not so far apart, because our understanding and characterisation of 'ecosystem services' includes the spiritual services we can experience through our contemplation of the natural world.

However this debate is resolved, it remains the case that, in our developed world, we are too separated from regular contact with the natural world, to the detriment both of people and wildlife. There is a strong drive from the environment sector, but particularly from voluntary organisations, to engage and involve people in our work. There are many examples on a broad spectrum, from passive interest through attendance at events such as the annual British Birdwatching Fair at Rutland Water, which attracts 20 000 people over three days in August, through visits to RSPB and Wildlife Trust reserves, to doing practical land-management tasks with the British Trust for Conservation Volunteers and active participation in national surveys of wildlife. This last category is important in collecting significant data and information about our wildlife and what is happening to it, and in helping the individual feel very much part of the national movement making a difference for nature. An important project currently underway that illustrates this well is the BTO's Bird Atlas 2007–11 in conjunction with the Scottish Ornithologists' Club and Birdwatch Ireland, mapping the distribution and abundance of all Britain and Ireland's birds over a four-year period. It is expected that 30 000 volunteers will be mobilised by the project to collect data, combining rigorous surveys to standard methods with casual records, and giving an unparalleled picture of our bird populations. The BTO has repeated this survey every 20 years from the late 1960s, and so can provide evidence of long-term trends in the status of birds. This time the innovation of the web and online applications means that the volume of data is potentially huge, and the BTO has received more than 1 million bird records during the first year of the project! The uses of these data and information are many and varied, ensuring that volunteers are able to contribute as individuals to organised and scientific conservation effort.

The theme of active participation has also been picked up by the BBC in their Breathing Places campaign supported by the regular seasonal evening TV slots, Springwatch and Autumnwatch. Having identified two important motivators for getting people involved – local and children – they aim to establish 50 000 local conservation projects around the country inspired by 'as seen on TV'. This initiative cleverly does two things: it tackles the trend for people engaging with nature only through television, and it will achieve some real, and local, gains for nature conservation.

What is not working

It is difficult to measure and record what has actually been achieved by all this nature-conservation effort, though the chapters of this book will provide an in-depth picture of the state of our wildlife. Here it is worth reflecting on the issues that, despite an active and apparently powerful sector, remain intractable. We have looked at the importance of evidence about biodiversity informing the policy- and decision-making processes, but there is still limited take-up of evidence-based approaches. There is simply a lack of evidence in many cases, particularly where new approaches such as coastal realignment and 're-wilding' have not yet built an adequate evidence base. Political, social and economic factors may override the evidence of damage to biodiversity, and there are plenty of examples of decisions not waiting for evidence to be collected, and the inertia of always doing things the same way. We have seen the power of the European Habitats and Birds Directives in halting inappropriate development at Dibden Bay, and this experience leading to a better approach, for example on the Humber, but this improvement is by no means universal. The UK Government's contribution to reducing the global carbon footprint relies on generating energy from renewable resources, and there are strong policies in favour of infrastructure developments to do this. The interaction between broad green policies and biodiversity conservation is well illustrated by the push for renewable energy sourced from wind. The RSPB's successful opposition to the Isle of Lewis wind farm in the Hebrides, on the basis of its likely impact on special features of the SPA such as the Golden Eagle (*Aquila chrysaetos*), has already been mentioned. Elsewhere, nature conservation interests have worked closely with wind-farm developers to identify and reduce or avoid damaging impacts, resulting in adjustment of the development to enable it to go ahead. The London Array in the Thames estuary is an example of this approach. Little Cheyne Court wind farm on Romney Marsh in Kent is a development underway, despite predicted damage to important bird populations (geese and swans) in that SPA. Uncertainty was a limiting factor in arguments put forward at this Public Inquiry – we simply do not know with enough certainty what the impacts will be, and in that context the inspector's decision weighed as more important than the Government's policy to get wind farms built. The arguments had more poignancy because the developers can argue environmental benefit in reducing CO_2 emissions.

At the time of writing, the Government is once again bringing forward new planning policies for major infrastructure projects, with the aim of speeding up and simplifying the process. The nature-conservation sector remains concerned that changes may weaken habitat and species protection, and make it likely that evidence about biodiversity is given less weight in decision-making. The current feasibility studies underway for proposed Severn Tidal Power will be a test of how biodiversity stacks up against the pressures to develop this particular contribution to renewable energy.

At the other end of the spectrum from an estuary of international importance affected by a £15 billion development, are the thousands of small areas of important habitat in Britain and Ireland that are not protected by the law and rely on, amongst other things, knowledge being made available to a sympathetic ear to enable them to be maintained as a vital resource for wildlife. Many are destroyed through ignorance or because other interests refuse to go the extra mile for wildlife. A recent example of this is Bramley Frith, a semi-natural ancient woodland in Hampshire with a rich flora, Hazel Dormouse

Figure 12.2 Ancient woodland at Bramley Frith, Hampshire – important habitats and species not protected by law, and threatened by infrastructure development (see colour plate).
(Photograph by Paul Sterry.)

(*Muscardinus avellanarius*), Willow Tit (*Poecile montana*), Great Crested Newt and a
diverse insect fauna (Figure 12.2). This site also houses an electricity sub-station operated by National Grid on behalf of the supplier. Clearly the demand for electricity in
southern England is not going to diminish, and an installation of this importance is
going to expand. Over the years this has happened most recently in 2007, when National
Grid pushed through the latest expansion, without due regard for the wildlife, simply
because they had the power to do so. It was debatable whether or not an Environmental
Impact Assessment was necessary – and National Grid chose to avoid that process – but
in any event for a national utility to refuse to go beyond compliance and use that process to demonstrate best practice shows their disregard for the biodiversity duty on all
public bodies enshrined within the CRoW Act. This example of poor practice is made
worse because for many years National Grid used the site to show off its environmental
credentials, operating a woodland classroom in partnership with the local authority, and
the ancient woodland at Bramley Frith was chosen by English Nature as a key site for
dormouse recovery. So not only has wildlife lost out, but children's appreciation of it has
suffered too. There will be hundreds of similar stories elsewhere, sometimes making it
into the local press, and sometimes going completely unnoticed.

Another example of an issue still searching for a solution is that of Hen Harrier
(*Circus cyaneus*) conservation, an example of the growing hot topic in global conservation of human–wildlife conflict (Macdonald and Service 2007; Thirgood and

Redpath 2008). In 2002, English Nature's Council decided they could not countenance the extinction of this bird as a breeding species in England. There is evidence that the species' population is limited by persecution in both England and Scotland and, at the time of the decision, there had been only a single breeding pair in the uplands of England. A project is underway, with a range of interested parties, to determine the likely causes of the decline, to search for a jointly owned solution and to protect pairs of birds attempting to breed. The stated problem with the birds, from the perspective of those involved with grouse moors, is that Hen Harriers eat Red Grouse (*Lagopus lagopus*) chicks and disturb grouse shoots. The nature-conservation sector view is that some grouse moor owners and their staff systematically break the law and disrupt or kill harriers attempting to breed. The interesting aspect from the perspective of nature conservation is the challenge presented by this polarisation of views in searching for a solution which has broad agreement. Enlightened moor owners recognise and value the full diversity their upland habitats support, and enjoy shooting grouse in a more natural and wild setting, complete with raptors. Moors that sell a day's shooting to European clients and city businessmen for very high sums are unwilling to put up with a single harrier. Perhaps the solution is to wait for the effects of climate change to shift the Red Grouse population northwards and out of the most contentious areas of harrier habitat! Meanwhile the talking should go on, in the belief that understanding each other and adjusting expectations may enable arrival at an eventual consensus. The Langholm 2 Project sited on the Langholm Estate in south-west Scotland is an attempt to do just this, and brings together all the stakeholders to look at the issues in detail.

A final example of an issue not yet working well universally is the impact of invasive non-native species. Birdlife International (2000) have drawn attention to the plight of the world's threatened birds, and say that around 300 species, roughly 25%, of globally threatened birds are currently affected by introduced mammals. The American Mink (*Mustela vison*) introduced into Britain mainly through escapes from fur farms is still a problem for ground-nesting birds in some parts of the country. A more positive story is how we are addressing the threat posed to White-headed Duck (*Oxyura leucocephala*) in southern Europe from potential hybridisation with the roving introduced population of North American Ruddy Duck (*Oxyura jamaicensis*). Government and the nature-conservation sector are working well together and making good progress towards the target of eradicating the Ruddy Duck in Great Britain. The learning from this sort of practical experience has helped to define strategy and action to address the general threat posed by invasive non-native species to native plants and animals (DEFRA 2008), and this gives cause for hope.

The future

Nature conservation now is very different from that practised 50 years ago. The networks of protected areas, knowledge about trends in, and status of, habitats and species and, most importantly, the will to work with all-comers and to encourage and enthuse the public, are all the instruments of change. There is a growing interest in the ecology of urban systems, strong policies that effect biodiversity conservation in the wider countryside and not just in protected areas, and ambitious and successful schemes to recreate habitats on a large scale. The RSPB fenland at Lakenheath, and the Wildlife Trusts' 'living landscape' in the Great Fen are good examples. Wildlife is much more accessible and popular through the virtual world of television and the internet, and the environment is hardly ever away from today's urgent news agenda because of the threat posed by climate change. But how should all this immediacy be turned into action for biodiversity that really turns things around and doesn't just preside over more declines? One of the key messages from Natural England's recent *State of the Natural Environment* report is the loss over the last 50 years of the specialists compared to the generalists, and it seems to apply across taxa. These are not the rarest specialist species, whose habitat needs are presumably well catered for by protected areas, but surely the widespread specialists that biodiversity action planning was supposed to save? We need to address the mismatch between our intentions and the results we can deliver.

A recurrent question has been why all this activity is undertaken. Are we conserving wildlife for its own sake or because of the value it brings to society and to humanity? Current thinking about the ecosystem providing services that we cannot live without – clean water, protection from flooding, carbon sequestration – makes this debate somewhat redundant. The service that brings these two camps together is the affect nature has on the human spirit. What is important is that, in the rush to take action to mitigate and adapt to climate change, we do so in a way that better protects biodiversity. Valuing the services it provides will be an important part of future strategies for nature conservation. Demonstrating the importance of intact and resilient ecosystems will be our crucial contribution. Climate change has moved from being an issue that raises scepticism to one where most agree that it is happening, and the questions now are only about how exactly it is caused and how to address it. This move has come about by communicating the evidence clearly, and this has made more compelling the idea that evidence, and not just opinion, is required before we act. Placing the evidence base at the heart of decision-making requires that biodiversity-conservation professionals get closer to the policy-making process in governments and industry. The Cambridge Conservation Initiative is doing just this, a powerful combination of the university and conservation organisations, both global and national, joining forces to identify the future issues and work in new and different ways to address them.

A useful test of any new approach is the marine environment, particularly offshore. At the time of writing, Marine Bills for England and Wales, and for Scotland are making their way through both parliaments and presenting many challenges, not least the alignment of cross-border marine protection with the 12 and 200 nautical mile limits. A key issue will be the selection, location and protection of Marine Protected Areas. We have learnt a lot through 50 plus years of terrestrial nature conservation – starting with a rarified scientific purpose and late in the day re-positioning for the support of society as a whole – and this learning must inform the urgent need to protect our seas. Institutional arrangements will play their part in government, its agencies and the voluntary sector, but ultimately we will succeed or fail because of our response to the way society expects us to act and, through that mandate, our influence on a wide range of activities so that they are undertaken in a way that helps to sustain the rich biodiversity of our seas.

References

Adams, W.M. (1996). *Future Nature*, London, Earthscan Publications Limited.

Birdlife International (2000). *Threatened Birds of the World*, Barcelona and Cambridge, UK, Lynx Edicions and Birdlife International.

DEFRA (2006). Measuring progress on the England Biodiversity Strategy: 2006 assessment. In *Working with the Grain of Nature – Taking it Forward*, Vol. II, London, DEFRA, Crown Copyright.

DEFRA (2008). *The Invasive Non-Native Species Framework Strategy for Great Britain*, London, DEFRA, Crown Copyright.

English Nature (2006). *Target 2010 – The condition of England's Sites of Special Scientific Interest in 2005*, Peterborough, English Nature.

Fry, M. (2008). *A Manual of Nature Conservation Law*, 2nd edn, Nottingham, NCWG Publishing Limited.

Macdonald, D. and Service, K. (2007). *Hot Topics in Conservation*, Oxford, Blackwell Publishing UK.

Millennium Ecosystem Assessment (2005). *Ecosystems and Human Well-being: Biodiversity Synthesis*, Washington DC, World Resources Institute.

Natural England (2008). *State of the Natural Environment Report*, Sheffield, Natural England.

Thirgood, S. and Redpath, S. (2008). Hen harriers and red grouse: science, politics and human-wildlife conflict. *Journal of Applied Ecology*, **45**, 1550–1554.

13

Wildlife in the UK Overseas Territories

Mike Pienkowski

Summary

UK Overseas Territories (UKOTs) are important parts of the UK, not foreign countries. Although small in size, they support far more endemic taxa and other globally important biodiversity than does Britain and Ireland.

The devastation of UKOT wildlife and ecosystems following their discovery by humans continues, with severe impacts, notably from:

- Loss of natural ecosystems
- Invasive species
- Over-exploitation and its side-effects
- Pollution, especially that leading to climate change.

UKOT- and British-based conservation bodies are brought together in the UK Overseas Territories Conservation Forum (UKOTCF), which has also encouraged interest by UK Government. This included finding ways, including 'Environment Charters', of addressing the problem that UK Government is responsible for international environmental commitments, but the UKOT Government is responsible for legislation and enforcement.

Endemic species – and endemic genera – are still becoming globally extinct on UK territory. Several species are down to the last few individuals, and 240 species remain at serious risk in the UKOTs (compared with 59 at risk amongst those occurring in Britain).

A major problem is lack of resources. The economies of the UKOTs are too small to address this alone. As UK territory, the UKOTs are ineligible for most international grant sources, but receive little support from the UK's conservation budget either. The UK Government spends around 500 times less on

Silent Summer: The State of Wildlife in Britain and Ireland, ed. Norman Maclean. Published by Cambridge University Press. © Cambridge University Press 2010.

conservation in UKOTs than in Great Britain and Northern Ireland. Per endemic species, the British Government spends about four orders of magnitude less.

A second major problem is lack of protection for natural areas, particularly in the wider Caribbean, and lack of insistence by the UK Government, under its responsibilities to good governance in the UKOTs, that proper spatial planning procedures are followed and participation by civil society is encouraged, rather than blocked.

Introduction

What and where are the UK Overseas Territories

The UK Overseas Territories (UKOTs) and Crown Dependencies include 21 administrations (Figure 13.1), differing in cultures, laws and relationships with the UK (e.g. FCO 1999; Pienkowski 1998, 2005). The populations of each inhabited UKOT have chosen to remain linked to the UK, rather than moving to independence (or, in the case of Gibraltar, a link to another country).

The Crown Dependencies of the Isle of Man, Jersey, Guernsey, Alderney and Sark (the last two linked to the Bailiwick of Guernsey for some purposes) are geographically close to Great Britain and, for most purposes, are included in the other chapters of this book. This chapter concerns mainly UKOTs in the more restricted sense, but some aspects relate also to the Crown Dependencies.

The people of UKOTs (except the Cyprus Sovereign Base Areas) and Crown Dependencies are British citizens, but they are not represented in the UK Parliament.

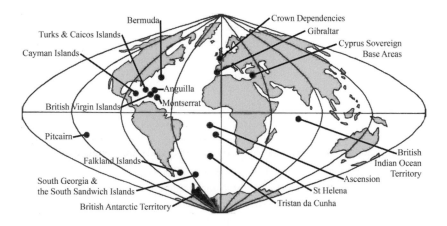

Figure 13.1 Locations of 16 UK Overseas Territories and the five Crown Dependencies (the Isle of Man, Jersey, Guernsey, Alderney and Sark).

All the UKOTs and Crown Dependencies are within the sovereign territory of the UK, but not funded through the British domestic budget. Only two UKOTs (St Helena and, since the start of the volcanic emergency of 1995, Montserrat) receive major overseas grant aid from the British budget. Most day-to-day governance in the inhabited UKOTs is devolved to a locally elected government.

The human population in Great Britain and Northern Ireland is about 59 million, whereas those of UK Overseas Territories range between 47 persons to 65 000, totalling about 200 000 (Table 13.1).

Some important differences from the situation in Britain and Ireland

The Introduction chapter sets out some generalisations about the UK's wildlife. Some do not apply to the UKOTs, on which most of the UK's globally significant wildlife depends.

The levels of prosperity between and within UKOTs vary greatly. Even those few with a higher per capita wealth than Britain lack economies of scale. A population of only a few thousand people means that the total budget is small, even if the wealth per capita is large. Also, whilst the government and population in Britain accept (in the words of our editor's Introduction) 'that the state of our wildlife is a barometer of our priorities, political, social and economic', this is not so in most UKOTs. There are forward-looking individuals in those territories (including some of those who have formed local conservation NGOs, as well as some local officials). However, these are gallantly struggling against a background which views the importance of wildlife in a way somewhat similar to that prevalent in Britain in the 1960s to the 1980s.

More positively, there are areas in UKOTs where the abundance of wildlife resembles that recalled by the editor and me in Britain at the time of our youth. These small areas hold a remarkable biodiversity. However, the land areas of the UKOTs are much smaller than even that of Britain. Modern machinery can destroy natural areas at a remarkable rate. In at least one Caribbean UKOT, the Turks and Caicos Islands, the bulldozing away of natural vegetation and soil, for replacement by concrete, is running at a rate equivalent to several % of the total land area of the territory each year. Such development is favoured by the taxation system; the main income for public spending comes from import taxes, particularly on building materials. Such taxes generate what economists call a 'perverse incentive' encouraging destruction of natural ecosystems – despite the fact that tourism agencies of the same governments recognise the natural beauty as main selling points for the major economic activity of tourism.

Other differences from Britain are the limited study of nature in UKOTs, and the shortage of amateur naturalists, partly a consequence of small human populations. These mean that both governmental departments and NGOs have few personnel

Table 13.1 *UK Overseas Territories and Crown Dependencies. These are grouped geographically, which has no legal significance.*

	Human population	Land area (km^2)
WIDER CARIBBEAN		
Bermuda	65 000	53
Cayman Islands	37 000	260
Turks and Caicos Islands	22 000	500
British Virgin Islands	19 000	153 (3445 sea)
Anguilla	12 000	90
Montserrat	4500 (normally 11 000)[a]	102
SOUTH ATLANTIC		
Ascension[b]	1100	90
St Helena[b]	5000	122
Tristan da Cunha[b]	300	159
Falkland Islands	2200	12173
South Georgia and the South Sandwich Islands	0 (60–250)[c]	4065
British Antarctic Territory[d]	0 (60)[c]	1 709 400
INDIAN OCEAN		
British Indian Ocean Territory	0 (3000)[e]	60 (54 400 sea)
PACIFIC		
Pitcairn Islands	50	44
EUROPE – UK Overseas Territories		
Gibraltar	27 000	6
Cyprus Sovereign Base Areas	0[f]	250
EUROPE – Crown Dependencies		
Isle of Man	70 000	572
Jersey	84 000	116
Guernsey[g]	59 000	64
Alderney[g]	2400	9
Sark[g]	600	5
TOTALS		
UK Overseas Territories	190 150	1 727 267
Total excluding BAT[d]		17 084

Table 13.1 (cont.)

	Human population	Land area (km^2)
Crown Dependencies	216 000	766
Great Britain and Northern Island	59 000 000	244 101

Notes:

[a] Montserrat's population is currently at the lower level indicated because of volcanic activity since 1995.

[b] Tristan da Cunha and Ascension are sometimes termed 'Dependencies' of St Helena, but this is misleading as they have separate administrations and economies, and do not depend on St Helena, although they share the British official serving as Governor, resident in St Helena.

[c] There are no permanent residents of South Georgia and the South Sandwich Islands nor of British Antarctic Territory. The numbers indicated are temporary residents, mainly scientists.

[d] The British Antarctic Territory is claimed also by Argentina and Chile. The expression of sovereignty by all parties to Antarctic claims is modified by the Antarctic Treaty. Most of the area indicated is ice-covered, stretching to the South Pole.

[e] British Indian Ocean Territory (BIOT) has no current permanent population. The total indicated consists of short-term US military personnel. The deportation of the inhabitants of BIOT by the UK Government in the 1960s and 1970s has now been found illegal by the English High Court and Court of Appeal. At the time of writing, the UK Government's Appeal to the House of Lords is pending.

[f] The Sovereign Base Areas of Cyprus were retained as UK territory as air bases when the rest of Cyprus became independent in 1960. They differ from the other UKOTs in that the Ministry of Defence, rather than the FCO, is responsible. The population of the Cyprus Sovereign Base areas is officially only that of the transient British military personnel. However, only the relatively small bases themselves are closed and most of the Areas are not demarcated from the adjacent Republic of Cyprus. Those using land in the SBAs are deemed to be citizens of the Republic, rather than of the SBAs.

[g] Alderney and Sark have separate governments, but are also part of the Bailiwick of Guernsey.

(*Sources:* Oldfield (1987), Pienkowski (1998), FCO (1999), updated.)

(Pienkowski *et al.* 1998). Each staff member has to cover a range of specialisms that would be the subject of several specialist NGOs or departments in Britain – as well as most management levels. Basic inventories of wildlife for many taxa are incomplete, and monitoring and detailed studies rare because of lack of resources (Cross and Pienkowski 1998).

In the Introduction chapter, the editor notes that even in Britain – a relatively environmentally aware country – we may not be spending enough of our GDP on our natural environment. It is even more shocking to note, as described below, that the UK Government spends several orders of magnitude less on its environmental responsibilities in the UKOTs than it does in Britain (and almost nothing in the Crown Dependencies).

Global biodiversity importance of UK Overseas Territories

Although UKOTs may be considered as rather peripheral, their global biodiversity importance reverses the usual relationship, with Britain being the minor partner – despite the importance of Britain's wildlife. There are many examples of this, such as proportions of world populations of various species supported. Some examples, centring on endemic species (i.e. those which occur nowhere else) are given below, before comments on each UKOT.

Endemic taxa

The incomplete nature of study in most UKOTs makes comparisons difficult. However, there is relatively complete cover for some taxa, summarised in Table 13.2.

Britain is internationally important for birds, notably breeding seabirds and wintering waders and wildfowl, but the UKOTs are even more so – yet largely overlooked. The number of bird species endemic to Britain is nil or one (depending on the current specific or sub-specific status of the Scottish Crossbill, *Loxia scotica*. On a conservative listing, there are at least 23 bird species endemic to UKOTs (Table 13.2). A further 41 species are nearly endemic, either because their area of endemism is smaller than that of Britain, but happens to be divided into several small countries, or because over 90% of their populations depend on the UKOTs. The high value of the UKOTs would be even more marked had humans not already devastated them. At least 14 former endemic species are now globally extinct – and this figure probably underestimates greatly the real total.

For reptiles and amphibians, Table 13.3 emphasises a high degree of endemism in the wider Caribbean. At least 23 endemic species, a further 24 near-endemics and 43 endemic sub-species compare with none in any of these categories in Britain. The UKOTs are important also for several turtle species, with the Green Turtle, *Chelonia mydas*, nesting in at least seven.

For other taxa, despite patchy coverage, more than 500 endemic invertebrates and more than 200 endemic plant species have been described so far. The global biodiversity importance of UKOTs is not restricted to endemic species. For example, a majority of the world population of many species of seabirds (including about half the world's breeding albatrosses) depend on UKOTs in the South Atlantic. The UKOTs hold substantial areas of sensitive ecosystems (Pienkowski 2005), including making the UK one of the world's most important coral nations.

Bermuda

The UK's oldest Overseas Territory, with over 150 limestone islands, sits on a volcanic seamount about 110 million years old. Influenced by the Gulf Stream, Bermuda's shallow-water platform covers about 1000 km^2, and supports the northernmost coral reef system in the world.

Mike Pienkowski

Table 13.2 *Endemic birds in the UK Overseas Territories and in Britain*

	Extinct endemic species[a]	Living endemic species	Living endemic sub-species[b]	Living near-endemic species[c]
WIDER CARIBBEAN				
Bermuda		1	1	
Cayman Islands	1		13	2
Turks and Caicos Islands			2	6
British Virgin Islands				6
Anguilla				4
Montserrat		1		9
SOUTH ATLANTIC				
Ascension	1	1		
St Helena	7	1		1
Tristan da Cunha	1	10	1	2
Falkland Islands		2	10	
South Georgia and the South Sandwich Islands		1	3	
British Antarctic Territory				
INDIAN OCEAN				
British Indian Ocean Territory				
PACIFIC				
Pitcairn Islands	4	5		2
EUROPE – UK Overseas Territories				
Gibraltar				
Cyprus Sovereign Base Areas				
TOTALS[d]	**14**	**23**	**30**	**41**
Great Britain and Northern Ireland	0	1	15	–

Notes:

[a] Extinct endemics will be underestimated, because only those noted in the incomplete historical record or leaving sub-fossil records (for which conditions in most areas are not suitable) will be recorded.

[b] Monotypic endemic species are not included in these numbers. Several of these endemic sub-species are expected to be given specific status when next reviewed.

[c] Britain is much larger than most UKOTs, so that comparisons are difficult. Therefore, species occurring in a UKOT and nearby areas, but limited to a total area of less than that of Britain are included here. Also included are species for which more than 90% of the population depend on the UKOT.

[d] The total of living endemic species is one more than the sum of the numbers above. This is because the tiny percentage of one species not breeding in one UKOT breed in another. The total of near-endemics has been adjusted down by one to correspond. The total for sub-species is not additive in a simple way to the totals of the others.

(*Sources:* Buden (1987), Oldfield (1987), Wragg (1995), Stattersfield (1998), Ashmole and Ashmole (2000), Shirihai (2002), Pienkowski (2002, 2005), IUCN *Red List*, unpublished UKOTCF material.)

Table 13.3 *Endemic reptiles and amphibians in the UK Overseas Territories and in Britain*

	Extinct endemic species[a]	Living endemic species	Living endemic sub-species[b]	Living near-endemic species[c]
WIDER CARIBBEAN				
Bermuda		1	0	0
Cayman Islands		7	18	9
Turks and Caicos Islands		5	12	5
British Virgin Islands		5	3	2
Anguilla		3	6	6
Montserrat		2	4	2
TOTALS[d]	**0**	**23**	**43**	**24**
Great Britain & Northern Ireland	0	0	0	0

Notes:

[a] Extinct endemics will be under-estimated, because only those noted in the incomplete historical record or leaving sub-fossil records (for which conditions in most areas are not suitable) will be recorded.

[b] Monotypic endemic species are not included in these numbers.

[c] Britain is much larger than most UKOTs, so that comparisons are difficult. Therefore, species occurring in a UKOT and nearby areas, but limited to a total area of less than that of Britain are included here. Also included are species for which more than 90% of the population depend on the UKOT.

[d] The total for sub-species is not additive in a simple way to the totals of the others.

(*Sources:* Oldfield (1987), Pienkowski (2002, 2005), IUCN *Red List*, unpublished UKOTCF material.)

Bermuda's low-rolling hills are largely suburban. Tourism and international business attract 500 000 visitors each year. Pressure for development and introduced species threaten the ecology.

About 250 of over 8000 plant and animal species known from Bermuda are endemic, including over 80 in the submerged caves. These, like the endemic Cahow (Bermuda Petrel), *Pterodroma cahow*, and Bermuda Skink, *Eumeces longirostris*, are endangered.

Cayman Islands

The three low-lying Cayman Islands are strung along a submarine mountain ridge south of Cuba and west of Jamaica. Business activities, concentrated in Grand Cayman, are destroying the sub-tropical dry forests and mangrove wetlands which originally clothed all three islands.

Endemic species include more than 20 plants, 30 land snails and the critically endangered Grand Cayman Blue Iguana, *Cyclura lewisi*. Birds include the endemic Grand Cayman Thrush, *Turdus ravidus* (extinct after 1938), 97% of the world population of the Vitrelline Warbler, *Dendroica vitellina* (the rest on nearby, tiny Swan Island), two endemic sub-species of Cuban Parrot, *Amazona leucocephala caymanensis* and *A.l. hesterna*, on Grand Cayman and Cayman Brac, respectively, and several endemic sub-species of forest birds.

Turks and Caicos Islands (TCI)

The TCI lies south-east of the Bahamas and 145 km north of Hispaniola. Two shallow banks hold 120 low limestone islands and cays, totalling 500 km^2 of land. Eight islands are inhabited (but resorts are being developed on most others). Most people reside on Providenciales, where wetlands and dry forest have been destroyed over about 30 years, by further development of real estate and tourism, now spreading increasingly rapidly across the other islands.

The East Caicos, Middle Caicos and North Caicos wetland complex forms one of the world's best natural transitions between dry- and wetland ecosystem complexes. It is one of the most natural amongst some 160 Wetlands of International Importance listed under the Ramsar Convention by the UK. The TCI's coral reefs, flats, mangroves, marshlands, tropical dry forest and salinas provide a haven for wildlife, and the natural basis of fisheries and tourism. The Grand Turk salt pans are important for migrant and breeding waders (shorebirds) and terns, and provide one of the best sites in the world for viewing wild birds at close range in an urban environment; they are currently being destroyed. Offshore cays hold the largest Caribbean breeding populations of several seabirds. The islands support five endemic reptile species, at least 14 unique plants and an unknown number of endemic invertebrates.

British Virgin Islands (BVI)

The BVI's 60 islands and cays are 60 km east of Puerto Rico. Most are hilly, but only small areas of the natural forest and coasts remain. The northernmost island, Anegada, is low and flat. The islands support a number of species of international importance, such as the endemic Anegada Rock Iguana, *Cyclura pinguis*, and plant species, some of which occur only on one or two islands, such as the Anegada-endemic Pokemeboy, *Acacia anegadensis*, and, occurring on Virgin Gorda and a few sites on Puerto Rica, *Calyptranthes kiaerskovii*, a woody understorey shrub of the myrtle family, all three critically endangered.

Anguilla

Tourism and off-shore finance are the major economic elements. The main island (with the entire human population) and several small cays are low and composed of limestone. The furthest islet, Sombrero, sits on its own long-isolated bank, lying midway between Anguilla and the BVI.

Endemics include several amongst the 520 recorded plant species, the Black Lizard, *Ameiva corvine*, on Sombrero Island and the Anole Lizard, *Anolis gingivinus*. Anguilla's salt ponds are important for wildlife and, during hurricanes and periods of heavy rains, act as flood control areas. They are threatened by built development. The breeding seabirds of some of the cays are at risk from introduced mammals.

Montserrat

Montserrat, one of the Leeward Islands in the Eastern Caribbean, lies 43 km southwest of Antigua and 64 km north-west of Guadeloupe. The island, 17 km long and 11 km wide, is known as the 'Emerald Isle of the Caribbean' due to both historical Irish influences and the lush greenness of tropical mountain vegetation, with streams and waterfalls.

In July 1995, the Soufriere Hills volcano in the south became active for the first time in 350 years. Increased pyroclastic activity killed 19 people on 25 June 1997. The capital, Plymouth, was destroyed in August 1997. More than half of the island will probably remain uninhabitable for decades or more. The volcano is monitored by geologists, and the still-inhabited area is safe. Since volcanic activity began, the human population on the island has declined from 11 000 to about 4500.

Despite its small size, Montserrat supports at least 132 tree, 59 bird and 13 mammal species. The Montserrat Oriole, *Icterus oberi*, is found nowhere else, as are several critically endangered lizards, including the Galliwasp, *Diploglossus montisserrati*. The critically endangered Mountain Chicken, *Leptodactylus fallax* (a frog), is found only on Montserrat and Dominica. Several other species are restricted to Montserrat and nearby islands.

Ascension

Ascension Island, with spectacular volcanic scenery, is isolated just south of the equator, in the mid-Atlantic. It was not settled until the nineteenth century, when Napoleon was captive on St Helena, 1300 km south. The main island, though barren, held huge seabird populations. Rats arrived by ship, and donkeys and cats were deliberately introduced. Many tropical flowers were planted. These introductions caused losses of endemic plants and the rapid decline in seabirds, so that, until very recently (see below), most could nest only on small stacks offshore.

Ascension is of world significance for 11 species of breeding seabird, especially the unique Ascension Island Frigatebird, *Fregata aquila*, one of the world's most important breeding Green Turtle populations, six unique species of land plants, nine of marine fish and shellfish and over 20 of land invertebrates. The recently introduced Mexican Thorn or Mesquite Bush, *Prosopis juliflora*, threatens

Ascension's Green Turtles, as well as the surviving unique desert wildlife and
geological features.

St Helena

St Helena lies 1960 km off south-west Africa and 2900 km east of South America.
The nearest land is Ascension. Its age and isolation have resulted in a remarkable land
and marine biodiversity (see Figure 13.2). Of the 60 known native species of plant, 45
occur nowhere else. Of 1100 land invertebrates, 400 are unique to St Helena; 61% of
256 beetle species are endemic. Ten shore fishes are found only around the island, and
16 more only here and on Ascension. The quite exceptional biodiversity of St Helena
has suffered greatly from human activities, but much remains.

Tristan da Cunha group

Tristan da Cunha, rising to over 2000 m above sea level, has nearby neighbours of
Nightingale and Inaccessible, with Gough Island 300 km south-east. Only Tristan da

Figure 13.2 Hugely different ecosystems occur over short ranges in some UK Overseas
Territories, as here in St Helena. The foreground is the cloud forest of Tree Ferns, *Dicksonia
arborescens*, and other endemics on the Peaks with, in the background, only 5 km away,
the desert of Prosperous Bay Plain with many endemic invertebrates (see colour plate).
(Photograph by Dr Mike Pienkowski.)

Cunha itself is inhabited, the most isolated inhabited island in the world, over 1900 km from St Helena and 2400 km west of Cape Town.

The Tristan Government is keenly aware of the need to live in balance with its environment because the economy of the community is dependent on sustainable harvests of lobster and fish. Over 40% of Tristan's territory is nature reserve, and Gough and Inaccessible Islands are a World Heritage Site.

Those islands still rodent-free support endemic land birds, including the Tristan Thrush, *Nesocichla eremite*, and the vulnerable Inaccessible Rail, *Atlantisia rogersi*, the smallest flightless bird in the world. Millions of seabirds, such as the vulnerable Spectacled Petrel, *Procellaria conspicillata* (see Figure 13.3), the endangered Yellow-nosed Albatross, *Thalassarche chlororhynchos*, the endangered Tristan Albatross, *Diomedea dabbenena*, the vulnerable Atlantic Petrel, *Pterodroma incerta* – all endemic – and the almost endemic Great Shearwater, *Puffinus gravis* (of which small numbers nest on the Falkland Islands) breed – as do Fur Seals, *Arctocephalus tropicalis*, and Elephant Seals, *Mirounga leonina*, now recovering from the hunting of the nineteenth century. There are 59 endemic species of moss among 126 species recorded on Tristan da Cunha.

Figure 13.3 Spectacled Petrel, *Procellaria conspicillata*, one of five seabird species which (together with six land-bird species) breed only in the Tristan da Cunha group, this species only on Inaccessible Island. Some of the seabirds range widely outside the breeding season (see colour plate). (Photograph by Dr Mike Pienkowski.)

Falkland Islands

The Falkland Islands, an archipelago of 700 islands totalling a land mass half the size of Wales, lie in the South Atlantic on the equivalent latitude to London, about 650 km off the coast of South America and 1600 km from Antarctica. The economy is now based on sustainable sea fisheries.

Exceptionally rich in marine life, the islands support vast colonies of seabirds – 85% of the world population of endangered Black-browed Albatrosses, *Thalassarche melan-ophrys*, and the world's largest concentration of vulnerable Rockhopper Penguins, *Eudyptes chrysocome*. The islands provide breeding grounds for Sea Lions, *Otaria flavescens*, Elephant Seals, *Mirounga leonina*, and Fur Seals, *Arctocephalus australis* Twenty-two cetacean species occur in the surrounding seas.

South Georgia and the South Sandwich Islands (SGSSI)

South Georgia lies 1300 km south-east of the Falkland Islands, and the South Sandwich Islands (SSI) a further 760 km south-east. South Georgia is mountainous with many glaciers (see Figure 13.4), permanent ice covering almost half of its total land area of 3755 km^2. The South Sandwich Islands are an uninhabited 240 km chain of active volcanic islands. The economy is now based on sustainable sea fisheries.

Figure 13.4 King Penguin, *Aptenodytes paragonicus*, colony and Tussac Grass, *Poa flabellate*, below glacier, South Georgia (see colour plate). (Photograph by Dr Mike Pienkowski.)

An estimated 53 million birds depend on South Georgia. The most numerous is the vulnerable Macaroni Penguin, *Eudyptes chrysolophus*, with over two million breeding pairs. It is an important nesting site for the largest seabird in the world, the vulnerable Wandering Albatross, *Diomedea exulans*. Further large seabird colonies in the SSI include the Chinstrap Penguin, *Pygoscelis antarcticus*, in vast numbers.

The South Georgia Pipit, *Anthus antarcticus*, is endemic. Several seal species breed on the two island groups. Whales are frequent offshore. There are few flowering plants, but many endemic mosses and lichens.

British Antarctic Territory (BAT)

This comprises 1 709 400 km^2 of land, including the Antarctic Peninsula, and ocean south of 60° S between 20° and 80° west. Although the UK claim overlaps those of Argentina and Chile, the Antarctic Treaty provides an agreed regime. There is no permanent population, but the British Antarctic Survey has two year-round and one summer-only research stations here. Other countries have research stations in this region. Management of fishing is by international agreement through the Convention for the Conservation of Antarctic Marine Living Resources (CCAMLR). Current issues include increasing tourism, the southern ocean whale sanctuary and climate-change.

On land, although vegetation is sparse, there are many types of lichen, moss and algae. In the seas, vast amounts of krill provide the basis for rich marine life, including whales, seals and huge numbers of birds, especially petrels and penguins, inhabiting the islands and coasts of the Peninsula. Adélie, *Pygoscelis adeliae*, and Emperor, *Aptenodytes forsteri,* Penguins both breed on the continent itself.

British Indian Ocean Territory (BIOT)

This comprises the 55 islands of the Chagos Archipelago – only 44 km^2 of land, but over 20 000 km^2 of one of the world's richest coral reefs. The Archipelago lies at the centre of the Indian Ocean, its only human inhabitants now being military personnel on the southernmost island, Diego Garcia.

Ocean currents bring fish and invertebrate larvae, which develop into adulthood and release progeny to regenerate the depleted stocks further west. The Government sets a protective framework, with the declared intention of treating the area with all the strictness applicable to World Heritage Sites, although it considers that its treaty with the USA prevents formal declaration as such.

The islands support large seabird colonies, nesting endangered Green Turtles and the critically endangered Hawksbill Turtles, *Eretmochelys imbricata*. Major challenges are aiding regeneration of indigenous wildlife, including dealing with introduced invasive species.

Pitcairn Islands

This group of four small, varied South Pacific islands include Pitcairn itself (4.5 km^2, the haven for the mutineers from HMS Bounty over 200 years ago) to Henderson Island – a 37 km^2 raised coral atoll – and tiny, low-lying coral atolls of Oeno and Ducie. The nearest land masses are over 4500 km away, New Zealand to the west-south-west and South America to the east. Only Pitcairn is inhabited; 47 people at Adamstown, isolated by more than a day's sail from French Polynesia, around 500 km north-west.

The other islands support a range of endemic species. The vulnerable Chicken Bird, *Porzana atra* (a jet black, flightless rail confined to Henderson Island – a World Heritage Site), seems to be less vulnerable to predation by rats than are the petrels. Of special concern is the recently described and endangered Henderson Petrel, *Pterodroma atrata*. UK funds have helped develop local conservation skills and a successful rat eradication programme on Oeno and Ducie.

Gibraltar

Gibraltar is a narrow peninsula 7 km long, attached to Iberia by a low, sandy isthmus. Wildlife survives on the limestone cliffs and slopes, with scrub, patches of woodland, caves and rocky shoreline. Steep cliffs rise from the Mediterranean on the east to 398 m. On the west, the Rock slopes more gradually through scrubland, with the city (where most of the people live) nestled at the foot, partly on land claimed from the sea. To the south are a series of stony terraces.

Soaring birds pass over twice a year, on one of two major migration routes between Europe and Africa. Gibraltar's waters are home to dolphins and many other animals. Species confined to Gibraltar include sea slugs, snails and plants. Within Europe, several plant species, e,g. Candytuft, *Iberis gibraltarica*, are unique to Gibraltar, as are Barbary Macaques, *Macaca sylvanus* (the famous 'apes') – opinions differ as to whether their original occurrence is natural.

Cyprus Sovereign Base Areas (SBA)

These remained British territory when the Republic of Cyprus was created in 1960. They cover 254 km^2, 123 around Akrotiri, the Western Sovereign Base Area (WSBA) and 131 around Dhekelia, the Eastern Sovereign Base Area (ESBA).

The SBA Authority is responsible for environmental protection, working closely with the Cypriot Republic, e.g. to protect breeding endangered Loggerhead, *Caretta caretta*, and Green Turtles on the beaches within the WSBA. The most important wetland on the island of Cyprus, Akrotiri salt lake, lies within the WSBA and is a Ramsar Convention Wetland of International Importance. Rare orchids (endemic to the island), colonies of birds of prey, such as Eleonora's Falcon, *Falco eleonorae*, and various reptiles and amphibians are also found within the Bases, as well as many migrant songbirds. The latter are subject to illegal hunting.

Economic importance of biodiversity

Apart from their intrinsic importance, natural ecosystems underpin the economies of most UKOTs. For example:

- Natural vegetation and soils provide the main freshwater reservoirs in several UKOTs
- Coastal waters provide the nurseries for fisheries, an important food resource in many territories
- Licencing sustainable sea fisheries is the main source of income for at least three UKOTs
- Mangroves and coral reefs provide shoreline protection against hurricanes and sea surges, as do forests for terrestrial areas
- Wildlife and unspoilt ecosystems provide opportunities for 'eco-tourism'.

Historical context

The early years

The history of European discovery was not glorious. In 1586, Sir Francis Drake's fleet called at the Cayman Islands; unable to find fresh water, the sailors set the forest on fire and departed. For over 300 years, ships passing here depleted probably the largest Green Turtles colony that has ever existed to very limited numbers (Oldfield 1987). The crocodiles which gave the islands their name are extinct.

Similar unsustainability was general, but space allows only one other example. Massive destruction of native plants and animals had followed St Helena's discovery in 1502, as did the introduction of goats and pigs, for passing ships. The sub-fossil record shows that at least six unique land birds once occurred on St Helena, but only one, the Wirebird, *Charadrius sanctae-helenae*, survives (Ashmole and Ashmole 2000).

Recent times

Over-exploitation, habitat destruction and introduction of alien, invasive species continue into modern times. This is linked to the British Government's apparent desire to accept as little responsibility for UKOTs as possible. After the Second World War, the British government developed a presumption that all former colonies would go independent; those that did not want this had to struggle to achieve the right to stay linked to the UK.

The invasion of the Falkland Islands by Argentina in 1982 and their subsequent liberation had a side benefit of a more constructive approach by open-minded British officials working with local initiatives, to re-invigorate the islands, to put them on a sound economic basis, particularly using sustainable fisheries. In contrast, a removal in Ascension in 2005 of the rights of inhabitants announced in 2000 to a say in their governance and even to residency has led to a reduction in a sense of local ownership of the islands, and this has adversely affected some conservation initiatives.[1]

In both uninhabited and inhabited UKOTs, the (largely successful) wish by the UK Government to minimise expenditure from the UK's main budget has had major negative environmental consequences. Unfortunately, the small former colonies which became the UKOTs never seemed to generate enough attention in the UK Government for it to give strategic thought to their futures. Instead, a rather ad hoc and piecemeal approach dominated.[2] In the Caribbean, the urge to generate short-term income and the perverse economic incentives noted earlier lead to essentially unplanned developments, with buildings sprawling over larger – and less suitable – areas than would be the case with adequate spatial planning. Theoretically adequate planning procedures have, in practice, become hidden from public scrutiny. The rate of habitat destruction has tended to increase in recent years, rather than decrease.

Conservation organisations' efforts

Early conservation actions in territories

Although the development pressures in the last 50 years increased impacts on wildlife in UKOTs, there has also been an increase in local environmental awareness and conservation action (Oldfield 1987; Pienkowski *et al.* 1998).

An outstanding example comes from Bermuda. The endemic Cahow Petrel nested in super-abundance, digging its nesting burrows in soil under the forest. It flies to and from its nest-burrows at night, but has no defences against mammal predators introduced after colonisation. Despite a protection proclamation as early as 1616, the Cahow was thought extinct by 1630, a mere 20 years after settlement! It was rediscovered in 1951, surviving on five tiny offshore islets, totalling less than 1.2 ha, which the mammals did not reach (Wingate 2001). Nest boxes to supplement the shortage of soil for burrowing nests and to overcome competition with the White-tailed Tropicbird, *Phaeton lepturus*, have helped the 18 pairs surviving in the 1950s to treble to 55 nesting pairs by 2000. The government declared the larger adjacent island of Nonsuch (6 ha) as a nature reserve in 1961. Introduced rats were eliminated and quarantine arrangements ensured

---

[1] UKOTCF (2006). *Forum News*, **28**, 1–3; **29**, 2–3 (http:// www.ukotcf.org/forumNews/index.htm); also footnote 2.

[2] House of Commons Foreign Affairs Committee (2008) Overseas Territories. Seventh Report of Session 2007–08 (http://www.publications.parliament.uk/pa/cm200708/cmselect/cmfaff/147/147i.pdf).

that it remained free of potential predators. Cahows are being encouraged to colonise Nonsuch, which has deep soil for nest excavation. The need is urgent: sea-level rise is increasing the rate of flooding and erosion on the islets where the petrels survived 300 years of presumed extinction, 40% of nest-sites having been destroyed there (fortunately outside the nesting season) in storms three times since 1995.

Of 37 known endemic species of flowering plant on St Helena, seven are extinct. Ten genera are endemic, one of these becoming extinct as recently as 2003. Endemics include also 13 ferns and an unknown number of mosses, liverworts, algae and lichens (Ashmole and Ashmole 2000). In the 1950s, active individuals on St Helena (both from Britain and St Helena) recognised the importance of the natural vegetation. They persuaded the government to establish a nature reserve in the Peaks ridge, started removing invading exotics, found remaining examples of native plants and established legal protection. However, activity – depending on individuals – flagged, so that in the 1980s losses of native plants were occurring on the Peaks as a result of invading New Zealand Flax, *Phormium tenax* (abandoned after planting from 1870 in an attempt to find an economic base for the island as its shipping role declined). The effectiveness of flax removal and assistance to the re-establishment of native vegetation has recently been demonstrated. However, limitations on costs and labour mean that this has been limited to small areas.

A third example of early local conservation initiatives comes from Gibraltar (Cortes 2001). With 28 000 inhabitants on 7 km^2, this has limited resources and tremendous pressure on space. The Gibraltar Ornithological and Natural History Society (GONHS) has grown since 1976 from a small club of four birdwatchers, to a society with about 400 members, a £200 000 pa budget, seven staff and five premises. Largely NGO-led conservation has proved effective. GONHS's willingness to state views frankly, while continuing to work constructively, has led to a successful relationship with Government – which has contracted GONHS to take on wildlife management work. Within the Development and Planning Commission, GONHS has prevented losses of natural rocky shoreline, prevented quarrying of sand slopes (the huge former water catchment) and saved an endemic plant, Gibraltar Campion, *Silene tomentosa*, from extinction.

Co-ordinating and collaborating actions across UKOTs and Crown Dependencies

In the previous section, the importance of co-ordination, exchange of ideas and continuity will have been apparent, both by example and absence. Until the end of the twentieth century, there was surprisingly little exchange of expertise between UKOTs, partly due to the UK Government tending to treat them almost as foreign countries, rather than parts of the UK. Until the mid-1990s, the lead UK Government ministry, the Foreign and Commonwealth Office (FCO), did not even have a department to deal with them; it simply grouped them with neighbouring foreign countries.

The UK has responsibility under international commitments to environmental conservation in the UKOTs – because they are UK territory, not foreign. It was in recognition of this, the under-resourcing of conservation in the UKOTs and their global importance to wildlife that the UK Overseas Territories Conservation Forum was formed in 1987. It brings together conservation and science bodies and individuals in the UK and UKOTs concerned with conservation in the UKOTs. It works closely with the governments of the UK and UKOTs. Because of a lack of available funding, it works on a largely volunteer basis.

It has followed a successful strategy of: (1) helping local people form a conservation NGO where one did not already exist – now largely achieved; (2) helping that NGO (and often the UKOT Government environment department) develop its capacity to manage itself and (3) evolving a programme of jointly run conservation projects; this is complemented by (4) raising awareness in the UK of UKOTs, their conservation importance and needs, and the UK's shared responsibility in this regard (Pienkowski *et al.* 1998; www.ukotcf.org).

Overcoming the divided responsibility for international environmental commitments

The UK Government (HMG) is responsible for international relations of UKOTs and Crown Dependencies, including environmental conventions, and for ensuring good governance. Thus, conservation of biodiversity in the UKOTs is a shared responsibility. Inclusion in the UK's ratification of international environmental conventions (Table 13.4) is not automatic, but depends on the agreement of the territory government.

In its 1999 White Paper,[3] HMG adopted UKOTCF's suggestion on addressing the problem that HMG is responsible for international environmental commitments, but that UKOT Governments are responsible for legislation and enforcement. The Environment Charters,[4] signed on 26 September 2001 by HMG and most UKOT Governments, include commitments by both parties to integrate environmental conservation into all sectors of policy, planning and implementation. At the request of UKOTs, in 2002–5, UKOTCF facilitated the development of strategies to implement the Charters in pilot UKOTs.[5] Several UKOTs have taken alternative routes, such as Bermuda's Biodiversity Strategy and Action Plan (Glasspool *et al.* 2003).

In August 2007, UKOTCF published its first review of progress on Environment Charter implementation (Pienkowski 2007). Whilst progress was apparent, a great deal remained to be done to meet commitments, for example, to development planning, to environmental impact assessment and to the openness of these processes. Disappointingly, one UKOT (Turks and Caicos Islands) has actually decreased the extent of protected areas since the Charters were signed, in order to allow more built development.

---

[3] UK Government White Paper on the UK Overseas Territories, Partnership for Progress and Prosperity, March 1999 (www.ukotcf.org/pdf/charters/WhitePaper99full.pdf).
[4] The Charters can be seen at http://www.ukotcf.org/charters/index.htm.
[5] http://www.ukotcf.org/charters/charterStrat.htm.

Table 13.4 Inclusion of UK Overseas Territories and Crown Dependencies in Multilateral Environmental Agreements

Biodiversity and other heritage MEAs	Ramsar Convention on Wetlands	World Heritage Convention	Convention on Biological Diversity	Convention on International Trade in Endangered Species (CITES)	Bonn Convention on Migratory Species (CMS)	CMS Agreement on European Bats (Eurobats)	CMS Indian Ocean Turtles MOU	CMS Agreement on the Conservation of Albatrosses and Petrels (ACAP)	Specially Protected Areas and Wildlife (SPAW) Protocol to the Convention for the Protection and Development of the Marine Environment of the Wider Caribbean Region (Cartagena)
Bermuda	Y	Y	N	Y	Y				
Cayman Islands	Y	Y	Y	Y	Y				N
Turks and Caicos Islands	Y	Y	N	N	Y				N
British Virgin Islands	Y	Y	Y	Y	Y				N
Anguilla	Y	Y	N	N	N				N
Montserrat	Y	Y	N	Y	Y				N
Ascension	Y	Y	Y	Y	Y				
St Helena	Y	Y	Y	Y	Y				
Tristan da Cunha	Y	Y	Y	Y	Y			Y	
Falkland Islands	Y	Y	N	Y	Y			Y	
South Georgia and the South Sandwich Islands	Y	Y	N	Y	Y			Y	
British Antarctic Territory	N	N	N	N	N			Y	
British Indian Ocean Territory	Y	N	N	Y	Y		Y		
Pitcairn Islands	Y	Y	N	Y	Y				

(*Sources*: Coffey and Pienkowski (1998) updated by unpublished UKOTCF material.)

Threats and trends

Threats

Space allows mention of only a few examples of each of the severe impacts occurring in several UKOTs.

Over-exploitation and side effects

UKOT Exclusive Economic Zones (EEZs) constitute a high proportion of South Atlantic, and other waters (Cooper 2007). Well-managed, sustainable fisheries underpin the economies of the Falkland Islands, South Georgia and the South Sandwich Islands, and Tristan da Cunha. Responsible fishing companies work with conservationists and authorities to minimise by-catches of albatrosses, which are threatening the survival of some species. However, some fisheries outside the EEZs and illegal, unregulated and unreported fishing in the unpatrolled waters of Ascension, St Helena and parts of those of Tristan da Cunha pose serious threats to marine ecosystems. This means that not only is potential income from licensing being lost, but also that the UK is failing in its responsibility to conserve these ecosystems. The internal economies of these UKOTs are inadequate to fund vessels (nor, in the case of Tristan, a suitable harbour), but the UK Government has proved unwilling to meet the responsibility.

Destruction of natural ecosystems

Urban development has been dramatic in Gibraltar since the early 1900s (Cortes 2001), and may become so in St Helena, with the construction of the airport scheduled for 2010. However, the biggest threats of this nature are in the wider Caribbean, including rapid development and inadequate planning controls, often related to an unsustainable reliance on resort-based tourism, leading to habitat loss and degradation.[6] For example, in the Cayman Islands, built development is causing deforestation of both mangrove wetlands and ancient dry forests, and anchoring of cruise liners has devastated the coral reefs.

In the Turks and Caicos Islands, unplanned development has converted the island of Providenciales in 30 years from three fishing villages to an urban sprawl. From the start of this millennium, such development has spread to the other islands, each of which still has its own character – which would, if retained, form an effective basis for long-term tourism. A further great threat to the habitats for endemics such as Rock Iguanas and the remaining breeding sites for turtles is posed by major developments on uninhabited islands and cays. Even statutory protected areas are not safe, with several current developments impacting on those, without available EIAs or public debate. The public are strongly discouraged from raising objections to these developments, and concern has been expressed by the House of Commons Foreign Affairs Committee[7] at restriction of free speech in TCI.

---

[6] UKOTCF (2007). *Forum News*, **31**, 1 and 18 (http://www.ukotcf.org/pdf/fNews/31.pdf).
[7] House of Commons Foreign Affairs Committee (2008) Overseas Territories. Seventh Report of Session 2007–08 (http://www.publications.parliament.uk/pa/cm200708/cmselect/cmfaff/147/147i.pdf).

In the British Virgin Islands, development continues to undermine the environment on which it is based, with marinas destroying mangroves, sea-grass beds and reefs. Citizens of BVI report a virtual collapse in the assessment, monitoring and enforcement mechanisms, with constant violations by some developers. In Anguilla, local concern has been expressed at a current 700% increase in hotel rooms, impacting natural or other heritage features. In Bermuda, planning regulations have been by-passed to build a hotel on coastal woodlands, also removing cliff coastal defences and seabird nest sites.

Invasive species

The introduction of rats and mice in the 1880s destroyed many of Tristan Island's indigenous birdlife. Fortunately the adjacent islands of Nightingale and Inaccessible, home to several endemic birds, remain rodent-free. However, introduced mice on Gough Island (also in the Tristan group) are potentially causing the extinction of several endemic albatrosses and petrels by eating the nestlings.

On Ascension Island, the one conservation project in the UKOTs that has ever been funded at levels appropriate to recovery plans was successful in restoring seabird breeding by the removal of feral cats. However, major threats to conservation remain from other introduced species, particularly Mesquite Thorn, *Prosopis juliflora*, and Black Rats, *Rattus rattus*.

On St Helena, the remaining, scattered patches of native vegetation are too small to allow those endemics which escaped extinction so far to survive. Successful experimental work in clearing invasive vegetation needs extending.

In the Pitcairn Islands, some endemic plants survive in remnants of indigenous vegetation. Globally important seabird populations (including Murphy's Petrel, *Pterodroma ultima*) on the other islands (having been extirpated on Pitcairn itself) are threatened by Pacific Rats, *Rattus exulans*, introduced by Polynesians during their settlement from about 800 to about 1600 AD (Wragg 1995).

On many other UKOTs, such as in the wider Caribbean, introduced mammals including feral pet cats and dogs, pose serious threats to endemic reptiles, and introduced plants threaten natural vegetation.

Thoughtless introductions continue. In 2005 the Caicos Pines, *Pinus caribaea* var. *bahamensis*, the national tree of the Turks and Caicos Islands, which formed characteristic stands in the water/land margin zone, were virtually wiped out by a newly introduced Pine Tortoise Scale Insect, *Toumeyella parvicornis*. This almost certainly arrived on Christmas trees brought from North America.

Pollution and climate change

The most wide-ranging aspect of pollution affecting UKOTs is via climate. Most of the Cayman Islands, the Turks and Caicos Islands, Anguilla and the British Indian Ocean Territory, as well as significant parts of Bermuda, the British Virgin Islands and the Pitcairn Islands would be submerged by the sea-level rises currently predicted. It is thus surprising to see the higher parts of several of these being quarried out of existence. Sea-level rise has already been noted as affecting the rate of flooding of the nest sites of the Bermuda Cahow Petrel.

Climate change can interact with other factors. For example, glacier reduction on South Georgia is linking the formerly isolated patches of unglaciated land. This reduces the practicability of removing the introduced rats, which threaten the endemic pipits and hugely important breeding seabird populations.

Trends

Unfortunately, some losses are so large that patterns are clear, despite the lack of systematic numeric monitoring.

The IUCN *Red List* records 39 global extinctions in the UKOTs in historical times, compared with one (the Great Auk, *Pinguinus impennis*, in the nineteenth century) in Britain. Limitation to very visible species and those which leave evidence in the sub-fossil record means that the numbers of extinctions in the UKOTs are greatly underestimated; additionally, several published extinctions are not listed by IUCN. Thirty recorded extinctions relating to St Helena include many from the early days of colonisation in the sixteenth century, but they continued later, with a dwarf ebony, *Trochetiopsis melanoxylon*, and a cuckoo, *Nannococcyx psix,* probably becoming extinct in the eighteenth century, and a shrub, *Acalypha rubrinervis,* in the nineteenth – which saw also the loss to the world of a night heron, *Nycticorax* sp., and three plant species (the shrub, *Oldenlandia adscensionis*, the fern, *Dryopteris ascensionis*, and the grass, *Sporobolus durus*) on Ascension Island, the Tristan Moorhen, *Gallinula nesiotis*, and the Falklands Wolf, *Dusicyon australis*. The Grand Cayman Thrush, *Turdus ravidus*, became extinct in 1938 and another Ascension endemic fern, *Anogramma ascensionis*, some time after 1964. The probable extinction of the St Helena Giant Earwig, *Labidura herculeana*, has been linked by some to the huge numbers of invertebrates collected by Belgian expeditions of the 1960s, which did much to document the invertebrates.

The sorry story continues to the present, with the St Helena Olive, *Nesiota elliptica* – an ancient endemic genus, not just a species – dying out in December 2003 when the last tree in cultivation died (the last wild individual had died in 1994). On the same island, the endemic Bastard Gumwood, *Commidendrum rotundifolium*, has been reduced to two individuals in cultivation, both badly damaged in a storm in 2007. Several other species, including He Cabbage, *Phadaroxylon leucadendron*, another endemic single-species genus, are also down to a few individuals.

Of globally threatened species identified in the 2004 IUCN Red List, UKOTs hold globally threatened species:

- 74 critically endangered (cf 10 in GB and NI)
- 49 endangered species (cf 12)
- 117 vulnerable species (cf 37)
- Many of these are endemic.

If the UK is to have any credibility in meeting international commitments, we cannot afford to permit further extinctions of endemics in our UKOTs, yet at least 240 species are at high risk of this.

Why are endemic species still becoming globally extinct and natural ecosystems being destroyed on UK territory?

Lack of resources

Despite increased local funding for conservation, the lack of personnel and of economies of scale in UKOTs mean that this will not be enough. UKOTs are not eligible for international aid – because they are legally UK territory. The international community expects the UK to fund work in these parts of its territory to meet its international commitments. However, UKOTs are excluded from the budgets of most British Government departments, effectively also from most British charitable and commercial sources (because of a lack of awareness) and from the National Lottery (a major funding source for conservation bodies in Britain) because the operating body believes erroneously that UKOTs are foreign!

One UK Government Commitment in the Environment Charters is 'Use the existing Environment Fund for the Overseas Territories, and promote access to other sources of public funding, for projects of lasting benefit to the Territories' environments.' However, a few months after signing the Charters, the fund mentioned was closed; although later reinstated (after protests) as a new fund, its continued existence remains uncertain.

Major NGO contributions and the modest UK Government funding have proved invaluable for small or pilot projects. However, there is no dedicated fund for larger projects, such as to extend successful pilot work to the scale of species recovery plans (normal in Britain and other countries). The British Government estimates that it spends at least £460 million per year on biodiversity conservation in Great Britain and Northern Ireland, compared with about £1 million per year in the UKOTs (and none in Crown Dependencies). One conservative estimate is that there are at least 20 times as many endemic species in UK Overseas Territories as in Great Britain and Northern Ireland. (Other measures give similar results.) Using this as a factor to multiply the spending difference, it appears that the UK Government values its responsibilities to global biodiversity in its Overseas Territories about 9000 times less than it values its responsibilities to global biodiversity in Great Britain and Northern Ireland (which elsewhere in this book, others argue is not itself enough). This appears to run counter to the UK's commitments under the Convention on Biological Diversity and other international agreements.

Lack of UK Government fulfilment of its responsibility to ensuring good governance

The Environment Charters include commitments by UKOT Governments to:

(2) Ensure the protection and restoration of key habitats, species and landscape features... and attempt the control and eradication of invasive species.

(4) Ensure that environmental…impact assessments are undertaken before approving major projects…

(5) Commit to open and consultative decision-making on developments and plans which may affect the environment; ensure that environmental impact assessments include consultation with stakeholders.

However, this is failing, as noted above.

A view from Parliament

The UK Government routinely comments, for example in responses to Parliamentary Committees, that addressing conservation issues in UKOTs is a matter solely for UKOT administrations. In view of the lack of human populations in some UKOTs and the small populations in others, this is nonsense. Conservation NGOs in both Britain and the UKOTs are not alone in disagreeing with the Government's position, as the UK Parliament does also. The House of Commons Environmental Audit Committee[8] concluded, on 23 May 2007:

(83) We are disturbed that witnesses have stressed to us that departments other than FCO[9] and DFID[10] do not provide the level of support to the UKOTs that is required. Although DEFRA[11] does provide some direct and indirect support, the level of this does not fill the specialist environmental gaps that are apparent in the UKOTs. We recommend…DEFRA should be given joint responsibility towards the UKOTs. This should be reflected in an updated UK International Priority, to include environmental protection alongside security and good governance in the UKOTs…Finally,…the case for larger and more routine funding must be explored…

(84) If the Government fails to address these issues it will run the risk of continued environmental decline and species extinctions in the UKOTs, ultimately causing the UK to fail in meeting its domestic and international environmental commitments. Failure to meet such commitments undermines the UK's ability to influence the international community to take the strong action required for reversing environmental degradation in their own countries, and globally.

What can be done?

Evidence from what has already been done with limited resources

The success of the under-funded work by the UKOT and British member organisations of the UKOTCF network and UKOT government departments, supported by volunteer

---

[8] The Fifth Report of the House of Commons Select Committee on Environmental Audit, on Trade, Development and Environment: the role of the FCO (2007): http://www.publications.parliament.uk/pa/cm200607/cmselect/cmenvaud/289/289.pdf. Later reinforced by The Thirteenth Report of the House of Commons Select Committee on Environmental Audit, on Halting Biodiversity Loss (2008): http://www.publications.parliament.uk/pa/cm200708/cmselect/cmenvaud/743/743.pdf.

[9] Foreign and Commonwealth Office (with the policy lead on UKOTs).

[10] Department for International Development (which has certain financial support duties to UKOTs).

[11] Department of Environment, Food and Rural Affairs (which has UK Government's lead on environmental conservation matters).

effort and the UK Government small project grants, demonstrate the potential. Some examples below provide indications of how much more a proper funding mechanism could achieve.

At a strategic level

Initial reviews of challenges and progress (Oldfield 1987; Cross and Pienkowski 1998; Pienkowski *et al.* 1998) were followed by UKOTCF's facilitating development of strategies to implement Environment Charters by the UKOTs, Bermuda's developing through public consultation a Biodiversity Strategy and Action Plan (Glasspool *et al.* 2003), and the Environmental Management Plan for South Georgia providing a framework for waste management, protected areas and control of alien species.

Site management

At a site level, the British Virgin Islands National Parks Trust has developed and begun to implement plans for the protected areas of the BVI. Management plans have been developed and adopted for Gough and Inaccessible Islands, Tristan da Cunha[12] and Henderson Island, Pitcairn Islands.[13]

In the Turks and Caicos Islands, an integrated Plan for Biodiversity Management and Sustainable Development was developed for the area around the large Ramsar Wetland of International Importance (Pienkowski 2002). This linked biodiversity and sustainable use of this by local communities (who were involved in the plan development) with the development of an infrastructure to make it available to residents and (paying) visitors. This is being implemented, including an integrated package of a conservation centre, provision of nature trails (see Figure 13.5), interpretative material, guide-training and help to the local community in developing appropriate small businesses (Manco 2007).

Environmental education

The Turks and Caicos National Trust has developed, and trained teachers to implement, a primary school education course, making use (for the first time) of local material: Our Land, Our Sea, Our People.

The British Virgin Islands have developed an interactive electronic atlas, making material available to schools.

Further cross-territory initiatives are developing from discussions on environmental education at the UKOTCF-organised conference in Jersey in 2006.

---

[12] Ryan, P.J. and Glass, J.P. (2001). Inaccessible Island Nature Reserve Management Plan. Edinburgh, Tristan da Cunha: Government of Tristan da Cunha: http://www.ukotcf.org/asp/cpview/cpview.asp?FUNC=SEARCH&SCRN=HOME&DETL=.

[13] Henderson Island World Heritage Site Management Plan 2004–09. London, UK: Foreign and Commonwealth Office: http://www.ukotcf.org/pdf/henderson.pdf.

Figure 13.5 Biologically rich garden pond, Middle Caicos, Turks and Caicos Islands, one of the features on a new interpreted nature trail. Seasonal changes in the limestone aquifer raise the water table and create ephemeral ponds that are often deep (see colour plate). (Photograph by Dr Mike Pienkowski.)

Restoration

St Helena conservationists have demonstrated the practicability of clearing invasive plants and restoring the endemics. It has been pointed out that, had such successful pilot work been on an island of such importance that happened to be nearer to Britain, British resources would long ago have been made available to apply it throughout the island.

On Bermuda, the endemic cedar was nearly wiped out in the 1940s by an introduced scale insect (after transportation access to the island was hugely increased by war-time activities), but island-wide planting schemes have re-established many (Wingate 2001). The recent Buy Back Bermuda campaign has acquired and restored wetlands.

The Gibraltar Ornithological and Natural History Society is re-establishing native vegetation on the slopes previously providing the water catchment.

In the Falkland Islands, sheep farming led to reductions in giant Tussac Grass, important habitat for birds and insects in a treeless landscape. Re-planting Tussac Grass and rat removal from small islets is allowing increase in endemic and other native birds.

The endangered endemic Blue Iguana (see Figure 13.6) is recovering from the brink of extinction thanks to captive breeding and re-stocking of protected habitat by the National Trust for the Cayman Islands (Burton 2007).

At Ascension Island, the restoration of breeding seabirds by the removal of feral cats was a huge success. The contribution to this by the UK Government was by far

Figure 13.6 Endemic Blue Iguana, *Cyclura lewisi*, Grand Cayman – the subject of a current recovery programme (see colour plate). (Photograph by Frederic J. Burton.)

the largest to date, and the only one which reached the normal scale of a recovery programme; the £500k equalled the sum of all UKOT projects normally funded by the UK Government each year. The House of Commons Environmental Audit Committee pointed out that 'While the RSPB and other [UKOTCF] Forum members had developed the environmental and business case for this project over many years, this had been repeatedly rejected by HMG[14] on budgetary grounds. Ironically, the money was found from the FCO's[15] programme budget, when a non-environmental large UN-related project fell through and there was a risk of an embarrassing under-spend, which would have been clawed back by the Treasury.' The Committee advocated that UK Government funding for this sort of exercise should be normal, not exceptional.

Site safeguard

If species and ecosystems can be saved by conservation action, the need for later expensive restoration is reduced. One example is the successful efforts in Anguilla to reverse a decision to establish rocket-launching on the remote islet of Sombrero, and to protect this as a nature reserve.

---

[14] Her Majesty's Government (the name the UK Government gives itself).
[15] Foreign and Commonwealth Office, the UK Government's lead department for UKOTs.

Land owned by the National Trust for the Cayman Islands is protected in perpetuity. The Trust's protected area system includes Booby Pond, Little Cayman (a Ramsar Conservation Wetland of International Importance, home to 20 000 Red-footed Boobies, *Sula sula*), Cayman Brac's Parrot Reserve and Grand Cayman's Salina, Mastic and Central Mangrove Wetland Reserves, protecting pristine forest environments.

What is needed to reverse the loss of biodiversity?

The requirements to stop global extinctions on UK territory include:

- *Encouraging the involvement of civil society*, and a welcoming by UKOT governments of an open approach.
- *Raising awareness* of UK public, officials and politicians of the importance of biodiversity in UKOTs, and the UK's shared responsibility for it. This should include recognition by Ministers and senior officials that UKOTs are potential sources of 'good news stories' – about people wishing to remain British, about their global importance for biodiversity, about the UK helping these small countries within its territory, and in the examples that good joint conservation work by Britain and the UKOTs can provide internationally. The Department for Education and Skills in the Britain should be encouraged to include information on the UKOTs in the National Curriculum.
- *UK Government needs to commit to continue its small project fund for UKOTs*, and amend legislation to make other funding sources, such as the National Lottery, available to UKOT conservation projects.
- *Achieving a separate fund for large-scale conservation projects/sustainable usage issues*. In addition to species recovery plans, there are a range of project-types which require funding on this scale, including:
  - Ecosystem (rather than individual species-centred) approaches
  - Institutional strengthening – which takes several years (to underpin this, support is needed for the work of co-ordinating NGOs, especially as this is cost-effective in attracting other support, both financial and via major volunteer contributions)
  - Monitoring both natural resources and human impacts
  - Major issues, such as dealing with invasive species, aiding sustainable tourism or fisheries, adapting to climate change (see above)
  - Linking into local planning, physical, economic and human.

A prime role of the UK House of Commons is to oversee the budget derived from taxes that it authorises Government to collect. The need for the sort of funding outlined above is considered reasonable by the Environmental Audit Committee of the House of Commons.

Its 2006 report on the UN Millennium Ecosystem Assessment concluded (paragraph 32):

Considering the UKOTs lack of capacity, both financial and human, we find it distasteful that FCO and DFID stated that if UKOTs are 'sufficiently committed' they should support environmental positions 'from their own resources'. The continued threat of the extinction of around 240 species in the UKOTs is shameful. If the Government is to achieve the World Summit on Sustainable Development 2010 target to significantly reduce the rate of biodiversity loss within its entire territory, the Government must act decisively to prevent further loss of biodiversity in the UKOTs.

Determining the funds needed is difficult because of the starvation of funding. Combining information on priorities with capacity to deploy resources, a modest figure of £16 million pa has been calculated to make a significant start on this work – a tiny annual investment from the UK Government relative to most of the British budget. Combined with appropriate encouragement to UKOT Governments to strengthen environmental protection, this could make a massive contribution to meeting the UK's international commitments and enhance the UK's environmental credentials. Conservation in the UKOTs is a good news story waiting to happen – for want of modest resources.

Acknowledgements

I am grateful to many colleagues in the UKOTCF network for information and discussions, to Ann Pienkowski for assistance in new analyses for this chapter and to her, Andrew Lack, Norman Maclean and UKOTCF colleagues for comments.

References

Ashmole, N.P. and Ashmole, M.J. (2000). *St Helena and Ascension Island: A Natural History*, Oswestry, Anthony Nelson.

Buden, D.W. (1987). *The Birds of the South Bahamas: An Annotated Checklist (Checklist No. 8)*, Tring, British Ornithologists' Union.

Burton, F. (2007). The Blue Iguana Recovery Programme. In Pienkowski, M., ed., *Biodiversity That Matters: A Conference on Conservation in UK Overseas Territories and Other Small Island Communities, Jersey, 6th to 12th October 2006*, London, UK Overseas Territories Conservation Forum, pp. 259–262, http://www.ukotcf.org.

Coffey, C. and Pienkowski, M. (1998). Biodiversity laws in the EC's associated territories. *Ecos*, **19**, 36–41.

Cooper, J. (2007). Topic 4: Integration of conservation and sustainable livelihoods: Marine, including fisheries. In Pienkowski, M., ed., *Biodiversity That Matters: A Conference on Conservation in UK Overseas Territories and Other Small Island Communities, Jersey, 6th to 12th October 2006*, London, UK Overseas Territories Conservation Forum, pp. 109–139, http://www.ukotcf.org.

Cortes, J. (2001). Welcoming Address: Conservation as viewed from a Gibraltar perspective, Calpe 2000: Linking the fragments of paradise. In Pienkowski, M., ed., *Proceedings of an International Conference on Environmental Conservation in Small Territories, 28th September to 1st October 2000, Gibraltar*, London, UK Overseas Territories Conservation Forum, pp. 11–15, http://www.ukotcf.org.

Cross, S. and Pienkowski, M. (eds.) (1998). Overlooking Britain's greatest biodiversity? – The Convention on Biological Diversity and the UK Overseas Territories. Report to WWF-UK by the UK Overseas Territories Conservation Forum. (available at http://www.ukotcf.org).

Foreign and Commonwealth Office (1999). *Partnership for Progress and Prosperity: Britain and the Overseas Territories* (Cmnd 4264), London, The Stationery Office.

Glasspool, A.F., Ward, J.A., De Silva, H., Sterrer, W. and Furbert, J. (2003). A Biodiversity Strategy and Action Plan for Bermuda – a recipe for success. In Pienkowski, M., ed., *A Sense of Direction: A Conference on Conservation in UK Overseas Territories and Other Small Island Communities,* London, UK Overseas Territories Conservation Forum, pp. 34–38. http://www.ukotcf.org.

Manco, B.N. (2007). Building the TCI Biodiversity Management Plan with the local community and putting it into practice: surveying biodiversity, designing trails, recruiting guides, encouraging crafts. In Pienkowski, M., ed., *Biodiversity That Matters: A Conference on Conservation in UK Overseas Territories and Other Small Island Communities, Jersey, 6th to 12th October 2006*, London, UK Overseas Territories Conservation Forum, pp. 154–168. http://www.ukotcf.org.

Oldfield, S. (1987). *Fragments of Paradise*, Oxford, Pisces Publications.

Pienkowski, M. (1998). Paradise mis-filed? *Ecos,* **19**, 1–11.

Pienkowski, M.W. (ed.) (2002). *Plan for Biodiversity Management and Sustainable Development around Turks and Caicos Ramsar Site, version 1.00*, Providenciales, Turks and Caicos National Trust (available at http://www.ukotcf.org).

Pienkowski, M.W. (ed.) (2005). *Review of Existing and Potential Ramsar Sites in UK Overseas Territories and Crown Dependencies (Final Report on Contract CR0294 to the UK Department of Environment, Food and Rural Affairs)*, London, UK Overseas Territories Conservation Forum, http://www.ukotcf.org.

Pienkowski, M. (2007). Review of the progress of implementation of the Charters, based on current work to develop a system to monitor this. In Pienkowski, M., ed., *Biodiversity That Matters: A Conference on Conservation in UK Overseas Territories and Other Small Island Communities, Jersey, 6th to 12th October 2006*, London, UK Overseas Territories Conservation Forum, pp. 54–72, http://www.ukotcf.org.

Pienkowski, M., Minter, R. and Spray, M. (eds.) (1998). Dependent Territories – overseas, overlooked? *Ecos,* **19**, 1–66.

Shirihai, H. (2002). *A Complete Guide to Antarctic Wildlife*, Degerby, Finland, Alula Press.

Stattersfield, A.J., Crosby, M.J., Long, A.J. and Wege, D.C. (1998). *Endemic Bird Areas of the World. (BirdLife Conservation Series No. 7)*, Cambridge, BirdLife International.

Wingate, D. (2001). Strategies for successful biodiversity conservation and restoration on small oceanic islands: some examples from Bermuda. In Pienkowski, M., ed., *Calpe 2000: Linking the Fragments of Paradise: Proceedings of an International Conference on Environmental Conservation in Small Territories, 28th September to 1st October 2000, Gibraltar,* London, UK Overseas Territories Conservation Forum, pp. 16–24, http://www.ukotcf.org.

Wragg, G. M. (1995). The fossil birds of Henderson Island, Pitcairn Group: natural turnover and human impact, a synopsis. In Benton, T.G. and Spencer, T., eds., *The Pitcairn Islands: Biogeography, Ecology and Prehistory,* London, Academic Press, pp. 405–414.

14

The United Kingdom's role in international conservation

N. Leader-Williams and A.M. Rosser

Summary

Britain supports very little globally important biodiversity, but many of its wild habitats have been heavily modified by people to produce a beautiful, varied and much cherished countryside. However, Britain and Britons have exerted a probably disproportionate impact and influence, both positive and negative, on international efforts to conserve global biodiversity, which this chapter seeks to overview. We focus on the impacts and influence of the political unit of the United Kingdom to conserving global biodiversity, and avoid overlap with other chapters in this book that focus on Britain's international conservation role in the UK Overseas Territories (Chapter 13), or in Europe (Chapter 12) and its coastal waters (Chapter 34). In terms of negative impacts, Britain is estimated to go into ecological debt for some 75% of the year, no doubt contributing disproportionately to ongoing global losses of biodiversity, through threats such as habitat loss and global warming.

In terms of positive impacts, Britain has provided considerable support to international efforts to conserve biodiversity as a result of its convening power, the conservation organisations and conventions it has helped establish, the research undertaken by its learned societies and scientific institutions, the role it plays in maintaining dead and live collections, its role in promoting research to define global priorities and its role in building national capacity and in raising public awareness.

Nevertheless, given its ecological debt, we argue that Britain could further mitigate its global footprint by engaging even more in international efforts to conserve global biodiversity, which probably poses the greatest challenge facing humankind in the twenty-first century.

Silent Summer: The State of Wildlife in Britain and Ireland, ed. Norman Maclean. Published by Cambridge University Press. © Cambridge University Press 2010.

Introduction

Many Britons treasure their countryside and its wildlife, and much has been done to promote its conservation value, as chapters in this book attest. However, if Britain submerged tomorrow under rising sea levels, there would be very little loss of global diversity!! Nevertheless, Britain and Britons have exerted a probably disproportionate influence, both positive and negative, on international efforts to conserve biodiversity elsewhere on Earth, which this chapter aims to overview. Britain's current role in global conservation has been shaped by several historical factors. These include: Britain's early settlement by Celts and Vikings, and by Anglo-Saxons and Normans; its later expansionist and colonial periods which saw large areas of the Earth's land surface coloured red; the nation's resulting wealth and its technological development as an industrial nation; the subsequent and currently unprecedented levels of consumption by a single species, largely organised socially in Western democracies such as that in Britain; and a post-colonial phase in which many Britons still view the world as their oyster.

Perhaps the most important precedents for Britain's impact on global conservation were set in the nineteenth and twentieth centuries. Advances in British science, warfare and business exploration led to expansion of British influence. Britain used resources from elsewhere that contributed to its current patterns of wealth, but that also brought recognition of the need to preserve those resources for future use, and of the importance of cataloguing new scientific discoveries. Like other colonial powers of the nineteenth and twentieth centuries, Britain used its own and others' natural resources to further fuel its colonial expansion, to contribute to development at home and abroad and to fight its corner in twentieth century wars. Equally, Britain has increasingly exported its human and technical expertise, exploited its knowledge base and used its convening power to take a lead on various fronts in global efforts to conserve biodiversity. Endowed with advantages in business, science and in speaking an internationally accepted language, Britian has assumed considerable responsibility for maintaining scientific collections, disseminating learning and teaching, and encouraging best practice. Nevertheless, Britain continues to owe a large debt to the global community, and could do more to recognise and repay the full costs for its use of global environmental services.

Although it is difficult to compartmentalise often inter-related contributions, this chapter seeks to overview some of the positive and negative contributions that Britain has made historically, and is currently making, to international efforts to conserve biodiversity under 10 main headings. First, it sets the relative importance of British biodiversity in its global context. Second, it discusses Britain's heavy global footprint in the context of the resources it consumes. Third, it outlines some international convening and leadership roles that Britain and Britons have contributed to international conservation. Fourth, it discusses Britain's role in establishing various non-government conservation organisations that have contributed to implementing or understanding international conservation needs. Fifth, it reviews some aspects of the historical and ongoing legacy of British learned societies, and how their contributions have helped underpin our understanding of global patterns of biodiversity and aspects of the current biodiversity crisis. Sixth, it considers the role of Britain's dead and living collections for taxonomy, and for captive breeding and reintroductions. Seventh, it describes some of the repositories of international conservation data held in Britain. Eighth, it considers some of the contributions of British scientists seeking to set conservation priorities and make conservation action more effective. Ninth, it reviews Britain's role in training and building capacity to conserve biodiversity. Finally, the chapter considers some of the funding contributions that Britain makes, and some of the opportunities that are presented for Britain to step up its involvement in international efforts to conserve global biodiversity. The treatment devoted to each issue is necessarily brief, and will hopefully not appear too selective, too eclectic or too superficial!

Unremarkable biodiversity in a global context

The United Kingdom comprises only 0.7% of the Earth's land surface and supports only 3% of the recorded global total of terrestrial species (Anon 1994). The United Kingdom is poor in terrestrial species richness and supports few endemics (Table 14.1), the most charismatic of which is the Scottish Crossbill (*Loxia scotica*). Likewise, the United Kingdom does not encompass any global priority region schemes, such as Conservation International's Hotspots or WWF's Global 200 Ecoregions (Olson and Dinerstein 1998; Myers *et al.* 2000).

Nevertheless, seas around the United Kingdom are potentially rich in marine biodiversity (Chapter 34), and support internationally important populations of the Grey Seal (*Halichoerus grypus*) and populations of other marine mammals, such as the Harbour Porpoise (*Phocoena phocoena*), Common Dolphin (*Delphinus delphis*) and Bottlenose Dolphin (*Tursiops truncates*). Britain is also very important for around 25 species of seabirds, including 90% of the world's Manx Shearwaters (*Puffinus puffinus*), 68% of Northern Gannets (*Morus bassanus*) and 60% of Great Skuas (*Catharacta skua*). Several species of globally important migratory birds have their flyways over Britain, and many use the extensive estuarine habitats around the British coast, along with important populations of wintering waders. Furthermore, around 80% of the world population of Pink-footed Goose (*Anser brachyrhynchus*) over-winter in Scotland and England (Anon 1994).

An island nation, Britain's development was based on its maritime power, which has greatly contributed to hardwood use in southern England and elsewhere. Chatham Naval Dockyard is estimated to have produced around 150 large wooden warships, each of which required in the region of 1500–2000 English Oak (*Quercus robur*) trees and the felling of some 75 acres of ancient Oak woodland. Despite such heavy use of

Table 14.1 *Numbers of terrestrial, freshwater and endemic species in the UK compared with recent global estimates of described species in major groups (based on Anon 1994)*

Group	British species	World species	Endemic species
Bacteria	Unknown	>4 000	
Viruses	Unknown	>5 000	
Protozoa	>20 000	>40 000	
Algae	>20 000	>40 000	
Fungi	>15 000	>70 000	
Ferns	80	>12 000	
Bryophytes	1000	>14 000	~20
Lichens	1500	>17 000	
Flowering plants	1400	>250 000	~43
Non-arthropod invertebrates	>3000	>90 000	9
Insects	22 500	>1 000 000	
Arthropods other than insects	>3000	>190 000	
Freshwater fish	38	>8 500	
Amphibians	6	>4 000	
Reptiles	6	>6 500	
Breeding birds	210	9 881	1
Wintering birds	180	–	
Mammals	48	4 327	
Total	88 000	1 770 000	73

Oak woodlands for ships, and also for timber-framed houses, clearance of land for agriculture is mostly responsible for the loss of British woodlands (Rackham 1986). Thus, around 90% of Britain's original ancient woodlands have been lost over the course of some 5000 years. Other native habitats have been similarly impacted, in some cases more recently. In the 50 years to 1984, 97% of unimproved species-rich grasslands were estimated lost, whilst lowland heath in southern England decreased by 70% and has become increasingly fragmented over the 150 years to 1980. Today, around 77% of Britain's land surface is farmed and just 10% is woodland, much of this comprising recently planted, non-native species. Nevertheless, Britain's varied topography and its mosaic of natural and human-modified habitats have created a countryside of great natural beauty that many Britons cherish, and that its conservation designations recognise through a network of Areas of Outstanding Natural Beauty. Nevertheless, Britain is arguably responsible for much more globally important impacts on biodiversity, some positive and some negative, both in the past and today, that reach well beyond its boundaries.

A heavy global footprint

Historically, colonial expansion led to Britain imposing development and systems of governance across many areas of the globe during the 1800s and early 1900s. This expansion also provided access to natural resources, such as hardwoods, that were not available on Britain's increasingly crowded islands, and to new products, such as coffee, tea, rubber and palm oil. In turn, this has led to increasing rates of tropical deforestation and land clearance to develop plantation agriculture (Williams 2003) that today still impact threatened rainforest species such as Orangutans (*Pongo* spp.) (Goossens *et al.* 2006). Initially, an extensive supply of coal fuelled the production of Britain's manufactured goods, and much of the hard labour and resulting pollution was felt on Britain's shores. However, environmental standards greatly improved in Britain during the latter half of the twentieth century. In a post-colonial, yet increasingly globalised, world, much of Britain's environmental impact has moved abroad to exporting countries that provide the source of raw materials, as they now strive to add value to their manufactured export goods in support of their own national development.

Even with its greatly reduced Empire, Britain's consumption patterns still have negative impacts way beyond its boundaries. Thus, a recent report adapted the Living Planet Index (Loh *et al.* 2005) to assess human impacts of development on the biosphere, and estimated that British consumption, in terms of its global footprint, is disproportionately high. Although, such measures are inherently unreliable, it is telling that current estimates suggest the UK goes into ecological debt, having exhausted its own production capacity, on 16 April each year (Simms *et al.* 2006)! Hence, for just under three-quarters of the year, British patterns of consumption are supported by the natural resources produced by other countries. If all countries consumed resources at the same rate as Britain, just over three planets would be needed to support the Earth's current human population. Therefore, British consumers should become increasingly more aware of the total costs of their current consumption patterns, of the legacy of previous generations and of their responsibilities towards the Earth, which the more positive contributions that Britain makes to global conservation efforts start to address. Among these positive contributions are an eclectic mix of often inter-related activities and institutions that are outlined in the sections that follow.

International convening and leadership

Modern approaches to conservation began in the late nineteenth century, when the world's first National Park, were established at Yosemite in 1867, followed soon after by Yellowstone in 1872 (Runte 1990, 1997). A Scot, John Muir (1938–14), is credited as the father of the national-parks movement for the seminal role he played in persuading

President Roosevelt to create these early national parks in areas of the United States Muir believed to be pristine wilderness. Nevertheless, the history of establishing protected areas across the globe goes back much further than the nineteenth century. An early example of using legal restrictions to protect important areas dates from 1079, when King William I (*c.* 1056–1100) set aside the New Forest to preserve his royal hunting grounds. Meanwhile, the protection of areas established by custom and managed locally through a system of usufruct rights has an even longer history. The wheel has now turned a full circle for the New Forest, which was created as England and Wales' 12th National Park in 2005, despite concerns among local users of the New Forest over possible diminution of commoner's rights.

Early in the modern era, conservation abroad was of greater priority to many Britons than was conservation at home. Britain's role in establishing international and national regimes to conserve global diversity was stimulated by five eminent Britons led by Sir Clement Lloyd Hill (1845–1913), when various European colonial powers, including the United Kingdom, opened negotiations to protect African wildlife in 1897. The resulting Convention Concerning the Preservation of Wild Animals, Birds and Fish in Africa (London Convention of 1900) aimed to prevent uncontrolled killing of wildlife and ensure the conservation of a wide diversity of wild species across Africa. The agreement proposed measures to protect 'useful' species, those of economic value and of interest to sportsmen, and rare species, as well as to allow appropriate reductions of pest species. The agreement also encouraged the establishment of reserves. However, the agreement never entered into force because most signatories did not ratify the treaty (Onslow 1938). Nevertheless, the London Convention of 1900 laid the basis for the Convention Relative to the Preservation of Fauna and Flora in their Natural State (the London Convention of 1933), which entered into force in 1936, with signatories that included countries outside Africa such as Belgium, India, Italy, Portugal, South Africa and the United Kingdom. While still focusing on 'useful' species, the London Convention of 1933 rejected the concept of nuisance species, but extended its remit to include plants. This convention became the first binding legal instrument to provide for creating protected areas such as national parks and nature reserves in Africa. Following the Second World War, many African nations met in 1953 to review the London Convention of 1933, but its eventual revision did not materialise until 1968, once many African states had gained their independence (van Heijnsbergen 1997).

The resulting African Convention on the Conservation of Nature and Natural Resources (African Convention of 1968) adopted a more holistic approach than either London Convention. Indeed, the African Convention of 1968 stressed the present and future interests of the African people and a common responsibility for environmental management, and moved away from focusing only on the conservation of useful species, to a broader consideration of conserving natural resources, including both its living and dead components. Therefore, the African Convention of 1968 was something of a precursor for modern international wildlife law, and probably sewed the seeds for the raft of Multilateral Environmental Agreements (MEAs) developed in the 1970s, including The Convention on Wetlands (Ramsar) 1971; the Convention in International Trade in Endangered Species of Wild Fauna and Flora (CITES) 1973; and the Convention on Migratory Species (CMS) 1979.

Since then the United Kingdom has consistently played a strong leadership role in the establishment and activities of all existing and more recently agreed MEAs. This has come about for several reasons, including: strong public interest at home; responsibility for the UK Overseas Territories (Chapter 13); and a unique position in terms of her key role in a range of important international fora, including the EU, the G8 and the Commonwealth, all of which give access to a number of influential networks. It is also helpful that English has become the default language for most of the business transacted away from the floor of conference rooms. Thus various Britons played a key role in formulating the Convention on Biological Diversity (CBD), which was agreed at the Rio Earth Summit in 1992 and is now the largest UN Convention, with a total of 192 state signatories. Consequently, CBD has unrivalled convening power, and plays a key role in setting biodiversity targets and framing global biodiversity policies. The intellectual contributions to the CBD in which Britons have subsequently played a key role have included: the adoption of an ecosystem approach at the 5th Conference of the Parties in 2000; and the formulation of the Addis Ababa Principles and Guidelines (AAPG) for the Sustainable Use of Biodiversity, adopted at the 7th Conference of the Parties in 2004. More recently, the UK has been heavily involved in supporting The Economics of Ecosystems and Biodiversity (TEEB) initiative, which is assessing the economic consequences of the global loss of biological diversity. In a global study, TEEB will analyse the global economic benefit of biological diversity and its associated ecosystem services, and assess the costs of the loss of biodiversity and the failure to take protective measures against the costs of effective conservation. This will be a key item for discussion at the 10th Conference of the Parties in 2010.

The United Kingdom's contribution to the activities of the MEAs has taken various forms. British Ministers have attended meetings in person and have used their presence not only to press for UK interests, but also to act as mediator and catalyst in helping to resolve other global issues, such as the debate in 1989 over the future of the ivory trade. British civil servants have taken a number of the key posts in all the main convention secretariats and related bodies, as well as in the EU. Meanwhile, the UK has played a crucial role in taking forward some of the supporting, smaller, agreements, such as the Global Tiger Forum (GTF), where the UK was for some time the only non-range state to attend, the Great Ape Survival Project (GrASP) and the Agreement on the Conservation of Albatrosses and Petrels (ACAP), all of which might well have collapsed without a strong and sustained input from the UK. At one CMS meeting in Nairobi in 2005, the UK provided the Chair of the Standing Committee, the Chair of the Scientific Committee and the Chair of one of the key Working Groups, as well as chairing the daily co-ordination meetings of the EU delegations attending the conference (and providing the Executive Secretary of the Convention). While this showed a strong leadership role it was probably too UK-oriented for the good of the convention, and the UK has since stepped back from some of these roles, while continuing to play a key role in the business of the convention. Finally, the United Kingdom has facilitated international conservation debate through hosting major events, including the Global Flyway Conference in 2005, and in providing a steady stream of financial support and British expertise for international conservation work, most notably through the Darwin Initiative (see below).

Meanwhile, the earlier London Conventions of 1900 and 1933 established the early basis for national wildlife legislation and the establishment of protected areas in many former British colonies in Africa and elsewhere. Thus, well-known national parks such as Kafue, Hwange and Luangwa were established in Africa, as was Corbett National Park in India, during the 1920s and 1930s. Forest reserves were also established throughout India and Malaysia during the 1930s. Many of these forest reserves have subsequently formed the basis for national parks designated after independence. In this way Britain and its colonial administration played an important role in developing the protected area estate of many countries. What is not so clear is the value of this legacy. Thus, many protected area networks were established in areas unsuitable for agriculture due to disease or poor soils (Leader-Williams *et al.* 1990), and many global networks of protected areas do not capture representative elements of biodiversity (Rodrigues *et al.* 2004). Another concern arises from the restrictive legislation and resettlement that comes with establishing protected areas and that in turn leads to the development of negative attitudes among local people towards conservation initiatives. Arguments over the effectiveness of protected areas, and trade-offs between conservation and development, now wage back and forth. Some studies indicate that protected areas have served to reduce habitat and species loss (Bruner *et al.* 2001), while others argue that the disenfranchisement of local people is often associated with problems of stewardship that has led to loss of animal species (Borgerhoff-Mulder and Copollilo 2005).

Establishing conservation organisations

Britons have played a critical role in helping establish voluntary and non-government conservation organisations (NGOs) to support international efforts to conserve biodiversity, whether through implementing direct conservation action or promoting understanding that informs policy. British naturalists and American politicians founded the world's first international conservation organisation in 1903, in order to stem the losses of southern Africa's large mammal populations. Initially known as the Society for the Preservation of the Wild Fauna of the Empire, the Society was the forerunner of the present Fauna and Flora International (FFI), which has evolved to promote a much more sophisticated twenty-first century mission 'to conserve threatened species and ecosystems worldwide, choosing solutions that are sustainable, based on sound science and that take account of human needs' (Adams 2004). The loss of African wildlife also stimulated another Briton, Sir Julian Huxley (1887–1975), then Director General of UNESCO, to work with others to found IUCN, the International Union for the Conservation of Nature, in 1948, to bring together governments and NGOs to work for the conservation of natural resources across the globe. British influence in Africa waned as a wave of independence movements swept the continent in the late 1950s. In turn, this created something of a vacuum that led to a lack of progress in implementing provisions of the London Convention of 1933, and that allowed the influence of non-governmental conservation organisations to burgeon. The Britons, Sir Peter Scott (1909–89) and Sir Julian Huxley, together with some of their business contemporaries, were instrumental in establishing the World Wildlife Fund (WWF) in 1961, in part to help IUCN to fund emerging conservation needs and crises. Furthermore, Scott's artistic skills gave WWF the Giant Panda, *Ailuropoda melanoleuca*, perhaps the most distinctive and enduring logo in global conservation.

WWF, now known simply by its acronym, has since become a very successful membership organisation that both works in Britain and raises funds for international work as prioritised by WWF national offices, independent of IUCN. Meanwhile, IUCN has itself grown into a large inter governmental organisation outside the aegis of the UN, whose programmatic work is promoted through six commissions, supported by a wide range of inputs from an extensive volunteer network. Among IUCN's current key products are the influential Red Lists of Threatened Species, which grew out of the earlier Red Data Books for birds and mammals initially proposed and developed by Peter Scott (Fitter and Fitter 1987), as the need to prioritise conservation action became more pressing. Now compiled through collaborative inputs from a global network of scientists and specialists, Red Lists covering the different taxonomic groups are a widely used awareness-raising and lobbying tool. Indeed, the Red Lists now underpin a barometer of the state of global biodiversity and form the basis of much national and international legislation to protect species from anthropogenic threats. Red Lists are now also being used to support efforts to assess whether or not the CBD's 2010 Biodiversity Target is being met, as discussed further below.

Birds have played a prominent role in Britain's national conservation efforts, and Britain has exported this expertise to international efforts to conserve avian and wider biodiversity. British organisations that promote bird conservation range from Peter Scott's specialist Wildfowl and Wetlands Trust to Birdlife International. The Royal Society for the Protection of Birds (RSPB) was founded in 1889 and is one of Britian's largest membership organisations, currently with over 1 million members. The RSPB brings great experience, as well as considerable convening and fundraising power, and highly developed advocacy skills, to its international work. Birdlife International, originally established as the International Council for the Preservation of Birds in 1934, has supported the development of a global partnership of national organisations that collate scientific information on the status of bird species, to assess their threat status, and to prioritise species for conservation action. The policies of the Birdlife Partnership are based on sound science and analysis, and the network functions to support exchange of knowledge and expertise in conserving birds. More recently, Plantlife and Buglife have been established to redress the taxonomic imbalance and cater for a growing public interest in species other than birds. Plantlife has grown rapidly and developed an international profile through contributing to the Global Strategy for Plant Conservation (GSPC) along with Botanic Gardens Conservation International (BGCI).

In terms of understanding the human face of conservation and trade-offs between conservation and development, the London-based International Institute for Environment and Development (IIED) has played a significant role in informing Britain's approach to conservation and development policy through its syntheses and reports, often funded by Britain's bilateral donor, the Department for International Development (DfID). IIED was established in 1971 by the economist and policy advisor Barbara Ward (1914–81), and was amongst the first international organisations to link environment and development, and to question the widely accepted global policies among conservationists of forming exclusive protected areas. One key output was the Evaluating Eden project that researched the socio-economic aspects of conservation policy and practice, in particular by examining the effectiveness of community-based approaches as an alternative to protected-area approaches (Roe *et al.* 2000). More recently, IIED has taken a key role in examining links between poverty alleviation and biodiversity conservation, and in particular its possible contribution to meeting the UN's Millenium Development Goals to ending poverty by 2015.[1]

The scientific legacy of learned societies

Conservation needs and action should be informed by research, to which Britain has also made a distinctive contribution, through the historical and ongoing legacy of its learned societies. The world's oldest biological society was founded in 1788, as The Linnaean Society of London following purchase of the collections of the Swede Carl Gustav Linnaeus (1707–78), developer of the binomial classification system upon which the taxonomy of global biodiversity is now built. The later Victorian passion for collection, science, exploration and learning produced seminal figures during the nineteenth century, including Charles Darwin (1809–82) and Alfred Russell Wallace (1823–1913), who co-discovered the theory of evolution by natural selection and first presented their findings on evolution in the rooms of the Linnaean Society in 1858. Wallace's later work on the distribution of species in the Malay Archipelago led to identification of the Wallace Line, which contributed to him earning the title of the father of biogeography, another science that underpins modern attempts to conserve biodiversity. In the early twentieth century, emphasis and interest led to the founding of the world's oldest ecological society, the British Ecological Society (BES) in 1913. Following Darwin's lead as a fieldworker, the founding figures of British ecology

[1] http://www.undp.org/mdg: accessed on 27 November 2009.

included Arthur Tansley (1871–1955) and Charles Elton (1900–91), who established the tradition of detailed observational studies, field trials and experiments that was spread around the globe by biologists and foresters of the colonial service.

The Royal Society is Britain's scientific academy and was founded in 1660. The Royal Society elects eminent scientists, engineers and technologists to its fellowship. Our understanding of the environment, and of the processes of evolution and extinction, was initially led by scientists such as Darwin, Wallace and Henry Bates (1825–92), all Fellows of the Royal Society. For much of the twentieth century, the British scientific establishment was arguably slow to recognise the importance of the practical and applied science of conservation biology, instead perhaps subsuming it under other disciplines, such as ecology. However, a Royal Society volume on extinctions (Lawton and May 1995) helped underpin claims of the seriousness of the current extinction crisis. Since then, the Royal Society has held a series of meetings, the first on measuring biodiversity (Crane *et al.* 2003), the second on developing indicators to measure progress towards the internationally agreed 2010 Biodiversity Target (Balmford *et al.* 2005). Currently, the Royal Society is also promoting conservation through its public outreach series. It has recently established an International Science Policy Centre, one of whose themes will be climate change, environment and energy.

Britain's major zoos are also associated with learned societies. The best known is London Zoo, more formally called the Zoological Society of London (ZSL), founded by Sir Stamford Raffles (1781–1826) in 1826. ZSL has been a force for promoting knowledge related to conservation, both through its government-supported research institute, through its collections and publications, and through its growing contributions to *in situ* conservation. Other zoological collections that are based around learned societies include The Royal Zoological Society of Scotland, which was founded in 1909, and then opened Edinburgh Zoo in 1913, while Chester Zoo is associated with the North of England Zoological Society, founded in 1934.

The model of a learned society focusing on natural history and conservation has been exported internationally. For example, the world-renowned Bombay Natural History Society was founded in India in 1883 by a group of Indian and British naturalists. The Society is credited with undertaking in 1911, what may be the first collaborative natural history study in the world, a survey of the mammals of India undertaken by its membership that resulted in the collection of over 50 000 specimens and the publication of associated research. Likewise, the former East Africa and Uganda Natural History Society, was established in Kenya in 1909, by a group of amateur scientists and naturalists. The first museum room was opened in 1910 and moved in 1929 to its current site as the Museums of Kenya. The Society continues to produce a journal and bulletin, but changed its name at the start of the millennium to Nature Kenya.

In terms of scientific publishing, the BES has provided an international forum for scientists throughout the world to publish in its respected journals (*Journal of Ecology*, *Journal of Animal Ecology* and *Journal of Applied Ecology*). More recently, scientific publishing in conservation and related disciplines has burgeoned, and many journals have sprung up around the world. In Britain, these have included the international journals, *Biological Conservation* and *Biodiversity and Conservation*, founded in 1968 and 1992, respectively. Of the more practice-oriented conservation journals, FFI's journal *Oryx* is deservedly widely read by an international audience, while ZSL has recently launched a new journal, *Animal Conservation*. Among overseas organisations that produce their own journals, the *Journal of the Bombay Natural History Society* and the *African Journal of Ecology* are excellent sources of local information and knowledge.

Dead and living collections

Britain supports world-class collections of scientific specimens, both dead and alive. These are available largely thanks to Britain's history of global exploration and the Victorian passion for collecting and cataloguing specimens of natural history. The Natural History Museum (NHM) and the Royal Botanic Gardens Kew (RBGK) are amongst the world's premier collections of natural-history specimens and of scholarship associated with taxonomy. Furthermore, some holders of living collections have been at the forefront of pioneering reintroductions to establish locally extinct species that may have been held in captive breeding situations.

Collections and taxonomy

The NHM houses over 70 million reference specimens of biological and geological importance, collected over a period of 400 years. The NHM also supports probably the best natural-history library in the world, comprising over 1 million books, 20 000 scientific journals and 500 000 works of art, among which the earliest book dates from 1469. The NHM is gradually extending its online directory of collections to make its material more accessible throughout the world. Over 300 scientists work at the NHM, where the research is arranged around a series of themes related to conserving biodiversity. In addition to collaborating with scientists from institutions around the world to further knowledge on its research themes, the NHM also runs a globally active consulting and identification service.

Meanwhile, the Royal Botanic Gardens at Kew (RBGK) and Edinburgh (RBGE) curate some 5.5 million vascular plant and 600 000 fungi specimens, including around 400 000 type specimens (Anon 1994). RBGK holds the world's largest collection of living and dead fungi and was inscribed as a World Heritage Site in 2003. Of its 680 staff, around 60% are specialist scientists or horticulturalists. A recent review of RBGK's past work to allow development of a forward-looking science strategy noted that 'Kew's strengths lie in the general breadth of its collections, specifically across the tropics, particularly in parts of Brazil and the Old World, and in the breadth and depth of its research programmes in monocots and several major eudicot families.'[2] RBGK plays a major role in global plant conservation through its taxonomic work to understand the distribution of plant diversity, through collating information on the value and uses of plants in its Economic Botany Unit, and undertaking major syntheses of plant biodiversity information from around the world. Outputs, such as global checklists and provisional conservation assessments, are directly relevant to meeting the CBD's Global Strategy for Plant Conservation (GSPC) targets and will also help monitor progress towards the 2010 Biodiversity Target.

In terms of arboreta, botanic gardens and living plant collections, Britain supports the world's third largest number of accessions in cultivation, which are mostly exotic plants, including over 4000 specimens of orchids, 2300 specimens of threatened trees, with a further 35 000 woody, wild-collected plants recorded in the National Trust Plant Collection catalogue. In addition, many plants of economic importance are held at the Commonwealth Potato Collection, Barley Collection, Soft-Fruit Collection, the National Fruit Collection, the Vegetable Gene Bank and the Pea Gene Bank. There are also important collections of cultures of cells, viruses, bacteria, fungi and yeasts. The Millenium Seed Bank project run at Wakehurst Place by RGBK aims, with partners around the world, to collect and store seed from 10% of the world's most threatened and useful plants by 2010. As this deadline approaches, a new project aims to increase its work to secure 25% of the world's plants by 2020. Botanic Gardens Conservation International (BGCI), with its 700 members in 118 countries, and its headquarters at Kew, supports botanic gardens worldwide to undertake conservation work, and also aims to catalyse conservation action for plants by implementing the GSPC.

Members of the British and Irish Association of Zoos and Aquaria (BIAZA) make significant contributions to field conservation world wide. The UK's Zoo Licensing Act was used as a model for the EU's Zoos Directive, providing more evidence of the UK helping set an international conservation agenda. Both the EU Directive and the UK Act require that all licensed zoos make a contribution to conservation, whether directly in the field, or through education to raise awareness of the need for conservation. A 2001 survey showed that member collections of BIAZA supported 177 field conservation projects in 62 countries, and spent over £10 million from 1997–2000 (Leader-Williams *et al.* 2007). Members also supplied husbandry and management skills, staff and equipment for habitat and species conservation and essential materials for local education and awareness programmes in developing countries. Zoos such as London, Jersey, Chester, Marwell, Paignton and Bristol are well known for their pioneering conservation work. However, all members contribute to BIAZA's conservation objectives by raising awareness and essential funds for conservation at home and abroad. Zoos often form partnerships to increase their ability to conduct *in situ* work.

---

[2] http://www.kew.org/science/directory/strategy/in_depth.html: accessed on 27 November 2009.

Captive breeding and reintroductions

The 11th Duke of Bedford (1858–1940) laid the foundation for the approach of captive breeding and reintroduction of large species of social ungulates when he established a captive herd of Père David's Deer (*Elaphurus davidianus*) at Woburn Abbey. A small founder group was whisked out of China before they became completely extinct in their native country during the late 1880s. Once the species was lost from China, all the remaining captive individuals were brought to Woburn to establish a breeding programme. As numbers increased, Père David's Deer were once again redistributed amongst different collections, until it was safe to attempt reintroduction. Initially released into a fenced area in China in 1985, Père David's Deer have since increased and have now been released from the original enclosure (Zhigang and Harris 2008). Similar approaches were followed by various organisations, including the then Fauna Preservation Society (FPS) now under Fauna & Flora International (FFI) and ZSL in capturing the last remaining Arabian Oryx (*Oryx leucoryx*), breeding them in captivity at Phoenix Zoo initially and then reintroducing them to Oman in the 1970s (Stanley Price 1989). Since then, ZSL, Marwell Zoological Park and others have worked with local partners to breed and reintroduce several species of desert antelopes to various Arabian and North African countries, as well as to re-establish Przewalski Horses (*Equus ferus przewalskii*) in Mongolia. Despite the high profile and huge investment in many of these ungulate reintroduction programmes, their long-term success is by no means assured, as the sad case of the once successful reintroduction of Arabian Oryx to a former World Heritage Site in Oman testifies.[3]

Other UK-based zoological collections have been active in developing reintroduction science and practice, notable among which was the pioneering work of Jersey Zoo. Gerald Durrell (1925–95) fostered a passion for the approach of combining *ex situ* captive breeding with captive breeding in range through what might now be recognised as an ecosystem-based approach. In conjunction with the Mauritius Wildlife Foundation, the Durrell, formerly the Jersey, Wildlife Preservation Trust, has rescued the Mauritius Kestrel (*Falco punctatus*), Pink Pigeon (*Nesoenas mayeri*), Echo Parakeet (*Psittacula eques echo*) and Rodrigues Fody (*Foudia flavicans*), all of which were close to extinction with only a few pairs remaining in the wild. The same partners were also responsible for restoring Round Island's ecosystem, including the removal of invasive animal species, and the propagation and replanting of native plants. In Jersey, Durrell has also been successful at breeding several species in captivity for the first time, including Malagasy primates, birds and reptiles, Round Island reptiles, Mascarene bats, Caribbean birds and reptiles and giant jumping rats. In the country of origin, Durrell has worked with local partners to notch up breeding firsts for: the Echo Parakeet and Rodrigues Fody in Mauritius, the Pygmy Hog (*Porcula salvania*) in India, as well as the Ploughshare Tortoise (*Astrochelys yniphora*), Side-necked Turtle (*Erymnochelys madagascariensis*) and Flat-tailed Tortoise (*Pyxis planicauda*) in Madagascar.

---

[3] http://whc.unesco.org/en/news/362: accessed 27 November 2009.

ZSL has also been instrumental in developing invertebrate reintroduction programmes to restore species of *Partula* snails to the Society Islands, Tahiti and Morea in the Pacific. Since 1995, ZSL has co-ordinated 15 collaborating organisations in a breeding programme for 25 species of *Partula*. These tree snails are unique in giving birth to live young, rather than to eggs, as occurs in all other snail genera known to date. The genus *Partula* presented a remarkable example of adaptive radiation that was well known to biologists of the 1800s and 1900s. In the 1950s, the predatory Rosy Snail (*Euglandina rosea*) was introduced to the islands as a biological control agent for a plague of introduced Giant African Land Snails (*Achatina fulica*). Instead, the Rosy Snail attacked the native snails, resulting in the extirpation and even extinction of many species of *Partula*. The *Partula* were rescued and bred at ZSL and other zoos. An experimental introduction to semi-native habitat was undertaken in the Polynesian palms in the glasshouses at Royal Botanic Gardens Kew (RBGK) (Pearce-Kelly *et al.* 1995), before reintroducing the snails to their original home!

Repositories of international data

Cambridge is now home to a number of international conservation organisations that maintain globally important data sets. Among well-known sources of data used by conservationists are those held at the United Nations Environment Programme's World Conservation Monitoring Centre (UNEP-WCMC). WCMC was initially established in 1979 as part of the IUCN Secretariat, and in 1988 became an independent organisation jointly managed by IUCN, UNEP and WWF. Since 2000, UNEP-WCMC has been an executive agency of UNEP that collaborates with the UK-registered charity, WCMC 2000. UNEP-WCMC undertakes biodiversity assessment as well as supporting policy development and implementation. UNEP-WCMC currently hosts the World Database on Protected Areas (incorporating the UN List of Protected Areas) in conjunction with the IUCN World Commission on Protected Areas, which is now searchable via the web.[4] UNEP-WCMC also manages the CITES trade database and provides a variety of information on species through the EU/CITES species database acting as a major repository of biodiversity data.[5,6,7] UNEP-WCMC works with several multi-lateral environment agreements, governments, business and NGOs to manage its data holdings so as to provide information and analytical tools for decision-makers.

In addition to specific reports and atlases, UNEP-WCMC has also produced a number of blockbuster biodiversity assessments. For example, WCMC managed the Global Biodiversity Assessment that compiled the work of 1500 scientists to update

[4] http://www.wdpa.org/Default.aspx: accessed 27 November 2009.
[5] http://www.unep-wcmc.org/citestrade/trade.cfm: accessed 27 November 2009.
[6] http://www.cites.org/eng/resources/species.html: accessed 27 November 2009.
[7] http://quin.unep-wcmc.org/eu/taxonomy/: accessed 27 November 2009.

available knowledge of global biological diversity at the ecosystem, species and genetic levels (Heywood 1995). Likewise, WCMC staff compiled *Global Biodiversity: Earth's Living Resources in the 21st Century*, which assessed information on the health of the biosphere at the start of the new millenium (Groombridge and Jenkins 2001). UNEP-WCMC has also contributed to the production of UNEP's GEO 1–4 series from 1997–2008, which analyse environmental change, causes, impacts and policy responses (UNEP 2008). They have also hosted the Secretariat for the Conditions Working Group of the Millenium Ecosystem Assessment (2005).

TRAFFIC International was initially established in 1976 as a specialist group of the Species Survival Commission, originally based in the UK and USA, but chaired from the UK. On becoming independent in 1990, TRAFFIC has since grown into an international organisation with over 100 staff and nine regional programmes co-ordinated by the Cambridge-based TRAFFIC International. From its initial aim to provide a 'data bank' on wildlife trade, TRAFFIC has increased its expertise and operational focus to provide a technically sound independent source of information, analysis and action to address unsustainable wildlife trade, in particular to inform the deliberations of CITES (Broad 2001).

Birdlife International is also located in Cambridge near to WCMC, and maintains the premier collection of data on birds worldwide, from which it produces the Red List of Threatened Birds, and regional syntheses of the state of birds to highlight their conservation requirements (Collar 2001). Also associated with this complex of data repositories is the office of the IUCN Red List Programme that manages the data for, and checks updates to, the IUCN Red List of Threatened Species.

Research to set global conservation priorities

Faced with the daunting task of averting the sixth mass extinction crisis (Lawton and May 1995), British scientists have spent much effort on research to prioritise areas or species in greatest need of conservation action. Such research has encompassed setting priorities for conservation, establishing indicators, measuring the impacts of conservation actions and taking an interdisciplinary approach to conservation.

Peter Scott's original idea of Red Data Books of Threatened Species were given much needed scientific rigour and objectivity through research and development led by scientists at ZSL and IUCN, together with a number of British academics (Mace and Lande 1992; Mace *et al.* 2008). Theoretically based population models were subsequently refined through a series of broad consultative meetings organised by the Species Survival Commission of IUCN. These consultations provided the bedrock for the first complete assessment of all birds by Birdlife International, when it produced the first Red List of Threatened Birds using the new IUCN categories (Collar 1994). This was followed soon after by complete assessments by IUCN of mammals (Baillie and Groombridge 1996) and of trees (Oldfield *et al.* 1998).

While species are the building blocks of ecosystems, a species-by-species approach to conservation would not be cost-effective. A Briton-led team proposed focusing on biodiversity Hotspots, a conservation approach that was adopted and further developed with colleagues at the US-based Conservation International (CI) (Myers *et al.* 2000). CI has cleverly marketed hotspots as a means of prioritising conservation action, and raised large funds ($94 million have now been disbursed since 2000) from organisations such as the French Development Agency, the Global Environment Facility, the Government of Japan, the John D. and Catherine T. MacArthur Foundation and the World Bank. At Birdlife's Cambridge-based headquarters, scientists have prioritised their conservation efforts by promoting the use of Endemic Bird Areas, to focus scarce resources to protect the most biologically valuable species and habitats (Bibby *et al.* 1992). Furthermore, Durrell (Durrell Wildlife Preservation Trust DWPT) scientists have developed Topspots to rationalise their organisation's focus on mountain-top and island species (Fa and Funk 2007). All these global priority region schemes are based on an assessment of the numbers of endemic species in a given area and, in the case of Hotspots and Topspots, of the threats that their habitats face. More recently, Zoological Society of London (ZSL) have developed a means of quantifying genetic uniqueness and combining this with threat levels to prioritise species for conservation action, through EDGE species that are evolutionarily distinct (ED) and globally endangered (GE). The EDGE approach has allowed ZSL to develop a conservation programme that is itself distinct, fulfils its mission and fills a separate niche from other organisations (Isaac *et al.* 2007).

At the opposite extreme, in the Earth's coldspots, the frozen wastes of Antarctica have always fired the British public's imagination. It is not only the coldest, windiest and most remote continent on Earth, but also the highest and driest. Britain and Britons have played a key role in polar research and collaboration, perhaps most notably through their ~200-year involvement in Antarctica. Captain James Cook (1728–79) first crossed the Antarctic Circle in 1774 and came across icebergs that suggested the presence of a southern continent, later confirmed through expeditions of the heroic age led by Captain Robert Scott (1868–1912), Sir Ernest Shackleton (1874–1922), Sir Vivian Fuchs (1908–99) and others. Some of Britain's early impacts in the Antarctic were negative through participating in unsustainable whaling practices during the 1800s and 1900s. However, increasing losses of great whales in the Southern Ocean, documented by the Discovery Expeditions, and elsewhere led to the establishment of the International Whaling Commission with its secretariat in Cambridge. Ongoing land-based research started by the early expeditions and developed by organisations such as the Falkland Islands Dependencies, and now the British Antarctic Survey (BAS), led to increasing co-operation through the International Geophysical Year (IGY) of 1957–58, a multi-national research programme of co-ordinated geophysical observations undertaken by 67 nations. IGY highlighted the opportunity to establish bases on Antarctica and engage in scientific co-operation without conflicts arising over the different, sometimes overlapping, claims of sovereignty over the continent. In turn, this gave rise to the Antarctic Treaty, which was signed in 1959 by the

12 countries whose scientists had been active in Antarctica during IGY, of which seven, comprising Argentina, Australia, Chile, France, New Zealand, Norway and the United Kingdom, had territorial claims over parts of the continent. The Treaty came into effect in June 1961, and the 45 current signatories gather annually at the Antarctic Treaty Consultative Meeting. The value of investing in Antarctic research was perhaps best demonstrated through the discovery of the increasingly large hole in the ozone layer by BAS scientists (Farman *et al.* 1985) that led to a worldwide ban in the use of CFCs, an important contribution to efforts to mitigate global warming. More recently, long-term research on top predators in the Southern Ocean by BAS has played a major role in developing an ecosystem approach to managing the oceans under the Convention for the Conservation of Antarctic Marine Living Resources (CCAMLR). Meanwhile, campaigns run by Birdlife and informed by this science have stimulated action to address the losses of albatrosses to long line fishing,[8] including through Agreement on Conservation of Albatrosses and Petrels (ACAP), agreed under the Bonn Convention.

More recently, the UK has provided ongoing leadership in the climate-change debate through recent research legislation and target setting. A British-led team documented that the effects of climate change upon global biodiversity was a more serious threat than had been hitherto recognised (Thomas *et al.* 2004). The British Government commissioned a review of the Economics of Climate Change (Stern 2007) that sought to quantify the effect of climate change and global warming on the global economy. Britain was the first country to set a legally binding, long-term framework for reducing its carbon emissions, in April 2009. Carbon-emissions trading has increased dramatically since it was first attempted experimentally in the US in the 1990s. Carbon trading comprises emissions trading specifically for carbon dioxide and is one of the ways that countries can meet their obligations under the Kyoto Protocol to reduce carbon emissions and thereby mitigate global warming. With the support of green NGOs, business in the UK have come out strongly in support of emissions trading as a key tool to mitigate climate change, while the London financial marketplace has established itself as the centre of the carbon finance market. Nevertheless, considerable challenges remain in attempts to encourage carbon markets to reduce biodiversity losses through avoided deforestation (Swingland 2003).

Given the increasing threats facing biodiversity, an emerging issue for conservationists is to document the local impact of conservation actions and funding (Leader-Williams and Albon 1988). Following the lead of medical researchers, British conservation scientists have promoted research that seeks to move conservation practice onto a more informed and logical basis in which the success of different actions are evaluated in terms of their positive or negative impacts on biodiversity. Strategies proven to be successful can then be replicated with expectations of similar success in other areas (see Sutherland 2000; Pullin and Knight 2001; Sutherland *et al.* 2004). To assess success and compile evidence, it is necessary that conservation interventions

---

[8] http://www.surfbirds.com/news/albatross.html: accessed 27 November 2009.

are designed in such a way that outcomes can be measured. Thus, the Cambridge Conservation Forum, a novel group comprising the range of conservation organisations based in Cambridge and one of the world's leading universities (Kapos *et al.* 2008), has contributed to a transatlantic initiative to help practitioners design, manage and monitor good conservation projects, in conjunction with the US-based Conservation Measures Partnership.[9]

The Red List Index, and the Sampled Red List Index, have since been developed by Birdlife International, and latterly ZSL, and use sequential assessments of species threat data to measure the success of conservation interventions at a global scale (Butchart *et al.* 2004; Butchart *et al.* 2005; Butchart *et al.* 2007). These indices will provide a means of assessing trends in the status of biodiversity, functioning like the FTSE index of leading companies, and thus give decision-makers an indication of our progress in combating species loss and making progress in reaching the CBD's 2010 Biodiversity Target: to significantly reduce the rate of loss of biodiversity by 2010 in order to contribute to poverty alleviation and for the benefit of all life on Earth. Meanwhile, in 1997, WWF together with WCMC developed the Living Planet Index to measure the changing state of biodiversity, by compiling time-series data on a broadly representative sample of 3000 populations from 1100 species from terrestrial, freshwater and marine habitats (Loh *et al.* 2005). WCMC also originally contributed to calculations of the ecological footprint that now aims to compare the impact of nations with different consumption patterns on the biosphere (Wackernagel *et al.* 2002). The slow progress in achieving positive conservation outcomes has been investigated by British researchers and is often attributed to a lack of attention to socio-economic issues (Adams 2004, 2008), an inability to recognise the full costs of ecosystem services (Balmford *et al.* 2008) and a need for interdisciplinary studies (Milner-Gulland and Rowcliffe 2007).

Training and awareness

Key long-term goals for conservation are to ensure that the general public in developed nations is aware of the consequences of their patterns of over-consumption, while capacity to conserve biodiversity is built among nationals of biodiversity-rich countries poor in financial resources, in which Britain plays a leadership role.

Training to build national capacity

Britain has a long history of training foresters and fisheries experts, firstly for the colonial service and latterly to build global capacity to conserve biodiversity. The former

---

[9] http://www.conservationmeasures.org: accessed 27 November 2009.

Oxford Forestry Institute and forestry departments at the universities of Edinburgh, Aberdeen and Bangor trained countless colonial officers. Currently 18 universities run dedicated postgraduate programmes on aspects of conservation and produce a conservative estimate of ~300 graduates per year, many of whom are home students. However, the Durrell Institute of Conservation and Ecology (DICE) was founded at the University of Kent to focus on capacity building of international postgraduate students (Swingland 1995), and has trained over 500 alumni from 80 countries since 1989 (Swingland 1995). In addition, the more specialist and long-established MSc in Plant Genetic Resources at Birmingham University has trained over 400 students in 30 years. Meanwhile, the more recent MScs run by Imperial College and the NHM, and by the University of Edinburgh and RBGE help keep the fundamental sciences of animal and plant taxonomy afloat with trained personnel, of which the taxonomy profession is in short supply (Mace 2004). International MSc students following programmes of study in Britain can apply for the Foreign and Commonwealth Office's (FCO) Chevening Scholarships through the British Council, while international research students from former British colonies can apply for Commonwealth Scholarships and Fellowships offered by the Commonwealth Scholarship Commission.

Raising public awareness

The BBC's Natural History Unit is another jewel in the crown of British-based institutions that raise interest in natural history and awareness of the need for conservation. Several well-known collectors have made the transition to broadcasting, including Gerald Durrell and Sir David Attenborough. The Unit is well known for its carefully crafted films and blockbuster series on the environment and natural history (e.g. Attenborough 1979; Fothergill 2006).

However, there has been some concern that much of the Unit's early work did not challenge viewers with the conservation message, which Filmmakers for Conservation (FFC) has been set up to address.[10] However, a careful balance needs to be struck between entertaining a large audience and raising awareness of the conservation issues, without turning off the audience.

Likewise, funds have not been available to show the BBC Natural History Unit's films on television in many of the countries that support rich biodiversity. Another British-based organisation, the Great Ape Film Initiative (GAFI), aims to address this last concern by taking films back to the countries and communities who actually live with the wildlife. The BBC has since agreed to screen some of its films in selected areas of the world. In addition to film screenings, GAFI has also helped a local community in Indonesia to make a film calling on the President of Indonesia to address their conservation concerns.

---

[10] http://www.filmmakersforconservation.org/: accessed 27 November 2009.

Funding shortfalls

The conservation funding allocated to biodiversity conservation is rarely thought to be sufficient (Leader-Williams and Albon 1988; James *et al.* 2001), irrespective of whether that funding is spent effectively. According to the Joint Nature Conservation Committee (JNCC), the United Kingdoms total public sector spending on biodiversity was £525 million in 2008,[11] an welcome increase of 112% since 2001, whilst GDP has increased by. However, a recent report on the funding of conservation concluded that, while the Government spends an estimated £294 million per annum in pursuit of the UK's Habitat Action Plan, this is viewed as an under-spend of £27.6 million pa (Morling 2008).

Likewise, the estimated £2 million pa spent on conservation in the UK Overseas Territories is also felt to be woefully inadequate, and it is estimated that an additional £14 million pa is required (Morling 2008). So if the United Kingdom is judged to be under-spending on its own biodiversity, how is it doing in a global context?

As a developed country with a relatively high GDP, Britain makes proportionate contributions to development and environment issues and governance globally, compared with poorer countries. Thus, the UK government contributes financially to global conservation efforts through its own bilateral assistance agreements, through UN agencies and conventions such as the UK's voluntary contribution to CITES, and through multilateral aid to conservation projects through the CBD's Global Environment Facility (GEF). Such spending is one way to assess the national priority accorded to conserving global biodiversity within the UK public sector, and such funds are essential to implement the CBD in developing countries. In 2007/8, UK government funding for global biodiversity totalled £54 million, comprising support to GEF, support from DEFRA for the Darwin Initiative for the Survival of Species, and other schemes such as the Flagship Species Fund, the Overseas Territories Environmental Programme (OTEP) and the FCO's Global Opportunities Fund. While public sector spending by the United Kingdom on global conservation has shown a very welcome increase of 85% in real terms since 2000/1 (Figure 14.1), the UK's spending on global conservation is only 10% of public-sector funding on national conservation efforts. In absolute terms, this suggests that the United Kingdom does not come anywhere near meeting the scale of the unaccounted environmental costs arising from Britons' patterns of over-consumption, nor recognising differences in the relative importance of global vs. national biodiversity (Table 14.1). For example, if OECD countries agreed to meet half the costs of maintaining the global network of terrestrial and marine protected areas, then the British Government would need to find an additional £257.4 million pa. This additional spend to meet our own home-based conservation pledges, as well as growing international obligations would represent just 0.04% of planned Government expenditure for 2008/9 before the credit crunch of October 2008 (Morling 2008).

---

[11] http://www.jncc.gov.uk/page-4251: accessed 27 November 2009.

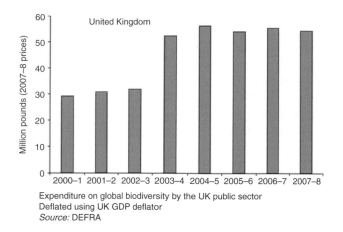

Expenditure on global biodiversity by the UK public sector
Deflated using UK GDP deflator
Source: DEFRA

Figure 14.1 UK Government funding for global biodiversity from 2000–1 to 2007–8.

Nevertheless, the Darwin Initiative illustrates a strategic approach to assisting countries that are rich in biodiversity, but poor in financial resources to meet their objectives under one or more of the three major biodiversity Conventions: CBD, CITES and CMS, through the funding of collaborative projects that draw on UK biodiversity expertise.[12] Since its launch in 1992, the Darwin Initiative has funded 672 projects to the tune of £73 million, partnering with 862 organisations in 148 host countries, and with 213 British organisations. Funding from the Darwin Initiative has arguably helped many of the UK-based NGOs to work abroad and export their expertise, while at the same time learning new lessons from others to bring back to their British constituency. Furthermore, Darwin Initiative funding has helped contribute to a growing interest in conservation-related research in British universities, which in turn supports the research-led postgraduate training programmes referred to above. According to monitoring and evaluation of projects by independent consultants, the progress of Darwin Initiative projects is generally very encouraging, and provides a distinctive and well-targeted approach to funding global conservation efforts, and very effectively counteracting some of the funding shortfall due to Britain's heavy global footprint.

Conclusions

Britain has probably made a disproportionate contribution to international efforts to conserve biodiversity, through using its global influence, its convening power, its

---

[12] http://darwin.defra.gov.uk/: accessed 27 November 2009.

science base and the international *lingua franca* that all Britons are fortunate enough to speak. However, as 2010 approaches, much still remains to be done to conserve global biodiversity and the Earth's life support systems upon which all humans depend. Equally, as a developed nation, Britain owes the world a large ecological debt through the resources it over-consumes. Thus British efforts to contributing to save global biodiversity should not flag, and the distinctive contributions that Britain makes to international conservation should be enhanced, both financially and in kind. Britons need to learn to curb or mitigate their patterns of over-consumption. British ingenuity is needed to help emerging initiatives such as carbon trading and efforts to reduce emissions from deforestation and degradation (REDD) to function effectively, both in the international marketplace and locally, where globally important forests, with their rich biodiversity and critical carbon stores, are being converted. British efforts to train an ever larger cadre of conservation professionals who can make a real difference in their home countries should re-double. Strategic funding initiatives such as the Darwin Initiative should be enhanced, especially in times of international economic crisis. The British public and its elected political representatives need to increasingly understand the importance of biodiversity and the services it provides, and to recognise that efforts to conserve biodiversity probably represent the most important global challenge of our time.

Acknowledgements

We thank Martin Brasher and Eric Blencowe of DEFRA for very helpful comments, but the authors bear responsibility for all the perspectives presented in this chapter.

References

Adams, W.M. (2004). *Against Extinction: The Story of Conservation*, London, Earthscan.

Adams, W.M. (2008). Thinking like a human: social science and the two cultures problem. *Oryx,* **41**, 275–276.

Anon (1994). *Biodiversity: The UK Action Plan*, London, HMSO.

Attenborough, D. (1979). *Life on Earth: A Natural History*, London, Collins and BBC Books.

Baillie, J. and Groombridge, B. (eds.) (1996). *1996 Red List of Threatened Animals*, Cambridge, UK and Gland, Switzerland, IUCN.

Balmford, A., Crane, P., Dobson, A.P., Green, R.E. and Mace, G.M. (2005). The 2010 challenge: data availability, information needs, and extraterrestrial insights. *Philosophical Transactions of the Royal Society Series B*, **360**, 221–228.

Balmford, A., Rodrigues, A., Walpole, M. *et al.* (2008). *Review on the Economics of Biodiversity Loss: Scoping the Science*, Brussels, European Commission.

Bibby, C.J., Collar, N.J., Crosby *et al.* (1992). *Putting Biodiversity on the Map: Priority Areas for Global Conservation*, Cambridge, International Council for Bird Preservation.

Borgerhoff-Mulder, M. and Copolillo, P. (2005). *Conservation: Linking Ecology, Economics and Culture*, Princeton, Princeton University Press.

Broad, S. (2001). TRAFFIC 25 years, News Section. *TRAFFIC Bulletin*, **19**, 1.

Bruner, A.G., Gullison, R.E., Rice, R.E. and da Fonseca, G.A.B. (2001). Effectiveness of parks in protecting tropical biodiversity. *Science*, **291**,125–128.

Butchart, S.H.M., Akçakaya, H.R., Chanson, J. *et al.* (2007). Improvements to the Red List Index. *PLoS ONE*, **2**, e140.

Butchart, S.H.M., Stattersfield, A.J., Baillie, J. *et al.* (2005). Using Red List Indices to measure progress towards the 2010 target and beyond. *Philosophical Transactions of the Royal Society Series B*, **360**, 255–268.

Butchart, S.H.M., Stattersfield A.J., Bennun, L.A. *et al.* (2004). Measuring global trends in the status of biodiversity: Red List Indices for birds. *PLoS Biology*, **2**, 2294–2304.

Collar, N.J . (ed.) (2001). *Threatened Birds of Asia: The BirdLife International Red Data Book*, Cambridge, BirdLife International.

Collar, N.J., Crosby, M.J. and Stattersfield, A.J. (1994). *Birds to Watch 2: The World List of Threatened Birds*, Cambridge, BirdLife International.

Crane, P., Balmford, A., Beddington, J.R. *et al.* (2003). *Measuring Biodiversity for Conservation*, London, The Royal Society.

Fa, J.E. and Funk, S.M. (2007). Global endemicity centres for terrestrial vertebrates: an ecoregions approach. *Endangered Species Research*, **3**, 31–42.

Farman, J.C., Gardiner, B.G. and Shanklin, J.D. (1985). Large losses of total ozone in Antarctica reveal seasonal ClOx/NOx interaction. *Nature*, **315**, 207–210.

Fitter, R. and Fitter, M. (eds.) (1987). *The Road to Extinction*, Gland, Switzerland, IUCN.

Fothergill, A. (2006). *Planet Earth: As You Have Never Seen it Before*, London, BBC Books.

Goossens, B., Chikhi, L., Ancrenaz, M. *et al.* (2006). Genetic signature of anthropogenic population collapse in orang-utans. *PLoS Biology*, **4**, 285–291.

Groombridge, B. and Jenkins, M.D. (2001). *Global Biodiversity: Earth's Living Resources in the 21st Century*, Cambridge, UNEP-World Conservation Monitoring Centre.

Heywood, V. (ed.) (1995). *Global Biodiversity Assessment*, Cambridge, Cambridge University Press.

Isaac, N.J.B., Turvey, S.T., Collen, B., Waterman, C. and Baillie, J.E.M. (2007). Mammals on the EDGE: conservation priorities based on threat and phylogeny. *PLoS ONE,* **2**, e296.

James, A.N., Gaston, K.J. and Balmford, A. (2001). Can we afford to conserve biodiversity? *BioScience*, **51**, 43–52.

Kapos, V., Balmford, A., Aveling, R. *et al.* (2008). Calibrating conservation: new tools for measuring success. *Conservation Letters*, **1**, 155–164.

Lawton, J.H. and May, R.M. (eds.) (1995). *Extinction Rates*, Oxford, Oxford University Press.

Leader-Williams, N. and Albon, S.D. (1988). Allocation of resources for conservation. *Nature*, **336**, 533–535.

Leader-Williams, N., Balmford, A., Linkie, M. *et al.* (2007). Beyond the ark: conservation biologists' views of the achievements of zoos in conservation. In Zimmerman, A., Hatchwell, M., Dickie, L.A. and West, C., eds., *Zoos in the 21st Century: Catalysts for Conservation?*, Cambridge, Cambridge University Press, pp. 236–254.

Leader-Williams, N., Harrison, J. and Green, M.J.B. (1990). Designing protected areas to conserve natural resources. *Science Progress*, **74**, 189–204.

Loh, J., Green, R.E., Ricketts, T. *et al.* (2005). The Living Planet Index: using species population time series to track trends in biodiversity. *Philosophical Transactions of the Royal Society Series B*, **360**, 289–295.

Mace, G.M (2004). The role of taxonomy in species conservation. *Philosophical Transactions of the Royal Society Series B*, **359**, 711–719.

Mace, G.M. and Lande, R. (1991). Assessing extinction threats: toward a reevaluation of IUCN threatened species categories. *Conservation Biology*, **5**, 148–157.

Mace, G.M., Collar, N.J., Gaston, K.J. *et al.* (2008). Quantification of extinction risk: IUCN's system for classifying threatened species. *Conservation Biology*, **22**, 1224–1242.

Millennium Ecosystem Assessment (2005). *Ecosystems and Human Well-being: Synthesis*, Washington DC, Island Press.

Milner-Gulland, E.J. and Rowcliffe, J.M. (2007). *Conservation and Sustainable Use: A Handbook of Techniques*, Oxford, Oxford University Press.

Morling, P. (2008). *Funding for Biodiversity: An Analysis of the UK's Spend Towards the 2010 Target*, Peterborough, IUCN UK Committee.

Myers, N., Mittermeier, R.A., Mittermeier, C.G., da Fonseca, G.A.B., and Kent, J. (2000). Biodiversity hotspots for conservation priorities. *Nature*, **403**, 853–858.

Oldfield, S., Lusty, C. and MacKinven, A. (1998). *The World List of Threatened Trees*, Cambridge, World Conservation Press.

Olson, D.M. and Dinerstein, E. (1998). The Global 200: a representative approach to conserving the Earth's most biologically valuable ecoregions. *Conservation Biology*, **12**, 502–515.

Onslow, Earl of (1938). Preservation of African fauna. *African Affairs*, **37**, 380–386.

Pearce-Kelly, P., Mace, G.M. and Clarke, D. (1995). The release of captive bred snails (*Partula taeniata*) into a semi-natural environment. *Biodiversity and Conservation*, **4**, 645–663.

Pullin, A.S. and Knight, T.M. (2001). Effectiveness in conservation practice: pointers from medicine and public health. *Conservation Biology*, **15**, 50–54.

Rackham, O. (1986). *The History of the Countryside,* London, J.M. Dent.

Rodrigues, A.S.L., Andelman, S.J., Bakarr, M.I. *et al.* (2004). Effectiveness of the global protected area network in representing species diversity. *Nature*, **428**, 640–643.

Roe, D., Mayers, J., Grieg-Gran, M. *et al.* (2000). *Evaluating Eden: Exploring the Myths and Realities of Community-Based Wildlife Management*, London, IIED Evaluating Eden Series No. 8.

Runte, A. (1990). *Yosemite: The Embattled Wilderness*, Lincoln and London, University of Nebraska Press.

Runte, A. (1997). *National Parks: The American Experience*, Lincoln and London, University of Nebraska Press.

Simms, A., Moran, D. and Chowla, C. (2006). *The UK Interdependence Report: How the World Sustains the Nation's Lifestyles and the Price it Pays*, London, New Economics Foundation.

Stanley Price, M.R. (1989). *Animal Reintroductions: The Arabian Oryx in Oman*, Cambridge, Cambridge University Press.

Stern, N. (2007). *The Economics of Climate Change: The Stern Review*, Cambridge, Cambridge University Press.

Sutherland, W.J. (2000). *The Conservation Handbook: Research, Management and Policy,* Oxford, Blackwell.

Sutherland, W.J., Pullin, A.S., Dolman, P.M. and Knight, T.M. (2004). The need for evidence based conservation. *Trends in Ecology and Evolution,* **19**, 305–308.

Swingland, I.R. (1995). The Durrell Institute of Conservation and Ecology. *Dodo,* **31**, 19–27.

Swingland, I.R. (2003). *Capturing Carbon and Conserving Biodiversity*, London, Earthscan.

Thomas, C.D., Cameron, A., Green, R.E. *et al.* (2004). Extinction risk from climate change. *Nature,* **427**, 145–148.

UNEP (2008). *GEO 4: Global Environment Outlook: Environment for Development*, Nairobi, Kenya, United Nations Environment Programme.

van Heijnsbergen, P. (1997), *International Legal Protection of Wild Fauna and Flora*, Amsterdam, IOS Press.

Wackernagel, M., Schulz, N.B., Deumling, D. *et al.* (2002). Tracking the ecological overshoot of the human economy. *Proceedings of the National Academy of Sciences USA,* **99**, 9266–9271.

Williams, M. (2003). *Deforesting the Earth: From Pre History to Global Crisis*, Chicago, Chicago University Press.

Zhigang, J. and Harris, R.B. (2008). *Elaphurus davidianus.* In 2008 IUCN Red List of Threatened Species. Available at http://www.iucnredlist.org. Accessed 16 May 2009.

PART III

The case histories

15

Mammals in the twentieth century

D.W. Yalden

Summary

Of the 49 or so terrestrial mammals in Britain (bats excluded), 14 have increased strongly in range and numbers over the last 50 years, five or six have declined, and the status of the others is variable or uncertain. The increases largely indicate recovery from more ancient declines due to persecution, while the declines reflect especially problems with introduced species (competitors or predators) and changes in land use. The biomass is overwhelmingly dominated by humans and domestic ungulates (97%), leaving little ecological room for wild species, but there is scope to restore a little more balance by reintroducing long-extinct species.

Introduction

The recent history of mammals in the British Isles has been reasonably well surveyed, and well reported. Summaries of recent (last 50 years) changes have been presented by, among others, Corbet and Yalden (2001) and Harris *et al.* (Chapter 2 in Harris and Yalden 2008). The longer history (back to 10 000 b.p.) has been summarised by Yalden (1999) and Yalden and Kitchener (Chapter 3 in Harris and Yalden 2008), allowing recent changes to be placed in a longer historical perspective. A national distribution atlas at the hectad (10 km) level was published first, tentatively, in 1971 (Corbet 1971), and updated three times (Arnold 1978, 1984, 1993). An attempt has been made to estimate the numbers of all species (Harris *et al.* 1995), their mass–abundance relationships have been discussed (Greenwood *et al.* 1996), their biomasses evaluated and, moreover, compared to plausible estimates of

Silent Summer: The State of Wildlife in Britain and Ireland, ed. Norman Maclean. Published by Cambridge University Press. © Cambridge University Press 2010.

Mesolithic biomasses, i.e. our native mammal fauna, before farming and persecution had a severe impact (Maroo and Yalden 2000; Yalden 2003). Three earlier editions of *The Handbook of British Mammals* (Southern 1964; Corbet and Southern 1977; Corbet and Harris 1991) summarised increasing knowledge of this section of our fauna, and the very recent 4th edition, albeit with a mutated title (Harris and Yalden 2008), includes summaries of changes and the balance of the fauna, as well as detailed accounts for each species; that is the source for otherwise unattributed comments here.

The balance of the mammal fauna

A tabulation of the British mammal fauna (Table 15.1) suggests a fauna of around 66 species, if one includes feral or semi-feral domestic species (e.g. Soay Sheep, Feral Goats, Chillingham Cattle, New Forest Ponies) and four species that are confined to small islands (assuming, too, that 'British Isles' includes the Channel Isles). There are another 11 vagrants (bats and seals that occur infrequently), six large native mammals (Bear, *Ursus arctos*, Wolf, *Canis lupus,* Lynx, *Lynx lynx,* Beaver, *Castor fiber*, Aurochs, *Bos primigenius*, Elk, *Alces alces*, and Boar, *Sus scrofa*) that became extinct in late prehistoric or historic times, and up to 25 cetaceans in the surrounding seas (15 regularly present, nine that occur occasionally, and one, the Gray Whale, *Eschrichtius robustus,* historically extinct). When to accept escapes and released mammals as wild species is a further cause of uncertainty (Baker, Chapter 13 in Harris and Yalden 2008). Adding the most established of these with all of those just mentioned suggests a potential mammal list of around 108 species.

   Table 15.1 summarises the mammal fauna in the traditional manner by taxonomic categories. For the purposes of this book, a series of five quasi-historical categories might be more relevant. There are: (1) a large group of species which had declined in recent (0.5–2) centuries, but which in the last 50 years have been recovering range and/or numbers steadily; (2) a group of species threatened, in various ways, by introduced species, which have consequently declined in the last 50 years; (3) species of agricultural land, whose status is uncertain or variable, certainly changing, but possibly in different directions in different parts of the country; (4) some species have increased, apparently responding very directly to legal protection and other conservation measures; (5) this leaves a number, especially of the smaller and moderately numerous species, for which our knowledge is too weak to indicate clear trends. These five categories are, in any case, not mutually exclusive.

Recovering species

The more recent history of a number of our more obvious and familiar larger mammals has been very positive, but these reflect a 'bounce back' from severe declines, from

Table 15.1 *A summary of numbers of British mammal species (from Harris and Yalden 2008, Table 2.2)*

	Native (+ Introduced)		Additional species (small islands only)	Vagrant	Feral	Extinct
	Great Britain	Ireland				
Insectivores	5	0 (+2)	3	–	–	–
Bats	17	9	–	6	–	–
Lagomorphs	1 (+2)	1 (+2)	–	–	–	–
Rodents	8 (+6)	2 (+4)	1	–	–	1
Carnivores	8 (+1)	4 (+2)	–	5	–	3
Pinnipeds	2	2	–	5	–	–
Ungulates	3 (+4)	0 (+3)	–	–	4	2
Marsupials	0 (+1)	0	–	–	–	–
Total	**44 (+14)**	**18 (+13)**	4	11	4	6
Cetacea	15	–	–	9	–	1

various causes, in earlier centuries. Our two native deer, Red Deer (*Cervus elaphus*) and Roe Deer (*Capreolus capreolus*) were hunted with increasing severity during the sixteenth and seventeenth centuries, as the formal hunting system, which protected them from poaching in the royal and other forests, fell into disuse and succumbed to agricultural pressures. Roe were extinct in England, Wales and southern Scotland by 1700, and Red Deer were barely more widespread (they possibly survived in the Lake District). During the nineteenth century, the spread of commercial forestry (especially for Roe) and the rise of sporting estates, especially in Highland Scotland, gave both species a chance to recover their numbers, and their range expansion continues to the present century. Roe spread naturally into southern Scotland about 1840, and then into northern England, but were also reintroduced into Dorset in 1800 (from Perth) and into East Anglia in 1888 (from Germany). They continue to spread out from these three foci towards the English Midlands; there seems also to have been a recent (1990s) surreptitious reintroduction into Wales. Red Deer recovered numbers and range in Highland Scotland during the nineteenth century; populations elsewhere (south-west England, East Anglia, the Peak District, southern Scotland) seem to be the result of introductions and escapes from parks, but all are currently expanding in range and numbers.

Carnivores were heavily persecuted by gamekeepers during the nineteenth century, additional to earlier harvesting for their furs (Yalden 1999). The Polecat (*Mustela putorius*) was exterminated everywhere except in an area of central Wales, possibly extending just into the Marches. The first signs of some range expansion were noted

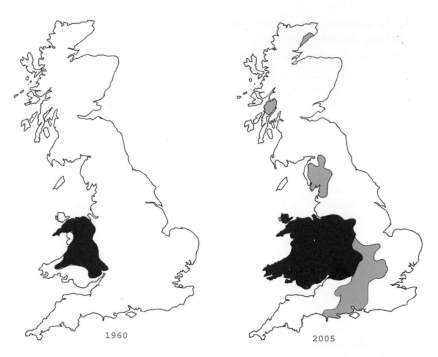

Figure 15.1 The apparent distribution of the Polecat, *Mustela putorius*, in 1960 (left) and 2005 (right) (simplified from Birks and Kitchener 1999). The grey tint on the 2005 map indicates populations which probably derive from reintroductions ahead of the natural spread indicated by the black shading.

as early as 1919, but until the 1960s it was still confined essentially to Wales. Since then, it has expanded its range considerably, into especially the English Midlands, so that its range, and presumed numbers, has at least doubled in the last few decades (Figure 15.1). Further, there have been several introductions further north and east, especially into Cumbria and Argyll, which have added further to its success (Birks and Kitchener, pp. 476–485 in Harris and Yalden 2008). The Pine Marten (*Martes martes*) was exterminated outside of small pockets in the Lake District, Snowdonia and the north-west Highlands. Its recovery in Scotland saw it spread south-east to the Great Glen by 1946, becoming widespread throughout the Highlands by the 1990s. A small introduced population in Galloway, started in the 1980s, also seems to be thriving. However, the remnant populations in Cumbria and North Wales show little sign of increase, and might even have died out. In Ireland, too, it survived in small pockets in the west, and has increased its range substantially. The Wildcat (*Felis silvestris)* was also reduced to a remnant range in the north-west Highlands, but, like the Pine Marten, expanded its range throughout the Highlands by the 1990s.

Table 15.2 *Summary of results of 11 Otter surveys, Great Britain 1977–2002 (from Jefferies and Woodroffe, in Harris and Yalden 2008, who give details of surveys and authors)*

Country	Sites visited	% occupied			
		1977–9	1984–6	1991–4	2000–2
England	2940	5.8	9.7	23.4	36.3
Wales	1008	20.5	39.0	52.5	73.8
Scotland	3556	67.0	73.0	87.2	–
Britain	7504	36.8	43.6	57.5	–

That in itself has caused problems of hybridisation, though, and merits its inclusion also in group (2). The Otter (*Lutra lutra*) was hunted by otter hunts and persecuted by angling interests throughout the nineteenth century and into the early twentieth century, but, unlike the previous three carnivores, remained widespread, even abundant, into the 1950s. However, it declined sharply from 1957, especially in England, as a result of poisoning by organochlorine pesticides. When structured distribution surveys were undertaken in the 1970s to ascertain its status, signs of its presence (droppings, mostly, but also tracks and other signs) were found at only 6% of English sites and 20% of Welsh sites, though it was rather more widespread in Scotland (67%) and remained common throughout Ireland (92%). There have been three subsequent surveys in England since then, and, with the reduction in organochlorine levels, the range has increased successively to 10%, 23% and 36%; the range in Wales has also increased (Table 15.2). It can be suggested, extrapolating from these results, that it will take about a century for the Otter to recover fully its range and status in the British Isles.

A similar, but agriculturally less welcome, recovery has been staged by the Rabbit (*Oryctolagus cuniculus*). Apparently introduced by the Plantagenets, probably from south-west France (Sykes 2007), it was carefully cosseted and cultivated in warrens until the eighteenth century, and did not become a pest until agricultural changes provided appropriate habitat, and persecution of its natural predators removed the checks on its population (see Chapter 4, this volume). By the 1950s, it was the major pest of agriculture and forestry in Britain. The deliberate release of the myxoma virus in France in a private estate in June 1952 led to its spread (natural, or with human assistance?) to south-east England in September 1953, and throughout Britain over the subsequent two years. It is thought that 99% of a Rabbit population estimated, retrospectively, at around 100 million, was killed. As a consequence, the Stoat (*Mustela erminea*) also declined, and both Field Voles (*Microtus agrestis*) and their principle predator, the Weasel (*M. nivalis*) increased. It required about a decade before the first suggestions of a recovery by the Rabbit population were noticed. Both more resistant Rabbits and more attenuated viruses were favoured by the disease, because Rabbits that survived longer in an infectious state were more likely to pass on the disease. Half a century on, naive young Rabbits still suffer periodically from outbreaks of the disease, but the population as a whole is believed to have reached about half its former abundance. The abundance of the Stoat has also partially recovered, apparently tracking the recovery of its main prey, while the Weasel appears to have become once more less abundant than its larger relative, though the population trends in both are uncertain, and depend on extrapolations from gamekeepers' vermin bags (McDonald and Harris 1999). Vermin bags also document the modest recovery in range and increase in abundance of the Fox (*Vulpes vulpes*); although always persecuted by gamekeepers, it was itself protected for hunting in some areas, and always remained reasonably common and widespread. Its successful invasion of suburban and urban habitats, often to reach much higher densities than in rural areas, means that its overall population is as high as ever; although estimated at 240 000 by Harris *et al.* (1995), it is thought that 260 000 was a more likely estimate around then. Outbreaks of sarcoptic mange have reduced numbers severely in some cities (notably Bristol) since then, but are believed not to have affected the population at the national scale.

Problems with introduced species

Four species at least have suffered from the effects of introduced species over the last 50 years. The best known case is the Red Squirrel (*Sciurus vulgaris*), which has been declining steadily since the 1920s as the introduced North American Grey Squirrel (*S. carolinensis*) has spread. The facts of the decline and its correlation with that spread are among the best documented of changes in our mammal fauna. As long ago as 1945, it was noted that Red Squirrels were scarce or absent wherever Grey Squirrels had been well established 15–20 years earlier. Then, Red Squirrels were still widespread in most of east, west and north England, as well as throughout Wales and Scotland. As Grey Squirrels spread into East Anglia, west England and Wales during the 1970s and 1980s, so Reds declined. Some small populations persisted, especially in areas of conifer plantation, long after they had been lost in the surrounding parklands and deciduous woodlands – in the Peak District and Cannock Chase to about 1994, in the Suffolk Sandlings to 1995 and in some of the Welsh forests. Even so, by 2008, the only populations in south England are on the Isle of Wight and some of the islands in Poole Harbour, and in the north, the species is still declining in the Lake District, Northumberland and Durham. In Wales, there are possibly three surviving populations (Anglesey, Clocaenog, Tywi/Crychan), though in Scotland the native is still reasonably widespread. It is also still widespread in Ireland, but even there, belatedly, is showing signs of a similar decline. The direct cause of the interaction has been less certain, and three factors seem to be involved. The Grey Squirrel is better adapted to deciduous woodland, in part because this is its natural habitat in the USA and in part because it is able to digest acorns efficiently, whereas the Red Squirrel, naturally a species of conifers, is unable to maintain weight on a diet of acorns. Grey Squirrels also have a disease-mediated advantage; they carry, but are resistant to, Squirrel-pox virus, which is usually fatal to Red Squirrels. Lastly, the larger Grey Squirrel seems to suppress breeding success of Red Squirrels, perhaps by reducing the recruitment and/or survival of young Red Squirrels. On Anglesey, a deliberate campaign of culling Grey Squirrels succeeded very quickly in enhancing recruitment of a small conifer-dwelling Red Squirrel population, which then spread into surrounding deciduous woodlands, even back into gardens. In Highland Scotland, Red Squirrels seem to maintain their range in coniferous woodland, and restrict Grey Squirrels to areas of deciduous woodland, though perhaps in the absence of the virus (which is widespread in England). (Grey Squirrels, which spend more time on the ground, are more susceptible to Fox predation and perhaps are less able to feed efficiently on the small seeds of conifers.) However, attempts to introduce Red Squirrels to areas of conifer in south England have not succeeded. While it may now be impossible to eliminate Grey Squirrels, stronger culling to defend remaining Red Squirrel populations, and maintaining isolated refuges, is essential.

The decline of the Water Vole (*Arvicola terrestris*) has been an extensive one, perhaps a response firstly to the introduction of Sheep 5500 years ago and then of Rabbits 800 years ago, and their combined reduction of the longer grasslands that Water Voles need; originally, they were not just waterside voles, but occurred more widely, as still they do elsewhere in Europe (Strachan and Jefferies (1993); Jefferies 2003). Within the last 50 years, it has been an essentially riparian species, confined to an increasingly narrow fringe of suitable vegetation by agricultural pressures, from both plough and livestock. In addition to these pressures, it has succumbed to predation from American Mink (*Mustela vison*) as that established itself across Britain since first breeding in the wild in 1956. Not only have detailed studies demonstrated its predation of voles, to the point of local extinction, but the efficacy of mink removal, by trapping, has also been clearly shown. The best results at restoring Water Voles have come from a combination of mink removal and habitat improvement, e.g. south of Chichester.

Two other species have suffered from genetic introgression with introduced relatives. The native Red Deer is closely related to the Sika (*Cervus nippon*), an Asian deer introduced originally to parks, which has very successfully established itself in conifer plantations, especially in Scotland (see Chapter 4, this volume). Despite the size difference, hybrids have sometimes been produced in captivity, and are then fully interfertile with both parent species. The earliest introduction of Sika was to Powerscourt in Ireland, in 1860, and probably the earliest escapes were also from there. Mixing with the Red Deer in the Wicklow Mountains, the result was a completely hybrid population there by the 1970s. A similar complete introgression was noted in the south Lake District, but introgression is also underway in Highland Scotland, where the majority of the British Red Deer population occurs. It is considered already that the process is irreversible, and the only 'pure' Red Deer by the end of this century are likely to be those on Scottish islands. The Wildcat is closely related to the Domestic Cat, itself tamed from the distinctive African sub-species, *F. silvestris lybica*. As the Wildcat recovered its range in Highland Scotland, it seems likely that young males, dispersing at the forefront of the range, encountered and mated with feral Domestic Cats (in the absence of wild relatives). The total population of Wildcats is thought to be about 3500, but possibly only 400 of these are pure Wildcats, the rest being hybrids of various degrees (Macdonald *et al.* 2004). It is unclear whether continued population increase will see wild genotypes thrive at the expense of hybrids or whether, like the deer, complete introgression will result.

Species of agricultural land

The decline of farmland birds has been well documented (see Chapter 17, this volume). One mammal most obviously fits with them, the Brown Hare (*Lepus europaeus*). Formerly widespread, its numbers have declined throughout the latter half of the twentieth century, as documented by game bags on the agricultural land most suited to them (Tapper 1992), and there seems also to have been a substantial reduction in range, particularly from west Britain (Hutchings and Harris 1996). The precise reasons for these declines are contentious. The simplification of farmland habitats, especially the loss of weeds, overwinter stubble and undersown crops, is one factor. Increasing numbers of predators is another. Possibly the combination of the two (simpler habitats, so less cover, more exposure to predation) has been critical. Certainly, experimental reduction of predators (especially Foxes) and increased diversification of farmland have both been shown to benefit Brown Hares. In Ireland, the Irish Hare, a well-marked race, *Lepus timidus hibernicus*, of the Mountain Hare (*Lepus timidus*), occupies similar farmland habitats; it is not confined to moorland, as is its Scottish relative. It too seems to have declined sharply in abundance, as a consequence of agricultural intensification, though it still remains widespread. The small mammal most closely tied to agricultural land is perhaps the Wood Mouse (*Apodemus sylvaticus*), which seems to have benefited in arable areas, but its largest populations are in woodlands and hedgerows. Simplification of farmland (fewer crops, larger fields, loss of hedgerows and field margins) is suspected to have reduced numbers of other farmland small mammals (Common Shrew, *Sorex araneus*, Bank Vole, *Myodes glareolus*, Field Vole, *Microtus agrestis*), but there is only marginal evidence (for example, from analyses of owl pellets) for this. The Scilly Shrew, *Crocidura suaveolens cassiteridum*, a sub-species of the widespread European Lesser White-toothed Shrew, *Crocidura suaveolens*, seems to be holding its own, but there is concern about the impact of agricultural changes on various Orkney suspecies of Common Vole, *Microtus arvalis*. The Harvest Mouse (*Micromys minutus*) must have declined in farmland, as the taller (cereal) vegetation it prefers has been changed, but it seems to survive well in reedbeds and similar tall grasslands. One extensive national resurvey suggested that many former sites had been lost, but more intensive local studies have found numerous new sites; it has probably always been an erratic species, responding very rapidly to the appearance of temporary patches of suitable habitat. The House Mouse (*Mus domesticus*) used to be common in cornfields when stooks and ricks were a regular feature of farmland. Now, it is rare in the countryside, but still common enough in towns, benefiting especially from 'houses in multiple occupation'. The Common Rat (*Rattus norvegicus*) seems to thrive, in farmland and urban habitats, despite the use of anti-coagulant poisons. The Ship Rat (*Rattus rattus*) appears to have completed its decline to extinction, which has taken 300 years, except for a few small island colonies. Moles (*Talpa europaea*) ought to have declined on farmland, suffering from persecution, ploughing and simplification of habitats, yet molehills remain a frequent sight in the countryside, and there is no quantitative evidence for any decline (nor any other method of documenting their continued abundance). The Hedgehog (*Erinaceus europaeus*) does seem to have declined, as suggested by vermin bags, now lapsed, and road casualty surveys. It is suspected that the simplification of farmland habitats has played a large part in this, but the possible impacts of pesticide use (slug pellets, particularly) and predation from increased numbers of Badgers (*Meles meles*) remain uncertain.

In the uplands, the heavy increases in livestock, especially sheep, have created tightly overgrazed pastures and rough grasslands, in which there is little habitat left for Field Voles or Brown Hares. The direct estimate of numbers lost is not possible, but a comparison of grazed uplands with ungrazed exclosures suggests that upland Field Voles in Britain number only half of what might be expected (Wheeler 2008). This has repercussions for numbers of predators (Weasels, owls and raptors especially) that might feed on them.

One special case of a species of agricultural land that has declined should be noted. The Coypu (*Myocastor coypus*) was introduced from South America to fur farms in the 1930s, and escaped from the 1940s. Originally limited by severe winters, it increased in numbers through the 1950s to become a perceptible threat to agriculture, especially root crops. An attempt to exterminate it from agricultural land and restrict it to Broadland in the 1960s, aided by the exceptional 1962–63 winter, reduced its numbers sufficiently to suggest success, but mild winters in the early 1970s allowed it to expand range and numbers again. The decision to attempt complete extermination was taken, and was vindicated; by 1987, some 35 000 had been, in a campaign that cost £2.5 million and employed 24 trappers deploying 216 000 trap-nights per year over the 7 years 1981–7. Coypu thus joined Muskrat (*Ondatra zibethica*) as one of the very few examples of successful elimination of an introduced species. Muskrat too was regarded as a serious threat to agriculture, and to drainage works, but was eliminated more promptly (Gosling and Baker 1989).

Gains from legal protection

Badgers (*Meles meles*), Grey Seals (*Halichoerus grypus*) (and Lesser Horseshoe Bats, see Chapter 16, this volume) are the species that have most clearly benefited from legal protection. It was argued in 1914 that Grey Seals numbered as few as 500 animals; certainly they had been heavily hunted throughout history. Closed seasons, protecting the breeding beaches, have allowed Grey Seals to increase at about 6% per annum for a century. When formal counts were first made in the 1930s, there were perhaps 8000; by the 1960s, 34 000; up to 69 000 in the 1970s and 93 000 by 1991 (Hammond *et al.*, Table 10.7 in Harris and Yalden 2008). Current estimates are more cautiously offered: 97–159 000, extrapolating from annual births of 46 000 pups. Badgers have also been persecuted, originally by gamekeepers and others. Badger baiting has been illegal since 1835, despite which, badger-diggers continued to persecute them. A succession of Badger Protection Acts, passed in 1973, 1991, 1991 and 1992, have given Badgers and their setts stringent protection. A national survey, structured by 1 km square and available habitats, suggested that there were 43 000 main setts and about 250 000 Badgers in 1986–7. A repeat survey 10 years later suggested 50 000 main setts and 309 000 Badgers. Areas where Badgers had increased most markedly were those where persecution in the 1980s had been most severe (as indicated by damaged setts) (Cresswell *et al.* 1990; Wilson *et al.* 1997). The recovery of Fin (*Balaenoptera physalus*) and Humpback (*Megaptera novaeangliae*) Whales, now seen regularly again in British waters, can also be regarded as a response to worldwide legal protection, after the excessive hunting of earlier last century.

Other recipients of legal protection have benefited less obviously. Common Seals (*Phoca vitulina*), for instance, also received legal protection under the Conservation of Seals Act 1970 during their breeding season, to give them some protection from serious legal harvesting, and, like Grey Seals, their populations increased in subsequent years. However, a severe viral disease reduced numbers of North Sea populations, at least by 40–60%, in 1988, and a partial recovery was reversed by a second disease outbreak in 2002, thus effectively negating any increase resulting from legal protection. The Hazel Dormouse (*Muscardinus avellanarius*) has suffered particularly from loss of coppicing and loss of hedgerows, so that it has apparently disappeared from about a third of the (more northern) counties in which it was recorded a century ago (Bright and Morris, pp. 76–81 in Harris and Yalden 2008). Legal protection does not of itself reverse the habitat losses, but has promoted an extensive captive breeding and reintroduction programme. This has at least returned it successfully to 10 of the 'lost' counties since 1992, though at the population level this has only a modest effect.

Uncertainties – little or no change?

This leaves a number of species 'in limbo'. Either we have insufficient knowledge of their abundance in the past to evaluate any possible changes in status, or we cannot perceive such changes on the basis of current monitoring efforts. The Pygmy Shrew (*Sorex minutus*) has always been thought widespread, but less abundant than its Common relative. That is still true. It is more widespread, perhaps more numerous, on moorlands than in the lowlands, and prefers taller vegetation. Whether, therefore, it has become less numerous, as postulated for upland Field Voles, is quite unknown. The Water Shrew (*Neomys fodiens*) is also, as it has always been, widespread, but erratic and sparsely distributed. Water pollution might have affected it adversely, as might drainage of wetlands, but there is no evidence for this. The Yellow-necked Mouse (*Apodemus flavicollis*) is a southern, old woodland, specialist, which has always been much less abundant, and more restricted in range, than the Wood Mouse, but there is little evidence that its relative numbers have changed. The Mountain Hare (*Lepus timidus*) might be vulnerable to climate change and overgrazing, given its northern range and upland habitat, but there is no obvious recent trend in numbers; current concerns about deliberate culling on grouse moors, to reduce the transmission of tick-borne diseases (hares being important alternative hosts for the ticks), are not yet well-enough documented to assess their effects at the population level.

Several of the smaller cetaceans have shown marked changes in the distribution of sightings and/or strandings around the British Isles. Some southern species (e.g. Common Dolphin, *Delphinus delphis*, Striped Dolphin, *Stenella coeruleoalba*) have at times become more common in northern parts of their range; conversely some northern species (e.g. White-beaked Dolphin, *Lagenorhynchus albirostris*) have sometimes extended their ranges southwards. However, it is thought unlikely that these changes reflect genuine increases in population, but rather indicate range changes as water temperatures and prey populations shift.

Overall balance of the fauna

The estimates by Harris *et al.* (1995) suggest a wild mammal fauna of 285 million mammals of 65 species in spring, totalling a biomass of 130 kt. Of these, the 16 bats are considered elsewhere. That leaves 49 species, of which at least 14 have increased substantially in range and numbers during the last 50 years. Unfortunately, these include six non-natives (three introduced deer (Sika, Muntjac *Muntiacus reevesi*, Fallow Deer *Dama dama*), Grey Squirrel, Mink and Rabbit). Still, the increasing species clearly outnumber the five or six that are certainly declining, leaving around 20 species whose status is equivocal, patchy or variable.

This is about half the number (535 million) and biomass (300 kt) estimated for the Mesolithic, albeit those totals omit bats and seals. The much higher biomass then reflects the presence of the large extinct species listed earlier. One of these might be reintroducing itself: Wild Boar (*Sus scrofa*) have reputedly escaped from boar farms (if they are not in fact hybrids with Domestic Pigs, *Sus domesticus*), but it is too early to know that this will be a successful restoration. Ultimately, it will be a politico-social decision whether to accept them back, and that decision is still pending. Also pending are the decisions to reintroduce Beavers to England and Wales, but the Scottish Executive has recently approved a trial reintroduction in Knapdale, Argyll. So far, serious thoughts about reintroducing Lynx and Wolf as well have only reached the stage of scientific discussions. The undoubted ecological and economic benefits of having these species back (improving wetlands and water storage, improving the structure of woodlands, limiting deer numbers, increasing tourism; Coles 2006, Nilson *et al.* 2007; Hetherington *et al.* 2008) have not so far outweighed the antipathy of farmers, sporting land-owners and walkers, nor the timidity of the politicians who must ultimately take the decisions to proceed (or not).

It must be carefully noted that these wild species, numerically and especially by biomass, are only a tiny minority of the mammals loose in the British countryside. It has been calculated that the wild mammals only provide 3% of the mammal biomass at large, dwarfed by the enormous contributions from humans, sheep, cattle, horses and pigs (Yalden 2003). There is not much ecological space left for wild mammals, and when they do become relatively abundant and conspicuous, it is not surprising that they are regarded as pests.

References

Arnold, H.R. (1978). *Provisional Atlas of the Mammals of the British Isles*, Abbots Ripton, Biological Records Centre, ITE.

Arnold, H.R. (1984). *Distribution Maps of the Mammals of the British Isles*, Abbots Ripton, Biological Records Centre, ITE.

Arnold, H.R. (1993). *Atlas of Mammals in Britain*, London, HMSO.

Birks, J.D.S. and Kitchener, A.C. (1999). *The Distribution and Status of the Polecat* Mustela putorius *in Britain in the 1990s,* London, Vincent Wildlife Trust.

Coles, B. (2006). *Beavers in Britain's Past*, Oxford, Oxbow Books.

Corbet, G.B. (1971). Provisional distribution maps of British mammals. *Mammal Review,* **1**, 95–142.

Corbet, G.B. and Harris, S. (1991). *The Handbook of British Mammals*, 3rd edn, Oxford, Blackwell's Scientific Publications.

Corbet, G.B. and Southern, H.N. (1977). *The Handbook of British Mammals*, 2nd edn, Oxford, Blackwell's Scientific Publications.

Corbet, G.B. and Yalden, D.W. (2001). Mammals. In Hawksworth, D.L., ed., *The Changing Wildlife of Great Britain and Ireland*, London and New York, Taylor and Francis, pp. 399–409.

Cresswell, P., Harris, S. and Jefferies, D.J. (1990). *The History, Distribution, Status and Habitat Requirements of the Badger in Britain*, Peterborough, Nature Conservancy Council.

Gosling, L.M. and Baker, S.J. (1989). The eradication of muskrats and coypus from Britain. *Biological Journal of the Linnean Society,* **38**, 39–51.

Greenwood, J.J.D., Gregory, R.D., Harris, S., Morris, P.A. and Yalden, D.W. (1996). Relations between abundance, body size and species number in British birds and mammals. *Philosophical Transactions of the Royal Society of London B,* **351**, 265–278.

Harris, S. and Yalden, D.W. (eds.) (2008). *Mammals of the British Isles: Handbook,* 4th edn, Southampton, The Mammal Society.

Harris, S., Morris, P., Wray, S. and Yalden, D. (1995). *A Review of British Mammals: Population Estimates and Conservation Status of British Mammals Other Than Cetaceans*, Peterborough, JNCC.

Hetherington, D.A., Miller, D.R., Macleod, C. and Gorman, M. (2008). A potential habitat network for the Eurasian lynx *Lynx lynx* in Scotland. *Mammal Review,* **38**, 285–303.

Hutchings, M.R. and Harris, S. (1996). *The Current Status of the Brown Hare (*Lepus europaeus*) in Britain*, Peterborough, JNCC.

Jefferies, D.J. (2003). *The Water Vole and Mink Survey of Britain 1996–1998, With a History of Long-Term Changes in the Status of Both Species and Their Causes*, Ledbury, Vincent Wildlife Trust.

Macdonald, D.W., Daniels, M.J., Driscoll, C., Kithchener, A. and Yamaguchi, N. (2004). *The Scottish Wildcat: Analyses for Conservation and an Action Plan*, Oxford, Wildlife Conservation Research Unit.

Maroo, S. and Yalden, D.W. (2000). The Mesolithic mammal fauna of the Great Britain. *Mammal Review,* **30**, 243–248.

McDonald, R. and Harris, S. (1999). The use of trapping records to monitor populations of stoats *Mustela erminea* and weasels *M. nivalis*: the importance of trapping effort. *Journal of Applied Ecology,* **36**, 679–688.

Nilson, E.B, Milner-Gulland, E.J., Schofield, L. *et al.* (2007). Wolf reintroduction to Scotland: public attitudes and consequences for red deer management. *Proceedings of the Royal Society B,* **274**, 995–1002.

Southern, H.N. (1964). *The Handbook of British Mammals*, Oxford, Blackwell Scientific Publications.

Strachan, R. and Jefferies, D.J. (1993). *The Water Vole* Arvicola terrestris *in Britain 1989–1990: Its Distribution and Changing Status*, London, Vincent Wildlife Trust.

Sykes, N.J. (2007). *The Norman Conquest: A Zooarchaeological Perspective*, BAR International Series 1656, Oxford, British Archaeological Reports.

Tapper, S. (1992). *Game Heritage*, Fordingbridge, Game Conservancy.

Wheeler, P. (2008). Effects of sheep grazing on abundance and predators of field vole (*Microtus agrestis*) in upland Britain. *Agriculture Ecosystems and Environment,* **123**, 49–55.

Wilson, G., Harris, S. and McLaren, G. (1997). *Changes in the British badger population, 1988 to 1997*, London, People's Trust for Endangered Species.

Yalden, D.W. (1999). *The History of British Mammals*, London, T. and A.D. Poyser.

Yalden, D.W. (2003). Mammals in Britain – a historical perspective. *British Wildlife,* **14**, 243–251.

16

Bats

Karen A. Haysom, Gareth Jones, Dan Merrett and Paul A. Racey

Summary

Throughout Europe, many species of bats experienced serious population declines during the last century. Bats have been affected by the same pressures that have caused the decline of many other taxa, for example, agricultural intensification, habitat fragmentation and land-use change. There have also been specific additional pressures, such as the widespread use during the 1970s and 1980s of timber treatments which had high mammalian toxicity, and the deliberate or accidental exclusion of bats from their roosts. The conservation of bats has been particularly challenging because they are difficult to study, hence many of their complex ecological requirements have been discovered only recently or remain uncertain. A further obstacle was the general unpopularity and misunderstanding of bats among the public, such that deliberate killing of bats at their roosts was once very common. The introduction of legislation to protect bats has been pivotal in improving the status of the group, both directly and indirectly, by inspiring the interest of professionals and amateurs.

This chapter introduces the bats of Britain and Ireland and provides an overview of their ecological requirements. We review the evidence for population declines and focus on two major pressures, agricultural intensification and timber treatment. We then explore the ways in which the conservation infrastructure has been improved for bats and how a handful of committed specialists has become a large, skilled network. Case-studies illustrate how science has underpinned the development of policy for 'flagship' species, such as the Greater Horseshoe Bat and the implementation of landscape-scale conservation projects. Finally we consider new threats and the challenges that bat conservationists will face in the twenty-first century.

Silent Summer: The State of Wildlife in Britain and Ireland, ed. Norman Maclean. Published by Cambridge University Press. © Cambridge University Press 2010.

Introduction

The combination of issues affecting the status of bat populations during the twentieth and twenty-first centuries and the resulting conservation challenges that have arisen are distinctive. Many pressures experienced by bats during this time have also driven population changes in other taxa, including agricultural intensification, pollutants, habitat fragmentation and land-use change. However, several additional factors have affected bats. These include: close contact and often direct conflict with humans; public unpopularity influenced by mythology and misrepresentation; nocturnality and flight that, until recent technological developments, limited the accessibility of the group to ecological researchers and a complex range of requirements such that conservation effort has often focused on particular aspects while neglecting others.

Over the past 50 years, the study and conservation of bats and their public perception has changed dramatically. As late as the 1960s–70s, when pressures acting on bats are believed to have driven some of the steepest population declines, only a handful of individuals were actively studying bats, and able to document population change or draw attention to key conservation issues. Today, although many threats remain and new concerns are emerging, the infrastructure to conserve bats has improved substantially. At least nine university research groups, two specialist NGOs, experts in each of the country statutory nature conservation organisations (SNCOs), more than 100 amateur bat groups and a large and well-organised network of volunteers, (including 1600, who supply data to the UK's National Bat Monitoring Programme (NBMP) or and 400 surveyors, who participate in Ireland's All Ireland Bat Monitoring Programme), contribute actively to the conservation of bats in Britain and Ireland. Bat protection is embedded within the legislation of all EU member states. So too is the obligation to work actively for bat conservation in all of the countries which, like the United Kingdom and the Republic of Ireland, have become signatories to the Agreement on the Conservation of Populations of European Bats (EUROBATS).

This chapter provides an overview of changes in the population size and conservation status of bats from the mid-twentieth century to the present day. The species known from Britain and Ireland (Table 16.1) include two species (Common, *Pipistrelle Pipistrellus pipistrellus* and Soprano Pipistrelle, *Pipistrellus pygmaeus*) that were considered until recently to be a single species, and one that has recently been confirmed resident (Nathusius' Pipistrelle, *Pipistrellus nathusii*); another (Greater Mouse-eared Bat, *Myotis myotis*) has an uncertain status, having been recorded occasionally in hibernation since it was declared absent from Britain in 1990. We focus on some of the issues considered to have been key drivers of change. To appreciate why bats have been vulnerable to these drivers, it is necessary to have a basic understanding of bat ecology, and for this reason we outline the main ecological requirements typical of the bat species resident in Britain and Ireland. (More detailed information on the status and ecology of particular species is summarised by Harris and Yalden 2008.) We then describe some of the pivotal actions that have been taken for the conservation of bats and consider what new challenges the twenty-first century may bring.

Table 16.1 *The distribution and status of the bats of Britain and Ireland. Status follows the European Mammal Assessment (EMA) (Temple and Terry 2007); abbreviations refer to the IUCN Europe Red List Category: LC Least Concern, NT Near Threatened, VU Vulnerable.*

Species	Latin name	Distribution					Status
		E	W	S	NI	RoI	
Greater Horseshoe Bat	*Rhinolophus ferrumequinum*	•	•				NT
Lesser Horseshoe Bat	*Rhinolophus hipposideros*	•	•			•	NT
Daubenton's Bat	*Myotis daubentonii*	•	•	•	•	•	LC
Brandt's Bat	*Myotis brandtii*	•	•			•	LC
Whiskered Bat	*Myotis mystacinus*	•	•	•	•	•	LC
Natterer's Bat	*Myotis nattereri*	•	•	•	•	•	LC
Bechstein's Bat	*Myotis bechsteinii*	•	•				VU
Greater Mouse-eared bat	*Myotis myotis*[a]	○					LC
Noctule	*Nyctalus noctula*	•	•	•			LC
Leisler's Bat	*Nyctalus leisleri*	•	•	•	•	•	LC
Serotine	*Eptesicus serotinus*	•	•				LC
Common Pipistrelle	*Pipistrellus pipistrellus*[b]	•	•	•	•	•	LC
Soprano Pipistrelle	*Pipistrellus pygmaeus*[b]	•	•	•	•	•	LC
Nathusius' Pipistrelle	*Pipistrellus nathusii*[c]	•	•	•	•	•	LC
Brown Long-eared Bat	*Plecotus auritus*	•	•	•	•	•	LC
Grey Long-eared Bat	*Plecotus austriacus*	•					LC
Barbastelle	*Barbastella barbastellus*	•	•				VU

Notes:

[a] The Greater Mouse-eared Bat was known to breed in the UK until the 1970s, but was declared absent in 1990. Since 2002 there have been occasional records of hibernating individuals and its status is currently uncertain, presumed non-breeding.

[b] At the time of BAP designation (see below), the Common and Soprano Pipistrelle were believed to be a single species, but taxonomic and autecological research led to their separation in 1999.

[c] Nathusius' Pipistrelle has been recognised as a resident species relatively recently, having previously been known only as a migrant.

Ecological requirements

Bats need suitable roosting locations within commuting distance of foraging habitat. Most species utilise several different types of roost over the course of a year. These include maternity roosts (sites used by groups of breeding females to give birth and rear their young), spring gathering roosts (where females of some species assemble before moving to maternity roosts), mating roosts (often used by a male and small numbers of females), night roosts (for resting and grooming during foraging excursions) and hibernation sites (including caves, other underground sites and man-made structures). These different roost types possess distinctive temperature or humidity conditions. For example, maternity roosts are generally warm, to promote the growth of young, while hibernation sites are cool and humid, aiding energy conservation during periods of extended torpor. Individual colonies often use many examples of each type of roost and sometimes spread among several roosts simultaneously. Species such as Common Pipistrelle, Serotine, *Eptesicus serotinus*, Natterer's Bat, *Myotis nattereri*, and Bechstein's Bat, *Myotis bechsteinii*, are particularly known for their frequent roost-switching behaviour. Roosts may be found in trees, domestic buildings or other built structures, such as barns and bridges, depending on species. The selection of a specific location for a roost may be governed by a combination of the microclimate it provides and its proximity to good quality foraging habitat. Swarming sites, often in the entrances of caves or other underground structures, may be visited by many hundreds of bats, often travelling tens of kilometres, mainly in the autumn. Turnover of bats at these swarming sites is high, individuals remaining for only a few nights, and they appear to facilitate gene flow among otherwise isolated bat populations (Parsons *et al.* 2003).

Foraging niches vary with five hunting strategies (fast hawking, slow hawking, trawling, gleaning, perch hunting) described for the different British species (Vaughan 1997). Dipteran and lepidopteran families dominate their diets, with nine British bats consuming mainly Diptera and all species eating Lepidoptera to some extent (Vaughan 1997). Coleopteran families are also taken by many species and a small number of other orders including Hemiptera and Trichoptera. Arachnida are taken in small quantities. Although bats utilise many natural and semi-natural habitats to hunt, woodland and riparian habitats are especially important, as these are associated with high densities of aerial invertebrates. For many species, connective features such as hedgerows and tree-lines are important as commuting routes between the foraging grounds and the roost. The removal of such features may render otherwise suitable habitat inaccessible.

Effective conservation measures for bats need to consider all three major requirements (roosting, foraging and commuting habitat) at a landscape scale. For the conservation of populations, delivery of these requirements across the wider countryside rather than solely within protected areas, such as nature reserves, is implicit, at least for the majority of species that are widely distributed and wide ranging. However, some of the constraints on working with bats may have led to past conservation actions being more site focused than landscape focused. For instance, the nocturnal activity of bats, coupled with their high mobility, meant that earlier studies were centred on locations where bats were comparatively easy to observe or protect, such as maternity and hibernation sites. Long-term studies that have marked bats using forearm bands have revealed that individuals are highly faithful to such locations. More recently, the improved affordability and sophistication of ultrasonic bat detectors and the availability of radio transmitters that are light enough to attach to even our smallest bat species now makes it possible to document the activities of species in the wider countryside. In combination with the use of genetics, such studies are building an increasingly sophisticated picture of how bats use landscapes. Species including Bechstein's Bat and Daubentons', Bat *Myotis daubentonii* appear to have sex-specific habitat associations, with females occupying prime habitat, presumably because such sites hold the high numbers of insects necessary to sustain the rearing of young. This type of research is likely to alter present understanding of the quantity and character of habitat required to sustain colonies and populations. The number of studies that have used radio-tracking, systematic approaches to surveying distribution or genetics is still quite small, however, so models derived from them need wider verification before they are extrapolated beyond the landscapes in which they were developed.

Certain aspects of bat biology and habitat associations make bats particularly vulnerable to human activities. Most species rear only one young in a breeding season, thus population recovery after a period of decline is intrinsically slow. The clustering of groups of animals at vulnerable stages (e.g. breeding, hibernation) means that a local event such as deliberate disturbance or the loss of a roost can have a severe impact on a colony. Maternity roosts of bats (which for some species can comprise several hundred individuals) may attract unwanted attention. During hibernation, the energetic costs of arousal caused by disturbance are high. Perhaps most significantly, the synanthropic habit (ecological association with humans) of the 13 British species that regularly use built structures for roosting brings bats near to people and at risk of deliberate or indirect interference.

The evidence for population declines

Bats experienced major declines throughout Europe during the last century. Unfortunately they were relatively understudied during the period of fastest decline, and much of the supporting information, though sufficiently compelling to result in government-level international agreements to protect and conserve populations, is based on local studies or anecdotal reports for individual species. Stebbings (1988) cites the losses of large colonies of the Greater Mouse-eared Bat, Greater Horseshoe Bat *Rhinolophus ferrumequinum* and other species from traditional cave and mine roosting sites across Europe and the contraction of range of the Greater Horseshoe Bat within Britain and mainland Europe during the twentieth century. The population status assessment conducted by Harris *et al.* (1995) reported general historical declines for Greater Horseshoe Bat, Lesser Horseshoe Bat, *Rhinolophus hipposideros*, Noctule, *Nyctalus noctula*, Pipistrelle and Brown Long-eared Bat, *Plecotus auritus*. The evidence supporting these assessments includes range contractions in which, despite the huge increase in biological recording effort, some species are no longer observed in areas where they used to be reported. For example, Barrett-Hamilton (1910) stated that the Lesser Horseshoe Bat was 'common in many parts of the south of England from Kent westwards, is widely distributed in the west and in Wales, and may be said with certainty to range as far north as Ripon in Yorkshire'. Although the species is still widely distributed in Wales and south-west England, it is no longer found in other areas.

A 26-year census of Greater Horseshoe Bats near Bristol (Ransome 1989) documented two steep declines (a 50% decline between the winters of 1962/3 and 1966/7, and another in 1986), which left the population 70% lower than its 1962 level. Although both declines were largely attributable to severe climatic events, long-term range contractions of this species are almost certainly due in part to anthropogenic factors, including habitat degradation and roost loss. British Pipistrelle populations (early studies do not separate *Pipistrellus pipistrellus* (Common Pipistrelle) and *P. pygmaeus* Solarano pipistrelle) were reported to have declined by 62% between 1978 and 1986 (Stebbings 1988) (Figure 16.1). Guest *et al.* (2002) found a significant 6% reduction in bat numbers in Greater London in a 15 year period between 1985–7 and 1999 and significantly lower species richness. Population change varied among species, however, and overall was considered to be a conservative estimate, with declines appearing greatest in Noctule/Leisler's Bats, *Nyctalus leisleri* and Serotine. A questionnaire survey of the Mammal Society (Racey and Stebbings 1972) contributed to the protection of bats, as it documented the disappearance of many bat roosts, declines in numbers of individuals at many roosts and incidences of bats being killed in large numbers by deliberate extermination. The survey also drew attention to the major loss of underground roosts and the importance of these for species such as the Greater Horseshoe Bat, then considered to be in danger of

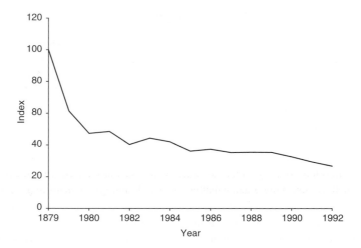

Figure 16.1 Population trends in summer counts of nursery roosts (mainly Pipistrelles). (R.E. Stebbings' data modified from Harris *et al.* 1995.) The line represents colonies counted since 1978 (mean colony size 119, $n = 81$).

extinction. Additional factors implicated in the decline of bats include landscape change and habitat loss, remedial timber treatment (Mitchell-Jones *et al.* 1989), insecticide poisoning (Jefferies 1972) and declines of their aerial insect prey (e.g. Benton *et al.* 2002); these are explored in more detail below.

The impact of agricultural intensification

Agriculture is the dominant influence on land management throughout the British Isles, with more than 76% and 72% of UK and Ireland, respectively, classed as farmed land. As for so many other species groups, the wide-scale intensification of farming that occurred through the second half of the twentieth century is considered to have been a major driver of population declines. Much of the evidence for this is indirect or fragmented, however, because of the paucity of bat studies dating from this period. Indeed, formal studies to assess the impact of agricultural intensification and farm systems on bat abundance and activity have taken place only recently, e.g. Wickramasinghe *et al.* (2003) and Fuller *et al.* (2005). However, the impact of intensification on habitats important to bats and, to a lesser extent, on populations of invertebrate prey is better documented. It is difficult to isolate which factors have been most critical for bats because so many of the changes to key habitats and invertebrate prey have occurred concurrently, but the collective evidence for agricultural intensification as a trigger for population decline in bats is convincing.

There has been considerable research in avian biology on the decline of 'farmland birds', i.e. granivorous passerines or game birds of arable habitats, and waders associated with mixed or grassland farms. All bats in the UK are insectivorous, but have nevertheless suffered from agricultural intensification, because all species forage in agricultural landscapes to some degree. Bat activity is generally (with a few exceptions) very low over arable land (Walsh and Harris 1996), but several species including Serotine, Natterer's Bat, Leisler's Bat, Greater Horseshoe Bat and Noctule forage selectively over pasture and Lesser Horseshoe Bats exploit insects attracted to or disturbed by the grazing animals themselves. The Greater Horseshoe Bat often forages over extensively managed cattle pasture, and tailored agri-environment agreements have been an important part of its population recovery (see Box 16.1). Much bat activity is associated with non-crop and edge habitats; woodland, hedgerows and riparian corridors all constitute important foraging and commuting habitat. Such habitats are also important for prey with adult stages commonly associated with damp, shady environments or decaying organic matter. Trees or buildings on farms may be used as bat roosts and one study of Greater Horseshoe Bats found 32% of roost sites in farm buildings.

Agricultural intensification is likely to have affected bats both directly and indirectly. Direct impacts include the loss of key commuting, foraging or roosting habitats, and reduced fitness through the accumulation of pesticide residues in fatty tissues. Indirect effects relate mainly to reduced availability of key prey items, caused again by habitat loss, habitat degradation or the action of pesticides. The scale of loss of key foraging and commuting habitats is very large: approximately 227 000 ponds were lost between 1945 and 1998; 250 000 km of hedgerow were removed between 1946 and 1990. Although the former decline has been halted and the latter reversed, the British landscape is essentially much more open, with fewer high-quality feeding sites and fewer of the linear features that enhance access by bats. Indeed, higher and more developed hedgerows were a major feature resulting in higher levels of bat activity on organic compared with conventional farms (Wickramasinghe *et al.* 2003). Loss of trees as a consequence of hedgerow removal and Dutch Elm Disease would have reduced roosting opportunities for tree-roosting species, and roosts in traditional buildings have also been lost as barns have been replaced or converted.

These landscape alterations are also relevant for the invertebrates on which bats prey. Invertebrate diversity is related to habitat heterogeneity and the persistence of certain less-mobile species can depend on the presence of less intensively managed crops or non-crop refugia. Such species often use different habitats as they pass through various life-history stages, so availability of a mosaic of habitats or microclimates within an insect's dispersal range is fundamental. There are relatively few long-term studies that demonstrate long-term declines in invertebrate populations relevant to bats, but those that do document declines in abundance of various aerial insects in Scotland (Benton *et al.* 2002) and Herefordshire (Harrington *et al.* 2003), and it is estimated that two-thirds of the moth species captured in the Rothamsted moth-trap network have declined since 1968 (Butterfly Conservation 2006). Causes of declines are many and varied, but include the impacts of a range of pesticides (insecticides, herbicides, fungicides) on non-target species, habitat loss, changes to drainage regimes, use of fertilisers, stocking and mowing rates and timings, and their impact on vegetation structure (e.g. conversion of hay meadows to silage), and diversity and changes in the availability and quality of other resources, such as dung and dead wood.

In comparison to major landscape changes, however, the precise impacts of pesticides and veterinary medicines on bats directly or indirectly are hard to quantify. A study by Jefferies published in 1972 found bats in one of the most intensively farmed areas of the UK were more heavily contaminated with residues of DDT than either insectivorous or carnivorous birds. The negative effects on bats of such exposure were revealed by Swanepoel *et al.* (1999). Subsequently, the number of general wildlife incidents associated with pesticide use has fallen since the early 1990s. The potential of veterinary medicines used to control livestock endo-parasites (warble-flies, nematodes) to disrupt supplies of prey invertebrates has also caused concern. For example avermectins, a group of synthetic pyrethroids that have been widely used for more than 20 years, decompose slowly, and so the chemicals remain active in dung for at least five weeks after treatment. Although various lethal and non-lethal effects of these chemicals have been demonstrated for a range of non-target invertebrates (dung beetles, dung flies) at a small scale, it is uncertain what the consequences are at higher trophic levels and at the landscape scale.

The impact of timber treatments

During the 1970s and 1980s, in order to obtain a mortgage on an older house, it was often necessary to provide evidence that any wood-boring beetle infestation had been effectively treated. This led to a proliferation of companies providing a certificate indicating that the property had been treated and guaranteed against reinfestation for a considerable period. The companies concerned sprayed chlorinated hydrocarbons, often lindane, against wood-boring beetles and pentachlorophenol (PCP) against timber-rotting fungi, in much higher concentrations than required for initial control of the infestations, in the hope that the treatments would last. In fact, it was later shown that the volatility of the chemicals used was such that they were soon lost to the atmosphere.

People familiar with the use of roof spaces as maternity roosts by bats were concerned that the high concentrations of chlorinated hydrocarbons would have an adverse effect on bats returning to their roosts in spring. The toxicity of chlorinated hydrocarbons was well known because before treatments could be marketed, tests were required on laboratory rodents. Bat biologists argued that chemicals that were highly toxic to rodents would also be highly toxic to bats, because both are mammals with fundamentally similar metabolisms. Timber-treatment companies would not accept this argument and required proof that their products killed bats before they would consider alternatives. Following the Wildlife and Countryside Act 1981, a question about the effects of remedial timber treatments on bats was asked in Parliament, prompting independently funded research on toxicity to bats. Researchers at Aberdeen University housed bats in cages with wooden liners that had been treated in exactly the same way as roof timber (Racey and Swift 1986). They compared commercial products containing lindane and PCP with alternative chemicals, in particular pyrethroids, which, though highly toxic to insects, had low mammalian toxicity. Whilst bats housed in cages treated with chlorinated hydrocarbons died, those in cages treated with pyrethroids did not. However, when these results were presented to the timber-treatment industry, it would not accept them because the bats had not been allowed to fly and, in the view of the industry, this invalidated the results.

In the late 1980s, the Department of the Environment (now the Department of the Environment of Food and Rural Affairs, DEFRA) established an ad hoc Committee for Bats and Remedial Timber Treatments, where industry representatives, members of the advisory committee for pesticides and bat biologists met regularly. The Institute of Terrestrial Ecology was commissioned to repeat the experiments of Racey and Swift, but this time with flight cages, enabling the bats to fly. Exactly the same results were obtained (Shore *et al.* 1990), and when published, the industry had no alternative but to accept them. At the same time, timber-treatment operatives were suing their companies for diseases ascribed to the effects of the chemicals. PCP was withdrawn from sale because dioxin (which is highly carcinogenic) was a by-product of its production. Ultimately, concerns about the use and effects of chlorinated hydrocarbons as remedial timber treatments, as well as health and safety considerations led to their withdrawal from sale and eventual banning throughout the EU. Effective alternatives were available and householders can still protect their properties against wood-boring beetles and timber-rotting fungi, but without adverse effects on any bats sharing their roof spaces.

The major approaches to bat conservation

Legislation and conservation infrastructure

Wildlife legislation (see Bat Conservation Trust 2008) has made bats among the best-protected mammals in Britain. For example, although a custodial sentence has yet to be delivered, it is now an imprisonable offence to kill or injure a bat or to damage or obstruct a roost. The predictable benefit of such legislation has been to reduce substantially the casual destruction of roosts and killing of bats described by Racey and Stebbings (1972), although bat crime still persists, with 170 incidents reported between July 2004 and April 2007. There are wider indirect benefits, however; crucially the legislation has encouraged contact with both the general public and professional sectors such as timber-treatment companies and forestry; Mitchell-Jones (1993) attributed the dramatic growth of interest in bats throughout the 1980s to the passing of the Wildlife and Countryside Act 1981. The Act required those seeking to carry out work likely to affect bats or their roosts to obtain advice from the SNCO (then the Nature Conservancy Council, NCC), inducing a role for amateur conservationists to train as licensed volunteer bat workers to assist in providing information to roost owners. The increase in both the number of roost visitor licences held and the number of bat groups established (Mitchell-Jones 1993) has continued such that volunteer delivery remains at the heart of the Natural England bat-roost visitor scheme, which is unique in an international context. It is estimated that there are now more than 850 licensed or trainee bat-roost visitors and approximately 3000 roost visits take place each year in England alone. More recently, the EU Habitats Directive of 1992, implemented in the UK by the 1994 Habitats Regulations and their subsequent modifications in 2007 and 2009 has refocused the attention of professional sectors, such as arboriculture, on bats and other European Protected Species (EPS). The relatively new service sector of 'ecological consultancy' has expanded rapidly to ensure that the potential impacts of developments on wildlife and natural heritage are considered and managed appropriately. New laws have clearly acted as a catalyst for amateur and professional sectors alike to deliver 'good practice'.

The rise in the number of bat workers and bat groups precipitated the establishment of the Bat Conservation Trust in 1990. It is the only UK organisation devoted solely to the conservation of bats and their habitats, and now has almost 5000 members. Bat Conservation Ireland was formed in 2003, following similar growth in interest. NGOs working for bat conservation have the difficult challenge of promoting a group of mammals which, through its diversity and synanthropic habits, has specific and often complex interactions with a wide range of other human interests. Thus much of BCT's work has focused on raising awareness of bats and providing technical training and advice on good practice for strategic target audiences, including planners, the construction industry and woodland managers. Supporting the recruitment and training of volunteer bat workers is a major part of this.

Aspects of bat conservation are very sensitive to the generation of goodwill among individuals and sectors whose primary interest is not biodiversity. This has much to do with the location of bat roosts in private buildings, such as houses, which means that species conservation is mainly achieved through influencing roost owners and sympathetically managing the wider countryside, rather than through the purchase of nature reserves. An exception to this is the work of the Vincent Wildlife Trust (VWT), which has focused on acquiring, protecting and enhancing key breeding roosts for rarer species, such as the horseshoe bats. VWT manages more than 50 sites in England, Wales and Ireland and the 11 Greater Horseshoe Bat roosts it owns now support a substantial proportion of the British population. BCT's national bat helpline exists to provide information and support to the public, over a third of callers being householders with bat roosts. The helpline now receives more than 10 000 enquiries each year, with a peak of approximately 100 calls per day during the summer months. While many callers are supportive, and the Natural England bat-roost visitor scheme is able to find solutions to ensure that most property maintenance work can proceed without affecting bats, inevitably some consider altering the timing or method of work for the benefit of wildlife an unwelcome constraint. The presence of bats in heritage or community buildings, such as churches, can provoke strong emotions and negative publicity. The National Trust has accrued particular experience of managing bats in historic buildings and one of BCT's earliest projects gathered information on bats in churches (Sargent 1995). So far, cross-disciplinary partnerships that share knowledge of managing species in such situations have enjoyed considerable success.

Such partnerships have been a key element of bat conservation under the UK Biodiversity Strategy and the Biodiversity Action Plan (BAP) framework that resulted from it. Between 1995 and 2008, seven bat species (Greater Horseshoe Bat, Lesser Horseshoe Bat, Barbastelle, *Barbastella barbastellus*, Bechstein's Bat, Greater Mouse-eared Bat and Common/Soprano Pipistrelle) were listed as priorities for conservation action. (The priority list has subsequently been revised in May 2008, with the addition of the Brown Long-eared Bat and Noctule and the removal of Common Pipistrelle and Greater Mouse-eared Bat from early 2009.) The species were so designated on the basis of knowledge of rates of decline and active threats to populations. The framework required the development of individual species action plans, outlining the status, ecological requirements, threats and prioritised actions and targets to be achieved over designated periods of time. Although the process has focused on only a few bat species, broad overlap in the ecological requirements of these with other species makes it likely that actions taken for these 'flagship' species will have had more general benefits. BCT was the lead partner for five of the original species and brought together a cross-sector steering group comprising partners able to influence the management of large areas of land. The precise structure of BAP target-setting has identified constraints, such as poor knowledge of a species' ecology or distribution, that have the potential to restrict the implementation of conservation action and the measurement of its success.

Improving the knowledge base

A detailed understanding of their ecology and changes in relative population size are fundamental tools for the effective conservation of bat species. Box 16.1 illustrates how science has guided the conservation effort that has contributed to an increase in the population size of Greater Horseshoe Bats. However, the Greater Horseshoe Bat is atypical, having been studied intensively over many years. For many other species, including BAP species, basic questions remain. For example, in the last BAP target-setting round (in 2006) it was not possible to set population increase targets for Barbastelle or Bechstein's Bat because neither population surveillance nor systematic distribution surveys were in place, and so progress towards a target could not be measured adequately. Updating national distribution data and developing surveillance have become priorities for these species. A detector survey for monitoring activity of Barbastelles has been piloted during the past three years at SAC sites and other selected woodlands. Following further development, this may be expanded to cover a much larger network of sites as part of the National Bat Monitoring Programme (NBMP).

The NBMP, begun in 1996, is now a partnership between BCT and the Joint Nature Conservation Committee (JNCC) and has become the principal tool for reporting on UK bat population trends. It is the longest-running, purpose-built, multi-species monitoring programme for mammals in the world, delivering statistically defensible trends for 11 species (Figure 16.2). Its surveillance techniques, which include standardised annual counts of bats at maternity and hibernation sites, and bat detector surveys, have been used as the template for other national bat surveys, such as the All Ireland Bat Survey. Nearly 1000 volunteers now gather data each year and, as more than 2200 people have participated since 1996, NBMP may also be considered as an engagement tool. The NBMP was designed to ensure 'red or amber alert' population declines could be detected, but has actually reported significant population increases for several species. In particular, the UK population of Lesser Horsehoe Bats has increased significantly, by approximately 49% at maternity roosts and 41% in hibernation sites since 1999.

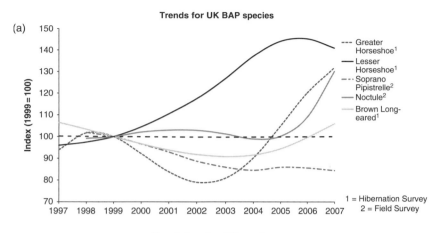

Trends for UK BAP species

(a)

Index (1999 = 100)

--- Greater
Horseshoe[1]

— Lesser
Horseshoe[1]

-·- Soprano
Pipistrelle[2]

— Noctule[2]

— Brown Long-
eared[1]

1 = Hibernation Survey
2 = Field Survey

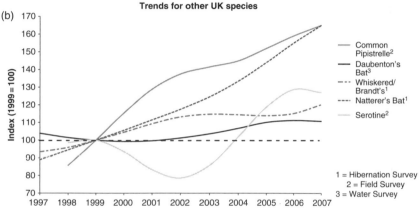

Trends for other UK species

(b)

Index (1999 = 100)

— Common
Pipistrelle[2]

— Daubenton's
Bat[3]

--- Whiskered/
Brandt's[1]

-·- Natterer's Bat[1]

— Serotine[2]

1 = Hibernation Survey
2 = Field Survey
3 = Water Survey

Figure 16.2 Trends from BCT's National Bat Monitoring Programme for (a) UK Biodiversity Action Plan (BAP) species and (b) other UK bat species.

Box 16.1 Using science to develop conservation policy: habitat management for greater horseshoe bats

Greater Horseshoe Bats, *Rhinolophus ferrumequinum*, underwent a substantial range reduction in Great Britain during the twentieth century, and a severe decline in numbers was part of this (Stebbings and Arnold 1987). They are now restricted largely to south-western areas of England and Wales. The bats were affected by exclusion from roosts, poisoning by toxic chemicals used to treat roof timbers, and by agricultural changes that presumably reduced the availability of insect prey. Currently, about 24 maternity colonies are known and the British population is now considered to be more than 6600 individuals (T. Mitchell-Jones, personal communication 2008). The Greater Horseshoe Bat has been studied in greater depth than any other British bat species, and a large volume of scientific research has been available to guide management programmes for it. Dr Roger Ransome has studied a colony of bats at Woodchester Mansion in Gloucestershire for over 50 years, and bats from several colonies have now been radio-tracked to foraging sites. Studies at the University of Bristol investigated the genetic structure of populations, diet, hibernal ecology and echolocation behaviour. The species has its own Biodiversity Action Plan, and hibernation sites are well protected: 23% of known hibernacula containing about 72% of this species are notified as Sites of Special Scientific Interest (Mitchell-Jones 1993).

Because agricultural intensification has been implicated in the decline of Greater Horseshoe Bats, research has been conducted to determine which habitats are used as prime feeding sites, and how these sites can be best protected. Greater Horseshoe Bats feed largely on large beetles (especially species that live as larvae in cowpats) and on moths. Radio-tracking showed that adults typically feed 2–4 km from the roost, and select cattle-grazed pasture and ancient semi-natural woodland habitats. Tall hedgerows and woodland edges are often exploited by foraging bats. Youngsters first leave the roost at 26–30 days of age, initially feeding over pasture within a few hundred metres of the roost, and extending their foraging ranges to distances similar to those travelled by adults by 55–60 days (Duvergé and Jones 1994).

These ecological data have been used to suggest appropriate habitat management to assist with the conservation of Greater Horseshoe Bats. Land managers who maintained land close to maternity colonies were encouraged to apply for grant aid through a Countryside Stewardship Scheme (CSS) administered by the Department for Environment, Food and Rural Affairs (Defra). The CSS proved popular with farmers, and its discretionary approach aimed to ensure best environmental value for money. Using findings from the radio-tracking studies, a 4 km 'sustenance zone' was identified around each maternity site, and land-management prescriptions rewarded under the CSS included:

- Retention and creation of permanent cattle-grazed pasture
- Maintenance of small fields and substantial hedges
- Replanting of broad, tall hedgerows along large open areas of permanent pasture
- Minimising insecticide use and managing stock without the use of wormers based on Avermectin compounds that may reduce the availability of insects that live in dung
- Leaving uncultivated arable field margins next to hedgerows to encourage insect prey.

English Nature (the SNCO in England at the time) initiated a Greater Horseshoe Bat project that visited and provided advice to over 160 land-owners managing about 13 200 ha of land in bat foraging sites around important maternity and hibernation sites over five years (Longley 2003). At least 46 farms (covering over 4000 ha) entered CSS agreements in Devon, Somerset and Cornwall. Over 30 applications covering 2300 ha were submitted by partner organisations, such as the Royal Society for the Protection of Birds (RSPB) and Wildlife Trusts within roost sustenance zones. 80 km of hedgerows close to roosts were designated for restoration or planting, and over 400 ha of grassland were brought under management to enhance bat foraging areas. The project was publicised by messages on milk products marketed by a large organic farm, with 7000 milk cartons distributed weekly across southern England.

Although the CSS no longer exists, the management agreements developed run for at least 10 years, and the replacement Environmental Stewardship schemes administered by DEFRA should prolong the success of this approach. A wide variety of farmland wildlife will have benefited from the CSS for Greater Horseshoe Bats. In Devon maternity roosts, bat numbers increased by 58% between 1995 and 2003 (Longley 2003). Some of this increase may be due to factors such as climate change, but there is little doubt that the success of CSS has made a major contribution to the impressive increase in numbers of a flagship conservation species.

Figure 16.3 The foraging habitat of the Greater Horseshoe Bat (inset) (see colour plate).

To expand the capacity of the programme to cover the remaining UK species requires technical innovation. The first systematic survey to determine the distribution of Bechstein's Bat across its entire known range (as prioritised by BAP) began in 2008, using the acoustic lure and harp trap technique previously developed by Hill and Greenaway (2005) in Hampshire and Sussex. The extent to which it is feasible to monitor the population of this species regularly remains to be seen, but the generation of such standardised data over a wide geographical area provides the framework for better understanding its ecological requirements and the drivers of change. This understanding is vital for all bat species and is stimulating exploration of new ways of utilising NBMP data in modelling approaches.

Bats in the twenty-first century: new threats and conservation approaches

There can be little doubt that the current position of bats is better in many respects than 30 years ago. From having been routinely treated as pests and actively persecuted, bats are heavily protected by legislation, supported by a large network of volunteer and professional specialists and the ecological requirements of many species are far better understood. Those species for which surveillance is in place appear mainly to be stable or increasing, albeit with an absolute population size that is suspected to be much lower than in the early twentieth century. There is greater public awareness and sympathy generally, despite the discovery of rabies in British bats (see Box 16.2), and the recent addition of bats to the small suite of groups that contribute population trend data to the UK biodiversity indicators may increase awareness among policy-makers. Whether the outlook for bats will remain as positive, however, depends on several emerging challenges.

Box 16.2 Rabies in British bats

It has long been known that bats are vectors of lyssaviruses, which cause rabies. Seven genotypes of lyssavirus have been recognised, including genotype 1, which is responsible for classical rabies and is carried by some New World bat species, including vampire bats. Across Europe, two lyssavirus genotypes, European bat lyssaviruses EBLV1 and EBLV2, have been identified in 12 bat species. Over 95% of EBLV1 infections are associated with Serotine. EBLV2 is associated with Daubenton's Bat and Pond Bat, *M. dasycneme*. The UK established an ongoing programme of passive surveillance to test bats for rabies in 1987. By 2004, the co-operation of bat workers and members of the public had enabled nearly 5000 bats found dead, and several grounded live bats that were behaving uncharacteristically, to be tested. Passive surveillance found no evidence of rabies in most bat species in Britain, including almost 3500 pipistrelles, the commonest bat found in association with humans. However Daubenton's bats were found to be infected with EBLV2 and by 2008 eight cases had been recorded.

Active surveillance, involving taking tiny blood samples and salivary swabs from about 1000 bats in Scotland and more than 600 in England to test for rabies seroprevalence and possible infection, has been undertaken since 2003. Seroprevalence involves tests for lyssavirus antibodies in blood, and positive results suggest that bats have been exposed to the virus at some stage. Although recorded levels vary from year to year, seroprevalence levels in Daubenton's bats average around 2.2% in England and 5% in Scotland. This shows that many bats have been exposed to lyssavirus, although few seemingly become infected by it. Clearly the paradigm until recently held by most scientists, that rabies is invariably fatal in all mammals, is flawed, because individual bats have remained seropositive year after year. Much remains to be learned about the pathogenicity of lyssaviruses.

In 2002, a batworker who had not received pre-exposure immunisation was bitten while handling bats in Scotland, developed rabies and died. The immediate reaction of politicians was to call for a cull of bats. However, the advice of the SNCO, Scottish Natural Heritage, was heeded and instead this tragic event resulted in a campaign of awareness-raising, spearheaded by the Bat Conservation Trust in collaboration with the country agencies, DEFRA, public health authorities and animal health agencies. Immunisation of all those who handle bats is now mandatory and members of the public who are bitten by bats or have a concern about close contact can receive up-to-date good practice advice from the Bat Conservation Trust helpline. Fears that the great advances in bat conservation which had occurred since the Wildlife and Countryside Act in 1981 would be reversed have proved groundless. Indeed, the combination of research, surveillance, education and being open about the potential risks has been powerful, gaining acceptance that bats and humans can co-exist in harmony, and that risks to humans are small and can be managed effectively.

Development and land-use change are strong pressures, and bats are vulnerable to such changes, due to their use of buildings and reliance on the continued availability of foraging habitats and connective features. Certain impacts of urbanisation are complex. For example, increased levels of lighting may concentrate insect prey at street lights, but may be detrimental for species adapted to foraging in woodland habitats. Under the Habitats Regulations, any changes that affect bats must only take place under licence, and must maintain the status of the population at a favourable level, either by avoiding disruptive activities or by appropriate mitigation. However, the legislative framework has developed faster than the science that supports the practical conservation activities. 'Favourable conservation status' is hard to define and its meaning widely debated, particularly its assessment over nested geographical scales (e.g. county, region, country, Europe). Individual losses of roosts may be judged unlikely to affect conservation status, but judgements are rarely taken with a full understanding of other recent losses, leaving the possibility of significant incremental erosion of population status. Mitigation, such as building artificial roosts for displaced colonies or green bridges across new roads, is widely practised, yet the outcomes are poorly researched and mainly unproven. Without investment in testing of mitigation approaches, including assessment of outcomes over the longer term, there is a risk that the letter, rather than the spirit, of the law is followed and that population status is ultimately diminished.

The potential impacts of climate change are uncertain. Climate envelope models suggest that certain species (some of which are on the edge of their European range) may extend their distribution. However these models do not consider barriers to changes in range. Species may be restricted geographically because of geology (which influences the availability of caves) or by barriers to dispersal, such as unsuitable habitat or lack of connective features. Nor do models consider changes to the ecological function of the habitats bats use, for example, the availability of mature woodland that may be essential for roosting, and riparian systems to provide sufficient invertebrate prey resources under future scenarios. Climate change will also impact on agriculture and insect populations, with additional dangers that peak prey abundance may move out of synchrony with bats' breeding seasons. Ironically, human responses to climate change may themselves pose dangers. For example, there is increasing concern that wind turbines could cause unacceptable mortality, though so far the evidence for this has been gathered outside the British Isles (e.g. Baerwald *et al.* 2008). There is an urgent need to assess risks to ensure energy generation schemes are guided appropriately. New building regulations and materials to improve energy efficiency may reduce substantially the availability of roosting opportunities in current and future buildings. Provision for biodiversity is possible, but needs to be incorporated at an early stage. Applied research is essential to underpin the guidance for such challenges. There are few responsive mode funders of research on the conservation biology of bats, however, and Mammals Trust UK deserves particular recognition for its work to date.

To address such complexities it is becoming increasingly important that conservation initiatives work at a landscape scale and take a wide view on changes that may affect biodiversity (e.g. for bats, buildings are often an important habitat, but lie outside the scope of more traditional general conservation approaches). Box 16.3 summarises a recent landscape-scale project that is being emulated in several other locations. The new BAP framework appears to be focusing on habitat and ecosystem approaches to the conservation of biodiversity and its success will depend on the degree to which the needs of species can be addressed at a range of scales. For bats, successful conservation is likely to require participation from sectors and people who have not traditionally concerned themselves with biodiversity. The past 30 years have seen substantial advances in bat conservation, which have included protective legislation, great expansion in the number of both amateur and professional bat experts, protection for vulnerable roosts and increased numbers of several species. The public, industries and governments are now far more aware of and sympathetic to bats. Fifty years ago it would have been unthinkable that bat walks would become the most oversubscribed activity at conservation centres, yet more than 100 events were held for European Bat weekend alone in 2008. This is surely a testimony to the ability of bats and their dedicated enthusiasts to highlight, and connect people to, environmental issues and the natural world. Bats will face new challenges from factors such as climate change in the twenty-first century. It is vital that bat numbers are monitored and that conservation measures are implemented to safeguard and enhance populations in the future.

Box 16.3 A landscape-scale approach to bat conservation: the Batscapes Project

The Batscapes Project was led by Bath and North-East Somerset Council, ran from 2003 to 2007, and applied across the council's district and that of neighbouring South Gloucestershire.

The project focused on awareness-raising and a landscape-scale approach to habitat improvements. Funding was secured from the Heritage Lottery Fund, Natural England and the Duchy of Cornwall. It had the overarching aim of involving all elements of the local community in the protection of horseshoe bats and local landscape features that support them. Fulfilment of these aims involved a broad partnership, including the county bat group and local environmental records centre.

To achieve landscape-scale habitat improvements, seconded officers from the Farming and Wildlife Advisory Group (FWAG) and Avon Wildlife Trust were employed to advise local land-owners and secure 10-year Environmental Stewardship agreements, which included horseshoe-bat-friendly management options within 5 km of key Greater Horseshoe Bat roosts. This approach followed earlier work done in Devon under the English Nature Greater Horseshoe Bat Project and was only possible because the foraging requirements and habitat use of the species had been well studied. The ideal landscape of insect-rich pastures surrounded by large hedgerows in a mosaic of woodlands, orchards, parkland and riparian habitats is of significant value for many other species, as well as being attractive to farmers and land-owners. Radio-tracking data were available for one of the main colonies, and the resultant maps facilitated targeted farm visits, and encouraged participation by land-owners.

In all, 35 landholdings entered into agreements, leading to around 70% of land targeted around key roosts being managed under stewardship. Farm open days were also held to promote bat-friendly farming practices which spread the information more widely.

Awareness-raising and community involvement featured strongly in the project, with the scope in this area broadened to include all bat species. The work supported and directed habitat improvements through increased surveying of roosts and key foraging areas, as well as directly through habitat-creation activities. Training was given to pest controllers, building surveyors, arboriculturalists and local planning officers, guidance notes were produced and numerous promotional events held. Public engagement ranged from simple bat talks to developing a trio of audio bat trails around local nature reserves in partnership with the local council and disability action group; the audio discs and bat detectors were available for loan from local libraries.

In order to increase recording of bats, a parish bat-warden scheme was developed, with the support of Avon Bat Group, whereby trained members of the public were allocated parishes to promote bats and survey for activity. Over 50 parish bat wardens were recruited and trained, a number which has continued to grow beyond the project under the auspices of the bat group. This led to numerous new flight and roost records. The project proved popular with both participants and funders, leaving a legacy of landscapes enhanced for horseshoe bats, a raised profile for bat conservation, increased understanding of local bats and a re-invigorated bat group. In its broader delivery, local communities benefitted from targeted participation and the opportunity to contribute to protecting their environment, while wider biodiversity gained through the land-management advice given and accepted.

Acknowledgements

We would like to thank all those who have contributed to this chapter, including Amy Coyte, Philip Briggs, Tony Mitchell-Jones, Jessa Battersby, Robert Stebbings, Tina Aughney, Conor Kelleher, Derek Yalden, Colin Galbraith and Norman Maclean. The National Bat Monitoring Programme is a partnership between BCT, JNCC and a large network of volunteer trainers and surveyors.

References

Barrett-Hamilton, G.E.H. (1910). *A History of British Mammals*, Vol. 1, London, Gurney & Jackson.

Baerwald, E.F., D' Armours, G.H., Klug, B.J. and Barclay, R.M.R. (2008). Barotrauma is a significant cause of bat fatalities at wind turbines. *Current Biology*, **18**, 695–696.

Bat Conservation Trust (2008). Bats and the law, http://www.bats.org.uk/pages/bats_ and_the_law.html.

Benton, T.G., Bryant, D.M., Cole, L. and Crick, H.Q.P. (2002). Linking agricultural practice to insect and bird populations: a historical study over three decades. *Journal of Applied Ecology*, **39**, 673–687.

Butterfly Conservation (2006). *The State of Britain's Larger Moths*, Dorset, Butterfly Conservation.

Duvergé, P.L. and Jones, G. (1994). Greater Horseshoe Bats – activity, foraging behaviour and habitat use. *British Wildlife*, **6**, 69–77.

Fuller, R.J., Norton, L.R., Feber, R.E. *et al.* (2005). Benefits of organic farming to biodiversity vary among taxa. *Biology Letters,* doi: 10.1098/rsbl.2005.0357.

Guest, P., Jones, K.E. and Tovey, J. (2002). Bats in Greater London: unique evidence of a decline over 15 years. *British Wildlife*, **13**, 1–5.

Harrington, R., Smith, E. and Hall, M. (2003). Assessing long-term trends in invertebrate biomass – a pilot study. Final Report to English Nature, Harpenden, Plant and Invertebrate Ecology Division, Rothamsted Research.

Harris, S. and Yalden, D.W. (2008). *Mammals of the British Isles*, Handbook, 4th edn., Southampton, The Mammal Society.

Harris, S., Morris, P., Wray, S. and Yalden, D. (1995). *A Review of British Mammals: Population Estimates and Conservation Status of British Mammals Other Than Cetaceans*, Peterborough, JNCC.

Hill, D.A. and Greenaway, F. (2005). Effectiveness of an acoustic lure for surveying bats in British woodlands. *Mammal Review*, **35**, 116–122.

Jefferies, D.J. (1972). Organochlorine insecticide residues in British bats and their significance. *Journal of Zoology Society of London*, **166**, 245–263.

Longley, M. (2003). The Greater Horseshoe Bat project: a species conservation success story. *British Wildlife*, **15**, 1–6.

Mitchell-Jones, A.J. (1993). The growth and development of bat conservation in Britain. *Mammal Review*, **23**, 139–148.

Mitchell-Jones, A.J., Cooke, A.S., Boyd, I.L. and Stebbings, R.E. (1989). Bats and remedial timber treatment chemicals – a review. *Mammal Review*, **19**, 93–110.

Parsons, K.N., Jones, G., Davidson-Watts, I. and Greenaway, F. (2003). Swarming of bats at underground sites in Britain – conservation implications. *Biological Conservation*, **111**, 63–70.

Racey, P.A. and Stebbings, R.E. (1972). Bats in Britain – a status report. *Oryx*, **11**, 319–327.

Racey, P.A. and Swift, S.M. (1986). Residual effects of remedial timber treatments on bats. *Biological Conservation*, **35**, 205–214.

Ransome, R.D. (1989). Population changes of Greater horseshoe bats studied near Bristol over the past twenty-six years. *Biological Journal of the Linnean Society*, **38**, 71–82.

Sargent, G. (1995). *The Bats in Churches Project,* London, Bat Conservation Trust.

Shore, R.F., Boyd, I.L., Leach, D.V., Stebbings, R.E. and Myhill, D.G. (1990). Organochlorine residues in roof timber treatments and possible implications for bats. *Environmental Pollution*, **64**, 179–188.

Stebbings, R.E. (1988). *Conservation of European Bats*, London, Christopher Helm.

Stebbings, R.E. and Arnold, H.R. (1987). Assessment of trends in size and structure of a colony of the greater horseshoe bat. *Symposium of the Zoological Society of London*, **58**, 7–24.

Swanepoel, R.E., Racey, P.A., Shore, R.F. and Speakman, J.R. (1999). Energetic effects of sub-lethal exposure to lindane on pipistrelle bats. (*Pipistrellus pipistrellus*). *Environmental Pollution,* **104**, 169–177.

Temple, H.J. and Terry, A. (compilers) (2007). *The Status and Distribution of European Mammals*, Luxembourg, Office for Official Publications of the European Communities.

Vaughan, N. (1997). The diets of British bats. *Mammal Review*, **27**, 77–94.

Walsh, A.L. and Harris, S. (1996). Foraging habitat preferences of vespertilionid bats in Britain. *Journal of Applied Ecology*, **33**, 506–518.

Wickramasinghe, L.P., Harris, S., Jones, G. and Vaughan, N. (2003). Bat activity and species richness on organic and conventional farms: impact of agricultural intensification. *Journal of Applied Ecology*, **40**, 984–993.

17

State of bird populations in Britain and Ireland

Robert A. Robinson

Summary

The bird fauna of Britain and Ireland has been studied for over 500 years and changes in numbers over the last 40 years are well documented by a range of surveys, mostly undertaken by volunteers. Britain and Ireland are home to internationally important numbers of seabirds in the breeding season and many species of wildfowl and waders in the winter. Although there has been little overall change in total bird numbers, about half of bird species in Britain and Ireland are of conservation concern because of small or declining populations. In the last 30 years, declines in farmland birds have been well documented, but declines in many woodland and migratory birds are just beginning to be recognised. Conversely, there have been increases in numbers of many raptors, seabirds and waterbirds. In general, habitat specialists have tended to decline most, while more adaptable, generalist species are increasing in number. Climate change threatens bird populations in all habitats, but loss of habitat and deterioration in habitat quality are more pressing threats. Conservationists have been successful at increasing populations of rarer species, but the greater challenge will be conserving birds in the wider countryside, which will require the integration of conservation goals with wider social and landscape policies.

Introduction

More is known about the birds of Britain than the vertebrate fauna of virtually any other country. This knowledge stretches back at least five centuries, with William Turner the first to publish original observations in his *Avium praecipuarum quarum apud Plinium et Aristotlem mentio est brevis & succinta historia* (a short and succinct

Silent Summer: The State of Wildlife in Britain and Ireland, ed. Norman Maclean. Published by Cambridge University Press. © Cambridge University Press 2010.

history of the principal birds noted by Pliny and Aristotle) in 1544 (Bircham 2007). Turner's 'succinct history' included just over 100 species that he recognised as occurring in Britain, including the Phesan (Pheasant, *Phasianus colchicus*), Bramlynge (Brambling, *Fringilla montifringilla*), Nut-jobber (Nuthatch, *Sitta europaea*) and Solend Guse (Gannet, *Morus bassana*). The first 'modern' ornithology was that of John Ray and Francis Willughby, which appeared in English (rather than Latin) in 1678 and which recognised around 200 species in Britain. By January 2009, 584 species had been recorded in Britain (and 460 in Ireland), representing an increase in knowledge and field effort as much as an increase in the number of species occurring.

The breeding population of birds in Britain is in the region of 75 million pairs of 220 species; a further 50 or so species visit regularly during the winter months or pass though in spring and autumn, though numbers of these are more poorly known (Appendix 1). About 200 species occur regularly in Ireland, reflecting its position further from the European mainland. Overall, populations of Britain's commoner breeding birds seem remarkably stable (Figure 17.1). This simple line, though, hides much variation, with some species (e.g. seabirds) increasing in numbers, whilst others (e.g. farmland birds) have fallen dramatically. The simplicity of this figure also belies the vast amount of effort, almost all unpaid, undertaken in survey work to produce the data on which it is based. However, its strength lies in its very simplicity: the clear decline in

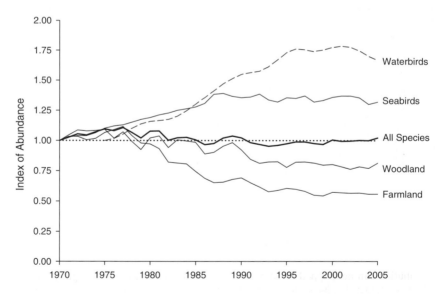

Figure 17.1 Trends in UK bird populations 1970–2005. The thick line represents the average trend of 116 species of breeding bird species, and the thinner lines 19 species of farmland, 38 woodland and 20 seabird species. The index for wintering waterbirds (68 spp., dashed line) is not part of the all species indicator. In each case the index (which is an unweighted average of the trends for each constituent species) is arbitrarily set to 1 in 1970 (1975 for waterbirds as earlier values are not available).

farmland birds it demonstrates, for example, was instrumental in stimulating a policy response to address the issues underlying the decline.

In comparison to other taxa, birds are relatively easy to monitor, being popular, visible, (mostly) diurnal and (generally) countable; consequently a large amount is known about their trends, at least in recent decades and for the commoner species (Appendix 1). Rather than pick out individual species, I have tried to identify common patterns that reflect the major patterns of environmental change in our islands over the last 40 years before going on to outline some of the major challenges for bird conservation in the coming decades. But first I would like to give a flavour of the range of monitoring efforts that exist, which mean we know so much about the state of our avian fauna.

Monitoring bird populations: approaches and scope

Birds vary greatly in number: from a single Long-billed Murrelet, *Brachyramphus perdix*, recorded off the Devon coast in 2006 to the Wren, *T. troglodytes*, which may, in some years, number tens of millions of individuals. They also vary greatly in their ecology, from Nightingales, *Luscinia megarhynchos*, inhabiting dense scrub of southern Britain to the Ptarmigan, *Lagopus muta*, of the windswept Scottish uplands, and in how easy they are count, from the Gannet which nests mostly on offshore stacks in Ireland and Scotland and whose population can be almost completely enumerated using aerial photography, to the cryptic and largely nocturnal Woodcock, *Scolopax rusticola*, for which population estimates are little more than educated guesses. Surveys of abundance therefore differ greatly in their aims and methods.

For some species, typically those with localised distributions, a complete, or almost complete, census can be contemplated; for commoner and widespread species, sample surveys must be undertaken, while for rarer species collation of reported sightings may be all that is possible (Table 17.1). Most monitoring of birds is undertaken by unpaid volunteers working in conjunction with professional scientists who direct the sampling and analyse the data collected to inform conservation and land-management policies (Figure 17.2). This arrangement not only allows schemes to operate over the long-term and extensive spatial scales at very low cost, it also encourages a greater appreciation of science and the environment by participants, facilitating democratic participation in research that often has a direct impact on wider policy (Greenwood 2007).

Britain and Ireland have a long tradition of recording birds stretching back into the nineteenth century; though this information is rarely quantitative, broad patterns of distribution can be mapped (Holloway 1996). Concerns over the use of pesticides in the 1950s, similar to those that led Rachel Carson to pen *Silent Spring*, prompted the Nature Conservancy (as it was then) to fund the British Trust for Ornithology (BTO) to organise an annual survey (the Common Birds Census, CBC) to measure both background variation in bird numbers and the extent of any changes as a result of pesticide poisoning, pollution or habitat change (Marchant *et al.* 1990). More recently this has been replaced by the Breeding Bird Survey (BBS), which provides more representative

Table 17.1 *Monitoring of Britain and Ireland's bird populations. Key schemes currently operating are listed with an indication of their geographic scope and year of commencement and survey interval. Results are published in books (first author, year of publication and publisher are given), annual reports (with lead organisation) or as journal articles (most recent cited).*

Breeding Season

All	Distribution Atlas	Britain and Ireland	1972, *c.* 20 yr	Sharrock (1976, Poyser); Gibbons *et al.* (1993, Poyser)
Common	Breeding Bird Survey	UK	1994, 1 yr	www.bto.org/bbs
	Countryside Bird Survey (CBS)	Ireland	1998, 1 yr	Coobes *et al.* (2009) (BirdWatch Ireland)
	Waterway Breeding Bird Survey (WBBS)	UK	1998, 1 yr	www.bto.org/survey/wbbs,htm
Grey Heron	Heronries Census	UK	1928, 1 yr	*Ibis*, **146**, 323–334
Seabirds	Seabird Colony Register	Britain and Ireland	1969, *c.* 15 yr	Cramp *et al.* (1974, Collins); Lloyd *et al.* (1991, Poyser); Mitchell *et al.* (2004, Poyser)
	Seabird Monitoring Programme (SMP)	UK	1986, 1 yr	www.jncc.gov.uk/page~1550
Scarce	Statutory Conservation Agency/RSPB Annual Breeding Bird Survey (SCARABBS)	UK	1961, various	
Rare	Rare Breeding Birds Panel (RBBP)	UK	1972, 1 yr	*British Birds*, **103**, 5–52
	Irish Rare Breeding Birds Panel	Ireland	2002, 1 yr	*Irish Birds*, **8**, 365–394
Non-native	Rare Breeding Birds Panel	UK	1996, 1 yr	*British Birds*, **100**, 638–649

Non-breeding Season

All	Distribution Atlas	Britain and Ireland	1983, *c.* 25 yr	Lack (1986, Poyser)
Seabirds	At-sea distribution	NW Europe		Stone *et al.* (1995, JNCC)
Waterbirds	Wetland Bird Survey (WeBS)	UK	1947, 1 yr	Annual report, BTO
	Irish Wetland Bird Survey (I-WeBS)	Ireland	1994, 1 yr	*Irish Birds*, **8**, 341–350
	Non-estuarine Coastal Waterbird Survey (NeWS)	UK	1984, *c.* 10 yr	*Bird Study*, **50**, 22–32

Table 17.1 (cont.)

Non-Breeding Season				
Gulls	Winter Gull Roost Survey (WinGS)	UK	1953, 10 yr	*British Birds*, **96**, 376–401
Scarce Migrants		Britain	1958, 1 yr	*British Birds*, **99**, 74–117, 129–173
		Ireland	2004, 1 yr	*Irish Birds*, **8**, 263–298
Rare	British Birds Rarities Committee (BBRC)	Britain	1958, 1 yr	*British Birds*, **102**, 528–601
	Irish Rare Birds Committee (IRBC)	Ireland	1953, 1 yr	*Irish Birds*, **8**, 395–416

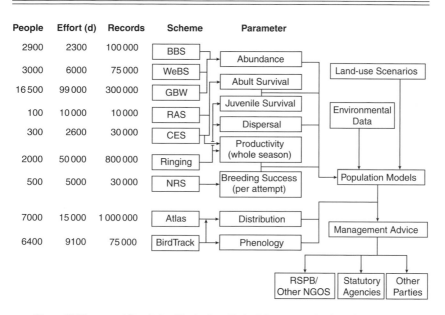

Figure 17.2 Integrated Population Monitoring. Each of the core monitoring schemes listed provides information on one or more key demographic parameters, which can be used to understand causes of population change through population modelling, which can then feed through into conservation or management advice to relevant stake-holders. For each scheme number of participants, estimated time spent each year (days) and approximate number of records contributed annually is indicated. The schemes represented are a selection of the core annual monitoring schemes, several others also exist.

Schemes listed are: BBS – Breeding Bird Survey, GBW – Garden BirdWatch, WeBS – Wetland Bird Survey, CES – Constant Effort Sites ringing scheme, RAS – Re-trapping Adults for Survival ringing scheme, NRS – Nest Records Scheme. For BBS, GBW, WeBS, Atlas and BirdTrack a record is one species at one site, for NRS and the ringing schemes a record is an individual bird or nest.

coverage of a greater range of species nationally, but less detailed information at each site (Newson *et al.* 2008).

For species that are too scarce to occur on a sufficient number of CBC or BBS sites, targeted surveys must be organised, often using specifically tailored methods. Species covered in this manner range from seabirds through Dartford Warbler, *Sylvia undata*, to Golden Eagle, *Aquila chrysaetos*, with an honourable mention to the Heronries Census which began in 1928 and is the longest-running annual single-species survey in the world. Summary results from these surveys are presented in the annual *State of the UK's Birds* report (published jointly by Britain's bird conservation organisations) and at http://www.bto.org/birdtrends. These specific surveys are supplemented, every 20 years or so, by national atlases which aim to record the distribution (and relative abundance) of all regularly occurring species. Most counties in Britain have also produced at least one local atlas (Ballance 2000) and the next atlas covering Britain and Ireland will be published in 2013 (http://www.birdatlas.net).

Monitoring of numbers (or relative abundance) is really just the first step. There is little point in monitoring unless appropriate action follows changes (up or down); determining the threshold at which action is required is a key conservation priority. Long-term quantitative data on trends mean that the status of species can be objectively assessed, resulting in much greater transparency in the conservation designation process (Eaton *et al.* 2009). Understanding the cause of population change is aided by knowledge of the demography of the population, i.e. reproductive output, survival and dispersal between populations (Figure 17.2), which can be critical in identifying the key environmental drivers of change and effective management actions (Baillie 1990). Such actions may be required, both if species are declining or if they increase to the extent where they cause economic impacts on other users of the countryside.

The changing state of Britain and Ireland's birds

Because they are islands, Britain and, especially, Ireland have smaller bird faunas than might be expected, with several species that are common on the near continent missing. Their oceanic position and extensive coastline mean our islands support large populations of breeding seabirds; more than 20% of the European population of nine species, and more than half of the world population of three: Gannet, Great Skua, *Stercorarius skua*, and Manx Shearwater, *P. puffinus*, breed in Britain or Ireland. In winter, Britain and Ireland also support internationally important populations of many geese and waders (Appendix 1). Only two species of global conservation concern occur regularly: Balearic Shearwater, *P. mauretanicus* (CRITICALLY ENDANGERED) and Aquatic Warbler, *Acrocephalus paludicola* (VULNERABLE), both on passage. A further six are classified as NEAR THREATENED: Sooty Shearwater, *P. griseus*, Red Kite, *M. milvus*, Corncrake, *C. crex*, Curlew, *Numenius arquata*, Black-tailed Godwit, *L. limosa*, and Dartford Warbler. Only one species, Scottish Crossbill, *Loxia scotica*, is endemic, but around 35 species have endemic races, four of which are restricted to Ireland.

One species occurring regularly in Britain and Ireland has become globally extinct: the last Great Auk, *Pinguinis impennis*, in Britain, was killed on Stac an Armin, St Kilda in the 1840s on the tragic presumption that it was a witch. Several species, though, have essentially disappeared as breeding birds in these islands, but remain common elsewhere, including: Great Bustard, *Otis tarda* (extinct by the mid-nineteenth century), Black Tern, *Chlidonias niger*, and Kentish Plover, *Charadrius alexandrinus* (mid-twentieth century), Wryneck, *Jynx torquilla*, Red-backed Shrike, *Lanius collurio*, and, in Ireland, Corn Bunting, *Emberiza calandra* (late twentieth century). In the last 50 years though, these have been offset by re-colonising former breeders, such as Avocet, *Recurvirostra avosetta*, new breeding species, notably Little Egret, *Egretta garzetta*, Collared Dove, *Streptopelia decaocto*, and, in England, Cetti's Warbler, *Cettia cetti*, and introduced, non-native, species such as Egyptian Goose, *Alopochen aegyptiacus* (Figure 17.3) and Rose-ringed Parakeet, *Psittacula krameri*.

Comprehensive accounts of changes in individual species' status are available in Brown and Grice (2005, England), Forrester and Andrews (2007, Scotland), Hutchinson (1989, Ireland) and Lovegrove *et al.* (1994, wales) and summarised in Parkin & Knox (2010). Because man has had such a huge influence on the British and Irish landscape, bird populations in particular habitats often exhibit similar trends in response to common environmental drivers (Fuller and Ausden 2008). I have structured the text around habitats to identify common themes among species inhabiting them. Most of the patterns

Figure 17.3 Numbers of Egyptian geese are booming as they spread from Holkham Hall, Norfolk where they were introduced in the eighteenth century, often using man-made reservoirs and water parks (see colour plate). (Photograph by Rob Robinson/BTO.)

described are common to both Britain and Ireland, as many of the drivers and trends are similar in these two countries; however, data are much more readily available for Britain, which has had a stronger, and longer, history of monitoring bird populations, so these are more often quoted.

Marine

Seabirds are mostly ground and burrow nesters and consequently tend to nest on remote cliffs and islands, where nest predators are few. Nowhere has this been more evident than in the west of Scotland, where breeding seabirds, such as Black Guillemot, *Cepphus grylle*, and Arctic Tern, *Sterna paradisaea*, have all but disappeared from many locations as a result of depredation by American Mink, *Mustela vison*. More widely, Brown Rat, *Rattus norvegicus*, predation has been associated with local declines of Manx Shearwater and Puffin, *Fratercula arctica*, colonies. Eradication of both predators is underway at some colonies, but is an arduous task.

Food availability is a strong driver of seabird population dynamics. An increase in the availability of food, particularly discards from the fishing industry, over the last century has been associated with dramatic increases in the numbers of Fulmar, *Fulmarus glacialis*, and Great Skua; Cormorants, *Phalacrocorax carbo*, meanwhile, have prospered on well-stocked inland waters used by anglers. The importance of food supply for seabird populations has been demonstrated by complete breeding failures in some areas in recent years when food has been scarce for species, such as Kittiwake, *Rissa tridactyla*, and Puffin, that rely on Sandeels, *Ammodytes*, to feed their chicks. When Sandeel stocks collapsed around Shetland between 1985 and 1990, very few chicks were reared successfully, leading to population declines in several species. Although over-fishing played a part in this decline, most fishing activity occurs beyond the foraging range of colonies and often targets bigger Sandeels than seabirds forage on. Increases in sea temperatures forcing the Sandeel spawning stock northwards, away from the colonies, seem to have been more important (Frederiksen *et al.* 2004).

Seabirds spend most of their lives at sea, only coming ashore to breed for two to three months each year. Despite the importance of offshore areas, relatively little is known about the status of seabirds at sea, although newly developed technologies, such as geo-locators and data-loggers are providing exciting insights into the use of marine habitats far from shore. During the breeding season, parents probably forage in hotspots near thermal fronts or areas of upwelling which tend to be rich in food, but in winter birds are much more dispersed. In recent years, oil spills have killed many thousands of birds, particularly Guillemots, *Uria aalge*, and other auks, but this seems to have had rather little impact on breeding populations due to the presence of a surplus of immature and non-breeding birds.

Coasts and estuaries

Populations of many wintering ducks and geese were limited by hunting in the first half of the twentieth century. However, increased protection, particularly following the 1954 Protection of Birds Act, and a decline in the popularity of wildfowling have meant that numbers of most species have increased. Some have grown dramatically; numbers of Pink-footed Goose, *Anser brachyrhynchus*, rose from 30 000 in the early 1950s to around 250 000 today, for example. Similarly, most wintering estuarine wader populations are stable or increasing. Numbers of birds on non-estuarine coastal sites (where there was less of a hunting tradition), however, have shown rather more mixed trends, with some species typical of rocky shores, such as Purple Sandpiper, *Calidris maritima*, Turnstone, *Arenaria interpres*, and Ringed Plover, *Charadrius hiaticula*, being recorded in smaller numbers more recently.

Habitat on the coastal fringe has been under threat since large-scale drainage of coastal marshes began in the late seventeenth century. Currently, the major threat comes from industrial development, such as new ports, renewable energy generation (offshore wind and tidal stream) and reclamation for amenity and other uses. Although populations of many waders are continuing to increase, probably from artificially low populations created by hunting pressure, this continued loss of habitat must limit their capacity for increase. In the future, coastal habitat will also be increasingly squeezed between rising sea levels, as a result of climate change, and sea defences, particularly in south-east England.

Climate change is already affecting shorebird populations. The Atlantic coasts of Britain and Ireland provide a mild climate, but good foraging habitat (invertebrate-rich mudflats) is scarce. Conversely, our eastern shores have large estuaries, but winters can be much more severe, with prolonged spells of cold weather resulting in large-scale mortality. In recent years, there has been a tendency for winters in Europe to become warmer and, consequently, we are seeing a shift in winter distribution eastward, as juveniles, particularly of Fennoscandian and Siberian breeding populations, settle on estuaries closer to their breeding grounds. Adult birds show high site fidelity, so are probably showing little change in distribution and introducing a lag in the population response of climate change. In itself, such redistribution does not pose a threat to populations providing sufficient habitat is present, but it does mean that site designations (usually based on numbers using a site) may need to be reassessed and that conservation strategies will increasingly need an international dimension, considering the flyway in its entirety.

Farmland

One of the most obvious changes in land use over the last 50 years has been the intensification of agriculture and the loss of mixed farming (Robinson and Sutherland 2002). Populations of farmland bird species mirror changes in agriculture: the area of agricultural land declined markedly between the 1870s and 1930s, but the post-war desire for food self-sufficiency saw a boom in cultivation and populations of many farmland species increased greatly in numbers, probably becoming more common in the 1970s than before or since. From around the point of Britain's entry into the European Community, advances in technology and generous production subsidies, such as guaranteed prices, meant that practices rapidly began to change: new crop varieties were

introduced, crop rotations changed, chemical inputs increased and farms became ever
larger, specialising in either arable crops or livestock because of the need for expensive machinery (Figure 17.4). Changes in pastoral farming have been equally marked
with increased fertiliser usage, a switch from hay to silage cropping and increased
stocking densities. The primary effect of these changes has been a decrease in habitat
heterogeneity at all scales, from within fields to across landscapes.

   These changes have had a catastrophic effect on farmland bird populations
(Figure 17.1), with a litany of declines in the last 40 years amongst the species most
closely associated with farmed land: Tree Sparrow, *Passer montanus*, 97%, Corn
Bunting 86%, Grey Partridge, *P. perdix*, 87% and Skylark, *Alauda arvensis*, 59%.
Declines in many once common species, such as Quail, *C. coturnix*, Corncrake and
Cirl Bunting, *Emberiza cirlus*, preceded these, but went unquantified (Newton 2004).
Of course, some species increased, notably Woodpigeon, *Columba palumbus*, (143%)
and corvids, such as Jackdaw, *Corvus monedula*, (87%), probably as a result of reduced
persecution and, in the case of Woodpigeon, extensive sowing of oilseed rape. Although
the general intensification of agriculture has undoubtedly been responsible for most of
these changes, disentangling the impacts of and relative importance of the different
facets of agricultural change is difficult. Doing so is, however, important for designing
effective conservation solutions and in the last 20 years it has been a major research area
that has fed directly into, and been informed by, policy. The long history of research on
Grey Partridge provides an exemplary study in unravelling the causes of these declines
(see Chapter 18).

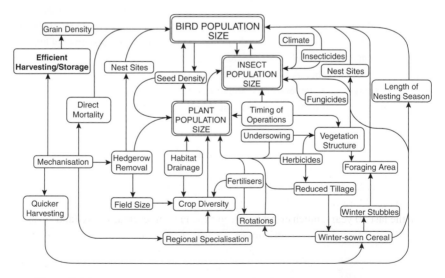

Figure 17.4 Potential causes of population change in plant, insect and bird populations
resulting from changes in arable management. (From Robinson and Sutherland 2002.)

Targeted conservation measures have proved easier to implement for species with restricted range than for more widespread species. So, for example, management agreements with farmers have increased the Cirl Bunting population fourfold since 1989 in south-west England and slowed the decline of Corncrakes in Ireland. Although agri-environment schemes can influence breeding populations, their success has been mixed (Ausden and Fuller 2009) and whether the recent stabilisation of farmland bird populations (Figure 17.1) is due to changes in policy, a recent run of mild winters, or because populations are simply reaching a new carrying capacity remains to be seen. The future of farmland bird populations will continue to depend on the economics of agriculture. Increases in cereal prices, for example, resulted in the abolition of set-aside for 2008, greatly reducing the availability of winter foraging habitat for many species. Ongoing monitoring, though, means the effects of such changes can be quantified and, because of this, biodiversity targets are increasingly being incorporated alongside production in framing agricultural policies.

Wetlands

A major component of agricultural intensification has been land drainage. Much lowland wet grassland has been lost, as well as unique habitats, such as reed and sedge fens in the south and east of Britain and the seasonally flooded callows and turloughs of Ireland. Consequently, some fen specialists, such as Black Tern and Bittern, *Botaurus stellaris*, have all but disappeared as breeding birds, and species associated with lowland wet grassland, notably breeding waders, such as Lapwing, *V. vanellus*, Snipe, *G. gallinago*, and Redshank, *Tringa totanus*, have declined significantly. In addition to direct habitat loss, wetlands are vulnerable to increased nutrient loads (eutrophication), mostly from non-point sources such as leaching from agricultural land, and scrub encroachment, particularly as a result of lowered water tables, often reducing habitat quality for those that remain.

The expansion of cities and towns in the south of England and elsewhere required the extraction of large amounts of sand and gravel for construction, holes that were often turned into reservoirs to supply water, such as those at Abberton, Chew and Rutland. Many of these newly created water bodies have since been managed, at least partly, with nature conservation in mind, both for species conservation and general amenity value. This has provided large amounts of new habitat for breeding and wintering waterbirds, such as Great-crested Grebe, *Podiceps cristatus*, Tufted Duck, *Aythya fuligula*, and Gadwall, *Anas strepera*, and inland breeding waders, notably Little Ringed Plover, *Charadrius dubius*.

In the last 20 years, much effort has been expended in re-creating wetlands in areas which have suffered large historic losses, such as the Thames estuary and East Anglia (see http://www.wetlandvision.org.uk). Projects are often targeted at 'flagship' species, particularly Bittern, but many other species (and not just birds) are also benefiting. Such habitat creation is likely to become commoner in the future as developers are increasingly required to compensate for lost habitat. Habitat creation schemes seem to be more successful for wetland (and coastal) habitats than terrestrial ones, though whether entire communities can be simply translocated and re-created elsewhere is a question that remains unanswered, both ecologically and morally.

Uplands

Despite their apparent bleakness, upland habitats, which range from unenclosed grazed pasture through bog and plantation forestry to arctic-alpine tundra on the high tops, support a diverse bird fauna, including many of our most emblematic birds, such as Golden Eagle, Raven, *Corvus corax*, and Red Grouse, *L. lagopus*. Open moor is itself the result of a long history of land use extending back nearly 4000 years in some regions; much of what might once have been montane scrub and wood is now sheepwalk or acid grassland. Britain, particularly Scotland, and Ireland are internationally important for blanket and raised bogs, despite the fact that less than 20% of their original area remains. They have been encroached by drainage for agriculture, afforestation and, especially in Ireland, large-scale extraction of peat for fuel and horticulture. Consequently, numbers of birds of open moor and bog, such as Curlew (Figure 17.5), Dunlin, *Calidris alpina*, and Red Grouse, have declined through habitat loss (Pearce-Higgins *et al.* 2008).

Although the uplands have long been grazed, they cannot withstand the current level of grazing pressure. High densities of Red Deer, *Cervus elaphus*, and sheep have

Figure 17.5 Recent declines in curlew populations mean it is one of six species occurring in Britain and Ireland considered as globally Near Threatened (see colour plate). (Photograph by Rob Robinson/BTO.)

greatly reduced vegetation diversity, diminishing both nesting and foraging habitat for birds. The number of sheep in upland areas is beginning to decrease with a shift away from headage payments, leading to scrub encroachment in some areas, which will benefit some species, such as Willow Warbler, *Phylloscopus trochilus*; deer numbers, on the other hand, are likely to continue to increase. Agriculture is also encroaching on the uplands, with marginal land being enclosed and improved (fertilised) for grazing, higher levels of drainage and an increase in silage cropping. These changes appear to have precipitated declines in a number of species associated with upland grassland, such as Whinchat, *Saxicola rubetra*, Wheatear, *O. oenanthe*, and Ring Ousel, *Turdus torquatus*. As in lowland areas, the fate of upland bird populations will depend on the degree of habitat diversity that can be maintained at different scales.

Although populations of moorland birds have suffered from loss of habitat due to afforestation, upland forests can provide important habitat for some species, particularly in the first 10–15 years before the canopy closes. The spread of young forest aided the re-colonisation of mainland Scotland by Hen Harriers, *Circus cyaneus*, from the Northern Isles in the 1940s, for example. Middle-aged plantations, with a dense, dark canopy, support relatively few species, but as the plantation matures, other species, such as Crossbill, *Loxia curvirostra*, can colonise, so one bird community is successively replaced by another. Consequently, as plantations have matured and the area of new planting fallen, we have seen declines in Tree Pipit, *Anthus trivialis*, and Lesser Redpoll, *Carduelis cabaret*, but increases in Goshawk, *Accipiter gentilis*, and Siskin, *C. spinus*, populations. Much of the conservation value of moorland communities, however, lies in their distinctness and rarity in a European context, while most species typical of conifer plantations are common throughout Europe, so increased diversity may not be a sufficient goal in itself. A key issue for the Scottish uplands is the extent to which we wish to encourage natural regeneration of broad-leaf and Scots Pine, *Pinus sylvestris*, woodland (replacing the presumed 'wood of Caledon'), which again will benefit some bird species, but be detrimental to others.

Birds of the high tops, such as Ptarmigan, Dotterel, *Charadrius morinellus*, and Snow Bunting, *Plectrophenax nivalis*, are at the southern edge of their range in Britain, and prospects for their continued existence in Britain look bleak, as the high tops are amongst the areas most likely to be affected by increasing global temperatures. In the past few decades, for example, the area of lying snow has decreased markedly and, although there is little hard evidence, it seems likely that the area suitable for breeding for most of these species will decline over the next two or three decades. Whether management actions can be identified to preserve these populations, which are also suffering from increased visitor pressure, remains to be seen.

While birds of prey were once widespread across Britain, ranges of many contracted into upland areas, away from human populations, as a result of persecution and poisoning from pesticides, particularly organochlorines such as dieldrin. The uplands still represent strongholds for many species, but the phasing out of organochlorine pesticides as their environmental impacts became clear and increased legal protection mean that most species have increased in number and expanded back into lowland areas (Greenwood *et al.* 2003). Persecution of raptors has often been greatest in areas of heather *Calluna* moor managed for driven Grouse shooting. Relationships between raptor numbers, Grouse production and habitat are complex and reductions in management intensity and overgrazing are leading to a general decline in the quality of Grouse moors, both in economic and biodiversity terms (Thirgood *et al.* 2000). Despite increased protection, continued persecution in some areas appears to be preventing further recovery of Hen Harriers and other raptors.

Woodland and scrub

Although much of lowland Britain and Ireland would once have been woodland (not necessarily with a continuous canopy), most of our woods have for a long time been relatively fragmented and heavily modified by man. The area of semi-natural woodland (and particularly ancient woodland) is gradually reducing, but the total area of woodland has steadily increased over the last 40 years, mostly through commercial planting of conifers. Population trends among woodland bird species have not been consistent over the last 40 years: scarce woodland specialists, such as the Lesser Spotted Woodpecker, *Dendrocopus minor*, and Willow Tit, *Poecile montana*, and long-distance migrants, such as Spotted Flycatcher, *Muscicapa striata*, and Tree Pipit, tend to be declining, while more generalist species tend to be increasing (Fuller *et al.* 2005).

Undoubtedly, greatly increased deer numbers, particularly of Roe Deer, *Capreolus capreolus*, and Muntjac, *Muntiacus reevesi*, are having a major impact on our woodlands, resulting in a reduction in habitat quality and changes in the structure of the woodland understorey, which many birds nest or forage in. In the last two to three decades there has also been a notable decrease in the intensity of woodland management; denser canopies have shaded out shrub layer plants, such as Bramble, *Rubus fruticosus*, to the detriment of species like Nightingale, which prefer a dense shrub layer (Fuller *et al.* 2005). Looking to the future, short-rotation coppicing, particularly of Willow, *Salix*, holds potential as a source of biofuel, but its impact on bird communities will depend on where it is planted and how it is managed.

Scrub is a bit of a Cinderella habitat, always on the boundary. Although there are places where scrub is probably the natural habitat, storm-lashed coastal heaths and in sub-montane areas above the treeline, it is more often a (usually unwelcome) stage in the succession of vegetation from open heath or marsh to young woodland. Yet scrub supports a distinctive community of birds, albeit one which is sensitive to the amount of cover available with, for example, Tree Pipit and Linnet, *Carduelis cannabina*, on more open heaths and Garden Warbler, *Sylvia borin*, and Dunnock, *Prunella modularis*, commoner in areas with continuous canopy. They also provide an important source of food for berry-eating thrushes and others in winter. The fortunes of such species undoubtedly reflect the amount of available habitat and many will have declined due to loss of habitat to agriculture or woodland succession. More recently active habitat management has seen a great improvement in the overall condition of Britain's shrub and heath stock, so many species, like Dartford Warbler and Nightjar, *Caprimulgus europaea*, are currently prospering.

Afro-Palaearctic migrants are an important component of woodland and scrub communities, and many species, particularly those that migrate to central Africa, are declining. The reasons for these declines are unclear, but could include: deterioration in habitat quality (either in Europe or Africa), increased competition from more abundant resident species as a result of milder winters or changes in seasonal phenology. Many bird species are breeding earlier in response to warmer springs, but so are their insect prey, which are emerging and maturing earlier (Crick 2004). Migrants may be constrained in the degree to which they can advance their timing of breeding because of the need to migrate back to breeding grounds, whereas insects can respond to warming temperatures more rapidly and to a greater extent. There is some evidence that in areas where insect phenology has advanced to the greatest extent, populations of Pied Flycatchers, *Ficedula hypoleuca*, are doing least well because their timing of breeding is no longer so closely matched with their prey. Though the extent to which these findings generalise to other regions and species is unknown, such decoupling has the potential to profoundly alter ecological systems in a way that will be difficult to mitigate.

Towns and gardens

Birds of towns and gardens are often overlooked in inventories of biodiversity, yet the area of private gardens is estimated to be approximately twice that of nature reserves (local, national and RSPB) in England and Wales (Cannon *et al.* 2005). Gardens support a significant proportion of the national population for some species; the BBS, for example, identifies eight species as characteristic of urban and suburban areas: House Sparrow, *Passer domesticus* (Figure 17.6), Starling, *Sturnus vulgaris*, Blackbird, *Turdus merula*, Magpie, *Pica pica*, Collared Dove, Greenfinch, *Charduelis chloris*, Carrion Crow, *Corvus corone*, and, increasingly, Woodpigeon. They can also provide an important refuge for some species of conservation concern, such as Song Thrush, *Turdus philomelos*, and Spotted Flycatcher.

Birds of gardens tend to be those that are common (or, well, garden!) and populations of such species are generally increasing, at least in part because of the increased provision (and in greater variety) of food. Food provision can also be important for species in the wider countryside, for example, Goldfinches, *Carduelis carduelis*, are increasingly exploiting garden feeders in winter as seed supplies in farmland decrease. Urban areas can also provide other resources, for example, the number of Herring Gulls, *Larus argentatus*, nesting on flat roofs is increasing markedly, in contrast to declining populations in coastal areas. Even within towns, though, suitable habitat can

Figure 17.6 House Sparrow has recently been placed on the Red List due to large population declines in both urban and rural areas (see colour plate). (Photograph by Rob Robinson/ BTO.)

be quite patchy; House Sparrows, once ubiquitous, now tend to be associated only with particular types of housing, for reasons which are unclear, but which may be related to the availability of nest sites or foraging opportunities.

Urban expansion still represents a threat of habitat loss and fragmentation. Over the next 20 years, around 200 000 new homes are expected to be required annually in England and there is a limit to how many can be built on brownfield sites. Such effects extend beyond habitat loss, for example the number of breeding Nightjars is lower on heathland closer to towns because of greater disturbance from visitors. How large an impact human disturbance actually has on population levels is unknown, but access to, and management of, the countryside will continue to increase, so quantifying such impacts will be important.

Summary

Overall, more bird species have increased than decreased over the last three to four decades (Figure 17.7); however, about half of Britain's and Ireland's breeding species are of conservation concern in a national context because of small, declining or concentrated populations (Lynas *et al.* 2007; Eaton *et al.* 2009). Declines amongst farmland birds have been well documented, but widespread declines in woodland and

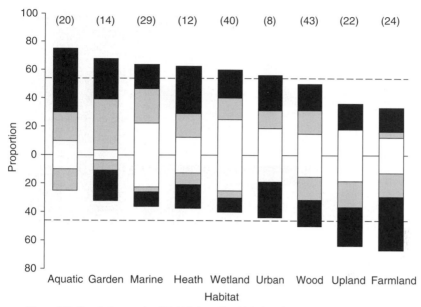

Figure 17.7 Population trends of British breeding birds in different habitats over the last 40 years. Species are indicated as strongly (black) or moderately (grey) increasing/decreasing or as stable/fluctuating (white). The dashed lines indicate the overall proportion of the 213 species that are increasing (38%) or decreasing (29%), also given is number of species included in each group. (From data in Appendix 1.)

migratory species are only just being recognised. Even populations of species once considered as pests, such as House Sparrow and Bullfinch, *P. pyrrhula*, have declined by as much as 50%. More generally, habitat specialists have tended to decline while commoner, more adaptable species have increased. Habitat specialists tend to be those of most conservation interest, precisely because they are often restricted in range or abundance. Historically, habitat loss and fragmentation have been major drivers of population change, but deterioration in habitat quality is now at least as important (Fuller and Ausden 2008).

Rarer species (those with fewer than 1000 individuals) have tended to fare better, while scarce species (those with fewer than 100 000 individuals) are doing worse (Figure 17.8).

Targeting rarer species, for example Cirl Bunting (agreements with farmers) and Goldeneye, *Bucephala clangula* (providing nest boxes), with conservation measures is relatively easy; increasing numbers of more widespread species that are currently declining will be much harder. Many species that suffered from persecution have benefited from increased legal protection, so most raptors, for instance, are increasing (although not in all areas). Many wildfowl populations are also increasing, though coastal habitats continue to be severely threatened both from human development and

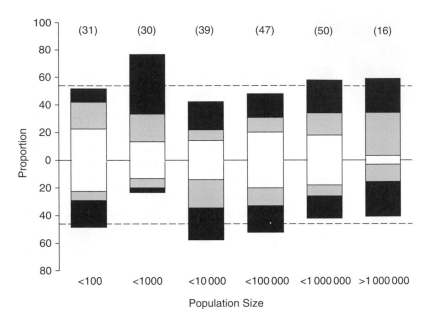

Figure 17.8 Population status of species breeding in Britain over the last 40 years. Species, grouped by population size, are indicated as strongly (black) or moderately (grey) increasing/decreasing or as stable or fluctuating (white). The dashed lines indicate the overall proportion of the 213 species that are increasing (38%) or decreasing (29%), also given is number of species included in each group. (From data in Appendix 1.)

a changing climate. Similarly, although seabird populations have increased in recent decades, whether this will hold true as climates change remains to be seen.

The future for Britain and Ireland's birds

Bird conservation has a long history in Britain: St Cuthbert created a sanctuary for birds on Inner Farne (Northumberland) in 676; the first Parliamentary Act (protecting game species) was passed in 1831 and the Society for the Protection of Birds was formed in 1889 (it gained its Royal Charter in 1904). An idea of the popularity (and influence) of bird conservation can be gained from membership of the RSPB, which currently stands at just over one million, nearly twice that of the combined membership of Britain's three main political parties (*c.* 560 000). Reflecting this interest and the availability of data, the UK Government has adopted an index of bird numbers Fig 17.1 as a surrogate for biodiversity generally in its measure of environmental sustainability, an initiative subsequently followed by the European Union (Gregory *et al.* 2005). Despite their flaws, such simple measures can be highly effective in communicating the need for action to policy-makers and others. High-profile reintroduction projects, such as those of Red Kite and White-tailed Eagle, *Haliaeetus albicilla*, have also been influential in engaging interest in conservation, as well as providing income for local economies. People have a greater interest in bird conservation if they see its benefits directly, and politicians need to know it matters to their electorate, as well as what solutions are available to particular problems.

Bird conservation is increasingly moving beyond the nature reserve. It is no longer just about protecting particular species on nature reserves (though this will, of course, remain an important challenge), but rather the much more difficult task of integrating conservation goals with other landscape planning priorities (Sutherland 2004). For example, wild geese often forage on farmland creating an economic conflict between conservationists and farmers, one that has increased as goose populations have grown. Is farmland solely for producing food, or should it also provide habitats for wildlife? More generally, should we have a smaller area of intensively farmed land, leaving room for undisturbed semi-natural habitat elsewhere, or more extensive areas of less-intensively managed land (e.g. Green *et al.* 2005)? The answers to such questions need to recognise that people value, and gain benefits from, the biodiversity immediately around them, and this often means birds as the most visible component of our fauna, but the balance between food production and biodiversity is one for society to determine.

The drivers of bird population change increasingly act at an international scale; trends in bird populations in Britain are similar to those in (north-western) continental Europe, for example the loss of farmland birds in Britain is mirrored across western Europe, reflecting common agricultural policies. Trends in migratory birds are also similar across Europe, perhaps reflecting changes in shared wintering quarters, similar patterns of land use across Europe, or a changing global climate. Increasingly, changes in climate will have an over-arching impact on bird populations, either directly, for example, rising sea levels reducing coastal habitat, or indirectly, perhaps by altering patterns of agriculture or development (Crick 2004). The most demonstrable effect of climate change on bird populations has been changes of range: the northern edge of bird distributions is moving north, both during the summer (on average by 20 km between 1970 and 1990) and winter (e.g. wader distributions have moved north-east by 85 km since the late 1970s) and these changes are predicted to continue (perhaps by as much as 550 km across Europe by the end of the century, Huntley *et al.* 2008). Such changes are clearly profound, and may result in new avian communities evolving, with complex, and unpredictable, consequences. Huntley *et al.* (2008) predict future ranges will only overlap by 40% with current ranges, so a key priority will be ensuring the landscape is sufficiently permeable to allow ranges to shift, and that suitable habitat is available to move into. This will be a challenging goal given the current intensity of land use over much of Europe.

In Britain, the main legislation protecting birds is the Wildlife and Countryside (1981, and amendments) and the Countryside and Rights of Way (2000) Acts. Increasingly, though, there is a need for internationally co-ordinated legislation, such as the European

Birds Directive (79/409/EEC), which provides for Special Protection Areas (SPAs) to protect bird populations which, along with Special Areas of Conservation (SACs) designated under the Habitats Directive (92/43/EEC), form the core of the Natura 2000 reserve network across Europe. This network has increased numbers of species listed under the Directive in countries where it has been developed (Donald *et al.* 2007). With changing climates, such co-ordinated networks of protected sites will increasingly be needed if species are to adapt their ranges appropriately.

Bird populations have changed dramatically over the last 200 years (Gibbons *et al.* 1996); future changes, both positive and negative, are inevitable and will be contingent on our management of the landscape. We cannot preserve our countryside or wildlife in aspic, so what is needed is a coherent vision of the mix of habitats we would like to see; that is, moving away from conserving 'original-natural' landscapes, which may be semi-mythical anyway, to creating 'future-natural' landscapes which support functioning ecosystems (Ausden and Fuller 2009). These will be expensive to create, so biodiversity goals need to be integrated with ecosystem services (such as carbon sequestration or flood management) to satisfy wider social and land-management aims. In broad terms, we probably have sufficient understanding to benefit populations of scarce specialists, especially within protected areas, and recent increases in Stone Curlew, *Burhinus oedicnemus*, Corncrake and Cirl Bunting, amongst others, show how effective evidence-based conservation measures can be (Aebischer *et al.* 2000). The greater challenge will be in maintaining landscapes that are sufficiently diverse that such intervention becomes unnecessary.

Acknowledgements

Most of the schemes referred to are partnerships between several organisations, notably the British Trust for Ornithology (BTO), Royal Society for the Protection of Birds (RSPB), Wildfowl and Wetlands Trust (WWT), the Joint Nature Conservation Committee (JNCC, on behalf of the statutory conservation organisations: Natural England, Scottish Natural Heritage, Countryside Council for Wales and the Council for Nature Conservation and the Countryside), and, in the Republic of Ireland, BirdWatch Ireland (BWI) and the National Parks and Wildlife Service. The Breeding Bird Survey is a joint scheme of BTO, RSPB and JNCC, the Wetland Bird Survey of BTO, RSPB, JNCC and WWT and BirdTrack of BTO, RSPB and BWI. None of this chapter could have been written without the dedication and support of the many thousands of volunteers who undertake these surveys and we all owe them our gratitude. I would also like to thank the many colleagues who supplied information or ideas and particularly Graham Appleton, Natasha Atkins, Andy Clements, Rob Fuller, Colin Galbraith, Jennifer Gill and Jeremy Greenwood, whose comments greatly improved earlier drafts.

Appendix 1   Population status of species regularly occurring in Britain

Conservation status (R[ed], A[mber] or G[reen], see Eaton *et al.* [2009]) and year of first successful breeding (after 1900) are given. Estimates of population size in 2000 (or the nearest available year) are taken from Baker *et al.* (2006), updated by Newson *et al.* (2008) and other sources (see http://www.bto.org/birdfacts); populations important (>20% of total) in a European or flyway context are highlighted in bold. A qualitative assessment of population trend since the 1960s is presented: extreme decline (– – –, >75%) or increase (+++, >100%), steep decline or increase (– – /++, >50%), moderate decline or increase (–/+, >25%), or as stable or fluctuating (~, <25% change); if the trend differs substantially before and after the 1980s these are indicated separately. Where a source is indicated trends are based on more or less quantitative data but the amount and quality of information varies hugely, so they are best regarded as indicative. Question marks indicate particular uncertainties.

Species	Status[a]	First Bred	Population[b]	Trend	Source[c]
Red-throated Diver *Gavia stellata*	RBWV	A	B: 1 200 p W: 17 000 1	+/–	2
Black-throated Diver *Gavia arctica*	RB WV	A	B: 170 P	?+	
Great Northern Diver *Gavia immer*	CB WV	A	1970	**W: 2800 I**	?	
Little Grebe *Tachybaptus ruficollis*	RB WV	A	B: 7500 P	?–	4
Great Crested Grebe *Podiceps cristatus*	RB WV	G	B: 23 000 I	++	6
Red-necked Grebe *Podiceps grisegena*	CB WV	A	1988	W: 200 I	~	6
Slavonian Grebe *Podiceps auritus*	RB WV	A	1908	B: 40 P	~/ – –	10
Black-necked Grebe *Podiceps nigricollis*	RB WV	A	1904	B: 50 P	+++	12
Fulmar *Fulmarus glacialis*	RB PV	A	1878	B: 500 000 P	++/~	11
Cory's Shearwater *Calonectris diomedea*	PV	–	P: 700 I	?++	9
Great Shearwater *Puffinus gravis*	PV	G	P: >150 I	?	

Table (cont.)

Species	Status[a]	First Bred	Population[b]	Trend	Source[c]
Sooty Shearwater *Puffinus griseus*	PV	A		P: >1000 I	?	
Manx Shearwater *Puffinus puffinus*	MB	A		**B: 300 000 P**	?	11
Balearic Shearwater *Puffinus mauretanicus*	PV	R		**P: >1000 I**	?+	
Storm-petrel *Hydrobates pelagicus*	MB	A		B: 26 000 P	?	11
Leach's Storm-petrel *Oceanodroma leucorhoa*	MB PV	A		**B: 48 000 P**	?	11
Gannet *Morus bassanus*	RB PV	A		**B: 220 000 N**	++	11
Cormorant *Phalacrocorax carbo*	RB WV	G		B: 8400 P W: 23 000 I	+ +	11 6
Shag *Phalacrocorax aristotelis*	RB	A		**B: 27 000 P**	~	11
Bittern *Botaurus stellaris*	RB WV	R	1911[d]	B: 50 M	–/~	8
Cattle Egret *Bubulcus ibis*	CB SV	–	2008	P: 10 I	+	13
Little Egret *Egretta garzetta*	RB PV	A	1995	B: 150 P	+++	8
Grey Heron *Ardea cinerea*	RB WV	G		B: 13 000 N	~/+	12
Purple Heron *Ardea purpurea*	PV	–		P: 20 I	~	9
Spoonbill *Platalea leucorodia*	CB PV	A	1998	P: 160 I	+	
Mute Swan *Cygnus olor*	RB	G		B: 45 000 P	+++	4
Bewick's Swan *Cygnus columbianus*	WV	A		**W: 8100 I**	+++/~	6
Whooper Swan *Cygnus cygnus*	CB WV	A	1910[d]	W: 5700 I	~/+++	6
Bean Goose *Anser fabalis*	WV	A		W: 500 I	~	6

Table (cont.)

Species		Status[a]	First Bred	Population[b]	Trend	Source[c]
Pink-footed Goose *Anser brachyrhynchus*	WV	A		**W: 240 000 I**	+++	6
White-fronted Goose *Anser albifrons*	WV	G		**W: 27 000 I**	++/–	6
Greylag Goose	RB	A		B: 130 000 I	+++	4
Anser anser[e]	WV			**W: 120 000 I**	++	6
Canada Goose *Branta canadensis*[e]	RB	–	1890	B: 82 000 I	+++	4
Barnacle Goose *Branta leucopsis*	WV	A		**W: 67 000 I**	+++	6
Brent Goose *Branta bernicla*	WV	A		**W: 67 000 I**	+++/~	6
Egyptian Goose *Alopochen aegyptiaca*[e]	RB	–	1700s	B: 1000 I	+++	6
Shelduck *Tadorna*	RB	A		**B: 35 000 P**	++/~	1
tadorna	WV			**W: 78 000 I**	~	6
Mandarin Duck *Aix galericulata*[e]	RB	–	1928	B: 7000 I	+++	
Wigeon *Anas*	RB	A		B: 400 P	?	
penelope	WV			**W: 410 000 I**	++	6
Gadwall *Anas*	RB	A	1850	B: 770 P	++	
strepera	WV			**W: 17 000 I**	+++	6
Teal *Anas crecca*	RB	A		B: 2000 P	–	
	WV			**W: 190 000 I**	++	6
Mallard *Anas*	RB	A		B: 660 000 P	+++	2
platyrhynchos	WV			W: 350 000 I	– –	6
Pintail *Anas acuta*	RB	A	1869	B: 20 P	~	8
	WV			**W: 28 000 I**	+++/~	6
Garganey *Anas querquedula*	MB PV	A	1862	B: 70 P	~	
Shoveler *Anas*	MB	A		B: 1200 P	+/–	
clypeata	WV			**W: 15 000 I**	++	6
Pochard *Aythya*	RB	A		B: 460 P	+/~	8
ferina	WV			W: 60 000 I	–	6
Tufted Duck *Aythya*	RB	A	1849	B: 42 000 P	+	4
fuligula	WV			W: 90 000 I	+	6
Scaup *Aythya marila*	CB WV	R	1897	W: 7 600 I	– – –/~	6

Table (cont.)

Species		Status[a]	First Bred	Population[b]	Trend	Source[c]
Eider *Somateria*	RB	A		B: 31 000 P	?~	
mollissima	WV			W: 73 000 I	++/~	6
Long-tailed Duck	WV	G		W: 16 000 I	?–	
Clangula hyemalis						
Common Scoter	RB	R	1855	B: 100 P	?–	
Melanitta nigra	WV			W: 50 000 I	?	
Velvet Scoter	WV	A		W: 3000 I	?–	
Melanitta fusca						
Goldeneye *Bucephala*	RB	A	1970	B: 200 P	+++/~	
clangula	WV			W: 25 000 I	~	6
Smew *Mergellus*	WV	A		W: 400 I	~	6
albellus						
Red-breasted	RB	G		B: 2200 P	?~	12
Merganser *Mergus*	WV			W: 9800 I	++/~	6
serrator						
Goosander *Mergus*	RB	G	1871	B: 2600 P	+++	4
merganser	WV					
				W: 16 000 I	+	6
Ruddy Duck *Oxyura*	RB	–	1960	B: <600 P	+++	6
jamaicensis[e]						
Honey-buzzard	MB PV	A		B: 50 P	~/+++	8
Pernis apivorus						
Red Kite *Milvus*	RB	A		B: 1000 P	+++	8
milvus[e]	WV					
White-tailed Eagle	RB	R	1983[d]	B: 40 P	+++	8
Haliaeetus albicilla[e]						
Marsh Harrier	MB PV	A		B: 360 F	+++	8
Circus aeruginosus						
Hen Harrier *Circus*	RB	R		B: 800 P	~	12
cyaneus	WV					
Montagu's Harrier	MB	A		B: 10 T	+	8
Circus pygargus						
Goshawk *Accipiter*	RB	G	1938[d]	B: 400 P	+++	8
gentilis						
Sparrowhawk	RB	G		B: 40 000 P	+++/~	2
Accipiter nisus	WV					
Buzzard *Buteo buteo*	RB	G		B: 38 000 T	~/+++	2
Rough-legged Buzzard	WV	–		W: 40 I	?+	9
Buteo lagopus						

Table (cont.)

Species	Status[a]	First Bred	Population[b]	Trend	Source[c]
Golden Eagle *Aquila chrysaetos*	RB	A		B: 440 P	~	12
Osprey *Pandion haliaetus*	MB PV	A		B: 150 P	+++	8
Kestrel *Falco tinnunculus*	RB WV	A		B: 55 000 P	~	2
Merlin *Falco columbarius*	RB WV	A		B: 1300 P	−−/++	12
Hobby *Falco subbuteo*	MB	G		B: 2200 P	+++	
Peregrine Falcon *Falco peregrinus*	RB WV	G		B: 1400 P	+++	8
Red Grouse *Lagopus lagopus*	RB	A		B: 160 000 P	−−	7
Ptarmigan *Lagopus muta*	RB	G		B: 10 000 P	?~	
Black Grouse *Tetrao tetrix*	RB	R		B: 5100 M	−−	12
Capercaillie *Tetrao urogallus*[e]	RB	R	1837[d]	B: 1200 I	−−	
Red-legged Partridge *Alectoris rufa*[e f]	RB	−	1770	B: 140 000 T	~	2
Grey Partridge *Perdix perdix*	RB	R		B: 72 000 P	−−−	2
Quail *Coturnix coturnix*	MB	A		B: 150 M	−	
Pheasant *Phasianus colchicus*[e f]	RB	−		B: 1 700 000 F	++	2
Golden Pheasant *Chrysolophus pictus*[e]	RB	−	1870s	B: 100 P	−−	
Lady Amherst's Pheasant *Chrys. amherstiae*[e]	RB	−	1890	B: 90 P	−−	
Water Rail *Rallus aquaticus*	RB WV	G		B: 700 P	?	
Spotted Crake *Porzana porzana*	MB	A		B: 70 M	+	8
Corncrake *Crex crex*	MB	R		B: 1100 M	−−− /+	8

Table (cont.)

Species		Status[a]	First Bred	Population[b]	Trend	Source[c]
Moorhen *Gallinula*	RB	G		**B: 160 000 T**	~	4
chloropus	WV			W: 750 000 I	?	
Coot *Fulica atra*	RB WV	G		B: 110 000 P	++	4
				W: 170 000 I	~	6
Crane *Grus grus*	CB	A	1981[d]	B: 5 P	+	
Oystercatcher	RB WV	A		**B: 110 000 P**	+++/~	4
Haematopus				**W: 320 000 P**	~	6
ostralegus						
Black-winged	CB	–	1945	B: <1 P		
Stilt *Himantopus*						
himantopus						
Avocet *Recurvirostra*	RB	A	1941[d]	B: 900 P	+++	8
avosetta	WV					
				W: 3400 I		
					~/+++	6
Stone Curlew	MB	A		B: 310 P	– –/++	8
Burhinus oedicnemus						
Lapwing *Vanellus*	RB	R		B: 150 000 P	++/– – –	2
vanellus	WV			**W: 1 800 000 I**	++	6
Golden Plover	RB	A		B: 46 000 P	–	12
Pluvialis apricaria	WV			**W: 250 000 I**	~/+++	6
Grey Plover	WV	A		**W: 53 000 I**	+++/–	6
Pluvialis squatarola						
Little Ringed Plover	MB	G	1938	B: 950 P	+	6
Charadrius dubius						
Ringed Plover	RB	A		B: 8400 P	– –	12
Charadrius hiaticula	WV			**W: 32 000 I**	–	6
Dotterel *Charadrius*	MB	A		B: 630 M	?~	
morinellus						
Knot *Calidris canutus*	WV	A		**W: 280 000 I**	~	6
Sanderling *Calidris*	WV	G		W: 21 000 I	~	6
alba						
Little Stint *Calidris*	PV	G		P: 450 I	~	
minuta						
Temminck's Stint	CB PV	R	1934	P: 100 I	~	9
Calidris temminckii						
Curlew Sandpiper	PV	G		P: 650 I		
Calidris ferruginea						
Purple Sandpiper	CB WV	A	1978	**W: 18 000 I**	~/– –	6
Calidris maritima						

Table (cont.)

Species	Status[a]	First Bred	Population[b]	Trend	Source[c]
Dunlin *Calidris alpina*	MB WV	R		B: 9500 P	– –	
				W: 560 000 I	– –	6
Ruff *Philomachus*	MB PV	R	1963[d]	B: 40 M	~	8
pugnax				P: 700 I	–	6
Jack Snipe	WV	A		W: 50 000 I	–/+	6
Lymnocryptes						
minimus						
Snipe *Gallinago*	RB	A		B: 52 000 P	– –	1
gallinago	WV			W: 100 000 I	~	6
Woodcock *Scolopax*	RB	A	1820s	B: 8800 P	– – –	
rusticola	WV					
Black-tailed Godwit	MB	R	1952[d]	B: 50 P	~	8
Limosa limosa	WV			**W: 15 000 I**	+++	6
Bar-tailed Godwit	WV	A		**W: 62 000 I**	~	6
Limosa lapponica						
Whimbrel *Numenius*	MB	R		B: 530 P	?–	
phaeopus	WV					
Curlew *Numenius*	RB	A		**B: 110 000 P**	–	2
arquata	WV					
Spotted Redshank	WV	A		P: 500 I	?–	6
Tringa erythropus						
Redshank *Tringa*	RB	A		B: 39 000 P	– –	4
totanus	WV			**W: 120 000 I**	~	6
Greenshank *Tringa*	RB	G		B: 1000 P	++	
nebularia	WV			P: 4300 I	++	6
Green Sandpiper	CB WV	A	1959	B: 2 P	+	
Tringa ochropus				P: 2000 I	+	
Wood Sandpiper	CB WV	A	1959	B: 10 P	++	8
Tringa glareola						
Common Sandpiper	MB	A		B: 50 000 P	~/–	4
Actitis hypoleucos						
Turnstone *Arenaria*	WV	A		**W: 50 000 I**	~	6
interpres						
Red-necked Phalarope	MB	R		B: 40 M	~	8
Phalaropus lobatus						
Grey Phalarope	PV	–		P: 300 I	~	9
Phalaropus fulicarius						
Pomarine Skua	PV	G		?		
Stercorarius						
pomarinus						

Table (cont.)

Species	Status[a]		First Bred	Population[b]	Trend	Source[c]
Arctic Skua *Stercorarius parasiticus*	MB PV	R		B: 2100 P	+++/–	11
Long-tailed Skua *Stercorarius longicaudus*	PV	G		?		
Great Skua *Stercorarius skua*	MB PV	A	1770s	**B: 9600 P**	+++	11
Mediterranean Gull *Larus melanocephalus*	MB WV	A	1968	B: 110 P	~/+++	8
Little Gull *Hydrocoloeus minutus*	CB PV	A	1975	?	++	
Sabine's Gull *Larus sabini*	PV	–		P: 150 I	~	9
Black-headed Gull *Chroicocephalus ridibundus*	RB WV	A		B: 128 000 P **W: 2 200 000 I**	~ +++/–	11 14
Common Gull *Larus canus*	RB WV	A		B: 48 000 P **W: 700 000 I**	++ +++	11 14
Lesser Black-backed Gull *Larus fuscus*	MB WV	A		**B: 110 000 P** W: 130 000 I	++ +++	11 14
Herring Gull *Larus argentatus*	RB WV	R		B: 130 000 P **W: 730 000 I**	– – ~	11 14
Yellow-legged Gull *Larus michahellis*	CB PV	–	1995	B: <1 P	+	
Iceland Gull *Larus glaucoides*	WV	A		?	?+	
Glaucous Gull *Larus hyperboreus*	WV	A		?	?–	
Great Black-backed Gull *Larus marinus*	RB WV	A		B: 17 000 P **W: 76 000 I**	~ ?++	11 14
Kittiwake *Rissa tridactyla*	RB WV	A		B: 370 000 P	~	11
Sandwich Tern *Sterna sandvicensis*	MB	A		B: 11 000 P	~	11
Roseate Tern *Sterna dougallii*	MB	R		B: 100 P	– – –	11
Common Tern *Sterna hirundo*	MB	A		B: 10 000 P	~	11
Arctic Tern *Sterna paradisaea*	MB	A		B: 53 000 P	+/–	11

Table (cont.)

Species	Status[a]	First Bred	Population[b]	Trend	Source[c]
Little Tern *Sternula albifrons*	MB	A		B: 2000 P	+/–	11
Black Tern *Chlidonias niger*	CB PV	A		?	?	
Guillemot *Uria aalge*	RB WV	A		**B: 1 300 000 I**	+++	11
Razorbill *Alca torda*	RB WV	A		B: 160 000 I	++	11
Black Guillemot *Cepphus grylle*	RB	A		B: 38 000 I	~	11
Little Auk *Alle alle*	WV	G		?	?	
Puffin *Fratercula arctica*	RB WV	A		B: 580 000 P	+	11
Feral Pigeon *Columba livia*	RB	G		B: 1 300 000 I	?	
Stock Dove *Columba oenas*	RB WV	A		**B: 310 000 T**	+++	2
Woodpigeon *Columba palumbus*	RB WV	G		B: 2 700 000 T	+++	2
Collared Dove *Streptopelia decaocto*	RB	G	1955	B: 800 000 T	+++	2
Turtle Dove *Streptopelia turtur*	MB	R		B: 44 000 T	– – –	2
Rose-ringed Parakeet *Psittacula krameri*[e]	RB	–	1971	B: 4300 I	+++	
Cuckoo *Cuculus canorus*	MB	R		B: 14 000 P	~/ – – –	2
Barn Owl *Tyto alba*	RB	A		B: 4000 P	– –/~	12
Little Owl *Athene noctua*[e]	RB	–	1879	B: 8700 P	?–	2
Tawny Owl *Strix aluco*	RB	G		B: 190 000 P	~	2
Long-eared Owl *Asio otus*	RB WV	G		B: 2400 P	?–	
Short-eared Owl *Asio flammeus*	RB WV	A		B: 2300 P	– –	

Table (cont.)

Species	Status[a]	First Bred	Population[b]	Trend	Source[c]
Snowy Owl *Bubo scandiacus*	CB	–	1967	B: <1 P		
Eagle Owl *Bubo bubo*	RB	–	1984	B: 1 P		
Nightjar *Caprimulgus europaeus*	MB	R		B: 4600 M	– – /+	12
Swift *Apus apus*	MB	A		B: 110 000 P	?/–	3
Kingfisher *Alcedo atthis*	RB	A		B: 5700 P	~	4
Bee-eater *Merops apiaster*	CB PV	–	1955	P: 20 I	++	9
Hoopoe *Upupa epops*	CB PV	G		P: 120 I	~	9
Wryneck *Jynx torquilla*	CB PV	R		B: <1 P	– – –	
				P: 300 I	~	9
Green Woodpecker *Picus viridis*	RB	A		B: 24 000 P	+++	2
Great Spotted Woodpecker *Dendrocopos major*	RB WV	G		B: 41 000 P	+++	2
Lesser Spotted Woodpecker *Dendrocopos minor*	RB	R		B: 2200 P	~/ – –	1
Woodlark *Lullula arborea*	MB	A		B: 3100 P	+++	12
Skylark *Alauda arvensis*	RB WV	R		B: 1 700 000 T	– –	2
Shorelark *Eremophila alpestris*	CB WV	–	1977	W: 300 I	?	
Sand Martin *Riparia riparia*	MB	A		B: 70 000 P	~	4
Swallow *Hirundo rustica*	MB	A		B: 780 000 T	~	2
House Martin *Delichon urbicum*	MB	A		B: 420 000 P	–	2
Tree Pipit *Anthus trivialis*	MB	R		B: 75 000 T	~/ – – –	2
Meadow Pipit *Anthus pratensis*	RB WV	A		B: 1 600 000 T	– –	2

Table (cont.)

Species	Status[a]	First Bred	Population[b]	Trend	Source[c]
Rock Pipit *Anthus petrosus*	RB WV	G	B: 34 000 P	?–	
Water Pipit *Anthus spinoletta*	WV	A	W: <100 I	+	
Yellow Wagtail *Motacilla flava*	MB	R	B: 19 000 T	– –	2
Grey Wagtail *Motacilla cinerea*	RB	A	B: 60 000 P	~	4
Pied Wagtail *Motacilla alba*	RB PV	G	B: 470 000 T	++/~	2
Waxwing *Bombycilla garrulus*	WV	G	W: 100 I	?	
Dipper *Cinclus cinclus*	RB	G	B: 13 000 P	~	4
Wren *Troglodytes troglodytes*	RB	G	B: 8 000 000 T	++	2
Dunnock *Prunella modularis*	RB WV	A	B: 1 800 000 T	–/~	2
Robin *Erithacus rubecula*	RB WV	G	B: 5 500 000 T	~/++	2
Nightingale *Luscinia megarhynchos*	MB	A	B: 6700 M	~	2
Bluethroat *Luscinia svecica*	CB PV	A	1968	P: 80 I	?	9
Black Redstart *Phoenicurus ochruros*	RB WV	A	1923	B: 50 P	++/–	8
Redstart *Phoenicurus phoenicurus*	MB	A	B: 100 000 P	~	10
Whinchat *Saxicola rubetra*	MB	A	B: 21 000 P	– – –	3
Stonechat *Saxicola torquatus*	RB	G	B: 15 000 P	– –/+	3
Wheatear *Oenanthe oenanthe*	MB	A	B: 550 000 I	–	3
Ring Ouzel *Turdus torquatus*	MB	R	B: 6900 P	– –	12
Blackbird *Turdus merula*	RB WV	G	B: 4 800 000 T	–	2

Table (cont.)

Species		Status[a]	First Bred	Population[b]	Trend	Source[c]
Fieldfare *Turdus pilaris*	CB WV	R	1967	W: 680 000 I	?~	5
Song Thrush *Turdus philomelos*	RB WV	R		B: 1 000 000 T	– –	2
Redwing *Turdus iliacus*	RB WV	R	1932	B: 60 P W: 650 000 I	~ ?~	8 5
Mistle Thrush *Turdus viscivorus*	RB WV	A		B: 250 000 T	–	2
Cetti's Warbler *Cettia cetti*	RB	G	1972	B: 650 M	+++	8
Grasshopper Warbler *Locustella naevia*	MB	R		B: 11 000 P	– –/~	3
Savi's Warbler *Locustella luscinioides*	CB	R	1960[d]	B: <10 P	++/ – – –	8
Aquatic Warbler *Acrocephalus paludicola*	PV	R		P: 30 I?	~	9
Sedge Warbler *Acrocephalus schoenobaenus*	MB	G		B: 300 000 T	~	4
Marsh Warbler *Acrocephalus palustris*	MB	R		B: 30 P	– – –	8
Reed Warbler *Acrocephalus scirpaceus*	MB	G		B: 91 000 P	?+	2
Icterine Warbler *Hippolais icterina*	CB PV	G	1992	P: 70 I	~	9
Dartford Warbler *Sylvia undata*	RB	A		B: 3200 P	+++	12
Barred Warbler *Sylvia nisoria*	PV	–		P: 200 I	+	9
Lesser Whitethroat *Sylvia curruca*	MB	G		B: 64 000 T	~	2

Table (cont.)

Species	Status[a]	First Bred	Population[b]	Trend	Source[c]
Whitethroat *Sylvia communis*	MB	A		B: 930 000 T	– – –/ ++	2
Garden Warbler *Sylvia borin*	MB	G		B: 190 000 T	~	2
Blackcap *Sylvia atricapilla*	MB WV	G		B: 920 000 T	+++	2
Pallas' Warbler *Phylloscopus proregulus*	PV	–		P: 110 I	+++	9
Yellow-browed Warbler *Phyll. inornatus*	PV	–		P: 430 I	+++	9
Wood Warbler *Phylloscopus sibilatrix*	MB	R		B: 17 200 M	~/ – –	3
Chiffchaff *Phylloscopus collybita*	MB WV	G		B: 750 000 T	+	2
Willow Warbler *Phylloscopus trochilus*	MB	A		B: 2 000 000 T	~/ – –	2
Goldcrest *Regulus regulus*	RB WV	G		B: 770 000 T	~	2
Firecrest *Regulus ignicapilla*	RB WV	A	1962	B: 170 M	++	8
Spotted Flycatcher *Muscicapa striata*	MB	R		B: 128 000 T	– – –	2
Red-breasted Flycatcher *Ficedula parva*	PV	–		P: 100 I	+	9
Pied Flycatcher *Ficedula hypoleuca*	MB	A		B: 38 000 P	+/–	3
Bearded Tit *Panurus biarmicus*	RB	A		B: 500 P	+++/~	10
Long-tailed Tit *Aegithalos caudatus*	RB	G		B: 260 000 T	++	2
Marsh Tit *Poecile palustris*	RB	R		B: 53 000 T	– –	2

Table (cont.)

Species	Status[a]	First Bred	Population[b]	Trend	Source[c]
Willow Tit *Poecile montana*	RB	R	B: 8500 T	− − −	2
Crested Tit *Lophophanes cristatus*	RB	A	B: 2400 P	?+	10
Coal Tit *Periparus ater*	RB	G	B: 600 000 T	++/~	2
Blue Tit *Cyanistes caeruleus*	RB	G	B: 3 300 000 T	+	2
Great Tit *Parus major*	RB	G	B: 2 000 000 T	++	2
Nuthatch *Sitta europaea*	RB	G	B: 140 000 T	+++	2
Treecreeper *Certhia familiaris*	RB	G	B: 200 000 T	~	2
Golden Oriole *Oriolus oriolus*	MB	R	B: <10 P	++/ − −	8
Red-backed Shrike *Lanius collurio*	CB	R	B: <1 P	− − −	8
			P: 200 I	−	9
Great Grey Shrike *Lanius excubitor*	WV	−	W: 100 I	−	9
Jay *Garrulus glandarius*	RB WV	G	B: 160 000 T	~	2
Magpie *Pica pica*	RB	G	B: 600 000 T	++/~	2
Chough *Pyrrhocorax pyrrhocorax*	RB	A	B: 450 P	++	12
Jackdaw *Corvus monedula*	RB WV	G	B: 1 000 000 T	++	2
Rook *Corvus frugilegus*	RB WV	G	B: 1 200 000 P	+	3
Carrion Crow *Corvus corone*	RB	G	B: 790 000 T	+++	2
Hooded Crow *Corvus cornix*	RB WV	−	B: 160 000 T	−	
Raven *Corvus corax*	RB	G	B: 12 000 P	?~	3
Starling *Sturnus vulgaris*	RB WV	R	B: 3 000 000 P	− − −	2
House Sparrow *Passer domesticus*	RB	R	B: 4 700 000 P	− − −	2
Tree Sparrow *Passer montanus*	RB	R	B: 68 000 T	− − −	2
Chaffinch *Fringilla coelebs*	RB WV	G	B: 5 600 000 T	+	2

Table (cont.)

Species	Status[a]	First Bred	Population[b]	Trend	Source[c]
Brambling *Fringilla montifringilla*	CB WV	G	1920	W: 920 000 I	?+	5
Serin *Serinus serinus*	CB PV	A	1967	P: 50 I	+++	9
Greenfinch *Carduelis chloris*	RB WV	G		B: 1 800 000 T	+	2
Goldfinch *Carduelis carduelis*	RB	G		B: 900 000 T	~	2
Siskin *Carduelis spinus*	RB WV	G		B: 360 000 T	++/?~	3
Linnet *Carduelis cannabina*	RB WV	R		B: 540 000 T	– –	2
Twite *Carduelis flavirostris*	RB WV	R		B: 10 000 P	– –	12
Lesser Redpoll *Carduelis cabaret*	RB	R		B: 25 000 P	– – –	2
Common Redpoll *Carduelis flammea*	CB WV	G		?		
Crossbill *Loxia curvirostra*	RB WV	G		B: 10 000 P	~	
Scottish Crossbill *Loxia scotica*	RB	A		**B: 780 P**	?+	
Parrot Crossbill *Loxia pytyopsittacus*	RB	A	1984	B: 30 P	?	
Scarlet Rosefinch *Carpodacus erythrinus*	CB PV	A	1982	P: 150 I	+++	9
Bullfinch *Pyrrhula pyrrhula*	RB	A		B: 160 000 T	– –	2
Hawfinch *Coccothraustes coccothraustes*	RB	R		B: 4800 P	~/ – –	12
Lapland Bunting *Calcarius lapponicus*	CB WV	A	1977	W: 350 I	~	
Snow Bunting *Plectrophenax nivalis*	RB WV	A		B: 90 P W: 11 000 I	++/– –	8
Yellowhammer *Emberiza citrinella*	RB WV	R		B: 790 000 T	– –	2
Cirl Bunting *Emberiza cirlus*	RB	R		B: 710 P	– – – /++	10
Ortolan Bunting *Emberiza hortulana*	PV	–		P: 60 I	~	9

Table (cont.)

Species	Status[a]	First Bred	Population[b]	Trend	Source[c]
Little Bunting PV	–		P: 30 I	++	9
Emberiza pusilla					
Reed Bunting RB	A		B: 190 000 T	+/ – –	2
Emberiza schoeniclus WV					
Corn Bunting RB	R		B: 10 000 T	– – –	2
Emberiza calandra					

Notes:

[a] RB: Resident Breeder, MB: Migrant Breeder, CB: Casual Breeder, PV: Passage Visitor, SV: Scarce Visitor, WV: Winter Visitor.

[b] I: individuals, P: pairs, F: Females, M: males, N: nests, T: territories, counts relate to breeding (B), passage (P) or winter (W) seasons.

[c] Source for trend information: 1 – Common Birds Census; 2 – Common Birds Census/Breeding Bird Survey; 3 – Breeding Bird Survey/Atlas; 4 – Waterways Bird Survey; 5 – Garden Bird Feeding Survey; 6 –Wetland Bird Survey; 7 – Game and Wildlife Conservancy Trust Game Bag Counts; 8 – Rare Breeding Birds Panel; 9 – Report on Scarce Migrants; 10 – RSPB data; 11 – Seabird 2000; 12 – Species-specific surveys; 13 – British Birds Rarities Committee; 14 – Winter Gull Survey.

[d] Had bred in historical times.

[e] Introduced species.

[f] It is estimated that at least 30 million Pheasant and 5 million Red-legged Partridge are released each year during the shooting season.

References

Aebischer, N.J., Green, R.E. and Evans, A.D. (2000). From science to recovery: four case studies of how research has been translated into conservation action in the UK. In Aebischer, N.J., Evans, A.D., Grice, P.V. and Vickery, J.A., eds., *Ecology and Conservation of Lowland Farmland Birds*, Tring, British Ornithologists' Union, pp. 43–54.

Ausden, M. and Fuller, R.J. (2009). Birds and habitat change in Britain: past and future conservation responses. *British Birds,* **102**, 52–71.

Baillie, S.R. (1990). Integrated population monitoring of breeding birds in Britain and Ireland. *Ibis,* **132**, 151–161.

Baker, H., Stroud, D.A., Aebischer, N.J. *et al.* (2006). Population estimates of birds in Great Britain and the United Kingdom. *British Birds,* **99**, 25–44.

Ballance, D.K. (2000). *Birds in Counties: An Ornithological Bibliography for the Counties of England, Wales, Scotland and the Isle of Man*, London, Imperial College Press.

Bircham, P. (2007). *A History of Ornithology*, London, Collins.

Brown, A.F. and Grice, P.V. (2005). *Birds in England*, London, T. & A.D. Poyser.

Cannon, A.R., Chamberlain, D.E., Toms, M.P., Hatchwell, B.J. and Gaston, K.J. (2005). Trends in the use of private gardens by wild birds in Great Britain 1995–2002. *Journal of Applied Ecology, 42*, 659–671.

Crick, H.Q.P. (2004). The impact of climate change on birds. *Ibis, 146*, S48–S56.

Donald., P.F., Sandrson, F.J., Burfield, I.J. *et al.* (2007). International conservation policy delivers benefits for birds in Europe. *Science, 317*, 810–813.

Eaton, M.A., Brown, A.F., Noble, D.G. *et al.* (2009). Birds of conservation concern 3: the population status of birds in the United Kingdom, Channel Islands and Isle of Man. *British Birds, 102*, 296–341.

Forrester, R. and Andrews, I. (2007). *The Birds of Scotland*, Edinburgh, Scottish Ornithologists' Club.

Frederiksen, M., Wanless, S., Harris, M.P., Rothery, P. and Wilson, L.J. (2004). The role of industrial fisheries and oceanographic change in the decline of North Sea black-legged kittiwakes. *Journal of Applied Ecology, 41*, 1129–1139.

Fuller, R.J. and Ausden, M. (2008). Birds and habitat change in Britain: a review of losses and gains in the twentieth century. *British Birds, 101*, 644–675.

Fuller, R.J., Noble, D.G., Smith, K.W. and Vanhinsbergh, D. (2005). Recent declines in populations of woodland birds in Britain. *British Birds, 98*, 116–143.

Green, R.E., Cornell, S.J., Scharlemann, J.P.W. and Balmford, A. (2005). Farming and the fate of wild nature. *Science, 307*, 550–555.

Greenwood, J.J.D. (2007). Citizens, science and bird conservation. *Journal for Ornithology, 148*, S77–S124.

Greenwood, J.J.D., Crick, H.Q.P. and Bainbridge, I.P. (2003). Numbers and international importance of raptors and owls in Britain and Ireland. In Thompson, D.B.A., Redpath, S.M., Fielding, S.H., Marquiss, M. and Galbraith, C.A., eds., *Birds of Prey in a Changing Environment*, Edingburgh, The Stationery Office, pp. 25–49.

Gregory, R.D., van Strein, A., Vorisek, P. *et al.* (2005). Developing indicators for European birds. *Philosophical Transactions of the Royal Society B, 360*, 269–288.

Holloway, S. (1996). *The Historical Atlas of Breeding Birds in Britain and Ireland: 1875–1900*, London, T. & A.D. Poyser.

Huntley, B., Green, R., Collingham, Y. and Willis, S.G. (2008). *A Climatic Atlas of European Breeding Birds*, Bareclona, Lynx Edicions.

Hutchinson, C.D. (1989). *Birds in Ireland*, Calton, T. & A.D. Poyser.

Lovegrove, R., Williams, G. and Williams, I. (1994). *Birds in Wales*, Calton, T. & A.D. Poyser.

Lynas, P., Newton, S.F. and Robinson, J.A. (2007). The status of birds in Ireland: an analysis of conservation concern 2008–2013. *Irish Birds, 8*, 149–168.

Marchant, J.H., Hudson, R., Carter, S.P. and Whittington, P. (1990). *Population Trends in British Breeding Birds*, Thetford, British Trust for Ornithology.

Newson, S.E., Evans, K.L., Noble, D.G., Greenwood, J.J.D. and Gaston, K.J. (2008). Use of distance sampling to improve estimates of national population sizes for common and widespread breeding birds in the UK. *Journal of Applied Ecology, 45*, 1330–1338.

Newton, I. (2004). The recent declines of farmland bird populations in Britain: an appraisal of causal factors and conservation actions. *Ibis, 146*, 579–600.

Parkin, D.T. and Knox, A.G. (2010). *The Status of Birds in Britain and Ireland*, London, Helm.

Pearce-Higgins, J.W., Grant, M.C., Beale, C.M., Buchanan, G.M. and Sim, I.M.W. (2008). International importance and drivers of change of upland bird populations. In Bonn, A., Hubacek, K., Stewart, J. and Allott, T., eds., *Drivers of Change in Uplands*, London, Routledge. pp. 209–227.

Robinson, R.A. and Sutherland, W.J. (2002). Post-war changes in arable farming and biodiversity in Great Britain. *Journal of Applied Ecology, **39**, 157–176.*

Sutherland, W.J. (2004). A blueprint for the countryside. *Ibis,* **146**, S230–S238.

Thirgood, S.J., Redpath, S.M., Haydon, D.T. *et al.* (2000). Habitat loss and raptor predation: disentangling long- and short-term causes of red grouse declines. *Proceedings of the Royal Society of London B,* **267**, 651–656.

18

The conservation of the Grey Partridge

N.W. Sotherton, N.J. Aebischer and J.A. Ewald

Summary

The Grey Partridge (*Perdix perdix*) is an iconic farmland bird that has declined on UK farmland by over 80% in the last 50 years. This decline was caused by poor levels of chick survival driven by agricultural intensification and primarily the use of insecticides and herbicides. These products reduce numbers of insects eaten by young chicks and the host plants that support these chick-food insects. Annual monitoring of such insects in cereal fields on a study area in Sussex, England over 40 years identified these insect declines and established how closely they mirrored pesticide use.

Mitigation measures were developed whereby the edges of cereal crops received only selective or seasonally restricted inputs of pesticides to facilitate insect recovery. These 'conservation headlands' were demonstrated to improve chick survival significantly and have now been made available (i.e. funded) in the UK's Agri-environment Schemes, whereby farmers are subsidised to help declining wildlife species recover.

Introduction

Over the last few decades, concerns have been expressed about the loss of wildlife from farmland (Gregory *et al.* 2001). The work by the Game and Wildlife Conservation Trust on the Grey Partridge (*Perdix perdix*) was some of the earliest research to voice and confirm these concerns, as well as quantify losses caused by pesticides (Potts 1986). The decline of the Grey Partridge is a well-studied example of a species of farmland wildlife under threat from the intensification of agricultural production (hedgerow removal, pesticide use, mechanisation). In this respect, the Grey Partridge is a good

Silent Summer: The State of Wildlife in Britain and Ireland, ed. Norman Maclean. Published by Cambridge University Press. © Cambridge University Press 2010.

species to study because it is the archetypal farmland bird. Grey Partridges spend their lives in fields and field edges, not in woodland, wetlands or around farm buildings. Their distribution and abundance are also well documented. As a quarry species, their numbers are noted and recorded, so our data sets go back a long way across a big acreage; for example, bag records from some very large estates go back continuously to the Victorian era (Tapper 1992).

Historically, the bird originated in the temperate Steppe grassland of Asia and Central Europe, adapted to open arable rather than forested landscapes. Its range grew with the expansion of agriculture over the last 8000 years. In Britain, a combination of land enclosure, increased cultivation for arable crops and intensive predator control in the eighteenth and especially nineteenth centuries increased Grey Partridge numbers considerably (Potts 1986). At the same time, sporting interest in the species developed, making it the most popular gamebird quarry species of the nineteenth century. Bag records show that around two million Grey Partridges were killed annually on a sustainable basis between 1870 and 1930 (Tapper 1992).

A declining species

The same bag records indicate that after the Second World War, numbers of Grey Partridges fell dramatically in nearly all countries in its range (Potts 1986). The declines were accompanied by a retraction in range from the periphery inwards and away from mountainous areas. Today, Grey Partridges have gone from Norway, and in Finland and Sweden are restricted to the south. They have also disappeared from Portugal and much of north-west Spain, southern Italy and southern Greece. In Ireland and Switzerland, they are almost extinct (Aebischer and Potts 1994). In the UK, the average bag declined by over 80% between 1940 and 1990 (Figure 18.1).

Such was the concern generated by this decline that in 1968, predecessors of the Game and Wildlife Conservation Trust began an intensive study in Sussex to identify the causes of the decline. This 'Sussex Study' gave us the necessary insight into Grey Partridge population dynamics and was responsible for shaping the various hypotheses regarding causes of decline that were subsequently tested elsewhere (Potts 1986). The annual monitoring of partridges and the condition of their arable habitats continues to this present day (Ewald *et al.* 2007). The monitoring in Sussex reflected the national decline. Density of spring pairs fell from over 16 pairs per km² to under 5 pairs per km² in the late 1980s (Figure 18.2). Such declines closely matched those detected nationally by the British Trust for Ornithology, which recorded an 87% reduction between 1967 and 2005.

Life cycle

The Grey Partridge life cycle is summarised in Figure 18.3. The species is monogamous and, after pairs form in the late winter to early spring, the hen seeks out a

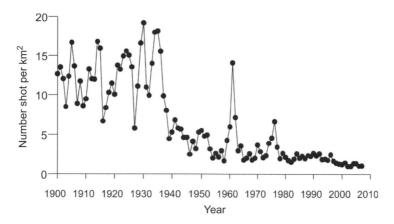

Figure 18.1 Mean annual number of Grey Partridges shot per km² from shoots through-out the UK contributing to the Game and Wildlife Conservation Trust's National Gamebag Census since 1900.

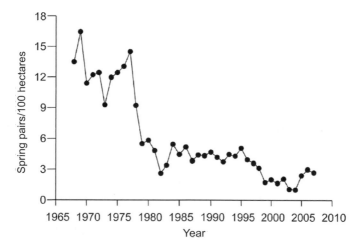

Figure 18.2 Changes in the annual abundance of Grey Partridges on the Game and Wildlife Conservation Trust's main study area in Sussex, 1968–2007. (From Potts and Aebischer 1995 updated.)

suitable piece of cover in which to nest. The nest is constructed on the ground and is typically a grass-lined scrape. The nest is usually well hidden by being built among rank dead grass found on uncut field margins, hedge bottoms or even autumn-sown cereals. The average clutch size is 15 eggs, the highest of any bird species. Incubation lasts 23–25 days and is done by the female alone. During this period, there is a high risk of predation by avian and ground predators. The main egg predators are Carrion

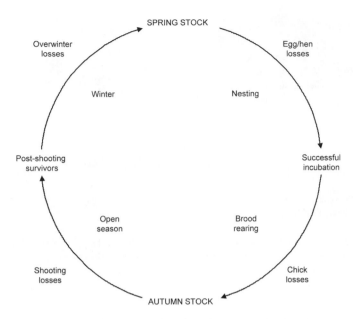

Figure 18.3 Schematic representation of the life cycle of the Grey Partridge.

Crows (*Corvus corone*) and Magpies (*Pica pica*), as well as Brown Rats (*Rattus rattus*), Hedgehogs (*Erinaceus europaeus*) and mustelids (Stoats, *Mustela ermina*, and Weasels, *Mustela nivalis*), while the sitting hen may be killed by Foxes (*Vulpes vulpes*), Stoats or Cats (*Felis catus*). However, a female whose clutch is lost will usually lay a replacement clutch.

Within a few hours of hatching, the chicks are mobile (precocious) and are led away from the nest by both parents (see Figure 18.4). They feed themselves, but require brooding by the adults to keep warm in cold weather. During the first two weeks after hatching, the chick diet consists almost entirely of insects, a rich source of protein (Ford *et al.* 1938). Laboratory experiments have shown that feather development is much faster for chicks on a high-protein diet than on a low-protein one (Potts 1986; Southwood and Cross 2002). After the first fortnight, the proportion of weed seeds and other vegetable material in the diet gradually increases to match that found in the adult diet. By the age of 12 weeks, the chicks are fully grown and begin to moult into adult plumage.

Causes of decline

The highest levels of chick mortality occur during these early weeks after hatching, during the stage of close dependency on insects. Annual rates of chick survival from the Sussex Study were positively correlated with an index of insect abundance (Potts and Aebischer 1991) taken from cereal fields in late June (Figure 18.5). Data from

Figure 18.4 Grey Partridge with newly fledged chicks (see colour plate). (Photograph by Jill Pakenham/BTO.)

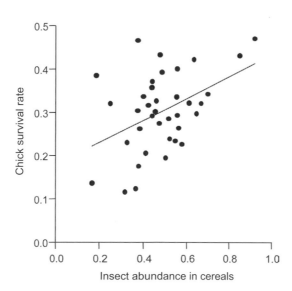

Figure 18.5 Relationship between annual Grey Partridge chick survival (to six weeks) and chick-food insects sampled in cereals in mid-June (time of peak chick hatch), 1970–2006.

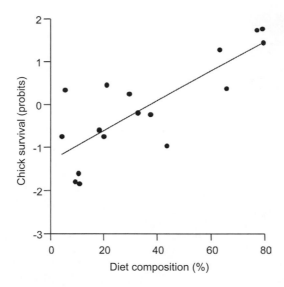

Figure 18.6 Survival of chicks in 17 radio-tracked broods (to six weeks) in relation to diet composition (percentage of caterpillars, Symphyta and Lepidoptera, leaf beetles, Chrysomelidae, and weevils, Curculionidae) determined by faecal analysis. (From Potts and Aebischer 1991; survival rates transformed to normal equivalent deviates (probits).)

radio-tracking in Hampshire and Norfolk show a positive correlation between survival of individual broods with the proportion of important chick-food insects in the diet, based on faecal analysis (Figure 18.6). These same radio-tracking studies also showed that broods spent 97% of their time inside cereal crops close to the crop edge (Green 1984).

The decline of the Grey Partridge was clearly brought about by a complex interaction of several factors, but driven primarily by the post-war intensification of agricultural production (Potts 1986). Potts (1986) identified the key factor responsible for population decline as chick mortality, occurring as a result of insufficient densities of chick-food insects in brood-rearing habitats in June/July.

The distribution and abundance of these chick-food insects is closely linked to the use of pesticides. The history of pesticide use in the UK's arable farming mirrors the temporal patterns of Grey Partridge decline. Herbicides were introduced in the early 1950s and it is estimated that over half of the UK cereal fields were treated by 1960 and nearly all were treated by 1965, a few years before the long-term monitoring study in Sussex began in 1970. Herbicides were thought to impact on chick-food insects, not because of any toxic properties to arthropods, but because a great many Grey Partridge

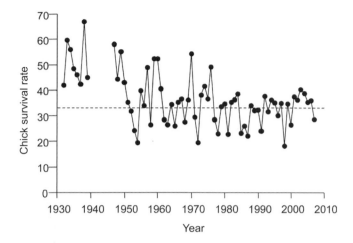

Figure 18.7 Annual chick survival rate (to six weeks) of Grey Partridges from the Game and Wildlife Conservation Trust's Partridge Count Scheme 1933–2007, corrected for weather and releasing of hand-reared birds. The thick line indicates the long-term trend; the dotted horizontal line is the minimum chick survival rate required to maintain the population.

chick-food insects were herbivores, feeding on cereal field weeds. Particularly at risk were the leaf beetles (Chrysomelidae), weevils (Curculionidae) and plant bugs (Heteroptera:Miridae) (Sotherton 1982).

These species fed on weeds in arable crops that were targeted by herbicides for removal. Southwood and Cross (1969) estimated that herbicides alone could reduce the abundance of invertebrates in cereal crops by 50%. Such insect declines match the long-term trends in annual rates of chick survival (Figure 18.7), which averaged over 40% in the early 1950s until 1960, but the long-term average since then has been below the 33% level needed to maintain numbers.

Population modelling has shown that decreases in annual average chick survival rates would have been responsible for only a relatively small decrease in spring stocks because it was partially compensated by lower overwinter losses (Potts and Aebischer 1995). The impact of low chick survival rates, however, was on autumn stocks and hence on the harvestable surplus and the associated loss of economic revenue from shooting. Many wild Grey Partridge gamekeepers either lost their jobs or turned towards the rearing of Pheasants (*Phasianus colchicus*) as the alternative quarry species. As a result, the reduction in numbers of predators that was a traditional role for the gamekeeper ceased or became less intensive. This led to an increase in predation during the nesting season, i.e. higher female mortality and egg losses. The situation was exacerbated by the removal of nesting cover, another manifestation of intensification, as greater mechanisation on farms led to the enlargement of fields by eliminating hedgerows and field boundaries. Further destruction of the amount of nesting cover and its quality resulted from the use of herbicides on hedge bottoms and field margins as farmers sprayed field margins to prevent invasion of the crop by pernicious weeds such as Couch Grass (*Elymus repens*) on its periphery.

Therefore the causes of the decline of the Grey Partridge in Britain were three-fold (the 'three-legged stool'): a fall in the abundance of cereal insects, an increase in predation pressure during nesting and a reduction in nesting cover. In retrospect, traditional management of Grey Partridge stocks for shooting before the Second World War sought to counteract the last two causes (the first cause was not an issue in the pre-intensification era).

The Sussex Study

The link between non-target insects in their role as food for Grey Partridge chicks and the decline of this once numerous and widespread farmland bird prompted the intensive study of the arable ecosystem that has become known as the Sussex Study. The Sussex Study area is located between the rivers Arun and Adur in West Sussex and takes in approximately 62 km² of farmland made up chiefly of chalk soils on the Sussex Downs. From 1970, and continuing to the present day, information regarding crop types, invertebrate densities and pesticide use has been collected each third week of June in approximately 100 cereal fields. Invertebrates are sampled using a D-Vac suction trap to take 5 s sub-samples, each of 0.092 m², along a diagonal transect into the field. Most chick-food invertebrates are identified to the family level, some to genus or species.

The pesticide data comprised information (products used, timing, dose rate) on the application of herbicides, fungicides and insecticides. These pesticide-use data were analysed twice, once for the period 1970 to 1996 (Ewald and Aebischer 1999) and then for an update from 1996 to 2004 (Ewald *et al.* 2007). Cropping information on a year-to-year and field-by-field basis, as well as pesticide, insect and weed information, were entered onto a geographical information system for ease of comparison.

The invertebrate taxa chosen for analysis were ones that figured prominently in the diet of farmland birds, especially at the chick stage. They included five broad taxonomic groupings and an index of Grey Partridge chick-food abundance.

- Araneae and Opiliones (all sizes of spiders and harvestman)
- Carabidae and Elateridae (adults of ground and click beetles)
- Symphyta and Lepidoptera (adults, larvae and shed skins of sawflies, butterflies and moths)
- Chrysomelidae and Curculionidae (adults and larvae of leaf beetles and weevils)
- Non-aphid Hemiptera (adults and nymphs of plant bugs/hoppers, excluding aphids)
- Grey Partridge chick-food index (CFI), defined as: CFI = 0.00 614 × plant bugs and leaf hoppers (adults and nymphs) + 0.0832 × leaf beetles and weevils (adults and larvae) + 0.000 368 × aphids (adults and nymphs) + 0.1199 × caterpillars − Symphyta

and Lepidoptera (adults and larvae) and Neuroptera + 0.1411 × ground and click beetles (adults) (Potts and Aebischer 1991).

Grey Partridges are surveyed post-harvest. Counting takes place at dawn and at dusk in late August, using a four-wheel-drive vehicle to drive around the edges and across fields so that all of each field area is examined (Potts 1986). By this time, Grey Partridges are found in coveys usually representing family groups of parents and young. Unsuccessful pairs or single adults may join up with other pairs or family groups. The number of young in each covey is recorded, as well as the number of adult males and females. All counts are entered into the Geographical Information System. Details of analyses are given in Ewald and Aebischer (1999).

Insecticides and Grey Partridges

Between 1970 and 1996 all measures of pesticide use increased. These included percentage of the arable crop area treated, intensity of use (expressed as percentage spray area) and number of treatments per field. None of these measures changed between 1996 and 2004. Insecticides were hardly used on cereal fields in Sussex in the 1970s, but use has increased with time so that in recent years, between 50 and 80% of fields are treated (Figure 18.8). The biggest increase has been the autumn/winter use of insecticides. However, use in spring/summer (the time most likely to impact on non-target chick-food insects) also increased over time. The autumn use has primarily involved sprays of the pyrethroid group of insecticides used to target aphid vectors of virus diseases and since the mid-1990s, practically every winter-sown cereal crop in Sussex gets such a spray.

The product choice and therefore the selectivity of insecticides used on the study area has also changed over time. The product of choice (most selective and therefore least damaging to chick-food insects) was a carbamate product called pirimicarb. Field trials had shown how much more selective it was compared to the alternative organophosphate and pyrethroid products on the market. In trials against sawfly larvae (Hymenoptera:Symphyta), pirimicarb caused significantly lower levels of mortality after six days (Figure 18.9). The use of pirimicarb has decreased over time in Sussex.

Examining invertebrate abundance and indices of bird food abundance, Araneae (spiders and harvestmen) and ground and click beetles declined over time in Sussex (Figure 18.10), whilst plant bugs/hoppers showed no change in abundance. Caterpillars and the chick-food index for Grey Partridges declined through the 1970s and 1980s, but have subsequently increased on the study area.

All invertebrate taxa and the CFI declined with insecticide use, number of insecticide applications and the use of insecticides in the autumn and spring. The use of organophosphate compounds was associated with declines in all nine taxa, whereas for

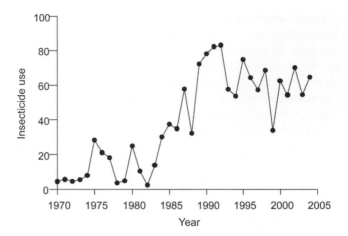

Figure 18.8 The long-term trend in the percentage of arable area treated with insecticide (all arable crops combined) showed an increase from 1970 to the early 1990s, then stabilised.

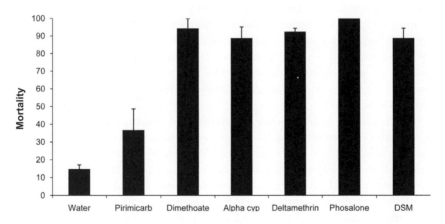

Figure 18.9 Percentage mortality (± one SE) of sawfly larvae (Hymenoptera:Symphyta) following exposure to treated foliage after six days sprayed with insecticides used in UK cereal crops. Comparisons are with water-treated control plants. Alpha cyp = alpha cypermethirn; DSM = demethrin -S-methyl.

pirimicarb, only leaf beetles and weevils showed a marginal but non-significant decline. No clear patterns emerged for invertebrate abundance in relation to use, intensity of use, timing of use or specificity of herbicides. Abundances of Araneae, caterpillars and plant bugs/hoppers were lower where insecticides were used in the previous year.

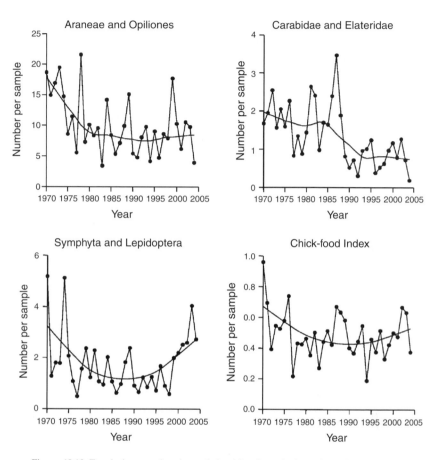

Figure 18.10 Trends in annual arthropod densities through time. Annual densities of Araneae and Opiliones, and Carabidae and Elateridae decreased with time. There was a u-shaped trend through time in the annual densities of Symphyta and Lepidoptera, and Chick-food Index with initial declines followed by increases in later years.

Conservation concern

The wide-scale national decline of the Grey Partridge has led to its heightened conservation status in the UK. Its designation as a Biodiversity Action Plan species and a red-listed bird in the Species of Conservation Concern classification means its decline in abundance and distribution has been recognised. Research studies to understand the causes of the decline have all been completed and experimental evidence confirms the important role played in the decline of this species by the removal of chick-food insects as a result of insecticides killing these prey items and herbicides removing their host plants. Experimental evidence has also confirmed how, on modern intensively managed farms, insect-rich brood-rearing covers can be created that reinstate insect levels and lead to high levels of chick survival within a single season. In the next section we review the applied aspects of this research and the implications for managing habitats on farmland for the Grey Partridge.

This has not meant turning the clock back and abandoning the technological gains provided by plant protection products that gave rise to the intensification of cereal production in the first place. Habitat management seeks to restore lost nesting cover and insect-rich brood-rearing cover and is designed to mitigate against the losses caused by agricultural intensification whilst remaining compatible with modern farming.

The road to recovery

Management of brood-rearing habitat

To tackle the problem of low densities of chick-food insects in cereal crops, which are responsible for low chick survival rates, the concept of 'conservation headlands' (Sotherton 1991) was developed. This involves selective herbicide use on the outer margins (usually at least 6 m) of a cereal crop (crop margins are known as 'headlands'), according to prescriptions that are regularly updated to take into account the availability of new selective herbicidal compounds. The aim is to encourage the development of annual arable weeds at ground level within the part of the crop most frequented by partridge broods, while preventing infestation by agriculturally pernicious and unacceptable weeds such as Barren Brome (*Anisantha sterilis*), Black-grass (*Alopecurus myosuroides*) and Cleavers *(Galium aparine)*. In this way chick-food insect host plants are allowed to survive on the edges of cereal fields. Thus non-residual herbicides that are specific to grasses or cleavers are allowed, as are fungicides (except the insecticidal pyrazophos) and insecticides up to 15 March (to enable the spraying of autumn crops against the aphid vectors of Barley Yellow Dwarf Virus). After this date all insecticides are forbidden, thus creating an insect-rich haven at the edges of cereal crops. The rest (most) of the field is fully sprayed as per normal agricultural practice. Agronomic costings have shown that financial losses incurred as a result of implementing Conservation Headlands are less than 1% (Boatman and Sotherton 1988).

Field experiments have shown that the percentage weed cover in Conservation Headlands is over four times as high as in fully sprayed headlands and that Conservation Headlands contain, on average, three times as many weed species (Sotherton 1991). In terms of insects, densities of the chick-food insect group can be between two and three times as high in Conservation Headlands than in equivalent fully sprayed headlands. The survival of partridge chicks follows suit: in each of eight experimental years, the survival rate was higher where Conservation Headlands were present than where they were absent (Table 18.1). With Conservation Headlands it exceeded 33%, i.e. the minimum required to maintain a stable population (Potts 1986), in five of those years, whereas without them it never reached that level.

Table 18.1 *Percentage of Grey Partridge chicks that survived the first six weeks after hatching, in relation to the management of cereal headlands (outer 6 m of the crop) on experimental farms in Norfolk, 1984–91. The headlands on one half of each farm were selectively sprayed (conservation headlands), and were conventionally farmed (fully sprayed) on the other half. (From Sotherton et al. 1993.)*

	1984	1985	1986	1987	1988	1989	1990	1991
Conservation headlands	52%	22%	60%	46%	39%	48%	25%	21%
Fully sprayed headlands	27%	13%	28%	22%	25%	30%	23%	18%
Number of farms	8	8	9	11	12	9	20	18

Management of nesting habitat

Traditional management of nesting cover has included the planting and mainte-nance of hedgerows on low grassy banks, thereby providing both cover and nest cup drainage at the same time. The hedges are kept below 2 m in height to pre-vent shading of the perennial vegetation at the base and avoid tall trees that could provide look-out perches for avian predators. The banks are cut every 2–3 years on a rotational basis, to avoid scrub encroachment while promoting nesting cover. Two new methods enable the control of pernicious weeds while safe-guarding the perennial grassy vegetation that provides Grey Partridges with nesting sites. The first is the sterile strip, which is simply a 1-m buffer between the crop and the field margin that is kept free of weeds by rotavation or herbicide use. The buffer prevents invasion of the crop by weeds growing in the margin, and also insulates to some extent the margin from crop fertilisers and spray drift (Boatman and Wilson 1998). The second is the use of selective herbicides in the margin, which eliminates perni-cious weeds without affecting the rest of the vegetation, thereby giving the farmer confidence to leave his crop headlands selectively sprayed. Experimental trials have identified compounds such as fluazifop-P-butyl, which has a high specificity against Barren Brome. Quinmerac, which targets Cleavers, has been particularly useful (Boatman 1992).

Where fields are large, additional nesting cover may be established by sub-dividing them in a non-permanent fashion using grass strips or 'Beetle Banks' (Thomas *et al.* 1991). These are strips or slightly raised banks constructed across a field by repeated passes with a plough, and sown with tussock-forming grasses such as Cock's-foot (*Dactylis glomerata*) or Yorkshire Fog (*Holcus lanatus*). The banks end 25 m away from the field margins to facilitate the use of farm machinery and prevent access by predators. Originally designed to create cover for wintering beneficial insects, they also provide excellent nesting cover.

The use of set-aside for Grey Partridge management

Set-aside was introduced into the European Union in 1988 to reduce cereal surpluses. In return for subsidies, farmers were paid to take land out of production. Initially this was of little value to Grey Partridges because land taken out of production quickly developed a dense, impenetrable perennial vegetation, hostile to small foraging chicks. This was replaced in 1992 with mandatory rotational set-aside on 15% of a farm's cultivated area. This was potentially of much greater use for Grey Partridges because it could be established after the cereal harvest, by leaving the stubbles over winter and allowing vegetation to regenerate naturally. Overwinter stubbles could provide feeding grounds for Grey Partridges (spilt grain and weed seeds) as well as leaving chick-food insects that overwinter in the soil undisturbed by cultivation. The regenerated vegetation could subsequently provide suitable brood-rearing habitat, especially in its first season after harvest.

In practice, the set-aside regulations obliged farmers either to plough the land shortly after 1 May, or cut the vegetation at least once before 1 July, to control pernicious weeds. This proved disastrous for nesting birds (Poulsen and Sotherton 1992). Changes to the regulations in 1993 enabled the full wildlife potential of set-aside to be realised. Cutting on rotational set-aside was delayed until 15 July or replaced by herbicide treatment that preserved the vegetational structure. New 'flexible' set-aside, lasting a minimum of three years, allowed the creation of gamebird habitats such as grass strips and banks for nesting and the use of unharvestable crop mixtures such as cereals and kale for brood-rearing and the provision of food in winter. These 'wild bird covers' recreated the open structure of a crop canopy full of weeds and chick-food insects. It was even possible to combine the two types of annual and longer-term set-aside to obtain an optimal configuration for game on each farm, strategically creating winter nesting and brood cover on a field-by-field basis (Sotherton 1998). Unintentionally, the opportunities for habitat creation on set-aside land became an extremely useful tool for Grey Partridge restoration schemes.

In the latest round of Common Agricultural Policy reforms, subsidies were redirected away from production foregone and towards environmental gain. Farmers are now offered a choice of management options, including habitat creation measures from a menu to gain sufficient points to become eligible for funding. All the Grey-Partridge-friendly measures to create nesting and brood-rearing habitat are on these menus and so UK farmers can now be paid to farm in ways that benefit Grey Partridges, funded by the Agri-Environment Scheme.

Predation management

The traditional role of the British gamekeeper has been to control predation on gamebirds and their eggs by killing predators. Trapping, shooting and poisoning predators was particularly widespread and intense during the 1800s and resulted in the local extinction of several raptor species and considerable reduction in numbers and range of many other predatory birds and mammals (Tapper 1992). Protective legislation during the twentieth century has restricted both the species that may be legally killed and the techniques that can be used to kill them. For instance, all raptors and owls have been protected since 1961 (and many of them well before that), while poisoning was outlawed already in 1911.

The question naturally arises whether nowadays predation control is still justifiable, not least because of the once widely accepted ecological belief (Errington's (1956) doomed 'surplus' theory) that predator numbers are controlled by the abundance of their prey and not vice versa. In fact, several scientific experiments have refuted that belief and demonstrated convincingly that generalist predators can (and do) depress numbers of their gamebird prey. Thus the experimental removal of mammalian predators increased reproductive success, autumn abundance and spring density of Woodland Grouse in Sweden (Marcström *et al.* 1988). Similarly in the case of the Grey Partridge, the experimental application of legal predation control in spring and early summer increased breeding success, post-breeding density, spring density and the shooting bag (Tapper *et al.* 1996); after three years, the autumn stock averaged 3.5 times higher when predation was controlled than when it was not and the breeding stock 2.6 times higher.

The predators that may legally be killed are common, and several are increasing in abundance in the UK, namely Foxes, small mustelids, Brown Rats, Grey Squirrels (*Sciurus cardinensis*) and corvids (birds of the Crow family) (Marchant *et al.* 1990; Corbet and Harris 1991). The highly seasonal predation control, carried out during the Grey Partridge nesting season, is directed at the period of greatest sensitivity to predation. The control methods that are currently legal are firearms (rifle or shotgun for Foxes, Brown Rats, Grey Squirrels and corvids), lethal devices designed to kill instantly and whose location avoids the capture of non-target species (tunnel traps for rats and mustelids), and non-lethal trapping or restraining devices that allow non-target animals to be released unharmed (cage traps for corvids, mustelids and Grey Squirrels, stopped snares for Foxes). Anti-coagulant poisons are permitted for use against rats and Grey Squirrels, under strictly defined conditions.

Conservation in action

All our management prescriptions (habitat creation, predation control) are tried and tested. This information has been synthesised down into user-friendly formats and is freely available in factsheet form and downloadable from the web (http://www.gwct. org.uk). The Game and Wildlife Conservation Trust also employs a team of advisors who can go on-farm and deliver one-to-one advice.

At the invitation of the Game and Wildlife Conservation Trust, groups of farmers across the UK meet regularly, all motivated by their desire to restore wild Grey Partridges to their farms. There are now 13 Regional Grey Partridge Groups in England

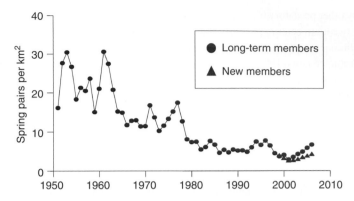

Figure 18.11 Changes over time in the average spring pair density on estates in the Game and Wildlife Conservation Trust's Partridge Count Scheme. Long-term contributors are shown as circles, recent contributors as triangles. Both show an increase since 2000.

and three in Scotland where, at each gathering, up to 60 farmers meet to learn how to plant cover crops, create insect-rich areas, control predators and increase Grey Partridge numbers. Each year these farmers count the numbers of Grey Partridges on their land and return the figures to the Game and Wildlife Conservation Trust. Examination of the figures shows that, for participating farmers, there have been heartening signs of recovery since 2000 (Figure 18.11).

And finally, for the last six years we have run a demonstration farm project near Royston in Hertfordshire where, on 2500 acres of farmland, the Grey Partridge management prescription in its entirety has been put into place and partridge numbers monitored. From an initial spring density of 2.9 pairs per km², densities have increased to 18.4 pairs per km² in only five years. On adjacent less well-managed lands densities changed from 1.3 to 3.7 pairs per km² over the same time period.

Conclusion

So, in conclusion, the future looks bright, despite having to overcome the apparent paradox that shooting conserves Grey Partridges by providing land-owners with the incentive and possible revenue to manage land appropriately. Knowledge is available, research is complete and land-owners are willing. However, the volatile nature of world farming means that in 2008, set-aside (the vehicle by which many farmers preferred to create insect-rich brood cover) has been set at 0% and the high world price of commodity foods means productive land that could grow wheat is unlikely to be sown to weedy covers for the improvement of biodiversity. For the Grey Partridge, it has always been a case of two steps forward, one step backward, but on balance the direction is positive and the future looks encouraging.

References

Aebischer, N.J. and Potts, G.R. (1994). Partridge *Perdix perdix*. In Tucker, G.M. and Heath, M.F., eds., *Birds in Europe: Their Conservation Status* (Birdlife Conservation Series No. 3), Cambridge, Birdlife International, pp. 220–221.

Boatman, N.D. (1992). Improvement of field margin habitat by selective control of annual weeds. *Aspects of Applied Biology*, **29**, 431–436.

Boatman, N.D. and Sotherton, N.W. (1988). The agronomic consequences and costs of managing field margins for game and wildlife conservation. *Aspects of Applied Biology*, **17**, 47–56.

Corbett, G.B. and Harris, S. (1991). *The Handbook of British Mammals*, 3rd edn, Oxford, Blackwell Scientific Publications.

Errington, P.L. (1956). Factors limiting vertebrate populations. *Science*, **124**, 304–307.

Ewald, J.A. and Aebischer, N.J. (1999). Pesticide use, avian food resources and bird densities in Sussex. JNCC Report No. 296, Peterborough, UK, JNCC.

Ewald, J.A., Aebischer, N.J., Moreby, S.J. and Potts, G.R. (2007). *A New Indicator to Measure Pesticide Impact on Farmland Wildlife*, London, UK, DEFRA.

Ford, J., Chitty, H. and Middleton, A.D. (1938). The food of partridge chicks (*Perdix perdix* L.) in Great Britain. *Journal of Animal Ecology*, **7**, 251–265.

Green, R.E. (1984). The feeding ecology and survival of partridge chicks (*Alectoris rufa* and *Perdix perdix*) on arable farmland in East Anglia. *Journal of Applied Ecology*, **21**, 817–830.

Gregory, R.D., Noble, D.G., Cranswick, P.A. *et al.* (2001). *The State of the UK's Birds 2000*, Sandy, UK, Royal Society for the Protection of Birds, British Trust for Ornithology and Wetland and Wildlife Trust, pp. 25.

Marchant, J.H., Hudson, R., Carter, S.P. *et al.* (1990). *Population Trends in British Breeding Birds*, Tring, British Trust for Ornithology.

Marcström, V., Kenward, R.E. and Engrén, E. (1988). The impact of predation of boreal tetraonids during vole cycles: an experimental study. *Journal of Animal Ecology*, **57**, 589–572.

Potts, G.R. (1986). *The Partridge: Pesticides, Predation and Conservation*, London, Collins.

Potts, G.R. and Aebischer, N.J. (1991). Modelling the population dynamics of the Grey Partridge: conservation and management. In Perrins, C.M., Lebreton, J.D. and Hirons, G.J.M., eds., *Bird Population Studies: Their Relevance to Conservation Management,* Oxford, Oxford University Press, pp. 373–390.

Potts, G.R. and Aebischer, N.J. (1995). Population dynamics of the Grey Partridge *Perdix perdix* 1793–1993: monitoring, modelling and management. *Ibis*, **137**, Supplement 1, 29–37.

Poulsen, J.G. and Sotherton, N.W. (1992). Crow predation in recently cut set-aside land. *British Birds*, **85**, 674–675.

Sotherton, N.W. (1982). The effects of herbicides on the chrysomelid beetle *Gastrophysa polygoni* (L.) in the laboratory and field. *Zeitschrift für Angewandte Entomologie*, **94**, 446–451.

Sotherton, N.W. (1991). Conservation Headlands: a practical combination of intensive cereal farming and conservation. In Firbank, L.G., Carter, N., Derbyshire, J.F.

et al., eds., *The Ecology of Temperate Cereal Fields*, Oxford, Blackwell Scientific Publications, pp. 373–397.

Sotherton, N.W. (1998). Land use changes and the decline of farmland wildlife: an appraisal of the set-aside approach. *Biological Conservation,* **83**, (3), 259–268.

Sotherton, N.W., Robertson, P.A. and Dowell, S.D. (1993). Manipulating pesticide use to increase the production of wild game birds in Britain. In Church, K.E. and Dailey, T.V., eds., *Quail III: National Quail Symposium,* Pratt, Kansas Department of Wildlife and Parks, pp. 92–101.

Southwood, T.R.E. and Cross, D.J. (1969). The ecology of the partridge III. Breeding success and the abundance of insects in natural habitats. *Journal of Applied Ecology,* **38**, 497–509.

Southwood, T.R.E. and Cross, D.J. (2002). Food requirements of Grey Partridge *Perdix perdix* chicks. *Wildlife Biology,* **8**, 175–183.

Tapper, S.C. (1992). *Game Heritage: An Ecological Review from Shooting and Gamekeeping Records,* Fordingbridge, Game Conservancy Limited.

Tapper, S.C., Potts, G.R. and Brockless, M.H. (1996). The effect of an experimental reduction in predation pressure on the breeding success and population density of Grey Partridges (*Perdix perdix*). *Journal of Applied Ecology,* **33**, 965–978.

Thomas, M.B., Wratten, S.D. and Sotherton, N.W. (1991). Creation of 'island' habitats in farmland to manipulate populations of beneficial arthropods: predator densities and emigration. *Journal of Applied Ecology,* **28**, 906–917.

19

Reptiles

Chris P. Gleed-Owen

Summary

The reptile fauna of the British Isles comprises six native species, and two additional species in the Channel Islands. Only one is present in Ireland. Two of them – the Sand Lizard and Smooth Snake – are rare and restricted by climate to areas where specific habitats exists. A third, the Grass Snake, is absent north of the Scottish border by climate. It is fair to say that all species have suffered major declines in the last century, primarily due to habitat loss and degradation, but conservation efforts have probably halted their decline on balance, and may even be reversing their fortunes. Realistically, their future is in the hands of habitat managers and conservation policies that may not always be sympathetic. The winter burning programme in the New Forest destroys many hectares of Smooth Snake habitat each year, albeit it temporarily. The constant battle with coniferous pine re-growth on heathlands is probably the biggest threat to sand lizards.

Agricultural intensification has made rural Britain's farmland largely uninhabitable to most reptiles. Ironically, one of the most widespread reptiles in Britain – the Adder – is the species causing the most concern. Widely reported as declining rapidly at the local population level, it has become extinct recently from whole counties. Although the rare species are subject to several decades of monitoring, a key problem for widespread species such as the Adder has been the lack of large-scale monitoring programmes. All are now the subject of national monitoring programmes, and for the Adder this includes raising awareness about its precarious dependance on traditional hibernation sites. Finally, it is worth speculating what the effects of anticipated climate change may be on the future of our reptiles. Curiously, global warming could widen the suite of habitats that reptiles are able to occupy, and this may even result in range expansion.

Silent Summer: The State of Wildlife in Britain and Ireland, ed. Norman Maclean. Published by Cambridge University Press. © Cambridge University Press 2010.

Introduction, distribution

The reptiles are an impoverished faunal group in Britain and Ireland. There are six native British terrestrial reptiles (eight including the Channel Islands), and only one Irish one. This conforms to island biogeography theory that the more isolated the land mass, the fewer the species inhabiting it. The British reptiles are: Sand Lizard (*Lacerta agilis*), Common Lizard (*Zootoca (Lacerta) vivipara*), Slow-worm (*Anguis fragilis*), Grass Snake (*Natrix natrix*), Smooth Snake (*Coronella austriaca*) and Adder (*Vipera berus*). The single Irish inhabitant is the Common Lizard. Jersey has three native reptiles: Common Wall Lizard (*Podarcis muralis*), Western Green Lizard (*Lacerta bilineata*) and Grass Snake. Guernsey and Alderney have one reptile species, the Slow-worm. The waters surrounding Britain and Ireland are also frequented by a marine reptile species that is considered native. Five out of the seven species of marine turtle in the world have been recorded in British and Irish waters, but only the Leatherback Turtle (*Dermochelys coriacea*) visits deliberately and habitually in order to feed.

Before understanding the status of these species and whether humans have contributed to any declines, a whole range of contributing factors underpinning their status must also be understood. The geographical distribution, ecological preferences, populations, abundance and conservation status of these species vary considerably. The most widely distributed species are also the most abundant, and they occupy the widest suite of habitats. Lizards are one step lower than snakes in the food chain, and an order of magnitude smaller in size and home range than snakes. It follows, therefore, that they are an order of magnitude more abundant and densely distributed, and their populations can persist in smaller habitat patches than snakes. Individual climatic and habitat tolerance also have a strong effect on species' distribution and resilience to change, particularly in determining macro-range. Four species (Common Lizard, Slow-worm, Grass Snake, Adder) can be considered widespread in Britain, if somewhat patchy according to habitat availability. The Common Lizard in Ireland is similarly widespread and patchy. The two British rare species (Sand Lizard and Smooth Snake) have restricted distributions owing to the narrow habitat tolerances that the British climate limits them to.

All species have undergone major declines within historic times, and particularly during the latter half of the twentieth century. These are predominantly the incidental results of human activity, rather than the deliberate persecution of reptiles. Despite a doubtful allegation from Mediaeval Ireland, humans have probably never extirpated any reptile from Britain or Ireland. We are certainly to blame for large-scale declines and local disappearances, but these patterns reflect an underlying patchiness due to natural factors. Geology and other factors determine where reptiles exist and at what densities, but they also dictate where we farm intensively, and where we have the greatest impacts on reptiles that may already be scarce in an area.

The geographical distribution of each species is primarily a function of their climatic tolerances, further refined by their habitat requirements. Adder, Common

Lizard and Slow-worm occupy the full latitudinal range of the British mainland. The Sand Lizard, Smooth Snake and Grass Snake have northern limits within Britain. The Grass Snake has a distinctly climatically induced northern limit approximating to the English–Scottish border, possibly with isolated records further north, but primarily controlled by summer temperature-limiting egg incubation. Sand Lizard and Smooth Snake are certainly restricted by climate to parts of Britain, but their distribution owes much to their reliance upon fragmented and patchily distributed habitats. Both species live on sandy heaths, and Sand Lizards also occupy some coastal dunes. This limitation to two habitat types is a climatic adaptation; in central Europe where summers are warmer, they occupy a much wider suite of habitats. If climate gets a degree or two warmer in southern Britain, we might start to see them spreading here too – provided corridors of newly suitable habitat exist. In fact, it may already be happening in Dorset.

The distribution of all herpetofauna species in Britain is also a product of a complex environmental history since the end of the last Ice Age (Gleed-Owen 1998). As climate ameliorated in northern Europe, species expanded northwards and westwards over a period of several thousand years. Reptiles arriving before sea-level rise cut off their last land bridge from the present-day Netherlands formed the British fauna. Likewise the rise of the Irish Sea cut off the island of Ireland so early that only Common Lizard appears to have made the crossing. Climate since then has included periods when summer temperature was several degrees warmer, and at times cooler than today. A seventh terrestrial reptile, the European Pond Terrapin (*Emys orbicularis*) actually colonised Britain since the last Ice Age, but climatic cooling probably caused its extinction around 5000 years ago.

The British reptile fauna is at its most diverse in lowland heaths of southern England, because this is the only habitat that supports both rare species, and such sites also tend to support all four widespread species. Common Lizards, Slow-worms and Adders are roughly equally distributed in uplands and lowlands, whereas the Grass Snake is a largely lowland species. The Common Lizard and Adder probably reach the highest altitudes as they are the least thermally demanding species and have arctic ranges. Most of the British species are associated with higher altitudes further south in their European range, for example the Sand Lizard is largely montane in Switzerland, and the Common Lizard is restricted to high mountains at its southern limit. Likewise, the habitats occupied by species change according to climate and latitude. The Sand Lizard is tied to sandy heaths and coastal dunes in Britain, whereas in France and Germany, for example, it is found in meadows and other habitats and does not need a sandy substrate. These are clearly all post-glacial adaptations achieved by shifting altitudinal and latitudinal range to fit the warming climate after the last Ice Age. This is important to understand, as it offers an insight into how species might react with changing climate in the future.

If summer temperatures were warmer in Britain (as anticipated in most global warming predictions), most reptiles would adapt in some or all of the following ways:

- Extend their range northwards (if geographically possible)
- Become less patchily distributed
- Colonise a wider suite of habitats
- Extend into higher altitudes (if topographically possible).

Conversely, if climate were to become cooler in Britain, most reptiles would:

- Contract their range southwards
- Become more patchy
- Become restricted to fewer habitats
- Contract to lower altitudes.

For example, if summer climate were to get warmer and sunnier, then Smooth Snakes might conceivably expand into neighbouring areas of grassland and scrubland and extend along corridors such as hedgerows, field margins and railway routes.

The Leatherback Turtle breeds in the Tropics, but migrates to higher latitudes to forage. As with many large marine vertebrates, relatively little is known about its life cycle and ecology. Uniquely in the reptile world, it can raise its body temperature metabolically; essential for its deep dives, but also enabling forays into cool British and Irish waters, where it feeds on jellyfish blooms.

Legal protection

In Britain, all of the British reptiles have some legislative protection, and the rare species are strictly protected. The two key measures are the Wildlife and Countryside Act 1981 (WCA), as amended by Amendment Acts and the Countryside and Rights of Way Act 2000 and the Conservation (Natural Habitats etc.) Regulations 1994 and 2007 (the 'Habitats Regulations'). The lowest level of protection under the WCA only prevents trade, killing and injury of the widespread species. The rare species are protected under European law from a range of potential impacts, including destruction of their habitat.

All native reptiles are listed on Schedule 5 of the WCA, although the widespread species only enjoy some of the provisions of Section 9. The two rare reptiles and the marine turtles are listed on Annex IV of the Habitats Directive and thus on Schedule 2 of the Habitats Regulations. These 'European-protected species' (EPS) enjoy much more protection than those only protected by the WCA. In fact, the history of the WCA is quite telling with respect to changing attitudes towards reptile conservation. Whilst the rare species were on Schedule 5 since 1981, the Common Lizard, Slow-worm and Grass Snake were only added in 1988, and legislators resisted inclusion of the Adder until 1992. Persecution of Adders still occurs, although probably less common than it was. Equally worrying are the effects on Slow-worms and Grass Snakes that are often mistaken for Adders through fear and ignorance.

The Common Lizard is protected in the Republic of Ireland by the Wildlife Act 1976 (and amendments). In Northern Ireland it is protected by Schedule 5 of the Wildlife Order 1985 (and amendments). The Leatherback Turtle enjoys protection in British and Irish waters.

Site protection

The British Sites of Special Scientific Interest (SSSI) series is meant to protect the best wildlife sites, and the site selection guidelines are quite specific about Sand Lizard and Smooth Snake sites. Nevertheless, it is an imperfect system and the SSSI series omits a significant proportion of Sand Lizard and Smooth Snake populations. The Amphibian and Reptile Conservation Trust (formerly the Herpetological Conservation Trust) (the ARC) developed inventories of rare herpetofauna populations, and assessed the contribution that the SSSI series makes to the conservation of individual species (Gleed-Owen 2004). Using GIS polygons to map all known populations, it was possible to calculate the proportion designated as SSSI interest features and therefore directly protected (in theory), as well as those that fell within a SSSI and received *de facto* protection.

Of the 521 Sand Lizard population 'foci' known in England, only 78% were designated as 'interest features', although 86% fell within a SSSI. In mitigation, reintroductions and the discovery of hitherto-unknown Sand Lizard populations have continued year on year (at least 530 populations by 2008), whereas new SSSIs are rarely designated. Many of the non-SSSI populations are found on forestry land, particularly with a trend towards reversion of some forestry blocks to conservation tenure, and these tend to fall outside statutory protection. For Sand Lizards, 63 of the 521 populations were outside Dorset and therefore should be notified by Nature Conservancy Council rules. In Wales, there are approaching 10 population foci, but all of them have been introduced in the last 15 years, and none of them are designated as 'interest features'. The single population in Scotland was an unofficial translocation beyond the natural range of the species, and thus unlikely to receive formal designation.

The situation for the Smooth Snake is even less satisfactory. Whilst 89% of the 163 known populations in England fall within a SSSI, only 36% of them are designated interest features. Thus, it remains hard to raise the importance of Smooth Snake conservation in the minds of land managers, when the emphasis is on species listed in site designation. About 85 Smooth Snake sites are on SSSIs with no formal obligation in the site's legal designation to look after the Smooth Snakes. This leaves their fate to other mechanisms, such as the Habitats Regulations and sympathetic land managers such as the ARC. The largest inhabited area of Smooth Snake habitat is the New Forest, and whilst the Forestry Commission is sympathetic to reptile conservation, they are under pressure to maintain a highly damaging burning programme that destroys many hectares of Smooth Snake habitat every year. Part of the problem, historically, has been a knowledge gap in the distribution of Smooth Snakes. Current and future survey is likely to identify more populations in the future, and this would alter the picture somewhat.

The GIS inventories created by the ARC demonstrated that whilst the vast majority of rare species populations fall within SSSIs, a considerable proportion of them are not notified interest features. Almost a quarter of Sand Lizard populations and two-thirds of Smooth Snake populations are not designated interest features. Of course, much of the problem described here has a historical explanation. There was a great rush to designate sites, and inevitably there were some omissions, not least due to data deficiencies, as well as a few erroneous inclusions. Nevertheless, even those populations that are designated are not immune to problems such as arson, overgrazing and unsympathetic management of various sorts. There are simply too many conflicting wildlife interests, and the policy bodies are too monolithic to rationalise them in a balanced way.

In sharp contrast, the widespread reptile species receive very little statutory protection through the SSSI system. There are eight reptile SSSI designations in England (out of a series of 4000 sites), and none in Wales (from a series of 1000 sites). SSSI designations of the widespread reptiles are meant to protect exceptional population assemblages, but at best they represent a miniscule and somewhat arbitrary sample, with little chance of ever designating most of the eligible sites. There are simply too many populations across Britain to feasibly survey, map or protect.

Pragmatically, the SSSI series can only ever make a significant contribution to the protection of the rare species, and even these cannot rely solely on site protection. The widespread species receive no meaningful site protection in their own right, and rely entirely on other mechanisms such as *de facto* protection on designated sites. The 'county wildlife site' series is increasingly important for them, as are agricultural and other land-use policies.

Pro-active conservation

Conservation action is directed towards all the reptile species, but the statutory emphasis is on the European-protected (i.e. rare) species. Most effort and resources are therefore targeted at the Sand Lizard, Smooth Snake and marine turtles, which enjoy strategic, centrally co-ordinated action. The UK Biodiversity Action Plan (BAP) drafted in 1995 is one key vehicle for this; although until recently, it did not include the Smooth Snake. Historically the British Herpetological Society carried out significant habitat management and protection work on various heathland sites in southern England, with the primary aim of safeguarding Sand Lizard and Smooth Snake populations. Since the ARC was formed 20 years ago, their heathland protection and management efforts have expanded to become a comprehensive and strategic programme of works. Alongside this, a programme of captive breeding and translocations of Sand

Lizards and Smooth Snakes has reintroduced them to many sites from which they had formerly been lost. The Sand Lizard has proved a particularly successful colonist, with over 50 translocations and a success rate of about 80%.

Publication of a revised BAP list in 2007 added the Smooth Snake and all of the widespread reptiles too. It is difficult to ascertain how much effort and resources have hitherto been applied to widespread species, though collectively they are probably substantial, albeit unco-ordinated. Conservation is generally delivered through local initiatives, the success of which depends on the existence of local activists, and is hampered by ephemeral funding.

Recent expansion of the BAP list through Section 40(I) of the NERC Act 2006 means theoretically greater strategic support and conservation in England and Wales, but in reality it could prove a dilution. Action plans may not be implemented for new species due to the added complexity and burden involved. Whether this will mean a diminution of the existing rare reptile action plans is difficult to say. Arguably the Adder is one reptile species that needs an urgent new focus, rather than the Sand Lizard and Smooth Snake, which are doing quite well and have strong legal protection anyway.

Trends in status

The title of this section is ambitious. We do not have robust time-series datasets to adequately demonstrate the reptile declines that most reptile workers are convinced have occurred, and for most species, continue to occur (Gleed-Owen *et al.* 2005). Monitoring of a sort has taken place for the rare species, and recently established schemes give hope for collecting better data for the widespread species, but the lack of comparable data from several decades ago is frustrating. A few national surveys have provided snapshots across Britain at various points in the last century; usually crude assessments from anecdotal reports rather than field survey. Stronger evidence comes from proxies, such as the loss of heathland habitat with its attendant loss of dependent reptile species. Real empirical time-series data are generally lacking, apart from a few local studies, and this has only recently been addressed by schemes such as the 'National Reptile Survey' and 'Make the Adder Count' as part of the National Amphibian and Reptile Recording Scheme (NARRS) initiative (http://www.narrs.org.uk). Some useful insights into trends are also buried within published data and datasets that have never been properly analysed or published.

The general distribution and abundance of British reptiles were described in early accounts such as Leighton (1903), based on anecdotal accounts rather than systematic surveys. Half a century later, Taylor's atlases were the first attempts to map distribution, again based on literature and anecdotes. He mapped them at a crude Vice County level, initially (Taylor 1948), and later as individual records (Taylor 1963). It is clear from these, and local accounts, that some parts of Britain have never been well endowed with reptiles. Some lowland agricultural counties, such as Warwickshire and Cambridgeshire, seem to have always been relatively thin on reptile sites. As will be discussed later, reptiles in such counties are in an inherently weaker position and more prone to further losses.

The first modern 10 km grid-based atlas was produced by the Biological Records Centre (BRC) following a period of pro-active solicitation of data (Arnold 1973). The data were split into pre- and post-1960 categories which, as always, give a superficial impression of decline. Of course, they do not permit comparison of data volumes, recording effort, density of records within 10 km squares etc. A revised atlas was published over 20 years later (Arnold 1995), which has yet to be superseded, although various county atlases have since been produced.

In terms of critical review and time-series analysis of reptile status, these have been ephemeral and rarely peer-reviewed. Prestt *et al.* (1974) gave a useful review of the status of British reptiles. The emphasis was on changes in status in the 1950s and 60s, with the loss of habitat addressed as a particular overall problem. For the Sand Lizard, they estimated that the Merseyside population had reduced from 8–10 000 to *c.*100 since the 1930s, mostly due to golf-course construction, and one important Dorset population had undergone about an 80% decline in recent decades. (It now seems that the Merseyside population never declined anywhere near as low as 100 individuals.) In parts of Surrey, where there had been 54 Sand Lizard colonies in the mid-1950s, only two remained by 1971, and none by 1974. Corbett (1988) assessed the national status of Sand Lizards, offering population estimates and trends in this and later reports. Whilst Sand Lizards undoubtedly declined in relation to heathland destruction and afforestation, this type of literature is short on satisfactory data and direct documentary evidence. Prestt *et al.* (1974) estimated the national population of Smooth Snakes to be between 1000 and 3000 adults, although the distributional knowledge at that time was even less complete than it is now.

Cooke and Arnold (1982) addressed the status of the widespread species, discussing apparent declines in relation to habitat loss since the 1930s. Again, the link with reptile declines is circumstantial and conjectural, although probably a fair representation of the truth. Cooke and Scorgie (1983) carried out a questionnaire-based survey of perceived abundance and distribution for the widespread species. Responses were divided into NCC regions, with some adjustments aimed at equalising coverage. An almost identical exercise was carried out by Hilton-Brown and Oldham (1991), thus presenting an opportunity for comparison. Both studies presented thematic maps of perceived status, with the latter also showing changes in perceived status over the preceding 10 years. All species showed some apparent decline, generally attributed to habitat loss. However, these exercises were too simplistic and subjective.

In the 1960s and 70s, the BRC collated distribution records into a national database, resulting in the atlas (Arnold 1973, 1995). The first pro-active field-based reptile survey was not carried out until the NCC commissioned Leicester Polytechnic to run one between 1990 and 1992 (Swan and Oldham 1993). Together with existing BRC records, the survey generated about 5000 observations. Geographical coverage was patchy, with vast differences between counties. The recording itself used standardised recording forms and parameters, but methods and effort were not standardised. The total number of new records per species was: 1083 Common Lizard, 742 Slow-worm, 823 Grass Snake and 817 Adder. The Common Lizard records came from 65% of 10 km squares in Britain, whereas the other three species had only 44–46% coverage. The data implied that the Common Lizard was more widespread than the other species, and all species were patchy, particularly the Adder, which was clearly less common in the Midlands. The authors were careful to point out that until a more detailed survey was carried out, the status of the widespread reptiles would remain essentially unknown.

In 2007, the NARRS national monitoring scheme was finally launched by the HCT (now ARC). It trains volunteers to survey random 1 km squares across the UK, using standard methodologies and effort. This generates occupancy-rate figures for individual species across the sample of squares surveyed. With sufficient sample size, it could be extrapolated to provide an index of reptile status across the whole UK. Results from the first season in 2007 showed that 103 squares were surveyed, and reptiles were detected in 55 squares, which is an incredible hit rate of 53%. This seems very high and probably hides some bias in the squares surveyed. Although survey squares were allocated randomly, there may have been a higher drop-out rate for squares perceived as unlikely to support reptiles. (Around 90% of volunteers expressing an interest did not take part.) Common Lizard was found in 27% of squares, Slow-worm 21%, Grass Snake 20% and Adder 8%. Preliminary results from the 2008 season showed broadly similar results, but it will take several more years to achieve a statistically adequate sample (www.narrs.org.uk).

The Leatherback Turtle is subject to a joint British–Irish research project (INTERREG) and there are several strandings databases. Global status assessments are carried out by monitoring nesting beaches in Latin America and other tropical breeding areas. A decline from 115 000 breeding females in 1980 to 26000–43000 in 2007 is widely reported, due to loss of breeding beaches, exploitation, bycatch and possibly ingestion of plastic and other marine debris.

Sand Lizard

The ARC Trust has co-ordinated a national monitoring programme for the Sand Lizard (see Figure 19.1) for nearly 20 years. It has never had a standardised sampling regime, and as such it has not produced consistent population indices or other measures that can be compared over time. Monitoring was originally carried out by the British Herpetological Society Conservation Committee (BHSCC) from the 1960s onwards, until the ARC took on the bulk of surveillance from 1989 onwards. Assessments of Sand Lizard status were based on the detailed personal knowledge of individuals

Figure 19.1 Male Sand Lizard in mature heathland habitat with moss–lichen understorey. This rare species suffered drastic declines due to habitat loss, but is probably stable now (see colour plate).

such as Keith Corbett, and strategic conservation measures were based on these. Such assessments were more intuitive than scientific, and academics might find the absence of source data disconcerting, although the conclusion that Sand Lizard populations were declining was undeniable. Count data were collected each year, but never systematically analysed, and these were only digitised by the ARC quite recently. Today the monitoring programme follows a similar methodology: recording counts and locations of all individuals seen on single or multiple visits to many different sites. Data are still not consistent in terms of effort and detectability, and have never been properly examined to ascertain trends in status or population sizes.

It is impossible to count the number of Sand Lizards in each population, but with an understanding of how lizard densities vary it would be possible to use habitat quality and extent as a proxy for population size. Some useful attempts have been made at estimating density figures (summarised in Gleed-Owen 2004). Keith Corbett proposed a maximum density of 300 adult Sand Lizards per hectare for the very best heathland patches in southern England. He later proposed up to 210/ha for prime Surrey heathland sites and 125/ha on sites with less exposed sand for egg-laying or less-favourable topography. Despite a comparable estimate of 240/ha coming from heathland in southern Sweden, Corbett's figures lack credibility to those who prefer more transparent methods such as mark-recapture and radio-tracking. These labour-intensive techniques give more defensible density figures, but, ironically, their inherent error margins compromise their superiority over intuitive estimates. One mark-recapture study calculated densities of around 50/ha on sub-optimal habitat, but the associated home range calculations varied from 40 m^2 to 1400 m^2. Radio-tracked lizards on another sub-optimal site yielded densities of 0.3/ha to 19/ha. Recent PhD work has used photo-recognition alongside detailed environmental monitoring to estimate population densities and detectability on nine intensively monitored Sand Lizard populations in Dorset. When the figures are published, we should be one step closer to a reliable habitat-based index of population size.

So with density figures ranging from zero to 300/ha, can we calculate a national population size for Sand Lizards and measure trends over time? In theory, yes we can. With good spatial knowledge of habitat extent and good typical density figures, we should be able to estimate the total UK population. Given that it is virtually impossible to count Sand Lizards directly, extrapolations based on the extent of occupied habitat are the only realistic option. The density figures above are certainly useful and give us brackets to work within. The key question now is how much occupied habitat is there and of what quality?

General views are that between 50 and 95% of Sand Lizards live within optimum habitat patches, often termed 'foci', within larger heathland or dune systems. Some Sand Lizard sites, particularly smaller ones, are almost completely occupied by a single focus; whereas some larger sites have narrowly defined foci surrounded by large areas of sub-optimal habitat that probably support low densities of Sand Lizards. Local topography is a key factor in determining Sand Lizard population density, but also the management of the site. Fire and heavy grazing destroy the mature undulating heather structure that is important to Sand Lizards. Bare sand is also essential for egg-laying, and on heathland, a rolling programme of bare sand provision is usually necessary to maintain optimal densities of Sand Lizards.

Between 2002 and 2004 the ARC created a Sand Lizard site inventory, based upon the mapping of population 'foci', i.e. areas of high population density usually related to prime habitat. It is difficult to say what proportion of Sand Lizards live within these foci, as the quality of sites vary greatly, but it is probably about 75% overall. The dataset currently contains about 580 extant foci with a total area of over 1000 ha. Even at a fairly modest density estimate of 50 adults per hectare, the Sand Lizard foci alone would imply the existence of 50 000 adult Sand Lizards in the UK. This figure is much higher than previous estimates of 7000 or so in the 1970s. Positive conservation has undoubtedly increased numbers, but the discrepancy reflects the inaccuracy of former estimates rather than a spectacular increase. In any case, the entire national population is still limited to a tiny area of about 10 km^2 of foci, less than four square miles.

Smooth Snake

The Smooth Snake has a rather patchy surveillance history. We still have an incomplete distribution knowledge, and little evidence of quantitative trends. The single most insightful parameter into Smooth Snake status is the proxy of heathland loss. Smooth Snakes are exclusively tied to heathlands and adjacent habitat patches. Therefore the loss and degradation of heathlands in southern England must have had a commensurate effect on Smooth Snakes. Phelps (2004) related his experiences from long-term studies on the dynamics of sub-populations in Dorset, but his data are insufficient to assess wider trends. Smooth Snakes are notoriously cryptic, and intensive mark-recapture or radiotelemetry studies yield as many questions as answers. Whilst those Smooth Snakes that are detected are often done so with ease, this tells us little about how many are going undetected. Generalisations are difficult for Smooth Snakes. Some seem to be strictly sedentary, never moving more than a few metres, whereas others range over hundreds of metres.

The difficulty of studying Smooth Snakes means density and population estimates are fraught with uncertainty. As for the Sand Lizard, the establishment of typical densities that can be extrapolated might be the best way forward. Goddard (1984) studied three Smooth Snake populations from 1976–8, using individual recognition by mark-recapture of 136 snakes in total. The sites were on mature heathland habitat in the New Forest, with areas of 80, 75 and 30 ha, respectively. The two larger sites enabled density calculations of one to two animals per hectare. Intuitively this seems extremely low, and almost certainly does not reflect the mean density across its English range. Smooth Snakes are often easy to detect using a very low density of corrugated metal sheets ('tins'), even with deployments of less than one tin per hectare on ARC reserves in Dorset, and Forestry Commission heaths in the New Forest. A single sheet of metal less than 1 m^2 in size occupies less that 0.01% of a hectare. This would suggest that Smooth Snakes are either more numerous than one or two per hectare on the whole, or they move around very rapidly indeed, thus discovering rare attractive metal objects under which to bask. Research by Breeds (1973) over a long period showed that some Smooth Snakes may go undetected for seven or more years before re-appearing; hence any density figures based on animals detected are probably an underestimate. Much higher density estimates have been made. Spellerberg and Phelps (1977) reported Smooth Snake density figures of 11–17 per hectare, which is probably more indicative of optimum habitat. Attempts have been made to standardise survey methods, such as an optimum density for laying the artificial refugia or 'tins' that provide sampling sites, but the prescriptions are impractical on a large scale. Existing monitoring efforts make do with very low sampling site densities and yet they produce comprehensive presence–absence data and consistent patterns of capture history. The capture histories of individual tins allow comparison between locations, and often pick out patterns of occupation that characterise whole areas rather than random variability between tins (unpublished

ARC data). For example, 'hotspots' exist where clusters of tins have 20–60% hit rates, whereas clusters of tins in other areas have zero encounters. Low-density deployment of tins may be imperfect, but it makes scant resources go a long way.

The ARC, and before it the BHSCC, have collected Smooth Snake data more or less continuously since the 1960s. Geographical coverage has never been complete, and there are gaps in distributional knowledge even today. Smooth Snakes are highly secretive and cryptic, and artificial refugia such as metal tins are essential to increase detection to a worthwhile level. The first attempt at a survey was by the British Herpetological Society (BHS) under contract from the NCC from 1984–7. It surveyed 196 sites in Dorset, Hampshire, Surrey and some peripheral areas. Coverage was not as complete as the team would have liked, but contemporaneous PhD research filled in some of the New Forest gaps. The final report summarised data from at least 261 individual snakes on 86 sites, presented as a 10 km square distribution map (Braithwaite *et al.* 1989). Security concerns prevented higher-resolution maps from being published.

Whilst no time-series analysis has ever taken place nationally, the ARC collects a great deal of data that would usefully permit some form of analysis. The ARC has tins on most of its 80 or so heathland reserves (generally between 10 to 50 tins per site), and also on many third party sites owned by the Forestry Commission, Defence Estates, local authorities etc.; more than 3000 tins in total. These are nearly always at densities of less than one tin per hectare and yet Smooth Snakes are detected at many of them. Most, but not all, of these are checked at least annually, and sometimes many times a year. The primary impetus for laying tins on heathland reserves is the Smooth Snake interest (although they generate data for widespread reptile species too).

As for the Sand Lizard, it would probably be easier to assess overall population status by multiplying typical density figures and extent of occupied habitat (notwithstanding the inherent variability in both parameters). The prerequisites are good knowledge of occupancy (i.e. all occupied sites known) and reliable density figures for a range of habitat qualities. An interim Smooth Snake habitat inventory has been created by the ARC in 2004, but it requires further work due to flawed habitat mapping and incomplete distribution knowledge. English Nature had created a GIS inventory of Lowland Heathland in England (version 1.2 in 2004), which enabled identification of all areas of lowland heathland within the Smooth Snake's range, and thus the mapping of Smooth Snake habitat. All areas greater than 5 ha provided the potential suite of sites, and those for which occupation data were available from recent historical times provided the actual current range. The population status at these sites were classed as 'potential', and for the sites with Smooth Snake records, it was categorised as either 'extant' (recorded since 1994) or 'unknown' (pre-1994 records). The 1994 cut-off point is somewhat arbitrary, although it reflects the date of the Habitats Directive's implementation. However, it does lump all pre-1994 sites together, including some early twentieth-century records, which may not be appropriate, as sites with more recent pre-1994 records are more likely to hold Smooth Snakes still. Some of the sites with older records are almost certainly extinct; nevertheless, as sites were only mapped in this exercise if suitable habitat still existed at (or very close to) the record location, presence/absence arguably remains unproven at all of the old sites.

No attempt was made to estimate population sizes or categorise population size classes for Smooth Snakes in the baseline datasets; there is insufficient information to do this. Clearly the continued presence of Smooth Snakes at any site needs to be established more often than every 10 years in order to keep an up-to-date distribution map, let alone to monitor population status.

Adder

Equally feared and revered, the Adder (see Figure 19.2) is perhaps the most enigmatic reptile of the British Isles. Also known as the viper, or northern viper, it is the only reptile that is truly a household name. Its bold dorsal zigzag marking stretches the entire length of its back and is unmistakable, yet countless Slow-worms and Grass Snakes are falsely 'accused' of being Adders every year, often by frightened householders who have

Figure 19.2 Male Adder basking on gorse in early spring. Adders are declining nationally due to habitat loss and degradation, such as insensitive scrub removal (see colour plate).

never seen a real Adder. The Adder has featured in folklore and literature more than any other British reptile, and as our only venomous snake, it has engendered fear and loathing throughout history. However, it is also one of our most threatened reptiles.

Whilst the Sand Lizard and Smooth Snake are rarer (their distribution is a tiny sub-set of the Adder's range), Adders seem to have been quietly disappearing from numerous sites. Even where Sand Lizards and Smooth Snakes flourish, the Adder has often disappeared entirely. Much of this is probably down to its tendency to hibernate communally in ground voids that can act as hibernacula for entire local populations, used faithfully for many generations. When they emerge sluggishly in the early spring, Adders can often be seen basking in groups for weeks on end. This leaves them at risk from predation (despite their powerful defence mechanism), but also to persecution by humans. Farmers, gamekeepers and the general public have all been implicated. Persecution has always been a problem for the Adder, but habitat loss and degradation through unsympathetic management is probably the most pressing problem for the Adder today. Again, empirical time-series data are thin on the ground.

Tony Phelps (2004) described his long-term studies of Adder populations in Dorset. These provide the longest-running population dynamics data for these species in the UK, with individuals being known to the author for up to 30 years. Sylvia Sheldon has also studied a population of Adders in Worcestershire for 20 years, monitoring population size and individuals for most of that time, and demonstrating an alarming decline (e.g. Sheldon and Bradley 1989). Yet the national status of this animal has been unproven and, until recently, subject to hearsay rather than systematically collected data.

English Nature commissioned a questionnaire survey in 2003 to identify long-term surveillance data for the Adder and Slow-worm, and assess their status (Baker *et al.* 2004). This provided a timely update since national status of these species had not been examined since Hilton-Brown and Oldham (1991) and Reading *et al.*'s (1996) questionnaire survey in Scotland. Baker *et al.* (2004) collected on 249 sites (roughly equal numbers for Adder and Slow-worm), of which about half were known to the recorder for over 15 years, and about a third constituted systematic surveillance. The respondents were unable to estimate population size for 40% of the Adder populations and 57% of the Slow-worm populations. Nevertheless, there were sufficient data to suggest a decline in Adder populations nationally, but not in Slow-worm populations. Interestingly, the results from non-systematic surveillance supported the conclusions drawn from systematically collected data. A worrying factor was the small size of many of the populations – a third of Adder populations were less than 10 adults – especially as the smallest populations included those most in decline. Factors such as public pressure and persecution were reported as having negative impacts on Adder status, whilst the Slow-worm was perceived as suffering most from development. No generalisations were possible for the impact of habitat management as there were contrasting stories from both sides. The report was limited by a disparity between types of data and collection methodologies, and by the unrepresentative site sample, but it does raise valid concerns, particularly for the Adder. A more systematic approach would be beneficial for assessing national Adder status, and perhaps other species such as the Slow-worm and Common Toad, whether thought to be in decline or not.

The most important outcome of the above assessment was that it precipitated the initiation in 2005 of a national Adder monitoring programme called 'Make the Adder Count'. Co-ordinated by the ARC as part of the over-arching NARRS scheme, around 30 volunteers at 100 sites make springtime head counts of Adder populations after their emergence from known hibernacula.

In addition to this, the ARC launched the 'Add an Adder' survey (http://www.adder. org.uk) to collate historical and current records from the general public, with a view to identifying how many populations have become extinct. Initial analysis indicates that up to 20% of recorded populations are now extinct in some southern English regions. In counties such as Warwickshire and Nottinghamshire, Adders have greatly declined or have become extinct.

Common Lizard, Slow-worm, Grass Snake

The other three widespread species can be grouped together here. The Common Lizard and Slow-worm are widely distributed across Britain. The Grass Snake is widespread in England and Wales, but apparently absent from Scotland. On the whole, these species are not as sensitive as the Adder. For a Common Lizard or Slow-worm population to be wiped out, the habitat typically has to be totally destroyed or at least heavily degraded. A small patch of habitat only tens of metres across is often enough to keep a population going at least in the short to medium term. Grass Snakes, on the other hand, are highly mobile, and the landscape is much more permeable to them. Loss of communal and traditional egg-laying sites is a real threat to individual populations, and loss of amphibian food sources could be a problem locally. However, as individuals can cross several kilometres of sub-optimal habitat, they are less likely to suffer the total eradication that habitat destruction can cause for other species. Contrast this with Adders, where even a small infraction on the integrity of the site, such as damage to a hibernation site, could put an end to Adder presence on the whole site.

Nevertheless, the picture is not rosy for Common Lizard, Slow-worm or Grass Snake. They are all equally exposed to the general attrition and fragmentation of habitat. Whilst they are more able than the other species to live alongside humans, sometimes in very small habitat patches, they are still being lost from sites that are managed unsympathetically or destroyed for development. The law protects them in theory, but not their habitat. In reality, saving just the animals is no use, and good-quality alternative habitat needs to be found to receive them. A large 'mitigation' industry has developed around the premise of no net loss: if a population will be destroyed, then an equivalent must be created elsewhere on a like-for-like basis. There is scope for imaginative solutions, provided the ecological status is not diminished. However, with woefully little regulation or guidance on best practice, there is little to stop anyone who wants to do so from becoming a practitioner. Even with good ecological understanding and the best will in the world, it is very difficult to prevent developers from simply instructing the capture and translocation of animals to any site – suitable or otherwise, occupied or unoccupied.

As the law protects the widespread reptiles themselves rather than their habitat, the focus of effort tends to be on the immediate welfare of the animals, and cynically on avoiding legal liability for the client. But the more important question is whether the strategic rationale behind the mitigation exercise is defensible. Will the translocation exercise compensate the lost population by create a new population on a previously unoccupied site?

The fate of the animals in question is very much down to the size and quality of the donor site habitat being lost, and the capacity of the receptor site habitat. Has an equivalent like-for-like receptor site been identified? Is the habitat really as good as the donor site? Is it already occupied by the target species? If so, then why not? And if so, then how can the exercise pass the no-net-loss test?

Mitigation exercises regularly move hundreds or even thousands of these reptiles from sites where several hectares of excellent habitat is being destroyed for housing, industry, roads etc. Ironically, some of the best sites for reptiles are those derelict post-industrial zones that are usually prioritised for building on, in order to save green-belt fields of monoculture.

Luckily these species seem to be more resilient than, for example, the Adder, and this bodes well for their future. However, some strategic measures are needed to improve the way mitigation is handled, and prevent too many wasted opportunities. Simply dumping reptiles on suitable habitat that is already occupied still means a net loss of occupied habitat. If occupied habitat became the currency for mitigation standards, it would help emphasise the need to survey receptor sites to ensure they are unoccupied, and if this means co-ordinated efforts to build up land banks of new habitat then so be it. Furthermore, if we are to maintain no net loss, then we may need to think beyond the current paradigm of keeping translocation on-site or as nearby as possible. If superior unoccupied sites lie further afield, then why can't we use them? Disease transmission risk is a potential concern, but the common perception is a rather arbitrary belief that we should maintain genetic 'purity' or 'integrity'. Provided a good database is held, to keep track of our interventions in the gene pool, then translocations should not have any deleterious effects. After all, when necessity dictates long-distance moves such as returning Sand Lizards to Cornwall, then it appears acceptable.

The situation for the Common Lizard in Ireland is difficult to assess. A survey by the Irish Wildlife Trust has gathered records showing that it is still widespread, but there seems a long way to go before any form of systematic status assessment could be made across the Irish Republic. NARRS operates in Northern Ireland, but with volunteer numbers so low it is difficult to gather much data. It can only be assumed that Common Lizards across Ireland are susceptible to the same pressures of modern human landscape manipulation as they are in Britain, and that this is more likely to induce a decline than an increase.

In Jersey, the Grass Snake is the rarest reptile and the Common Wall Lizard and Western Green Lizard are restricted to isolated coastal sites where they are intrinsically threatened. In an unusual partnership, the States of Jersey Environment Division has a Biodiversity Action Plan for the Western Green Lizard that is sponsored by a law firm. The Jersey Amphibian and Reptile Group has begun surveys as part of NARRS, and in due course this should tell us more about the status of the supposedly widespread Slow-worm as well as the rare species.

What is the prognosis?

So are the British and Irish reptiles still declining? Will they continue to decline in the next 50 years? What can we do about it?

It is clear that the rarest species – the Sand Lizard and the Smooth Snake – have undergone dramatic twentieth-century declines due to heathland and sand-dune loss and degradation. The causes are many: urban development (housing, industry, golf courses), afforestation, agricultural expansion and intensification, quarrying, unsympathetic management (burning, heavy grazing), accidental fire and arson have all had major impacts. The losses slowed down dramatically in the 1980s and 90s with the introduction of habitat-protection policies and international legislation. Nevertheless, major Dorset heathlands were still disappearing under houses well into this period, and agriculture was still taking over former heathland blocks. Even today, commercial forestry covers a large portion of former heathland. Arson and accidental fires still ravage heaths around Bournemouth and Poole, though establishment of the 'Urban Heaths Partnership' may be having a positive effect. Meanwhile, across the county border in the New Forest, a highly questionable burning regime is legitimately used to destroy large areas of Smooth Snake habitat on an annual basis.

But are Sand Lizard and Smooth Snakes still declining? Conservation efforts and expert assessment suggest that they ought not to be. Using the parameter of macro-range, the range of both species has certainly expanded due to translocations, particularly dramatically for the Sand Lizard. But have overall numbers increased or declined? Has the number of populations increased or declined? Has the overall extent of suitable habitat increased or declined? Both species have benefited greatly from heathland restoration and recreation over the last 10 years, but time will tell whether these benefits are permanent. With shrinking conservation budgets, expensive maintenance costs might not be easily met. A cynic might also question the wisdom of prioritising something that is not a naturally self-sustaining habitat. The wholesale destruction of heathland and sand dunes in southern Britain has probably halted, but the Trump case in Aberdeenshire is very worrying and the management of heathlands remains a moot point. In a drive towards attaining 'traditional' grazing on heathlands, there is a strong risk of over-grazing with respect to reptiles which prefer well-structured vegetation mosaics. Physical management will always be needed to control tree and scrub growth on many sites anyway, and heathland is always at risk of disappearing under vegetation succession. Maintaining the total area of habitat available to Sand Lizards and Smooth Snakes is therefore an ongoing struggle. Rather like climbing the wrong way up an escalator: unless we are constantly making steps forward, we slide backwards.

The New Forest burning regime remains a very contentious issue too. Sand Lizards became totally extinct in the New Forest in the latter twentieth century, most probably due to a combination of over-grazing, lack of exposed sand and the controlled burning regime. The annual programme of controlled burning physically destroys heathland habitat from a reptile perspective. The charred heather and gorse is simply no longer inhabitable, and it takes years to recover sufficiently for reptiles to recolonise. Well-developed heather structure and moss–lichen understorey are important requirements for the Sand Lizard (and other reptiles), and fire wipes the slate clean, setting the habitat structure back 20–30 years. It also kills reptiles hibernating close to the surface, and as the burning continues until March, it kills any reptiles that have emerged to bask in the early spring sun. When the remainder finally emerge, sluggish from hibernation, they too are subject to predation and starvation. A controlled New Forest burn may be applied to several hectares at a time, and as with fires caused by arson, it can wipe out an entire Sand Lizard population in one go. The Sand Lizard is probably more susceptible to such dramatic events than other reptiles, as it is particularly reliant on mature heather structure and moss–lichen understorey. It is also often tied to focal points within the landscape, such as a south-facing bank or other localised topographic feature. All areas of mature heather are burnt eventually in an ongoing cycle, and only animals that can speedily recolonise contiguous habitat patches have persisted. All things told, therefore, it seems that Sand Lizards were simply not ubiquitous or vagile enough in the New Forest to recolonise previously burnt areas. The cautious reintroduction programme has therefore had to be limited to a few fenced-off enclosures of un-burnt and ungrazed heather.

Common Lizards have suffered to a lesser degree from New Forest burning (owing to their wider habitat preferences) and they remain widespread in the New Forest, albeit at lower densities than in unburnt heathland sites. However, the impact of burning is strongly determined by its scale, and no doubt Common Lizards are much more severely affected in parts of northern Britain where large-scale burning of grouse moors takes place. In such areas, lizards are typically found at very low densities, although a trend towards smaller burns should be easing the pressure on them.

Still, the evidence is not all bad with respect to burning. Against all the odds, the Smooth Snake has remained relatively widespread in the New Forest. It appears to be absent from some sizeable areas where the heather is currently too short (due to burning or overgrazing), and its distribution seems to be patchy and unpredictable, but it still occupies most of the suitable heather blocks where it would be expected. It has certainly suffered from the burning regime – hectares of Smooth Snake habitat are knowingly burnt each year – but the species is evidently resilient enough to persist across most heathland areas of the New Forest. Although so little is known about its ecology, it is clearly able to re-colonise areas that were burnt in the past, once the vegetation matures sufficiently. The vagility of a snake would be expected to be greater than that of a lizard that is a fraction of its size, and this is clearly an important factor here.

So are we able to calculate a realistic estimate of Smooth Snake population size in Britain? Previous estimates have varied between 1000 and 30 000 individuals. The latter assumes that all heathland habitat within the Smooth Snake's range is occupied and of equally good quality, hence such high-end figures tend to be seen as reckless overestimates. However, they may not be that far from the truth if, for example, our density estimates are too low. Judging purely by the areal extent of occupied sites, this author feels that 10 000 is a justifiable estimate and it could even be quite a lot more.

Understanding and measuring Smooth Snake status is still difficult, due to gaps in our knowledge of seasonal habitat use, population densities and landscape-scale occupation patterns. The single safest bet is to preserve the habitat and the snakes will look after themselves. If we keep an eye on deleterious impacts by preventing overgrazing and ending the heathland burning prevalent across the New Forest, then Smooth Snakes should maintain and even improve their status.

Adders do not seem nearly as resilient as the rare species. Whilst Sand Lizards and Smooth Snakes do very well as long as the habitat is there, the presence–absence of Adders cannot be explained exclusively by the availability of habitat. Their distribution is much patchier than that of Smooth Snakes in the New Forest, Dorset and Surrey heaths. It seems, as a general rule, that the Adder is much more susceptible to extinction than the rare species, and it seems less able to recolonise than any of the other reptile species. Once the Adders have gone, they tend not to reappear. This may be a lot to do with their tendency to exist as small sub-populations that faithfully use traditional hibernation sites which are susceptible to destruction. Scrub clearance, fires and other stochastic events, whether deliberate or accidental, can wipe out an Adder hibernaculum and with it, a whole local population. This population strategy means fewer points from which to expand and colonise new areas, and it is a distinct disadvantage when compared to a species such as the Smooth Snake that seems permanently well dispersed rather than clustered. Genetic inbreeding is also a distinct risk for isolated populations of Adders, as demonstrated in a Swedish study.

The demise of Adders in the huge conurbation of Greater London represents a picture that is both depressing and potentially the eventual outcome for them elsewhere. Intensive competition with humans for a dwindling habitat has resulted in the decline of a once-widespread species to less than a handful of isolated (and ultimately doomed?) populations. The survival of Adders in Nottinghamshire, Buckinghamshire and other counties with scarce populations is in the lap of future trends in management of heath, scrub and other 'wild' habitats.

Adders aside, an interesting question is why are the other widespread reptiles present in some parts of the country and not others, and why are they scarcer and more thinly distributed in some areas? This characteristic is true of the distribution of Common Lizards, and Slow-worms in particular. Why are Slow-worms common in grassy and herbaceous habitats in Kent, but not Lancashire? Why are both Common Lizards and Slow-worms apparently functionally absent from the county of Buckinghamshire, except for a few scattered sites? There is no apparent reason, ecologically, why reptiles should not be present in many meadows, rough pastures and other longer-sward agricultural habitats, roadsides and field-edges in Buckinghamshire. But they are not present. Nevertheless, it is likely that this has not always been the case. Before set-aside and other more recent initiatives aimed at reducing intensive use of marginal land, strips and corridors of suitable reptile habitat may have been much rarer in the county. Furthermore, the intensive use of agricultural pesticides and herbicides in the latter part of the twentieth century could have effectively wiped out the invertebrate food source of Common Lizards and Slow-worms. Invertebrates are certainly not absent now, so it may be that wholesale reptile extinction took place, and recolonisation has not occurred to most areas once they became suitable later. Those places where reptiles thrive in Buckinghamshire, e.g. parts of Burnham Beeches, have always provided suitable habitat and management environments. Conversely, much of the agricultural land in the Chilterns is probably much more habitable now than it used to be. Yet there are too few extant reptile sites, and they are too isolated, to permit the recolonisation of the rest of the county.

The same sort of scenario probably exists in other counties. Within Dorset there are great extremes from reptile-perfect heathlands in the south-east of the county to agricultural vales to the north and west where reptiles are much patchier. Other counties such as Warwickshire, Cambridgeshire and Lancashire (except its coastal dunes), seem to be intrinsically less reptile-friendly. Perhaps it is down to the geology and habitats not being as conducive. With very few Adder populations persisting into modern times, Warwickshire appears to have lost all but one of them. There are very few areas of suitable habitat for Adders in the county anyway, and Adders only ever seem to occupy a fraction of those available to them. Nottinghamshire, on the other hand, has quite a few heathland sites, some of which have been recently recreated or restored. Yet it seems that Nottinghamshire has lost its last Adder population. Persecution, habitat loss, degradation or whatever other reasons caused its near-extinction in the past, are responsible for leaving it in a position too precarious to survive the present. Reintroduction may be the only solution.

Another possible problem for the future in Britain is the establishment of species such as the Common Wall Lizard, which is alien to Britain, but has become established along parts of the Dorset coast, and may threaten some populations of Sand Lizard and Common Lizard. Common Wall Lizards and Western Green Lizards (see Figure 19.3) from deliberate introductions breed readily in the climate of the southern English coast and have been spreading rapidly along the Bournemouth cliffs for over 15 years. Wall Lizards at the nearby Canford Cliffs area are already occupying Sand Lizard habitat and may be out-competing them. Similar scenarios in Germany seem

Figure 19.3 Male Green Lizard displaying defensive posture. Native only to Jersey, it has been introduced to southern England (see colour plate).

to suggest that Wall Lizards are deleterious to Sand Lizards and Common Lizards (Münch 2001). There are now more than 20 established Wall Lizard populations in southern Britain (S. Langham, personal communication) and this number is set to rise as people continue to release them illegally or captive lizards escape from gardens. They have become so well established that it is unrealistic to consider eradicating them. New populations are reported each year, and existing populations are spreading along railway lines in West Sussex and coastal cliffs in Dorset. Another species, the Aesculapian Snake (*Zamenis longissimus*), is established in London and North Wales, but is unlikely to spread far under current climatic conditions. Likewise, the formerly popular pet Red-eared Terrapin (*Trachemys scripta elegans*), which graces hundreds, if not thousands, of ponds and lakes across Britain, is probably not causing a major impact. They cannot breed in the current climate, but as they are long-lived chelonians, this might all change in a warmer climate.

It is also worth mentioning that the Slow-worm has been introduced to the west of Ireland where it is thought to be established locally. There have been historical introductions of Grass Snake and Green Lizard on Guernsey, but it is not known whether either species persists.

So what can we do to remedy the state of our reptiles? Historically and currently, it is our depletion of their natural habitats that poses the greatest threat to them. The future will bring more of the same, plus unknown influences (possibly even positive influences) of climate change. Habitat loss will almost certainly remain the biggest threat, and the best chance is to try and find some novel and clever ways of allowing reptiles to survive and thrive despite our competitive advantages. In terms of managing land sympathetically, most of this is completely out of the hands of individuals, except by influencing land managers. The policy-makers and conservation practitioners among us can do something directly, however, to influence land management. Simple prescriptions are the most effective. Leaving strips and corners uncultivated, uncut, unmanaged; leaving patches connected to other patches. Structural diversity of the vegetation is the key for reptiles. We should endeavour to integrate the needs of reptiles into everyday land management, whilst acknowledging the potential conflicts of interest that species-specific prescriptions inevitably cause. Whether this is on protected sites, farmland, urban fringes or even those increasingly important brownfield fragments of 'wasteland' scheduled for destruction – let us re-evaluate the real importance they can hold for reptiles.

As for loss of sites to development, there is no easy solution. An ever-increasing land-take for new developments needs an ever-increasing area of specially created reptile habitat to receive the evictees. In most counties where translocations occur, there simply aren't handfuls of sites waiting to receive translocated reptiles. If the habitat is right for reptiles, it is generally already occupied by reptiles. There are plenty of unoccupied sites in other counties that would be ideal for reptiles (for example, many agricultural fringes and roadsides in Buckinghamshire), but this would require a major change to current policy. To use good unoccupied areas of habitat as receptor sites for reptiles from other parts of the country is a can of worms that many people would rather not open. The argument is whether we should aim to preserve genetic purity and geographical integrity, or whether we could accept that mixing genes is actually good on the whole, and that the status quo is based on an arbitrary anthropocentric concept anyway. The paradigm in the UK until now has been to keep translocations as local as possible, and only to move further away as a last resort. But is this to benefit the reptiles or meet our arbitrary notion of what is right? Some pragmatic decisions might need to be made soon, and ultimately they may be the saviour of our reptiles.

Conclusions

In summary, the recent past has been bad for reptiles in the British Isles overall; the present sees a mixture of positive and negative influences, and the future depends very much on the direction that human policies take. The rarest species – the Sand Lizard and Smooth Snake – became drastically rarer in the twentieth century, but

Table 19.1 *Distribution of reptiles in the British Isles (introduced species in parentheses)*

Common Wall Lizard	(England, Wales), Jersey
Western Green Lizard	(England), Jersey
Sand Lizard	England, Wales, (Scotland)
Common Lizard	England, Scotland, Wales, Ireland
Slow-worm	England, Scotland, Wales, (Ireland), Channel Islands
Grass Snake	England, Wales, Jersey
Smooth Snake	England
Adder	England, Scotland, Wales
Leatherback Turtle	British and Irish waters

have hopefully now turned a corner. Outright habitat loss has more or less stopped, but they are still heavily dependent on sympathetic management policies on a tiny fraction of the British land mass. Ironically, they might even benefit from global warming, if increasing summer temperatures allow them to occupy more habitat types. Meanwhile, the widespread species have suffered a wholesale decline throughout the latter half of the twentieth century, partly through land-take for development, but most dramatically through agricultural land-use changes. Despite the efforts of an industry dedicated to rescuing them from development, it is debatable whether this mitigation is working, or whether the net effect is still 'death by a thousand cuts'. Ultimately, the extent of agricultural land is much greater than that which is developed, and the stewardship of agricultural land provides a much greater canvas upon which to achieve any conservation goals. Most worrying is the extent of reptile habitat that is under conservation tenure, but which does not include reptiles in its management regime. The Adder is quietly disappearing from sites all over Britain, largely through unsympathetic management of habitat. As a species that is more sensitive to habitat degradation than other reptiles, it is unfortunate that it receives so little attention. Simple measures such as incorporating Adders into management plans would go a long way to preserving them. Whereas the other reptiles respond well to prescriptive management and easily colonise new sites, Adders are very sensitive to change, and one wrong move can wipe them out locally. Stories abound of how many Adder populations have been lost in recent years due to conservation action: grazing projects that have destroyed habitat structure, scrub removal that has destroyed communal hibernation sites, and burning that has wiped out entire populations. Our reptiles are up against many competing land-use interests, often including conflicting wildlife interests; but if nature can sustain equilibrium between such interests, then so should our conservation policies. If reptiles are to thrive into the future, their interests must be given a fair hearing when formulating conservation policy. What's more, with scarce resources and competing land-use interests, conservation policy must be both brave and ingenious.

Acknowledgements

Professor Colin Galbraith and Sir Christopher Lever for reviewing earlier drafts.

References

Arnold, H.R. (1973). *A Preliminary Atlas of Amphibians and Reptiles in Britain and Ireland*, Huntingdon, BRC Monks Wood.

Arnold, H.R. (1995). *Atlas of Amphibians and Reptiles in Britain*, London, ITE Research Publication 10, HMSO.

Baker, J., Suckling, J. and Carey, R. (2004). *Status of the Adder* Vipera berus *and Slow-worm* Anguis fragilis *in England,* Peterborough, English Nature Research Report 546, English Nature.

Braithwaite, A.C., Buckley, J.B., Corbett, K.F. *et al.* (1989). The distribution of the smooth snake (*Coronella austriaca Laurenti*). *Herpetological Journal*, **1**, 370–376.

Breeds, J.M. (1973). *A Study of the Smooth Snake* (Coronella austriaca) *in the Purbeck Area*, Furzebrook, Nature Conservancy Council.

Cooke, A.S. and Arnold, H.R. (1982). National changes in status of the commoner British amphibians and reptiles before 1974. *British Journal of Herpetology*, **6**, 206–207.

Cooke, A.S. and Scorgie, H.R.A. (1983). *The Status of the Commoner Amphibians and Reptiles in Britain,* Peterborough, Nature Conservancy Council Report 3, Nature Conservancy Council.

Corbett, K.F. (1988). Distribution and status of the sand lizard, *Lacerta agilis agilis*, in Britain. *Mertensiella*, **1**, 92–99.

Gleed-Owen, C.P. (1998). Quaternary herpetofaunas of the British Isles: taxonomic descriptions, palaeoenvironmental reconstructions, and biostratigraphic implications, PhD thesis, Coventry, Coventry University.

Gleed-Owen, C.P. (2004). *Initial Surveillance Baseline Datasets for the Sand Lizard* Lacerta agilis, *Natterjack Toad* Bufo calamita *and Smooth Snake* Coronella austriaca *in England*, Bournemouth, The Herpetological Conservation Trust.

Gleed-Owen, C., Buckley, J., Coneybeer, J. *et al.* (2005). *Costed Plans and Options for Herpetofauna Surveillance and Monitoring,* The Herpetological Conservation Trust. English Nature Research Report No. 663, Peterborough, English Nature.

Goddard, P. (1984). Morphology, growth, food habits and population characteristics of the Smooth snake *Coronella austriaca* in Southern Britain. *Journal of the Zoological Society of London*, **204**, 241–257.

Hilton-Brown, D. and Oldham, R.S. (1991). *The Status of the Widespread Amphibians and Reptiles in Britain, 1990, and Changes During the 1980s*, Nature Conservancy Council Report 131, Peterborough, Nature Conservancy Council.

Leighton, G. (1903). *The Life History of the British Lizards and Their Local Distribution in the British Isles*, London, Blackwood.

Münch, D. (2001). Do allochthone Common Wall Lizards jeopardize autochtone Sand and Viviparous Lizards? *Dortmunder Beiträge zur Landesskunde*, **35**, 187–190.

Phelps, T.E. (2004). Beyond hypothesis – a long-term study of British snakes. *British Wildlife*, **15**(5), 319–327.

Prestt, I., Cooke, A.S. and Corbett, K.F. (1974). British amphibians and reptiles. In Hawkesworth, D.L., ed., *The Changing Flora and Fauna of Britain*, London, Academic Press, pp. 229–254.

Reading, C.J., Buckland, S.T., McGowan, G.M. *et al.* (1996). The distribution and status of the adder (*Vipera berus* L.) in Scotland determined from questionnaire surveys. *Journal of Biogeography*, **23**(5), 657–667.

Sheldon, S. and Bradley, C. (1989). Identification of individual adders (*Vipera berus*) by their head markings. *Herpetological Journal*, **1**, 392–396.

Spellerberg, I.F. and Phelps, T.E. (1977). Biology, general ecology and behaviour of the snake, *Coronella austriaca*. *Biological Journal of the Linnéan Society*, **9**, 133–164.

Swan, M.J.S. and Oldham, R.S. (1993). *Herptile Sites Volume 2: National Common Reptile Survey Final Report*, English Nature Research Report 38, Peterborough, English Nature.

Taylor, R.H.R. (1948). The distribution of reptiles and amphibia in the British Isles, with notes on species recently introduced. *British Journal of Herpetology*, **1**, 1–38.

Taylor, R.H.R. (1963). The distribution of amphibians and reptiles in England, Wales, Scotland and Ireland and the Channel Islands: a revised survey. *British Journal of Herpetology*, **3**(5), 95–115.

20

Amphibians

Tim Halliday

Summary

Great Britain and Ireland have a very small amphibian fauna compared with
many parts of the world, especially the tropics. In this chapter, I consider the
current status of our seven native species in the context of the global amphibian
decline phenomenon, asking to what extent our amphibian fauna is vulnerable to
the same threatening processes as amphibians elsewhere in the world. Detailed
studies of the impact of various threats on Britain's amphibians are few in
number and so the level of threat must be inferred from studies carried out
elsewhere, particularly in the USA. All of our seven native species also occur
widely in western Europe and I draw extensively on the results of research from
other European countries to infer the level of risk.

Biodiversity on planet Earth is undergoing a mass extinction event, the sixth during the
history of life on Earth. Amphibians, which survived the previous four mass extinction
events better than many animal groups (they did not exist during the first), are among the
most severely affected by this current event (Wake and Vredenburg 2008). The global
amphibian decline phenomenon, first noted in 1989, has since been the subject of intensive research (Alford and Richards 1999; Halliday 2007). A recent global assessment of
the world's known amphibian species (currently numbering 6453 and increasing rapidly,
due to the discovery of new species) concluded that around a third of amphibian species
are threatened with extinction and that an estimated 168 amphibian species have become
extinct in the last four decades (Stuart *et al.* 2004). It has been estimated that current
extinction rates among amphibians are 211 times greater than the background extinction
rates; if all the currently threatened amphibian species become extinct, the extinction
rate will be 25 000 to 45 000 times greater than the background rate.

Silent Summer: The State of Wildlife in Britain and Ireland, ed. Norman Maclean. Published by Cambridge
University Press. © Cambridge University Press 2010.

A number of features of amphibians, such as their thin, moist skin and their shell-less eggs, are often implicated in making them particularly vulnerable to a variety of environmental insults, such as pollution and climate change, and amphibians are often regarded as 'canaries in the coalmine', their decline portending global environmental collapse (Halliday 2000). A recent study of global patterns of amphibian and bird distributions supports the hypothesis that amphibians will be more susceptible than birds to slight environmental changes, such as those caused by climate change. Amphibians are declining more rapidly than other vertebrate groups (Stuart *et al.* 2004), but it remains to be seen whether they are declining more rapidly than other taxa elsewhere in the animal kingdom. Amphibian declines are a complex process, not attributable to any single cause, and are indicative of a major decline in biodiversity in freshwater habitats worldwide (Halliday 2001).

Britain's amphibian species

Great Britain is home to seven indigenous amphibian species, Ireland only two, all of which are also widely distributed across western Europe. All seven species are protected, to different degrees, in Great Britain; two species are protected in Europe (Table 20.1). Under the IUCN Red List criteria, all seven species are listed as of least concern.

The status of the Pool Frog (*Pelophylax lessonae*) in Britain has changed recently. Previously regarded as an introduced species, in one location the Pool Frog is now considered to be a native, surviving in a single relic population in Norfolk. Other populations of Pool Frogs in Britain are the result of introductions from mainland Europe. These and other introduced amphibian species are discussed below.

All of Britain's amphibians breed in ponds; Common Toads (*Bufo bufo*) and Great Crested Newts (*Triturus cristatus*) generally use larger, permanent ponds but, for the other species, smaller, ephemeral ponds that dry out, if only occasionally, are the optimal breeding habitat. All seven species are long-lived and breed several times during their lives and their reproductive success typically varies considerably from year to year. Variation between years in the reproductive success of amphibian populations presents a serious challenge to conservationists. The natural fluctuations that occur in the population sizes of amphibians means that only long-term studies, over many years, can detect real population declines, unless they are very rapid. A major cause of inter year variation in the breeding success of Common Frogs (*Rana temporaria*) in Britain and Ireland is pond-drying. In dry years, when ponds dry out early, mortality of frogspawn or tadpoles can be total.

The landscape of Britain and Ireland is substantially dominated by agriculture, and the long-term future of our native amphibians may largely depend on their ability to thrive in agricultural habitats. In the past, the 'traditional' pattern of small fields, separated by wide hedgerows, and each field containing a pond to provide water for livestock, provided an ideal habitat for many amphibians, providing both breeding sites and abundant terrestrial habitat. Since World War II, this pattern of land use has been replaced over much of Britain by a large-field system, with hedgerows destroyed and

Table 20.1 *Amphibian species native to Great Britain and Ireland*

Species[a]	Common name	European status	UK status
Triturus cristatus	Great Crested Newt	+	2
Lissotriton (Triturus) helveticus	Palmate Newt		1
Lissotriton (Triturus) vulgaris[b]	Smooth Newt		1
Bufo bufo	Common Toad		1
Epidalea (Bufo) calamita	Natterjack Toad	+	2
Rana temporaria[b]	Common Frog		1
Pelophylax (Rana) lessonae	Pool Frog		2

Notes:

[a] Nomenclature reflects new generic names, together with former names (in brackets).

[b] Native to Ireland as well as Great Britain.

+ Listed in Appendix II of the Bern Convention.

1 Protected in the UK only against commercial trade.

2 Protected in the UK against killing, collection and habitat disturbance.

ponds replaced by stand pipes. A number of surveys have revealed widespread declines among Britain's amphibians in the 1960s and 1970s and the loss of farmland ponds has been identified as a major cause of these declines. It is important to note, however, that our amphibians spend only a small proportion of their lives in water; the loss of suitable terrestrial habitat is likely to be just as important as the loss of breeding sites. More recently, a marked decline in numbers of the Common Toad in central, southern and eastern England has been reported. Factors other than habitat loss are believed to be responsible for this (see below).

The most widely distributed amphibian in Britain and Ireland is the Common Frog, which occurs in all parts of the British Isles (Beebee and Griffiths 2000). The Common Toad is absent from Ireland and, in the rest of Britain, is common in lowland areas, but is largely absent from mountainous areas. The Natterjack Toad (*Epidalea calamita*) is confined to heath and sand-dune habitats; its distribution is much less extensive than in the past and it is now confined to a few coastal sites in England and south-west Ireland (Beebee 1983). Of the three British newts, the Smooth Newt (*Lissotriton [Triturus] vulgaris*) has the widest distribution, being common in England and Ireland, especially in lowland areas. It prefers ponds with neutral pH that are rich in vegetation, and it thrives in garden ponds. The similarly sized Palmate Newt (*Lissotriton [Triturus] helveticus*) is most common in ponds with low pH, is more common in western parts of Britain and is absent from Ireland. The known distribution of the Great Crested Newt in Scotland, Wales and south-west England suggests that it is restricted to just a few areas and it is entirely absent from Ireland. It is not at all unusual to find three or four amphibian species breeding in the same pond.

Are Britain's amphibians at high risk of extinction?

In all past major extinction events there have been winners as well as losers. A feature of the current amphibian decline phenomenon is that, while many species are heading for extinction, others continue to thrive. Indeed a few species, notably the Cane Toad (*Bufo marinus*) in Australia, and the North American Bullfrog (*Rana catesbeiana*), in many parts of the world, are serious, invasive pests.

While there is widespread agreement that habitat destruction, largely driven by encroaching agriculture and urbanisation, is the primary cause of amphibian declines and extinctions worldwide, much research has focused on so-called 'enigmatic' declines, that is those for which habitat destruction can be discounted as a cause (Gardner *et al.* 2007). The most disturbing aspect of the global amphibian decline phenomenon is that many species have declined, some to extinction, in areas set aside to protect biodiversity, such as nature reserves and national parks. In such places, for example in Australia and Central America, it is clear that some species have declined, while others have not. As more data are gathered on the occurrence of amphibian declines, it is becoming possible to compare species that have declined in protected habitats with those that have not, and to identify specific 'risk factors'. These include: living at high altitude, breeding in streams, small clutch size, a high degree of habitat specificity and small geographic range.

None of Britain's amphibian species show any of these ecological or life-history risk factors. All mostly live at low altitude, all breed in ponds, all produce large clutches of eggs, most live in a wide range of habitats and all have large geographic ranges covering much of western Europe. It thus appears unlikely that Britain's amphibians are threatened by whatever causes 'enigmatic' declines and that the most significant threat to them is habitat loss.

A recent taxonomic analysis of amphibian declines reveals that species showing enigmatic declines are concentrated in a particular clade of frogs, the super-family Hyloidea. The Hyloidea includes the family Bufonidae, however, suggesting that Common Toads and Natterjacks may be more susceptible to decline than other British species, even in areas where their habitat is protected.

Habitat loss, degradation and fragmentation

Britain's amphibians are generally regarded as pond-dwelling animals, but they are better thought of as terrestrial animals that breed in ponds, as the time they spend in water represents only a small proportion of their lives. In particular, newly metamorphosed newts, frogs and toads spend two or three years on land before breeding for the first time and it is during this period that mortality is very high. Unfortunately, very little is known about the habitat requirements of amphibians when they are terrestrial, either as juveniles or as adults. Limited evidence suggests that they move considerable

Table 20.2. *Loss of ponds (actual or potential amphibian habitats) in the UK over the last 50 years*

Location	% Ponds lost	Annual rate (% per year)
All UK	20% of *c*. 350 000 ponds between 1958 and 1988	0.7
Sussex downland (rural)	18% of 33 ponds lost between 1977 and 1996	0.9
Huntingdonshire (rural)	99% lost over 40 years	2.5
Milton Keynes (urban)	68% of 22 ponds lost between 1975 and 1997	3.1

distances away from ponds, indicating that they may require much more extensive terrestrial habitat than many conservation projects allow for.

Ponds provide not only breeding sites for our amphibians, but also habitat in which their larvae and tadpoles can grow and develop to metamorphosis. Eggs and larvae are subject to heavy predation by fish and the larvae of such insects as dragonflies and diving beetles. Toad tadpoles and Great Crested Newt larvae are thought to gain some protection from predators by being distasteful, and this may be why they fare better in permanent ponds that support such predators. The use of ephemeral ponds by frogs and the smaller newts reduces the risk from predators, but exposes them to risk of catastrophic mortality if a pond dries out before their tadpoles or larvae reach metamorphosis.

A high proportion of ponds in Britain and Ireland are artificial, created by farmers to provide water for livestock. Pond numbers in Great Britain reached a peak around 100 years ago; since then, urban expansion and changes in agricultural practice have caused a steady decline. A number of surveys have quantified the extent to which ponds in Britain have been destroyed since World War II (Table 20.2). These indicate a steady decline of around 1% per year in rural areas, with a higher rate in counties such as Huntingdonshire, where a shift to intensive farming methods has been particularly marked. Where rural habitats have become urbanised, as in Milton Keynes, rates of pond loss have been much higher. While ponds have been destroyed in rural areas, many new ponds have been created in urban areas to adorn gardens. Apart from the Natterjack, all our amphibians thrive in garden ponds, especially frogs and the smaller newts, and gardens now represent an important habitat for Britain's amphibians.

Monitoring of amphibian populations at the national level in Britain has been negligible until recently. Consequently, historical changes in the status of amphibians can only be determined by questionnaires that depend on memory. One such study examined the status of the Common Frog and the Common Toad in the fenland of East Anglia. Severe declines, beginning in the 1940s, caused both species to have become very rare by the 1970s. This was attributed to improved drainage, which meant that fewer ponds and dykes now hold water long enough for tadpoles to reach metamorphosis, and a switch from pasture to arable land use. It is likely that increasing use of pesticides also contributed to this decline.

Britain's rarest amphibian, the Natterjack Toad, is confined to two kinds of habitat, coastal dunes and inland heaths. Between the 1930s and 1970s, it declined much more markedly on heaths than on dunes (Beebee 1983). This decline was due, not to loss of heathland to urbanisation or agriculture, but to vegetational changes due to reduced grazing and increased forestry activity. This has led to encroachment by taller vegetation, creating a more shaded habitat unsuitable for the Natterjack, but very suitable for its competitor, the Common Toad.

Pond-breeding amphibians, like all the species native to Britain, show strong philopatry (highly localised dispersal), returning each year to their natal ponds, so that each breeding site is the focal point of a population that, to varying degrees, is distinct from neighbouring populations. They thus show a metapopulation structure, in which movement of individuals, and of genes, between one local population and another depends on the distance and the nature of the habitat between adjacent ponds. In a metapopulation, sub-populations are subject to extinction, especially if they are small, and the probability of their being re-established depends on immigration from neighbouring populations. Consequently, the viability of amphibian populations across a landscape depends, not only on the existence of breeding ponds, but also on the nature of the terrestrial habitat between them.

A number of recent studies of European amphibians have investigated the genetic consequences of increased isolation of individual populations, either by the loss of neighbouring ponds or by factors that make the habitat between ponds less favourable to amphibians. A study of the Common Toad in Leicestershire examined genetic diversity across 20 semi-isolated breeding populations. The level of inbreeding within a population was significantly related to the presence of other ponds nearby. A comparison of toads living in rural and urban habitats in south-east England revealed lower heterozygosity in urban populations separated by small distances, but by habitat that inhibits toad dispersal, than in more widely separated rural populations. Studies of Common Frogs in Germany and of Moor Frogs (*Rana arvalis*) in the Netherlands found evidence of reduced gene flow between ponds separated by major roads and railways.

Small, isolated breeding populations are vulnerable to extinction by traumatic events, such as pond-filling and pollution, but, even if protected, are subject to more subtle effects that threaten their long-term existence as a result of their reduced genetic diversity. Isolated populations of the Italian Agile Frog (*Rana latastei*) proved to be more susceptible to experimental infection by a frog virus than populations near the centre of the species' range. This is significant in view of the fact that disease is a major threat to amphibian populations (see below). In northern Finland, reduced heterozygosity in Common Frog populations is correlated with small body size at metamorphosis, and thus reduced adult fitness. A comparison of Common Frogs in continuous and fragmented landscapes in Sweden found that breeding populations in fragmented landscapes were smaller, had lower genetic diversity, and showed a reduction in two fitness-related traits, survival and body size.

In much of Europe, and particularly in Britain, the landscape within which amphibian populations occur is agricultural. This raises an important question: does agricultural land provide suitable terrestrial habitat for amphibians, or is it a barrier to dispersal between populations? A study on the Swedish island of Gotland suggests that agricultural land use has a negative impact on three amphibians, the Moor Frog, the Common Toad and the Smooth Newt. A study in the Netherlands investigated the 'permeability' of agricultural landscape to adult and juvenile Common Frogs. Juvenile frogs showed stronger preferences for particular habitat types, such as meadows and hedgerows, and more strongly avoided others, such as arable land. Thus, intensively farmed landscapes appear to be a greater barrier for juvenile amphibians than they are for adults.

There is much variation in agricultural methods and some are more hostile to amphibians than others. A comparison across different regions in Sweden found that agricultural landscapes reduced occurrence, population density and genetic diversity among Common Frogs in the south, but had no effect in the central region. In a more northerly region, agriculture had a positive effect on frog populations. In southern Sweden there is a higher density of roads and more intensive land use provides less suitable micro-habitat for frogs.

Chemical contamination

An enormous number and diversity of chemical compounds of human origin are released into the natural environment, deliberately or inadvertently, and many of these find their way into amphibian habitats, especially into the ponds where they breed. The toxic effects on amphibians of only a tiny fraction of such compounds have been studied, primarily in the USA and continental Europe. There is a perception that chemical contamination is not an important factor in amphibian declines in the UK and only a few detailed studies of the effect of chemicals on amphibians have been conducted in the UK. Given the accumulating wealth of evidence from elsewhere about the effects that chemical contaminants have had on amphibian populations in many parts of the world, it is surely time that this perception was reassessed.

The aquatic larvae of amphibians are highly vulnerable to chemical contaminants dissolved in water. The tadpoles of *Xenopus* have long been used in laboratory toxicology tests of potentially harmful dissolved compounds. Such tests are crude and simplistic, involving as they do single compounds dissolved in pure water, and using mortality rate as the measure of toxicity. Recent work, in the field of ecotoxicology, examines the effects of chemical compounds in natural pond water, in ecologically realistic concentrations, often in mixtures of two or more compounds, and in the presence of such natural features as plants, food and predators, and generally uses sublethal effects, such as reduced growth or delayed metamorphosis as measures of toxicity. A tadpole does not have to die in order to suffer a significant loss of fitness. Other sub-lethal effects revealed by ecotoxicological studies include behavioural abnormalities, physical deformities appearing at metamorphosis (e.g. missing limbs, extra limbs etc.), disruption of the adult reproductive system, including hermaphroditism and sex reversal, and impairment of the immune system.

An early example of an ecotoxicological study, carried out in the UK, examined the effects of low doses of pesticides, including DDT, on the spawn and tadpoles of Common Frogs, Common Toads and Smooth Newts. Among other effects, frog tadpoles became hyperactive and developed physical deformities; toad tadpoles were much less susceptible to DDT. The erratic movements of treated frog tadpoles made them more conspicuous to a common predator, adult Smooth Newts. Thus a sub-lethal effect led to greater mortality through predation.

The chemical stressors that have been most intensively studied in relation to amphibians are those that are applied directly to the land, such as pesticides, herbicides and fertilisers, and those of industrial origin, such as acid rain and heavy metals.

Acidification is a serious threat to amphibians in some parts of the world and certain characteristics of the ponds that many amphibians use for breeding, such as their ephemeral nature, make them especially vulnerable to acid rain. Marked amphibian declines in Scandinavia in the 1960s were attributed to acid rain that originated in industrial Britain. In Britain, acidification is implicated in the decline of Natterjack Toads at heathland sites. Tadpoles of the Common Frog reared at pH levels, combined with aluminium, comparable to those found in parts of Britain showed delayed metamorphosis and reduced size at metamorphosis.

While acidification may have adversely affected amphibian populations in Britain in the past, the fact that the industrial emissions that produce acid rain are now controlled makes it unlikely to be a major factor in current amphibian declines. Moreover, there is evidence from studies of the European Moor Frog that amphibians, through both genetic changes and maternal effects, adapt rapidly to low pH.

Agricultural pesticides have been implicated in amphibian population declines, sometimes on a large spatial scale. For example, a study of declines among several species over a very large area in California concluded that pesticides, drifting downwind from agricultural regions, were responsible for these declines, and that other factors, such as habitat deterioration, elevated UV-B radiation and climate change, were not. At high concentrations, pesticides kill amphibian larvae; lower concentrations have sublethal, but equally devastating effects. For example, there is experimental evidence that low doses of a variety of pesticides affect the immune response of amphibians, reducing their ability to resist parasitic infection. Application of low doses of the widely used insecticide malathion to mesocosms (artificial experimental enclosed systems for studying ecology) containing zooplankton, phytoplankton and periphyton, as well as amphibian larvae did not kill the larvae, but initiated a trophic cascade in which zooplankton died, phytoplankton bloomed and periphyton declined, leading to heavy mortality among the larvae. Only a few such studies have been carried out in Europe.

A study of the effects of six pesticides on Common Frog tadpoles in Sweden found negative effects at high concentrations, but no or very weak effects at concentrations found in natural water bodies.

Polychlorinated biphenyls (PCBs) are toxic compounds, released by a variety of industrial processes, that have become persistent and ubiquitous environmental contaminants. Common Frogs exposed at different life stages to PCBs showed a variety of responses, including mortality, physical deformities and reduced size at metamorphosis, depending on the dose and the time of exposure during development. This was a laboratory study and cannot be extrapolated to the natural situation, but it does suggest that amphibians may be adversely affected by PCBs.

Arguably the most serious chemical threat to the natural environment, and particularly to aquatic habitats, is nitrogen. Such large quantities of nitrogen compounds are being released, in the form of fertilisers, sewage, animal manure etc., that the natural nitrogen cycle has been swamped by a 'nitrogen cascade'. An assessment of the likely impact of nitrogen pollution on amphibians across the USA concluded that, in several watersheds, nitrate concentrations are high enough to cause death and developmental abnormalities in amphibians.

The effect of sodium nitrate on the tadpoles of Common Toads in Britain has been investigated in two laboratory studies. Both reported behavioural changes, reduced size at metamorphosis and increased mortality; these were more marked in the earlier study, which used pure water, than in the later study, which used pond water. Other research reveals that the response of amphibian larvae to nitrates is very dependent on the chemical composition of the water. There is also much variation in the response of amphibians to nitrates between species, and between different life-cycle stages. In general, research on European amphibians suggests that the adverse effects of elevated nitrogen are very slight at current environmental levels; these include Natterjack Toads in Spain, the Common Frog in Sweden and the Smooth Newt in Britain. It is important to recognise, however, that elevated nitrogen has major ecological effects in freshwater habitats, notably eutrophication, and the impact of this on amphibians has not been studied. There is evidence that, globally, nitrification increases the incidence of parasitic and infectious diseases associated with freshwater habitats. The trematode parasite *Ribeiroia ondatrae* infects amphibians, causing major morphological deformities, and aquatic eutrophication in the USA increases both the density of snails, its intermediate host and its per-snail parasite production.

Herbicides are assumed to have little effect on animals because they primarily function to disrupt the photosynthetic pathways of plants. Atrazine is the most widely used herbicide in the world; 30 000 tons of it are sprayed onto farmland in the USA each year and it is widely used in many other countries. It can be detected at quite high levels in streams and rivers that collect run-off from farmland and has been detected at high levels in rain. In a laboratory study, tadpoles of the African Clawed Frog (*Xenopus laevis*) were reared in water containing atrazine at concentrations similar to those found in natural water bodies in the USA. The tadpoles grew, developed and metamorphosed into frogs, at which point they were examined in detail. Many of them were hermaph-rodites, their gonads containing both egg- and sperm-producing tissues. Many of those that were unequivocally male had a poorly developed larynx, the organ with which males produce mating calls. Males that were allowed to develop to adult age showed a 10-fold decrease in testosterone level compared to untreated males. More recent work on *Xenopus* has shown that tadpoles exposed to atrazine at an early developmental stage, when the organs are being formed, exhibited abnormalities in the circulatory system, the kidney, the digestive system and the brain. As with other chemical con-taminants, there is evidence that amphibian species vary considerably in their response to atrazine. While it appears that it has little effect on tadpole growth, there is evidence that it adversely affects the immune system, making amphibians more susceptible to parasites. While atrazine is widely used in the USA and many other parts of the world, its use in the European Union has been severely restricted since 2003.

Atrazine is but one of a large and diverse array of chemicals, released into the envi-ronment by agriculture and industry, that disrupt the endocrine systems of aquatic animals. Endocrine disruptors include hormones from humans and from farm animals, and a wide variety of chemicals that bear no resemblance to natural hormones, but which bind onto hormone receptors in animals and thus mimic the effect of natu-ral hormones. These chemicals are called hormone mimics or endocrine-disrupting chemicals (EDCs). There is accumulating evidence that EDCs are affecting wildlife, particularly fish (see Chapter 9).

Agriculture is a major source of EDCs and an Australian study provides evidence that agrochemicals have an adverse effect on the reproductive biology of amphibians. The Cane Toad is an invasive species in Australia, spreading rapidly across both farm-land and natural habitats. Animals collected on farmland show significant signs of feminisation. In contrast, a study looking for physical abnormalities in Common Frogs in Finland found no evidence for a higher frequency of abnormalities in agricultural habitats.

There is no direct evidence that EDCs are affecting Britain's amphibians. However, given that much of Britain is agricultural, and that there is strong evidence that EDCs are affecting freshwater fish in Britain, there is an urgent need for more research in this area.

Climate change

Globally, climate change is affecting amphibians in a variety of ways. Where fall-ing levels of precipitation cause prolonged drought, breeding sites become increas-ingly ephemeral and may disappear altogether. Climate change causes the geographic ranges of some species to shift; this is most apparent in mountainous areas, such as the Andes, where the range of some amphibians is moving vertically. A predictive study of the likely effects of climate change on European amphibians concludes that some species will expand in range, and that others will contract. Amphibians typically have poor powers of dispersal and this will likely have a profound effect on their long-term response to climate change. A long-term study of two water frogs (*Rana ridibunda* and *R. lessonae*) in Poland found that, between 1963 and 2003, adult body size increased significantly. Because the pathogen that causes the deadly amphibian disease chytridiomycosis, *Batrachochytrium dendrobatidis*, is markedly affected by temperature, it has been suggested that its spread in many parts of the world is linked to climate change, though this hypothesis is disputed. Finally, several amphibian species in northern temperate latitudes are breeding earlier in the year, part of the general phenomenon of earlier springs.

The timing of migrations to their breeding ponds by Britain's amphibians is highly variable from year to year and is strongly influenced by temperature and, to a lesser degree, rainfall (Beebee and Griffiths 2000). A recent study suggests that it may also be influenced by the lunar cycle. There are reports of newts and Natterjack Toads breeding earlier in the year in south-east England, and of earlier breeding by toads in Dorset in the decade 1989 to 1998 than in the preceding decade. Analysis of several sites across Britain reveals a long-term trend for migration and spawning by Common Frogs to occur earlier in the spring, but there is no such trend for the hatching of frogspawn. Taken together, these results suggest that that the reproductive cycles of most, if not all, of Britain's amphibians have been starting earlier since the late 1970s. An eight to nine day shift, over 25 years, towards earlier breeding in Common Frogs and Common Toads has been reported in Poland. There is no particular reason for supposing that earlier breeding will have a significant effect, negative or positive, on the reproductive success of amphibians. In toads, earlier spawning tends to lead to increased duration of the tadpole stage. At a site in mid-Wales, the arrival dates of Smooth and Palmate Newts are changing in response to higher spring temperatures, such that males are increasingly arriving earlier than females. The impact of such subtle changes on fitness is unknown and this is clearly a topic that requires detailed research.

A long-term study of Common Toads in Dorset has revealed more subtle, and more disturbing, effects of climate change on their physiology and reproductive success (Reading 2007). Between 1983 and 2005 there were several abnormally mild winters. Following such winters females were in markedly less good condition than following cold winters; moreover, they subsequently showed reduced survival. In addition, females laid fewer eggs following milder winters. Reduced condition may have other effects; research on mammals suggests that animals in poor condition are more susceptible to pathogens. It appears that milder winters cause toads, and probably other amphibians, to be more active during the winter than they otherwise would be and so to draw on their fat reserves, so that they arrive at breeding sites with reduced amounts of fat. Body condition on arrival at breeding sites not only affects the fecundity of female toads, but also the development of secondary sexual characters of male Great Crested Newts.

Ultraviolet radiation

The thinning of the ozone layer in the Earth's stratosphere has led to increased levels of ultraviolet (UV) radiation reaching the Earth's surface; this is particularly marked in regions where there are 'holes' in the ozone layer. Such radiation, especially UV-B, is potentially harmful to living organisms because is causes DNA to mutate. There is accumulating evidence that this is a factor in the decline of some amphibian species, especially those living at high latitudes and at high altitudes, where incident levels of UV-B are highest. Because water is a very effective filter of UV-B, only those amphibian species that lay their eggs close to the water surface arc particularly susceptible to increased levels. Although there is considerable evidence that ambient levels of UV-B radiation are harmful to the early stages of amphibians, causing them to develop abnormally and sometimes to die, a number of studies have failed to find such an effect and there is considerable debate about the extent to which elevated UV-B has been a factor in the decline of amphibian populations (Alford and Richards 1999). Some biologists have rejected the hypothesis that UV-B causes amphibian mortality and population declines altogether. A recent meta-analysis concluded that such differences of opinion have arisen from there being marked variation in susceptibility to UV-B among amphibian species and, within a species, among different life stages and populations; it concludes that UV-B is a significant threat to amphibians, especially when combined with other environmental stressors (Bancroft *et al.* 2008).

Amphibians possess a number of adaptations that protect them from UV-B. These include the black pigment that is characteristic of many frogs' eggs, which filters out UV-B. The jelly surrounding amphibian eggs filters out UV-B and a study of frogspawn across an altitude gradient suggests that, at higher altitudes, female common frogs invest more in egg jelly. European newts protect their unpigmented eggs from UV-B by wrapping them individually in folded plant leaves. Many species produce an enzyme called photolyase, which repairs DNA damage of the kind caused by UV-B. It is likely that UV-B affects amphibians most potently by acting synergistically with other adverse environmental factors, such as acidification and pathogens. There is evidence, for example, that it reduces the ability of amphibians to make an adequate immune response to pathogens. Climate change, where it has reduced water levels in breeding ponds, acts synergistically with UV-B, by forcing amphibians to lay their eggs in shallow water.

A number of studies have looked at the effects of elevated UV-B on European amphibians. A study in Sweden found no effects on five species, with the exception of the Great Crested Newt, which showed reduced hatching rate and larval survival when their eggs were removed from their protective leaves. Early life stages of the Common Frog were found to be unaffected in Finland, though those of Common Toads and Moor Frogs were. However, another study in Sweden found that Common Frog embryos are not tolerant of elevated UV-B, and that it can be lethal in combination with low pH, an effect that was more pronounced in northern than in southern populations. Further studies in Sweden have revealed that, in Common Frogs, exposure to UV-B during the embryonic and larval stages of development causes metamorphosis both to be delayed and to occur at a smaller body size. Both these effects are likely to reduce fitness during the adult phase of frogs. These studies of Common Frogs reveal an important point about UV-B: in an animal with a complex life cycle, the effects of exposure to UV-B may not be apparent at the stage when the exposure occurs, but may be manifested in loss of fitness at a later stage. Common Frogs may, however, be affected by UV-B in the presence of other stressors; one study has demonstrated a synergistic effect of UV-B and cadmium pollution on frogs' eggs. In Spain, the Natterjack Toad seems to be very resistant to UV-B, but the Common Toad is affected by UV-B at high altitudes.

The meta-analysis by Bancroft *et al.* (2008) concluded that salamanders are more susceptible to elevated UV-B than frogs and toads. Only two studies have looked at European tailed salamanders. The larvae of Alpine Newts (*Mesotriton alpestris*) are extremely sensitive to UV-B under laboratory conditions, where it causes skin damage and high mortality, and this may account for their absence from very shallow ponds at high altitudes. As described above, the eggs of Crested Newts are damaged by UV-B if removed from protective leaves.

It is not possible to say anything about the impact of elevated UV-B on amphibians in the UK, because no studies have been carried out. Levels of ambient UV-B are measured in the UK, because of their link to increased skin cancer risk in humans, and significant increases have been reported. Ozone levels in the stratosphere above the UK decreased from 350 to 320 Dobson units between 1980 and 2006. UV-B levels rise by 8% for every 5% drop in the ozone level, indicating that ambient UV-B levels are now around 16% higher in the UK than they were in 1980. Ozone depletion over the UK is particularly marked in the spring, just when amphibians are breeding, and it must be considered as a potential threat to amphibians breeding in clear, shallow water at higher altitudes in Britain.

Alien species

Animal species that have been introduced, deliberately or accidentally, to parts of the world where they do not normally occur often pose a threat to native species, especially if they become invasive. In many parts of the world, invasive alien species have had a serious negative impact on native amphibians. Such aliens fall into two categories: non-amphibians, particularly fish, that prey on amphibian larvae, and amphibian species which compete with native species.

There are no reports of non-amphibian aliens having a negative impact on any of Britain's amphibians. However, the Mink (*Mustela vison*), which is widespread in Britain, is a serious predator of Common Frogs in parts of Finland; it has no impact on Common Toads which it finds distasteful.

Table 20.3 *Alien amphibian species living in the UK*

Species[a]	Status and threat to native species
Italian Crested Newt *Triturus carnifex*	Restricted to a few sites in England, e.g. Surrey and Birmingham. Hybridises with native *T. cristatus*, but progeny are infertile.
Alpine Newt *Mesotriton (Triturus) alpestris*	Several populations in England, mostly in gardens and parks. May compete with native newts.
Pool Frog *Pelophylax (Rana) lessonae*	Many populations in England. Not thought to pose a threat to native species.
Marsh Frog *Pelophylax (Rana) ridibunda*	Extensive populations in south-east England. Occupies habitat that is little used by native frogs. Not thought to pose a threat to native species.
Edible Frog *Pelophylax (Rana) esculenta*	Many populations in England. Not thought to pose a threat to native species.
Midwife Toad *Alytes obstetricans*	A few small populations in England. Not thought to pose a threat to native species.
European Treefrog *Hyla arborea*	A few small populations in southern England. Not thought to pose a threat to native species.
African Clawed Frog *Xenopus laevis*	A few small populations in England and Wales. Not thought to pose a threat to native species.
American Bullfrog *Lithobates catesbeianus (Rana catesbeiana)*	A viable breeding population in southern England. Poses a severe threat to native amphibians as competitor, predator and carrier of disease.

Note: [a] Nomenclature reflects new generic names, together with former names (in brackets).

Several amphibian species have been introduced to Britain and have established viable populations (see Table 20.3). With the exception of the African Clawed Frog and the North American Bullfrog, all of these are native to mainland Europe. Few of the species listed in Table 20.3 pose a threat to native amphibian species and such adverse effects as they may have are very localised in nature. In contrast, the North American Bullfrog does pose a serious threat to native species, as it does in many parts of the world, including mainland Europe, where it has been introduced at least 25 times and where it is proving very hard to eradicate. The Bullfrog is a threat to native species for three reasons. First, as an adult, it is a voracious predator and feeds on native amphibians. Secondly, it is a very fecund species that produces large numbers of larvae that grow faster and out-compete the tadpoles of native species. Thirdly, it carries, but is not affected by, the fungus *Batrachochytrium dendrobatidis* (*Bd*) that causes the lethal disease chytridiomycosis. This pathogen has recently appeared in southern England, carried by Bullfrogs, and the Bullfrog is now the subject of a vigorous eradication programme in Britain. At the time of writing, intensive research is under way to determine the distribution of *Bd* in the United Kingdom and whether any of our native amphibian species are susceptible to it.

Diseases

Infectious diseases and parasites are natural causes of morbidity and mortality among animals and, recently, they are increasingly perceived as a major threat to biodiversity. There is no more dramatic example of this than the disease chytridiomycosis that is currently affecting amphibians throughout the world, causing the total collapse of populations and the extinction of several species, particularly in Central America and eastern Australia. It is, however, one of many diseases that causes serious mortality in amphibians, several of them occurring in Britain.

Saprolegnia is a ubiquitous water mould that feeds on dead animal material and which also invades animals that are injured or compromised in some way. It causes high mortality among Natterjack Toad eggs following very cold nights and, through its effect on eggs, is largely responsible for the decline of a once very large population of Common Toads at Lysdinam in Wales (Beebee and Griffiths 2000). It also commonly infects newt eggs (personal observation). It is not unusual to find adult amphibians, particularly frogs, suffering from the disease 'red leg', which is caused by the bacterium *Aeromonas hydrophila* (Beebee and Griffiths 2000). In the 1980s, there were many outbreaks of a disease causing severe skin lesions among adult Common Frogs in southern and eastern England; these occurred frequently in garden ponds and caused mass mortality at a local level. This is caused by one or more ranaviruses.

Disease outbreaks among amphibians around the world have led to the suggestion that the immune systems of amphibians are being compromised by one or more environmental factors. These include climate change, chemical pollution and elevated UV-B radiation, and there is accumulating evidence that these factors are involved in increased susceptibility of amphibians to pathogens and parasites. A recent study of the distribution of two pathogens, *Batrachochytrium dendrobatidis* (*Bd*) and ranavirus FV3, in 11 populations of the Green Frog (*Rana clamitans*) in Canada found that the incidence of the ranavirus was strongly associated with anthropogenic influences, such as human disturbance, and proximity to housing and industry. The distribution of *Bd* showed no such association. As described above, there is also evidence that inbreeding, resulting from amphibian populations becoming isolated, increases susceptibility to disease.

Bd causes the disease chytridiomycosis, which is lethal to many, but not all amphibian species. There is debate as to whether *Bd* is a novel pathogen which has somehow rapidly achieved a virtually global distribution, or whether it is an endemic that has changed its host range and/or its pathogenicity. There is evidence that *Bd* is a long-established pathogen in Africa and that it may have been spread around the world by the international trade in African Clawed Frogs. It is now widely distributed in Europe, where American Bullfrogs have acted as a carrier of the disease. It has recently been found in Bullfrogs in a population in southern Britain. As yet, there are no reports that *Bd* has infected any of Britain's native species, and it remains to be seen whether chytridiomycosis will have as devastating an effect in the UK as it has elsewhere. One reason for predicting that it may not is that all Britain's amphibians are pond breeders and, in Queensland, Australia, pond-breeding species are significantly less likely to be infected with *Bd* than stream-breeding species. In central Spain, the Common Toad becomes infected with *Bd*, but has not declined as a result, as has the Midwife Toad (*Alytes obstetricans*). Indeed, Common Toads have increased in number at sites where previously they were found co-habiting with Midwife Toads. This example shows that the impact of chytridiomycosis at the amphibian community level can be complex and unpredictable.

Amphibians and roads

Roads have a major impact on the ecology of many animal species, being a major cause of mortality. Amphibians are especially vulnerable; they are slow-moving and migrate each year, sometimes over large distances, to and from their breeding ponds. As described above, there is much genetic evidence that roads represent a major barrier between adjacent amphibian populations. It has been suggested that the recent decline of Common Toads in southern England may be largely due to mortality on roads.

A detailed study of Common Toad mortality on roads has been made in Spain; this indicates that mortality is highest where streams run under a road. Another study in Spain found that Natterjacks suffer even higher mortality than Common Toads and that, across several species, females suffer higher mortality than males. This study also identified 'hotspots', where the density of amphibians, live and dead, was especially high. A study of Common Toad mortality in Poland found that mortality rate was highest on roads with the lowest traffic volume and that the best predictor of mortality was proximity to toad breeding sites. Annual levels of road-kill mortality among toad populations ranged from 2% to 18%. While it is widely assumed that toads suffer higher mortality than other amphibians on Europe's roads, a meta-analysis of all the data available for Europe concludes that this is true only in suburban areas. Across both urban and rural habitats, the impact on Common Frogs is greater than that on toads, and mortality among newts is underestimated.

Mortality on roads is typically estimated by counting corpses, but this may seriously underestimate true mortality. Looking at the fate of road-kills of a variety of vertebrate species, including frogs and toads, a study in Wales has shown that many corpses are removed by scavengers before they are found by a researcher. Among amphibians, migratory movements towards breeding sites typically peak shortly after nightfall and it is likely that many road-kills will be removed by nocturnal scavengers, such as hedgehogs and badgers before daybreak. It is likely, therefore, that the carnage wrought among amphibians on Britain's roads is even worse than it appears to be.

Roads also present a chemical hazard to amphibians, in the form of de-icing salt. Studies in the USA and Nova Scotia have revealed that some species of frogs and salamanders have reduced populations in, and may be totally absent from, ponds close to roads. The latter study revealed considerable variation among amphibian species in their tolerance to road salt. A study of Wood Frogs (*Rana sylvatica*) in Alaska found that the incidence of skeletal deformities was very high in populations close to roads. The possible impact of road salt on Britain's amphibians has not been investigated.

Mortality on roads is an area of amphibian conservation where the general public can make a simple and effective contribution. Under such slogans as 'Help a toad across the road', there are many places in Britain where groups of volunteers gather at dusk in the spring to carry amphibians across the road, many of them marked by road signs. The conservation charity Froglife currently lists no less that 670 registered toad crossings in the United Kingdom (http://www.froglife.org/ToadsOnRoads/ToR.htm). The data reviewed above suggest that such schemes should pay attention, not only to toads, but also to frogs and newts.

The conservation of amphibians

This chapter has examined a number of threats to Britain's amphibians in the broader context of the global amphibian decline and extinction phenomenon. This is a process that defies a simple explanation; rather, amphibians are threatened by a wide variety of environmental insults that interact in complex and, sometimes unexpected, ways. Of the various specific threats to amphibians, some can only be sensibly addressed by changes in human behaviour on a global scale; these include climate change, elevated UV-B radiation and, to some extent, the release of toxic chemicals into the environment. Amphibians provide some very striking examples of the adverse effects of these threats to biodiversity, but there is little that the amphibian conservationist can do at a local level. There is a great deal that can be done locally, however, about two major threats to Britain's amphibians, habitat loss and mortality on roads.

As described above, groups of volunteers can be very effective in identifying where amphibians cross roads in the spring and organising groups of volunteers to help them to cross safely. Local groups can also help to protect and preserve existing breeding ponds, and to create new ponds. A study of 78 new ponds created on farmland in southern England revealed that they were quickly colonised by amphibians, particularly by toads (Figure 20.1). This study also found that Smooth Newts and Crested Newts did not colonise new ponds that were more than 400 m from existing populations of these

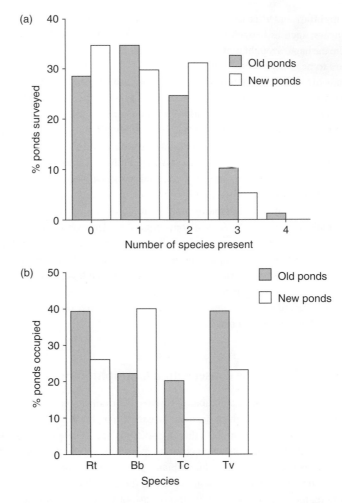

Figure 20.1 (a) The number of amphibian species occupying old and newly constructed farm ponds. (b) The percentage of old and newly constructed ponds occupied by *Rana temporaria* (Rt), *Bufo bufo* (Bb), *Triturus cristatus* (Tc) and *Lissotriton vulgaris* (Tv). (From Baker, J.M.R. and Halliday, T.R. (1999). Amphibian colonisation of new ponds in an agricultural landscape. *Herpetological Journal*, **9**, 55–63.

species. In contrast, Common Frogs and Common Toads colonised ponds up to 950 m from existing populations.

This study emphasises the importance, in habitat creation and restoration, of considering amphibian breeding ponds, not as single entities, but as clusters, separated from one another by distances that allow amphibians to disperse from one pond to another. Equally important, but somewhat neglected, is to insure that amphibian ponds are separated by habitat that is suitable for them. For several of Britain's amphibians, it is desirable that some ponds created for amphibians are ephemeral, temporary ponds being ideal breeding habitat for some species.

The creation of new breeding ponds for amphibians brings the additional benefit of a substantial increase in other components of biodiversity. Comparative studies of aquatic habitats of all sizes have revealed that small water bodies support very high levels of biodiversity and are likely to be home to rare species; they are particularly rich in macroinvertebrates and plants. Thus, creating habitat for amphibians creates habitat for a wide range of species belonging to other taxa.

Given that Britain is a small, overcrowded country, in which truly wild country-side is scarce, amphibian conservationists need to explore the potential for conserving amphibians within both urban and agricultural habitats. As described above, urban habitats present problems for amphibians, especially in the context of movement between breeding sites. A study in Australia, however, has revealed an unexpected benefit of living in the urban environment. Sites in urban habitats around Blue Mountains National Park showed higher amphibian abundance than in protected, non-urban sites within the park. It is suggested that the salts, detergents and other chemicals that pollute urban sites protect amphibians from chytridiomycosis.

The fact that all our native amphibians readily colonise new ponds is a reason for being optimistic about their conservation in the long term. A campaign, launched in 2008, called the Million Ponds Project, seeks to replace many of the ponds lost in Britain's countryside over the last 60 years. Though not directly targeted at amphibians, it is likely to increase considerably the number of viable amphibian populations in Britain. It is important, however, that equal attention be given to protecting and creating terrestrial habitat suitable for amphibians. At present, the distribution of amphibians across Britain is not well-known, but this situation is being addressed by the National Amphibian and Reptile Recording Scheme (NARRS), which was launched in 2007 and the results of which will appear at the NARRS website (http://www.narrs.org.uk).

References

Alford, R.A. and Richards, S.J. (1999). Global amphibian declines: a problem in applied ecology. *Annual. Review of Ecology and Systematics,* **30**, 133–165.

Bancroft, B.A., Baker, N.J. and Blaustein, A.R. (2008). A meta-analysis of the effects of ultraviolet B radiation and its synergistic interactions with pH, contaminants, and disease on amphibian survival. *Conservation Biology,* **22**, 987–996.

Beebee, T.J.C. (1983). *The Natterjack Toad,* Oxford, Oxford University Press.

Beebee, T.J.C. and Griffiths, R.A. (2000). *Amphibians and Reptiles. A Natural History of the British Herpetofauna,* London, Harper Collins.

Gardner, T.A., Barlow, J. and Peres, C.A. (2007). Paradox, presumption and pitfalls in conservation biology: the importance of habitat change for amphibians and reptiles. *Biological Conservation,* **138**, 166–179.

Halliday, T. (2000). Do frogs make good canaries? *Biologist*, **47**, 143–146.

Halliday, T.R. (2001). The wider implications of amphibian population declines. *Oryx*, **35**, 181–182.

Halliday, T. (2007). Amphibian decline. In *Encyclopedia of Life Sciences (ELS)*, Chichester, John Wiley & Sons.

Reading, C.J. (2007). Linking global warming to amphibian declines through its effects on female body condition and survivorship. *Oecologia*, **151**, 125–131.

Stuart, S., Chanson, J.S., Cox, N.A. *et al.* (2004). Status and trends of amphibian declines and extinctions worldwide. *Science*, **306**, 1783–1786.

Wake, D.B. and Vredenburg, V.T. (2008). Are we in the midst of the sixth mass extinction? A view from the world of amphibians. *Proceedings of the National Academy of Sciences, USA*, **105**, 11466–11473.

21

Freshwater fishes: a declining resource

Peter S. Maitland and John F. Craig

Summary

The freshwater fish fauna of Britain and Ireland is an impoverished one compared to much of the rest of Europe, due to the effect of the last Ice Age some 10 000 years ago and to the more recent separation of Britain from the continental land mass. For the same reasons there is a significant difference from north to south in local fish faunas. The major pattern of change in freshwater fish populations in these islands over the last 200 years has been a decline in native, especially northern, species and a parallel increase in non-native and some southern species. Some native species like Burbot and Houting are now extinct, whilst others, for example Vendace, Smelt, Allis and Twaite Shad, and even European Eel, are declining. In contrast, southern species like Ruffe, Dace and Rudd are extending their range into northern catchments, thanks to introductions by coarse anglers, and increasing numbers of non-native species, for example Sunbleak, Topmouth Gudgeon and Black Bullhead, are being successfully introduced. Climate change appears to be enhancing these changes. Of the 57 freshwater fish species known from Britain and Ireland, 14 are alien. Only in the last few decades has there been any attempt to reverse these changes through legislation, habitat restoration, catchment management and conservation management of rare species. It is emphasised that habitat protection and restoration are the principal means through which successful sustainable fish conservation and restoration of biodiversity will be achieved.

Silent Summer: The State of Wildlife in Britain and Ireland, ed. Norman Maclean. Published by Cambridge University Press. © Cambridge University Press 2010.

Introduction

Fishes are a heterogeneous group of animals defined by Nelson (2006) as 'aquatic vertebrates that have gills throughout life and limbs, if any, in the shape of fins'. Worldwide, about 28 900 fish species were listed in FishBase in 2005, but some experts feel that the final total may be considerably higher. Freshwater fishes comprise almost 13 000 species (including only freshwater and strictly peripheral species), or about 15 000, if all species occurring in fresh and brackish waters are included (Leveque *et al.* 2008); note that only 2.5% of the water on Earth is fresh water, the rest is salt water. Nomenclature used in this chapter follows that of Maitland (2004).

Marine habitats are, in general, continuous, whereas freshwater habitats are frequently broken up, or fragmented, into isolated units, making the latter more vulnerable to perturbations. The freshwater fish fauna of Britain and Ireland is an impoverished one compared to much of the rest of Europe, due to the effect of the last Ice Age some 10 000 years ago and to the subsequent and more recent separation of Britain from the continental land mass that occurred as a result of post-glacial rises in sea level. For the same reasons there is a significant difference from north to south in local fish faunas. Islands like Ireland are especially impoverished since, for the most part, only fishes with marine affinities were able to reach them. The major pattern of change in freshwater fish populations in these islands over the last 200 years has been a decline in native, especially northern, species and a parallel increase in non-native and some southern species. Some native species like Burbot, *Lota lota*, and Houting, *Coregonus oxyrhincus*, are now extinct in Britain, whilst others, for example Vendace, *Coregonus albula*, Smelt, *Osmerus eperlanus*, Allis Shad, *Alosa alosa*, and Twaite Shad, *Alosa fallax*, and even European Eel, *Anguilla anguilla*, are declining. In contrast, southern species like Ruffe, *Gymnocephalus cernuus*, Dace, *Leuciscus leuciscus*, and Rudd, *Scardinius erythrophthalmus*, are extending their range into northern catchments, thanks to introductions by freshwater anglers, and increasing numbers of non-native species, for example Sunbleak, *Leucaspius delineatus*, Topmouth Gudgeon, *Pseudorasbora parva,* and Black Bullhead, *Ameiurus melas*, are being successfully introduced, some of them through the pet trade. Climate change, through, for example, an increase in mean atmospheric temperature and alterations in the amount of precipitation, appears to be enhancing these changes. Of the 57 freshwater fish species known from Britain and Ireland, 14 are alien. Only in the last few decades has there been any attempt to reverse these changes through legislation, habitat restoration, catchment management and conservation of rare species.

For many years, fishes were greatly neglected in terms of conservation, and most attention was given to animals and plants of more appeal to the public, for example birds, mammals and flowering plants. Starting in the 1970s, however, it was gradually realised that, all over the world, freshwater fishes were facing severe threats and many species were declining or becoming extinct. Gradually, more and more countries started to assess the status of the members of their fish fauna and appropriate legislation and Red Data Books started to appear. Unfortunately, much of the action taken so far is too little too late, for Red Data Books and the IUCN Red List of Threatened Species (http://www.iucn.org) are only the beginning and not the end of the conservation process. Ireland is fortunate in having had a Red Data Book for fishes for many years (Whilde 1993), whereas Britain, in spite of criticism (Maitland and Lyle 1991), has so far failed to produce one. The development of global assessments of the conservation status of species throughout their known range (rather than restricted to regional or political boundaries) has been an important step forwards in developing a better understanding of the relative importance of threats to species (Hoffman *et al.* 2008). For example, a species that is severely threatened in one country at the edge of its range may be common elsewhere. Although attempts to protect all populations of a species should be made, it may be important to set priorities for conservation action (and commitment of limited financial support) based on those species that face the greatest threats globally (32 of the 43 native species of Britain and Ireland have been globally assessed).

In most countries, freshwater fishes are a significant part of the biodiversity, and many of them are also the subject of important fisheries of a wide variety of types (see FAO publications and FishStat for further information). Altogether, there are over 300 freshwater fish species found in Europe, as defined by Maitland (2004). Kottelat and Freyhof (2007), however, believe there are many more than this (i.e. 546 native species in European fresh waters), including several which are diadromous and a few which are mainly brackish, but do come into fresh water for significant periods. A number of international agreements have come into effect over the last 30 years and these are aimed at protecting Europe's most threatened species. Without such agreements it is unlikely that many countries would have taken action to protect their native fish fauna. Most countries face the same problems as the United Kingdom, notable among these being pollution, alien species and climate change; some countries are in advance of the United Kingdom in terms of conservation and management, others are well behind.

Ichthyofauna of Britain and Ireland

There are 43 species of freshwater fishes native to Britain and Ireland (Maitland and Linsell 2006). The dominant fishes were originally the salmonids, and Scotland and Ireland are still notable strongholds in Europe for populations of Atlantic Salmon, *Salmo salar*, Brown Trout, *Salmo trutta* (both of considerable economic importance) and Arctic Charr, *Salvelinus alpinus*. For over 100 years the taxonomic status of salmonids in Britain and Ireland, especially of Charr (*Salvelinus*), has been controversial. Some early taxonomists named a multiplicity of species. Some early authors agreed that there were 16 species of Charr in Britain and Ireland. These were reduced to one polymorphic species (*S. alpinus*) by most later authors. Maurice Kottelat, in 1997, however, surprisingly resurrected all but two of the former species and this was accepted by Wheeler *et al.* (2004). Kottelat and Freyhof (2007) have confirmed this and added

Arctic Charr in Irish loughs

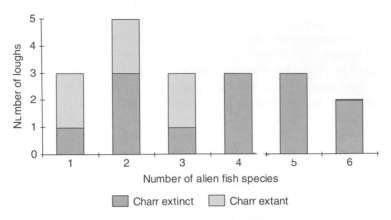

Number of alien fish species

■ Charr extinct   □ Charr extant

Figure 21.1 Arctic Charr and alien fish species in Irish loughs (data from Igoe and Hammar, 2004).

Figure 21.2 Arctic Charr: populations of this species have disappeared in England, Wales, Ireland and Scotland (see colour plate).

several other British charr species, some of them as yet un-named. This surprising reversal of opinion is not accepted by the present authors.

With the decline of many other species elsewhere in Europe, populations of, for example, River Lamprey, *Lampetra fluviatilis*, Brook Lamprey, *Lampetra planeri*, and

Sea Lamprey, *Petromyzon marinus*, are also important as stocks of conservation concern. These and several other species are now given some protection by the EU Habitat and Species Directive.

During the last Ice Age, which ended some 10 000 years ago, most of Britain was covered by ice and therefore its fish fauna would have been largely removed. Therefore, the present freshwater fish fauna is almost entirely based on colonisation events that occurred as the ice receded. Some salmonids, notably Arctic Charr, used any running water available and migrated to and from ice lakes. Gradually, as the ice cap continued to retreat, just as it is doing today in northern latitudes, more and more rivers and lakes became available for colonisation by those fishes which had the capacity for life in both fresh and salt water. Purely freshwater fishes found only in the unglaciated parts of south-east England and originally connected to the Rhine, however, were unable to disperse along the coasts and so had difficulty moving north. Nevertheless, 42 out of the 57 species found in Britain and Ireland are now found in Scotland. This number is very gradually increasing, however, through human activity as more species are introduced from the south and abroad.

Thus, the only fishes which were able to colonise truly fresh waters in the north and west after the last ice receded were those which were also tolerant of marine conditions, allowing them to make coastal dispersals between river networks. At most there were then probably only approximately 12 species common in fresh water, most notable among which were River, Brook and Sea Lampreys, Atlantic Salmon, Brown Trout, Arctic Charr, Powan, *Coregonus lavaretus*, Vendace, Common Eel, Three-spined Stickleback, *Gasterosteus aculeatus,* Nine-spined Stickleback, *Pungitius pungitius*, and Flounder, *Platichthys flesus*. In the larger estuaries and coastal waters, making regular visits to fresh water for spawning or feeding, were another nine species: Sturgeon, *Acipenser sturio*, Allis and Twaite Shad, Smelt, Thick-lipped Grey Mullet, *Chelon labrosus*, Thin-lipped Grey Mullet, *Liza ramada*, Golden Grey Mullet, *Liza aurata*, Sea Bass, *Dicentrarchus labrax* and Common Goby, *Pomatoschistus microps*. Some or most of these 21 species probably dominated the ichthyofauna of various parts of Britain and Ireland for many thousands of years. By the end of the eighteenth century, various native species had moved from the unglaciated corner of south-east England to the north and west and were well established in many parts of mainland Britain. Notable among these were Pike, *Esox lucius*, Minnow, *Phoxinus phoxinus*, Roach, *Rutilus rutilus*, Stone Loach, *Barbatula barbatula*, and Perch, *Perca fluviatilis*. It seems probable that all of these were often dispersed by natural means (perhaps connections across watersheds, egg transfer by birds and transfer in waterspouts), but it is certain that many have also been introduced by humans to different parts of the country.

Thus the present freshwater fish fauna of Britain and Ireland is a mixture of natural immigrants from the sea and from fresh waters in the south-east, along with many more recent exotic fishes which have been brought in by humans from continental Europe, Asia and North America. The situation is by no means a stable one and other arrivals can be expected in future years. Though these apparently add to the diversity of our fish communities, they may bring with them threats in the form of diseases, competition and predation, which in turn may eliminate our more sensitive, and commercially valuable, indigenous fishes, thus reducing natural biodiversity.

Pressures and problems

Humans have been interacting with fish populations for many thousands of years, and it is often difficult to separate the effects of human impact from changes which have taken place due to natural processes where there has been no human intervention (e.g. ecological succession). Over the last 200 years, particularly the last few decades, various new and intense pressures have been applied to fresh waters and very many species have declined in range and in numbers (Harrison and Stiassny 1999). Many of the pressures are interlinked, the final combination often resulting in a complex and sometimes unpredictable situation. An example might be a river system where the blocking effect of physical and chemical obstructions to fish migrations varies greatly according to river flow, itself affected by weather and abstraction.

Worldwide, human impact has destroyed fish habitat on a wide scale and many populations of rare species have disappeared over the last two centuries. In addition, numerous distinct stocks of common species and a number of important fish communities have become extinct. For example, in the Columbia River, USA, >200 stocks of salmonids have become extinct, mainly as the result of building large dams.

The pollution of fresh waters is a significant factor in causing major declines in the populations of many fish species. Most pollution comes from domestic, agricultural or industrial wastes and can be either totally toxic, thereby killing all the fish species present or selective, destroying a few sensitive species or so altering the environment that some species are favoured and others are not (for example, in some waters which have become eutrophic, cyprinid species now do better than salmonids). Some pollutants can have an indirect effect, e.g. cause oxygen depletion (hypoxia) of the water, leading to fish mortality. Some can have sub-lethal effects, e.g. endocrine-disrupting chemicals affecting the reproductive physiology of fishes. Considerable research has been carried out on the subject of pollution and criteria for environmentally acceptable water quality for fishes are now available. Many pollutants are present at sublethal levels and can raise the susceptibility thresholds of fishes to other threats, such as heated effluents. Eutrophication is sometimes thought of as a form of pollution (and is often a product of pollution from fertilisers and other chemicals), whilst the recent acidification from atmospheric pollution (acid rain) of waters in various parts of Britain, Scandinavia and elsewhere (e.g. Canada) has shown the global nature of human impacts, with the effects being felt often very remotely from the source of the pollution. Thus, rivers and lakes far away from urbanisation are not necessarily safe.

Fish farming has also had a detrimental effect on fish stocks, especially Atlantic Salmon and Sea Trout (anadromous Brown Trout) in catchments associated with fish

Atlantic Salmon catches by rod and line

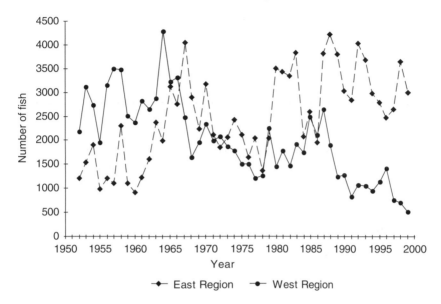

Figure 21.3 Rod catches of Atlantic Salmon in north-east Scotland, where there are no fish cages, and in north-west Scotland, where there are many fish cages.

cages. The main threats are from extensive populations of fish lice, e.g. *Lepeophtheirus salmonis*, which build up around cages, pollution below the cages and the large numbers of escapes of domesticated farmed fishes, which then compete and interbreed with wild stocks.

The impact of land use on many species of fishes can be considerable. Land drainage schemes can totally alter the hydrology of adjacent river systems and lead to problems of siltation. The type of crop grown on the land can also have a major effect; for instance, the recent development of extensive monoculture forests of spruce or other conifers has led to concern about excessive water loss from catchments through evapotranspiration together with increased acidification of run-off to the streams. A problem in many low-land areas is wetland drainage or reclamation, involving the filling in of ponds which were formerly important sites for fishes. Land disturbance, especially in upland peat areas, can cause increased levels of turbidity and loss of carbon normally held in the peat as dissolved organic carbon in the water. These perturbations can persist for a considerable time after the initial disturbance, clogging salmonid spawning grounds and upsetting the global carbon balance (which is tied to global climate change).

River and lake engineering has been responsible for the elimination of fish species in fresh waters all over the world. Migratory species are particularly threatened by dams (McAllister *et al.* 2001) and other obstructions, such as those controlling flood-ing laterally into floodplains, and, if they are unable to reach their spawning grounds, may become extinct in a few years. Stretches of severe pollution in rivers can act in the same way. Obstacles which can be surmounted by active leaping salmonids have been regarded as satisfactory, but they can be complete barriers to less agile species and have been a major factor in the decline of Sturgeon, Allis Shad, Twaite Shad, Houting and Smelt across the whole of their European distribution. Engineering works can also completely destroy the habitat for some species by dredging or siltation, or by creating intolerable fluctuations in water level. The technology of fish-pass design and other ways of ameliorating the impact of such works, such as reducing the use of culverts, has improved in recent years and most problems can now be solved if the will or appro-priate legislation is there.

The impact of fisheries (both sport and commercial) on the stocks which they exploit can range from the virtual extinction of populations to, ideally, a stable relationship of recruitment and cropping. The essence of success in management is to have a well-regulated fishery where statistics on the catch are consistently monitored and used as a basis for future management of the stock. Where there is any exploitation of a threatened species, it is essential that monitoring and control of this type is exerted. Only then can both fishes and humans be successful in the long term. Management of a fishery, in particular for salmonids, often includes enhancement by stocking with hatchery bred fishes. In cases where the fishes have been bred for several generations in a hatchery, the genetic diversity of the natural stock can decline through inbreeding and it is a better management practice to breed from local native fishes.

Apart from physical and chemical habitat alterations created by humans, there are also various biological perturbations. Of major importance among these is the intro-duction of new fish species. If these establish themselves they can alter the commu-nity structure radically and lead to the extinction of sensitive native species. In spite of existing legislation there are still potential dangers from disease introduced with ornamental fishes. Most of these fishes are of tropical origin and destined for private indoor aquaria; there is probably very little risk here. With temperate species, however, there are definite disease and parasite risks associated with their introduction, and both fishes and parasites could become established in the wild. Moreover, even if the host fishes were unable to establish a permanent population in the wild, a parasite might well do so by transferring to native species.

There is increasing evidence that human activities are altering the atmosphere to such an extent that global warming may create major climatic changes over the next few decades. The most certain changes seem to be rising sea levels and atmospheric temperatures, especially at high latitudes. These changes are almost certain to affect fishes. Everywhere there is likely to be a shift of southern species to the north and a retreat northwards of northern species. In the open sea, changing temperature and circulation patterns will probably affect pelagic, demersal and migratory species. In fresh waters, as well as the latitudinal changes, there will probably be parallel changes related to altitude, with cold-water species moving into higher cooler waters and their place being taken in the lowlands by warm-water species. Many fish species confined to lakes will be eliminated since they have no migratory options. In rich, eutrophic lakes in summer there will be an increasing tendency towards deoxygenation in deeper water (i.e. anaerobic conditions in the hypolimnion), with 'summer kill'; there will be less freezing in winter and so a lesser tendency to 'winter kill' in these lakes.

Thus fishes face a number of problems, some particular to themselves, some common to other forms of wildlife. In addition, there has been habitat loss on an enormous scale, right across the wide range of aquatic habitats, not only in Britain and Ireland, but across the whole of Europe. This has included infilling or drainage of ponds and other wetlands, canalisation of and damming of rivers, and abstraction and pollution on a wide scale.

Native species of Britain and Ireland in decline

With one exception, there has been relatively little national monitoring of freshwater fishes and so few data are available on current trends. The exception relates to the economic value of Atlantic Salmon and Sea Trout and so, for many decades, catch statistics have been collected centrally for these two species. There has also been other useful and more accurate monitoring of Atlantic Salmon using traps and electronic fish counters. There is very little information for other species, apart from some catch statistics for Brown Trout and other species in a few systems, for example Perch and Pike in Windermere.

The number of discrete, reproductively self-sustaining populations is a crucial aspect of survival for rare fish species. For instance, a population of, say, one million individuals in one lake is much more vulnerable to pollution, disease and other catastrophic events than, say, ten thousand individuals in each of ten lakes. The presence of multiple populations provides a potential source of individuals to recolonise any one of the lakes where the native population has declined (assuming connectivity between lakes or translocation by humans).

Hundreds of fish communities and individual stocks of fishes have been lost from Britain's fresh waters over the last 200 years (Maitland 1977), largely due to the human activities described above. Severe domestic and industrial pollution caused the extirpation of all fishes from the lower reaches of some rivers (e.g. Rivers Clyde and Thames), and migratory species from their middle and upper reaches, because of the pollution barrier to migration. Acidification has eliminated the entire fish populations of many lakes and streams in base poor upland areas (e.g. Galloway) (Maitland *et al.* 1987), exacerbated by blanket afforestation in some places (e.g. the Trossachs). Piscicides used by fishery managers have poisoned populations of native fishes in several lakes, to be replaced mainly by salmonid species, most commonly non-native Rainbow Trout, *Oncorhynchus mykiss*, which have to be restocked regularly, as they do not normally reproduce naturally in the wild (Campbell *et al.* 1994).

Figure 21.4 Vendace: three out of the only four original populations in England and Scotland of this species are extinct (see colour plate).

More localised species have been less fortunate. The Vendace, known in recent times in Scotland only from the Castle and Mill Lochs near Lochmaben, finally became extinct there in about 1975 due to eutrophication and other human pressures. In England, only two populations were known and one of these, in Bassenthwaite Lake, is now believed to be extinct. The Smelt, formerly recorded from at least 16 rivers in southern Scotland, is now found in only three of them (Rivers Cree, Tay and Forth), thanks to overfishing and pollution. In England too it has disappeared from many rivers. Populations of Arctic Charr, a species for which Scotland is a stronghold in Europe, have disappeared from most of their southern sites (Lochs Grannoch, Dungeon, St Marys and Leven) and are continuing to do so further north (e.g. Heldale Water in Orkney).

Other species, where data are more fragmentary, but which appear to have suffered significant decline over the last hundred years, are diadromous species, and include the migratory Common Sturgeon, Allis Shad, Twaite Shad, River Lamprey, Sea Lamprey and European Eel. Of these, the Common Sturgeon in particular has suffered a notable decline; whereas several specimens were taken almost every year off the British coasts by commercial fishermen during the middle of the twentieth century, virtually none are seen now and this species is almost extinct worldwide.

The situation in Ireland is similar to that in Great Britain. Several native species have declined (e.g. Arctic Charr and Smelt), whilst introduced species are widespread

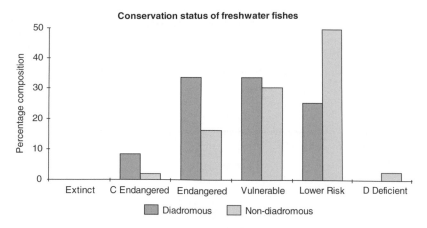

Figure 21.5 Conservation status of diadromous and non-diadromous fishes in Europe. The classes are: extinct, critically endangered, endangered, vulnerable, lower risk and data deficient.

in some catchments. Two threatened Irish fishes are of particular note: the Pollan, *Coregonus autumnalis*, and the Killarney Shad, *Alosa fallax killarnensis*.

The Irish populations of Pollan are the only stock of this species in Europe and are landlocked relics of post-glacial colonisation by anadromous forms (Rosell *et al.* 2004). In Ireland, Pollan are found in habitats and temperature ranges atypical for the species as a whole. They are threatened with extinction by a range of potentially detrimental factors, including eutrophication and competition with introduced non-indigenous species. All but one of the four populations is critically endangered. Rosell *et al.* (2004) summarise current knowledge of this species, the status of the four populations and actions proposed to protect and enhance the remaining stocks.

A landlocked sub-species of the Twaite Shad, the Killarney Shad, which Kottelat and Freyhof (2007) recognise as a distinct species, occurs in Lough Leane in south-western Ireland. The ecology of the Killarney Shad has been reviewed by Doherty *et al.* (2004); its number of gill rakers and adult body size easily separates this sub-species from the normal form. The perceived threats to the Killarney Shad in Ireland are eutrophication and competition from introduced species. It is categorised as endangered by Whilde (1993).

Native species expanding

The distribution of several native species, however, has expanded over the last 200 years, some of it through natural means, the rest through introductions by humans. Though suffering from attempts to eradicate them in some waters, Pike, Perch, Stone

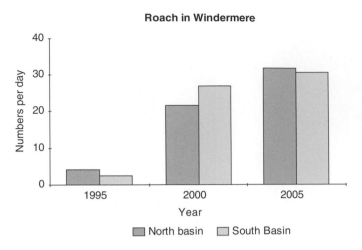

Figure 21.6 Increase of Roach in Windermere (data from Winfield *et al.*, 2008). The numbers are catches per unit effort by gillnetting.

Loach and Minnows have successfully extended their distribution from southern England towards the north of Scotland, thanks to their natural powers of dispersion and some help from humans. These fishes are often considered to be extremely variable or 'plastic' in choice of prey types, prey size and response to prey behaviour (Craig, 2000, 2008). Roach and various other purely freshwater species have shown fewer powers of dispersal, but have recently become successful in several Cumbrian lakes where they have been introduced by anglers. Thanks to introductions by humans and canal waterways, the majority of our cyprinid species have managed to extend their ranges in recent years. This has been augmented by regional introductions made by humans.

Some species have been deliberately introduced by anglers, and the Grayling *Thymallus thymallus*, is a notable example. Previously absent from Scotland it was introduced to several Scottish rivers, starting in the 1850s, and is now a widespread and successful species in the southern half of the country. The Ruffe too is an alien in Scotland, but introductions, probably by pike anglers in the 1970s, mean that it is now one of the most abundant fish in Loch Lomond. It is now widely distributed in Britain south of this, for example in Bassenthwaite Lake, England, and Llyn Tegid, Wales.

Alien species

At the end of the eighteenth century, very few alien fish species were established in Britain or Ireland. Although there had been some translocations by humans by this

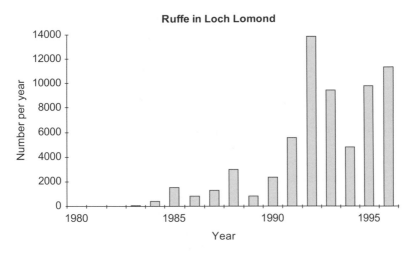

Figure 21.7 Explosive increase of introduced Ruffe in Loch Lomond. The numbers are those taken from the screens at a water supply system.

time, it seems likely that almost all of the species present had arrived, and largely dispersed, naturally and can be regarded as having become secondarily established as native species. During the latter half of the nineteenth century, however, it was very fashionable to introduce fishes (and other) species from abroad, mainly for ornamental use, such as aquaria and garden ponds, and sport fishing, and by 1950 several alien species were known to be established or stocked regularly, mostly in England (Copp *et al.* 2007). These included Rainbow Trout, Brook Charr, *Salvelinus fontinalis*, Rock Bass, *Ambloplites rupestris*, Pumpkinseed, *Lepomis gibbosus*, and Largemouth Bass, *Micropterus salmoides* (from North America), Pikeperch, *Sander lucioperca*, Danube Catfish, *Silurus glanis*, Common Carp, *Cyprinus carpio*, Goldfish, *Carassius auratus*, Bitterling, *Rhodeus sericeus*, and Orfe, *Leuciscus idus* (from Eurasia). The status of Crucian Carp, *Carassius carassius*, as a native or alien is still a matter of some debate. Recent alien fishes which have become established are Black Bullhead, Sunbleak and Topmouth Gudgeon.

Several of these fishes must now be regarded as a permanent part of the British fauna for few of them could ever be eliminated from the waters in which they have become established. It is likely that some of them will disperse further into new catchments and no doubt other species will be introduced in the future, probable candidates being Channel Catfish, *Ictalurus punctatus*, and Fathead Minnow, *Pimephales promelas*, from North America and Asp, *Aspius aspius*, and Japanese Weatherloach, *Misgurnus anguillicaudatus*, from mainland Europe and Asia. Many of the introduced species, especially cyprinids, are tolerant of some pollutants and favoured by warming due to climate change (Maitland 1991) and eutrophication (Maitland 1984), in contrast to indigenous British fish fauna, especially its salmonids, which require cool, unpolluted, well-oxygenated water.

Discussion and conclusions

The overall conclusion from a study of trends in both native and non-native fishes is that, though some native species are relatively stable, the general trend is a decline and loss of populations and stocks. Non-native species, in contrast, are continuing to be introduced from abroad, and are expanding north, east and west, thanks to the actions of coarse anglers and aquarists. Whereas it was thought until recently that many fishes in Britain, especially cyprinids, had already reached their northern limits and were unlikely to disperse much further, this is clearly not the case, as the successful moves made recently by several species (e.g. Gudgeon, *Gobio gobio*, Chub, *Leuciscus cephalus*, Dace and Ruffe) have resulted in the establishment of thriving new populations considerably further north of their previous areas of distribution. For example, 35 years ago only native fish species were found in Loch Lomond and its catchment; since then, five alien species have become established there. All of these new stocks appear to have resulted from deliberate introductions by anglers, either intentionally to initiate new populations or by discarding excess live bait.

The success of invasive species appears to be higher in disturbed native habitats or where there are vacant niches. New, alien species can change the trophic dynamics of the system further down the food chain, i.e. zoobenthos, zooplankton and phytoplankton. This can be illustrated by introducing predators such as Pike in biomanipulation of lakes. In extreme cases, Pike have been know to eliminate other fish species, their subsequent survival depending on the large Pike eating smaller ones, which themselves feed on zoobenthos (Munro 1957).

There is still substantial work to be done in the field of fish conservation. In addition to establishing the status of fishes in each geographic area, much effort must go towards identifying the specific conservation needs of the most endangered species and implementing appropriate measures as soon as possible. As well as habitat restoration, one of the most positive areas of management lies in the establishment of new populations, either to replace those which have become extinct or to provide an additional safeguard for isolated populations. Any species which is found in only a few waters is believed to be in potential danger, and the creation of additional independent stocks is an urgent and worthwhile conservation activity.

As well as strong legislation to protect species and habitats, some would say in spite of it (for example, the Burbot was already extinct in Britain by the time it was placed on Schedule 5 of the Wildlife and Countryside Act, 1981), most threatened species require practical 'hands on' management of some kind. The processes involved have been described in greater detail elsewhere (Maitland and Lyle 1991, 1992) and only a brief outline is given here.

Habitat management. Obviously extensive damage has been done to many fish habitats and the situation is often not easy to reverse, especially in the short term, where fish species or communities are severely threatened. In many cases, unique stocks have completely disappeared. Even where habitat restoration is contemplated, stock transfer (discussed below) could be an important interim measure. There are a number of important examples of habitat restoration in temperate areas, however, and it should be emphasised that habitat protection and restoration are the principal long-term means through which successful sustainable fish conservation and restoration of biodiversity will be achieved.

There have been significant strides in pollution control over the last few decades and a number of the worst rivers are now much cleaner. In Britain, for example, the Rivers Clyde and Thames are now so much better than 50 years ago that previously extirpated fishes have been returning to them in increasing numbers. At their worst, both rivers were virtually fishless in their lower reaches and because of the pollution no migratory fishes could pass through to reach the clean upland waters. Among the final arbiters of water quality are surely the fishes themselves and the return of the Atlantic Salmon to these rivers after an absence of >100 years is a marvellous tribute to decades of work by the pollution-control authorities.

Translocation. Where rare fishes are threatened, stock transfer can be done without any threat to the existing stocks, but it is important that certain criteria are taken into account in relation to any translocation proposal. With most of the stocks of fishes concerned it should be possible to obtain substantial numbers of fertilised eggs by catching and stripping adults during their spawning period. These fishes can then be returned safely to the water to spawn in future years. Fortunately, most fishes are very fecund and so substantial numbers of eggs can be taken at this time without harm. Having identified an appropriate water in which to create a new population, the latter can be initiated by placing the eggs there, or hatching the eggs in a hatchery and introducing the young.

Translocation projects for threatened fish species have proved to be one of the most realistic immediate ways to help to conserve several species, assuming that additional habitat is available and can be conserved. In general, these are likely to be less expensive and have a greater chance of success than many habitat-restoration proposals, especially in the short term. All translocation proposals should follow IUCN guidelines.

Captive breeding. Captive breeding is widely used throughout the world for a variety of endangered animals, including fishes. For most animals, however, it can really only be regarded as a short term emergency measure, for a variety of genetic and other difficulties are likely to arise if small numbers of animals are kept in captivity over several generations or more. Captive breeding in the long term does not seem appropriate to any of the freshwater fish species at present under threat in Britain or Ireland, unless the numbers of fishes which can be obtained for translocation from some sites are very small.

Short term captive breeding involving only one generation does have some advantages for a number of species and has already been carried out with Arctic Charr (P.S. Maitland, personal data). It is especially relevant where translocations are desirable, but it is difficult to obtain reasonable numbers of eggs or young because of ecological or logistic constraints. In such cases there are considerable advantages to be gained in rearing small numbers of stock in captivity and then stripping them to obtain much larger numbers of young for release in the wild. Due to genetic problems related to the 'bottleneck' effect and inbreeding it should not be carried out for more than one generation from the wild stock and as many parent fishes as possible should be used.

Cryopreservation. Modern techniques for rapid freezing of gametes to very low temperatures have proved successful for a variety of animals, including fishes. After freezing for many years and then thawing the material is still viable. The technique, however, is successful only for sperm and though much research is at present being carried out on eggs, no successful method of cryopreservation for them has yet been developed. The technique is therefore of only limited value in relation to the conservation of fish species.

Acknowledgements

We are grateful to Ian Harrison and Colin Galbraith for useful comments on a draft of this chapter and to Fran Igoe and Ian Winfield for permission to use the data shown in Figures 21.1 and 21.4.

References

Campbell, R.N., Maitland, P.S. and Campbell, R.N.B. (1994). Management of fish populations. In Maitland, P.S., Boon, P.J. and McLusky, D.S., eds., *The Fresh Waters of Scotland*, Chichester, Wiley, pp. 489–513.

Copp, G.H., Templeton, M. and Gozlan, R.E. (2007). Propagule pressure and the invasion risks of non-native freshwater fishes: a case study in England. *Journal of Fish Biology*, **71** (Supplement D), 148–159.

Craig, J.F. (2000). *Percid Fishes Systematics, Ecology and Exploitation*, Oxford, Blackwell Science.

Craig, J.F. (2008). A short review of pike ecology. *Hydrobiologia*, **601**, 5–16.

Doherty, D., O'Maoiléidigh, N and McCarthy, T.K. (2004). The biology, ecology and future conservation of twaite shad (*Alosa fallax* Lacépède), allis shad (Alosa alosa L.) and Killarney shad (*Alosa fallax* killarnensis Tate Regan) in Ireland. *Proceedings of the Royal Irish Academy*, **104B**(3), 93–102.

Harrison, I.J. and Stiassny, M.L.J. (1999). The quiet crisis: a preliminary listing of freshwater fishes of the world that are either extinct or 'missing in action'. In MacPhee,

R.D., ed., *Extinctions in Near Time: Causes, Contexts, and Consequences*, New York and London, Plenum Press, pp. 271–331,

Hoffmann, M., Brooks, T.M., Fonseca, G.A.B. *et al.* (2008). Conservation planning and the IUCN Red List. Endangered Species Research. http://www.int-res.com/articles/esr2008/theme/IUCN/IUCNpp3.pdf.

Igoe, F. and Hammar, J. (2004). The Arctic Char *Salvelinus alpinus* (L.) species complex in Ireland: a secretive and threatened ice age relict. *Proceedings of the Royal Irish Academy*, **104B**, 73–92.

Kottelat, M. and Freyhof, J. (2007). *Handbook of European Freshwater Fishes*, Cornol, Switzerland, Publications Kottelat.

Leveque, C., Oberdorff, T., Paugy, D., Stiassny, M.L.J and Tedesco, P.A. (2008). Global diversity of fish (Pisces) in freshwater. *Hydrobiologia*, **595**, 545–567.

Maitland, P.S. (1977). Freshwater fish in Scotland in the 18th, 19th and 20th centuries. *Biological Conservation*, **12**, 265–278.

Maitland, P.S. (1984). The effects of eutrophication on wildlife. *Institute of Terrestrial Ecology Symposium*, **13**, 101–108.

Maitland, P.S. (1991). Climate change and fish in northern Europe: some possible scenarios. *Proceedings of the Institute of Fisheries Management Annual Study Course*, **22**, 97–110.

Maitland, P.S. (2004). Keys to the freshwater fish of Britain and Ireland, with notes on their distribution and ecology. *Freshwater Biological Association Scientific Publication*, **62**, 1–248.

Maitland, P.S. and East, K. (1989). An increase in numbers of Ruffe, *Gymnocephalus cernuus* (L.), in a Scottish loch from 1982 to 1987. *Aquaculture and Fisheries Management*, **20**, 227–228.

Maitland, P.S. and Linsell, K. (2006). *Guide to Freshwater Fish of Britain and Europe*, London, Philip's.

Maitland, P.S. and Lyle, A.A. (1991). Conservation of freshwater fish in the British Isles: the current status and biology of threatened species. *Aquatic Conservation*, **1**, 25–54.

Maitland, P.S. and Lyle, A.A. (1992). Conservation of freshwater fish in the British Isles: proposals for management. *Aquatic Conservation*, **2**, 165–183.

Maitland, P.S., Lyle, A.A. and Campbell, R.N.B. (1987). *Acidification and Fish Populations in Scottish Lochs*, Grange-over Sands, Institute of Terrestrial Ecology.

McAllister, D.E., Craig, J.F., Davidson, N., Delaney, S. and Seddon, M. (2001). *Biodiversity Impacts of Large Dams*. Background Paper No. 1, Gland, Switzerland, IUCN/UNEP/WCD.

Munro, W.R. (1957). The Pike of Loch Choin. *Freshwater and Salmon Fisheries Research, Scotland*, **16**, 1–16.

Nelson, J.S. (2006). *Fishes of the World*, 4th edn, Hoboken, NJ, John Wiley & Sons, Inc.

Regan, C.T. (1911). *The Freshwater Fishes of the British Isles*, London, Methuen.

Rosell, R., Harrod, C., Griffiths, D. and McCarthy T.K. (2004). Conservation of the Irish populations of the pollan *Coregonus autumnalis*. *Proceedings of the Royal Irish Academy*, **104B**, 67–72.

Wheeler, A.C., Merrett, N.R. and Quigley, D.T.G. (2004). Additional records and notes for Wheeler's (1992) List of the Common and Scientific Names of Fishes of the British Isles. *Journal of Fish Biology*, **65** (Supplement B), 1–40.

Whilde, A. (1993). *Threatened Mammals, Birds, Amphibians and Fish in Ireland*, Belfast, HMSO.

Winfield, I.J., James, J.B. and Fletcher, J.M. (2008). Northern pike (*Esox lucius*) in a warming lake: changes in population size and individual condition in relation to prey abundance. *Hydrobiologia*, **601**, 29–40.

22

Riverflies

Cyril Bennett and Warren Gilchrist

Summary

Riverflies (mayflies, caddisflies and stoneflies) have shown a serious decline
in the United Kingdom over the past few decades, most of which has been
identified by anglers. This decline has been attributed to a number of causes,
including pollution, siltation, abstraction, poor land management, loss of aquatic
weed and climatic changes. Whilst there is little quantitative data to demonstrate
declines, two surveys have shown a serious decline in one mayfly species and a
change in the life cycle of another. The mayfly parasite, *Spiriopsis adipophila*,
new to the UK, could also be restricting the growth rates of certain mayfly
species.

The Riverfly Partnership has brought together a large number of organisations
with a common interest to conserve and protect riverfly populations. Working
in partnership with the Environment Agency, the Anglers Monitoring Initiative
(AMI) has been devised for anglers (and others) to check water quality by
monitoring riverfly populations. This provides an alert of pollution events that
may otherwise go undetected. One-day workshops give anglers the basic training to carry out this simple monitoring procedure and a fully funded PhD study
on riverflies is planned to run from 2010.

Reintroductions and improvements to aquatic environments can also help to
increase riverfly populations; the mayfly, *Ephemera danica*, was successfully
reintroduced to the River Wey in Surrey and the River Wye in Derbyshire after
two serious pollution incidents.

Working with the Field Studies Council, the Riverfly Partnership publishes
simple keys to the riverflies to aid identification and encourage anglers to feed
information into the National Riverfly Recording Schemes.

Silent Summer: The State of Wildlife in Britain and Ireland, ed. Norman Maclean. Published by Cambridge
University Press. © Cambridge University Press 2010.

Introduction

'Riverflies' is the term used to describe three orders of aquatic insects, mayflies (Ephemeroptera), caddisflies (Trichoptera) and stoneflies (Plecoptera), with 279 species in total (Figure 22.1). The mayflies and stoneflies are ancient orders long pre-dating the dinosaurs and, having an incomplete metamorphosis (no pupa stage), the final moult becomes the adult. Mayflies are also unique in having two winged stages, the subimago and the imago. Whilst seldom noticed by most people, they have for centuries been studied by anglers, as these are the groups of natural flies that fly fishermen imitate with their artificial fly lures. Anglers therefore have a strong vested interest in riverflies and have contributed much to the biological literature, e.g. Lunn (see Hills 1934); Sawyer 1970; Goddard 1976) together with the common names used. This is particularly so with the mayflies, for which anglers have developed artificial copies of most of the common species and in some cases copies of both the males and females. Much of this chapter is therefore written from the angler's perspective.

Riverflies are a vital part of the river ecology, providing food for fish, birds, bats and predatory insects. They also act as a sensitive indicator of the health of the river and, together with other freshwater invertebrates, they are used to monitor the quality of the water. The Biological Monitoring Working Party (BMWP) scoring system is the standard method used for measuring the biological quality of rivers, and a simplified version of this, using riverfly groups, is being used by anglers to highlight changes in water quality and pollution problems (see below).

Mayflies	Caddisflies
Blue Winged Olive (*Serratella ignita*)	Grannom (*Brachcentrus subnubilus*)

Stoneflies

February Red (*Taeniopteryx nebulosa*)

Figure 22.1 The riverflies (see colour plate).

Decline of riverflies

Despite numerous reports of improving water quality, dramatic declines in many of our riverfly species have been observed by anglers and river-keepers over the past few decades, but this decline has generally gone unnoticed by most people, as has the lack of fly-splattered car windscreens when driving anywhere near a river on a warm summers' evening. A survey carried out by the Wiltshire Fisheries Association and the Environment Agency (Frake and Hayes, 2001) teased out records and general observations of anglers and river-keepers over many years which indicated a huge decline in the abundance of many of our riverfly species. Reduced numbers of emerging adults have resulted in a change in the feeding habits of trout, such that they have become less discerning about which species of fly they will take. This means the art of river fly-fishing has, to a great extent, been lost. No longer does the angler have to put up a good copy to tempt a trout preoccupied with feeding on Iron Blue Duns (*Alainites muticus*) or Blue Winged Olives (*Serratella ignita*) and his choice of artificial fly can therefore be general rather than specific.

This decline in riverflies has been widely attributed to a number of factors, particularly pesticides, such as the sheep dip cypermethrin and cattle carrying permethrin-impregnated ear tags (for fly-transmitted summer mastitis). If sheep or cattle are allowed to enter the river after treatment, the entire invertebrate population can be wiped out for many miles downstream; cattle shaking their heads will distribute the insecticide, and cattle dung in the river will release a hefty dose of permethrin. Due to the enormous pollution problems caused by the misuse of sheep dips, the sale of cypermethrin has been temporarily banned.

Poor land management can lead to diffuse pollution with 'run-off' increasing the levels of nutrients in the river and causing siltation of the river bed. Climatic changes can also reduce riverfly populations with low river flows, increased water temperatures and loss of aquatic weed. Whilst there has been considerable work done on the feminisation of fish due to oestrogens from sewage-treatment works, little has been done on what effects these may be having on invertebrates. Figure 22.2 (photographed in 1990) shows what appear to be eggs in a male Large Dark Olive Mayfly (*Baetis rhodani*).

Apart from the obvious catastrophic wipe-outs due to point-source pollution events, such as the misuse of sheep dip, there is very little hard quantitative data to show any general declines over time and it is very easy to become complacent about the somewhat meagre numbers of riverflies that are now considered as 'normal' on many of our rivers. On the River Wey in Surrey, a *3 minute* kick sweep sample currently produces perhaps a few hundred Ephemeropteran larvae. In 1979, a similar sample produced so many larvae that this had to be reduced to just *10 seconds* to facilitate counting (Figure 22.3).

The once large emergence of the Grannom Caddisfly (*Brachycentrus subnubilis*) in mid-April has now all but disappeared on many of our rivers and can be very patchy on others. Whilst vast 'clouds' of this fly continue to emerge from the River Avon in the centre of Salisbury each year, it is almost absent a few miles upstream. As the larvae

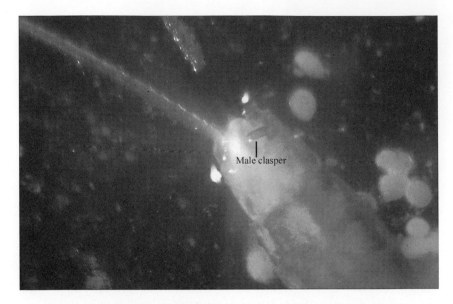

Figure 22.2 Male Large Dark Olive (*Baetis rhodani*) with eggs (River Wey – 7 September 1990).

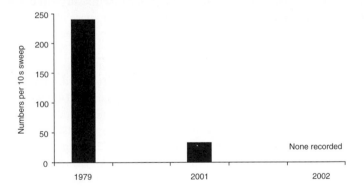

Figure 22.3 Numbers of mayfly larvae recorded in weed beds on the River Wey at Frensham in 1979, compared with those in 2001/2002.

of this species attach themselves to strands of weed, particularly Water Crowfoot (*Ranunculus* spp.), this decline could be due to the loss of this plant on many stretches of water; in recent years there have been stretches of the Rivers Test and Itchen in Hampshire with no weed at all and this is often due to over-grazing by increasing numbers of swans. It has also been suggested that the decline in riverflies could be due to excessive weed cutting, but with the expense and reduction in manpower, it is probable that weed cutting was more thoroughly done in past years when there was no shortage of riverflies. Also gone are the large populations of the March Brown Mayfly (*Rhithrogena germanica*) from many of the South Wales rivers such as the River Usk, where a spectacular emergence used to be common during March. A two-day search for larvae on both the River Usk and the River Taff in March 2008 revealed none. It is also thought that the mayfly, *Heptagenia longicauda*, no longer occurs in the British Isles (Elliott *et al.* 1988) and there is growing concern that other uncommon species may also have disappeared.

Two mayfly species that are of extreme importance to the fly fisherman on the southern chalk streams are the angler's 'Mayfly' (*Ephemera danica*) and the Blue Winged Olive and for this reason a long-term survey was carried out on each of these species. This confirmed anglers' observations that a considerable decline in the Blue Winged Olive had occurred, and whilst it also confirmed anglers' observations that *E. danica* had not declined (perhaps due to the burrowing habit of its larva), there was strong evidence to show that increased water temperatures had reduced its life cycle from two years to one year.

Decline of the Blue Winged Olive *(Serratella ignita)*

The Blue Winged Olive is one of the most common mayflies found in the British Isles; it has a univoltine (one generation a year) life cycle with over wintering eggs, although in the warmer southern lowland rivers some are now over wintering as larvae. Probably more than any other, this fly provides the angler with most of his sport during the summer months. Subimagos usually emerge in the evening and female imagos return to lay their eggs just before dark. This enables the angler to 'catch the evening rise' as the surface of the water is covered with both emerging and egg-laying insects.

A survey on the Bere Stream in Dorset (Bass 1976) recorded a population of over 1500 larvae per square metre, but a more recent survey carried out at Leckford on the River Test in Hampshire over a ten-year period (Bennett, unpublished) shows a rapid decline in this species, which correlated with reducing flow rates (Figure 22.4).

Change in the life cycle of the Mayfly *(Ephemera danica)*

The anglers 'Mayfly' (*Ephemera danica*) usually emerges in vast numbers on many lowland rivers for a two-week period in the spring (commonly known as 'duffer's fortnight'), providing the angler with unique sport as the trout cast caution to the wind while rising to take the adult of this large mayfly. This species does not seem to have suffered the same decline as other species and on some rivers may even have increased; this was confirmed in a seven-year survey at Leckford (Bennett 2007). However, when this population was compared to a population at Tilford on the River Wey in Surrey it was clear that the latter had a shorter life cycle.

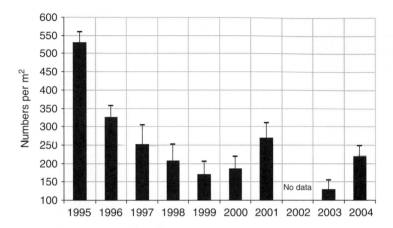

Figure 22.4 Decline in the Blue Winged Olive (*Serratella ignita*) on the River Test at Leckford. (Error bars indicate 95% confidence limits.)

While there has been much debate on the length of the life cycle of *E. danica* (one, two or three years), it has generally been recorded as having a two-year life cycle (Elliott *et al.* 1988). A nine-year study by Wright *et al.* (1981) on the River Lambourn in southern England also found a two-year cycle and Tokeshi (1985) has suggested that, based on the degree-days of growth, at least the larger females cannot reach a mature size in less than two years. However, the River Wey study shows that, depending on water temperatures, both males and females can reach maturity in a single year (Bennett 2007).

Higher summer water temperatures at Tilford (compared with those at Leckford) result in faster egg development and increased early larval growth rates; this leads to a much earlier recruitment of small larvae, up to six weeks before those at Leckford. This results in a predominantly one-year cycle at Tilford whereas at Leckford, where summer water temperatures are lower, there is a mainly two-year cycle (Figure 22.5). It has also been shown that the normal two-year life cycle of the stonefly *Leuctra nigra* can be shortened to one year at high temperatures in the laboratory (Elliott 1987).

Although there are no reliable data to show the extent to which summer water temperatures may have increased, earlier work on *E. danica* (Hills 1934; Courtney Williams 1949) indicates that water temperatures were generally lower than those recorded during this study. This would have meant that during that period, it would have been unlikely for *E. danica* to complete its life cycle in less than two years, but with increasing water temperatures on many of our rivers, populations are probably moving more towards a one-year cycle.

This can have serious consequences, because those females that do complete their development in a year are usually significantly smaller than those taking two years.

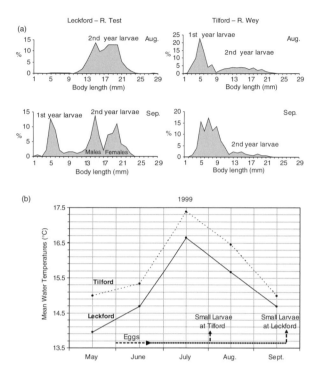

Figure 22.5 Growth rates of *Ephemera danica* on the River Test at Leckford and the River Wey at Tilford. (a) Growth rates at each site in August and September showing a large percentage of larvae entering a second year at Leckford (and separating into male and female size classes), whereas at Tilford very few larvae enter a second year. (b) Mean monthly temperatures at both sites during egg development and early larval growth; eggs at Tilford hatch two days before those at Leckford. Temperatures were recorded at 30-minute intervals, using permanently sited equipment.

This results in the production of fewer eggs, from around 6000 in a 24 mm female down to 3000 in an 18 mm female (Bennett 1996). Also, a period of bad weather during the relatively short emergence period, when most of the population would be in the adult stage, could severely reduce or even wipe out a population. This was seen at Tilford in 2000, when most of the population was lost after prolonged high winds and heavy rain prevented most of the female imagos from returning to the water to lay their eggs. Samples taken in September showed that there was very little recruitment of first-year larvae, resulting in a very low population the following April. Whilst losses also occurred at Leckford, the high proportion of larvae entering a second year ensured that a near normal population remained the following April.

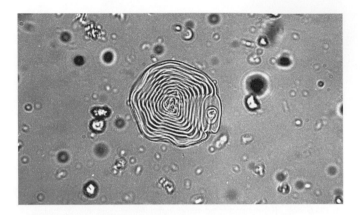

Figure 22.6 *Spiriopsis adipophila* (diameter = 70 μm).

Appearance of the parasite *Spiriopsis adipophila* in *E. danica* populations

In common with other freshwater insects, riverflies quite normally carry a community of parasites. One, *Spiriopsis adipophila* (previously *Spirinella adipophila*), is a species new to the UK; previously it was only recorded in France, Luxemburg and Poland. This parasite is specific to the *Ephemera* species of mayfly and has so far only been recorded in the Thames catchment area (Bennett 1994, 1996). It is a micro-organism of unclear systematic position; the full life cycle is unknown and the definitive host still remains to be identified (Figure 22.6).

It was initially detected in the *E. danica* population on the River Wey in February 1993 (Bennett 1994, 1996), where it rapidly increased and moved upstream. Usually the whole population carries the parasite and, in some cases, over 5000 parasites can be found in a single larva. Infection is mostly restricted to the parietal and visceral fat bodies of the larvae (Soldan 1980), and large infestations can totally destroy the adipose tissue (Arvy 1979). Although it generally appeared to have little detrimental effect on the River Wey population as a whole, growth rates may be restricted and numbers of the parasite increase dramatically when larvae are under stress, caused by lack of food or during a moult (Bennett 1996).

Reintroductions and improvements

Even when populations of riverflies were large, there were problems. Over 100 years ago *E. danica* was (for some reason) lost on the River Test, but after a number of failures, the world-renowned river-keeper William Lunn was able to reintroduce this species using large numbers of eggs taken from fertilised females (Hills 1934). A similar project, following Lunn's basic procedures, albeit with more modern techniques, was recently used on the River Wey.

Two pollution incidents on the River Wey in 2002 and 2004 resulted in a drastic reduction in the invertebrate community, together with a total loss of the *E. danica* population. Although a typical community of invertebrates remained in the headwaters above the pollution site, *E. danica* populations are never large in the headwaters of a river, and whilst downstream invertebrate drift did result in a certain amount of recovery of some species, this was unlikely to be the case with *E. danica*, which, due to its burrowing habit, does not normally enter the drift. Frequently when this mayfly is lost from a site it does not return unless given a helping hand (e.g. Hills 1934). Therefore a reintroduction programme was planned using mature larvae and eggs taken from the River Test at Leckford after these were carefully screened for unwanted pathogens. As *E. danica* was being moved into a site with *S. adipophila* (see above) rather than out, this did not pose a problem.

Introduction of mature larvae

Around 3000 mature male and female larvae were collected from Leckford in early May and immediately introduced at two sites; some were placed into isolation tanks containing water and sediments from the South Wey in order to check if reintroduction was successful. As these larvae were released just before the main adult emergence period for this species, a high proportion will have emerged and been capable of reproduction within a matter of days, thus reducing losses due to predation.

Introduction of eggs

Under natural conditions, fewer than 0.5% of mayfly eggs will normally develop through to the adult stage, with 95% of losses occurring during the egg and early larval stages (Elliott *et al.* 1988). However, previous work on the River Wey (Bennett 2002) had shown that well over 90% of *E. danica* eggs, reared artificially in an experimental stream, hatched successfully; the eggs from around 500 adult females should therefore produce several million larvae. In late May and early June, fertilised females were collected at Leckford and the eggs 'milked' onto microscope slides; each slide contained about 30 000 eggs (Figure 22.7).

Over two million eggs were collected and incubated at 20 °C, and development was monitored daily using a high-powered microscope. When the eggs were about to hatch (after about 10 days), the slides were placed in bottomless trays and suspended just above the river bed. This kept the eggs up out of the reach of bottom-feeding predators and allowed the newly hatched larvae to drop out of the trays and quickly reach cover in the sediments below. The trays were regularly checked and only removed when all the eggs had hatched. Monitoring in the following October showed that significant numbers of small larvae were present, and further monitoring

(a)   (b)

(c)

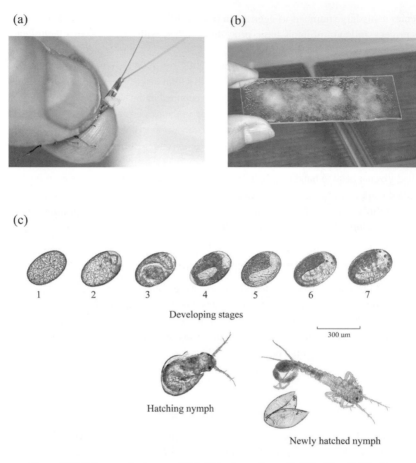

1   2   3   4   5   6   7

Developing stages

300 um

Hatching nymph

Newly hatched nymph

Figure 22.7 *Ephemera danica* eggs: (a) 'milking' eggs from a fertilised female (b) micro-scope slide containing about 30 000 eggs and (c) developing stages of eggs; eggs were introduced to the river at stage 6–7.

in early April of the following year showed that these were approaching maturity. Adults were seen emerging in the middle of May, confirming that a population of *E. danica* had been re-established. After a spillage of creosote on the Derbyshire Wye, a full population of *E. danica* has also been re-established after just two years, using the same methodology.

Fly boards

Lunn also observed that females of many of the *Baetis* species of mayflies descend under the water to lay their eggs using partially submerged rocks and emergent vegetation.

To increase the populations of these species he used 'fly boards' (long planks of wood) suspended from footbridges to increase the sites for egg-laying females (Hills 1934). Within a very short time these fly boards were covered in countless millions of eggs. However, as large populations of riverflies have been taken very much for granted on most rivers, these were generally seen to be of limited value, but with the huge declines now being seen, fly boards are increasingly being used (Figure 22.8).

The Riverfly Partnership

Just a small amount of insecticide entering a river can wipe out an entire invertebrate population for many miles downstream, and this can happen without anyone even noticing that they have gone. However, as they are at the bottom end of the food chain, fish, frogs, bats and birds will surely follow. Whilst the river may look in perfect condition, a quick look below the surface will reveal the sad truth, but with the never-ending cutbacks in the frequency of statutory biological (invertebrate) monitoring on our rivers, this type of pollution will often go unrecorded. However, because anglers spend so much time by the river they will quickly notice that 'something' is wrong and only too often they will be the only ones to notice. Therefore a simple method for anglers (and other interested people) to monitor the biological quality of their local river was developed in order to alert the Environment Agency to a possible pollution problem.

After a highly successful Riverfly Conference at the Natural History Museum in 2004, the Riverfly Partnership (RP) representing anglers, fishery managers, riverkeepers, scientists, conservationists and government agencies was established. The RP work to conserve, protect and raise awareness of the importance of riverflies in the aquatic environment and at the 2nd Riverfly Conference in the spring of 2007, the Angler's Monitoring Initiative was launched. This is a simple monitoring procedure (pioneered at Leckford on the River Test) which uses seven easily identified riverfly groups plus the Freshwater Shrimp, *Gammarus pulex* (all of which anglers are familiar with) to highlight changes in water quality and associated pollution problems. RP tutors, in conjunction with local statutory agency biologists, carry out one-day workshops throughout the UK to give anglers the simple skills needed.

Within 10 months of the launch of the initiative over 200 monitoring sites were registered throughout the UK, with this number rapidly growing. In the same period, four serious pollution incidents were detected by the monitoring groups in South Wales and two on the River Wey in Surrey which may otherwise have gone unnoticed. This led to investigations by the Environment Agency (EA) and, in two incidences, successful EA prosecutions of the polluters responsible.

Working with the Field Studies Council (FSC), the RP have also published simple keys of the mayflies, caddisflies and stoneflies to aid identification and encourage anglers (and other naturalists) to feed information into the National Riverfly Recording Schemes.

(a)

(b)

(c)

Figure 22.8 Fly boards: (a) fly board in position, (b) bottom of fly boards covered in eggs and (c) female laying eggs on the board (see colour plate).

The Future

The future of riverflies will very much depend on the continued fight against pollution, over-abstraction and inappropriate management of aquatic environments. Anglers are in a unique position to conserve their riverflies and indeed they have a vested interest in doing so. AMI will continue to monitor the water quality of local rivers, highlighting pollution problems that may otherwise go unnoticed and, working closely with the statutory bodies, the RP will continue to expand the initiative each year, which will include a Masters degree at the University of London leading into a fully funded PhD on Riverflies to run from 2010.

Other groups within the RP (e.g. The Salmon and Trout Association and The Wild Trout Trust) are working closely with the EA to improve aquatic environments to ensure that our rivers achieve a 'Good Ecological Status' (EQS), required by the European Water Framework Directive.

Perhaps then we may once again see the vast swarms of riverflies dancing in the evening sun which we once took so much for granted.

References

Arvy, L. (1979). *Nouvelles Donees Sur Spiriopsis adipophila* (Arvy et Delage, 1966) (*Spirinella adipophila*, Arvy et Delage), Sporozoaire probable. Proceedings of the second International conference on Ephemeroptera.

Bass, J.A.B. (1976). Studies on *Ephemerella ignita* (Poda) in a chalk stream in S. England. *Hydrobiologia*, **49**, 117–121.

Bennett, C.J. (1994). The first reported occurrence of the mayfly parasite *Spirinella adipophila* (Sporozoa) in a British river. *Freshwater Forum,* **4** (2) 89–96.

Bennett, C.J. (1996). The ecology of mayflies (Ephemeroptera) in the upper reaches of the River Wey in Surrey. PhD thesis, University of London, UK (unpublished).

Bennett, C.J. (2002). A seven year study of the life cycle of the mayfly *Ephemera danica* (Ephemeroptera) on two rivers in southeast England. The John Spedan Lewis Trust for the Advancement of the Natural Sciences – Record No. 7 (unpublished).

Bennett, C.J. (2007). A seven year study of the life cycle of the mayfly *Ephemera danica. Freshwater Forum,* **27**, 3–14.

Courtney Williams, A. (1949). *A Dictionary of Trout Flies*, London, A. & C. Black Publishers Ltd, pp. 235–236.

Elliott, J.M. (1987). Temperature-induced changes in the lifecycle of *Leuctra nigra* (Plecoptera: Leuctridae) from a Lake District stream. *Freshwater Biology,* **18**, 177–184.

Elliott, J.M., Humpesch, U.H. and Macan, T.T. (1988). *Larvae of the British Ephemeroptera. A Key with Ecological Notes*, Scientific Publication No. 49, Ambleside, Freshwater Biological Association.

Frake, A. and Hayes, P. (2001). Report on the millennium chalk streams fly trends study. Environment Agency publication ISBN 1 85 705759 7.

Goddard, J. (1976). *Trout Fly Recognition*, London, A. & C. Black Publishers Ltd (ISBN 0 7136 1698 9).

Hills, J.W. (1934). *River Keeper, The Life of William James Lunn*, London, Geoffrey Bles Ltd, pp. 30–37.

Sawyer, F. (1970). *Nymphs and the Trout*, London, A. & C. Black Publishers Ltd (ISBN 0 7136 1074 3).

Soldan, T. (1980). Host and tissue specificity of *Spiriopsis adipophila* (Arvy et Delage) (Protozoa, Coccidia) and its distribution in the Elbe Basin of Czechoslovakia. *Folia Parasitologica (Prague),* **27**(1), 77–82.

Tokeshi, M. (1985). Life-cycle and production of the burrowing mayfly, *Ephemera danica*: a new method of estimating degree-days for growth. *Journal of Animal Ecology*, **54**, 919–930.

Wright, J.F., Hiley, P.D. and Berrie, A.D. (1981). A nine-year study of the life cycle of *Ephemera danica* Müller (Ephemeridae: Ephemeroptera) in the River Lambourn, England. *Ecological Entomology*, **6**, 321–331.

23

Bumblebees

Dave Goulson

Summary

Since bumblebees are a group associated with cool climates, Britain supports a large proportion (~10%) of the world's bumblebee fauna. However, three of our 25 species have become extinct, and seven species are Biodiversity Action Plan (BAP) listed, a higher proportion than for any other insect group. Declines are primarily driven by habitat loss and declines in floral abundance resulting from agricultural intensification, notably the loss of ~97% of all species-rich grasslands (haymeadows, calcareous grasslands) in the last 60 years. The decline in the abundance of Red Clover, once a common fodder and ley crop and a major source of pollen and nectar for many bumblebee species, is likely to have had a significant impact. Effects of habitat degradation and fragmentation are compounded by the social nature of bumblebees and by their largely monogamous breeding system, which means that they have a very low effective population size (most bumblebees are sterile workers). Hence, populations are susceptible to chance extinction events and inbreeding. Given the importance of bumblebees as pollinators of crops and wildflowers, their declines have broad ecological and economic significance. Suggested measures for their conservation include tight regulation of commercial bumblebee use and targeted use of agri-environment schemes to enhance floristic diversity in agricultural landscapes.

Introduction

The drone of bumblebees busily collecting nectar and pollen is, for me, the sound of summer: I have fond memories of childhood days spent in our garden in Shropshire catching bumblebees and imprisoning them temporarily in jam jars. With their clumsy

Silent Summer: The State of Wildlife in Britain and Ireland, ed. Norman Maclean. Published by Cambridge University Press. © Cambridge University Press 2010.

flight and large, furry, striped bodies they are among the most familiar and endearing of British insects, but like many other organisms they have not fared well in recent decades. The world bumblebee (*Bombus*) fauna consists of approximately 250 known species, largely confined to temperate parts of the northern hemisphere. Bumblebees are social insects, and the vast majority have an annual life cycle. Mated queens emerge from hibernation in spring, and attempt to found a nest in which they rear daughter workers. If all goes well, the number of workers may reach as many as 400 in some species by mid-summer, when new queens and males are reared. These leave the nest, mate and the new queens enter hibernation, while the rest of the population dies off.

An interesting consequence of the large size of bumblebees is that they must beat their wings exceedingly fast to remain in the air (~200 times per second) and it takes an enormous amount of energy to do so. Estimates of the metabolic costs of flight suggest that flying bumblebees have one of the highest metabolic rates recorded in any organism, being 75% higher than that of Hummingbirds. For comparison, a jogging human male burns the energy in a Mars bar in roughly one hour. A bumblebee of equivalent mass would burn the same energy in just 30 seconds. For this reason bumblebee survival depends on the ready availability of nectar-rich flowers, and this lies at the crux of the problems facing bumblebees in modern Britain.

Causes of bumblebee declines

There is mounting evidence that many bumblebee species have declined in recent decades, particularly in developed regions, such as western Europe and North America, but the most detailed records available are from Britain. The data reveal a dramatic reduction in the populations of many species during the second half of the twentieth century. Three of the 25 British species having become nationally extinct (the Apple Bumblebee, *Bombus pomorum*, Cullum's Bumblebee, *B. cullumanus*, and the Short-haired Bumblebee, *B. subterraneus*) (although it should be noted that the Apple Bumblebee became extinct over 100 years ago and may never have been a resident species). A further eight species having undergone major declines (the Great Yellow Bumblebee, *B. distinguendus* (Figure 23.1), the Red-shanked Carder Bee, *B. ruderarius*, the Ruderal Bumblebee, *B. ruderatus*, the Shrill Carder Bee *B. sylvarum* (Figure 23.2), the Brown-banded Carder Bee, *B. humilis*, the Moss Carder bee, *B. muscorum*, the Bilberry Bumblebee, *B. monticola*, and the Broken-belted Bumblebee, *B. soroeensis*). The first six of these, along with the extinct Short-haired Bumblebee, have BAP status.

More so than for most other taxonomic groups, declines in bumblebees have potentially serious ecological and economic consequences. Many wild plants are pollinated predominantly or exclusively by bumblebees. Most bumblebees are generalist pollinators and most insect-pollinated plants use multiple pollinators, so it could be argued that loss of a few pollinator species will have little effect on plant reproduction, but simulating the effects of removal of individual pollinators from pollination networks

Figure 23.1 A Great Yellow Bumblebee worker collecting pollen from Red Clover on unimproved flower-rich grasslands on South Uist, Outer Hebrides. This is probably Britain's rarest bumblebee, and is now confined to the far north and west of Scotland (see colour plate). (Photograph by Dave Goulson.)

has demonstrated that removal of highly linked pollinators (those that provide a pollination service to many different plant species) such as bumblebees produces the greatest rate of decline in plant-species diversity. Reduced pollination services can be particularly detrimental when plants are already scarce and threatened directly by the same changes in land use that threaten the bees. Hence, we ought to be particularly concerned by the state of our bumblebee fauna.

Figure 23.2 A Shrill Carder bee. This species is associated with flower-rich unimproved grasslands in southern Britain, a habitat which has been all but entirely eradicated leading to precipitous declines in several bumblebee species (see colour plate). (Photograph by Dave Goulson.)

Aside from the implications for conservation, there are good financial reasons for conserving bumblebees. The yields of many field, fruit and seed crops are enhanced by bumblebee visitation. For example, field beans are largely pollinated by longer-tongued species, such as the Common Carder Bee, *B. pascuorum*, and the Garden Bumblebee, *B. hortorum*, without which, yields are poor. Many crops rely primarily on honeybee pollination, but beekeeping in Britain has declined due to problems with disease (notably also in North America where, since 2006, an epidemic of unknown cause has destroyed a significant proportion of managed and almost all wild honeybee colonies). The impoverished bumblebee communities often associated with agricultural landscapes may be insufficient to replace the pollination services currently provided by honeybees, and many soft-fruit growers in Britain now buy in commercially reared colonies of the Buff-tailed Bumblebee, *B. terrestris*, from eastern Europe to boost natural bee populations (although there is actually no evidence that wild bumblebee populations have fallen so low in Britain that soft-fruit crops need imported bumblebees to set a good crop).

It is pretty clear that the primary cause of bumblebee declines in Britain is the intensification of farming practices, particularly in the period from ~1945–90. The drive for self-sufficiency in the wake of the Second World War led to a number of major changes documented elsewhere in this book, some of which are particularly pertinent to bumblebees. Permanent unimproved grassland was once highly valued for grazing and hay production, but the development of cheap artificial fertilisers and new fast-growing grass varieties meant that farmers could improve productivity by ploughing up ancient grasslands. Hay meadows gave way to monocultures of grasses which are directly grazed or cut for silage. In the second half of the twentieth century, ~97% of unimproved lowland grassland was lost. Grants were introduced to grub out hedgerows, to plough and re-seed pasture and to drain marshy areas. This led to a steady decline in the area of unfarmed land and of unimproved farmland. There is evidence to suggest that bumblebee forage plants have suffered disproportionate declines. A recent study in Britain found that of 97 preferred bumblebee forage species, 71% have suffered range reductions and 76% have declined in abundance over the past 80 years, exceeding declines of non-forage species.

On farmland, the crops themselves may provide an abundance of food during their brief flowering periods. Leguminous crops (notably clovers, *Trifolium* spp.) used to be an important part of crop rotations in much of Europe, and these are highly preferred food sources, particularly for long-tongued bumblebee species, such as the Ruderal Bumblebee and the Great Yellow Bumblebee. Since the introduction of cheap artificial fertilisers, rotations involving legumes have been almost entirely abandoned, and it is probable that this is one of the primary factors driving the decline of long-tongued bumblebees. Flowering crops such as oilseed rape may contribute to supporting bumblebee populations in arable landscapes, but in order for bumblebee colonies to thrive, they require a continuous succession of flowers from April until August, and crops alone are unlikely to provide this. Farms must contain areas of wildflowers if they are to support bumblebee populations.

Uncropped areas of farmland, such as hedgerows, field margins and borders of streams may provide flowers throughout the season, and therefore support greater numbers of foraging bumblebees than cultivated areas. However, these areas will be adequate only if there are enough of them, and if they have not been degraded by drift of herbicides and fertilisers. Insufficient flower-rich uncropped areas may lead to gaps in the succession of flowering plants, during which bumblebee colonies may starve and die. With a decline in bees, the plants that they pollinate set less seed, resulting in less forage for the bees in subsequent years. The feedback process by which mutually dependent species drive each other to extinction is known as an 'extinction vortex'. We do not as yet know whether this process is really occurring, but it is clear that farmland provides less food for bees than it once would have done, and it seems probable that reduced pollinator abundance in turn has had negative effects on farmland plant populations.

In addition to floral resources, bumblebees need suitable nesting sites, the precise requirements for which vary between species. The carder bees (*Thoracobombus*) such as the Common Carder tend to nest in dense grassy tussocks, while other species such as the Buff-tailed Bumblebee nest underground in cavities. Both groups often use abandoned rodent nests. The loss of hedgerows and of unimproved pastures is likely to have reduced availability of nest sites for both above- and below-ground nesting bumblebee species (3). Those species that nest above ground frequently have their nests destroyed by farm machinery, particularly by cutting for hay or silage. The scarcity of weeds and field-margin flowers on modern intensive farms means that there are less seeds, and therefore less food for voles and mice. Lower populations of these mammals will lead to fewer nest sites for both above- and below-ground nesting bumblebee species.

Impacts of pesticides

An obvious potential contributor to bumblebee declines is the use of pesticides, but we have very little information on whether they cause substantial bumblebee mortality. Pesticide risk assessments are routinely carried out for honeybees, but the results of these are probably not directly applicable to bumblebees since both their behaviour and physiology are different. For example, to avoid honeybees, pyrethroids are commonly applied to flowering oilseed rape in the early morning or evening, but being better able to forage in cool conditions, bumblebees are often active at this time. Laboratory and field-based bioassays appropriate to bumblebees have been developed in response to the growing use of bumblebees for the pollination of greenhouse crops, but these are not widely used and few toxicological data are available. Almost all tests conducted so far have been on Buff-tailed Bumblebees, and suggest that toxicity is similar to that found in honeybees. Tests with dimethoate and carbofuran (the latter now banned in Britain) suggest that these chemicals are selectively transported into the nectar where they can reach high concentrations. Given the large volume of nectar consumed by bumblebees, this could prove to be the most important route of exposure to pesticides.

When colonies are large, it is likely that they can tolerate the loss of some of their workers. However, in the spring, when queens are foraging, and subsequently when nests are small and contain just a few workers, mortality may have a more significant effect. Thus, spring applications of pesticides are of particular concern.

Despite risk assessments, widespread poisoning of honeybees has been reported. Such effects are obvious in domestic hives, where dead bees are ejected and form piles by the nest. It seems probable that pesticides would have similar effects on bumblebees, but they are unlikely to be noticed in most situations, since the nests are tucked away and generally not observed. However, bumblebee deaths have been reported following applications of the insecticides dimethoate or α-cypermethrin to flowering oilseed rape, and of λ-cyhalothrin to field beans.

A growing appreciation of the damaging effects of broad-spectrum pesticides has led to the development of a new generation of more target-specific compounds. EU law now demands that oral and acute toxicity tests are carried out on honeybees prior to the registration of any new pesticide. However, there is no obligation to study sub-lethal effects on any bees, or to look at specific effects on bumblebees. Some of these substances cause no mortality in bumblebees if used appropriately, but there is evidence that supplementary trials for non-lethal effects are needed. For example, spinosad is a commonly used insect neurotoxin which, based on studies of honeybees, has been deemed harmless to bees. However, it has recently been shown that bumblebee larvae fed with pollen containing this pesticide give rise to workers with reduced ability to gather food. Screening of chitin synthesis inhibitors that are used as pesticides found that although they had no lethal effect on adult bumblebees, the use of these pesticides has strong effects on colony growth and the development of larvae. Diflubenzuron and teflubenzuron were found to be the most harmful to bumblebees, greatly reducing reproductive output at concentrations far below the recommended field concentrations. In summary, it is likely that many pesticides currently in use do impact on bumblebee populations, but hard data are largely lacking.

The global trade in commercial bumblebees

A final potential threat to bumblebees is posed by the global trafficking of commercial bumblebee hives. Around 60 000 colonies of a south-eastern European sub-species of the Buff-tailed Bumblebee, *Bombus terrestris dalmitinus*, are imported each year into Britain. Britain has an endemic sub-species of the Buff-tailed Bumblebee, *Bombus terrestris audax*. Evidence suggests that there are dangers to the British sub-species in the form of parasite transmission and competition. Also, *B. terrestris dalmatinus* and *B. terrestris audax* readily interbreed, at least under laboratory conditions, so the native sub-species could be lost through introgression.

Effects of habitat fragmentation

As a consequence of the various factors discussed above, populations of a number of bumblebee species have become increasingly small, fragmented and separated from one another by large distances. Declines appear to have followed a characteristic pattern. The last bumblebee species to disappear from Britain, the Short-haired Bumblebee, was once widespread across southern England, but declined rapidly in the years after World War II. By the 1980s, the few remaining populations were small and isolated, surviving on habitat islands (mostly nature reserves) that had escaped agricultural intensification. However, these populations subsequently disappeared, despite the protected status of the remaining habitat. The species was last recorded at Dungeness in 1988. Several other species, such as the Great Yellow Bumblebee and the Shrill Carder Bumblebee are in the late stages of a similar process (Figure 23.3), and are likely to go extinct in Britain in the near future. Why do isolated populations go extinct? Understanding the consequences of the fragmentation of remnant populations of bumblebees is of great importance to conservationists, given the current distributions of many rare species.

Small populations of all organisms are inherently more vulnerable to extinction due to chance events. If these populations form part of a broader network of interlinked

(a)   (b)

Figure 23.3 Distribution of *Bombus distinguendus*: (a) pre-2000; (b) post-2000. (Data from NBN, largely collected by the Bees, Wasps and Ants Recording Society and the Highland Biological Recording Group.)

populations, then local extinctions can be balanced by subsequent recolonisation, but if fragmentation is severe, then extinct patches may never be reoccupied. In addition, if habitat fragmentation results in the isolation of populations, then they may face an additional extinction threat through inbreeding. Small populations inevitably lose genetic diversity over time, a process known as genetic drift, and after a few generations it becomes inevitable that all individuals within the population will be related to one another and will be genetically similar. This loss of genetic diversity and forced interbreeding between relatives usually results in a general reduction of population fitness. There are a number of reasons to believe that bumblebees may be particularly badly affected by such processes. It is the effective population size (often known as N_e) which determines the rate of genetic drift in a population, and N_e may be several orders of magnitude lower than the actual number of individuals present (because not all individuals in a population manage to produce offspring). In bumblebees, as in many other social insects, N_e depends on the number of successful colonies. Each colony contains one breeding female, the queen (ignoring occasional egg-laying by unmated workers). Queens of most bumblebee species mate only once, so each colony effectively represents two breeding individuals. Hence a flower-filled meadow may contain many foraging bumblebees and give the impression of a large population, but the vast majority are sterile; the actual number of nests present may be tiny. It seems therefore that population sizes of bumblebees may be low, making them particularly susceptible to inbreeding and to chance extinction events (for example, a hungry badger might consume several nests in a single night, and could conceivably wipe out a small population very swiftly).

Inbreeding may be especially costly to bumblebees because of their rather unusual sex-determination mechanism. Bumblebees (along with many other hymenopterans, the bees, ants and wasps) can be either haploid (have a single copy of each chromosome) or diploid (have two copies of each chromosome, the usual number in most animals including humans). Haploid individuals are produced from unfertilised eggs, diploids from fertilised eggs. In general, haploids are male and diploids are female. However, the mechanism that determines sex is actually based on a single gene: if the bee is heterozygous at this locus (it has two different alleles of the gene) it is female; if not, it is male. In large populations the sex-determining gene tends to be very variable, so diploid individuals are almost always heterozygous, and hence female, while haploids must always be male (they have only one copy of the gene). However, problems arise in small populations which have lost genetic diversity through drift. As diversity at the sex-determining locus declines, the odds of a queen mating with a male carrying the same allele as one of her own increases. If this happens, she produces a colony in which 50% of her workforce are diploid males. Diploid males have low fertility and all males do little or no work in the nest, so this is a major handicap and it seems probable that most such colonies are doomed to die off before they can produce new queens.

Diploid males represent a clear example of inbreeding depression, and have been detected in numerous wild populations of hymenopterans. Their frequency has been suggested to provide a reliable indicator of population fitness and recent modelling work has shown that diploid male production, where present, may initiate a rapid extinction vortex. However, only very recently has diploid male production been detected in naturally occurring populations of bumblebees.

Until recently, studying the population genetics of rare bee species was extremely difficult, as lethal sampling was necessary. Work in this area was greatly aided by the development of a non-lethal DNA sampling technique. This approach has recently been applied to studies of fragmented populations of some of our rarest species: the Moss Carder Bee, Shrill Carder Bee and Great Yellow Bumblebee. All three studies found high levels of population structuring, which suggests that populations are small (and hence subject to rapid genetic drift) and isolated from one another (movement of individuals between populations keeps the populations from becoming genetically different over time). All three rare species appear to have much lower genetic diversity (measured as either allelic richness or heterozygosity) than common British bumblebee species. For example, in the Moss Carder Bee, all populations >10 km apart were significantly genetically different from one another, as were some populations just 3 km apart. Low frequencies of diploid males were found in three of the 16 studied populations. Use of DNA markers can also enable us to group workers into sisterhoods and so estimate the number of colonies (and hence N_e). This has been done for remaining populations of the Shrill Carder Bee. Estimates of N_e were very low (range 21–72) suggesting that these populations are very vulnerable to loss of genetic diversity through drift, and also that they are likely to be prone to chance extinction events. Significant differentiation was found between all populations, suggesting that they are genetically isolated, which in turn suggests that if a population becomes extinct, there is little chance of the site being recolonised from elsewhere. In addition, diploid males were found at low frequency, suggesting that the surviving populations may be suffering from inbreeding.

We do not as yet have unequivocal evidence that inbreeding plays a major role in driving small, isolated populations of bumblebees to extinction, but it seems likely. If reductions in the genetic diversity of neutral markers found in rare species are indicative of reductions in the diversity of functional genes, then there will be serious consequences for population fitness and evolutionary potential. If fragmented populations of rare bumblebee species are suffering from reduced fitness through inbreeding then we must take steps to conserve what genetic diversity remains. Management strategies in vertebrates routinely consider genetic factors, and we may need to adopt similar measures in the management of rare bumblebee populations. In short, the genetic evidence suggests that the Shrill Carder Bee has a bleak and probably short future in Britain unless action is taken. Similar patterns appear to be evident in the Great Yellow Bumblebee.

Why have some species declined more than others?

Interestingly, some bumblebee species appear to have been largely unaffected by habitat loss, fragmentation and degradation. In most of Britain, six species are widespread and common: the Buff-tailed Bumblebee, White-tailed Bumblebee (*B. lucorum*), Red-tailed Bumblebee (*B. lapidarius*), Early Bumblebee (*B. pratorum*), Garden Bumblebee and Common Carder Bee. How do these species differ from those that have declined? Based on studies of forage use, it has been argued that the rare species (which includes all seven BAP species) tend to have narrower diets, with a very large proportion of the pollen they collect being from the pea family (the Fabaceae, vetches, trefoils and clovers, many of which have deep flowers). This group seems to be primarily associated with Fabaceae-rich unimproved grasslands, a habitat which has been very largely eradicated in western Europe. In contrast, the common species tend to have broad foraging preferences and readily encompass non-native garden plants and mass-flowering crops, such as oilseed rape in their diets. It is also noticeable that the common species tend to emerge early from hibernation (February to April), and utilise spring flowers, such as bluebells, that flower early before the trees come in to leaf. In contrast, the rare species emerge later from hibernation (April to June). This would make sense if they are indeed open grassland species, since most grassland plants do not flower until mid-spring. Where nesting habitat is scarce, those species in which queens emerge early in the season may be able to monopolise available nest sites, reducing the chances of colony founding for later emerging queens. Rodent holes may limit bumblebee abundance, and it could be that the earliest emerging species monopolise nest sites.

The apparent dependency of a number of late-emerging bumblebee species on pollen from Fabaceae may prove to have a simple explanation. Fabaceae pollen tends to be rich in protein and in essential amino acids compared to the pollen of other plants frequently visited by bumblebees, such as Asteraceae (daisy family, thistles, knapweeds etc.) or Rosaceae (roses, bramble etc.). This may reflect the fact that Fabaceae are able to obtain atmospheric nitrogen via mutualistic bacteria in their root nodules, and so have a supply of nitrogen from which to build proteins that is not available to most herbaceous plant species. In turn, this explains why Fabaceae thrive in nutrient-poor unimproved grasslands, where growth of most other plant species is limited by the low fertility.

Despite the evidence that most of our rarer species tend to have narrow diets, it seems that most bumblebee species are not strongly associated with particular habitat types. For example, prior to its extinction in Britain, the Short-haired Bumblebee occurred in habitats as diverse as shingle, saltmarshes, sand dunes, and calcareous and neutral unimproved meadows (the one factor these habitats tend to share is low fertility). Although some of the rarer species do appear to exist in very specific habitats, historical records show that most once existed across a much wider range of biotopes (39). For example, the Great Yellow Bumblebee now has a strongly coastal distribution in the far north and west of Britain, and several of the strongest surviving populations are found on coastal machair in the Hebrides. However, 100 years ago, this species was found across Britain at inland locations such as Warwickshire, which conspicuously lack coastal habitat, so it is clearly not a machair or coastal specialist.

The species that are rare and declining in Britain are also declining elsewhere in Europe. It seems that species such as the Shrill Carder Bee and Great Yellow Bumblebee have always had small geographic ranges across Europe, perhaps because they have narrower climatic niches. Their declines in Britain show marked latitudinal shifts, although in opposite directions (the Great Yellow has contracted northwards, the Shrill Carder southwards). This corresponds to a shift towards their range centres in Europe. It seems probable that populations that are near the edge of a species range are more susceptible to environmental degradation (e.g. declines in floral abundance), and so are the first to disappear. Indeed, the one notable feature of all the remaining sites that support Great Yellow Bumblebees in Britain (Hebrides, north coast of Caithness and Sutherland, Orkney) is climatic: they are all windy, cool, damp sites. It is possible that only under these conditions does this species have a competitive edge over other less-hardy bumblebees. Of course the likely consequences of a warming climate for this species need hardly be explained.

In recent years it has become apparent that there are major differences between bumblebee species in their foraging range. Species such as the Buff-tailed Bumblebee and Red-tailed Bumblebee have been found to forage further afield than so-called 'doorstep foragers' such as the Carder Bees. It is perhaps significant that the former two species remain ubiquitous in much of Europe, while four of the five British Carder Bee species are on the BAP list. A larger foraging range would give a greater chance of colony survival in areas where the average density of flowers is low, or where resources are highly patchy. Intensively farmed arable landscapes with occasional fields of mass-flowering crops provide just such a landscape, and it is probably no coincidence that Buff-tailed and Red-tailed Bumblebees are among the species most commonly recruited in large numbers to such crops.

Fortunately, the future for bumblebees in Britain is not all doom and gloom. Agricultural policy in Europe now places an emphasis on combining the goals of agriculture and conservation. Demand for organic food is growing rapidly, and it seems highly likely that organic farming methods (particularly reduced pesticide use and use of leguminous ley crops to boost soil fertility) will be beneficial to bumblebees and many other organisms. Subsidies are currently available for various agri-environment schemes, including maintaining and restoring flower-rich grassland. Most of the management options promote floral abundance and diversity. It has been found that a 6 m wide field margin kept free of crops and agrochemicals may contain six times as many flowering plants and ten times as many flowers than the equivalent cropped area. The effects of field-margin management options on bumblebee communities have been the focus of many studies in recent years. The most valuable form of field-margin management for bumblebees has been found to be the sowing of either a wildflower meadow mix or a pollen and nectar mix, consisting of agricultural cultivars of legume species. Simple pollen and nectar mixes produce the highest flower abundance, with a seasonal succession of forage plants flowering over at least three years following sowing. Wildflower mixtures produced few flowers in the first year, but flower abundance tends to increase over time as they become established. Either seed mixture leads to a rapid increase in bumblebee species richness and abundance. The duration for which these seed mixes remain effective is likely to depend on soil fertility and fertiliser treatment of adjacent crops. If fertility is low, then wildflower mixes can theoretically persist indefinitely. In contrast, agricultural legume cultivars have been selected to grow fast and tall, but are short-lived, and will probably need re-sowing within five years. The trade-off is that agricultural cultivar seed is very cheap compared to wildflower mixtures. Whichever approach is used, creation of flower strips in field margins will undoubtedly provide benefits for a broad range of other flower-visiting insects, in addition to bumblebees.

Studies of forage use by bumblebees suggest that it is not necessarily important to provide a great diversity of flowers. In studies of 15 bumblebee species across a broad range of habitats in Britain, 80% of all pollen collecting visits were to just 11 plant species. Similarly, in studies of bumblebee foraging in sown wildflower strips along field margins, 92% of visits were to just six flowering plant species. It has been found that a diverse sown wildflower field-margin option consisting of 18 herb species is no

Figure 3.3 The applied ecology of corncrakes. These birds nest in grass fields, where they become vulnerable to mowing operations (a) that destroy eggs (b) and chicks. Payments to farmers have led to more sympathetic mowing practices and corncrake populations are recovering as a result. (Photos: Glen Tyler, RSPB.)

Figure 4.1 First introduced to Britain *c.* 1874, the Little Owl is the only naturalised vertebrate that is of practical benefit to man. (Jill Pakenham/BTO.)

Figure 4.2 The Red Kite has been widely and successfully reintroduced in England, Scotland and Ireland, and by 2050 is likely to be widely established. (Jill Pakenham/BTO.)

Figure 5.1 Fritillaries in their classic locality, water meadows by the River Cherwell, Magdalen College, Oxford.

Figure 5.2 'Wild' Rhododendron covering a hillside near Beddgelert, N. Wales.

Figure 5.3 Himalayan Balsam growing as an almost pure stand, Boundary brook, Oxford.

Figure 7.1 The Red Grouse affords the most prestigious and expensive shooting in Britain. To thrive it depends on skillfully managed heather moorland. (Photograph by Laurie Campbell.)

Cormorant (*Phalacrocorax carbo*) in Europe – Breeding Colonies

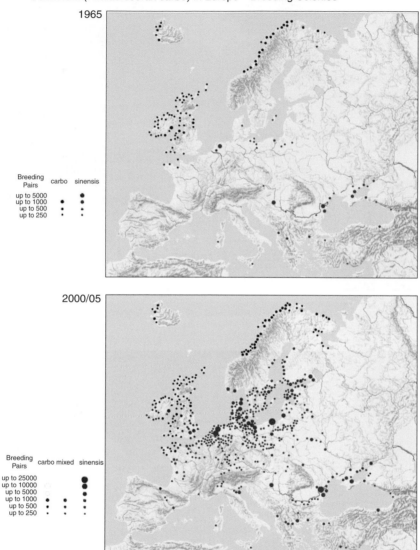

Figure 8.2 Maps of 1965 and 2005 Cormorant distribution across Europe. (Maps compiled from multiple sources by Franz Kohl, Austria.)

Figure 8.3 The Bristol Avon at Limpley Stoke. (Photograph courtesy of the Environment Agency.)

Figure 9.1 Dipper (*Cinclus cinclus*) eggs in Wales are amongst the most highly contaminated with polychlorinated biphenyls anywhere in Europe. (Photograph by Charles R.Tyler.)

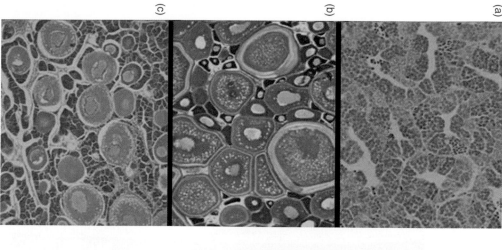

(a)

(b)

(c)

Figure 9.2 Gonadal intersex in Roach (*Rutilus rutilus*), characterised by the presence of developing eggs in the testis of 'male' fish. Panel A shows a section taken through a normal testis with the tiny sperm developing within lobules. Panel B shows a section through a normal ovary illustrating the huge developing eggs (compared with the sperm cells). Panel C shows an intersex gonad, where both male and female sex cells are present in the same gonad.

Figure 9.3 Chemicals with hormone-disrupting activity contributed to the declines in the Otter (*Lutra lutra*) populations in Britain in the 1950s–80s. (Photograph by Charles R Tyler.)

Figure 12.1 Maintaining the biodiversity of our seas will be a test of new marine legislation. (Photograph by Paul Sterry/Nature Photographers Ltd.)

Figure 12.2 Ancient woodland at Bramley Frith, Hampshire – important habitats and species not protected by law, and threatened by infrastructure development. (Photograph by Paul Sterry.)

Figure 13.2 Hugely different ecosystems occur over short ranges in some UK Overseas Territories, as here in St Helena. The foreground is the cloud forest of Tree Ferns, *Dicksonia arborescens*, and other endemics on the Peaks with, in the background, only 5 km away, the desert of Prosperous Bay Plain with many endemic invertebrates. (Photograph by Dr Mike Pienkowski.)

Figure 13.3 Spectacled Petrel, *Procellaria conspicillata*, one of five seabird species which (together with six land-bird species) breed only in the Tristan da Cunha group, this species only on Inaccessible Island. Some of the seabirds range widely outside the breeding season. (Photograph by Dr Mike Pienkowski.)

Figure 13.4 King Penguin, *Aptenodytes paragonicus*, colony and Tussac Grass, *Poa flabel-late*, below glacier, South Georgia. (Photograph by Dr Mike Pienkowski.)

Figure 13.5 Biologically rich garden pond, Middle Caicos, Turks and Caicos Islands, one of the features on a new interpreted nature trail. Seasonal changes in the limestone aquifer raise the water table and create ephemeral ponds that are often deep. (Photograph by Dr Mike Pienkowski.)

Figure 13.6 Endemic Blue Iguana, *Cyclura lewisi*, Grand Cayman – the subject of a current recovery programme. (Photograph by Frederic J. Burton.)

Figure 16.3 The foraging habitat of the Greater Horseshoe Bat (inset).

Figure 17.3 Numbers of Egyptian geese are booming as they spread from Holkham Hall, Norfolk where they were introduced in the Eighteenth century, often using man-made reservoirs and water parks. (Photograph by Rob Robinson/BTO.)

Figure 17.5 Recent declines in curlew populations mean it is one of six species occurring in Britain and Ireland considered as globally Near Threatened. (Photograph by Rob Robinson/BTO.)

Figure 17.6 House Sparrow has recently been placed on the Red List due to large population declines in both urban and rural areas. (Photograph by Rob Robinson/BTO.)

Figure 18.4 Grey Partridge with newly fledged chicks. (Photograph by Jill Pakenham/BTO.)

Figure 19.1 Male Sand Lizard in mature heathland habitat with moss–lichen understorey. This rare species suffered drastic declines due to habitat loss, but is probably stable now.

Figure 19.2 Male Adder basking on gorse in early spring. Adders are declining nationally due to habitat loss and degradation, such as insensitive scrub removal.

Figure 19.3 Male Green Lizard displaying defensive posture. Native only to Jersey, it has been introduced to southern England.

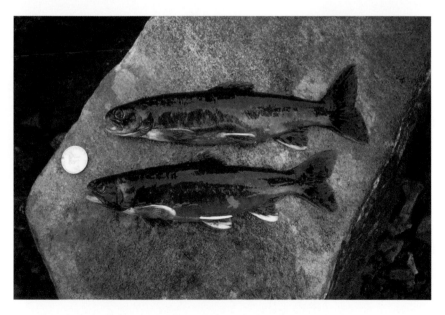

Figure 21.2 Arctic Charr: populations of this species have disappeared in England, Wales, Ireland and Scotland.

Figure 21.4 Vendace: three out of the only four original populations in England and Scotland of this species are extinct.

Mayflies

Caddisflies

Blue Winged Olive (*Serratella ignita*)

Grannom (*Brachcentrus subnubilus*)

Stoneflies

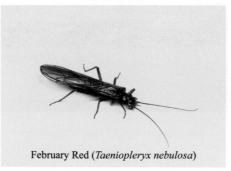

February Red (*Taeniopleryx nebulosa*)

Figure 22.1 The riverflies.

(a)

(b)

(c)

Figure 22.8 Fly boards: (a) fly board in position, (b) bottom of fly boards covered in eggs and (c) female laying eggs on the board.

Figure 23.1 A Great Yellow Bumblebee worker collecting pollen from Red Clover on unimproved flower-rich grasslands on South Uist, Outer Hebrides. This is probably Britain's rarest bumblebee, and is now confined to the far north and west of Scotland. (Photograph by Dave Goulson.)

Figure 23.2 A Shrill Carder bee. This species is associated with flower-rich unimproved grasslands in southern Britain, a habitat which has been all but entirely eradicated leading to precipitous declines in several bumblebee species. (Photograph by Dave Goulson.)

Figure 25.4 Population trends of four widespread moths in Britain 1968–2002: (a) Blood-vein (*Timandra comae*) 79% decrease 1968–2002, (b) White Ermine (*Spilosoma lubricipeda*) 77% decrease, (c) Rosy Footman (*Miltochrista miniata*) 299% increase and (d) Green Silver-lines (*Pseudoips prasinana*) 157% increase. (Photographs by Robert Thompson and Roy Leverton.)

Figure 25.6 Populations of the Garden Tiger (*Arctia caja*) decreased by 89% in Britain over the period 1968–2002. Population levels of this moth are closely correlated with winter temperature and humidity and the species is predicted to decline further as climate change continues. (Photograph by Alan Barnes.)

Figure 28.1 Nymph of *Nezara viridula*, a shieldbug that has recently established in Britain.

Figure 26.1 (a) Female Orange-spotted Emerald, *Oxygastra curtisii* (photograph by David Chelmick). (b) Male Black-tailed Skimmer, *Orthetrum cancellatum* (photograph by Barbara Murphy). (c) Male Southern Damselfly, *Coenagrion mercuriale* (photograph by Phill Watts). (d) Male Northern Damselfly, *Coenagrion hastulatum* (photograph by Dave Smallshire).

(a)

(b)

Figure 26.4 (a) Male White-faced Darter, *Leucorrhinia dubia* (photograph by Helen Wake). (b) Male Brilliant Emerald, *Somatochlora metallica* (photograph by Steve Cham). (c) Male Small Red-eyed Damselfly, *Erythromma viridulum* (photograph by Ann Brooks). (d) Male Red-veined Darter, *Sympetrum fonscolombii,* with zygopteran exuvia on its perch (photograph by Steve Cham).

(c)

(d)

Figure 26.4 (cont.)

Figure 26.9 (a) Male Banded Demoiselle [Banded Jewelwing], *Calopteryx splendens* (photograph by Dave Smallshire). (b) Female White-legged Damselfly, *Platycnemis pennipes* (photograph by Steve Cham). (c) Male Club-tailed Dragonfly, *Gomphus vulgatissimus* (photograph by Dave Smallshire). (d) Female Scarce Chaser, *Libellula fulva* (photograph by Steve Cham).

(c)

(d)

Figure 26.9 (cont.)

Figure 28.2 *Athysanus argentarius*, a leafhopper that has recently expanded its range inland and northwards from its formerly southern coastal distribution.

Figure 29.1 Southern Oak Bush-cricket (*Meconema meridionale*) male (left) and female (right). (Photograph courtesy of Ted Benton.)

Figure 31.1 Wasp Spider, *Argiope bruennichi*. First recorded in Sussex in 1922, this species has spread since the 1970s. By 2008 there was at least one substantial breeding colony in Cambridgeshire, with individual records as far north as Derbyshire. (Photograph by Philip Precey.)

Figure 32.1 Freshwater Pearl Mussel (*Margaritifera margaritifera*). (Photograph by Pete McCullough.)

Figure 33.2 (left) The Elmer sea defence system near Bognor Regis on the south coast of England. These defences have modified sedimentary habitats (Martin *et al.* 2005) and provided new habitat for rocky shore species (Moschella *et al.* 2005) – as well as preventing flooding to nearby homes.

Figure 33.3 (right) Plastic debris littering the strandline providing an unsightly environment and a hazard to marine and terrestrial wildlife, as well as a danger to the public (Thompson *et al.* 2004). (Picture courtesy of Dr R.C. Thompson.)

(a) 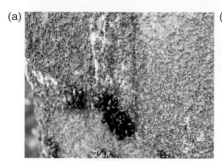 (b)

Figure 33.4 Homogenisation of assemblages on artificial structures: barnacles (*Elminius modestus*) and mussels (*Mytilus* spp.) (a) Quay wall in Nelson Harbour, New Zealand and (b) sea defences on the Wirral, Merseyside, UK. *Elminius* was introduced to Britain from Australasia in the mid-1940s and *Mytilus* is currently thought to have been introduced to Australasia. Both species are successful invaders and are now common sights on artificial structures.

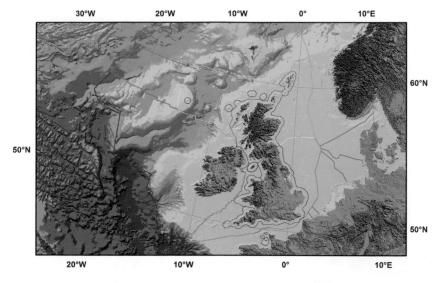

Figure 34.1 Continental Shelf Area boundaries (red line Territorial sea limit, yellow line UK CSA, pink line Ireland CSA).

Figure 34.3 Mixed sediment seabed on the steep slopes of the tributaries at around 140 m depth with dense aggregations of the crinoid, *Leptometra celtica*, and the squat lobster, *Munida* spp.

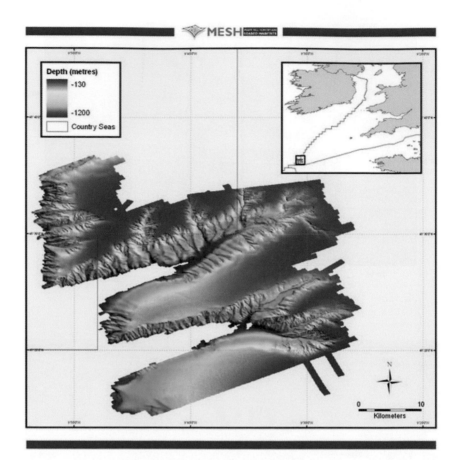

Figure 34.2 High-resolution topographic image of the seabed in the south-west approaches showing a series of canyons that varied in depth from 138 m to 1165 m with a complex network of tributary valleys.

Figure 35.1 Corn Cockles at a reintroduction site.

Figure 35.2 Cowslips in one of the few remaining 'unimproved' hay meadows of southern England, Yarnton, Oxfordshire.

Figure 35.3   A flower-rich hay meadow in June with Greater Burnet, Red Clover, Knapweed, Rough Hawkbit, Ox-eye Daisy and other plants, Oxfordshire.

Figure 36.1 Young Gannet entangled in nylon ropes from discarded fishing tackle. (Reproduced by kind permission of James Fair.)

more beneficial to bumblebees than a simple sown wildflower option consisting of only three herbaceous species. All studies concur in that Red Clover is an important pollen source for many rare species and also some of the common ones (including all of the Carder Bees, the Great Yellow Bumblebee and the Ruderal Bumblebee). Studies of the only surviving population of British origin of the Short-haired Bumblebee, in New Zealand (to which they were introduced in 1895) show that this species, too, has a strong dependency on Red Clover. As mentioned earlier, one feature of the agricultural changes that have occurred in Britain is the loss of Red Clover ley crops, and this single change could have played a major role in driving declines of bumblebees. There is clear evidence that Red Clover is now much less common than it once was in Britain. Also, it is notable that parts of eastern Europe, such as southern Poland still retain high bumblebee diversity (although now declining), and their agricultural systems still include Red Clover leys, which swarm with both rare and common bumblebees.

Bumblebees not only require a suitable source of forage, but also nest and hibernation sites. A popular agri-environment scheme in Britain is the sowing of field margins with tussocky grasses, or creation of such strips across the centre of fields ('beetle banks'). These habitats attract the small mammals whose abandoned holes are used by bumblebees for nest sites, so it is likely that this form of management is of value to bumblebees. It has been found that it is possible to combine wildflowers and tussocky grasses in a single mix that provides both nest sites and flowers for bumblebees.

Urban areas as bumblebee hotspots

Urbanisation is generally viewed by conservationists negatively, but there is evidence that gardens and urban parks are particular strongholds for some species of bumblebee. Young nests of the Buff-tailed Bumblebee placed in suburban gardens have been found to grow more quickly and attain a larger size than nests placed in arable farmland. It is likely that gardens provide favourable habitat for several bumblebee species as a result of the density, variety and continuity of flowers that they provide, and recent studies suggest that bumblebee nest densities are higher in gardens than in farmland. However, many commonly used garden plants are unsuitable for bumblebees. Artificial selection has often resulted in modern flower varieties which provide little or no reward (such as sterile F1 hybrid flowers), or which are inaccessible to insects. Similarly, some exotic plants, such as those pollinated by hummingbirds, provide rewards that are inaccessible to native species. It is clear that urban gardens can provide a refuge for several bumblebee species, but encouraging gardeners to choose their plants appropriately could make them much better. This said, it is notable that although gardens can support high densities of the common bumblebee species, rarer bumblebees do not seem to thrive in gardens, unless the gardens are immediately adjacent to high-quality semi-natural habitat (for example, Great Yellow Bumblebees commonly visit garden flowers in the Uists). The reasons for this remain unclear.

Perhaps unexpectedly, urban areas provide another benefit for bumblebees in the form of brownfield sites. Some of the strongest surviving populations of the Shrill Carder, Moss Carder and Brown-banded Carder in southern England are on brown-field sites along the Thames Estuary. These sites are often rather less than scenic, with burnt-out cars and abandoned buildings, but a combination of low soil fertility and little disturbance over several decades have often led to the development of rich wild-flower swards and exceptionally high invertebrate diversity. Sadly, these sites are rarely recognised as important to biodiversity and are targeted for development. Further loss of habitat could easily prove fatal to species such as the Shrill Carder that are close to extinction in Britain.

Bumblebees new to Britain

There is one notable bumblebee success story in Britain. In 2001, the Tree Bumblebee, *B. hypnorum*, was first recorded in Britain (in Hampshire), having somehow crossed the channel from mainland Europe, where it is widespread. It has since spread steadily northwards as far as Hull, with unconfirmed sightings in Scotland. So far as we know, it was a natural invasion, and there is no reason to believe that it threatens our native species (the Tree Bumblebee is short-tongued and seems to thrive alongside our com-mon species in gardens). There has been a second addition to the British Bumblebee fauna in recent years, although not the result of an invasion. Genetic and pheromonal studies provide compelling evidence that *B. cryptarum* (the Cryptic Bumblebee?), a species known from Europe and with a very similar appearance to the White-tailed bumblebee, is alive and well in Britain. It would appear to be widespread and possibly common, occurring from southern England to the Hebrides. However, it is virtually indistinguishable from the White-tailed Bumblebee, with only very subtle morpho-logical differences in the queens, and no known morphological differences between workers or males, so it seems that this species is native, but has simply been overlooked until now. This is quite remarkable that in a country such as Britain, with a long his-tory and tradition of entomological study, that we have been unaware of the existence of a large and abundant insect species for so long. One must wonder how many other cryptic species await identification.

Conclusion

In summary, widespread declines of bumblebee species threaten pollination services to both wildflowers and crops. It is clear from studies of population structure that most bumblebee species cannot be conserved by managing small protected 'islands' of habi-tat within a 'sea' of unsuitable, intensively farmed land. Large areas of suitable habitat are needed to support viable populations in the long term. Also, studies of foraging range indicate that bumblebees exploit forage patches at a landscape scale, so that the scale of management must be appropriate. An integrated approach across large areas or several farms is more likely to succeed than localised efforts. Where small, isolated populations of rare species remain in habitat fragments, targeting the adjacent farms for uptake of suitable agri-environment schemes could increase the population size and so reduce the likelihood of chance extinction events and inbreeding. Similarly, such schemes could be used to provide linkage between habitat islands. Unimproved flower-rich grassland is one of the most important habitats for bumblebees, but has been largely lost to agriculture. Restoration of areas of this habitat will boost bumblebee populations and has been shown to provide improved pollination services on nearby farmed land. Substantial benefits could also be obtained by reintroducing clover ley crops into rotations, since this is a key forage source for many declining bumblebee species. Finally, long-term monitoring of bumblebee populations (not just distributions) is required in order to build up a picture of the current status of bumblebee species and to establish baselines to which future studies can refer.

References

Carvell, C., Roy, D.B., Smart, S.M. *et al.* (2006). Declines in forage availability for bumblebees at a national scale. *Biological Conservation,* **132**, 481–489.

Goulson, D., Hanley, M.E., Darvill, B., Ellis, J.S. and Knight, M.E . (2005). Causes of rarity in bumblebees. *Biological Conservation,* **122**, 1–8.

Goulson, D., Lye, G.C. and Darvill, B. (2008). Decline and conservation of bumblebees. *Annual Review of Entomology,* **53**, 191–208.

Williams, P.H., Araujo, M.B. and Rasmont, P. (2007). Can vulnerability among British bumblebee (*Bombus*) species be explained by niche position and breadth? *Biological Conservation,* **138**, 493–505.

24

Butterflies

J.A. Thomas

Summary

The average rate of decline of butterfly species in the British Isles has been high in recent decades, exceeding that of breeding birds or native vascular plants. Nearly a third of species, however, has increased, and several have expanded their ranges northwards. Some clear patterns are evident from these changes. Most losses are attributable to a decline of the specialised habitats required by the caterpillar stages in species' life cycles, either through fundamental ecosystem destruction, for example through intensive farming, or more subtle degradation, when surviving ecosystems have become shadier or more overgrown. The fragmentation of extensive breeding sites into small isolated patches has also been a major obstacle for some species. Climate warming, to date, has benefited all but the few northern species of butterfly, but is likely to become a major driver of decline in future decades. It was only after conservationists began to understand the causes of change in British butterflies that they were able to restore populations, through targeted land management, to former ecosystems. This process began successfully in the 1970s, and is probably responsible for the survival today of the Heath Fritillary, Silver-spotted Skipper and Adonis Blue.

Introduction

Just 71 species of butterfly have regularly been recorded in the British Isles since the first list of native insects was published in 1634, by Thomas Moffett in *Insectorum Theatrum*. Eight of these, moreover, are such rare vagrants from abroad that even the most diligent naturalist is unlikely to encounter them more than once or twice in a lifetime. And sadly, a further five species are extinct, although one, the Large Blue

Silent Summer: The State of Wildlife in Britain and Ireland, ed. Norman Maclean. Published by Cambridge University Press. © Cambridge University Press 2010.

(*Maculinea arion*), has been successfully reintroduced and has spread to 30 carefully managed sites in the West Country. That leaves 59 butterfly species that currently breed each year in the British Isles, a trivial number compared with the roughly 27 000 species of other insect that have been recorded in the British Isles or indeed with the 20 000 butterfly species known worldwide. Yet British butterflies are of considerable interest. Not only are they an extremely popular group, almost the only insects that many naturalists notice or enjoy; they are also – and not unconnectedly – the most thoroughly monitored and scientifically studied taxon of insects in the world. For example, every week from 1 April to the end of September, about 1500 predominantly amateur UK recorders take part in a strictly regulated 1–2 hour census, or 'Pollard Walk', for the Butterfly Monitoring Scheme, counting the numbers of every species seen along fixed transects on over 400 sites from Lands End and Ventor to Co. Tyrone and the northern Highlands. This has provided an accurate time series of changes in population size in every generation and year since 1976 for the large majority of native species across the United Kingdom. In addition, no fewer than 10 000 naturalists submitted a staggering 1.8 million records of sightings to the national butterfly recording scheme during the past decade, making British butterflies four times more intensively mapped, per species, than either plants or breeding birds, and 14 times more so per species than dragonflies, the next most thoroughly recorded British insect group (Thomas 2005). Indeed, due to the rigour with which they have been monitored, coupled with their sensitivity to environmental change and their usefulness as indicators for other terrestrial invertebrates, the British butterfly fauna is frequently referred to as the 'miner's canary' of the insect world.

Changes in the abundance of British butterflies

Fifty years ago, in the early days of conservation, it was widely assumed that insects would be less vulnerable than larger, slow-breeding vertebrates or plants to the impacts of human-induced environmental changes, such as habitat destruction, degradation and fragmentation; pollution; overexploitation and, more recently, climate change. This view prevails in much of the world today, and it seems probable that the megafauna – which in Britain included Bison, Auroch, Wild Horse, Bear, Wolf, Lynx and, from an earlier age, Irish Elk, Mammoth and Saber-toothed Cats – did experience national or global extinctions associated with hunting and the habitat changes inflicted by early humans at a greater rate than was the case with prehistoric invertebrates. Probable, but not certain: for the two groups to experience most recorded extinctions following the clearance of the South American Atlantic Rain Forest in recent centuries have been parrots and butterflies (Brown and Brown 1992).

In modern times, it became evident during the 1970s that British butterfly populations were disappearing from individual sites, including many nature reserves, at rates that were an order of magnitude higher than those reported for our current vertebrate or plant species (Thomas 1984). To take an extreme, but unexceptional, example: the 157 ha broad-leaved National Nature Reserve of Monks Wood in Cambridgeshire supported populations of 35 butterfly species when it was declared a reserve in 1953, yet within 30 years, 11 of these butterflies were locally extinct, including all but four of the 15 national or local rarities for which the wood had been famed. In contrast, none of these butterflies' larval food plants declined noticeably during the same period, while just two out of 48 breeding birds and one out of 25 mammal species disappeared. Similar scales of loss were reported for butterflies in their other principal ecosystems of heathland, fen and most types of semi-natural grassland (Thomas 1991).

The realisation that most (but by no means all) butterfly species were experiencing disproportionately high declines dismayed conservationists, who had hitherto assumed that the modern British countryside, whilst perhaps ill-suited for certain large birds and mammals, could nonetheless provide adequate habitats for our flora, insects, fish and other small animals through the strategy of conserving numerous, mainly 10–100 ha-sized nature reserves across the lowland landscapes of Europe. This seemed a reasonable assumption at the time. For example, about 80% of British butterfly species live in predominantly closed populations (rather than in open or migratory ones), and large populations of 93% of the colonial species can be supported by a patch of suitable habitat that is less than 10 ha in size; a third of species frequently exist in patches of 0.5–1 ha (Thomas 1984).

By the 1980s it was clear that amplified losses among butterflies had occurred, not just in single sites, but across whole landscapes and regions. For example, in the county of Suffolk, 42% of resident butterfly species became extinct between the 1850s and 1980s, compared with a 5% loss of plant species and 3% of mammals, whilst there had actually been a net gain of 14% in breeding bird species over the same period, thanks partly to enlightened conservation measures (Thomas 1991). A landmark towards understanding the full scale of these changes was provided by Heath *et al.*'s (1984) first *Atlas of Butterflies in Britain and Ireland*, which drew upon more than a quarter of a million past and current records of the distribution of every species through an unprecedented survey organised by John Heath at the Biological Records Centre. It confirmed not only that the majority of our butterfly species was in decline, but also that many declines were widespread across the British Isles and were of greater magnitude than anyone had perceived.

Gloomier still were the results of a yet more comprehensive second survey of butterfly distributions, organised by the Butterfly Conservation Society in 1995–2000, which resulted in the magnificent *Millenium Atlas of Butterflies in Britain and Ireland* (Figure 24.1, Asher *et al.* 2001). Records from Ireland in the Heath atlas were too few to make an accurate comparison between the two surveys, but the data for Scotland, Wales and England were more or less complete, allowing a precise assessment of change to be made for every butterfly species native to Great Britain in the 25 years up to the millennium. Moreover, the publication of twin atlases for both breeding birds and plants over roughly similar periods meant that changes in butterflies could be

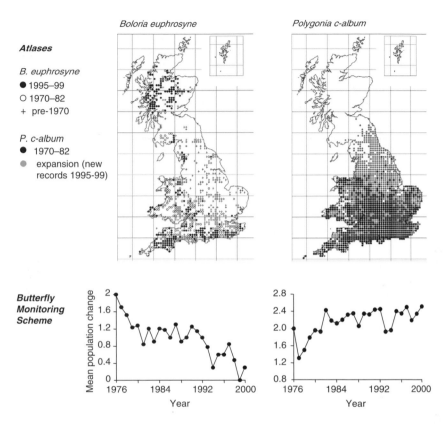

Figure 24.1 Changes in distribution, detected through atlases, and in population sizes (log scale) of surviving populations, measured through the Butterfly Monitoring Scheme, of the declining Pearl-bordered Fritillary (*Boloria euphrosyne*) and the expanding Comma (*Polygonia c-album*). (From Thomas 2005.)

directly compared with them. The results made sober reading (Figure 24.2, Thomas *et al.* 2004). They showed that 70% of UK butterfly species had declined during that period, and that the median decline in species' distributions (–13%) was an order of magnitude more severe than the median changes in birds (–2%) and native vascular plant species (+7%), when plotted at the same scale of species' presence or absence in 10-km grid squares.

This analysis was supported by a more sensitive measure of changing butterfly abundances, the Butterfly Monitoring Scheme (BMS), which generates trends in most species' population sizes long before they manifest themselves as losses (or expansions) in the 10-km squares of the national grid (Figure 24.1). As expected, there is a strong correlation between the average size a species' trend in numbers on fixed

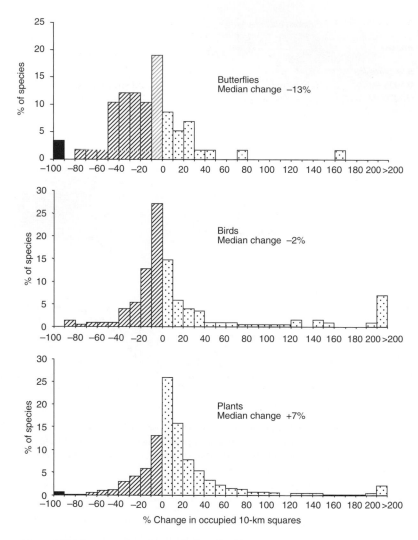

Figure 24.2 The proportion of butterfly, breeding bird and native vascular plant species that increased or decreased in the United Kingdom during the last decades of the twentieth century. Black = extinct; diagonal hatch = declining species; stipple = increasing species. (From Thomas *et al.* 2004.)

sites since 1976 and the range changes measured between the two atlases: thus, over and above the roughly 50% loss in distribution of the Pearl-border Fritillary (*Boloria euphrosyne*) over the 25 years up to the millenium, the average number flying in those populations that still survived in 2000 was roughly 5% the density at which they had existed on the same sites in 1976 (Figure 24.1). On the other hand, it is important to note that not every butterfly species is in decline in the British Isles. About 30% were stable or have increased during the past 30 years, none more spectacularly than the Comma (*Polygonia c-album*), which expanded its range northwards by several hundred kilometres, reaching deep into Scotland by 2008, and simultaneously increased in density by about threefold in its former stronghold of southern England (Figure 24.1). It is worth noting too that these changes are by no means confined to the British Isles. Although less precisely monitored, there is burgeoning evidence that regional butterfly extinctions have been as great, and in many cases greater, across much of Europe, particularly in the more intensively managed western nations and at lower altitudes north of the Mediterranean. Although in most cases not strictly comparable due to their smaller sizes, Belgium, the Netherlands, Denmark, Luxemburg, Poland and the Czech Republic have all experienced a higher percentage of national butterfly extinctions than the British Isles; in the case of the Netherlands, 21% of former species are extinct compared to 8% since 1664 in Britain.

Are butterflies indicators of change in other insects?

There has been considerable debate as to whether the dramatic changes seen in butterfly ranges and abundance are typical of other less-well-monitored insect groups. Some argue, correctly, that the proportion of butterfly species that is known to have become extinct in the British Isles during the twentieth century is substantially higher than that recorded for most other insect taxa, and have concluded, in my view incorrectly, that butterflies are atypically sensitive to environmental changes, whereas other insects are more robust. The counter-argument is that nearly every other group of insect is so poorly recorded in Britain and Ireland that many rare species have yet to be discovered, and – as has been demonstrated across the world for all organisms studied in this way (including British butterflies) – it is the rarest species on national lists that are most prone to extinction. In other words, although the reported national extinction rate of hoverfly species was lower than that of butterflies during the twentieth century, the former is likely to have been underestimated because accumulation curves show that dipterists are today discovering new British hoverfly species at a similar rate to the additions made in the early 1900s, whereas lepidopterists had discovered more or less all our butterfly species by the mid-nineteenth century (Figure 24.3a). This implies not only that there is still an appreciable number of rare hoverfly species that await discovery in the British Isles, but that several of these will, and have, become extinct before they are ever found. A critical examination of other invertebrates, ranging from weevils to spiders, bears this argument out. Apart from butterflies, only dragonflies and bumblebees were so well recorded by early entomologists that more than 90% of the currently recognised British species had been discovered by 1900, and in both groups a slightly higher proportion of species were

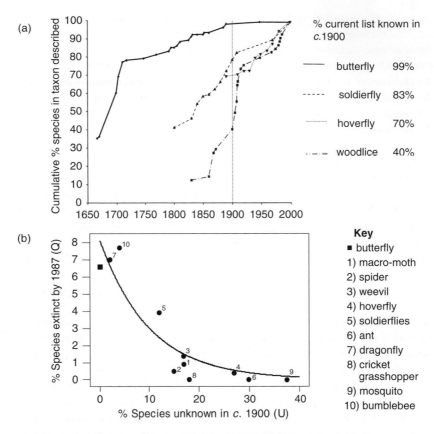

Figure 24.3 (a) Accumulation curves of the rates of discovery of four species of terrestrial invertebrate in the British Isles since records began. (b) The proportion of recorded species extinctions in 11 groups of invertebrate in the Great Britain between 1900 and 1987, compared with the state of recording of each species in 1900. (From Thomas and Clarke 2004; Thomas 2005.)

extinct in the British Isles a hundred years later than was the case with butterflies. Furthermore, when the proportion of species that was undiscovered a century ago is factored into the recorded extinction rates of eight other insect groups between 1900 and 1987 (the date of the first Red Data Book of British insects), butterfly extinction rates appear, alas, to be closely in line with those of other taxa (Figure 24.3b, $r^2 = 0.92$, $n = 11$). Further support for this still tentative conclusion comes from the steep declines in moth populations recorded in the Rothamsted trapping scheme, which match those of butterflies (Conrad *et al.* 2006), and from recent surveys of the status of bumblebees.

Patterns in the recent changes of British butterflies

Within the wide spectrum of change, from the extinction of the Large Blue and Large Tortoiseshell (*Nymphalis polychloros*) to the extraordinary expansion of the Comma and Speckled Wood (*Pararge aegeria*), clear-cut patterns emerge associated with the lifestyles of different species. These, in turn, shed light on the drivers of change, discussed more fully below. Extending Hodgson's (1993) perceptive analysis of the different ecological characteristics of the larval food plants of rare vs. common butterflies, Pollard and Eversham (1995) observed that a dichotomy existed in British species, and that local or rare butterflies were getting rarer, whilst the common and widespread ones were getting commoner. The two atlas surveys confirmed that there had been an almost universal decline among specialist (i.e. the rarer) butterfly species whose larval food plant(s) are generally adapted to nutrient poor soils (e.g. violets, vetches, fine or moorland grasses, *Primula*, Rockrose, Devil's-bit Scabious, Wild Strawberry, Cow-wheat) and which, also as larvae, exploit much narrower and more specialised niches within ecosystems than their uncompetitive food plants. In contrast, most butterflies that have increased are more generalist in their larval resources, and typically feed on two or more abundant plants, especially on the coarser species of grass and nettles that flourish in nutrient-rich soils (Warren *et al.* 2001). This latter group of increasing species encompasses most, but not quite all, of the roughly one-third of butterflies that has historically been common and widespread, at least in the southern half of England. Two exceptions are the Small Heath (*Coenonympha pamphilus*) and Wall (*Lasiommata megera*), once common, but much diminished today; it is probably no coincidence that, unlike most widespread butterflies, their caterpillars feed, respectively, on fine grasses and in a narrow niche.

Comparing ecosystems, those butterflies that breed predominantly in woods have declined considerably more than the so-called 'grassland species' during the past 30 years (Thomas 2005). Among the former, species whose larvae feed on plants of the woodland floor, rather than on the leaves or flowers of shrubs or trees, have generally experienced the steepest falls (see 'Habitat degradation'). This is not to say that there have not been extraordinary declines, too, in Britain's surviving semi-natural grasslands. On limestone and chalk, which provide the richest grassland habitats for butterflies, it is again the more specialised species that have borne the greatest losses. For example, seven species of Blue and another lycaenid (Blues, Coppers, Hairstreaks), the Green Hairstreak (*Callophrys rubi*), possess remarkable adaptations that allow their caterpillars and pupae to interact with ants. All possess glands that secrete sugars and amino acids that are particularly attractive to Red (*Myrmica*) and Yellow Meadow or Black (*Lasius*) Ants; in exchange for nutritious secretions, the worker ants protect the feeding larvae during their later instars, and may bury and tend them and the pupae in loose earthen cells. Some species of Blue are more intimately adapted to ants than others. Thus, the Silver-studded Blue (*Plebejus argus*) lays eggs on suitable food plants growing only along the edges of Black Ant, *Lasius niger*, nests, in whose colonies the caterpillars and pupae spend most of their lives, while the Large Blue (*Maculinea arion*) has eschewed a phytophagous (plant-eating) life-style in the final (10 month) larval stage and has evolved as a mimic of one species of Red Ant, *Mymica sabuleti*, in whose societies it lives and feeds by preying on the ant brood. As semi-natural grasslands have deteriorated in quality, there has been a consistent order of population extinctions among butterflies, with the most closely integrated myrmecophiles, notably Large, Silver-studded and Adonis (*Polyommatus bellargus*) Blues, typically becoming extinct first, whereas species with weak (e.g. Common Blue, *Polyommatus icarus*) or no interaction with ants have been more persistent (Thomas *et al.* 2005).

A final pattern among the recent changes in butterfly distributions is that about a quarter of species has spread northwards in recent decades, in some cases reoccupying regions from which they retreated during the nineteenth century, in others extending beyond historical ranges. In addition to the expansions of the Comma and Speckled Wood described above, notable extensions north have occurred in Large (*Ochlodes venata*), Small (*Thymelicus sylvestris*) and Essex Skippers (*T. lineola*) (the latter also westwards), the Peacock (*Inachis io*), Orange Tip (*Anthocharis cardamines*), Gatekeeper (*Pyronia tithonus*), Wall and Marbled White (*Melanargia galathea*). Not all these species have increased in absolute terms; the Wall, for example, has simultaneously become much rarer within its original British range, where numerous local extinctions have occurred (Fox *et al.* 2006). These shifts reflect the fact that most native butterfly species, unlike their food plants, are living near the northern limits of their global (climatic) ranges in the British Isles, and have traditionally been confined to the warmer climates of the south. The modest degree of global warming experienced across the British Isles in recent decades has permitted some, but not all, of the warmth-loving species to colonise northern landscapes that were previously too cool for them (see 'Climate Change'). A similar pattern of northwards shifts has occurred across the continent of Europe, accompanied by a retraction in range by the same species at their southern climatic limits, especially in Mediterranean ecosystems (Parmesan *et al.* 1999). Only four British butterflies are northern or alpine species, which reach their southern limits in the northern half of the British Isles (Large Heath, *Coenonympha tullia*, Scotch Argus, *Erebia aethiops*, Mountain Ringlet, *Erebia epiphron*, Northern Brown Argus, *Aricia artaxerxes*). Although all four have declined in recent years, population losses to date are largely attributable to habitat changes; only the Mountain Ringlet, which has disappeared from many lower-altitude sites, while persisting at high altitudes, shows a pattern of losses consistent with climate warming. All four northern species, however, are predicted to retreat as climate warming continues, and, indeed, the hitherto beneficial effect on our more thermophilous butterfly species is also predicted to break down under more extreme change. These possibilities are discussed further in the section 'Climate Change'.

Causes of change in the abundance
and ranges of butterflies

The ecology of British butterflies is sufficiently well understood to generalise about the main drivers of recent population changes, even though knowledge about the precise ecological requirements of several species is still inadequate for their successful conservation. Nearly every decline can be attributed to fundamental habitat loss or to the degradation and increased isolation of surviving patches of habitat, whereas most increases are attributable to a combination of moderate climate warming and an increase in the butterfly's specific habitat within semi-natural ecosystems.

With three of the above four drivers of change, the critical stage in the life cycle is the caterpillar. Almost without exception among species whose population dynamics have been rigorously studied, the adult stage was found to have more catholic (generalist) requirements than had previously been supposed, whereas the (usually inconspicuous) caterpillar was much more specialised. From apparently generalist, common species such as the Small White (*Pieris rapae*) and Common Blue (*Polommatus icarus*), to more specialist ones such as the Wood White (*Leptidea sinapis*), White Admiral (*Ladoga Camilla*) and Brown Argus (*Aricia agestis*), the caterpillar typically feeds only on a sub-set of its food plant(s) growing under highly specific ecological conditions, for example in a narrow (often ephemeral) successional stage of its ecosystem that may be associated with an optimum microclimate for that species, or on a particular growth form or physiological state of its plant, such as very young or mature growth, or plants with exceptionally nitrogen-rich or lush leaves or flowering parts (Thomas 1991). As described above, certain Blues survive only if their food plant also co-exists with a single species of ant. Thus, by and large, the caterpillar stage is restricted to a much narrower niche within ecosystems than had once been assumed, and a population often exploits less than 1% of its caterpillars' food plants growing in a woodland, grassland or heathland. In most cases, the average population size of a butterfly species on a site is closely correlated with the number of suitable food plants that are present, which may bear little relationship to (and indeed can be inversely correlated with) the absolute population size of its plant species. In contrast, although the adult butterflies may have favourite nectar sources (particular flowers or aphid honeydew), in all well-studied examples, the adults will switch to less-favoured sources with no detectable impact on their numbers (Thomas 1984, 1991).

In two respects the adult stage can, however, be the limiting factor in determining the local status of butterflies. Some species require a certain amount of shelter; windswept sites may be unsuitable for a colony even if the caterpillar's food plant is growing under optimum conditions. More importantly, the adult is the only significant stage for dispersal in the life cycle of a butterfly. For reasons discussed more fully in the section 'Habitat patch fragmentation and isolation', many species of butterfly have surprisingly sedentary adults, and when former sites become less suitable, they are often unable to track the generation of new patches of habitat in a landscape or region quickly enough for the species to persist.

Fundamental habitat loss

It is undisputed that the agricultural 'improvement' of most land in the British Isles has caused fundamental losses of ecosystems, and with them their characteristic butterflies. For example, The Rev. F.O. Morris (1853) wrote of the extinction of the Large Copper (*Lysandra dispar*) following the draining of the Fens and their conversion to arable:

> Science, with one of her many triumphs, has here truly achieved a mighty and a valuable victory, and the land that was once productive of fever and ague, now scarce yields to any in broad England in the weight of its golden harvest... The entomologist is the only person who has cause to lament the change, and he, loyal and patriotic subject as he is, must not repine even at the loss of the Large Copper Butterfly in the face of such vast and magnificent advantages. Still he may be pardoned for casting 'one long lingering look behind,' and I cannot but with regret recall the time when almost any number of this dazzling fly was easily procurable.

During the twentieth century, the intensification of agriculture resulted in the fundamental loss of the large majority of neutral, chalk and limestone grasslands, and lowland heathlands as breeding sites for butterflies (Thomas 1991). Most combinations of drainage, ploughing, reseeding with modern cultivars, spraying with herbicides and the application of artificial fertilisers caused more or less every native wild food plant used by caterpillars to be eliminated from intensively farmed ley fields, apart from those of the Clouded Yellow (*Colias croceus*), which feed readily on sown clovers. In arable, only the two 'Cabbage Whites', *Pieris brassicea* and *P. rapae*, are able to breed, and then only as pests on Brassica crops. Weedy meadows, containing ruderals, such as thistles and nettles, may also support the Painted Lady (*Cynthia cardui*) and Small Tortoiseshell (*Aglais urticae*), but, otherwise, butterflies are restricted to a few common species on intensive farmland that can breed on hedge and ditch-side plants.

Habitat degradation

As described in earlier sections, numerous local extinctions of butterflies have also occurred on sites that appear not to have changed in obvious ways, and where the larval food plants and other resources remain abundant. Nor have conservation areas or nature reserves been exempt. Thomas (1991) lists four species (Large Copper, Large Blue, Heath Fritillary, *Mellicta athalia*, Chequered Skipper, *Carterocephalus palaemon*) that became extinct on every nature reserve that supported their populations during 1960–80. Fortunately, following the application of detailed research into their ecology, the last three species flourish again on certain reserves, where their specialised larval habitat requirements have been restored through targeted site management.

There were, in fact, two subtle changes that occurred within the large majority of semi-natural terrestrial ecosystems of the British Isles during the second half of the twentieth century, and in many cases since the late nineteenth century. Grasslands, fen, heathlands and woodlands all shifted to predominantly later stages of vegetational succession, especially at low altitudes, due to new practices in agriculture and forestry. And whereas traditional forms of management generated a diversity of seral stages that co-existed within an individual down-, wood- or heathland, modern land usage generates more homogeneous islands of habitat.

On farmland (including heathland), the agri-chemical revolution that enabled farmers to increase production on flat, fertile terrain was accompanied by the partial or complete abandonment of most of the semi-natural ecosystems that were spared, the majority being steep or thin-soiled hillsides that had become uneconomical to farm. This trend occurred across western Europe, although on many British sites, the reduction of domestic grazing was temporarily replaced by that of vast rabbit populations. When myxomatosis eliminated rabbits as a significant grazing force in the 1950s, the shift from open, early successional, herb-rich swards to denser, taller ones was almost universal. This caused a clear-cut sequence of local extinctions among butterflies starting, typically, within 2–5 years of abandonment, with the Grayling (*Hipparchia semele*), Silver-spotted Skipper (*Hesperia comma*), Adonis, Large and Silver-studded Blues. All five species bred exclusively in the earliest stages of grass- and heathlands, not because they required small or close-cropped growth-forms of their larval food-plants per se, but because under prevailing British climates they survived only in the warmest spots where the turf was sufficiently short for the sun to bake the ground. For these five butterflies, the average daytime temperature in the micro-habitats used by their larvae falls by about 5 °C during their spring or autumn growth periods if the average height of the sward increases from 1 cm to 5 cm tall (Thomas 1991). From the mid-1950s onwards, this swiftly rendered most former breeding grounds unsuitable, years or decades before their larval food plants were shaded out, although the ants with which the Blues interact declined as rapidly as the butterflies. Indeed, in the case of the Silver-spotted Skipper and Grayling, the fine grass species on which they depend generally increased in abundance as the butterflies disappeared from sites, when these grew from the sparse small tufts favoured for egg-laying into taller denser swards (Thomas 1991). Longer periods of abandonment saw the loss of most other characteristic 'short' or 'medium grassland' butterflies (Anon 1986), again usually several years before the larval food plants experienced noticeable declines. Not every grassland species was a loser. Species of Brown that bred in taller swards generally increased, although some, including the Marbled White (*Melanargia galathea*) and Meadow Brown (*Maniola jurtina*) were gradually supplanted a decade or two later as coarse grass species began to dominate swards. These are the habitats of four of our five 'Golden' Skippers – the Large (*Ochlodes venata*), Small (*Thymelicus sylvestris*), Essex (*Thymelicus lineola*) and Lulworth (*Thymelicus action*). All increased greatly from the 1960s onwards on many unfarmed downs and hillsides, although only the Lulworth Skipper, which is restricted to steep southern south-facing slopes, showed a net gain; local increases by the other three species were more than offset by the destruction of colonies on intensively farmed, flatter land.

The area of woodland in the United Kingdom has roughly doubled in the two centuries since its nadir during the Napoleonic Wars, yet local extinctions of its characteristic butterflies have been greater than the losses in other biotopes. A major factor has been the changed structure of most British woods. Whereas a high proportion of woodland was managed as coppice, or coppice with low-density standards, for hundreds or thousands of years before the early twentieth century, commercial coppicing is now virtually obsolete. Many broad-leaved woods and twentieth-century plantations have been left to grow into high forest, with the result that the woodland floor is much shadier, and very much cooler, than in the past. Since 32 of the 42 species of butterfly that regularly bred in woods possess caterpillars that feed on the forest floor (the six and four other species breed, respectively, on shrubs and trees), the impact has been dramatic (Warren and Thomas 1992). Particularly vulnerable have been 11 species whose larval food plants flourish briefly in clearings after trees or scrub are harvested, as opposed to the 21 ground-dwelling species that breed mainly in glades and rides. As in other biotopes, each species exploits a distinct, typically narrow niche. For example, there is little or no overlap at any one time within a wood in the distribution of eggs (and hence larvae) of the five Fritillaries that feed on violets; all have declined greatly with the cessation of coppicing, but the first species to be lost were typically the Pearl-bordered (*Boloria euphrosyne*) (Figure 24.1) and High Brown (*Argynnis adippe*) Fritillaries, both of which select violets growing in the warmest, earliest micro-habitats available after a clearing (Thomas 1991). Nevertheless, as in grassland, a minority of species benefited from the changed structure of British woods: the White Admiral (*Ladoga camilla*) and Speckled Wood (*Pararge aegeria*) oviposit on semi-shaded examples of their food plants, and both spread substantially as coppicing declined and canopies began to close.

Habitat patch fragmentation and isolation

A combination of fundamental habitat losses and the degradation in quality of most surviving fragments has also meant that, for many species, any surviving patch of habitat in a landscape tends to be more isolated from neighbouring patches than was formerly the case. This is exacerbated by the fact that modern farmland and woodland are generally more homogeneous in structure than the patchworks of early to late successional vegetation that co-existed within single sites under pastoral grazing or rotational coppicing. For the many butterflies whose larval stage is confined to a narrow seral stage, it is increasingly necessary for the adults regularly to colonise new distant sites in a landscape instead of perpetually 'following the woodman', as fritillaries used to do within a single coppiced wood. Unfortunately, several butterflies are too sedentary to track the generation of new breeding areas across modern British landscapes. There may even be selection for less-mobile adults once the chances of an emigrant discovering a new site becomes low; this was recognisable in Swallowtail (*Papilio machaon*), Silver-spotted Skipper and Large Blue populations by an increase in individuals with narrow thoraxes (Dempster 1991). Among the most sedentary of all British butterflies are the Silver-studded Blue and the Black Hairstreak (*Satyrium pruni*), both of which have spread, after introductions to unoccupied landscapes containing many patches of optimum habitat, at roughly 1 km a decade (Thomas 1991). Fortunately the process can be reversed, resulting in more dispersive adults, if the number of habitat patches increases and the distances between them decrease. This has occurred over the past decade in the Large Blue as a result of conservation management, and in the Speckled Wood and Silver-spotted Skipper as a result of climate warming and, in the latter case, also of conservation management.

Climate change

In theory, the recent warming of the British climate should have benefited 58% of native butterfly species that were formerly absent, due to temperature constraints, from cool ecosystems in the north. In practice, only 22% and 29% of species, respectively, have shifted north or experienced net population increases within former ranges (see 'Patterns in the recent changes of British butterflies'), either because they were too sedentary to spread to higher latitudes or because the local cooling experienced by caterpillars due to the shift towards late vegetational stages in ecosystems negated any rise in local temperature due to climate warming. Indeed, Warren *et al.* (2001) concluded that the declines of most butterfly species during the 25 years up to the millennium would have been substantially greater had it not been for the ameliorating effect of warmer springs and summers. This is supported by population models constructed from the BMS time series, which suggest that all but one British species studied will increase on current sites under predicted scenarios of climate change for the next two decades, the exception being the Large White (Roy *et al.* 2001). For the many warmth-loving species that are confined, at their northern range limits, to examples of their larval food plant(s) growing both in early seres and on sheltered south-facing slopes, the amount of habitat available in a landscape can also increase by more than 50-fold, and the distance between suitable sites decrease to an eighth, simply because an elevated temperature enables more patches of food plant to be used for breeding (Thomas 1991). Unfortunately, as we have seen, many species of butterfly have proved too sedentary, to date, to exploit new habitats near their current range edges, and three other provisos are necessary:

For our few northern species the situation occurs in reverse: climate warming results in fewer, smaller, more isolated patches of habitat.

Throughout the British Isles, populations of several butterflies, including the Large Blue and Small Tortoiseshell, decline severely following a drought. If spring and summer droughts are more prevalent than UK climatologists currently predict, then the benefits gained from an ameliorating climate will be sharply reversed.

If, as predicted, average temperatures rise by more than about 3 °C in future decades, current extrapolations for butterfly populations are invalid. It is likely that the composition of entire ecosystems will change, and that much of the British Isles will instead be suited to more thermophilous communities, including butterflies.

Conservation

We have seen that the broad-brush strategy of simply establishing nature reserves across the British Isles largely failed to conserve our more specialised butterfly species during the first three-quarters of the twentieth century. More targeted conservation of butterflies was equally unsuccessful, not because their declines went unnoticed, but because the ecological changes that were driving populations to local extinction were poorly understood. Instead different factors were blamed, resulting, with hindsight, in inappropriate measures.

For many years, butterfly collectors were blamed for the disappearance of populations from semi-natural ecosystems where larval food plants remained abundant. This was a reasonable hypothesis, given the large number of collectors who used to congregate on favourite sites throughout the flight periods of the Large Blue, Black Hairstreak and other rarities. However, early measures to ban or regulate collecting had no impact on declines, and it is now recognised that collectors have little or no impact on butterfly populations, except on the smallest sub-optimal sites (Thomas 1984).

Another popular measure was to reintroduce species to nature reserves from which they had previously disappeared. In the large majority of cases this failed, because the ecological changes that had caused a species to become extinct in the first place were unknown; in practice, most releases were onto sites where the habitat was no longer suitable for the young stages (Warren and Oates 1990). Even when there was knowledge of a species' ecological requirements, early attempts with the Large Copper and Swallowtail also ultimately failed because it was impractical to regenerate sufficiently large areas of optimum habitat to support an isolated population. In contrast, early twentieth-century introductions of the Black Hairstreak across the East Midlands forest belt were highly successful, as were recent introductions of the Large Blue and Heath Fritillary to carefully restored ecosystems.

The realisation that most butterflies exploit narrow definable niches within biotopes has led to a switch to more targeted management of sites in recent decades. Initially it was a matter of restoring degraded habitats to more suitable conditions, often through ensuring continuity of early successional stages, coupled with the establishment of networks of managed reserves to allow metapopulations to persist in a landscape. As yet there are relatively few examples, but for some species the success rate has been high, notably the Adonis Blue, Silver-spotted Skipper, Large Blue, Heath Fritillary and

Black Hairstreak. The first two species were aided by the return of rabbits and warmer weather, but without targeted conservation to improve their habitats on both their extinct and the few occupied sites that existed at their nadir in the early 1980s, it is probable that both they and the Heath Fritillary would have been lost to the British Isles by the early years of the twenty-first century. Conservation was too late to prevent the extinction of the Large Blue in 1979, but its habitat requirements, which were becoming understood, were swiftly restored and the species was reintroduced using indistinguishable populations from Öland, Sweden in 1983. Today the Large Blue flies on carefully managed grasslands in four of its former regions, notably the Polden Hills, Somerset, where it has spread to about 25 new sites, some of which support the largest known European populations of this globally threatened species (Thomas *et al.* 2009).

Following the successful demonstration that degraded ecosystems could be restored to support rare butterflies, more ambitious schemes were initiated in the past two decades, aimed at creating new communities on arable or other land that had been fundamentally changed. A disadvantage of recreation projects is that they are costly and, as yet, largely experimental; one advantage is that they can sometimes be located in strategic positions in landscapes, providing stepping stones between otherwise isolated sites, as has occurred for the Large Blue. Some examples originated as compensation for new road or railway constructions. The more successful include the creation of new scrub habitats for Black and Brown Hairstreak (*Thecla betulae*) populations near the M40 in Oxfordshire and fine calcareous grassland for Chalkhill (*Polyommatus coridon*) and Small Blues (*Cupido minimus*) at Twyford Down, both on former arable fields, and for the Large Blue on new railway embankments and arable fields in Somerset and Devon. A further cause for optimism is that the targeted restoration or creation of new habitat for one declining species usually results in increases in a diversity of other species which require similar, but not identical conditions, and which had been declining due to the same general changes in land management. For example, the restoration of rotational scrub burning and intensive grazing for the Large Blue in Devonshire has resulted in new or greatly increased populations of such Biodiversity Action Plan species as the Pearl-bordered, Small Pearl-bordered, High Brown and Dark Green Fritillaries, Grayling and other rarities, including the Western Beefly (*Bombylius canescens*), Wood Lark (*Lullula arborea*) and Pale Heath Violet (*Viola lactea*).

Today, our relatively recent understanding of specific habitat requirements, coupled with increased knowledge about their persistence as metapopulations, provides the knowledge to conserve several, but not all, of the declining species of butterfly in the British Isles under current climates. The extent to which this knowledge will be applied to the wider countryside, for example through agri-environmental schemes, rather than restricted to a scattering of nature reserves, depends largely on political and socio-economic policies, which in turn are influenced by the lobbying of conservation bodies supported by the general public, such as Butterfly Conservation, Buglife, the National Trust and the County Wildlife Trusts. In parallel, there is much research still to be done before ecologists fully understand the drivers of change affecting all our butterfly species, and how these may alter under a changing climate and under future land usage.

References

Anon (1986). *The Management of Chalk Grassland for Butterflies*, Peterborough, Nature Conservancy Council.

Asher, J., Warren, M.S., Fox, R., Jeffcoate, G. and Jeffcoate, S. (2001). *The Millenium Atlas of Butterflies in Britain and Ireland*, Oxford, Oxford University Press.

Brown, K.S. and Brown, G.G. (1992). Habitat alteration and species loss in Brazilian forests. In Whitmore, T.C. Sayer, J.A., eds., *Tropical Forest Deforestation and Species Extinction*, London, Chapman & Hall, pp. 119–142.

Conrad, K.F., Warren, M.S., Fox, R., Parsons, M. and Woiwod, I.P. (2006). Rapid declines of common, widespread British moths provide evidence of an insect bio-diversity crisis. *Biological Conservation,* **132**, 279–291.

Dempster, J.P . (1991) Fragmentation, isolation and mobility of Insect population. In Collins, N.M. and Thomas, J.A., eds., *The Conservation of Insects and their Habitats*, London, Academic Press, pp. 143–154.

Fox, R., Asher, J., Brereton, T., Roy, D. and Warren, M.S. (2006). *The State of Butterflies in Britain and Ireland*, Newbury, Pisces.

Heath, J., Pollard, E. and Thomas, J.A. (1984). *Atlas of Butterflies in Britain and Ireland*, Harmondsworth, Viking.

Hodgson, J.G. (1993). Commonness and rarity in British butterflies. *Jounal of Applied Ecology,* **30**, 407–427.

Morris, F.O. (1853). *History of British Butterflies*, London, Groombridge & Sons.

Parmesan, C., Rytholm, N., Stefanescu, C. *et al.* (1999). Poleward shifts of species' ranges associated with regional warming. *Nature,* **399,** 579–583.

Pollard, E. and Eversham, B. (1995). Butterfly monitoring 2 – interpreting the changes. In Pullin, A., ed., *Ecology and Conservation of Butterflies,* London, Chapman & Hall, pp. 23–36.

Pollard, E. and Yates, T.J. (1993). *Monitoring Butterflies for Ecology and Conservation*, London, Chapman & Hall.

Roy, D.B, Rothery, P., Pollard E., Moss, D. and Thomas, J.A. (2001). Butterfly numbers and weather: the potential for predicting historical trends in abundance and the effects of climate change. *Journal of Animal Ecology,* **70**, 201–217.

Thomas, J.A. (1984). The conservation of butterflies in temperate countries: past efforts and lessons for the future. In Vane-Wright, R.I. and Ackery, P., eds., *Biology of Butterflies,* Symposia of the Royal Entomological Society, Vol. 11, London, Academic Press, pp. 333–353.

Thomas, J.A. (1991). Rare species conservation: case studies of European butterflies. In Spellerberg, I., Goldsmith, B. and Morris, M.G., eds., *The Scientific Management of Temperate Communities for Conservation*, BES Symposium, Vol. 29, Oxford, Blackwell, pp. 149–197.

Thomas, J.A. (2005). Monitoring change in the abundance and distribution of insects using butterflies and other indicator groups. *Philosophical Transactions of the Royal Society B,* **360**, 339–357.

Thomas, J.A. and Clarke, R.T. (2004). Extinction rates and butterflies. *Science,* **305**, 1563–1564.

Thomas, J.A. and Morris, M.G. (1994). Patterns, mechanisms and rates of decline among UK invertebrates. *Philosophical Transactions of the Royal Society of London B*, **344**, 47–54.

Thomas, J.A., Clarke, R.T., Randle, Z. *et al.* (2005). Maculinea and myrmecophiles as sensitive indicators of grassland butterflies (umbrella species), ants (keystone species) and other invertebrates. In Settele, J., Kuehn, E. Thomas, J.A., eds., *Studies in the Ecology and Conservation of Butterflies in Europe 2. Species Ecology Along a European Gradient: Maculinea Butterflies as a Model*, Sofia, Pensoft, pp. 28–31.

Thomas, J.A., Telfer, M.G., Roy, D.B. *et al.* (2004). Comparative losses of British butterflies, birds and plants and the global extinction crisis. *Science,* **303**, 1879–1881.

Thomas, J.A., Simcox, D.J. and Clarke, R.T. (2009). Successful conservation of a threatened Maculinea butterfly. *Science,* **325**, 80–83.

Warren, M.S., Hill J.K., Thomas, J.A. *et al.* (2001). Rapid responses of British butterflies to opposing forces of climate and habitat change. *Nature,* **414**, 65–69.

Warren, M.S. and Oates, M. (1990). *A Review of Butterfly Introductions in Great Britain*, Peterborough, Nature Conservancy Council.

Warren, M.S. and Thomas, J.A. (1992). Butterfly responses to coppicing. In Buckley, P., ed., *Ecology and Management of Coppice Woodland*, BES Symposium Volume, London, Chapman & Hall, pp. 249–270.

25

Moths

Richard Fox, Kelvin F. Conrad, Mark S. Parsons,
Martin S. Warren and Ian P. Woiwod

Summary

Moths are a diverse group of insects (around 2500 species in Britain and Ireland) that make a significant contribution to our biodiversity. Despite being a species-rich group, the popularity of moth recording has made it feasible to assess rates of species colonisation and local extinction, conservation status and, for hundreds of macro-moth species, long-term population trends in Britain.

The moth fauna of Britain is constantly changing, with small numbers of species colonising the country or becoming extinct each decade. Set against this small turnover of species is the dramatic evidence of a severe decline in moth numbers, most notably in the south-east of Britain. The unique monitoring data available from the Rothamsted light-trap network show that the total number of moths captured nationally declined by almost a third between 1968 and 2002, although there was no overall decline evident in northern Britain. Two-thirds of the 337 individual species of common larger moth examined in detail had declined in abundance during that period. Over 20% of these common species have decreased so severely that they qualify as nationally threatened species under internationally recognised criteria. Such widespread declines are likely to have serious detrimental knock-on effects on other organisms and signal a wider biodiversity crisis.

Introduction

The significance of moths

Moths are one of the largest insect groups both in Britain and globally, and thus make up a significant part of our biodiversity. About 2500 species have been recorded in Britain and Ireland. Moths are traditionally divided into larger (or macro-) moths and

Silent Summer: The State of Wildlife in Britain and Ireland, ed. Norman Maclean. Published by Cambridge University Press. © Cambridge University Press 2010.

smaller (or micro-) moths, although this separation was born of convenience rather than scientific rationale. There are approximately 900 species of larger moth in Britain, and these are the main focus of this review.

They are found in almost all habitats, from the shoreline to the mountain top, and occupy a wide variety of ecological niches. In addition to feeding on the leaves, stems, flowers and seeds of terrestrial plants, there are British moths whose caterpillars feed on roots and wood, as well as on aquatic plants, lichens and algae, honeycomb, fungi, dung, fur and feathers, and even other caterpillars (Young 1997; Leverton 2001). Moths' reputation for eating clothes and other textiles is greatly overstated. There are very few species amongst all this diversity that can cause such damage, and most of these are now very scarce. A few moth species are crop pests, but again there are only a relatively small number in Britain that require regular control.

Moths are an important element of many ecosystems. Many other organisms depend upon them either for pollination or for food (Proctor *et al.* 1996; Wilson *et al.* 1996). Moths and their caterpillars are an important component of the diets of many birds. A few birds catch adult moths on the wing, such as Nightjar (*Caprimulgus europaeus*) and Spotted Flycatcher (*Muscicapa striata*), but many collect caterpillars, particularly when feeding their young. Examples include almost all the familiar garden species, such as Blue Tit (*Parus caeruleus*) and Great Tit (*Parus major*), House Sparrow (*Passer domesticus*), Wren (*Troglodytes troglodytes*), Robin (*Erithacus rubecula*) and Starling (*Sturnus vulgaris*), as well as many birds that have undergone severe declines, such as Grey Partridge (*Perdix perdix*), Stone Curlew (*Burhinus oedicnemus*) and Corn Bunting (*Miliaria calandra*) (Wilson *et al.* 1996). Blue Tit chicks alone are estimated to eat at least 50 000 000 000 caterpillars in Britain and Ireland each year!

All 16 British species of bat feed on moths to some extent, and moths make up a substantial part of the diet for Greater Horseshoe Bat (*Rhinolophus ferrumequinum*), Lesser Horseshoe Bat (*Rhinolophus hipposideros*), Brandt's Bat (*Myotis brandtii*), Bechstein's Bat (*Myotis bechsteinii*), Leisler's Bat (*Nyctalus leisleri*), Noctule (*Nyctalus noctula*), Serotine (*Eptesicus serotinus*), Barbastelle (*Barbastella barbastellus*), Grey Long-eared Bat (*Plecotus austriacus*) and Brown Long-eared Bat (*Plecotus auritus*) (Vaughan 1997). Many other small mammals, including Hedgehog (*Erinaceus europaeus*), Wood Mouse (*Apodemus sylvaticus*) and shrews (*Sorex* spp.), eat moth caterpillars and pupae. Moths and their immature stages are preyed upon by many other invertebrates and are unwilling hosts to numerous species of parasitic wasps and flies, fungi, bacteria and viruses.

The study of moths

We are fortunate in Britain and Ireland to have a long tradition of recording and study by amateur naturalists, dating back over 300 years. Collecting moths and butterflies was a social, even a fashionable, pursuit in the early 1700s and many of the vernacular names still in use today were coined at this time. Outside of northern Europe, the study and conservation of moths, together with most invertebrate taxa, remain neglected issues relative to vertebrates (New 2004; Dunn 2005).

The study of moths was revolutionised during the twentieth century by the invention of light traps. These traps, which are used by the vast majority of moth recorders today, all utilise a light source to attract moths, which are then funnelled into a box in which they settle, enabling them to be identified before release. While such traps have greatly facilitated the recording of moths, some species are rarely caught in light traps. Light traps also do not provide direct evidence of breeding status (unlike searching for caterpillars), because it is not always possible to tell whether a captured moth has bred locally or originated from much further away.

Moth recording is more popular today than it has ever been. There are at least 2000 active moth recorders in Britain at present, and almost certainly many more. Interest is growing rapidly, spurred on by national initiatives (e.g. Butterfly Conservation's Moths Count project and National Moth Night) and local moth groups. Despite much recording activity at the county level (resulting in the publication of local moth lists and atlases), there has not been a national distribution recording scheme for the larger moths for several decades. At the beginning of 2008, a new National Moth Recording Scheme was launched by Butterfly Conservation, and the collation of recent and historical records of larger moths in Britain, Northern Ireland, the Isle of Man and Channel Islands commenced. In due course, up-to-date distribution information and assessments of change over time will be available for all larger moths to underpin biodiversity conservation.

The Rothamsted Insect Survey (RIS) light-trap network

Rothamsted Research began a national network to monitor moths systematically from 1964 (Woiwod and Harrington 1994; Harrington and Woiwod 2007). Since then, standard Rothamsted light traps (Figure 25.1) have been operated by volunteers at more than 430 sites, with an average of over 80 traps running per year. The traps are run every night at a wide range of sites, including private gardens, coastal habitats, woodland, moorland and farmland. Rothamsted traps tend to catch small, representative numbers of moths, which makes the samples effective and manageable without affecting the moth populations being studied (Conrad *et al.* 2004; Woiwod *et al.* 2005). The RIS light-trap network has generated one of the longest-running and geographically extensive data sets on insect populations anywhere in the world. The RIS also operates a network of 12 m suction traps, and results from that network on aerial populations of other insect groups are described in Chapter 30.

From the nightly counts of moth species at each RIS light-trap site, indices of abundance at regional and national levels were calculated for the period 1968–2002, using generalised linear modelling within the TRIM software package (Pannekoek and Van Strein 2001). By convention, the estimated annual abundance index was set to one in the first year of the monitoring time series. Subsequent annual indices are relative to the first, so that TRIM measures relative changes in population size rather than changes in

Figure 25.1 Rothamsted light trap. (Photograph by Rothamsted Research.)

absolute abundance. Long-term trends were estimated as the slopes (change in abundance index per year) of the regression of the annual TRIM indices as provided by the TRIM package (Conrad *et al.* 2004). These annual rates of population change were converted to 10-year rates to comply with the IUCN criteria. TRIM is a flexible and robust method of estimating population trends for individual species and also enables comparisons of long-term trends across species. This methodology has been widely used and is part of a proposed indicator of changes in European bird diversity (Gregory *et al.* 2005).

The changing moth fauna of Britain and Ireland

Extinctions and colonisations

The number of moth species living in Britain changes as some species cease to be resident here and new ones colonise from continental Europe or further afield. Parsons (2003) summarised these changes, concluding that 62 resident moth species were lost from Britain during the twentieth century (e.g. Lesser Belle, *Colobochyla salicalis*, and Viper's Bugloss, *Hadena irregularis*). Several other species have not been seen for a number of years (e.g. Bordered Gothic, *Heliophobus reticulata*, and Brighton Wainscot, *Oria musculosa*).

In contrast, 89 species colonised successfully during the twentieth century (Parsons 2003). For example, Light Brown Apple Moth (*Epiphyas postvittana*), a micro-moth native to Australia, was first recorded breeding in the wild in Britain in Cornwall in 1936. Since the 1980s it has expanded rapidly and is now recorded widely across England and Wales, and has been reported recently in Scotland and Ireland (Porter 2001; Lee 2003). It is a generalist herbivore with a wide range of larval food plants, but many other recent colonisers are specifically associated with non-native plants in our gardens and parks, for example Firethorn Leaf Miner (*Phyllonorycter leucographella*) on Pyracantha shrubs (Agassiz 1996; Parsons 2003). South-east England has borne the brunt of these changes, with more losses and more colonisations than any other region (Parsons 2003). Since 2000, over 60 moth species have been recorded as new to Britain and several of these are now breeding and spreading rapidly (e.g. *Ectoedemia heringella* and Horse Chestnut Leaf-miner, *Cameraria ohridella*).

Moths in decline

In addition to those that have been lost from Britain, many moths have declined severely and are now nationally threatened. For example, New Forest Burnet (*Zygaena viciae*) survives at a single British site, Marsh Moth (*Athetis pallustris*) is now known from only two sites and Dark Bordered Beauty (*Epione vespertaria*) at only four. There are many other examples. The conservation status of many such moths has been recognised in the UK Biodiversity Action Plan (see 'Moth conservation') and significant progress has been made towards improved understanding and protection of these species over the past decade.

The decline of moths at the local level has been highlighted in many county moth books, which include long lists of locally extinct and declining species. For example, in Cornwall, 135 moth species are listed as not recorded since 1906 (Smith 1997) and 112 species have been judged likely to be extinct in Hertfordshire (Plant 2004). However, the most convincing evidence of widespread moth declines comes from the analysis of 35 years of data from the RIS light-trap network (Figure 25.2). This shows that between 1968 and 2002 the total number of larger moths had decreased significantly, by 31% overall in Britain and by 44% in the south of Britain (south of the 4500 N gridline of the Ordnance Survey National Grid, Conrad *et al.* 2006). Interestingly, in the north of Britain there was no significant change over this period.

Long-term (35 year) population trends (1968–2002) were obtained from the Rothamsted dataset for 337 common, larger moths based on annual indices of abundance calculated using the TRIM modelling procedure. In this context, 'common' relates to species with sufficient captures for the calculation of national trends. Two-thirds (226 species) showed a decreasing population trend and one-third (111 species) an increase in population over the 35-year study (Figure 25.3) (Conrad *et al.* 2006).

The population trends for 71 species (21% of the sample) of these 'common' moths met the criteria for endangered or vulnerable Red Data Book status according to IUCN

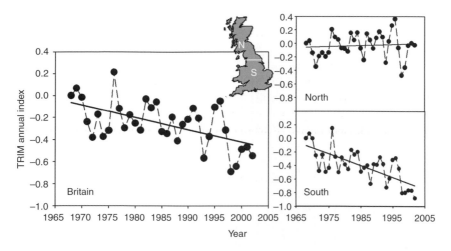

Figure 25.2 Total larger moth catches in the Rothamsted light-trap network 1968–2002. The total number of moths recorded has decreased significantly by 31% in Britain as a whole. There has also been a significant 44% decrease in southern Britain, in contrast to a 5% increase in the north (although the latter trend is not statistically significant). (Reprinted from Conrad *et al.* 2006, with permission from Elsevier.)

criteria (50% or greater decrease over 10 years and 30% or greater decrease over 10 years, respectively) (IUCN 2001). Fifteen species met the criteria for endangered status and 56 species for vulnerable status (Table 25.1 and Figure 25.3) (Conrad *et al.* 2006). These species have not been proposed for inclusion in a Red Data Book and we recognise that there is ongoing debate about the application of global threat categories at different spatial scales (Gardenfors *et al* 2001; Dunn 2002; Eaton *et al.* 2005; Keller *et al.* 2005). Rather, we have used the IUCN criteria to provide an independent and objective benchmark to indicate a suitable level of conservation concern appropriate for these moth population trends.

None of these moths has been listed as Red Data Book species before in Britain and none was previously thought to warrant any conservation priority. For example, Figure of Eight (*Diloba caeruleocephala*), a woodland, hedgerow and garden moth described in a recent field guide as 'common' and 'well distributed' (Waring and Townsend 2003), declined by 95% over the 35-year study and meets the IUCN criteria for a Red Data Book endangered species. This moth was caught in over 30% of Rothamsted traps in the early years of the monitoring scheme, but had declined to only around 10% during the final years of the twentieth century. Other once very familiar moths that have undergone dramatic declines include V-moth (*Macaria wauaria*) (97% decrease 1968–2002), Garden Dart (*Euxoa nigricans*) (97% decrease) and Spinach (*Eulithis mellinata*) (95% decrease).

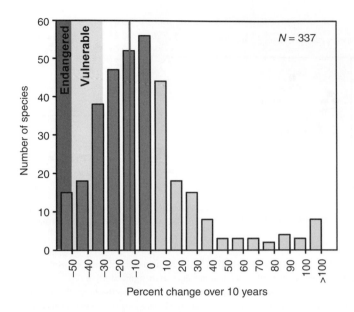

Figure 25.3 Frequency distributions of population change of 337 British moth species. The size of population change is the percentage change over a 10-year period, calculated from the annual rate of change estimated from long-term trends from 1968–2002. The vertical line shows the median 10-year change. *x*-axis labels are the upper limits of each class. Shaded areas correspond with the IUCN criteria thresholds for the endangered and vulnerable status.

These findings are extremely alarming. Few naturalists had noticed or predicted the dramatic population declines of many of these larger moths, some of which are still recorded very regularly in gardens across Britain (e.g. Blood-vein, *Timandra comae*, 79% decrease 1968–2002, and White Ermine, *Spilosoma lubricipeda*, 77% decrease) (Figure 25.4). There are obvious parallels (and in some cases possible causal links) with the dramatic and well-publicised declines of common birds such as Skylark (*Alauda arvensis*), House Sparrow and Starling, as well as with butterflies (Warren *et al.* 2001; Thomas *et al.* 2004).

The proportion of declining common moths (66%) is very similar to the proportion of declining British butterflies (72%, Fox *et al.* 2006) and substantial decreases in the distribution of day-flying moths have been recorded in the Netherlands (87% of species had declined, Groenendijk and van der Meulen 2004). However, it should be noted that, at present, high-quality national-level information exists for only about half of the larger moths in Britain. The advent of the National Moth Recording Scheme and continued recording by the RIS light-trap network will make it possible to assess the status and trend of all larger moth species in the future.

Table 25.1 *The 20 larger moths with the greatest decreases in population 1968–2002 from a study of 337 widespread species*

Species	% change over 35 years
Dusky Thorn *Ennomos fuscantaria*	−98
Hedge Rustic *Tholera cespitis*	−97
V-moth *Macaria wauaria*	−97
Double Dart *Graphiphora augur*	−97
Garden Dart *Euxoa nigricans*	−97
Grass Rivulet *Perizoma albulata*	−96
Dark Spinach *Pelurga comitata*	−95
Spinach *Eulithis mellinata*	−95
Figure of Eight *Diloba caeruleocephala*	−95
Anomalous *Stilbia anomala*	−93
Dusky-lemon Sallow *Xanthia gilvago*	−92
Autumnal Rustic *Eugnorisma glareosa*	−92
White-line Dart *Euxoa tritici*	−92
Dark-barred Twin-spot Carpet *Xanthorhoe ferrugata*	−92
September Thorn *Ennomos erosaria*	−91
Feathered Gothic *Tholera decimalis*	−90
Beaded Chestnut *Agrochola lychnidis*	−90
Deep-brown Dart *Aporophyla lutulenta*	−90
Lackey *Malacosoma neustria*	−90
Brindled Ochre *Dasypolia templi*	−90

Moths on the increase

Although the majority of larger moths display decreasing population trends in the RIS dataset, some species have increased over recent decades (Table 25.2 and Figure 25.3). Forty-six species have more than doubled their population levels and a further 23 species have increased by more than 50% over the 35-year period (1968–2002). Two species have been particularly successful, Least Carpet (*Idaea rusticata*) and Blair's Shoulder-knot (*Lithophane leautieri*), both of which have increased enormously (41 696% and 20 798% increases in TRIM index, respectively). Blair's Shoulder-knot is a recent colonist and successful invader; from the first recorded individual on the Isle of Wight in 1951, the species has spread northwards to reach Scotland by 2001 (Agassiz 2004). This moth is associated primarily with non-native cypress trees (including the ubiquitous Leyland Cypress, *X Cuprocyparis leylandii*) and Britain's gardens and parks provide a large area of potential habitat for the species to colonise.

Figure 25.4 Population trends of four widespread moths in Britain 1968–2002: (a) Blood-vein (*Timandra comae*) 79% decrease 1968–2002, (b) White Ermine (*Spilosoma lubrici-peda*) 77% decrease, (c) Rosy Footman (*Miltochrista miniata*) 299% increase and (d) Green Silver-lines (*Pseudoips prasinana*) 157% increase (see colour plate). (Photographs by Robert Thompson and Roy Leverton.)

The footman moths (sub-family Lithosiinae) have fared very well over the period 1968–2002. Eight species in this group were included in the analysis of Rothamsted data, and all had increased population levels, for example Scarce Footman (*Eilema complana*) 2035% increase, Buff Footman (*Eilema depressa*) 815% increase and Dingy Footman (*Eilema griseola*) 737% increase.

Immigrant moths have also fared well in Britain over recent decades, both in the Rothamsted analysis (e.g. the TRIM index for Vestal, *Rhodometra sacraria*, increased by 674% despite considerable annual fluctuations in the population index) and in other studies (e.g. Sparks *et al.* 2005).

Table 25.2 *The 20 resident larger moths with the greatest increases in population 1968–2002 from a study of 337 widespread species*

Species	% change over 35 years
Least Carpet *Idaea rusticata*	41 696
Blair's Shoulder-knot *Lithophane leautieri*	20 798
Satin Beauty *Deileptenia ribeata*	3856
Treble Brown Spot *Idaea trigeminata*	3061
Scarce Footman *Eilema complana*	2035
Peacock Moth *Macaria notata*	2022
Juniper Carpet *Thera juniperata*	1241
Grey Shoulder-knot *Lithophane ornitopus*	1055
Broad-bordered Yellow Underwing *Noctua fimbriata*	954
Devon Carpet *Lampropteryx otregiata*	937
Spruce Carpet *Thera britannica*	861
Buff Footman *Eilema depressa*	815
Dingy Footman *Eilema griseola*	737
Dotted Carpet *Alcis jubata*	732
Least Black Arches *Nola confusalis*	689
Red-green Carpet *Chloroclysta siterata*	587
Marbled Beauty *Cryphia domestica*	467
Blue-bordered Carpet *Plemyria rubiginata*	426
Dwarf Cream Wave *Idaea fuscovenosa*	419
Vine's Rustic *Hoplodrina ambigua*	413

Some 'common' moths appear to have increased their range in northern Britain and this is reflected in their long-term population trends (see 'Geographical patterns'). The recently launched National Moth Recording Scheme will provide much more information on range change for moths in Britain, but we would expect a substantial minority of species to be spreading northwards due to climate change, as has been found for a wide range of other taxa, including butterflies (Hill *et al.* 2002; Hickling *et al.* 2006).

Patterns of change

Ecological patterns

Univoltine (single-brooded) species tend to have fared worse on average than double- or multiple-brooded ones, though this was not statistically significant (Conrad *et al.* 2004). Species that overwinter in the egg stage, such as Spinach, Pale Eggar (*Trichiura crataegi*) and Scalloped Oak (*Crocallis elinguaria*), appear to have fared particularly badly.

Species that fly through the winter from autumn into spring (e.g. Spring Usher, *Agriopis leucophaearia*) have, on average, increased, whereas species with flight periods in other seasons have decreased, on average. Moths that fly in the autumn, such as Beaded Chestnut (*Agrochola lychnidis*), appear to be faring worst of all. It is worth noting, however, that flight period season and overwintering stage are not independent. Many of the autumn-flying moths that have declined severely also overwinter as eggs. Examples include Flounced Chestnut (*Agrochola helvola*) (88% decrease 1968–2002) and Green-brindled Crescent (*Allophyes oxyacanthae*) (79% decrease).

Moths that are relatively specialised, in that they occur in only one or two broad habitat types (e.g. woodland, grassland, heathland, wetland etc.) (Emmet 1991), declined on average. However, no significant differences were found between groups of moths occupying different broad habitat types (Conrad *et al.* 2004).

Species utilising lichens/algae (such as the footmen moths mentioned in 'Moths on the increase') and coniferous trees as larval food plants (such as the Spruce Carpet, *Thera britannica*, and Pine Beauty, *Panolis flammea*) generally increased, whereas moths using food plants in the categories of deciduous trees, grasses, shrubs and low-growing herbs declined on average. The differences between the groups of species that had increased and those that had declined were statistically significant (Conrad *et al.* 2004).

Geographical patterns

As previously discussed, the total abundance of moths decreased significantly in southern Britain (44% decrease 1968–2002, south of the 4500 N grid line, which runs through York and just to the south of Lancaster). The moth abundance index showed a small (5%) increase in northern Britain over the same period, but this was not statistically significant. Despite this major difference, a similar proportion of species had declined severely in both regions. In northern Britain, 21% of species with long-term population trends met the IUCN criteria for endangered or vulnerable, while in southern Britain, 26% qualified (Figure 25.5). Some of the most rapidly decreasing species, such as Hedge Rustic (*Tholera cespitis*), Figure of Eight, Garden Dart and Spinach appear to be declining across the whole of Britain.

While there was consistency between northern and southern Britain with regards to the most rapidly declining species, there were substantial differences among other species. Overall, 75% of species decreased in southern Britain compared to 55% in the north (Conrad *et al.* 2006). In northern Britain 45% of the 'common' moths assessed had increased (Figure 25.5). This difference leads to the greater stability in the overall numbers of moths caught in the north (i.e. declines have been balanced out by increases) and the sharply decreasing trend in the south (where declining species are driving the overall trend). This pattern of moths faring better in northern Britain has been confirmed by a more recent analysis using RIS light-trap data for

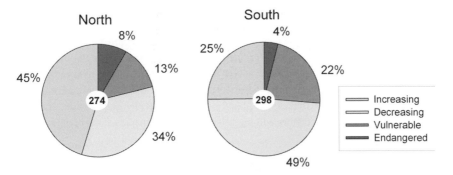

Figure 25.5 Moth population changes in northern and southern Britain. Categories are based on percentage population changes over a 10-year period, calculated from the annual rate of change estimated from long-term trends from 1968–2002. Endangered: decrease >50%; Vulnerable: decrease 30–49%; Decreasing: decrease >0% and <30%; Increasing: increase >0%. Numbers at the centre of each chart indicate the total number of species in each analysis.

Scotland alone for the years 1975–2004 (Scottish Government 2007). That analysis included 185 species for which there were sufficient data and found an overall increase of 2.6% over the 30-year period. A separate analysis of records from a single RIS light trap located in central Scotland found that both abundance and diversity of larger moths had increased significantly over a similar period (1968–2003) (Salama *et al.* 2007).

The difference between regions also means that there are many species that have different trends in the north and south. Examples include Lilac Beauty (*Apeira syringaria*) (697% increase in northern Britain, 77% decrease in southern Britain) and Scorched Wing (*Plagodis dolabraria*) (472% increase in north, 52% decrease in south). The national increases of some common moths are also being driven by changes in northern Britain. For example, Satin Beauty (*Deileptenia ribeata*) has only increased by 32% in southern Britain, but by 2438% in the north and Common Footman (*Eilema lurideola*) by 32% in the south and 1678% in the north.

A further geographical division of the southern Britain area was made, to look for differences between eastern and western parts. This was done along the 4500 E grid line of the Ordnance Survey National Grid, which runs through the Isle of Wight, Oxford and Nottingham. Population indices and trends were recalculated for species in these south-west and south-east regions and compared along with the trends for northern Britain. Northern Britain had the greatest proportion of increases, with the south-west and south-east approximately equal. South-west Britain had the greatest proportion of species with relatively stable populations, while south-east Britain had the greatest proportion (74%) of moths displaying substantial declines.

Causes of change

The causes of decline are known for a small proportion of our rarest and most threatened moth species. Further research is needed urgently to determine the underlying causes of the widespread declines of larger moths and suggest ways of reversing the trends. It seems very likely that agricultural intensification and other land-use changes will have had significant impacts on many moths of the wider countryside, and that climate change and other factors will be influencing some species at the same time.

Habitat change

Over the last 60 years, agricultural intensification, commercial forestry and urban development have wrought massive change upon the British landscape. The widespread destruction, modification and fragmentation of semi-natural habitats have had a severe impact on many specialist moths, leading to severe decline at the national level. Examples include *Pyrausta sanguinalis* in sand dunes, Straw Belle (*Aspitates gilvaria*) and Black-veined Moth (*Siona lineata*) on unimproved grassland, Shoulder-striped Clover (*Heliothis maritima*) and Speckled Footman (*Coscinia cribraria*) on lowland heath and Barberry Carpet (*Pareulype berberata*) in hedgerows (Waring 2004; Allen and Mellon 2006; Natural England 2008).

Often, subtle aspects of habitat quality are vital for population persistence. The abandonment of traditional management can quickly lead to loss of specialist moth species, even though the habitat remains superficially similar. For example, increased intensity of livestock grazing in Scotland almost led to the loss of New Forest Burnet from Britain (Young and Barbour 2004 and see 'Moth conservation'), while decreased gazing and abandonment of traditional pasture has caused losses of species such as Forester (*Adscita statices*) and Narrow-bordered Bee Hawk-moth (*Hemaris tityus*). The general reduction in woodland management leading to increasing shade, fewer open spaces and changing plant communities is a major problem for many taxa, including moths such as *Anania funebris* and Drab Looper (*Minoa murinata*).

There is insufficient evidence at present to determine the level of impact of habitat change on the declines of 'common' moths. However, the substantial loss of hedgerows, destruction of field margins and re-seeding and fertilisation of pastures are likely to have been major factors. A recent comparison of organic and conventional mixed farms in southern Britain found significantly more moths on the organic farms (Wickramasinghe *et al.* 2004). This supports a previous analysis of data from a very long-running light trap on the Rothamsted Farm, which found that agricultural intensification during the 1950s had caused a significant decrease in moth numbers and diversity (Woiwod 1991; Woiwod and Gould 2008).

In some cases, we can speculate about the specific impacts of habitat change on common larger moths. For example, the increase of many conifer-feeding moths is hardly surprising, given the massive expansion of conifer plantations (a 20-fold increase in Britain 1800–1980). Two rapidly declining species (V-moth and Spinach) utilise currants (*Ribes* spp.) as their larval food plants, and their declines may be due to fewer people growing these plants in their gardens (Waring and Townsend 2003). While many declining moths use native food plants that are unlikely to be affected by trends in gardening, the success of some rapidly increasing moths is strongly related to their ability to make use of exotic garden plants. Blair's Shoulder-knot is a prime example (see 'Moths on the increase') as its caterpillars feed primarily on cypresses, which are not native to Britain. Another example is Juniper Carpet (*Thera juniperata*), which was formerly restricted to semi-natural habitats where its food plant Juniper (*Juniperus communis*) grows. However, in recent decades, the moth has successfully colonised many gardens in which ornamental juniper varieties have been planted.

Pesticides

Agricultural use of pesticides (insecticide and herbicide) increased enormously as a key part of agricultural intensification during the latter half of the twentieth century, and may have played an important role in the declines of many common moths. Nowadays, insecticide use may be having less influence in this respect, as modern chemicals are less persistent than previously. However, herbicides have enabled farmers to reduce weed populations greatly, no doubt having profound effects on the availability of larval food plants for many common moths.

The total weight of pesticides sold for use in domestic gardens increased by 70% between 1992 and 1997 alone (Ansell *et al.* 2001) and this may have hastened the decline of garden specialists such as V-moth and Spinach.

Air pollution

There are no clear instances of air pollution directly causing the decline or increase of any moth species in Britain (although there is the famous example of 'industrial melanism' – changes in the frequency of melanic forms of moths such as Peppered Moth, *Biston betularia*, Cook 2000). Eutrophication (increased fertility of soil and water caused by inputs of nitrates from the air as well as agricultural fertilisers) is altering the plant composition and vegetation structure of many habitats, with unknown impacts on herbivores such as moths (Pollard *et al.* 1998; Preston *et al.* 2002; WallisDeVries and van Swaay 2006). The increases seen amongst lichen-feeding moths, such as the footman moths and Marbled Beauty (*Cryphia domestica*), may be linked to increases in some lichen species, which are in turn attributed to the reduction of sulfur dioxide air pollution and hence acid rain in many areas (Gilbert 1992).

Climate change

Over the period that the Rothamsted network has been operating, climate change has become evident. Numerous impacts are already apparent on the distribution and phenology of species (see Wilson *et al.* 2007 for a recent review). There have been many recent observations of 'early' or 'late' moths and changing moth phenology (e.g. Visser and Holleman 2001; Visser *et al.* 2006; Salama *et al.* 2007; Woiwod and Gould 2008), of moths extending their ranges northwards in Britain and of increased immigration (see 'Moths on the increase'), always consistent with a climatic explanation. The recent colonisation of Britain by moths such as Tree-lichen Beauty (*Cryphia algae*) may be related directly to climate change.

Several results from our analysis of common moths suggest a climatic cause. The group of 56 species classified as having southern distributions had increased on average, whereas northern species and ubiquitous species had declined on average, although this finding was not quite statistically significant (Conrad *et al.* 2004). Similarly, the observed relationship between positive population trend and species with winter flight periods hints at an underlying climatic cause (e.g. warmer winters are favouring these species).

The study by Salama *et al.* (2007) in central Scotland found that increasing moth diversity was positively correlated with mean annual temperature and that several of the most abundant species at their study site had experienced significant increases in flight period and earlier emergence. They concluded that climate change was at least in part responsible for the changes to moth populations and phenology.

Furthermore, in the one example of a 'common' moth that has been examined in considerable detail, Garden Tiger (*Arctia caja*), climate seems to be playing a significant role (Figure 25.6). Overall, its population decreased by 89% over the period 1968–2002, but the moth appears to have declined in the south of Britain, particularly in south-east England, and increased in northern Scotland (Conrad *et al.* 2002). Population levels of the moth decreased after wet winters and warm springs and were strongly correlated with the East Atlantic teleconnection pattern, a large-scale climatic pattern in the Atlantic basin, which is thought to influence winter weather in Britain (Conrad *et al.* 2002, 2003). This species is predicted to decline further in many areas as climate change continues.

Light pollution

Outdoor lighting can have disruptive effects on moth behaviour and increase exposure to predators. However, such effects seem to vary between species, populations and even individuals, as well as with the type of lighting used (Eisenbeis 2006; Frank 2006). More importantly, it is very difficult to separate out the direct impact of light pollution on moth populations from the other impacts of urbanisation and development that usually accompany an increase in lighting levels. This potentially serious problem is receiving increasing interest amongst ecologists working on various animal groups, particularly bats, and would certainly benefit from further research

Figure 25.6 Populations of the Garden Tiger (*Arctia caja*) decreased by 89% in Britain over the period 1968–2002. Population levels of this moth are closely correlated with winter temperature and humidity and the species is predicted to decline further as climate change continues (see colour plate). (Photograph by Alan Barnes.)

aimed specifically at its potential and actual impact on moth populations (Sutherland *et al.* 2006).

The attractiveness of moth-trap lights depends partly upon the level of background lighting, as well as the type of bulb used. It could be argued that increased light pollution over recent decades may thus have decreased the efficacy of Rothamsted traps, resulting in spurious population trends. We investigated this using satellite data on the change in illumination levels of each 1 km square in Britain. The decrease in total moths captured was as great or greater at traps in areas that remained unaffected by increasing background light levels than at sites that had become measurably brighter. We concluded, therefore, that the population trends of 'common' moths in our study had not been biased significantly by light pollution (Conrad *et al.* 2006).

Moth conservation

In Britain, the conservation of larger moths has had a relatively high profile over the past decade. Fifty-three moth species were afforded the top priority status under the original UK Biodiversity Action Plan (UK BAP), with all but one of these being larger moths. Actions and targets were set for each species and a huge amount of work undertaken, largely co-ordinated by Butterfly Conservation. Progress was reviewed by Parsons (2004) and showed that 27 priority moths had benefited substantially from action under the auspices of the UK BAP, 15 had no overall change, eight were in a worse position and there was insufficient information for the remaining three. Improvements have included the discovery of previously unknown colonies, better knowledge of species distribution, implementation of annual monitoring, increased understanding of ecological requirements, the provision of appropriate habitat management and, in some cases, the creation of new habitat. In a few cases, reintroductions have been carried out to restore moth populations to areas within their former range.

There are good examples of successful moth conservation, including New Forest Burnet, which survives at a single British site, in western Scotland. The colony had declined severely until, in 1990, the total British population was estimated to be only 20 individuals. Conservation action to reduce sheep grazing led to a spectacular recovery, with adult moth numbers increasing to over 8500 in 2003 (Young and Barbour 2004). Research into the ecological requirements and life history of Fisher's Estuarine Moth (*Gortyna borelii*), a rare moth of coastal grassland in south-east England, led to successful habitat-management trials, species translocations and the involvement of farmers and private land-owners in securing a long-term future for the moth in a sustainable network of habitat patches (Ringwood *et al.* 2004). Other successful examples of moth conservation include Netted Carpet (*Eustroma reticulatum*) in the Lake District and Barberry Carpet in southern England (Waring 2004; Thomas 2007).

The UK BAP priority list has been revised recently, with considerable changes to the moths included (Parsons and Davis 2007). Eleven of the former UK BAP moths were downgraded. In two cases this was because the species are no longer considered to be resident here. For the remainder, survey work undertaken over the past decade has shown the species to be more widespread than was previously realised (e.g. Buttoned Snout, *Hypena rostralis*) or increasing in distribution (e.g. Toadflax Brocade, *Calophasia lunula*). An additional 39 moths have been added to the priority list, giving a new total of 81 species (including 25 micro-moths). The actions and targets for these species have yet to be developed, and it remains to be seen whether sufficient resources will be made available by government to implement effective conservation of these threatened species.

The decline of 'common' moths identified from the analysis of RIS data demands further research and conservation action. Indeed, it was recently listed among the 100 most important research priorities for informing conservation policy in Britain (Sutherland *et al.* 2007). The short life cycles, reproductive potential and mobility of moths, and many other insects, lends hope that populations can increase quickly if conditions are favourable (e.g. species listed in Table 25.2). However, reversing the observed decline of 'common' moths cannot be achieved through standard conservation activities developed to protect rare species. The fact that so many common and widespread species are declining so rapidly points strongly to patterns of large-scale environmental deterioration that will require large-scale solutions. Only measures that act at the landscape scale and improve agricultural and woodland habitats over large areas are likely to be successful. It is crucial, therefore, that measures to conserve moths and other widespread insects are integrated into Habitat Action Plans and new agri-environment schemes such as Entry Level Stewardship in England. Because 71 'common' moths met the population decline criteria for red listing, these have also been included in the new UK BAP priority list, but for research action only (Parsons and Davis 2007).

Moth conservation has developed considerably over the past decade and some significant successes have been achieved (Parsons 2006). Nevertheless, the analyses presented in this chapter signify an even greater challenge than was previously recognised for moths. Almost all conservation efforts are underpinned by data from recording and monitoring programmes, so long-term biodiversity programmes such as the RIS light-trap network and the National Moth Recording Scheme are more important than ever.

Wider implications of moth declines

Insects make up the largest portion of UK biodiversity, comprising over half of terrestrial species. Monitoring insects presents a major challenge, even in temperate, developed nations where the taxonomy is relatively well established and there is a large pool of interested and knowledgeable amateurs (Thomas 2005). The analysis of 'common' moths is therefore important, as it is the first time that population trends have been available for such a large group of insects in Britain (Conrad *et al.* 2007). The declines uncovered by the analysis of RIS light-trap data are dramatic and alarming. The total number of moths caught by the traps has decreased by almost a third in 35 years and two-thirds of the 337 common, larger moth species examined have declined. The findings support other research that showed that 72% of butterfly species have declined since the 1970s, substantially more than the declines recorded for British birds and plants (Thomas *et al.* 2004). Moreover, the results for moths are even more startling because they relate only to trends in widespread, common species. Together, the declines of so many common moths, and of butterflies, signal a severe crisis for British biodiversity (Conrad *et al.* 2006).

In addition to acting as an indicator of wider biodiversity change, the moth declines may have other serious implications. Moths are important in ecosystems (see 'The significance of moths') and such widespread declines are likely to have detrimental knock-on effects on other organisms. Although the link between the decline of common moths and their predators and parasitoids has not been proven conclusively, there is a growing body of research that demonstrates such links amongst farmland birds and their insect prey (Vickery *et al.* 2001; Benton *et al.* 2002; Barker 2004). Another recent study found a strong correlation between farmland moth abundance and the activity of bats that feed mainly on moths (Wickramasinghe *et al.* 2004).

Common moths are part of the fabric of the British countryside. They occur in countless millions across the landscape from urban gardens to wild stretches of moor or coast. And yet, like the House Sparrow and other common species that we once took for granted, we now know that many larger moths are declining at alarming rates and overall numbers are decreasing rapidly, with unforeseen, but potentially serious consequences for ecosystems throughout Britain, particularly in the south.

Acknowledgements

We wish to acknowledge the foresight of L.R. (Roy) Taylor for instigating the Rothamsted Insect Survey and the efforts of Joan Nicklen, Peter Hugo, Adrian Riley and Phil Gould for co-ordinating the national light-trap network at various times over the years. We would also particularly like to thank the numerous volunteers and other members of the Rothamsted Insect Survey team who continue to be so vital for maintaining and running traps and identifying the samples. Joe Perry, Suzanne Clark and Peter Rothery offered statistical advice and discussion, and Arco van Strien provided excellent advice and support for TRIM. We would also like to take this opportunity to thank the many individuals and organisations who have supported work on the UK BAP moths, particularly Natural England, the Countryside Council for Wales, Scottish Natural Heritage, and the Northern Ireland Environment Agency. The analysis of Rothamsted data was funded by the Esmée Fairbairn Foundation and the UK Biotechnology and Biological Sciences Research Council.

References

Agassiz, D.J.L. (1996). Invasions of Lepidoptera into the British Isles. In Emmet, A.M., ed., *The Moths and Butterflies of Great Britain and Ireland*, Vol. 3, Colchester, Harley Books, pp. 9–36.

Agassiz, D.J.L. (2004). Cypress trees and their moths. *British Wildlife*, **15**, 265–268.

Allen, D. and Mellon, C. (2006). Survey of *Pyrausta sanguinalis* (Linn.) in Northern Ireland in 2005 with notes on other selected species. *Atropos*, **28**, 19–25.

Ansell, R., Baker, P. and Harris, S. (2001). The value of gardens for wildlife – lessons from mammals and herpetofauna. *British Wildlife*, **13**, 77–84.

Barker, A.M. (2004). Insects as food for farmland birds – is there a problem? In van Emden, H.F. and Rothschild, M., eds., *Insect and Bird Interactions*, Andover, Intercept Ltd, pp. 37–50.

Benton, T.G., Bryant, D.M., Cole, L. and Crick, H.Q.P. (2002). Linking agricultural practice to insect and bird populations: a historical study over three decades. *Journal of Applied Ecology*, **39**, 673–687.

Conrad, K.F., Fox, R. and Woiwod, I.P. (2007). Monitoring biodiversity: measuring long-term changes in insect abundance. In Stewart, A.J.A., New, T.R. and Lewis,

O.T., eds., *Insect Conservation Biology*, London, Royal Entomological Society, pp. 203–225.

Conrad, K.F., Warren, M., Fox, R., Parsons, M. and Woiwod, I.P. (2006). Rapid declines of common, widespread British moths provide evidence of an insect biodiversity crisis. *Biological Conservation,* **132**, 279–291.

Conrad, K.F., Woiwod, I.P., Parsons, M., Fox, R. and Warren, M. (2004). Long-term population trends in widespread British moths. *Journal of Insect Conservation,* **8**, 119–136.

Conrad, K.F., Woiwod, I.P. and Perry, J.N. (2002). Long-term decline in abundance and distribution of the garden tiger moth (*Arctia caja*) in Great Britain. *Biological Conservation,* **106**, 329–337.

Conrad, K.F., Woiwod I.P. and Perry, J.N. (2003). East Atlantic teleconnection pattern and the decline of a common arctiid moth. *Global Change Biology,* **9**, 125–130.

Cook, L.M. (2000). Changing views on melanic moths. *Biological Journal of the Linnean Society,* **69**, 431–441.

Dunn, E.H. (2002). Using decline in bird populations to identify needs for conservation action. *Conservation Biology,* **16**, 1632–1637.

Dunn, R.R. (2005). Modern insect extinctions, the neglected majority. *Conservation Biology,* **19**, 1030–1036.

Eaton, M.A., Gregory, R.D., Noble, D.G. *et al.* (2005). Regional IUCN red listing: the process as applied to birds in the United Kingdom. *Conservation Biology,* **19**, 1557–1570.

Eisenbeis, G. (2006). Artificial night lighting and insects: attraction of insects to streetlamps in a rural setting in Germany. In Rich, C. and Longcore, T., eds., *Ecological Consequences of Artificial Night Lighting*, Washington DC, Island Press, pp. 305–344.

Emmet, A.M. (1991). Chart showing the life history and habits of the British Lepidoptera. In Emmet, A.M. and Heath, J., eds., *The Moths and Butterflies of Great Britain and Ireland*, Vol. 7, Part 2, Colchester, Harley Books, pp. 61–303.

Fox, R., Asher, J., Brereton, T., Roy, D. and Warren, M. (2006). *The State of Butterflies in Britain and Ireland*, Newbury, Pisces Publications.

Frank, K.D. (2006). Effects of artificial night lighting on moths. In Rich, C. and Longcore, T., eds., *Ecological Consequences of Artificial Night Lighting*, Washington DC, Island Press, pp. 305–344.

Gärdenfors, U., Hilton-Taylor, C., Mace, G.M., and Rodriguez, J.P. (2001). The application of IUCN red list criteria at regional levels. *Conservation Biology,* **15**, 1206–1212.

Gilbert, O.L. (1992). Lichen reinvasion with declining air pollution. In Bates, J.W. and Farmer, A.M., eds., *Bryophytes and Lichens in a Changing Environment*, Oxford, Clarendon Press, pp. 159–177.

Gregory, R.D., van Strien, A., Vorisek, P. *et al.* (2005). Developing indicators for European birds. *Philosophical Transactions of the Royal Society B,* **360**, 269–288.

Groenendijk, D. and van der Meulen, J. (2004). Conservation of moths in the Netherlands: population trends, distribution patterns and monitoring techniques of day-flying moths. *Journal of Insect Conservation,* **8**, 109–118.

Harrington, R. and Woiwod, I. (2007). Foresight from hindsight: the Rothamsted Insect Survey. *Outlooks on Pest Management,* **18,** 9–14.

Hickling, R., Roy, D.B., Hill, J.K., Fox, R. and Thomas, C.D. (2006). The distributions of a wide range of taxonomic groups are expanding polewards. *Global Change Biology,* **12,** 450–455.

Hill, J.K., Thomas, C.D., Fox, R. *et al.* (2002). Responses of butterflies to 20th century climate warming: implications for future ranges. *Proceedings of the Royal Society B,* **269,** 2163–2171.

Howe, M.A., Hinde, D., Bennett, D. and Palmer, S. (2004). The conservation of the belted beauty *Lycia zonaria britannica* (Lepidoptera, Geometridae) in the United Kingdom. *Journal of Insect Conservation,* **8,** 159–166.

IUCN. (2001). *IUCN Red List Categories and Criteria: Version 3.1,* Gland, IUCN Species Survival Commission.

Keller, V., Zbinden, N., Schmid, H. and Volet, B. (2005). A case study in applying the IUCN regional guidelines for national red lists and justifications for their modification. *Conservation Biology,* **19,** 1827–1834.

Lee, M. (2003). The Light Brown Apple-moth *Epiphyas postvittana* and the spread of alien species. *Atropos,* **18,** 9–13.

Leverton, R. (2001). *Enjoying Moths,* London, T & A.D. Poyser.

Natural England (2008). *The State of the Natural Environment 2008,* Peterborough, Natural England.

New, T.R. (2004). Moths (Insecta: Lepidoptera) and conservation: background and perspective. *Journal of Insect Conservation,* **8,** 79–94.

Pannekoek, J. and Van Strein, A.J. (2001). *TRIM3 manual (Trends and Indices for Monitoring Data),* Voorburg, Statistics Netherlands.

Parsons, M.S. (2003). The changing moth fauna of Britain during the twentieth century. *Entomologist's Record and Journal of Variation,* **115,** 49–66.

Parsons, M.S. (2004). The United Kingdom Biodiversity Action Plan moths – selection, status and progress on conservation. *Journal of Insect Conservation,* **8,** 95–107.

Parsons, M.S. (2006). Recent developments in moth recording and conservation. *Atropos,* **28,** 45–55.

Parsons, M.S. and Davis, T. (2007). Revisions to the moths included within the UK Biodiversity Action Plan. *Atropos,* **32,** 4–11.

Plant, C.W. (2004). The lost moths of Hertfordshire. *Transactions of the Hertfordshire Natural History Society,* **36,** 47–68.

Pollard, E., Woiwod, I.P., Greatorex-Davies, J.N., Yates, T.J. and Welch, R.C. (1998). The spread of coarse grasses and changes in numbers of Lepidoptera in a woodland nature reserve. *Biological Conservation,* **84,** 17–24.

Porter, J. (2001). Range expansion in the Light Brown Apple-moth *Epiphyas postvittana. Atropos,* **14,** 42–46.

Preston, C.D., Pearman, D.A. and Dines, T.D. (2002). *New Atlas of the British and Irish Flora,* Oxford, Oxford University Press.

Proctor, M., Yeo, P. and Lack, A. (1996). *The Natural History of Pollination,* London, Harper Collins.

Ringwood, Z., Hill, J. and Gibson, C. (2004). Conservation management of *Gortyna borelii lunata* (Lepidoptera: Noctuidae) in the United Kingdom. *Journal of Insect Conservation,* **8**, 173–183.

Salama, N.K.G., Knowler, J.T. and Adams, C.E. (2007). Increasing abundance and diversity in the moth assemblage of east Loch Lomondside, Scotland over a 35 year period. *Journal of Insect Conservation,* **11**, 151–156.

Scottish Government (2007). *Scotland's Biodiversity Indicators*, Edinburgh, The Scottish Government.

Smith, F.H.N. (1997). *The Moths and Butterflies of Cornwall and the Isles of Scilly*, Wallingford, Gem Publishing Company.

Sparks, T.H., Roy, D.B. and Dennis, R.L.H. (2005). The influence of temperature on migration of Lepidoptera into Britain. *Global Change Biology,* **11**, 507–514.

Sutherland, W.J., Armstrong-Brown, S., Armsworth, P.R. *et al.* (2006). The identification of 100 ecological questions of high policy relevance in the UK. *Journal of Applied Ecology,* **43**, 617–627.

Thomas, J.A. (2005). Monitoring changes in the abundance and distribution of insects using butterflies and other indicator groups. *Philosophical Transactions of the Royal Society B,* **360**, 339–357.

Thomas, K. (2007). Cattle grazing of woodland to conserve the Netted Carpet moth. *British Wildlife,* **18**, 325–326.

Thomas, J.A., Telfer, M.G., Roy, D.B. *et al.* (2004). Comparative losses of British butterflies, birds, and plants and the global extinction crisis. *Science,* **303**, 1879–1881.

Vaughan, N. (1997). The diets of British bats (Chiroptera). *Mammal Review,* **27**, 77–94.

Vickery, J.A., Tallowin, J.R., Feber, R.E. *et al.* (2001). The management of lowland neutral grasslands in Britain: effects of agricultural practices on birds and their food resources. *Journal of Applied Ecology,* **38**, 647–664.

Visser, M.E. and Holleman, L.J.M. (2001). Warmer springs disrupt the synchrony of oak and winter moth phenology. *Proceedings of the Royal Society B,* **268**, 289–294.

Visser, M.E., Holleman, L.J.M. and Gienapp, P. (2006). Shifts in caterpillar biomass phenology due to climate change and its impact on the breeding biology of an insectivorous bird. *Oecologia,* **147**, 164–172.

WallisDeVries, M.F. and van Swaay, C.A.M. (2006). Global warming and excess nitrogen may induce butterfly decline by microclimatic cooling. *Global Change Biology,* **12**, 1620–1626.

Waring, P. (2004). Successes in conserving the Barberry Carpet moth *Pareulype berberata* (D. & S.) (Geometridae) in England. *Journal of Insect Conservation,* **8**, 167–171.

Waring, P. and Townsend, M. (2003). *Field Guide to the Moths of Great Britain and Ireland*, Hook, British Wildlife Publishing.

Warren, M.S., Hill, J.K., Thomas, J.A. *et al.* (2001). Rapid responses of British butterflies to opposing forces of climate and habitat change. *Nature,* **414**, 65–69.

Wickramasinghe, L.P., Harris, S., Jones, G. and Jennings, N. (2004). Abundance and species richness of nocturnal insects on organic and conventional farms: effects of agricultural intensification on bat foraging. *Conservation Biology,* **18**, 1283–1292.

Wilson, J.D., Arroyo, B.E. and Clark, S.C. (1996). The diet of bird species of low-land farmland: a literature review, unpublished report to the Department of the Environment and English Nature, Oxford, University of Oxford.

Wilson, R.J., Davies, Z.G. and Thomas, C.D.T. (2007). Insects and climate change: processes, patterns and implications for conservation. In Stewart, A.J.A., New, T.R. and Lewis, O.T., eds., *Insect Conservation Biology*, London, Royal Entomological Society, pp. 245–279.

Woiwod, I.P. (1991). The ecological importance of long-term synoptic monitoring. In Firbank, L.G., Carter, N., Darbyshire, J.F. and Potts, G.R., eds., *The Ecology of Temperate Cereal Fields*, Oxford, Blackwell, pp. 275–304.

Woiwod, I.P. and Gould, P.J.L. (2008). Long-term moth studies at Rothamsted. In Plant, C.W., ed., *The Moths of Hertfordshire*, Welwyn Garden City, Hertfordshire Natural History Society, pp. 31–44.

Woiwod, I.P. and Harrington, R. (1994). Flying in the face of change: the Rothamsted Insect Survey. In Leigh, R. and Johnston, A., eds., *Long-term Experiments in Agricultural and Ecological Sciences*, Wallingford, CAB International, pp. 321–342.

Woiwod, I., Gould, P. and Conrad, K. (2005). The Rothamsted Light-trap Network – shedding light on a common moth problem. *Atropos, 26*, 5–18.

Young, M. (1997). *The Natural History of Moths*, London, T. & A.D. Poyser.

Young, M.R. and Barbour, D.A. (2004). Conserving the New Forest burnet moth in Scotland; responses to grazing reduction and consequent vegetation changes. *Journal of Insect Conservation, 8*, 137–148.

26

Dragonflies (Odonata) in Britain and Ireland

Peter Mill, Steve Brooks and Adrian Parr

Summary

Although three species of dragonfly became extinct in Britain and Ireland in the 1950s, the outlook for most of the present resident species is favourable, providing that appropriate freshwater habitat is increased and pollution reduced. A number of species are extending their range northwards, mostly as a result of overall temperature increase, but at least one also as a result of reduction in river pollution. Three northern species are showing some sign of a retraction northwards of their southern range margins and this could lead to a serious problem if temperatures continue to rise. A further species currently restricted to the East Anglian coast is threatened by projected sea-level rise. According to IUCN criteria, of our 39 breeding species (17 zygopterans (damselflies) and 22 anisopterans (typical dragonflies)) two are classed as 'endangered', four as 'vulnerable' and six as 'near threatened' in Britain. One of these 'near threatened' species is classed as 'vulnerable' in Ireland and Ireland has a further species classed as 'vulnerable'. One resident species in Britain has become established only this century and a further two species have begun breeding on a regular basis and may become established as permanent residents in the near future.

Introduction

Dragonflies inhabit an aquatic environment as larvae and a terrestrial one as adults, and are extremely useful as indicator species of both climate change and of pollution (Corbet 1999; Brooks *et al.* 2007), with some species being particularly susceptible to the latter. They spend from one to five years as aquatic larvae, the duration depending on the species and on temperature, with the life cycle being shorter where conditions

Silent Summer: The State of Wildlife in Britain and Ireland, ed. Norman Maclean. Published by Cambridge University Press. © Cambridge University Press 2010.

are warmer (Corbet 1999). They are large insects and hence easy to observe and they are now well recorded (e.g. Merritt *et al.* 1996). Their ranges are limited by the availability of suitable habitat and by climate, particularly temperature, and they respond rapidly to temperature changes over time by shifting their broad-scale distribution, provided suitable habitat is available.

A brief history

The odonate fauna of Britain is a typical island fauna, having fewer species than on the adjacent continent; Ireland has even fewer species. In the early accounts in particular, it is not always possible to determine which species were breeding in Britain and Ireland and which were migrants. This is especially the case for the anisopterans as they are stronger fliers and hence are much more common as migrants. One of the first annotated lists of the British and Irish odonates was that of Sélys Longchamps (1846) who added three species to the list of 48 species that had been compiled earlier by Stephens (1835–37); however, both authors included synonyms and vagrant species that cannot be considered as part of the British fauna. This was followed by an annotated list of British Odonata by McLachlan (1884) (see also Baker 2007). McLachlan listed 14 species of zygopterans (damselflies) that were resident in Britain and one, the Willow Emerald Damselfly (*Lestes viridis*), as an occasional migrant. He also listed 22 or 23 anisopteran species (typical dragonflies in the narrowest sense[1]) that were probably resident in Britain at that time and a further five migrant species, two of which, the Red-veined Darter (*Sympetrum fonscolombii*) and the Yellow-winged Darter (*Sympetrum flaveolum*), are, as we shall see later, of particular relevance. Lucas in his book on *British Dragonflies* (Lucas 1900) recorded the same number of resident zygopteran species as had McLachlan (1884) and 23 anisopterans. King (1889) produced a checklist of Irish Odonata containing 25 species, two more than in Sélys Longchamp's list (Sélys Longchamps 1846). However, a more detailed species account for Ireland was provided by King and Halbert (1910), who considered that only 23 species should be accepted as resident.

There was then a long gap until Longfield's book on *The Dragonflies of the British Isles* was published (Longfield 1937) in which she described 16 breeding zygopteran species in Britain. The extra two were the Northern Damselfly [Northern Bluet][2] (*Coenagrion hastulatum*) and the Norfolk Damselfly (*C. armatum*). The former is confined to Scotland and it is almost certain that it has been breeding there for some considerable time and was simply not known to either McLachlan (1884) or Lucas (1900). The same may be the case for the Norfolk Damselfly, which was first

---

[1] Recently Corbet and Brooks (2008) have suggested the term 'Warriorflies'.
[2] Where the Irish common name differs from the English common name, the former is given in square brackets.

discovered by Balfour-Browne at Stalham, Norfolk in 1903 (Balfour-Browne 1904). However, Longfield (1937) stated that it was 'exceedingly rare' and only found in Norfolk, and later noted that it was confined to just two areas in one localised region of the Norfolk Broads (Longfield 1949). It is thus quite possible that it was a relatively recent migrant from the near continent. By the time of the second edition of Longfield's book (Longfield 1949) a seventeenth breeding species had been added to the list, following the discovery of the Dainty Damselfly (*Coenagrion scitulum*) in south-east Essex in 1946 by Pinniger (1947), its main site (a pond near Hadleigh) being found later (Merritt *et al.* 1996). Longfield (1949) noted that it is 'extremely rare' and confined to one locality. Like the Norfolk Damselfly, it may have been present for a considerable time or have been a fairly recent coloniser from the continent.

Longfield (1937, 1949) listed 23 breeding species of anisopterans, the same number as Lucas (1900). However, by the time Hammond's book on *The Dragonflies of Great Britain and Ireland* was published (Hammond 1977), the number of breeding dragonflies in Britain had been reduced to 15 zygopterans and 22 anisopterans due to three extinctions (see below). The current number of resident species in Britain stands at 38 and includes 16 zygopterans and 22 anisopterans (Table 26.1).

Longfield (1937, 1949) described 10 zygopterans resident in Ireland. However, in 1981, the Irish Damselfly [Irish Bluet] (*Coenagrion lunulatum*) was discovered (Cotton 1982), bringing the number of breeding species to 11 (Nelson and Thompson 2004). Since this species is quite widespread in Ireland (but does not occur in Britain) it is unclear why it had not been recorded earlier. In the first edition of Longfield's book (Longfield 1937) only eight anisopteran species were recorded as breeding in Ireland, but recent information brings this up to a possible 13 (Nelson and Thompson 2004).

Of the species that breed in England, Lucas (1900) refers to five that have been recorded from the Channel Islands, but breeding records from there were not well documented. More recent information, including details of breeding, has been summarised by Silsby and Silsby (1988). This reveals a much larger list, but with an indication that some species may have been lost during the second half of the twentieth century. Askew (1988) lists 29 species for the Channel Islands; however this includes migrants and non-British species. An upturn in interest in recording Odonata in the Channel Islands over the last decade will help to clarify the exact current situation. Only two species are definitely known to breed in the Isles of Scilly, the Blue-tailed Damselfly [Common Bluetip] (*Ischnura elegans*) and the Common Darter (*Sympetrum striolatum*) (Parslow 2007).

The Joint Nature Conservation Committee (JNCC) Red List for British dragonflies has been revised recently (Daguet *et al.* 2008; Taylor 2008). Four species are now listed as 'endangered', two as 'vulnerable' and six as 'near threatened' (Table 26.2). In Ireland, two species are listed as 'vulnerable' (Nelson and Thompson 2004) (Table 26.2).

Table 26.1 *Resident species in (a) Britain and Ireland, (b) Britain only and (c) Ireland only.*

(a) Britain and Ireland.

Zygoptera	*Anisoptera*
Banded Demoiselle	Brown Hawker
Beautiful Demoiselle	Common Hawker
Scarce Emerald Damselfly	Migrant Hawker
Emerald Damselfly	Emperor Dragonfly
Azure Damselfly	Hairy Dragonfly
Variable Damselfly	Downy Emerald
Large Red Damselfly	Northern Emerald
Common Blue Damselfly	Four-spotted Chaser
Blue-tailed Damselfly	Black-tailed Skimmer
Scarce Blue-tailed Damselfly	Keeled Skimmer
	Black Darter
	Ruddy Darter
	Common Darter

(b) Britain only

ZYGOPTERA	ANISOPTERA
Northern Damselfly	Azure Hawker
Southern Damselfly	Southern Hawker
Red-eyed Damselfly	Norfolk Hawker
Small Red-eyed Damselfly	Common Club-tail
Small Red Damselfly	Golden-ringed Dragonfly
White-legged Damselfly	Brilliant Emerald
	White-faced Darter
	Broad-bodied Chaser
	Scarce Chaser

The Red-veined Darter has bred in England continuously for about six years but, as a migrant species, it is uncertain whether it can yet be classed as 'resident'.

(c) Ireland only

ZYGOPTERA
Irish Damselfly

Table 26.2 *Species on the IUCN Red Data List in the categories endangered, Vulnerable and Near Threatened in (a) Britain (Daguet et al. 2008; Taylor 2008) and (b) Ireland (Nelson and Thompson 2004).*

(a) Britain

Species	IUCN Category
Northern Damselfly	Endangered
Southern Damselfly	Endangered
Norfolk Hawker	Endangered
White-faced Darter	Endangered
Azure Hawker	Vulnerable
Brilliant Emerald	Vulnerable
Scarce Emerald Damselfly	Near Threatened
Variable Damselfly	Near Threatened
Scarce Blue-tailed Damselfly	Near Threatened
Common Club-tail	Near Threatened
Northern Emerald	Near Threatened
Scarce Chaser	Near Threatened

(b) Ireland

Species	IUCN Category
Downy Emerald	Vulnerable
Northern Emerald	Vulnerable

Recent changes in odonate distribution

Thus, from the latter part of the nineteenth century up until about 1950 there was a fairly stable situation in Britain, with no recorded losses. However, since the Second World War, an increase in the amount of arable farming and the ready availability of piped water meant that there was less need for farm ponds for the livestock and this led to a marked reduction in the number of such ponds through neglect, resulting in them becoming nutrient enriched and shaded, and drying out through succession, the process often hastened by improved drainage (Moore 1987). Indeed Moore (1987) noted that studies in the late 1960s showed a loss of 35% of the ponds in Huntingdonshire and 30% in Leicestershire. Many of the ponds and ditches that did remain became polluted through agricultural run-off of nutrients and pesticides. Furthermore, many areas were drained to increase land for agriculture and vast amounts of peat were extracted for horticultural use, with the consequent loss of important habitat for dragonflies. In

Figure 26.1 (a) Female Orange-spotted Emerald, *Oxygastra curtisii* (photograph by David Chelmick). (b) Male Black-tailed Skimmer, *Orthetrum cancellatum* (photograph by Barbara Murphy). (c) Male Southern Damselfly, *Coenagrion mercuriale* (photograph by Phill Watts). (d) Male Northern Damselfly, *Coenagrion hastulatum* (photograph by Dave Smallshire) (see colour plates).

addition, many of our rivers had become severely polluted through agricultural run-off adding to poor sewage treatment and industrial waste. Indeed some of our rivers had become anoxic and supported little wildlife, particularly in their lower reaches. Since all dragonflies are dependent on good-quality water, there have been some serious consequences and it is perhaps surprising that only one anisopteran, the Orange-spotted Emerald (*Oxygastra curtisii*) (Figure 26.1a), and two zygopterans, the Norfolk Damselfly and the Dainty Damselfly, have become extinct in Britain. At the beginning of the twentieth century, the Orange-spotted Emerald had been recorded in Hampshire, Dorset and Devon, but was clearly not an abundant species (Lucas 1900). Longfield (1937) noted that it was the rarest of the Emeralds and was confined to two localities in Hampshire. In her second edition (Longfield 1949) she records that, in Hampshire, it had become restricted to one locality, two previously occupied habitats having been destroyed, but that it also occurred in one locality in Devon, having been rediscovered there in 1946. Its last suitable habitat in Britain was the Moors River in Hampshire, and it became extinct in 1963, possibly as a result of accidental pollution of the river (Merritt *et al.* 1996). The Norfolk Damselfly was first recorded by Balfour-Browne in 1903 (Balfour-Brown 1904) at Stalham Broad and was recorded on both Sutton and Stalham Broads by Porritt (1912); it was present at the former until the 1950s (Merritt *et al.* 1996). Longfield (1954) noted that the ponds and ditches in which it bred were drying out, and the last record was probably in 1958 by Beaufoy (Brownett 2005). The Dainty Damselfly was last recorded in 1952 by Gardner. However, its demise was a result of the flooding of its habitat by the sea in 1953 (Merritt *et al.* 1996).

Towards the end of the twentieth century, several species had declined due to this loss of habitat. However, in the latter part of the twentieth century and in this century, there has been some improvement in habitat provision in that there has been an increase in the number of garden ponds, and many disused gravel extraction sites have become flooded. Also there has been an attempt to reduce the levels of pollution in our rivers. This has clearly had a positive effect on odonates by providing more and varied habitat. Although there is evidence that climate change is having an effect on the range of some species, in others an increase in range may be due to an increase in suitable habitat, due, e.g. to reduced levels of pollution, or to a combination of both factors. Furthermore, although warmer climatic conditions are generally associated with increased odonate diversity, they can have a negative effect on species with primarily a northern distribution.

By the 1970s our knowledge of the distribution of most of the dragonfly species in Britain had become well known, thanks to a large number of recorders. As a result of this enthusiasm the British Dragonfly Society was founded in 1983 and there are many active recorders among the 1400 current members. We can now be confident that, since that time, our recording system indicates the true distribution of our dragonflies, rather than the distribution of the recorders, although some caution does still need to be exercised for some regions of northern England and Scotland. In Ireland there has recently been a concerted effort to map dragonfly distribution there and the project DragonflyIreland 2000–03 culminated in a detailed analysis by Nelson and Thompson (2004). The records for Britain are available on the NBN Gateway (http://www.search-nbn.net). An initial analysis of the range changes of 37 resident species of British dragonfly between 1960–70 and 1985–95, which attempted to take into account changes in recorder effort between the two periods, indicated that all but three had shifted their northern range margins northwards by, on average, 74 km (Hickling *et al.* 2005). However, the significance of some of the more subtle changes is unclear. Two northern species that are restricted to Scotland, the Northern Emerald [Moorland Emerald] (*Somatochlora arctica*) and the Northern Damselfly (*Coenagrion hastulatum*) were stated to show a retraction northwards of their southern range margins, while also expanding their northern range margins northwards. However, two other species, the Azure Hawker (*Aeshna caerulea*), which is also restricted to Scotland, and the White-faced Darter (*Leucorrhinia dubia*) were both shown to have an overall range reduction

(Hickling *et al.* 2005). There is now data available up to and including 2006. It is clear that some of the trends noted by Hickling *et al.* (2005) have continued (Brooks *et al.* 2007) and the current situation with regard to the Odonata of Britain and Ireland is outlined below.

Lentic species (inhabiting still water)

Common species

There are 11 species (five zygopterans and six anisopterans) that are relatively common and most of which are widespread. The Emerald Damselfly [Common Spreadwing] (*Lestes sponsa*), the Large Red Damselfly [Spring Redtail] (*Pyrrhosoma nymphula*), the Common Blue Damselfly [Common Bluet] (*Enallagma cyathigerum*) and the Four-spotted Chaser (*Libellula quadrimaculata*) are all widespread throughout most of Britain and Ireland. The Azure Damselfly [Azure Bluet] (*Coenagrion puella*) is widespread, except that it is absent from northern Scotland; likewise the Blue-tailed Damselfly [Common Bluetip] (*Ischnura elegans*), which is absent in some parts of central and north Scotland. The Common Darter (*Sympetrum striolatum*) and the Black Darter (*Sympetrum danae*) are common in most of the region, but the former is absent from parts of central and east Scotland and the latter from parts of the Midlands and east England and is rather scarce in south and east Ireland (Nelson and Thompson 2004). The Common Hawker [Moorland Hawker] (*Aeshna juncea*) is common throughout except in south-east England. The Golden-ringed Dragonfly (*Cordulegaster boltonii*) is found in west and south-west England, in Wales and in much of Scotland and has also recently been seen in Ireland. The Brown Hawker [Amber-winged Hawker] (*Aeshna grandis*) is common in England from Yorkshire southwards and is found in a few localities further north, but is generally absent from the south-west and from much of Wales. It is also common and widespread in Ireland, apart from in the extreme north and south-west, where it is scarce, possibly because of the lack of suitable habitat in these areas (Nelson and Thompson 2004).

Southern species extending northwards

There are several primarily southern species that inhabit ponds and lakes, and are relatively non-specialist, that have shown a particularly striking northward range expansion, which appears to be a result of rising temperatures rather than an increase in the availability of suitable habitats or other factors. These are the Southern and Migrant Hawkers (*Aeshna cyanea* and *A. mixta*), the Emperor Dragonfly [Blue Emperor] (*Anax imperator*), the Black-tailed Skimmer (*Orthetrum cancellatum*) (Figure 26.1b) and the Ruddy Darter (*Sympetrum sanguineum*). The Southern Hawker has spread northwards into Northumberland and Cumbria, and has expanded its range in Scotland; it has also become well established in some western parts of Scotland and in the north around Aberdeen (Brooks *et al.* 2007) (Figure 26.2a). The Migrant Hawker has been expanding its range northwards and westwards for some time, and in the last few years has become common in Yorkshire and has spread well up the east side of Britain,

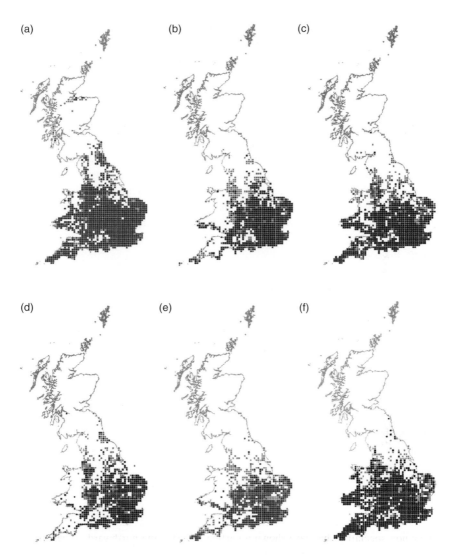

Figure 26.2 The distributions of six southern species: that have extended their ranges north-wards in recent years. (a) Southern Hawker, *Aeshna cyanea*, (b) Migrant Hawker, *Aeshna mixta*, (c) Emperor Dragonfly, *Anax imperator*, (d) Ruddy Darter, *Sympetrum sanguineum,* (e) Black-tailed Skimmer, *Orthetrum cancellatum* and (f) Broad-bodied Chaser, *Libellula depressa* ■: all records up to and including 1996; ▓: new records in the 10 years from 1997 to 2006 inclusive.

even reaching into Scotland (Brooks *et al.* 2007). On the west it has spread as far north as Cumbria (Clarke 2001) (Figure 26.2b). It was first reported in Ireland in 2000 (Nelson *et al.* 2003) and has since spread north and west, mainly in coastal areas, and has become well established (Nelson and Thompson 2004). The Emperor Dragonfly and the Ruddy Darter have extended northwards into Yorkshire, Tyne and Wear and Cumbria in recent years, with some individuals indeed reaching Scotland (Smith 2004; Perrin 2005; Batty 2007; Brooks *et al.* 2007) (Figure 26.2c, d) and the Ruddy Darter is widespread across the central region of Ireland (Nelson and Thompson 2004). The Emperor Dragonfly, like the Migrant Hawker, was first reported in Ireland in 2000 (Nelson *et al.* 2003) and has again spread north and west along the coastal region (Nelson and Thompson 2004). The Black-tailed Skimmer has also extended the northern limit of its range in Britain further north, but not to quite the same extent as the others (Kitching 2004) (Figure 26.2e). It is fairly scarce in Ireland, but is quite widely distributed in the centre and west of the country (Nelson and Thompson 2004). A sixth species, the Broad-bodied Chaser (*Libellula depressa*) has shown some tendency to extend its range northwards, but largely by increasing its distribution within the northern part of its range and is now common in much of Yorkshire, for example (Figure 26.2f). It is absent from Ireland.

Southern species at risk

Three other species with a southern distribution in Britain, the Small Red Damselfly (*Ceriagrion tenellum*), the Scarce Blue-tailed Damselfly [Small Bluetip] (*Ischnura pumilio*) and the Southern Damselfly (*Coenagrion mercuriale*) (Figure 26.1c) are relatively rare odonates and have not obviously responded to temperature change, probably because they have specialised habitat requirements which are not readily available outside their limited ranges. The Small Red Damselfly and the Scarce Blue-tailed Damselfly have very similar ranges in the south and south-west of England and in south-west and west Wales, the latter species being considered 'near threatened'. They both require shallow water, the former needing oligotrophic (nutrient-poor, but oxygen-rich) conditions, and the latter water bodies with little vegetation (Brooks 1997). In Ireland the Scarce Blue-tailed Damselfly is considered to be scarce, but probably widespread (Nelson and Thompson 2004). The Southern Damselfly inhabits slow-flowing base-rich streams and is confined to a few localities in southern England and southern Wales, with one 'outpost' in Anglesey, its two main localities being in the New Forest in Hampshire and the Prescelli mountains in Pembrokeshire (Brooks 1997). Indeed, even as early as 1900, Lucas (1900) noted that it had already been lost from its locality in Dorset due to drainage of the site. According to IUCN criteria it is 'endangered' and it has been lost from several sites in Britain since 1985 (D.J. Thompson, personal communication) (Figure 26.3). Although temperature increase may ultimately help these species to increase their ranges, provision of suitable habitat within their existing ranges is of much greater importance at present.

The Red-eyed Damselfly (*Erythromma najas*) is another mainly southern species, being largely confined to the Midlands and south-east England, although it does seem to have become more common within this range. Also, there are a few established colonies further north, e.g. in East Yorkshire.

Figure 26.3 Southern Damselfly, *Coenagrion mercuriale*. The distribution of an endangered species that has been lost from a number of sites in recent years.
■: records from 1997 to 2006 inclusive; ■: sites where it was present at some time up to 1996, but after which time it has not been recorded.

Northern and western species at risk

There are three species, the Northern Damselfly (*Coenagrion hastulatum*) (Figure 26.1d), the Northern Emerald (*Somatochlora arctica*) and the Azure Hawker (*Aeshna caerulea*), that are clearly northern species confined to Scotland within Britain. The first two were reported by Hickling *et al.* (2005) to have expanded their ranges in spite of them retracting northwards at their southern margin. However, the latest information shows that there has been virtually no recent change in the range of either of these species; indeed some of the recent records for the Northern Emerald, a 'near threatened' species, are south of previous records, which may be a result of increased recorder effort. This species is also found at just two localities in the south-west of Ireland where it is classed as 'vulnerable'. The Northern Damselfly is 'endangered' in Britain and is to be found in only four locations. For the Azure Hawker, which is 'vulnerable', there is evidence for a slight northwards contraction of its southern range boundary while it has

Figure 26.4 (a) Male White-faced Darter, *Leucorrhinia dubia* (photograph by Helen Wake). (b) Male Brilliant Emerald, *Somatochlora metallica* (photograph by Steve Cham). (c) Male Small Red-eyed Damselfly, *Erythromma viridulum* (photograph by Ann Brooks). (d) Male Red-veined Darter, *Sympetrum fonscolombii*, with zygopteran exuvia on its perch (photograph by Steve Cham) (see colour plates).

expanded its range to the north and west (Brooks *et al.* 2007). It is possible that further global warming could result in the extinction of these three species in Britain.

The White-faced Darter (*Leucorrhinia dubia*) (Figure 26.4a) has a western and northern distribution with a predominance of localities in Scotland. It is a rare species, particularly in England, and is one of our four 'endangered' species. It was lost from its Surrey habitat and from parts of Cheshire towards the end of the last century (Taylor 2008) (Figure 26.5a) and is now extinct in the south of England. This apparent northward contraction of the southern boundary of its range may in part be a response to climate warming; if so this could ultimately result in it being restricted to Scotland. It has shown some infilling within its range (Figure 26.5b). Another species with a largely western distribution in Britain is the Keeled Skimmer [Heathland Skimmer], (*Orthetrum coerulescens*), being found in England, Wales and Scotland. It is scarce in Ireland, where again it is predominantly found in the extreme west and south-west (Nelson and Thompson 2004).

Other species at risk

The Scarce Emerald Damselfly [Turlough Spreadwing] (*Lestes dryas*) and the Norfolk Hawker (*Aeshna isosceles*) both have a south-eastern distribution in Britain, but, to varying degrees, have limited distributions. Thus the Scarce Emerald Damselfly, which is

(a) (b)

Figure 26.5 White-faced Darter, *Leucorrhinia dubia*. The distribution of an endangered species that has retracted its southern boundary northwards in recent years (a) but has managed to colonise a few new sites in the northern parts of its range (b).

(a) ■: records from 1997 to 2006 inclusive; ▨: sites where it was present at some time up to 1996, but after which time it has not been recorded.

(b) ■: all records up to and including 1996; ▨: new records in the 10 years from 1997 to 2006 inclusive.

'near threatened', is confined to Norfolk, Essex and north Kent, while the 'endangered' Norfolk Hawker has a very restricted range and is only found in one area of East Anglia centred on the Norfolk Broads, having had many colonies destroyed by sea encroachment (Hammond 1977). Neither of them has shown any major indications of range expansion in recent years, though the Norfolk Hawker has recently been seen along parts of the Suffolk coastal strip, and they remain very vulnerable to habitat damage. The current proposal to surrender part of the Norfolk Broads to the sea as sea levels rise due to climate change (P. Taylor, personal communication) may result in the Norfolk Hawker becoming extinct in Britain. The Scarce Emerald Damselfly is the rarest damselfly in Ireland, where it is found in the centre and the west. It was formerly found in the east of the country, but it has been lost from most of its sites there (Nelson and Thompson 2004).

Figure 26.6   The distribution of the Variable Damselfly, *Coenagrion pulchellum*, showing new sites from which it has been recorded since 1996.
■: all records up to and including 1996; ▪: new records in the 10 years from 1997 to 2006 inclusive.

The Variable Damselfly [Variable Bluet] (*Coenagrion pulchellum*), which is 'near threatened' in Britain, occurs sporadically in the south of England and East Anglia, but is also found in south-west Scotland. It has disappeared from many localities over the last few decades and its numbers in the Norfolk Broads have become very much reduced (Hammond 1977), though it is still locally common in parts. It has shown no indication of range expansion in recent years, but there has been some infilling (Figure 26.6). It is quite common in most of Ireland; less so in the north and south-east of the country. There are concerns that decreasing water quality could adversely affect its distribution (Nelson and Thompson 2004). The Brilliant Emerald (*Somatochlora metallica*) (Figure 26.4b), classed as 'vulnerable', has similarly shown no indication of recent range expansion in Britain. It has a very odd distribution in Britain in that it is found in two disjunct regions, one in the Great Glen region of Scotland, the other in Surrey. The Hairy Dragonfly [Spring Hawker]

(*Brachytron pratense*) has recently shown some infilling within its range. It has an unusual distribution, being found in parts of south-west, south and east England and in south and north Wales, but is also found in some localities in northern England and south-west Scotland. However, in Ireland, although somewhat scarce, it is widely distributed. The Downy Emerald (*Cordulia aenea*) also has a disjunct distribution; it is primarily a western species, occupying localities in the south of England as well as in Cumbria, north Scotland and south-west Ireland. It is one of the rarest Irish anisopterans and is only present at three sites, all in the south-west, at two of which it is thought to breed. It is classed as 'vulnerable' here, being a considerable distance from any other breeding populations (Nelson and Thompson 2004).

The Irish Damselfly [Irish Bluet] (*Coenagrion lunulatum*) is found at small, slightly nutrient-enriched water bodies with floating-leaved plants in the northern half of Ireland (Nelson and Thompson 2004), but does not occur in Britain. It was first discovered in Ireland in 1981 (Cotton 1982). Since then many new sites have been discovered, but it does appear to have been lost from some sites (Nelson and Thompson 2004). The species has a mainly northern distribution in Europe and the population in Ireland is one of the largest outside Finland.

Colonising species

In this category are included species where there is evidence of confirmed breeding in at least five of the ten years up to 2008. A notable recent addition to the English dragonfly fauna is the Small Red-eyed Damselfly (*Erythromma viridulum*) (Figure 26.4c). This species has been extending its range on the continent in recent years and first appeared in Essex in 1999 (Dewick and Gerussi 2000). There was a particularly large migration from the continent in 2001 into south-east England and as far north as Norfolk. Breeding was confirmed at several sites in 2002 (although it may well have bred even before this) and it has since spread throughout much of south-eastern England, reaching as far north as Yorkshire and as far west as Devon and Derbyshire by 2006 (Parr 2007) (Figure 26.7).

The Red-veined Darter (*Sympetrum fonscolombii*) (Figure 26.4d) and the Yellow-winged Darter (*Sympetrum flaveolum*) have been regular migrants from the continent for well over a century, both having been mentioned by McLachlan (1884). The Red-veined Darter has been recorded particularly from south-west England although migrant individuals have been recorded as far north as the Scottish border and there has been an increase in the number of records in recent years (Figure 26.8). In the latter part of the twentieth century it occasionally bred in England, although most populations lasted for a few years at most (Brooks 1997). More recently it has attempted to breed in most years and there is good evidence that the duration of breeding colonies is increasing (Hursthouse 2007). This species can have two generations per year and such rapid larval development is unknown in other species that breed here. In 2006, 16 breeding sites were recorded (Parr 2007). Thus there is a real possibility that, as temperatures have increased, this species has now become a permanent addition to the British list. Migrants have also been recorded from Ireland and the Channel Islands (Parr 2007) but,

Figure 26.7 The distribution of the Small Red-eyed Damselfly, *Erythromma viridulum*, a new resident in Britain.
■: all records from 1999 to 2002 inclusive; ▨: new records in the four years from 2003 to 2006 inclusive.

as yet, there have been no confirmed breeding records from Ireland. The Yellow-winged Darter sometimes occurs in large numbers and, in the large migration that occurred in 2006, most sightings were in eastern England, but there were also some in the north-west (Parr 2007). This species has occasionally established breeding populations but, to date, these have always been short-lived (Brooks 1997). Again, increasing summer temperatures may well mean that this species will become a permanent resident in Britain at sometime in the near future. Certainly the winters are not harsh enough to be a problem, as it breeds in southern Norway, Sweden and Finland, where the continental climate provides warmer summers (Brooks 1997). The Lesser Emperor [Yellow-ringed Emperor] (*Anax parthenope*) is a relatively recent migrant, having been first recorded in England in 1996 (Brooks 1997) and in Ireland in 2000 (Nelson and Thompson 2004). In Britain it has become more common in recent years and is known to have bred successfully on one occasion in Cornwall (Brooks 2002), with circumstantial evidence for sporadic breeding in other areas over the last few years. Although its range is mainly

Figure 26.8 The distribution of the Red-veined Darter, *Sympetrum fonscolombii*, a migrant species that, in recent years, has become a more frequent visitor and which has bred in Britain in several successive years.
■: all records up to and including 1996; ▪: new records in the 10 years from 1997 to 2006 inclusive.

in southern Europe and it is rare in northern Germany and France (Brooks 1997), it is possible that it too may be on its way to colonising Britain (Parr 2007).

Lotic (riverine) species

Common species

We have relatively few riverine species in Britain and many of these showed range contraction before the mid-1970s, probably resulting from poor water quality (Brooks *et al.* 2007). Two of these, the Beautiful Demoiselle [Beautiful Jewelwing] (*Calopteryx virgo*) and the Banded Demoiselle [Banded Jewelwing] (*Calopteryx splendens*) (Figure 26.9a) are not in any current danger. The Beautiful Demoiselle has not shown any evidence of range expansion in recent years. However, it is quite common in Wales and south-west England and also occurs in south-west Scotland and the southern half

Figure 26.9 (a) Male Banded Demoiselle, *Calopteryx splendens* (photograph by Dave Smallshire). (b) Female White-legged Damselfly, *Platycnemis pennipes* (photograph by Steve Cham). (c) Male Common Club-tail, *Gomphus vulgatissimus* (photograph by Dave Smallshire). (d) Female Scarce Chaser, *Libellula fulva* (photograph by Steve Cham) (see colour plates).

of Ireland. It requires faster-flowing water than the Banded Demoiselle (see below) and inhabits clean, pebble or sandy-bottomed streams (Siva-Jothy 1997; Nelson and Thompson 2004). Although more tolerant of shade than the Banded Demoiselle (Siva-Jothy 1997), such streams in northern England are often heavily tree-lined and hence the lack of range expansion in this species may be due to lack of suitable habitat.

Southern species extending northwards

The Banded Demoiselle, which has a primarily southern distribution, has extended its range in a similar way to the above five anisopterans mentioned in 'Lentic southern species extending northwards', in recent years extending into Yorkshire and Northumberland (Jeffries 2001; Ward and Mill 2004) and expanding northwards from its north Cumbrian sites (Clarke 1999) (Figure 26.10). However, in this case the reasons are less clear-cut. Although temperature increase cannot be ruled out, it is quite probable than increase in available habitat as a result of cleaning up our river systems may be primarily responsible (Gibbins and Moxon 1998) and indeed there has been

Figure 26.10 The distribution of the Banded Demoiselle, *Calopteryx splendens*, a southern riverine species that has extended its range northwards in recent years.
■: all records up to and including 1996; ■: new records in the 10 years from 1997 to 2006 inclusive.

some 'infilling' within its range which tends to support this conclusion. Certainly the range of this species extends some 10° of latitude further northwards on the continent than it does in Britain (Merritt *et al.* 1996; Ward and Mill 2004). However, this species appears to have less stringent habitat requirements than other British riverine species, and it may well be the combination of both temperature increase and improvement in water quality that has resulted in its rapid northwards spread. It is a widespread species in Ireland.

Southern species at risk

Other riverine species, the White-legged Damselfly (*Platycnemis pennipes*) (Figure 26.9b), the Common Club-tail (*Gomphus vulgatissimus*) (Figure 26.9c) and the Scarce Chaser (*Libellula fulva*) (Figure 26.9d) are all very much southern species. The first two show no clear evidence of range expansion, but there has been infilling within their current ranges since 1995 (Brooks *et al.* 2007) (Figure 26.11). The White-legged Damselfly is found in central and southern England, and has recently been found as far north as Cheshire (D. Kitching, personal communication) (Figure 26.11a), while the Common Club-tail, which is classed as 'near threatened', is found in the west Midlands and south-central England and in south-west Wales (Figure 26.11b). The 'near threatened' Scarce Chaser, which tends to breed in rather slow-flowing water, is now less abundant in the Norfolk Broads due to pollution (Hammond 1977) and has been lost from some of its southern and south-eastern sites. However, there has been some recent infilling, as well as evidence of a westward extension of its range (Brooks *et al.* 2007; D. Smallshire, personal commiunication) (Figure 26.12).

Conclusions

The main general threat to dragonfly populations is the loss of habitat due to either drainage or pollution leading to eutrophication. Climate change will certainly also have an effect, and an overall increase in temperature could lead to the loss of northern species such as the Northern Damselfly, the Northern Emerald, the Azure Hawker and possibly the White-faced Darter. It will also lead to the range of southern species shifting northwards. This could include such species as the Banded Demoiselle, the Southern and Migrant Hawkers, the Emperor Dragonfly, the Black-tailed Skimmer, the Ruddy Darter and the Broad-bodied Chaser. Furthermore, a rise in sea level will threaten the low-lying sites in East Anglia that support the Norfolk Hawker. Overall there is likely to be an increase in the number and frequency of migrants from mainland Europe, some of which will probably establish breeding populations, as indeed is already happening in the case of the Small Red-eyed Damselfly, the Red-veined and Yellow-winged Darters and the Lesser Emperor. In the European context, the Southern Damselfly and the Scarce Chaser are of particular importance in that both of these

(a)   (b)

Figure 26.11 The distributions of two riverine species: that have not shown any extension of their ranges in recent years but have shown infilling. (a) White-legged Damselfly, *Platycnemis pennipes*, and (b) Common Club-tail, *Gomphus vulgatissimus*.
■: all records up to and including 1996; ▩: new records in the 10 years from 1997 to 2006 inclusive.

species tend to be only local in continental Europe as well as in Britain, even though their ranges are quite large.

The conservation measures required for dragonflies include the continuing clean-up of existing water bodies, both lentic and lotic, and preventing any run-off that may lead to eutrophication. This should be accompanied by sympathetic maintenance of such habitats, such as restricting shading, preserving areas of open water and maintaining the presence of a range of aquatic macrophytes. Also new ponds (which should not be stocked with fish) should be established to off-set the loss of this habitat that occurred in the second half of the twentieth century.

In conclusion, whereas a number of species are expanding their ranges and new colonisers from the adjacent continent are becoming more frequent, nevertheless several

Figure 26.12 The distribution of the riverine dragonfly the Scarce Chaser, *Libellula fulva*, showing new sites from which it has been recorded since 1966.
■: all records up to and including 1996; ▨: new records in the 10 years from 1997 to 2006 inclusive.

of our odonate species are clearly under threat and much needs to be done to improve existing habitat and to increase the amount of suitable habitat available to them.

References

Askew, R.R. (1988). *The Dragonflies of Europe*, Colchester, Essex, Harley Books.

Baker, R.A. (2007). What was the British list like 120 years ago? Robert McLachlan's list of Odonata compared with today's list. *Journal of the British Dragonfly Society,* **23**, 52–57.

Balfour-Browne, F. (1904). A bionomical investigation of the Norfolk Broads. *Transactions of the Norfolk and Norwich Naturalists' Society,* **7**, 661–673.

Batty, P. (2007). Scottish dragonfly news. *Darter: Newsletter of the Dragonfly Recording Network,* **24**, 5.

Brooks, S. (1997, 2002). *Field Guide to the Dragonflies and Damselflies of Great Britain and Ireland,* 1st and 3rd edns, Hook, Hampshire, British Wildlife Publishing.

Brooks, S., Parr, A. and Mill, P.J. (2007). Dragonflies as climate-change indicators. *British Wildlife,* **19**, 85–93.

Brownett, A. (2005). A re-examination of the status of the Norfolk Damselfly *Coenagrion armatum* (Charpentier): a species of Odonata now presumed extinct in Britain. *Journal of the British Dragonfly Society,* **21**, 21–26.

Clarke, D. (1999). The outpost populations of the Banded Demoiselle *Calopteryx splendens* (Harris) in the Solway Firth area, Cumbria: historical perspective and recent developments. *Journal of the British Dragonfly Society,* **15**, 33–38.

Clarke, D.J. (2001). First occurrence of the Migrant Hawker Dragonfly (*Aeshna mixta* Latreille) in Cumbria. *Carlisle Naturalist,* **9**, 40–41.

Corbet, P.S. (1999). *Dragonflies: Behaviour, and Ecology of Odonata,* Colchester, Essex, Harley Books.

Corbet, P. and Brooks, S. (2008). *Dragonflies,* London, HarperCollins.

Cotton, D. C. F. (1982). *Coenagrion lunulatum* (Charpentier) (Odonata: Coenagrionidae) new to the British Isles. *Entomologist's Gazette,* **33**, 213–14.

Daguet, C.A ., French, G.C . and Taylor, P. (eds.) (2008). *The Odonata Red List of Great Britain. Species Status,* No. 11, Peterborough, Joint Nature Conservation Committee.

Dewick, S. and Gerussi, R. (2000). Small Red-eyed Damselfly *Erythromma viridulum* (Charpentier) found breeding in Essex – the first British records. *Atropos,* **9**, 3–4.

Gibbins, C.N. and Moxon, J.B. (1998). *Calopteryx splendens* (Harris) at edge of range sites in North-East England. *Journal of the British Dragonfly Society,* **14**, 33–45.

Hammond, C.O. (1977). *The Dragonflies of Great Britain and Ireland,* London, Curwen Books.

Hickling, R., Roy, D.B., Hill, J.K. and Thomas, C.D. (2005). A northward shift of range margins in British Odonata. *Global Change Biology,* **11**, 502–506.

Hursthouse, D. (2007). Red-veined Darters *Sympetrum fonscolombii* at Lound, Nottinghamshire in 2006. *Journal of the British Dragonfly Society,* **23**, 1–9.

Jeffries, M. (2001). The Northumbrian Frontier of the banded Demoiselle *Calopteryx splendens* (Harris). *Journal of the British Dragonfly Society,* **17**, 55–58.

King, J.J.F.X. (1889). A contribution towards a catalogue of the neuropterous fauna of Ireland. *Transactions of the Natural History Society of Glasgow,* **2**, 259–292.

King, J.J.F.X. and Halbert, J. N. (1910). A list of the Neuroptera of Ireland. *Proceedings of the Royal Irish Academy,* **28B**, 29–112.

Kitching, D. (2004). News from Cheshire. *Newsletter of the Dragonfly Recording Network,* **21**, 8–9.

Longfield, C. (1937, 1949). *The Dragonflies of the British Isles,* 1st and 2nd edns, London, Frederick Warne.

Longfield, C. (1954). The British dragonflies (Odonata) in 1952 and 1953. *Entomologist,* **87**, 87–91.

Lucas, W.J. (1900). *British Dragonflies (Odonata),* London, L. Upcott Gill.

McLachlan, R. (1884). The British dragon-flies annotated. *Entomologist's Monthly Magazine,* **20**, 251–256.

Moore, N. (1987). *The Bird of Time: The Science and Politics of Nature Conservation*, Cambridge, Cambridge University Press.

Merritt, R., Moore, N.W. and Eversham, B.C. (1996). *Atlas of the Dragonflies of Britain and Ireland*, ITE Research Publication No. 9, London, HMSO.

Nelson, B. and Thompson, R. (2004). *The Natural History of Ireland's Dragonflies*, Belfast, The National Museums and Galleries of Northern Ireland.

Nelson, B., Ronayne, C. and Thompson, R. (2003). Colonization and changing status of four Odonata species, *Anax imperator, Anax parthenope, Aeshna mixta and Sympetrum fonscolombii*, in Ireland 2000–2002. *Irish Naturalists' Journal,* **27**, 266–272.

Parr, A. J. (2007). Migrant and dispersive dragonflies in Britain during 2006. *Journal of the British Dragonfly Society,* **23**, 40–51.

Parslow, R. (2007). *The Isles of Scilly*. The New Naturalist Library, Vol. 103, London, Collins.

Perrin, V.L. (2005). Dragonflies. *British Wildlife,* **16**, 356.

Pinniger, E.B. (1947). *Coenagrion scitulum*, Rambur, a dragonfly new to Britain. *London Naturalist,* **26**, 80.

Porritt, G.T. (1912). *Agrion armatum*, Charp, in the Norfolk Broads. *Entomologist's Monthly Magazine,* **23**, 163.

Sélys Longchamps, E. de (1846). Revision of the British Libellulidae. *Annals and Magazine of Natural History,* **18**, 217–227.

Silsby, J.D. and Silsby, R.I. (1988). Dragonflies in Jersey. *Journal of the British Dragonfly Society,* **4**, 31–36.

Siva-Jothy, M. (1997). Description of the Beautiful Demoiselle *Calopteryx virgo* (Linnaeus). In Brooks, S., *Field Guide to the Dragonflies and Damselflies of Great Britain and Ireland*, Hook, Hampshire, British Wildlife Publishing, pp. 59–61.

Smith, B. (2004). Report from Scotland 2002/2003. *Newsletter of the Dragonfly Recording Network,* **21**, 5–6.

Stephens, J.F. (1835–37). *Illustrations of British Entomology: A Synopsis of Indigenous Insects: Containing their Generic and Specific Distinctions: with an Account of their Metamorphoses, Times of Appearance, Localities, Food, and Economy*, 11 Vols., London, Baldwin and Craddock.

Taylor, P. (2008). Comments on the Odonata Red List for Great Britain. *Journal of the British Dragonfly Society,* **24**, 37–44.

Ward, L. and Mill, P.J. (2004). Distribution of the Banded Demoiselle *Calopteryx splendens* (Harris) in northern England: an example of range expansion? *Journal of the British Dragonfly Society,* **20**, 61–69.

27

Flies, beetles and bees, wasps and ants (Diptera, Coleoptera and aculeate Hymenoptera)

Alan Stubbs

Summary

These large insect groups have a huge range of lifestyles, ecological niches and habitats. Their fate over the last 50 years has been a response to the many well-documented environmental changes, but these insects have also responded to more subtle ecological factors which are less obvious. Large declines in whole assemblages of species have gone largely unreported in conservation reviews, and many species fall into the modern definition of Species of Conservation Concern. An important message is that these insect groups have declined even on many nature reserves, since their requirements are often not met by general-ised habitat management. The term Favourable Conservation Status for SSSIs can readily misrepresent the status of the invertebrate fauna, a key issue for the future. In covering such a large subject, examples can only give a partial picture, and issues raised are to varying degrees applicable to more than one group of insects.

Introduction

In Britain and Ireland, these groups of insects between them include about 11 500 species: 7000 flies (Diptera), 4000 beetles (Coleoptera) and some 500 aculeate Hymenoptera. They cover a huge range of lifestyles and ecological niches, major components of the ecological web of life. Apart from larvae eating plants and adults being pollinators, life histories can be dependent on rotting wood, decaying vegetation, carrion, mud and peat, soil, commensalism, parasitism (including parasitic 'cuckoo' types) and blood-sucking, and fly species can occur in all environments, on land, in fresh water and at the marine fringe. Whilst there are many charismatic species, most are easily overlooked. By the end of the nineteenth century, the British fauna was monographed for beetles and aculeates, but it took until the end of the twentieth century before the fly fauna was listed to a similar level.

Silent Summer: The State of Wildlife in Britain and Ireland, ed. Norman Maclean. Published by Cambridge University Press. © Cambridge University Press 2010.

The Second World War marked a tipping point in the fortunes of these insect groups. Government policies towards maximising home-grown food and timber, and with it insecticides and herbicides, has led to much of the countryside becoming hostile to many insects.

Plants have seed banks or can survive vegetatively without reproduction. Birds are very mobile and find habitat created for them. To some extent these species are buffered against discontinuity of breeding habitat. However, most invertebrates need the right conditions all the time (for both adults and early stages) and often have poor mobility, making them much more vulnerable to local extinction. Moreover, as well shown with butterflies, meta-population structure and habitat size/population viability are strong factors in their survival.

Ironically, in the 1990s and 2000s, just when agricultural and forestry policies were becoming more favourable, the big government drive has been to build on 'brown-field' (the last refuge for important invertebrate assemblages) rather than on now sterile 'greenfield' sites. Late in the day 'Open Mosaic Habitats on previously developed land' is now a Biodiversity Action Plan (BAP) Priority Habitat, the insect groups in this chapter contributing to these key assemblages.

Expertise

Much of the knowledge of the British fauna is derived from about two centuries of dedication by amateur entomologists. By the late 1800s, beetles had been well worked as a popular group, and the aculeates (bees, wasps and ants) had been well studied by a small band of entomologists. However flies (Diptera) were still considered to be too difficult for most entomologists. In essence, it took another 100 years before knowledge of flies was up to an equivalent level.

The notion of recording schemes took hold with some flies in the 1970s (craneflies and hoverflies, for instance). It took rather longer for other recording schemes to arise, and also for specialist societies and journals to appear. The outcome has been a dramatic increase in recording activity. The Dipterists Forum (flies) has over 300 members (also known for its journal *Dipterists Digest*), the Bees, Wasps and Ants Recording Society over 400 members (its journal is *BWARS News*) and the beetle enthusiasts have *The Coleopterist* journal, with 400 subscribers.

There has thus been a dramatic increase in interest in these groups of insects, but interest groups remain small relative to the size of the faunas being studied and recorded, compared with ornithologists or botanists.

Climate change

Britain has always been noted for its unpredictable climate, lying between the North Atlantic and the continental land mass. The literature refers to poor insect seasons well before pesticides could be the main causal factor. While 'traditional' low-intensity land use prevailed (as indeed during the agricultural depression prior to the Second World War), and good-quality habitats were widespread or large, a poor season or two could be buffered by a fresh surge of large population numbers.

A significant climatic change occurred in the early 1960s when there was a succession of cool summers, including a period of exceptionally low summer temperatures for three months running. Thus southern warm-climate species, which had done well into the late 1950s, rapidly declined. This was a strong tipping point in the fortunes of solitary bees and wasps, and for some of the charismatic flies such as the bug parasite, *Gymnosoma rotundatum*. The ant, *Formica pratense*, has never been seen since and it has taken the succession of hot summers of the early 2000s to detect recovery (or recolonisation from the continent) and for some of the lost species to appear again.

However, the pattern is not always simple. Not only are there fluxes of insect populations caused by climate, but other environmental factors have had severe and generally negative impact since the 1950s, including insecticides, which for some years were applied very liberally and were especially prone to drift onto non-target habitat, both land and water.

More recently, exceptional climatic events have also upset the norm. The hot drought summer of 1975, and dry conditions continuing into the even hotter drought of 1976 proved to be a major threshold. Warmth-loving species benefited, though within the limitations of temperatures becoming too hot, including the drying up of nectar sources and food plants. But it was a distinct disadvantage for moist- or wet-habitat groups. Certainly the cool, wet conditions of the 1960s suited craneflies (350 species), but they did much less well in the more drought-prone districts. It took at least 10 years before numbers were respectable again. Anecdotal evidence suggests that about 1990s snail-killing flies (nearly 70 species) declined sharply and have never recovered. By 2000, a sequence of exceptionally warm years again affected the seasonal norms. Then in the later 2000s, summers switched to become cooler and wetter; aculeates declined, many fly groups became scarce and some of the beetle groups were much more unpredictable. Regrettably, for the most part there have been no monitoring schemes to provide data for critical scientific analysis.

A European-wide view is desirable. An ever larger number of species are changing their European range rapidly, with ever more reaching the western continental belt. Some of these can fly across the Channel unaided, but there are also many ways of being accidentally imported. Various flies and beetles from New Zealand and other distant countries have taken up residence in our compatible climate; options will change as our climate changes.

Flies (Diptera)

In 1901, after much re-evaluation, 2578 species had been recorded in Britain. By 1945 that figure was 5219 species as a result of more serious attention to the taxonomy of flies, and this reached 5728 species by 1974. As flies have became more accessible to enthusiastic amateurs, as a result of better keys to identification, the number of people recording Diptera has risen considerably, especially with the institution of recording schemes from the 1970s, plus the promotion of workshops and other means of assistance via the Dipterists Forum. Thus the British list of Diptera now exceeds 7000 species (inclusive of some as yet known only from Ireland). Historic evaluation of species status needs care, since while many species have become scarcer due to habitat loss, the great increase in recording can result in a disproportionate percentage of recent records that masks the true situation. There has, however, been a determined effort since 1974 to hold long field meetings in poorly recorded parts of Britain, thus giving a more representative knowledge of the distribution of species, and locating many new species, including ones new to science, in the process.

Shirt (1987) categorised 13.8% of the then-known flies as Red Data Book species, of which three were extinct before 1900 (many more species may have died out depending on the evaluation of records without a properly labelled voucher specimen). Those figures are deceptive, since only the better-known families of flies were considered.

Losses and declines

Hoverflies have always been one of the most-studied families of flies, monographed in 1901, yet there has not been a decade when further additions have not been made. Indeed there were 47 additions by the year 2000, and more since. Whilst many additions have been due to refinements of taxonomy that have recognised new cryptic species, there have been new colonists from mainland Europe. Most other families of flies have also proved to be far more species rich than earlier thought possible, and that trend continues.

The future of the more specialist saproxylic fauna (feeding on dead wood) is causing much concern. The Scottish Highlands provide prime BAP examples among hoverflies. Thus *Blera fallax* used to be widespread in eastern Caledonian pine forest, but now it is reduced to two very small populations: there are no longer enough veteran trees to provide the right rot conditions, so artificial rot holes are being made. The Aspen Hoverfly (*Hammerschmidtia ferruginea*) depends on continuity of supply of newly fallen mature Aspen; only 11, mainly small, sites in Britain have this continuity, all in the Scottish Highlands (and an associated fauna of equally rare flies has been found). The importance of dead wood lying in streams and seepages was overlooked. Hence four species of *Lipsothrix*, a cranefly genus that specialises in saturated decaying wood, were placed on the BAP list and it has become apparent that their restricted distribution correlates with past woodland management regimes, since continuity of habitat is vital to their survival (Hewitt and Parker 2005).

Land drainage has seriously impoverished fly faunas. Craneflies are a good example of flies that require wet or moist ground, so they were particularly vulnerable to the massive programmes of field under-drainage and ditching; moor-gripping in the uplands has led to similar deprivation (Stubbs 2001). Many of the places in which craneflies were recorded in the past are now greatly impoverished or sterile. The dredging and straightening of lowland rivers has also removed exposed riverine sediment (ERS) and other riparian habitats. It is now evident that whole assemblages of flies have been eliminated from some catchments before they were recorded. Recent studies have revealed the local presence of surviving rich fly faunas dependent on ERS, some representative species being listed under the BAP, such as the stiletto flies *Cliorismia rustica* and *Spiverpa lunulata* and yellow species of the cranefly *Rhabdomastix* (which has proved to be two species). Shallow flood-plain pools on unimproved grasslands are a special habitat for the soldierfly, *Odontomyia argentata*, but suitable habitat has become scarce. A study in Surrey revealed that even ditching a stream within sallow carr by six inches reduced the cranefly fauna from 31 species to 13 species (Stubbs 2001): Wisley Common SSSI used to have the second richest cranefly fauna in Britain in the 1960s, with over 100 species, yet now it is little more than an average site; the construction of the adjacent M25 added to the problems by intercepting shallow groundwater while public pressure on the rich marginal habitats at Boulder Lake has not been adequately controlled.

Grazing levels provide an old style of land drainage via ditch systems which act as fences between fields. From the early 1980s, renewed interest has revealed the true importance of this habitat. In particular, most special flies live along the ditch margins where cattle trampling creates a wet, poached shelf. Moreover, a high concentration of Red Data Book fly species has been found at the transition from brackish water to fresh water. Thus changes in hydrology and management can have serious consequences. Sheep are not heavy enough to create and maintain a poached wet berm (a shelf at the ditch margin at about summer water level). Deep drainage to allow cereal culture has created deep sharp-sided ditches and the application of fertilisers led to the ditch water being covered in a blanket of algae that shaded out the water plants required by some aquatic flies. Special species include the cranefly, *Limnophila pictipennis*, found in wet margins and the soldierfly, *Odontomyia ornata*, whose larvae live among Ivy-leaved Duckweed, *Lemna trisulcata*. Usually the grasslands are improved, but on parts of Pevensey Levels NNR, Sussex, there are unimproved meadows that grade up to land which does not flood for long periods – it is here that the rare horsefly, *Atylotus rustica*, has one of its few last strongholds.

Whilst exploitation of surface springs and bore-hole abstraction of groundwater is not new, the post-war demand for water has substantially increased. Thus even on some high-grade conservation sites, the surface flow has greatly declined and groundwater seepage habitats have become drought prone. In most such cases the tragedy is that the fly fauna was not recorded prior to abstraction, which also remains the case even now, as new resources are exploited. Recording in recent decades has revealed some extraordinarily special sites, such as two for the soldierfly, *Odontomyia hydroleon*, and three for the cranefly, *Ellipteroides limbatus*. It is apparent that habitat for a number of other species is nowadays extremely rare and vulnerable to loss. For instance, the cranefly, *Ellipteroides alboscutellatus*, was known from very few sites: a survey of all known tufaceous sites (sites rich in tufa, a porous calcareous rock) with potential, extending from Somerset to Lancashire and Yorkshire revealed only 12 sites supporting this species (Heaver 2006). The habitat is flushed *Palustriella* (= *Cratoneuron*) moss beds on spring-line tufa seepages, most of which are now in lowland woodland. The patches of habitat are small, some without conservation designation, and some are vulnerable hydrologically and to other ecological change.

Open mosaic habitat on previously developed land is now a recognised BAP priority. 'Brownfield', which includes the abandoned parts of quarries, provides for species which require ruderal plants, such as the tephritid picture-winged flies whose larvae live in flower heads or as leaf-miners in Ragwort, Mugwort and other wild plants. The key plant for some species is Hoary Ragwort, *Senecio erucifolius*, for the tephritids, *Merzomyia westermannii* and *Tephritis malaris*. Some species of *Homoneura* (Lauxaniidae) are mainly found under sallows on brownfield. In fact there is large fly fauna whose main or sole refuge is here rather than in the semi-natural vegetation sites catered for by the conservation movement.

The larvae of tephritid picture-winged flies specialise in particular food plants, mainly living in the flower/seed heads of Asteracea, while some are leaf-miners or berry feeders. Species of chalk grassland flora and other such habitats have clearly suffered from habitat declines. There is also the issue of grassland management, such as periods when conservation grazing has been too intensive for the occupants of stems and flower heads to survive, applying also to mowing, since even overwintering stages of these insects can be in galled seed-heads.

Sciomyzids are called snail-killing flies because the larvae are parasitoids of snails, mainly found in marshes and water sides, but also in dry habitats. In the early 1990s, this fauna declined sharply and has not recovered to its former numbers; the explanation is not clear. It is easier to appreciate why craneflies were plentiful in the 1960s, since a cool, wet climate suited many of them, and why the heat and droughts of 1975–6 caused a major decline in the southern areas of Britain, from which these insects have only slowly recovered. In the hot years of the early- to mid-2000s, the beneficiary was *Tipula helvola*, a dry ground specialist, but this also declined, together with many other craneflies, from 2006 onwards when summers were again cool and wet. In 2007 Dolichopodidae was spectacularly reduced for no obvious reason, and many other types of fly did poorly; 2008 was not much better. As yet it is difficult to say whether these changes are part of the normal fluctuations in status or whether something more fundamental is happening.

In 1992, Britain declared that it had eradicated cattle warble fly (*Hypoderma bovis* and *H. lineatum*; the Deer Warble Fly, *H. diana* remains). This is the only significant case of the successful deliberate extinction of British fly species. Of course, there have been other campaigns, as against the House Fly, *Musca domestica*, in the 1940s and 50s, leading to it becoming immune to DDT and other such chemicals. This latter species has undergone an enormous decline, almost to rarity status in many districts, mainly due to environments becoming so hygienic, and it is now often replaced by the Lesser House Fly, *Faunia canicularis*.

Additions and increases

The great increase in conifer afforestation in Britain and Ireland has enabled some species to extend their distribution. This is evident with some hoverflies formerly confined to the native pine woods of the Scottish Highlands; the conifer aphid-dependent *Eupeodes nielseni* is now present even in southern England. Other conifer aphid-dependent species prefer spruce and fir rather than native Scots Pine and would seem to have colonised from Europe, such as *Dasysyphrus friuliensis* and *Eriozona syrphoides*, whilst others, such as *Parasyrphus vittiger*, are much more plentiful than in the past. The larvae of *Xylota jakatorum* live under the bark of stumps where conifers have been recently felled, so there was a time lag awaiting the felling of the initial plantings before this fly spread widely from Scotland.

The tachind flies that are parasitic on shield bugs (Acanthosomidae and Pentatomidae) underwent a major decline in the poor summers of the early 1960s, but were able to recover in the hot summers of the 2000s; these include *Phasia hemiptera, Subclytia rotundiventris* and *Gymnosoma nitens* (the latter had seemingly become extinct and may have re-colonised from mainland Europe).

The significance of climate applies to many additions. Thus the large and spectacular hoverfly, *Volucella zonaria*, colonised Britain in the 1940s and persisted on the south coast and in the urban heat island of London. Not until the 2000s did it spread north of London, but by 2008 it had reached Cheshire. The larvae are scavengers in the nests of social wasps and it is thought that longer, milder autumns have given more time for the large larvae to mature (not simply a matter of high summer temperatures).

It is important to recognise that many flies are quite dramatically increasing their range in Europe (apparently related to changing climate), poising them for the next jump into Britain. A good hoverfly example is *Sphegina siberica*, which in recent decades expanded its range across Europe and then into Britain where it is now a very common species in some districts; its larvae live in wet, rotting wood. About a third of the hoverfly British fauna have larvae that feed on aphids, the supply and quantity of which is unreliable, so some species of hoverfly are very mobile. Thus, in the 1990s, species such as *Epistrophe melanostoma* colonised Britain, following good years in mainland Europe, and are dependent on aphids on deciduous trees.

Tehritid flies have been discussed under losses among semi-natural flora habitats. However, there have been remarkable gains and increases in species associated with various ruderal weedy Asteraceae. A number of these species have spread from southern England to much further north in recent decades. Thus *Tephritis cometa* on Creeping Thistle (*Circium arvense*) had only three records for the London area in 1956, and that was its stronghold, yet now it is plentiful around London and extends into Scotland. On Mugwort (*Artemesia vulgaris*), the flies, *Campiglossa absinthii* and *C. misella*, are no longer unusual. In 1974 *Campiglossa malaris* was found near Folkstone on Hoary Ragwort and has now spread into the Midlands. One of the latest newcomers on the south coast is *Tephritis divisa* that specialises on Bristly Ox-tongue (*Picris echiodes*), so it is very likely that it will soon spread more widely onto this locally common plant of disturbed land.

Various other flies seem to have been introduced into Britain via the horticultural trade. The scathophagid, *Norellia spinipes*, was first found in Surrey in 1965; now this leaf-miner of daffodils (*Narcissus*) has extended its range into the Midlands. *Rhagoletis meigeni* larvae live in the berries of Barberry, *Berberis*, (which was almost eliminated in the wild since it is a vector for a cereal rust fungus); after many years 'absence' this fly has now been found on ornamental *Berberis* in Battersea Park, London so it may become a beneficiary of urban planting. The leaf mines of the agromyzid, *Phytomyza hellebori*, were found in gardens in the early 2000s; searches in nearby garden centres revealed similar leaf-mines on imported plants of *Helleborus foetidus* from Holland (the mines were also found on wild plants, thus confusing the source). In 2007, leaf mines were found in House Leek (*Sempirvirens tectorum*) obtained from a Surrey garden centre; this proved to be the first record of the hoverfly, *Cheilosia caerulea*, that may now establish in British gardens, even though the plant on which it is dependent is a native of mountains in central and southern Europe.

Beetles (Coleoptera)

Though regarded as one of the historically best-studied large groups of insects, additional species of beetles are regularly discovered. Taxonomic advances have resulted in species splits and extra species have found their way into Britain by range extension or accidental introduction. In 1945, the British list stood at 3690 species, but by 1974 the figure had risen to 3811 (excluding doubtful ones) (Hammond 1974). Now the total is about 4030, the increase reflecting, in part, a resurgence in the number of able recorders.

The Red Data Book lists 14% of the fauna of the UK (Shirt 1987), including 54 species regarded as extinct prior to 1900; a number of endangered species may have become extinct since, but there is a time lag before confirming this. About 250 species of beetle were recorded prior to 1970, but have not been recorded since.

Losses and declines

As with flies, the destruction of veteran trees and tidying away of fallen branches and larger timber has caused the decline of many beetle species. The sites with a really rich saproxylic beetle fauna are the old classic localities such as the New Forest, Windsor Forest and Epping Forest. After the Second World War, the first two localities suffered massive losses of veteran trees to make way for conifer plantations, but, fortunately, some conservation areas were set aside; a major concern is whether enough trees remain to provide continuity of rare niches for rare beetles, such as the BAP click beetle, *Limoniscus violaceus*, which received provision of articifical breeding habitat. The prospect of tree generation gaps (in the case of Oak it may take 400–500 years before providing the right conditions) is worrying. In all three of the above sites excessive removal of fallen timber for firewood has been a problem in the past. Britain also has many old deer parks, some of which contain populations of veteran Oaks, and indeed it is thought that Britain has the highest remaining representation of such trees in Europe. Improvement of documentation has helped to make ecological information more accessible (Alexander 2002).

The aquatic beetle fauna associated with good-quality water margins has suffered badly, including ditches on grazing levels. In the days of hand clearing of choked ditches, the pace was gradual compared with modern machinery that can rapidly dig deep channels over a large area. A four-year rotation may suit some open-water beetles, but not those of emergent vegetation. The dytiscids and related water beetles now have much reduced suitable habitat (except those of gravel pits). The fauna of shallow pools on fen has become of particular concern because of drainage. The donacine leaf-beetles have aquatic larvae with breathing spiracles plugged into air spaces in plants. Some species have suffered major decline, and the position is even worse in some European countries, where a substantial proportion of species have become extinct. The British distribution maps of *Donacia* in Cox (2007) do not display declines since 1970, *Donacia aquatica*, for instance, now being BAP because it is reduced to so few sites. Aquatic weevils of the genus *Bagous* were revealed as a particularly vulnerable genus in the Red Data Book (Shirt 1987). The statuses were confirmed or revised by Hyman (1992) who defined two species as extinct, seven endangered, two vulnerable and one status insufficiently known, plus two rare and six in the non-RDB category notable (= nationally scarce). This is a high proportion of the 21 British species, and indeed the only representatives of the sub-family Bardinae.

Terrestrial leaf beetles (Chrysomelidae and allies) have proved to be a very vulnerable group, very evidently so with the Pot Beetles, *Cryptocephalus*: of the 20 British species, one is extinct, six are so endangered as to be on the BAP list and another two are graded as vulnerable (Cox 2007). Various other leaf beetles are in decline, such as those associated with young-growth Aspen, which used to thrive when coppicing woodland was commonplace. When coppice management ceases, even for a few years, the early-coppice-cycle fauna can all too easily die out, especially if rides with Aspen also become shaded. Such species might survive on sunny woodland edges, especially where Aspen sucker growth is allowed space to naturally extend outwards, but generally there are sharp edges between woodland and fields, and those directing conservation measures are often intolerant of scrub invasion. Many insects specialise in this transitional mid-pioneer zone between grassland and woodland. The weevil tribe Lixini has only six species in Britain; of the five species in the genus *Lixus*, four are listed as of Red Data Book status by Hyman (1992), of which three were classified as endangered (in fact no post-1970 records, even of the one whose larvae live in the stems of thistles; the other two are associated with water margin or aquatic plants).

The earliest pioneer seral, onto bare ground, succession is vulnerable to neglect or mismanagement. Some ground beetles (Carabidae), for instance, require bare ground, which does not register in the National Vegetation Classification (NVC) that conservationists use to classify ecological representation. Britain has five tiger beetles (Cicindellinae), four of which are very restricted in distribution, and the Wood Tiger Beetle (*Cicindella sylvestris*) has declined rapidly in recent decades, causing it to have endangered/BAP status. In fact, the bare ground has to be within a habitat mosaic, either as small patches between pioneer plants or as larger patches adjacent to more mature vegetation, since predatory beetles need conditions that suit prey.

Dung is not a high-profile habitat in conservation circles, yet it supports a substantial invertebrate fauna, including various types of dung beetles. The widespread decline and loss of grazing cattle has had major implications in some regions. Also, silage and improved grassland is lower in roughage, and dung quality has further suffered though the use of avermectins, which result in the dung containing toxins. The resurgence of the horse also carries with it the avermectin limitations. Hyman (1992) reviews the status of scarabaeid dung beetles, listing eight as extinct and eight as endangered (of which one had no post-1970 records, and that was before avermectins). Fortunately some dung beetles can also use rabbit dung, such as the large *Typhaeus typhoeus*.

Some beetles have a complex life cycle, for instance oil beetles (Meloidae) whose larvae are kleptoparasites of bees. Since the host populations of bees have declined, oil beetles have become very prone to local extinction, and indeed three of the nine species recorded in Britain are already extinct. Declines in occurrence over the 25 years or so are about 50–60% in *Meloe rugosus* (with few records), 25–50% in *Meloe proscarabaeus and* 20–30% in *Meloe violaceus*, these figures not taking into account the massive habitat loss and degradation prior to 1980. Hence, these species are categorised as BAP.

Rising sea levels will also be an increasing issue. Increased rates of erosion of soft-rock cliffs could make the cliff too devoid of the niches required by the associated beetles and other insects; the staphyilinid beetle, *Bledius filipes*, occurs only in one small patch of cliff in Norfolk. On accretionary coasts the main habitats will adjust to modified circumstances, even if lost in some places and building up in others. The greatest risk is to those beetle assemblages which are currently very localised, such as those of saline seepage gravel on the East Anglian coast.

Additions and increases

Ladybirds prove a good example of beetle species which have increased. The Cream-streaked Ladybird (*Harmonia quadripunctata*) was first found in Suffolk in 1939 and spread, thanks to the availability of pines (arguably not native outside the Scottish

Highlands); for instance, it is now quite common in Surrey. The Orange Ladybird (*Halyzia 16-punctata*) used to be a rare species of ancient woodlands, but it showed a marked increase in the 1980s, and by the 1990s was common over parts of southern England and Wales (it feeds on mildew, most frequently on non-native sycamore) (Majerus 1994). In May 1997 the Bryony Ladybird (*Eiplachia argus*) was discovered in Surrey and was soon established in a part of that county (Hawkins 2000); as the name suggests, it lives on White Bryony (*Bryonia dioica*), a widespread native plant of the southern half of England. A far less welcome arrival of the 2000s has been the Harlequin Ladybird (*Harmonia axyridis*), which has fast colonised England and Wales and is still progressing northwards. It is of Asian origin, though probably routed via the Netherlands; the big concern in some quarters is that this voracious species will out-compete native aphid-feeding ladybirds and its varied diet could lead to a threat to populations of many other invertebrates.

Bark beetles also illustrate patterns of increase (Foresty Commission website, http://www.forestry.gov.uk/). Dutch Elm Disease has struck Britain several times, the Elm Bark Beetles fluctuating accordingly. Prior to the devastating disease that was accidentally imported into Britain in the mid-1980s, the main vector, *Scolytus scolytus*, had 'disappeared', but then reappeared and exploded in numbers. The Smaller Elm Bark Beetle, *Scolytus multistriatus*, populations reacted similarly, though this beetle was regarded as a poor vector. These species now survive on the varying fortunes of Elm sucker growth. Other bark beetles attack forestry trees, including introduced beetles that attack non-native trees such as Spruce. In 1982 the Great Spruce Bark Beetle (*Dendroctonus micans*) was found, causing major concern and the introduction of measures to try to confine it to Wales and adjacent English counties; in 1996 it appeared in Kent. *Ips typographicus* was found in 1997, probably via imported timber, another potential major threat to economic forestry. A varied array of other types of beetles turn up as accidental imports, including destructive timber-burrowing longhorn beetles, Cerambycidae. The big question is which species are capable of establishing themselves in the British environment. Future higher temperatures may allow more species to successfully colonise; some will be 'harmless', others may have significant economic and ecological impact unless prompt control measures prove effective.

Bees, wasps and ants (aculeate Hymenoptera)

Note that the sawflies and parasitic wasps are not covered in this account. Historically, the aculeates have been well recorded, including a monograph on bees and wasps in 1898. The situation with ants is complex, since there have been some taxonomic revisions in recent decades, including splits in common species. Felton (1974) noted that there had been an average of one species per year added since the beginning of the century, a 28% increase since 1898, giving a total of 483 species (excluding Bletharidae and Chrysidae). For Felton's home county of Kent, species added to the county list and apparent losses roughly balanced out, leading him to the general statement that aculeates in Britain were stable. However, Kent did not suffer the degree of the massive intensification of farming characteristic of wide swaths of England in the 1960s–80s. It is now known that there were massive declines in many species (as with bumblebees). From doom and gloom, the picture altered during the sequence of hot summers in the early to mid-2000s when various 'extinct' and near extinct species did well, some possibly having re-colonised Britain, reaching a wider range than the historic picture. Then came a series of poor summers, 2007 and 2008 in particular, when in many parts of Britain aculeate numbers crashed, so there is now considerable uncertainly as to the current status of many species.

The Red Data Book (Shirt 1987) treated 28.3% of the aculeates as meeting the criteria. This is an exceptionally high figure, in excess of butterflies (21.4%) and dragonflies (22%) and with aculeates, a far greater number of species were of concern. Statuses were updated by Falk (1991).

In evolutionary terms, the aculeates are the most advanced insects (plus Hymenoptera Parasitica). Many have specialised multi-niche requirements, together with specialised behaviour. That makes them especially vulnerable if even one piece of their ecological jigsaw is not correct. It is not surprising that aculeates have suffered very badly from the intensification of land management and simplification of ecological niches and habitat mosaic.

Such ecological and resulting faunal simplification is nothing new. For instance, Hampstead Heath, now enveloped by North London, was well surveyed for aculeates in 1830, revealing that nearly half the British fauna was present. Later surveys indicated that by 1946 the average decline was one species per year (Stubbs 1982). For the most part, the losses were of the most ecologically fussy species, leaving the generalist ones (regrettably there is no recent re-survey). Yet the 'site' is protected (as a public open space). The graver concern is that many nature reserves and SSSIs have been mirroring a similar decline of aculeates (and often other types of insects). The loss of one species a year does not sound much, and may not be noticed, but over the decades it leads to a substantial impoverishment of biodiversity.

Losses and declines

The last known nests of the ant, *Formica pratense*, were seen in East Dorset in the late 1950s. More recent searches at the exact spots and locality in general have been unsuccessful. After a 50-year gap with no records, this species is effectively regarded as extinct.

Solitary bees are dependent on their favoured flower resources. Nesting sites can be very specialised, either in the ground or in hollow stems and beetle burrows in wood. Some genera are cuckoos, vulnerable to populations of their hosts falling below a critical threshold. Tongue length is one of the factors that define flower-type requirements, and some species obtain nectar and pollen from different flower species. The large species, *Andrena hafforfiana*, is mainly dependent on Field Scabious, *Knautia arvensis*; this bee has retreated to the very few districts with sufficient flowers, and its cuckoo bee, *Nomada armata*, is further reduced to parts of Salisbury Plain within a large unimproved area of chalk grassland. *Nomada errans* was first recorded at a locality on the Dorset coast in 1878, but was last seen there in 1982; after over 100 years with suitable habitat, amenity management proved to be its downfall.

The woodland Hymenopteran fauna is largely restricted to rides and other sunny positions, thus subject to decline as coppicing and other woodland management became neglected. This is most easily observed with the Wood Ant, *Formica rufa*, whose present residual distribution is an indicator of woods that have not had a period of complete dense shade. Coniferisation of woodland was often at the expense of ground flora and scrub flowers used by bees. Actually, in the larger forests it was coniferisation and ride management that saved the aculeate fauna from being completely lost. Some aculeates nest in beetle burrows in dead trees or logs, which are very prone to being tidied away in management procedures. A problem of recent decades has been the massive increase in deer populations in some regions, such as the east Midlands, causing the drastic loss of flowering herbs used by aculeate insects, and their replacement by grasses and sedges.

Many roads have been widened, reducing or eliminating the verge grassland. During the 1960s, in some districts, chemicals were also applied to verges in order to restrict growth, and this was also the period when mowing road verges became very widespread. The periodicity and timing of cutting or mowing off all the flowers on which aculeate insects depend can be critical, including the availability of any flowers persisting after treatment. Often a strip nearest the road is cut more regularly, which can usefully suit low-growing yellow composites. It remains the case that some very floristic road verges are important remnants of grassland habitat useful to solitary bees. The protected-road-verge principle has been adopted in some counties for flowers, but needs extending for the interests of aculeate insects.

Lowland heath includes some of the richest aculeate habitats, but there have been massive losses of open heath. Traditionally, fire was used in some vague rotation. However, by the 1960s arson had become widespread, reaching a critical level in the drought summers of 1975 and 1976, when vast areas were burnt, creating landscape bereft of nectar sources. Thus mowing became the prime option, but this allowed peaty litter to build up so that mineral soil was no longer available for burrowing solitary bees and wasps. In the 1990s came the idea to reintroduce cattle grazing in the hope that the flora might recover to the former richness apparent prior the age of the car. However, cattle are prone to selectively eat plants with flowers, causing concern that nectar sources are insufficient for solitary bees. That principle also applies to the mowing or grazing of grassland.

Access for all has become an increasing theme, as pleasing habitat sites are expected to cater for more visitors. More visitors mean greater trampling of paths, leading to loss of plant cover and erosion on slopes. Within reason, many aculeates require the bare soil and sand created by trampling. However, such niches are often regarded as unsightly and unsuited to the urban visitor in town shoes. Hence, erosion protection is put in place and paths grassed or hard surfaced. The intent may be laudable, but the net result can be impoverishment of the aculeate fauna, especially where such measures are adopted on high-grade aculeate sites, including National Nature Reserves. The immense increase in recreational riding has also resulted in some tracks being too churned up for burrowing aculeates, especially when riding schools are using the same routes very regularly.

Some species of aculeate have retracted their range to the last unaffected refuge, coastal cliffs. The last large populations of the bee, *Eucera longicornis*, are here, but its cuckoo bee, *Nomada sexfaciata*, is reduced to only one section of cliff. Even on such coasts, agricultural improvement has often removed the cliff-top flowery margins. Also, some eroding soft-rock cliffs have deteriorated as a result of sea defences. Sea defences at the bottom of such a cliff result in the cliff stabilising at an incline, or engineered as a stable slope, leading to the loss of the bare ground on which the aculeates depend. Or sea defences on the adjacent coast may lead to increased cliff erosion on aculeate-rich cliffs, resulting in erosion becoming too fast to provide for a proper representation of pioneer vegetation habitat, nectar and pollen sources; at the extreme, cliff erosion can cause the loss of whole populations within nesting burrows in a cliff.

The other main refuge is 'brownfield' sites, especially where these coincide with a biodiversity hot spot for aculeates, as in the Thames Gateway. A mile-wide strip along the estuary edge has an especially favourable climate, including high sunshine figures, and there used to be extensive abandoned quarries in chalk, gravel and other substrates which provided a range of soils and a wealth of flowers. In the 1990s, and especially 2000s, much of the best aculeate habitat has been built upon, creating a tip-point in the survivability of the most special species: the loss of some species is a real probability unless policies change soon.

Additions and increases

A good number of rare species have suddenly done well and expanded their range beyond the past historic limits, such as the bee, *Sphecodes niger*. Some formerly widespread species which had become scarce have been showing an impressive recovery, such as the bee, *Andrena flavipes*, in turn enabling the cuckoo bee, *Nomada fucata*, to thrive. But some strange changing distributions are puzzling: *Andrena cineraria* was regarded as a northern and western bee of cooler conditions yet in recent decades it has spread south-eastwards even to the London area, and moreover its cuckoo, *Nomada lathbruiana*, has almost kept pace. Thus it can be difficult to predict which will be the future climatic winners among the long-standing native fauna, especially since some range expansions have been sudden and unexpected.

But the 1990s and 2000s have also been a period of primary colonisation of Britain or re-colonisation by species long gone. The Bee Wolf Wasp, *Philanthus triangularum*, caused great excitement when it re-established in Britain and has since spread widely, including Wales, and in some districts has large populations. The social wasps, *Vespula media* and *V. saxonica*, were entirely new residents that soon spread, and very recently a species of *Polistes* has colonised. The spectacular new colonists include *Xylocopa violacea*, which was first noted to overwinter in 2007 (like a large black bumblebee with violet wings, so not easy to overlook). There seems little doubt that if the British climate continues to warm, many more aculeates will colonise and spread as part of the re-adjustments in European range.

The most enigmatic aculeates are the ants, mainly because there have been so many taxonomic splits and re-valuations. Also better surveys have revealed that some of the great rarities are more widespread than was apparent when ants were rather casually considered. The Black Bog Ant, *Formica candida*, was thought to be confined to some bogs in the New Forest and east Dorset, yet now it has been located even in South Wales and some other districts. The common ants, *Lasius niger* and *L. alienus*, have each been split into two species and nests of the genus *Myrmica* proved to contain some very elusive related species that live in the nests of the common species. These examples are 'false increases', due only to increased understanding and recording.

The challenge for the future

- Terms such as Favourable Conservation Status, as applied to SSSIs, for instance, should not have narrow objectives (confined to features highlighted in the schedule), but include favourable conditions for their invertebrate fauna, so that both biodiversity and functional ecology are maintained. Otherwise the term 'favourable' is meaningless as regards the hidden majority of wildlife and the interdependent ecological girder systems.
- Greater attention needs to be given to habitat structure, including unvegetated ground. The National Vegetation Classification as a site description and monitoring tool does not easily translate into invertebrate attributes.
- Better awareness of niches important to these insect groups is required, including habitat mosaic structure and the interdependences entailed at ecological guild level.
- Habitat management mistakes must be reduced if invertebrates are to be safe from needless impoverishment.
- Water-supply policy is at a threshold. Meeting further resource demands threatens spring and seepage sites which have not been evaluated for their invertebrate significance.
- Unless the conservation movement takes 'brownfield' invertebrate faunas more seriously, and the Government changes its rush into building on brownfield as a policy mantra, whole assemblages of species will almost certainly be eliminated from some regions, and probably nationally.

- BAP status for some habitat categories and species is currently almost meaningless on the ground. A mechanism for regular updating and dispersal and application of knowledge of invertebrate requirements is required.
- There is shortage of expertise in the identification of flies, beetles and aculeates relative to the need for sound information; there remain worries about how to generate the next generation of such entomologists. There is an even more acute shortage of people with the required level of expertise in applied invertebrate conservation.
- Climatic change has always been a factor in the changing fortunes of species. The difference is the scale of anticipated change, and there are bound to be winners and losers. Unless we can get a better grip on preventing unnecessary declines and extinction under present circumstances, we shall be very ill prepared to cope with the implications of adjusting to the land-management implications of major climate change.

References

Alexander, K.N.A. (2002). *The Invertebrates of Living and Decaying Timber in Britain and Ireland*, English Nature Research Reports No. 467, Peterborough, English Nature.

Cox, M.L. (2007). *Atlas of the Seed and Leaf Beetles of Britain and Ireland (Coleoptera: Bruchidae, Chrysomelidae, Megalopodidae and Orsodacinidae)*, Peterborough, CEH, JNCC, NHM.

Falk, S. (1991). *A Review of the Scarce and Threatened Bees, Wasps and Ants of Great Britain*, Research and Survey in Nature Conservation, No. 35, Peterborough, Nature Conservancy Council.

Felton, J.C. (1974). Some comments on the Aculeate Fauna. In Hawksworth, D.L., ed., *The Changing Flora and Fauna of Britain*, London, Academic Press, pp. 399–418.

Hammond, P.M. (1974). Changes in the British Coleoptera fauna. In Hawksworth, D.L., ed., *The Changing Flora and Fauna of Britain*, London, Academic Press, pp. 323–369.

Hawkins, R.D. (2000). *Ladybirds of Surrey*, Pirbright, Surrey Wildlife Trust.

Heaver, D. (2006). The ecology of *Ellipteroides alboscutellatus* (von Roser, 1840) in England. *Diptera Digest,* **13**, 67–86.

Hewitt, S.M. and Parker, J. (2005). Craneflies of the genus *Lipsothrix* Loew (Diptera, Limoniidae) in Cumbria. *Diptera Digest,* **12**, 151–157.

Hyman, P.S. (1992). *A Review of the Scarce and Threatened Coleoptera of Great Britain,* Part 1, Peterborough, UK Joint Nature Conservation Committee.

Majerus, M.E. (1994). *The New Naturalists Series: Ladybirds*, London, HarperCollins.

Piper, R. and Hodge, P. (2002). *The Rare Species of* Cryptocephalus*: The Current State of Knowledge*, English Nature Research Reports No. 469, Peterborough, English Nature.

Shirt, D.B. (1987). *British Red Data Books: 2. Insects*, London, Nature Conservancy Council.

Smith, K.G.V. (1974). Changes in the British Dipterous fauna. In Hawksworth, D.L., ed., *The Changing Flora and Fauna of Britain*, London, Academic Press, pp. 371–391.

Stubbs, A.E. (1982). Conservation and the future for the field entomologist. *Procedings and Transactions of the British Entomological & Natural History Society*, **15**, 55–68.

Stubbs, A.E. (2001). Flies. In Hawksworth, D.L., ed., *The Changing Wildlife of Great Britain and Ireland*, London, Taylor Francis.

28

Hemiptera

Alan J.A. Stewart and Peter Kirby

Summary

The Hemiptera are a diverse order of sucking bugs, but reliable data on the
geographical distributions of species in Britain, and changes therein over the
last 50 years, exist only for the Heteroptera (so-called 'true bugs') and the
Auchenorrhyncha (leafhoppers and related groups). Greatly increased recording
activity and more efficient sampling techniques have improved our knowledge
of many species in these two groups, making it important to distinguish species
that have genuinely expanded their ranges from those that are now simply better
recorded. Nevertheless, there is little doubt that considerable changes have taken
place in the distribution of individual species in the last half century and that these
changes are accelerating. The rapid spread of a number of species with previously
restricted ranges, sometimes by switching to a novel host plant or adopting a new
habitat or a wider habitat range, may be a signal of climate change. Fifty-one
species have been added to the British list since 1990, their arrival, usually from
the immediate continent, facilitated by a number of factors, including climatic
warming and the importation of ornamental plant stock. In some cases, new waves
of immigrants have enabled previously scarce or locally extinct species to spread
rapidly. Measured against these positive changes, approximately one-quarter of
the species in both the Heteroptera and the Auchenorrhyncha are of conservation
concern by virtue of being classified as nationally notable or rarer. These species
are associated with a wide range of habitats, but seral grasslands, mires and a
variety of open disturbed ruderal habitats predominate. In summary, the overall
picture is one of an expanding species list, a trend that is likely to continue and
possibly accelerate in future. At least in southern Britain, the hemipteran fauna is
richer now than at any time in the recently recorded past. Measured against this,
very real concerns still exist about a large number of specialist species associated
with vulnerable and declining habitats.

Silent Summer: The State of Wildlife in Britain and Ireland, ed. Norman Maclean. Published by Cambridge
University Press. © Cambridge University Press 2010.

Background

The Hemiptera, collectively known as 'bugs', comprise the fifth largest insect order, both globally and in Britain. They are a very diverse group, the common feature linking them being the possession of piercing and sucking mouthparts in the form of a rostrum used for the extraction of liquids from plants and/or animals. They can be extremely numerous and widespread, a feature that has caused certain species to become pests. They are normally divided into the Heteroptera (often referred to as 'true bugs'), in which the forewings are neatly divided between a thickened basal two-thirds and a membranous tip, and the Homoptera, in which the structure of the forewing is uniform throughout (either hardened or membranous). The latter group is further divided between the Auchenorrhyncha (a term that includes the leafhoppers, planthoppers, froghoppers, treehoppers and cicadas) and the Sternorrhyncha (that include the aphids, whiteflies, scale insects and psyllids or jumping plant lice). The precise taxonomic status of these major groupings and the relationships between them is somewhat controversial and subject to periodic change, but they are nevertheless robust and workable terms for the purposes of biological recording. The Homoptera are exclusively herbivorous, feeding on plant sap, the majority tapping into the phloem stream, but a small number have evolved to exploit xylem sap, while others empty the contents of mesophyll cells. Most Heteroptera are also herbivores, but some families are predatory and some species are omnivorous.

There are some 1600 species of Hemiptera in Britain. The largest groups are the Heteroptera (approx. 577 species) and the Auchenorrhyncha (approx. 390 species). These are the two groups for which the most data exist on distribution and ecology in Britain, although in both cases there is a heavy bias towards records from southern England. Perhaps because of the need for specialist techniques for identification and study, the Sternorrhyncha tend not to be popular amongst amateur naturalists, and consequently distributional data for this group are still sparse, although a long-running network for monitoring aerial aphid populations exists (see Chapter 30). For this reason, we confine our attention in this chapter to the Heteroptera and the Auchenorrhyncha.

In certain habitats, such as grasslands, the Hemiptera can be both species-rich and extremely numerous. Their abundance means that they are an important component in many food webs, supporting a diverse parasitoid community and providing an important resource for both invertebrate and vertebrate predators. Their style of feeding can facilitate the spread of pathogens between plants with significant effects on vegetation composition. Also, the profuse production of liquid excreta, especially by leafhoppers, contributes substantially to nutrient cycling. Their diversity and abundance, together with our increasing knowledge of their habitat requirements and responses to management, has allowed ecologists to use them as indicators of habitat quality, level of disturbance and restoration success (Biedermann *et al.* 2005). Data from multi-site surveys have begun to show the potential for using assemblage composition of

Hemiptera to monitor large-scale environmental change (Eyre *et al.* 2005) and habitat condition (Maczey *et al.* 2005).

Both the Heteroptera and the Auchenorrhyncha are supported by active national recording schemes that produce periodic newsletters, organise field meetings and run websites (e.g. http://www.hetnews.org.uk). To date, however, only one species-distribution atlas has been published (Huxley 2003), although others are in preparation, and selected distribution maps have appeared periodically (e.g. Stewart 1999). An interesting recent development has been a growth in interest amongst amateur wildlife photographers in the challenge of photographing small insects such as the Hemiptera. This has generated a lot of new records, including a number of significant ones, and has prompted the development of a photographic gallery of images devoted to the Hemiptera occurring in Britain (http://www.britishbugs.org.uk).

The first insect Red Data Book listed 79 species of Heteroptera in Britain (Shirt 1987). None of the Auchenorrhyncha was listed due to the limited knowledge of their status at the time. Revised RDB and Nationally Notable conservation statuses were subsequently assigned to 143 rarer species of Heteroptera and 98 Auchenorrhyncha in Britain by Kirby (1992) in a review of their general ecology, distribution and habitat requirements. This represents 24.8% and 25.1% of species in these two groups, respectively. In 2007, seven Auchenorrhyncha and three Heteroptera were added to the UK Biodiversity Action Plan (BAP) list of priority species for conservation action (Table 28.1).

Only one programme of standardised monitoring exists in Britain that includes species in either of these two groups. Larval and adult population densities of two froghoppers (*Philaenus spumarius* and *Neophilaenus lineatus*) are included in the core measurements for monitoring invertebrate numbers within the Environmental Change Network (http://www.ecn.ac.uk/), a long-term environmental monitoring programme covering 12 terrestrial sites across the UK since 1993. Likewise, very few long-term quantitative datasets exist from which it is possible to draw conclusions about trends. Population densities of *Neophilaenus lineatus* have been monitored at a single exposed upland site in Cumbria since 1961 (Whittaker and Tribe 1998). Densities of adults and larvae were highly variable between years, being mainly influenced by the weather. The only multi-species study over a long time period compared numbers of Heteroptera caught in a single light trap at Rothamsted at various intervals between 1933 and 2000 (Southwood *et al.* 2003). Catches from the opposite ends of this time series show remarkable similarity in species diversity, but also profound changes in species composition, reflecting changes in land use in the immediate vicinity of the trap. Interestingly, there is evidence for a trough in diversity in the middle of this time span (1950s to 1970s) that the authors suggest may reflect a period of intense pesticide usage.

In the absence of long-term population-monitoring data comparable to those collected for butterflies and moths (see Chapters 24 and 25), the rest of this chapter will focus on what conclusions can be drawn from data on apparent expansions and contractions in the ranges of individual species and the addition of new species to the British list. Such information has to be treated with some caution, since, as explained

Table 28.1 *The status of Hemiptera species in Britain (Heteroptera and Auchenorrhyncha only)*

Category	Definition	Heteroptera	Auchenorrhyncha
RDB1	Endangered, in danger of extinction if causal factors continue to operate	8[a]	1[a]
RDB2	Vulnerable, likely to move into RDB1 category in near future	3[a]	0[a]
RDB3	Rare, but not presently vulnerable or endangered	38[a]	0[a]
RDBK	Insufficiently known, but suspected to fall within one of the RDB categories	4[a]	22[a]
Notable A	Thought to occur in less than fifteen 10-km squares	15[a]	20[a]
Notable B	Thought to occur in less than a hundred 10-km squares	66[a]	55[a]
Extinct	Former populations now thought to have died out	7[a]	0[a]
Sub-total	Total species of conservation concern	143	98
Local	Restricted distribution and/or habitat	153	115
Common	Widespread and generally common	247	160
Recent[b]	Recent additions to British list	34	17
TOTAL	Total species in Britain	577[c]	390
BAP	Biodiversity Action Plan priority species, 2007	3[d]	7[e]

Notes:

[a] Data from Kirby (1992); note that the statuses of Hemiptera are in need of revision in the light of recent range changes.

[b] Recent additions (since 1990) to British list for which insufficient data currently exist to determine status.

[c] Total does not include casual imports, non-established occasional vagrants or species with transient indoor populations.

[d] *Hydrometra gracilenta, Physatocheila smreczynskii, Saldula setulosa.*

[e] *Chlorita viridula, Cicadetta montana, Doratura impudica, Eurysa douglasi, Euscelis venosus, Macrosteles cyane, Ribautodelphax imitans.*

below, some of these changes may reflect increased recording effort or improved collection techniques as much as real changes in the distribution of the species themselves. However, changes are so widespread, and some of them on such a large scale amongst conspicuous insects, that there is no doubt that there has been a considerable change in the British bug fauna and in the distribution of individual species in recent years. Here, we outline some of the more pronounced changes and discuss possible causative agents. Further details are provided in our earlier review (Kirby *et al.* 2001), though the rate of change in the fauna and in the status of individual species means that it is already substantially out of date.

Apparent changes in range

Species with very low population densities

As a general principle when dealing with relatively small and inconspicuous insects, it is easier to chart the expansion of a species' range than it is to be confident about range contraction, because it is hard to prove that a species has definitely disappeared from formerly occupied sites. The recent re-discovery of species that had not been recorded in Britain for 50 or more years should encourage us to be cautious about declaring species to be extinct too readily. Thus, the leafhoppers *Platymetopius undatus* and *Metalimnus formosus* had not been reported for over 50 and 100 years, respectively, but have nevertheless recently been found at single sites. Only further focused survey will establish whether these are isolated relict populations or simply represent species that typically occur at very low population densities below the normal detection threshold. Similarly, the Pondweed Leafhopper, *Macrosteles* (= *Erotettix*) *cyane*, a species that feeds exclusively on Broad-leaved Pondweed, *Potamogeton natans*, had been recorded from four sites in southern England, but had not been seen for over 40 years. The old locations had proved impossible to trace, but since then three new populations have been found. Scarce species which form transient populations could conceivably change substantially in frequency and range over a period of a few years as a result of habitat availability, quite independently of any long-term shift in abundance: the leafhopper, *Macrosteles quadripunctulatus*, for example, is typically found amongst very sparse grasses on recently disturbed ground; such conditions may be rapidly lost through successional change, and there is never sufficient recording to gain a picture of its status at any one time.

Better methods/more fieldwork in suitable habitats

The phenomenon that the recorded ranges of certain species increase with more recording effort is widely recognised amongst entomologists. In the absence of evidence to the contrary, the assumption must be that the true distribution of the species has not changed appreciably, but that the apparent expansion in range is due to a better detection rate. Certainly, the larger number of fieldworkers that routinely record Hemiptera, as the focal group or as part of wider entomological surveys, has greatly enhanced our knowledge of the distribution of many species. Some species that were previously thought to be rare have in fact turned out to be more common than was originally thought, purely as a result of greater recording effort. The completion of certain large-scale surveys focused on particular habitats has contributed significantly to this. Cryptic species which have specialised habitat requirements and small scattered populations are particularly prone to having a recording history of a gradual accumulation of records giving an apparent increase or infilling of known range, with few repeat records from individual sites, from which no conclusions can in practice be drawn. *Ceratocombus coleoptratus*, for example, lives in permanently damp leaf litter, and might be expected to be sensitive to changes in management, hydrology and climate, but is rarely captured during routine recording: it is not even entirely clear what its current status is, much less how it may have changed.

Under-recording in those parts of Britain and Ireland that are remote from the well-worked areas of southern England means that foci of important rare species may have been missed. An interesting case in point is the recent discovery of substantial populations of the planthopper, *Paraliburnia clypealis*. For many years, this species was regarded as exceptionally rare in Britain, being known initially only from Wicken Fen and then from a handful of other wetland sites, and specialised on Purple Small-reed, *Calamagrostis canescens*. However, Helden and Sheridan (2006) reported it in substantial numbers in intensively managed dairy grassland in Ireland, and it has recently been recorded as a frequent component of upland wet pasture in the Scottish Highlands (N. Littlewood, personal communication), in both cases showing previously unreported host-plant associations. These recent developments serve to demonstrate that more recording effort in such under-worked areas could provide significant further insights into the ecology and biogeography of some of our rarest species.

A further contributory factor has been the adoption of novel or improved collecting or sampling techniques. The increasingly widespread use of modified garden leaf-blowers as insect suction samplers (Stewart and Wright 1995) has enabled fieldworkers to collect species that live close to the soil and are therefore passed over by conventional sweep-netting. These machines also facilitate sampling of otherwise inaccessible microhabitats such as woody vegetation and the bases of coarse tussock-forming grasses that preclude the use of a sweep net. Likewise, pitfall trapping of Hemiptera, either as part of general invertebrate surveys or as 'by-catch' from sampling directed at groups such as ground beetles or spiders, has extended the known range of several scarce ground-dwelling species. Thus, the Welsh Peatland Invertebrate Survey (1985–7) of 118 sites across Wales considerably extended the known range of species that were previously considered rare (such as the delphacid planthopper, *Struebingianella litoralis*) or confined to the wettest parts of bogs (such as *Tyrphodelphax distinctus*, *Oncodelphax pullulus* and *Delphacodes capnodes*).

Gains and expansions of range

Evidence for increases in frequency and range of Hemiptera varies in quality, and the scale of the suggested change is enormously different in different species. There is, however, at least a suggestion of increase for such a large number of species, particularly of southern species being found further north, that it can be considered a general phenomenon. For many of these species, the reported changes are relatively small or the species sufficiently poorly known that it is uncertain whether the reported change represents a true spread. For others, it is unambiguous, either because of its scale, or because the insect is conspicuous and not easily overlooked, or both. The Green Shieldbug, *Palomena prasina*, for example, until recently occurred commonly only in southern, and especially southern coastal, counties, with local populations somewhat more widely spread. In the space of a few years it has become a common species through extensive areas of southern and midland counties. The increase is the more apparent and dramatic because it is a large insect and because it occurs in very 'ordinary' habitats such as gardens and hedgerows; the numerical increase in the population of this species in the last decade must have been immense.

Most of the species for which expansion of range has been recorded are, like *Palomena prasina*, simply doing much as they have always done, but in more places in Britain. The tentative assumption tends to be made that this is a result of climate change, and this seems certainly the likeliest explanation for the general phenomenon of increase in southern species. The general climate-related shift, however, may mask changes that would have happened without it. There are, however, several categories of increased species which are more special, because the increase involves the adoption of new food plants, new habitats or new countries.

Range expansion due to adoption of new host plant species or habitats

Some species have been able to extend their ranges considerably through the adoption of a novel host-plant species. Thus, the Box Bug (*Gonocerus acuteangulatus*) was traditionally known only from Box Hill in Surrey, where it lived exclusively on scattered bushes of Box, *Buxus sempervirens*. Since the mid-1990s, it has widened its host plant range to include Hawthorn, *Crataegus monogyna*, and other woody shrub species, thus enabling it to spread widely through much of south-east England (Hawkins 2003) and to become an increasingly suburban species. This example of 'ecological release' also explains the considerable range expansion in recent years of the Juniper Shieldbug (*Cyphostethus tristriatus*). This species was previously confined to living on Juniper, *Juniperus communis*, growing in small isolated populations on southern chalk downland. Since the middle of the twentieth century, it has switched onto Lawson's Cypress (*Chamaecyparis lawsoniana*) and is now a common inhabitant of suburban gardens throughout southern England, where the new host is grown as an ornamental tree (Hawkins 2003). Such species are at the northern edge of their range in southern Britain. Narrow habitat or host plant specialisation is a commonly observed ecological pattern at range margins which would be relaxed as the climate warms and ranges move north. Whether or not this is the explanation for the genuine ecological and geographical range expansion in these species is impossible to say, but it seems plausible.

The other shieldbug exclusively associated with Juniper, *Chlorochroa juniperina*, also at the northern edge of its range in Britain, but presumed to have become extinct before 1900, was presumably lost too early to take advantage of this alternative resource.

A less plant-specific change has been shown by the plant bug *Lygus pratensis*. This bug was considered to be of Red Data Book status as recently as 1992, and seemed to be restricted to sunny spots in ancient woodland rides in southern England, though in mainland Europe it has always been a polyphagous species found in a wide range of open habitats, including waste ground and arable field margins. In recent years, its British habitat range has become essentially the same as that on the continent, and it is now a common or abundant species in the south-east.

New arrivals

Some 51 new species have been added to the British list of Heteroptera and Auchenorrhyncha since 1990 (Table 28.2). A number of these are, more or less unambiguously, new colonists. It is not always easy to distinguish those that have arrived through natural dispersal from those that have been brought in by human agency, though undoubtedly both processes have been involved.

The recent increase in importation of mature specimen trees and shrubs for the ornamental horticultural trade has introduced a number of new species to Britain from continental Europe, presumably as eggs laid inside the plant tissue. Thus, the recent discoveries of the leafhoppers *Synophropsis lauri* on Bay Laurel, *Laurus nobilis*, and *Fieberiella florii* on a range of trees and woody shrubs were made in synanthropic or 'brownfield' habitats. *S. lauri* originates from the Mediterranean area, so has been introduced substantially outside its climatic optimum. Against this background, it may be relevant that neither of these species has yet been found outside Greater London in which the local climate is known to be significantly warmer than in surrounding areas.

Movement and planting of trees by the horticultural trade may also explain the arrival and considerable geographical spread since the early 1990s of the leafhopper *Idiocerus ustulatus*. This species is confined to White and Grey Poplars (*Populus alba* and *P. canescens*), two species that have been widely planted as amenity trees and that readily spread by suckering. *I. ustulatus* is now well established on these trees as far north as Northamptonshire and west to Wales and Cornwall, although is not yet as abundant as other idiocerine leafhoppers on the same hosts.

Over a longer time frame, importation and distribution of plant stock may explain the arrival and spread of the Rhododendron Leafhopper, *Graphocephala fennahi*. This species was first reported in Surrey in 1933 and has since spread widely, although not as extensively as its host plant, *Rhododendron ponticum*, has been planted. Where it occurs, it can be extremely abundant, to the extent that many gardeners regard it as a pest, so its arrival at new sites is unlikely to have gone unnoticed. Its further spread may be limited either by climatic intolerance or the patchy distribution of his host. By contrast, the Rhododendron Lacebug, *Stephanitis rhododendri*, was first recorded in

Table 28.2 *Additions to the British Hemiptera list, 1990 onwards*

Taxon	Date of first capture	New arrival	Tax. split	New-found resident	Notes
Anthocoridae					
Buchananiella continua	1995	+			
Coreidae					
Leptoglossus occidentalis	2007	+			
Corixidae					
Cymatia rogenhoferi	2005	+			
Micronecta griseola	2000	+			Possibly previously overlooked
Sigara iactans	2005	+			
Sigara longipalis	2006	+			
Lygaeidae					
Arocatus longiceps	2006	+			
Emblethis denticollis	1991	+			
Megalonotus emarginatus	n/a		+		
(Metopoplax ditomoides)	(1992)				One old record, almost certainly transient and absent until recent re-colonisation
Metopoplax fuscinervis	1995?	+			Dubiously distinct from *M. ditomoides*
Nysius cymoides	?	+			Vagrant?
Nysius huttoni	2007	+			
Nysius senecionis	1992	+			
Sphragisticus nebulosus	1997	+			
Microphysidae					
Loricula ruficeps	(1999)			+	First record 1999, but location and character suggest long-established
Miridae					
Brachynotocoris puncticornis	2006	+			
Deraeocoris flavilinea	1996	+			
Dicyphus escalerae	2008	+			
Europiella decolor	n/a		+		Pre-1990 specimens known

Table 28.2 (cont.)

Taxon	Date of first capture	New arrival	Tax. split	New-found resident	Notes
Hypseloecus visci	2003	+			
Macrotylus horvathi	2003	+			
Orthotylus caprai	2006	+			
Psallus pseudoplatani	2001	+			
Reuteria marqueti	2006	+			
Trigonotylus coelestialium	n/a		+		Pre-1990 specimens known
Tuponia brevirostris	2001	+			
Naucoridae					
Naucoris maculatus	2004	+			
Pentatomidae					
Eurydema ornata	1997?	+			
Nezara viridula	2003	+			
Reduviidae					
Oncocephalus pilicornis	1990			+	
Rhopalidae					
Brachycarenus tigrinus	2003	+			
(*Stictopleurus abutilon*)	(1996)				Old records, but almost certainly a re-colonist after extinction
(*Stictopleurus punctatonervosus*)	(1997)				Old records, but almost certainly a re-colonist after extinction
Saldidae					
Saldula melanoscela	n/a			+	Pre-1990 specimens known
Tingidae					
Corythuca ciliata	2006	+			Tree-nursery import; extent of spread into the wild?
Stephanitis takeyai	C. 1995	+			Subject to eradication attempts
TOTAL HETEROPTERA		28	3	3	

Table 28.2 (cont.)

Taxon	Date of first capture	New arrival	Tax. split	New-found resident	Notes
Cicadellidae					
Balclutha saltuella	1993	+			
Batracomorphus allionii	2005 ?			+	
Dryodurgades antoniae	2008	+			
Elymana kozhevnikova	1996		+		
Eupteryx decemnotata	2002	+			
Fieberiella florii	1998	+			
Idiocerus ribauti	2008		+		
Idiocerus ustulatus	1991	+			
Liguropia juniperi	2007	+			
Oncopsis appendiculata	2008		+		
Psammotettix helvolus	1998		+		
Synophropsis lauri	2006	+			
Zyginella pulchra	2001	+			
Delphacidae					
Delphax crassicornis			+		
Eurysa brunnea	1991			+	
Kelisia occirega	1998		+		
Prokelisia marginata	2008	+			
TOTAL AUCHENORRHYNCHA		9	4	4	

Notes: New arrival: species which are almost certainly recent arrivals.

Tax. split: species previously mixed with related taxa, or split by recent revisions.

New-found resident: species that were probably long-established residents, but have only recently been discovered or recognised.

The table includes all species established outdoors in Britain, or captured in situations which suggest that they are or were established. There can be no guarantee that all still are. Casual imports are not counted. Entries are for the British mainland and islands only: species previously established in the Channel Isles and colonising Britain are counted as new arrivals. Three species of Heteroptera are also included (in brackets in the table, and not counted in the totals) which are not technically additions to the British list, but which were almost certainly absent for decades from Britain before re-establishing.

1901 and quickly increased to pest status by the 1920s. Since then, it has all but disappeared and was thought for some time to have become extinct, until it was rediscovered in the 1990s. Quite why one hemipteran on this host plant should flourish and the other species should fare so badly remains a mystery.

In some cases, the establishment of imported species in recent years may be dependent on climate change. The shieldbugs, *Nezara viridula* (Figure 28.1) and *Eurydema ornata* have been occasionally imported into Britain with vegetables from southern Europe for a substantial time, suggesting that they have had ample opportunity in the past for colonisation, but only in recent years have they become established, and in the case of *E. ornata* probably without human assistance.

The extent to which natural dispersal has played a part in the arrival and spread even of species associated with woody plants is uncertain. The extent of cross-channel traffic makes the inadvertent introduction of species by other means relatively easy. However, there is no doubt that a large number of insects arrive in Britain by active flight or passive drift from mainland Europe, and a number of recent arrivals are most likely to have come in this way, including water bugs such as *Sigara iactans, S. longipalis, Cymatia rogenhoferi* and *Naucoris maculatus*, and ground-dwelling bugs such as *Emblethis denticollis, Sphragisticus nebulosus, Nysius senecionis, N. huttoni* and *N. cymoides*.

Most of the recent arrivals, by whatever means, are unsurprising, in that the colonisation of Britain can be seen as part of a more general spread in Europe, typically of formerly southern species moving gradually north into a wider, but continuous, range. A few have originated from further afield: the groundbug, *Nysius huttoni*, comes from

Figure 28.1 Nymph of *Nezara viridula*, a shieldbug that has recently established in Britain (see colour plate).

New Zealand and the squashbug, *Leptoglossus occidentalis*, from North America. Both these species have, however, spread to Britain via mainland Europe. The salt-marsh planthopper, *Prokelisia marginata*, which lives on cordgrass (*Spartina* spp.), may be a more direct long-distance colonist. This native of saltmarshes along the eastern seaboard of the USA was recently reported from the Portuguese Algarve coast and sites around the northern Mediterranean. In 2008, it was recorded at a few sites along the Channel coast of England in densities that match the very high population levels found in the USA. Whether the British and southern European populations arose from separate colonisation events directly from the USA, or whether the appearance in Britain arose simply from a northward extension up the Atlantic coast from the south, is unknown. Either way, it looks set to spread rapidly in saltmarshes around the British coastline where *Spartina anglica*, itself a non-native invasive species, has already colonised.

It is possible that arrivals from mainland Europe have facilitated the increase of some species which are long-term residents. Although, for the most part, this must be merely a hypothetical possibility, it seems likely that for species which are scarce and localised within Britain, cross-channel dispersal from more populous colonies is easier than spread from existing British colonies. The most convincing case of such a secondary arrival is that of the shorebug, *Saldula arenicola*. Though associated with bare sandy water margins in mainland Europe, in Britain this species was historically confined to seepages and trickles on soft-rock cliffs in the south-west. In recent years it has been recorded in Britain in more 'continental' habitat at the margins of gravel and sand pits. The earliest records in such situations are from the convenient land-fall of Dungeness, Kent, with subsequent records more widely scattered in southern counties.

A special case is afforded by two large bugs associated with ruderal vegetation, *Stictopleurus abutilon* and *S. punctatonervosus*. Though there is good evidence that they were established in Britain in the past, both were considered extinct in Britain when the group was reviewed in 1992, almost certainly correctly, as these are large and conspicuous insects. Since then, both have re-colonised and spread to become frequent or, in the case of *S. punctatonervosus*, common over a large area of the south-east.

The rate of spread and eventual abundance of recent arrivals varies greatly, but can be impressive. The groundbug, *Nysius senecionis*, spread extensively in disturbed habitats through southern England to become frequent and widespread within a decade of establishment, and is now an expected species in brownfield sites and at arable field margins throughout the south-east. However, another groundbug, *Metopoplax dito-moides*, after a period of abundance in which it could be found in many thousands in suitable areas, appears now to be somewhat less frequent. The plantbug *Deraeocoris flavilinea*, has shown a similar rapid spread on shrubs, and is now generally distributed along hedges and wood margins and in scrub, and can be the commonest bug in the foliage of suburban shrubberies.

Formerly coastal species spreading

One biological signal of a gradually warming climate may be the inland spread of species that were previously confined to strictly coastal areas. The rhopalid bug, *Chorosoma schillingi*, previously had a strongly maritime distribution with a single inland stronghold in the East Anglian Breckland. From here it has spread widely since the late 1960s to inland locations in sandy, chalky and other ruderal habitats. A similar expansion since the 1960s away from a previously exclusively coastal distribution has been shown by the leafhopper, *Athysanus argentarius* (Figure 28.2) that now inhabits a variety of dry grasslands in ruderal and waste-ground habitats. It is tempting to draw parallels with some of the Orthoptera such as the Long-winged Conehead, *Conocephalus discolor*, and Roesel's Bush Cricket, *Metrioptera roeselii,* which have also undergone substantial inland extensions of their range over a similar time period. Other predominantly coastal species which have increased in frequency in inland locations, but in more recent years, include the shieldbug, *Odontoscelis lineola*, and the squashbug, *Arenocoris falleni*, both feeding, in Britain, only on Common Stork's-bill, *Erodium cicutarium*, and the groundbugs, *Megalonotus praetextatus* and *M. sabulicola*.

Figure 28.2 *Athysanus argentarius*, a leafhopper that has recently expanded its range inland and northwards from its formerly southern coastal distribution (see colour plate).

Species associated with ruderal habitats

'Brownfield' sites (disused quarries, ex-mineral workings, urban waste ground etc.), can contain rich faunas with a significant proportion of rarities. These sites contain various habitats, from wetland to drought-stressed dry ground, and from early successional stages to mature scrub and woodland, but the most significant for Hemiptera are early successional and open-structured habitats, often in highly disturbed and stressed environments. Though sites of this type have long been recognised as supporting interesting insects, it is only in recent years that their importance has been fully realised; in part this is because conservation and recreational entomology has tended to focus more on the traditional countryside, in part because many of the most substantial sites are themselves of only recent origin and perhaps in part because the interest they supported may have increased in recent years. The sort of species most likely to colonise brownfield sites (efficient colonists with a preference for partly bare ground) are precisely those most likely to have benefited from climate change.

Conditions in such sites can mimic those found only sporadically, or in small areas, under more natural conditions. Early successional stages which might usually be restricted to a few square metres of recent disturbance in more natural grassland may extend over hectares of brownfield; very large populations of host plants may occur in high concentration and quarries in particular can mimic some coastal features – for example partly vegetated sand and soft-rock cliffs – very well. The planthopper, *Reptalus panzeri*, is one beneficiary of brownfield. It is often found where soils dry out and crack in summer, perhaps because these cracks provide egg-laying females with access to plant roots on which the juvenile stages develop. The coarse soil and rubble substrates that are found in many brownfield sites may provide analogous conditions. Heteroptera in such sites can include a large number of groundbugs (Lygaeidae) and squashbugs (Coreidae) in particular; species such as *Graptopeltus lynceus* and *Bathysolen nubilus* are probably now more frequent in brownfield than in non-brownfield sites.

Losses and range contractions

Well-documented cases

Whilst we have to be careful about declaring species to be extinct in Britain, this may indeed be the case for some. Probably the best known candidate is the New Forest Cicada (*Cicadetta montana*). This species has a life cycle that extends over at least six to eight years, the majority of which is spent as an underground larva. After a recorded population peak of one hundred singing males in 1962, the last definite sighting of this species at one of its traditional New Forest sites was in 1993. Nevertheless, its long life cycle, difficulty in detection and history of enigmatic appearances at new sites within the Forest means that declaration of its extinction in Britain may still be premature. Only time will tell if we have lost this species, but even if it still survives, there is little doubt that its population size and distribution is greatly reduced from what it was. Certainly, there is good evidence that its traditional sites are no longer suitable for it, having become overgrown as a result of natural succession (Pinchen and Ward 2002). Paradoxically, if sufficient suitable habitat became available, it is a species that would probably benefit from climatic warming.

The data for some species do appear to demonstrate substantial range contraction over the last 50–100 years. Thus, old records for *Platymetopius undatus* exist from a broad sweep of scattered sites across southern and eastern England. At some sites, substantial series of specimens were taken in a single year, suggesting that the species was not uncommon. Many of the sites were, and still are, mature Oak (*Quercus* spp.) woodland, although changes in the field and ground vegetation may be more pertinent to the survival of the leafhopper as it is one of several species that feed on herbaceous plants and grasses in the larval stages and then migrate up into the canopy as adults.

However, when considering individual species, interpretation of data is hampered by uncertainty as to what normal long-term variation in populations might be. The distinctive planthopper, *Asiraca clavicornis*, was at one time recorded widely across southern and eastern England, but declined in the mid-twentieth century until it was apparently confined to London and the Thames basin. This restriction was particularly puzzling given that most records were from waste ground, roadside verges and other ordinary disturbed habitats. In the 1980s and early 1990s, this might have been considered an excellent example of a declining 'wider countryside' species. In recent years, however, *A.clavicornis* has again been more widely recorded, with records extending into Norfolk, Suffolk, Cambridgeshire and Northamptonshire. The reasons for the decline and subsequent upturn are not known.

Species under threat

The Hemiptera contain their fair share of species about which we should be concerned. A small number of species have been recorded only infrequently at a limited number of sites and so may never have had permanent populations in Britain. They can be omitted from further consideration. The remaining rare species are vulnerable to a range of potential threats across a wide variety of habitats, many of which are recurrent themes in the conservation of several groups of insect. Thus, changes in management of grasslands, especially cessation of grazing and the resultant succession to scrub, threaten important leafhopper faunas associated with southern calcareous grasslands, the richest grassland habitat for Hemiptera generally. Heathlands also support important assemblages of rare Hemiptera that are subject to the familiar problems of fragmentation, succession to Birch (*Betula* spp.) and Scots Pine (*Pinus sylvestris*) woodland, public pressure and loss to peri-urban development, agriculture and forestry. Mire habitats, from base-rich fens to acid bogs, contain a significant number of important species which are vulnerable wherever the hydrological regime of their habitat is threatened, whether as a result of deliberate drainage, drying out through succession or, in the longer term, changes in rainfall pattern resulting from climate change. Coastal species are liable to suffer from habitat loss and change as sea levels rise and as measures are taken to limit marine incursion and erosion. Upland habitats have been extensively lost or damaged through afforestation, drainage or over grazing, with inevitable damage to Hemiptera as a result. Increasing eutrophication of the British countryside and high nitrogen content in rain encourage the growth of coarse vegetation and make it difficult to maintain open-structured vegetation and early successional stages. There can be no doubt that these changes must have produced population declines, and sometimes extinctions, at individual sites, but the extent of these declines and their effect on overall distributions is unclear.

Brownfield sites provide recently created habitat which can substitute for some of these losses, or in some cases improve on anything which occurred naturally, but they are not necessarily present on a sufficient scale to provide adequate replacement habitat, and are themselves subject to heavy pressures: they are often selectively developed, and even where retained there may be pressure for recreational use, for the development of lakes of interest only for fish and birds, or for planting and seeding to develop 'wildflower grasslands', woodlands or reed beds, with resultant loss of immediate interest and long-term potential.

Perversely, though lack of management has probably been a major cause of decline in many habitats, well-intentioned conservation management can also lead to damage. For example, scrub-associated species such as the groundbug *Eremocoris podagricus*, typically found under Hawthorn bushes on calcareous grassland, may be lost through scrub clearance, or tussock-dwelling species may be lost through increased grazing pressure.

The warming climate which is presumed to be a major cause for the increase in many previously restricted southern species should logically also threaten northern species. Since the Hemiptera fauna is richer in the south (more so for Heteroptera than for Auchenorrhyncha), gains may still outweigh losses, even amongst long-established species. As yet, however, there appears to be no strong evidence for decline in northern species. It may be that the impact of climate change has not yet been sufficient for a change to appear; equally, it may be that recording activity in the north is not high enough to detect convincing changes. However, it is also the case that even the most northerly of British Hemiptera are not associated with extreme climatic conditions; if anything, they tend either to be found in relatively sheltered areas buffered from the worst extremes of climate, or to be very tolerant species found in a wide range of conditions. It may well be that, so far, the impact of habitat changes greatly outweighs any influence of climate change.

Conclusion

So what is the balance between these gains and losses? As we have explained, it is hard to disentangle real changes in the fortunes of individual species from changes that have arisen as a result of a general increase in the number and activity of recorders. Nevertheless, there is unquestionably a net gain in the number of species, at least in southern England where the rate at which new species are arriving from the near continent seems to be accelerating. Many species of formerly restricted southern distribution have increased in range, and often in frequency within their pre-established range. The extent to which this is due to climatic warming, as opposed to various other possible influences, is hard to say, but it is undoubtedly a contributory factor. We can expect a continuing steady flow of new arrivals recruited from the much richer continental fauna. There is no doubt that in southern and midland counties, at least, the suburban fauna, and the fauna of brownfield sites, is already richer than at any point in the recent past, and possibly at any time. Measured against this, species associated with certain habitats are undoubtedly vulnerable and may be lost if positive action is not taken to secure them. Pre-eminent amongst these must be the rich faunas found in grasslands and wetlands, together with assemblages associated with an eclectic collection of southern coastal habitats from sand dunes to salt marshes and eroding cliffs.

References

Biedermann, R., Achtziger, R., Nickel, H. and Stewart, A.J.A. (2005). Conservation of grassland leafhoppers: a brief review. *Journal of Insect Conservation,* **9**, 229–243.

Eyre, M.D., Woodward, J.C. and Sanderson, R.A. (2005). Assessing the relationship between grassland Auchenorrhyncha (Homoptera) and land cover. *Agriculture, Ecosystems and Environment,* **109**, 187–191.

Hawkins, R.D. (2003). *Shieldbugs of Surrey,* Woking, Surrey Wildlife Trust.

Helden, A.J. and Sheridan, H. (2006). An Irish population of the little-known planthopper *Paraliburnia clypealis* (Hom., Delphacidae) in a very unexpected habitat. *Irish Naturalist's Journal,* **28**, 232–239.

Huxley, T. (2003). *Provisional Atlas of the British Aquatic Bugs (Hemiptera, Heteroptera),* Huntingdon, Biological Records Centre.

Kirby, P. (1992). *A Review of the Scarce and Threatened Hemiptera of Great Britain,* UK Nature Conservation, No. 2, Peterborough, Joint Nature Conservation Committee.

Kirby, P., Stewart, A.J.A. and Wilson, M.R. (2001). True bugs, leaf- and planthoppers and their allies. In D.L. Hawksworth, ed., *The Changing Wildlife of Great Britain and Ireland,* London, Taylor & Francis, pp. 262–299.

Maczey, N., Masters, G.J., Hollier, J.A., Mortimer, S.R. and Brown, V.K. (2005). Community associations of chalk grassland leafhoppers (Hemiptera: Auchenorrhyncha): conclusions for habitat conservation. *Journal of Insect Conservation,* **9**, 281–297.

Pinchen, B.J. and Ward, L.K. (2002). The history, ecology and conservation of the New Forest Cicada. *British Wildlife,* **13**, 258–266.

Shirt, D.B. (ed.) (1987). *British Red Data Books: 2. Insects,* Peterborough, Nature Conservancy Council.

Southwood, T.R.E., Henderson, P.A. and Woiwod, I.P. (2003). Stability and change over 67 years – the community of Heteroptera as caught in a light trap at Rothamsted, UK. *European Journal of Entomology,* **100**, 557–561.

Stewart, A.J.A. (1999). Twenty years of recording the distribution of Auchenorrhyncha (Hemiptera: Homoptera) in Britain and Ireland: progress, achievements and prospects. *Reichenbachia,* **33**, 207–214.

Stewart, A.J.A. and Wright, A.F. (1995). A new inexpensive suction apparatus for sampling arthropods in grassland. *Ecological Entomology,* **20**, 98–102.

Whittaker, J.B. and Tribe, N.P. (1998). Predicting numbers of an insect (*Neophilaenus lineatus*) in a changing climate. *Journal of Animal Ecology,* **67**, 987–991.

29

Grasshoppers, crickets and allied insects

Judith Marshall

Summary

The term orthopteroid insects is here used in the wide sense to include both the saltatorial Orthoptera, the true 'jumpers' with well-developed hind legs (grasshoppers, ground-hoppers, crickets, bush-crickets and camel-crickets), and the cursorial or running Orthoptera – several distinct groups of insects now treated as separate orders: the Blattodea (cockroaches) and Mantodea (praying mantids) (sometimes linked together as the Dictyoptera), the Phasmida (stick- and leaf-insects) and the Dermaptera (earwigs). The Mantodea are only represented in the UK by occasional adventive specimens. By 1974 there were 38 native species of orthopteroid insects recognised as breeding in the UK, the majority inhabiting southern England and Wales, with three species restricted to the Channel Islands. A further 14 species which were known to be established introductions or aliens brought the total to 52. Additional established introductions are now recognised, and since 2001, at least two Continental European species have been breeding successfully in the UK, resulting in a current total of about 60 species. However the number of native species is unchanged and whilst several of these have increased their known range, others have been less successful; in 1987 three Orthoptera species were recognised in the British Red Data Book as endangered and two as vulnerable, some of which became the subject of Species Recovery Programmes – though with only limited success. More detailed and up-to-date distribution information is always needed, and hopefully will be forthcoming following the 2008 launch by the Biological Records Centre (BRC) of their online Recording Scheme for Orthopteroids of the British Isles: http://www.orthoptera.org.uk/.

Silent Summer: The State of Wildlife in Britain and Ireland, ed. Norman Maclean. Published by Cambridge University Press. © Cambridge University Press 2010.

Introduction

Native insects of the British Isles are considered to have arrived here independently of human activity, after the last Ice Age and before the Neolithic period; 'aliens' or non-native species are those whose presence here is as a consequence of the activities of humans. Many alien orthopteroid species are cosmopolitan pests which arrive as casual introductions, often with imported fruit, vegetables and other goods, and if such introductions have been or are still successfully breeding here they are regarded as 'established' species. All such species are identifiable by reference to Marshall and Haes (1988) or Marshall (1999). However, since 2001 the category of established non-natives has been extended to include species from Continental Europe previously only encountered as occasional migrants, identifiable from the BRC website though not from earlier references.

The six orthopteroid groups (superfamilies or orders) are discussed below, listing the known major changes in distribution.

Tettigonioidea: bush-crickets and camel-crickets

Ten native species were recognised in the British Isles by 1936 with confirmation of the presence of the Long-winged Cone-head (*Conocephalus discolor*), although until the 1970s this was still known only as a rare and localised species in southern coastal areas. New records from Hampshire were reported in the 1970s; by the early 1980s it was found to be widely distributed in the New Forest and even common in quaking bogs, and during the 1990s it extended inland to Surrey and Oxfordshire and westwards to Cornwall and is now widespread in Essex and expanding through East Anglia. Normally a long-winged species, the extra-macropterous form occurs more frequently in hotter summers, and single new distribution records have often been of this form – though it is possible that Continental specimens may be involved, particularly for the extreme south-western records in Cornwall and the Scilly Isles.

The Short-winged Cone-head (*Conocephalus dorsalis*) has been more fully recorded in recent years, and has also extended its range in the Thames Valley area, again with the macropterous fully winged form (*burri*) found mainly during hot summers.

Roesel's Bush-cricket (*Metrioptera roeselii*) has also shown a considerable increase in distribution in recent years particularly in the London area, taking advantage of urban wasteland and road and railway verges. Originally considered to be a strictly coastal or estuarine species, it has now extended its range from the Thames northwards through Suffolk and Bedfordshire, westwards through Oxfordshire and southwards through Sussex and Kent. Increased numbers of the fully winged form (*diluta*) are observed in very hot summers and have probably contributed to the spread of the species.

The Grey Bush-cricket (*Platycleis albopunctata*) was known only from coastal habitats in southern Britain until the late 1990s, when it was discovered on a chalk ridge at least 2 km inland in Dorset, and 14 km inland on dry waste ground in Hampshire (Widgery 1999). Colonies have since been recorded in Suffolk in 1996 and in Essex in 2004 (Gardiner 2009).

Although it has a relatively restricted distribution it seems likely that the species is still under-recorded. The Grey Bush-cricket on the Channel Islands was originally described as a separate sub-species (*P. albopunctata jerseyana*), a slightly smaller form with more slender wings.

By contrast, the Wart Biter (*Decticus verrucivorus*) is a species recognised as vulnerable, listed as protected under Schedule 5 of the Wildlife and Countryside Act, 1981, and made the subject of a Species Recovery Programme, even though in 1974 it was reported as having a wider known distribution than at any time since 1800 (Marshall 1974). Nevertheless, it is known to survive at only a few sites and at very low densities and its ultimate survival in the country probably depends upon appropriate site management; the ideal habitat for the species would seem to be formed of a mosaic of short turf and grass tussocks (Cherrill 1993).

The Bog Bush-cricket (*Metrioptera brachyptera*) has a very rare long-winged form (*marginata*) which does not seem to contribute to extension of its range, since its distribution has changed little in recent years. The Great Green Bush-cricket (*Tettigonia viridissima*), notable for its loud and penetrating stridulation, may now be less widespread in inland areas.

Two southern species which are fairly well known as garden inhabitants are the Speckled Bush-cricket (*Leptophyes punctatissima*) and the Oak Bush-cricket (*Meconema thalassinum*); very young nymphs of both species may be mistaken for green aphids and both species are probably under-recorded. The Dark Bush-cricket (*Pholidoptera griseoaptera*), whose young nymphs have a spider-like appearance, has gradually extended its range in recent years.

The discovery of the Southern Oak Bush-cricket (*Meconema meridionale*) (see Figure 29.1) in Surrey (Hawkins 2001) was exciting, though not totally surprising; originally thought of as a southern European species, it has gradually extended its range northwards, reaching France, Holland and Belgium during the 1990s. It is highly brachypterous (forewings maximally 2 mm long) and hence flightless, and, like its fully winged relative the Oak Bush-cricket, it may be found around houses. It has also been found on motor vehicles, thus extending its range by assisted travel – so may have reached southern England by this route, though perhaps more likely is its introduction with garden shrubs imported from mainland Europe. Whatever the means of its arrival, it is now known from a number of locations in Surrey and also Berkshire, Hampshire, Greater London and Essex, and is likely to continue its expansion, though recognition of its presence may be lagging behind. Early in the season, the young nymphs are not distinguishable from those of the Oak Bush-

Figure 29.1 Southern Oak Bush-cricket (*Meconema meridionale*) male (left) and female (right) (see colour plate). (Photograph courtesy of Ted Benton.)

cricket, but any 'nymphs' observed from September onwards are likely to be the brachypterous adults of the Southern Oak Bush-cricket.

A colony of a second Continental central European species, the Sickle-bearing Bush-cricket (*Phaneroptera falcata*), was discovered in East Sussex in 2006 (Collins *et al.* 2007). This southern, warmth-loving species may not become a permanent resident, given the variability of climate here. It is even more unlikely that its close relative from southern Europe (*Phaneroptera nana*), known to have been brought into the London area with imported shrubs and trees, will become established. Sightings of the Large Cone-head (*Ruspolia nitidula*) continue on the Isles of Scilly (Hathway *et al.* 2003) and in southern England, and occasional colonies of the cosmopolitan Greenhouse Camel-cricket (*Tachycines asynamorus*) continue to be found in heated environments. With the continued importation of shrubs and trees and occasional wind-assisted immigration, more such introductions are possible.

Grylloidea: true crickets and mole crickets

In 1987 there were three Orthoptera recognised in the British Red Data Book as endangered, all crickets; two of them, the Field Cricket (*Gryllus campestris*) and the Mole Cricket (*Gryllotalpa gryllotalpa*), have since become the subject of Species Recovery Programmes.

In Britain, the Field Cricket (*Gryllus campestris*) survives only in very restricted habitats in southern England. Its requirements are short grass and a light, sandy or chalk soil suitable for the nymphs to burrow into; crickets overwinter as penultimate instar nymphs and need the protection of burrows to survive. By 1988 the Field Cricket survived at only one site in the Coates Castle area of West Sussex, however the launch in 1991 by English Nature of their Species Recovery Programme has enabled this species to be helped back from the very brink of extinction. The captive-breeding programme with the Invertebrate Conservation Centre, London Zoo enabled nymphs to be released at selected sites in the following years, and although with varying degrees of success, three separate populations are now well established (Edwards 2008).

The Mole Cricket (*Gryllotalpa gryllotalpa*) used to be a well-known insect of marshy areas, living in the warm, sandy areas along the edges of bogs and marshes, but since the 1950s it has declined dramatically on mainland Britain. In 1994 it became the subject of a special project under English Nature's Species Recovery Programme and in 1996 a survey was launched. Sadly this large and distinctive insect has proved extremely elusive, and occasional sightings have not resulted in the location of colonies of the British Mole Cricket. In 2005 hopes were raised by the presence of a thriving colony in a compost heap in a garden in Oxfordshire – but chromosome analysis proved that the colony had been introduced, possibly from Italy. Mole Cricket chromosome numbers range from $2n = 12$ to $2n = 23$, but all specimens so far examined from northern Europe, including Britain, France and Guernsey, possess only $2n = 12$ chromosomes. With no known breeding sites, even excellent habitat management will make no difference to the status of the species, and the continued commercial exploitation of peatland could result in the serious reduction or loss of potential sites for such moisture-dependent species as the Mole Cricket.

The third endangered species listed in 1987, the Scaly Cricket (*Pseudomogoplistes vicentae*), was first collected from Chesil Beach, Dorset in 1949 and thought to be dubiously native (Marshall and Haes 1988). It has since been discovered at new localities and shown to exist in larger numbers than was previously thought possible; its history in Britain up to the end of 1998 was fully described and reviewed by Sutton (1999). The name 'Scaly Cricket' (with a locality prefix) is applied to several closely related members of the Mogoplistinae, separable only on examination of the male genitalia, as the females are identical. The identity of males from Chesil Beach and Sark was confirmed (as *P. vicentae*) by Gorochov and Marshall (2001).

The House-cricket (*Acheta domesticus*) has been established in dwellings here for many centuries, possibly having travelled back from the eastern Mediterranean region with the returning crusaders (Marshall 1974).

The fully winged Southern Field Cricket (*Gryllus bimaculatus*) is widely reared as a food source for reptiles and birds, as well as being an occasional accidental immigrant with fruit and vegetables from the Mediterranean area. Occasional specimens of this species have been seen and heard in various locations in southern England, giving rise to confusion with our native short-winged Field Cricket, though permanent colonies have not yet been recorded.

Acridoidea: grasshoppers and ground-hoppers

There have been no grasshopper additions to the British list since the Lesser Mottled Grasshopper (*Stenobothrus stigmaticus*) was found on the Isle of Man in 1962, and some species have been in decline.

The Large Marsh Grasshopper (*Stethophyma grossum*) is regarded as a vulnerable species, because, as with the Mole Cricket, its habitat is at risk through changing land use (Brown and Cheesman 1997).

The Heath Grasshopper (*Chorthippus vagans*) was listed in 1987 as rare, and has a very restricted range in dry heathlands in Hampshire and Dorset. On Jersey it occupies a wider range of dry, often exposed grassy habitats, some, however, threatened by recreational or road-building activities. The continuing extension of urbanisation may restrict the available habitat for many British species, although disused railway land has aided the range extension of the Lesser Marsh Grasshopper (*Chorthippus albomarginatus*).

In recent years, the widening of field margins in southern England under the 6-m wide Countryside Stewardship Scheme has had some benefits for grasshoppers. Several studies have been summarised by Gardiner (2008), mostly on the Meadow Grasshopper (*Chorthippus parallelus*) and the Field Grasshopper (*Chorthippus brunneus*) (also including bush-crickets, where relevant), and such surveys are continuing. Wider borders may produce more grasshoppers, but annual cutting of margins in summer can lead to high grasshopper mortality and dispersal. Grass composition may also be unfavourable, but the presence of hedgerows, particularly if a grass margin is located on the sheltered side of the hedgerow, may be highly beneficial.

In the Channel Islands, the Jersey Grasshopper (*Euchorthippus elegantulus elegantulus*) is at the extreme north of its range, as also is the Blue-winged Grasshopper (*Oedipoda caerulescens*); this and other Continental species are unlikely to travel further north.

The short-winged Common Ground-hopper (*Tetrix undulata*), though widely distributed, is probably under-recorded, as also are the fully winged species – which are more difficult to identify in the field.

Locusts, both the Desert Locust (*Schistocerca gregaria*) and the Migratory Locust (*Locusta migratoria*), are cultured commercially as a food source and for teaching purposes, so that stray specimens encountered outdoors may be introductions or have been released – deliberately or otherwise. Both these species may also reach our shores under their own power, flying from Europe or even North Africa; specimens may be carried for many miles with the easterly trade winds – though are unlikely to breed here. The large Egyptian Grasshopper (*Anacridium aegyptium*) occasionally finds its way here as a stowaway with goods from the Mediterranean area.

Blattodea: cockroaches

The three native species are confined to southern England and Wales and are rarely seen unless searched for, though males of the Dusky Cockroach (*Ectobius lapponicus*) will fly readily if disturbed from herbage. Regrettably, the charm of these small cockroaches and indeed all other cockroach species is disregarded by the majority who know only of the horrors of the few (but prolific) pest species.

The Common Cockroach (*Blatta orientalis*) has been an established pest here since the 1500s, invading from south-eastern Europe, probably accompanying the House-cricket. The American or Ship Cockroach (*Periplaneta americana*) and the Australian Cockroach (*P. australasiae*), (both African in origin) arrived in the 1800s, though the small, but very persistent, German Cockroach (*Blattella germanica*) (of Oriental origin) was probably earlier. The Brown-banded Cockroach (*Supella longipalpa*) continues to establish occasional colonies in heated premises.

The status of a live, alien cockroach found in Britain may range from that of a well-established cosmopolitan pest species to a one-off importation of a single tropical insect – and, depending on where the specimen is captured, the exact status may be extremely difficult to determine. Specimens captured in domestic environments are normally pest species, but may have been imported; insects, particularly cockroaches, are easily transportable in a variety of ways, many come in with bananas, but may transfer to other goods – so appear in shops with local-grown vegetables. Occasionally the casual introduction of a gravid female or a fertile ootheca may result in a temporary infestation, sometimes on domestic premises. Tropical species may establish breeding colonies in protected sites; the Surinam Cockroach (*Pycnoscelus surinamensis*) is parthenogenetic and a burrowing root-feeder, so a stray imported with plants may rapidly build up a thriving and potentially damaging colony. Many tropical species of cockroach are kept in culture both as food sources and as pets, and escapees may result in temporary infestations in homes and sheds; not a popular occurrence!

Phasmida: stick-insects

There are no native stick-insects, but New Zealand species were accidentally introduced here with plants in the early 1900s and have become well established in gardens in the Scilly Isles, Cornwall and Devon. These New Zealand species and the long-cultured Laboratory (or Indian) Stick-insect (*Carausius morosus*) have a well-documented history here for nearly a century (Brock 1991; Haes and Harding 1997). Although the New Zealand species are difficult to rear in captivity, they have long shown their ability to survive where appropriate food plants are available.

The Laboratory Stick-insect is only one of many tropical and sub-tropical species reared in culture here, often very successfully. Of the many other species in culture, at least two – the Corsican Stick-insect (*Bacillus rossius*) and the Pink-winged Stick-insect (*Sipyloidea sipylus*) – have been reported as surviving for a number of years after being deliberately released. Other tropical species may be unlikely to be able to survive for very long if released, even when ample stocks of food are apparently available. However, culture material discarded (by accident or design) may well result in the future survival here of other species.

Dermaptera: earwigs

The Common Earwig (*Forficula auricularia*) is widely distributed and a well-known (though generally unpopular) species, and probably under-recorded; though western Palaearctic in origin, it now occurs throughout the world. The Lesser Earwig (*Labia minor*) is easily recognisable as it flies readily; less easy to confirm are records of the Short-winged or Hop-garden Earwig (*Apterygida media*) and Lesne's Earwig (*Forficula lesnei*), and confusion with imported material is always a possibility.

The future

British Orthopteroids perform a key role as habitat and climatic indicators because they comprise a limited number of species at the edge of their European ranges, and the majority are readily identifiable.

The collation of 10-km-square distribution records of Orthoptera began in 1967, with the first Provisional Atlas of Orthoptera published in 1978 (Skelton 1978). The culmination of many years of effort was the definitive *Atlas of Grasshoppers, Crickets and Allied Insects in Britain and Ireland* (Haes and Harding 1997), incorporating current, recent and historical data from over 1500 individual recorders; they summarised the history of recording in Britain and Ireland with a comprehensive list of the many people involved in the scheme from its inception. Recording has since continued, often on a county level, e.g. Surrey, where the use of a bat-detector has contributed significantly to orthopteroid recognition (Baldock 1999).

The online Recording Scheme for Orthopteroids of the British Isles (Sutton *et al.* 2008) lists native and non-native species and also many of the casual introductions and occasional migrants, with photographs and, where appropriate, sound recordings, to aid identification.

Instantly accessible up-to-date taxonomic and other information on orthopteroid insects is also available online from the Species Files (http://software.speciesfile.org/Files/Files.aspx); available for the saltatorial orthopteroids (OSF), the Phasmida (PSF), Blattodea (BSF) and Mantodea (MSF), whilst the Dermaptera file is under development.

References

Baldock, D.W. (1999). *Grasshoppers and Crickets of Surrey*, Woking, Surrey Wildlife Trust.

Brock, P.D. (1991). *Stick Insects of Britain, Europe and the Mediterranean*, London, Fitzgerald Publishing.

Brown, V.K. and Cheesman, O.D. (1997). English Nature Species Action Plan, *Stethophyma grossum* (L.) (*Mecostethus grossus* (L.), (Orthoptera: Acrididae), Peterborough, Report for English Nature.

Cherrill, A. (1993). The Conservation of Britain's Wart-biter Bush-cricket. *British Wildlife*, **5**, 26–31.

Collins, G.A., Hodge, P.J., Edwards, M. and Phillips, A. (2007). Sickle-bearing Bush-cricket, *Phaneroptera falcata* (Poda) (Orthoptera: Tettigoniidae), breeding in south-east England. *British Journal of Entomology and Natural History Society*, **20**, 133–137.

Edwards, M. (2008). English Nature Species Recovery Programme, Field Cricket, *Gryllus campestris*, Project Report for 2008, Peterborough, Report for Natural England.

Gardiner, T. (2008). Grass field margins and Orthoptera in eastern England. *Entomologist's Gazette*, **59**, 251–257.

Gardiner, T. (2009). Essex Grasshopper Recording, http://www.essexfieldclub.org.uk/portal/p/Essex+Grasshopper+Recording.

Gorochov, A.V. and Marshall, J.A. (2001). New data on *Pseudomogoplistes* from Atlantic islands (Orthoptera: Mogoplistidae). *Zoosystematica Rossica*, **9** (2000), 76.

Haes, E.C.M. and Harding, P.T. (1997). *Atlas of Grasshoppers, Crickets and Allied Insects in Britain and Ireland*, London, The Stationery Office.

Hathway, R., Stancliffe, P. and Goodey, M., (2003). The discovery of Large Cone-head Bush-cricket in the Isles of Scilly. *British Wildlife*, **15**, 45–46.

Hawkins, R. (2001). The southern oak bush-cricket, *Meconema meridionale* Costa (Orthoptera: Tettigoniidae) new to Britain. *British Journal of Entomology and Natural History*, **14**, 207–213.

Marshall, J.A. (1974). The British Orthoptera since 1800. In D.L. Hawksworth, ed., *The Changing Flora and Fauna of Britain*, London and New York, Academic Press, pp. 307–322.

Marshall, J.A. (1999). *Guide to British Grasshoppers and Allied Insects* (AIDGAP key), Preston Montford, Field Studies Council.

Marshall, J.A. (2001). Grasshoppers, crickets and allied insects. In D.L. Hawksworth, ed., *The Changing Wildlife of Great Britain and Ireland*, Systematics Association Special Volume Series 62, London, Taylor & Francis, pp. 328–339.

Marshall, J.A. and Haes, E.C.M. (1988). *Grasshoppers and Allied Insects of Great Britain and Ireland*, Colchester, Harley Books.

Skelton, M.J. (ed.) (1978). *Provisional Atlas of the Insects of the British Isles*, Part 6, Orthoptera, Huntingdon, Biological Records Centre.

Sutton, P.G. (1999). The Scaly Cricket in Britain – A complete history from discovery to citizenship. *British Wildlife*, **10**, 145–151.

Sutton, P., Beckmann, B. and Roy, H. (2008). *Recording Scheme for Orthopteroids of the British Isles*, Wallingford, Biological Records Centre, http://www.orthoptera.org.uk/.

Widgery, J. (1999). Orthoptera Recording Scheme for Britain and Ireland. *Orthoptera Recording Scheme Newsletter*, **25**, 1–13.

30

Aerial insect biomass: trends from long-term monitoring

Richard Harrington, Chris R. Shortall and Ian P. Woiwod

Summary

Insects are a key component of natural biodiversity, providing food for birds, mammals and other invertebrates, and pollinating many natural and cultivated plants. Despite this importance, there is a real lack of long-term data across Britain on the general abundance of most insect orders. An important source of information on aerial insect populations comes from the national network of 12.2 m high suction traps of the Rothamsted Insect Survey, which started operation with the first site in 1965. All aphids have been identified and counted from these samples and, of the 12 longest-running sites, seven show no trends, three increases and two overall declines in total aphid numbers. Recently a small subset of stored samples from these traps has been analysed for biomass and added to the aphid biomass to estimate total aerial biomass across all insect orders for four sites in southern Britain. At three of these sites there are no long-term trends, but the total biomass has declined severely at one site, Hereford. A more detailed analysis of the Hereford samples has been done, which indicated that the major component of the biomass decline is in the larger insects, particularly the Diptera (flies). Such declines may have been more widespread before the present sampling system was initiated, and may have had important conservation consequences, particularly for insectivorous birds and mammals.

Insects as service providers

In taxonomic terms, Britain has one of the best-studied insect faunas in the world and with about 24 000 species there is no denying that the group is a major component of our biodiversity. With such a large number of species, often only identifiable by professional

Silent Summer: The State of Wildlife in Britain and Ireland, ed. Norman Maclean. Published by Cambridge University Press. © Cambridge University Press 2010.

or dedicated amateur entomologists, it is hardly surprising that most conservation concern and effort until now has been directed at the more local or rare species, particularly from the more charismatic and popular groups such as the butterflies and moths, dragonflies and bumblebees (Chapters 23–26). This enormous species diversity, alongside their general abundance and range of lifestyles, also make insects a key group within the terrestrial ecosystem for a wide variety of reasons. These days, the importance of biodiversity is often considered from the perspective of its role in ecosystem functioning, or the sub-set of functions known as ecosystem services, which are of direct benefit to mankind and can be valued in economic or other terms. Of course we need to set against such benefits the disservices, such as competition with us for food, or the spread of plant, animal and human diseases. In an agricultural context this has recently been discussed by Zhang *et al.* (2007) who point out that insects provide vital ecosystem services to agriculture, such as pollination, pest control and dung burial. Indeed, for pollination alone, it has been estimated that insect services are worth over £122 billion worldwide, or 9.5% of the value of the world agricultural food production in 2005 (Gallai *et al.* 2008), and in this respect there has been a lot of concern recently about possible pollinator decline in Britain and elsewhere in Europe (Biesmeijer *et al.* 2006). In this chapter we are going to focus on another important service that insects provide: as a source of food, particularly for animal groups higher up the food chain such as birds and mammals. To assess changes in this service it will be important to assess changes in the amount of insect food, or biomass, available, as well as having some idea of changes in abundance of taxa. Although it has often been claimed that insect populations have been declining overall in recent years, and this might be the reason for the current declines in some common birds, good evidence for such declines in the amount of food being provided across all the main insect groups has largely been lacking, with the possible exception of the larger moths (Conrad *et al.* 2006; Chapter 25). In Britain we are more fortunate than in most countries throughout the world in having three large-scale, long-term schemes for monitoring populations of particular insect groups. These are the national Butterfly Monitoring Scheme, run jointly by the Centre for Ecology and Hydrology, and Butterfly Conservation (Chapter 24), the Rothamsted Insect Survey's (RIS) national light-trap network, which routinely monitors the larger moths (Chapter 25) and the RIS national suction-trap network, primarily for monitoring aphids. It is largely the information from the last of these three schemes that will be the subject of this chapter, as recent studies have started to make use of stored samples from this network to begin to answer the difficult, but very important, question of what has been happening overall to Britain's aerial insect populations.

The Rothamsted Insect Survey's suction-trap network

Interestingly in the context of this book, the origins of the RIS national suction-trap network can be traced back to the publication *Silent Spring* (Carson 1963). This stimulated public awareness of possible environmental hazards of widespread pesticide use and led to funds being made available for research relevant to reduction of pesticide applications. It was largely as a result of this that in 1964 it was possible to begin developing a network of suction traps for monitoring aerial populations of aphids to complement the light-trap network being developed to monitor moth populations. It was these two networks that became known collectively as the Rothamsted Insect Survey (Taylor 1986, Harrington and Woiwod 2007). Aphids, colloquially known to gardeners as greenfly and blackfly, include some of the most important agricultural insect pests in Britain. Their basic biology, which for many species involves long periods of asexual reproduction, very short overlapping generations and the regular production of very mobile wind-borne migrants, means that pest populations can readily invade crops and very rapidly build up large populations, causing feeding damage. As important is the fact that many aphid species are also very effective vectors of serious crop viruses.

The initial purpose of setting up the aphid monitoring network was to provide current information to the farming community about the timing of aphid immigration into crops and the size of their populations, to aid crop-protection decisions and ultimately reduce unnecessary prophylactic insecticidal sprays. For this purpose, a weekly bulletin of the main pest aphid species is produced and provided to the industry. In addition, the data have been widely used for basic research on aphid biology and ecology (Harrington and Woiwod 2007). A specially designed 12.2 m high suction trap was developed for the RIS network (Figure 30.1) (Macaulay *et al*. 1988). These traps are effectively upside-down vacuum cleaners, sucking 50 m^3 air per minute. The insects entering the traps are filtered out for later sorting, counting and identification in the laboratory. Suction traps have an advantage over many other methods because, rather than being dependent on the attraction of the insect to the trap, the sampling is passive. As a result, aerial insect density can be estimated and the aerial populations of all insect groups sampled can be compared directly. The sampling height of 12.2 m (40 ft) was chosen to be above the height of most local insect flight, sampling instead those species involved in more long-distance, often wind-borne, movement. This is particularly appropriate for aphids, many species of which have migratory stages in their life histories. A further advantage of sampling at height is the large amount of mixing, in effect randomisation, of the aerial insect fauna due to wind run and thermal turbulence. As a result, a single sample gives a very good representation over a large area. For example, it has been shown that aphid samples are highly correlated over at least 50–100 km (Taylor 1973; Cocu *et al*. 2005b). For this reason, relatively few sampling sites are needed to give a good coverage. The first RIS suction trap was set up at Rothamsted in 1965 and a national network of such traps was rapidly developed. Currently there are 16 traps in operation in England and Scotland (Figure 30.2). The RIS suction trap has been widely adopted for pest aphid monitoring in Europe and elsewhere in the world, and because of this standardisation it has been possible to carry out very large spatial scale analyses of aphid abundance and phenology (e.g. Cocu *et al*. 2005a, b, c; Harrington *et al*. 2007). Only aphids are routinely sorted, identified

Figure 30.1 Rothamsted Insect Survey 12.2-m suction trap at Hereford.

and counted from all of the RIS suction-trap sites, but other groups have been taken out for particular studies, and the aphids and other insects have been stored from many of the sites, allowing us to study retrospectively long-term changes in many of the dominant insect groups. Let us start with the group we know most about, the aphids themselves.

Changes in aphid abundance

Aphids are relatively small sap-feeding insects that range from 1–7 mm in length. In Britain there are over 550 species recorded, of which about 350 have been identified from RIS suction traps. Of these only about 20 species are regarded as important agricultural pests, although these can often dominate the samples at certain times of the year. Throughout their varied life cycles, aphids are often wingless, but most

Figure 30.2 Location of suction traps in the UK. Filled stars indicate sites used in more detailed biomass studies.

species produce winged migrant forms, either in response to overcrowding and low plant-nutrient status, or when they use day-length cues to migrate to and from overwintering host plants. Because of their enormous potential rates of population increase, these migrant aphids can be very abundant and sometimes comprise over 50% of the aerial insect fauna. As such, they are undoubtedly an important component of the diet of aerial feeding birds such as swifts, swallows and martins. Because most aphids in the RIS trap network are identified to species or species group, it would be possible to describe in detail trends for all the regularly caught species, but here we are mainly concerned with their role as food for predators, where individual species identity is less important. As they are all in the same general size category, the total number of aphids trapped per year will give a good estimate of the total aphid biomass available to predators. We therefore selected for linear trend analysis current RIS sites that have been running for at least 20 of the years between 1965 and 2006. This provides 12 sites which have run for periods between 27 and 42 years, depending on starting date. The logged total numbers per year were regressed against year and the results are rather surprising (Figure 30.3). At only two sites, Hereford and Wye, were there significant declines in aphid numbers, whereas at three sites, Ayr, Preston and Newcastle, there were significant increases. The remaining seven sites showed no significant trends, in nearly all cases convincingly so. These results go rather against two common perceptions: that most insect groups have been declining over the past 20 years, but that pests have been getting more abundant. The RIS data support neither of these propositions, at least for total aphids across the whole year, with the majority of sample sites showing no change and the two declining sites, Wye and Hereford, only changing by 13% and 15% per decade, respectively. This may be because aphids comprise both pest and non-pest species. The changes in aphid abundance at the two north-westerly sites of Preston and Ayr are more impressive, with 22% and 49% increases per decade, respectively, and a more modest 14% increase per decade at Newcastle. If annual geometric mean abundance is calculated across all 12 sites, then there is no overall trend, suggesting that increases and decreases are approximately balancing each other out at the national scale. As can be seen from the graphs, there are large year-to-year fluctuations in total aphid numbers, even when log transformed. This is not unexpected with this insect group, as nearly all aphid species have enormous potential population growth rates if unchecked, and this is the reason that runs of at least 20 years are required to detect meaningful trends. The reason for the long-term increases at Preston, Ayr and Newcastle is unknown, but may be a combination of agricultural land-use change and climate. The decline at Hereford will be discussed in more detail later, but for aphids it might not be coincidental that Hereford and Wye are in the two areas which used to be main centres for hop growing in England and hops have their own pest species, the hop aphid, *Phorodon humuli*. This species has certainly declined significantly at both sites, presumably as a result of the reduction in the land area under hops in both areas. When this species is removed from the total aphids then there is still a decline in total aphids, but it is barely significant.

Total aerial insect biomass

In addition to aphids, a wide range of insects disperse at height, both passively, using air currents if they are small, and actively, under their own power if they are larger and their flight speed is higher than the background wind speed. All these insects are likely to end up in RIS suction-trap samples in proportion to their aerial abundance at 12.2 m. For many species, aerial density will also reflect relative abundance at ground level. This was confirmed by a recent study linking temporal changes in invertebrates with bird numbers and agricultural practice, which successfully used a 26 year run of data from a RIS-type suction trap in Stirling to measure insect populations and

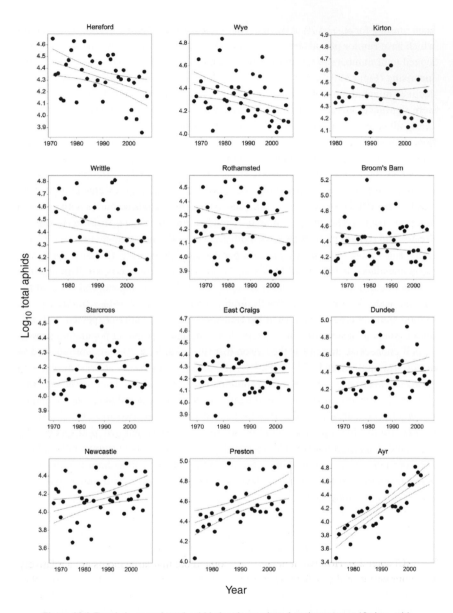

Figure 30.3 Trends in annual total aphid abundance plotted against year at 12 sites, with 95% confidence intervals. (Note: insect population data are routinely log transformed to normalise variance and because population processes are inherently multiplicative.)

show that they were related to the local breeding success of many bird species (Benton *et al.* 2002). Many birds have undergone well-documented declines in recent years (Chapter 17). For example, 83% of UK farmland bird species declined between 1970 and 1990 (Fuller *et al.* 1995) and over a longer period (1966–99) almost a third of woodland bird species declined (Fuller *et al.* 2005). These declines have coincided with a period of rapid agricultural intensification, which almost certainly has reduced farmland populations of some insect groups (Aebisher 1991; Woiwod 1991). Although bird populations are very well documented in Britain, we know much less about most insect groups, so the long-term data from the RIS suction traps provide a particularly important resource for trying to understand the links between long-term population trends in birds and insects. Fortunately, the non-aphid portions of the samples from many of the RIS traps have been stored and so it has been possible to go back and sort these into various taxonomic and/or size classes in order to reconstruct long runs of aerial biomass. Sorting and identifying insects is very labour intensive and with the limited resources available so far it has only been possible to reconstruct total aerial biomass from four RIS sites, Rothamsted, Hereford, Wye and Starcross (Figure 30.2). Even for this limited set of southern sites, it has been necessary to sub-sample within years to reduce the amount of material to be examined. Full details of sub-sampling regimes and the way total biomass has been reconstructed, by weighing or estimating the weights of various insect fractions, are given elsewhere (Harrington *et al.* 2003; Moore *et al.* 2004; Shortall *et al.* 2006; Shortall *et al.* 2009). Regressions of logged total aerial biomass against year for the four sites over the 30 year period 1973–2002 are shown in Figure 30.4. Only at the Hereford site is there a significant overall decline in biomass, with the other three sites showing no discernible trends. However, it should be noted that Hereford starts from an overall higher aerial density and the importance of this will be discussed later. Only one other insect group, apart from aphids, has been analysed for all years from these four sites, the macro-moths (Harrington *et al.* 2003; Shortall *et al.* 2006, 2009). Adult macro-moths are relatively large insects and therefore are important individual food items for crepuscular and nocturnal predators such as bats and nightjars. Significant declines in moth biomass at Hereford, Starcross and Wye were found, but not at Rothamsted (Figure 30.5). This confirms the general downward trend of this group in southern Britain that was found from the more extensive network of RIS light traps, as described and discussed in detail elsewhere in this book (Chapter 25). However it needs to be pointed out that large moths are a relatively rare component of the aerial insect fauna and so numbers, even in the powerful RIS suction traps, are always low, although individual macro-moths include some of the heaviest insects. This relative rarity is one of the reasons that light traps are widely used in moth monitoring, as sample size is increased by attraction to the light source. As a result, the findings from the RIS light traps probably give a better representation of large-scale population changes in this important group of insects (Chapter 25). The other group for which we have some information is social wasps, largely thanks to the work of Michael Archer, who has been identifying and counting this group from the

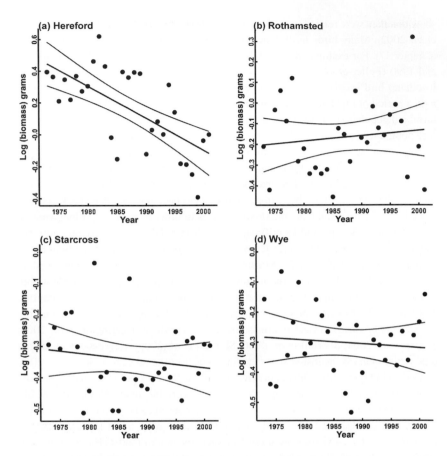

Figure 30.4 Trends in total insect biomass ($\log_{10}$ mean weight in grams of insects per sample) plotted against year, with 95% confidence intervals.

RIS suction-trap samples for many years (Archer 2001). For the two sites for which there are full estimates of biomass, Hereford and Rothamsted, there were no significant long-term trends in samples for this group, which is mainly composed of the two common wasp species, *Vespula germanica* and *V. vulgaris* (Shortall *et al.* 2009).

A detailed investigation of the Hereford decline

With the strongest trend being the decline in total insect biomass at Hereford, it was decided to examine this effect in more detail to see if it was possible to tie down the main groups responsible. Preliminary analysis suggested that smaller-sized insects

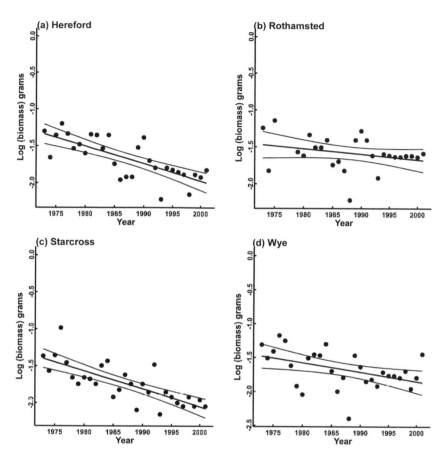

Figure 30.5 Trends in macrolepidoptera (macro-moths) biomass (log$_{10}$ mean weight in grams of moths per sample) plotted against year, with 95% confidence intervals.

were not the main culprits; in fact, total numbers of the smaller insects showed a significant overall increase (Moore *et al.* 2004). It was therefore decided to concentrate the more detailed taxonomic study on the larger insects. This was done by passing stored samples through a 2 mm × 2 mm sieve and only analysing the samples of insects too large to pass through the mesh. Weekly samples from April to September were then selected to provide 26 sample dates from every year from 1973 to 2004. The sample selected for analysis in a particular week was from the day with the highest maximum temperature to ensure optimum conditions for flight. The taxonomic separation was taken as far as practicable; this was usually to insect order and family, but in some cases to genus and species (Shortall *et al.* 2009). As with the total biomass for all species (Figure 30.4a) the total biomass for just the larger insects at Hereford showed a strong and significant downward trend, confirming that it was indeed changes in populations of the larger insects that had mainly contributed to the general biomass decline at this site. It should be noted that aerial biomass of these larger insects is not evenly spread throughout the year, but has two distinct peaks, a large spring peak around May (weeks 18–22), with a smaller autumn peak in September (weeks 36–39) (Figure 30.6). The major insect orders in the samples were Diptera (flies) and Coleoptera (beetles), with Hymenoptera (bees and wasps) and Lepidoptera (moths) having a large percentage of the counts in some years. The Diptera families with the highest counts, in order of decreasing abundance, were Bibionidae, Chironomidae, Empidae, Anthomyiidae, Calliphoridae, Tipulidae and Anisopodidae. The main Coleoptera families by decreasing abundance were Curculionidae, Staphylinidae and Carabidae. In terms of numbers, the Bibionidae dominated the catches in nearly all of the spring samples and a high proportion of the autumn samples across all years. Because of the dominant role of bibionids in the Hereford samples, further taxonomic work was done and it turned out that the majority were of a single species, the Fever Fly, *Dilophus febrilis* (Shortall *et al.* 2009). There was a significant decline in the biomass of bibionid flies on their own, as well as the remainder of the sample of large insects with all bibionids removed (Figure 30.7). The rate of decline of these two portions of the catch was not significantly different (Shortall *et al.* 2009). When

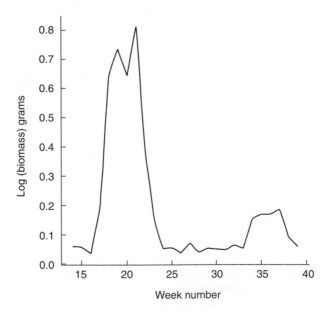

Figure 30.6 Mean weekly biomass index (1973–2004) of larger invertebrates from Hereford suction trap.

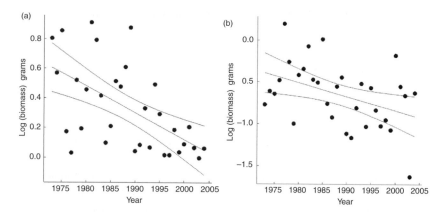

Figure 30.7 Total annual biomass of: (a) Bibionidae and (b) other large insects, in samples from Hereford suction trap plotted against year, with 95% confidence intervals.

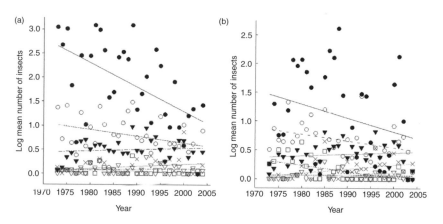

Figure 30.8 Total number of larger insects in: (a) spring and (b) autumn samples, from the Hereford suction trap plotted against year. —●— Bibionidae ···▼··· Coleoptera —⊖· Diptera —✕— Hymenoptera - ·⊟· Lepidoptera - ▽- Hemiptera.

the data were analysed separately for the two biomass peaks of spring and autumn, it was found that the decline of bibionids was particularly evident in the spring, but that both bibionids and Diptera excluding bibionids declined significantly in both the spring and autumn flight periods (Figure 30.8). None of the other insect groups had significant trends, but this may have been partly because of the small sample sizes of these groups after sub-sampling, which would have reduced statistical power for detecting trends. We know this is so for the macro-moths, where there was a significant decline at Hereford when all samples were analysed (Figure 30.5), whereas the decline evident in Figure 30.8b is not significant because of the large number of years with zero catches as a result of sub-sampling a relatively rare group of insects.

Discussion and conclusions

The insect trends apparent from the RIS suction-trap samples analysed so far should help to dispel some of the myths and simplifications that tend to surround the subject. There is clearly no straightforward message of universal decline across all insect groups (as often reported in the popular press), at least over the last 20 to 30 years analysed here. The group for which we have the most detailed records, the aphids, seem free of strong annual trends, except at two sites, Preston and Auchincruive, both near the north-west coast of Britain, where climate or land-use change might be factors. This lack of aphid trends is perhaps surprising, particularly as several species are now flying earlier because of climate change, and this usually goes hand in hand with larger numbers in spring and early summer. The reason this is not feeding through to larger annual totals is probably down to natural enemies responding and keeping populations controlled later in the year (Harrington and Woiwod 2007). This may be particularly relevant with aphids and their enemies, as they usually have short life cycles with many generations and hence time for natural enemy populations to build up within years. The total biomass results are surprising, with only one in four of the sites so far examined having a significant downward trend. This suggests that at three sites, increases and decreases in populations of particular species are, on average, cancelling each other out. The strong decline in biomass at Hereford is therefore of particular interest and the first thing to note is that in 1973, Hereford started at a much higher level and it may well be that similar declines had already taken place at the other sites before systematic RIS sampling began. Unfortunately, there is little evidence available to confirm this, but some support comes from light-trap data from the Rothamsted estate in Hertfordshire that go back to the 1930s. At that site a very large decline in moth population took place during the major phase of agricultural intensification in the 1940s and 50s, in response to food shortages after the war, and it is likely that this reflected a much more widespread decline in overall insect abundance at that time (Woiwod 1991; Woiwod and Gould 2008). The more detailed analysis of the Hereford samples provides some insights into the insects implicated in the decline and how this might affect bird food resources more generally. The first important finding was that the fraction of catch that contained the relatively larger insects was declining, rather than smaller insects. The fraction of the samples that did not pass through the 2 mm × 2 mm sieve made up only 16% of the total number of insects sampled (Moore *et al.* 2004), although its contribution to total biomass is much higher. This also confirms the general inverse relationship between size and abundance in insects. Further it seems that the Diptera are the main component of the larger insects sampled and that there was a general decline in these, both when including and excluding the dominant family, the bibionids. On top of that there has almost certainly been a decline in larger moths at the Hereford site, although suction traps are not ideal for monitoring this group because of its generally lower population levels. Although we can speculate, the causes of the insect declines at Hereford are unknown. Amongst possible factors could be regional changes in farming practice (Benton *et al.* 2002). This might just be a general intensification, with its implication of increased insecticide and herbicide use, or it might be a more major change in the pattern of crops under cultivation, for example a switch from grassland to arable in the area. The larvae of the dominant Fever Fly, *Dilophus febrilis*, feed in the soil on decaying organic matter, so it may be a change in either the quality or quantity of this resource that is implicated, at least for some of the larger Diptera. The decline in macro-moths seems to be part of a larger-scale phenomenon in southern England and may be related to additional factors such as climate change and pollution, although this also requires further study (Conrad *et al.* 2006). Larger insects are a component of the diet of many birds, and Diptera have been identified as particularly important, with bibionids making up a significant part of the diets of partridges, dunnocks, swifts and other species (Moreby 2004). Tipulids (crane flies), together with aphids, weevils, spiders, ants, grasshoppers and moths, have been highlighted as important food for newly hatched sparrow chicks (Seel 1969; Peach *et al.* 2008). The declines at Hereford are therefore likely to have at least some effect on the bird populations of the surrounding area.

There is clearly much work still to be done in understanding patterns of insect population change and the relationships between these and other components of the ecosystem. At Hereford, the next step will be to quantify changes in land use and agricultural practice in the area and see whether these can help explain the observed declines. It would also be interesting to examine bird census trends in the surrounding countryside and relate these to the insect trends discussed here. With only four sites examined so far, and only one of those in any detail, we still know far too little about wider changes in general patterns of abundance of the vast majority of the insect fauna of Britain. Their importance as service providers and key components of most terrestrial ecosystems make further studies imperative. Stored RIS suction-trap samples are available from other sites and these will need studying as a priority if we are to get any further in understanding how our insect populations are changing and in predicting how they might respond to future change.

Acknowledgements

We thank English Nature (currently Natural England), especially David Sheppard, for supporting much of this work. We are also indebted to the trap operators and RIS staff for keeping the network functioning over the years and helping with these biomass studies in many ways. The RIS trap networks are supported by the Lawes Agricultural Trust Company Ltd. Rothamsted Research is grant-aided by the UK Biotechnology and Biological Sciences Research Council.

References

Aebischer, N.J. (1991). Twenty years of monitoring invertebrates and weeds in cereal fields in Sussex. In Firbank, L.G., Carter, N., Darbyshire, J.F. and Potts, G.R., eds., *The Ecology of Temperate Cereal Fields*, Oxford, UK, Blackwell Scientific Publications, pp. 305–331.

Archer, M.E. (2001). Changes in abundance of *Vespula germanica* and *V. vulgaris* in England. *Ecological Entomology, 26*, 1–7.

Biesmeijer, J.C., Roberts, S.P.M., Reemer, M. *et al.* (2006). Parallel declines in pollinators and insect-pollinated plants in Britain and the Netherlands. *Science, 313*, 351–354.

Benton, T.G., Bryant, D.M., Cole, L. and Crick, H.Q.P. (2002). Linking agricultural practice to insect and bird populations: a historical study over three decades. *Journal of Applied Ecology, 39*, 673–687.

Carson, R. (1963). *Silent Spring*, London, Hamish Hamilton.

Cocu, N., Conrad, K.F., Harrington, R. and Rounsevell, M.D.A. (2005a). Analysis of spatial patterns at a geographical scale over north-western Europe from point-referenced aphid count data. *Bulletin of Entomological Research, 95*, 47–56.

Cocu, N., Harrington, R., Hullé, M. and Rounsevell, M.D.A. (2005b). Spatial autocorrelation as a tool for identifying the geographical patterns of aphid abundance. *Agricultural and Forest Entomology, 7*, 31–43.

Cocu, N., Harrington, R., Rounsevell, M.D.A., Worner, S.P., Hullé, M and the EXAMINE project participants (2005c). Geographic location, climate and land use influences on the phenology and abundance of the aphid, *Myzus persicae* in Europe. *Journal of Biogeography, 32*, 615–632.

Conrad, K.F., Warren, M.S., Fox, R., Parsons, M. and Woiwod, I.P. (2006). Rapid declines in common moths underscore a biodiversity crisis. *Biological Conservation, 132*, 279–291.

Fuller, R.J., Gregory, R.D., Gibbons, D.W. *et al.* (1995). Population declines and range contractions among lowland farmland birds in Britain. *Conservation Biology, 9*, 1425–1441.

Fuller, R.J., Noble, D.G., Smith, K.W. and Vanhinsbergh, D. (2005). Recent declines in populations of woodland birds in Britain: a review of possible causes. *British Birds, 98*, 116–143.

Gallai, N., Salles, J.-M., Settele, J. and Vaissière, B.E. (2008). Economic valuation of the vulnerability of world agriculture confronted with pollinator decline. *Ecological Economics, 68*, 810–821.

Harrington, R. and Woiwod, I.P. (2007). Foresight from hindsight: the Rothamsted Insect Survey. *Outlooks on Pest Management, 18*, 9–14.

Harrington, R., Clark, S.J., Welham, S.J. *et al.* (2007). Environmental change and the phenology of European aphids. *Global Change Biology, 13*, 1550–1564.

Harrington, R., Smith E. and Hall, M. (2003). Assessing long-term trends in invertebrate biomass – a pilot study. English Nature and Rothamsted Research (unpublished report).

Macaulay, E.D.M., Tatchell, G.M. and Taylor, L.R. (1988). The Rothamsted Insect Survey 12-metre suction trap. *Bulletin of Entomological Research,* **78**, 121–129.

Moore, A., Harrington, R., Hall, M. and Woiwod, I. (2004). Temporal changes in abundance of insects of importance as bird food. English Nature and Rothamsted Research (unpublished report).

Moreby, S.J. (2004). Birds of lowland arable farmland: the importance and identification of invertebrate diversity in the diet of chicks. In van Emden, H.F. and Rothschild, M., eds., *Insect and Bird Interactions,* Andover, UK, Intercept, pp. 21–35.

Peach, W.J., Vincent, K.E., Fowler, J.A. and Grice, P.V. (2008). Reproductive success of house sparrows along an urban gradient. *Animal Conservation,* **11**, 1–11.

Seel, D.C. (1969). Food, feeding rates and body temperature in the nestling house sparrow at Oxford. *Ibis,* **111**, 36–47.

Shortall, C., Harrington, R., Hall M. and Clark, S. (2006). Long-term trends in aerial insect populations. English Nature and Rothamsted Research (unpublished report).

Shortall, C.R., Moore, A., Smith, E. *et al.* (2009). Long-term changes in the abundance of flying insects. *Insect Conservation and Diversity,* **2**, 251–260.

Taylor, L.R. (1973). Monitoring change in the distribution and abundance of insects. Rothamsted Report for 1973, Part 2, pp. 202–239.

Taylor, L.R. (1986). Synoptic dynamics, migration and the Rothamsted Insect Survey. *Journal of Animal Ecology,* **55**, 1–38.

Woiwod, I.P. (1991). The ecological importance of long-term synoptic monitoring. In Firbank, L.G., Carter, N., Darbyshire, J.F. and Potts, G.R., eds., *The Ecology of Temperate Cereal Fields,* Oxford, UK, Blackwell, pp. 275–304.

Woiwod, I.P. and Gould, P.J.L. (2008). Long-term moth studies at Rothamsted. In Plant, C.W,, ed., *The Moths of Hertfordshire,* Welwyn Garden City, The Hertfordshire Natural History Society, pp. 31–44.

Zhang, W., Ricketts, T.H., Kremen, C., Carney, K. and Swinton, S.M. (2007). Ecosystem services and dis-services to agriculture. *Ecological Economics,* **64**, 253–260.

31

Other invertebrates

Richard Chadd and Brian Eversham

Summary

This chapter involves those orders of invertebrates which are not insects – including crustaceans, spiders, myriapods and worms – which, though frequently overlooked, are useful indicators of the state of our wildlife, because of their profound response to environmental pressures.

The chapter is arranged in two broad sections – terrestrial and fresh water – but it will be seen that the pressures are common to both environments. Habitat destruction, climate change (with the secondary effects, such as drought, flood and changes in life cycle), changing agricultural practices and introduction of alien species have all played a part in forcing change in the British fauna, at broad scales, such as national distribution of species, and local scales, such as changes at a community or population level.

Among terrestrial invertebrates, colonists and introduced species tend to live mainly in gardens and other man-made habitats in southern or south-eastern England, where temperatures are higher, and competition may be reduced. In recent years, several of these species have begun to expand their range northward and westward, and at the same time to colonise semi-natural habitats.

Included in the case studies are examples of the contraction in distribution or population size of cold-loving species (e.g. highland flatworms, montane spiders) and the concomitant rise of those which prefer warmer climates (e.g. the colourful Wasp Spider, *Argiope bruennichi*), superimposed against the other pressures outlined above. Individual cases of the impact and spread of non-natives (e.g. Signal Crayfish, *Pacifastacus leniusculus,* or the harvestman, *Opilio canestrinii*), the potential loss of rare species (e.g. spiders and pseudoscorpions dependent on coastal shingle banks and sand dunes), and life cycle or population changes (e.g. zooplankton in the English Lake District) are presented.

Silent Summer: The State of Wildlife in Britain and Ireland, ed. Norman Maclean. Published by Cambridge University Press. © Cambridge University Press 2010.

Terrestrial invertebrates

The terrestrial non-insect invertebrates are a diverse and species-rich assortment, but many groups are too poorly known to interpret their past or present distribution accurately, let alone predict their future. Some groups, such as the nematodes, are of great agricultural and horticultural importance. The main sources of information on distribution are academic research, agriculture and amateur naturalists. Of these, only naturalists are enthusiastic about species identification and detailed patterns of distribution.

Amateur naturalists have studied and recorded invertebrates for over 200 years, and began mapping them in the early twentieth century, initially using county or vice-county distribution. Since the introduction of Ordnance Survey maps showing the national grid in 1948, naturalists' efforts have concentrated on mapping species distributions in 10 km grid squares. Since the pioneering *Atlas of the British Flora* (Perring and Walters 1962), national recording schemes have been launched for many groups of invertebrates, and their distributions have been mapped.

Most naturalists depend on the availability of literature in English, so the absence of a modern identification guide prevents more than a handful of enthusiasts from studying a group. Lack of useable British keys, coupled with the need for elaborate preparation of specimens for microscopic examination, has meant that little information is available on the following organisms in Britain: nematodes, rotifers, tardigrades, potworms (Annelida: Enchytraeidae), Symphyla, Pauropoda and mites (Acarina). These groups have therefore been omitted from this account.

Land flatworms – Platyhelminthes: Tricladida: Terricolae

All the known British species are reviewed and almost all are illustrated in colour by Jones (2005). The four species considered likely to be native, *Microplana humicola*, *M. scharffi*, *M. terrestris* and *Rhynchodemus sylvaticus*, are all small (usually less than 30 mm long, and only 1–2 mm wide), and are easily overlooked, often being mistaken for insect larvae or slugs. All four are widespread in Britain, and are unlikely to respond strongly to climate change, though they may be less abundant during periods of prolonged drought.

About 10 species of land flatworm have been accidentally introduced into Britain or Ireland through the international horticultural trade. Three of these, *Dolichoplana striata*, *Coenoplana coerulea* and *Bipalium kewense*, are confined to heated greenhouses or vivaria, having come originally from Sri Lanka/south-east Asia, Australia and south-east Asia, respectively. Though they may become more widespread indoors, it is unlikely they will establish outside. Seven or so species have already been recorded living outside, mostly in gardens: 2–3 come from New Zealand, and 4–5 from Australia, though some have yet to be found in their presumed country of origin. One conspicuous species, the so-called New Zealand Flatworm, *Arthurdendyus triangulatus* (= *Artioposthia triangulata*), which can grow to 20 cm long and 10 mm wide, was first found in Scotland and Northern Ireland in the 1950s or 1960s. It has attracted much research since the 1980s, when it became abundant, because it feeds on earthworms and was perceived to be a potentially serious pest. It now appears that its impact is mainly on the larger, longer-lived, deep-burrowing earthworms, and that it has little effect on smaller, more rapidly reproducing, shallow-burrowers.

It is likely that further species of flatworm (see Figure 31.2) will be imported to, or discovered in, Britain, and that some of the established species will spread. Although rather little information is available on their ecophysiology, most species are likely to be more abundant in years of higher rainfall and humidity, and to decline during prolonged droughts.

Terrestrial Nemertea

The Nemertea are a predominantly marine group, with moderate numbers of freshwater species, and 10–20 terrestrial species. Most of the world's terrestrial nemerteans are forest species with restricted distributions in Australia, New Zealand and on oceanic islands. Several species appear to be in decline or even extinct (Moore *et al.* 2001). The only species which has been introduced and is now widespread in Britain is *Argonemertes* (= *Geonemertes*) *dendyi*, from Australia, which has been transported by horticulture to several parts of Europe and North America. It is seldom recognised, but appears to be widely distributed, but rarely abundant. It is mainly southern and coastal at present, a distribution which it has been suggested may be temperature-related (Pantin 1961). If so, the species may become more widespread and frequent in a warmer climate, though it may be intolerant of prolonged droughts.

Leeches: Annelida: Hirudinea

The only quasi-terrestrial leeches in Britain, the two introduced *Trocheta* species, which forage on damp ground up to several metres away from water, are dealt with in the freshwater section of this chapter.

Earthworms: Annelida: Lumbricidae

Almost all of the *c.* 400 species of the family Lumbricidae (the only earthworms native to Britain) have small geographic ranges, being confined to those parts of southern Europe which escaped the permafrost and ice sheets of the Pleistocene/ Quaternary glaciations. Hence, Britain has a relatively very species-poor fauna.

Presumably, a much more diverse earthworm fauna existed in the early Pleistocene, but became extinct at the onset of the first of the present series of glaciations, about three million years ago. Most, perhaps all, of the earthworm species in Britain today may have been assisted in their arrival by human activity, though some may have colonised via the post-glacial land bridge which linked Britain to the continent until about 8000 years ago.

About 26 species of earthworm are well established outdoors in Britain, of which three are considered fairly recent introductions (Sims and Gerard 1985). Although none of these are likely to be threatened by climate change, many are intolerant of prolonged waterlogging, so will contract their range if floods become more widespread. The future of some of the larger, deeper-burrowing species may be partly dependent on the extent to which the New Zealand Flatworm, *Athurdendyus triangulates*, spreads and becomes their dominant predator.

Of the 17 or more casual or greenhouse introductions, few are able to survive outside heated greenhouses or waste-processing units. One species, *Microscolex phosphoreus*, from temperate South America, was previously known from a handful of market gardens in Britain, and was reported new to Ireland in 1992 (Cotton 1992). It has recently become sufficiently abundant in places to cause concern to the managers of golf courses and bowling greens because of its numerous wormcasts. It could potentially become more frequent in a warmer climate. As it is strongly phosphorescent when disturbed, it may attract attention if it does spread.

Woodlice: Crustacea: Isopoda

Thirty-seven species are native or naturalised out of doors in Britain and Ireland, and a further 10 have been reported from heated greenhouses (Hopkin 1991; Oliver and Meechan 1993). Some scarce species, such as *Halophiloscia couchi* and *Stenophiloscia zosterae*, are largely confined to coastal shingle, so may be vulnerable to sea-level rise in future. One species characteristic of ancient fens and ancient woodlands, *Ligidium hypnorum*, might be thought vulnerable to climate warming and especially to droughts, but laboratory studies suggest it is actually surprisingly tolerant of dry conditions (Hopkin 2003).

One large slate-grey pill-woodlouse, *Armadillidium depressum*, appears to have expanded its range north and east in the last 20 years, from an original geographic range in the south-west peninsula. Another, the small, hairy purple-brown pill-woodlouse, *Eluma purpurascens*, previously known from two small populations, has now been found to be widespread in parts of east Kent. Given that these are both distinctive species, the range expansions may be genuine, though it is difficult to rule out the effect of increased recorder effort.

Additional species may colonise Britain in future: for instance, *Hyloniscus riparius* was recently found in the Netherlands for the first time (Hopkin 2003).

Terrestrial Amphipoda

The British amphipods include several species of freshwater shrimp, and a diverse marine and brackish-water fauna of shrimps and sand-hoppers. Two species of amphipod live more or less on land, and both may be increasing. The landhopper, *Arcitalitrus dorrieni*, was introduced to Cornwall, the Scilly Isles and to Ireland from Australasia (Sutton and Harding 1988), and is spreading gradually from the south-west, at least as far as Dorset and Bristol. It is now abundant in parts of Bristol, where it was absent 20 years ago (Hopkin 2003). It occurs in gardens, under stones, rocks and plant pots, among leaf litter etc.

Rather less terrestrial, the sandhopper, *Orchestia cavimana* (= *bottae*) occurs on mud, sand and shingle beside rivers and canals, usually just above the water's edge, and can be locally extremely abundant, although it sometimes disappears from sites where it was plentiful. It was first found in Britain in 1942, and appears still to be spreading (Gledhill *et al.* 1993; Fryer 1993).

Centipedes: Chilopoda

The 52 British species include several synanthropic (associated with human occupation) introductions mostly from further south in Europe. One species which is almost domestic is the long-legged and extremely fast-moving House Centipede, *Scutigera coleoptrata*. There have been several casual records of this species being imported, but no evidence of it yet becoming established. It lives out of doors in southern France, so with a warming climate may have a better chance of establishment in Britain. Some other species which are frequent in gardens in urban areas, such as the two large centipedes, *Cryptops anomalans* and *C. parisii* (Scolopendromorpha, with 22 pairs of legs at all stages of their life), have begun to occur in woodlands and other semi-natural habitats since 1990.

Millipedes: Diplopoda

As with the centipedes, the 53 species recorded in Britain include several synanthropic introductions, and several casuals which are not yet established. Heated greenhouses support one of the smallest species, *Prosopodesmus panporus*, less than 5 mm long and probably of Asiatic origin, and the larger, glossy brown and cream, flat-backed, *Oxidus gracilis*, which has occasionally been found in gardens and compost heaps near heated greenhouses, but cannot overwinter without heat (Blower 1985). Recent arrivals include the conspicuously hairy cylindrical millipede, *Unciger foetidus*, which was found in a garden at Dereham, Norfolk in 1993, but does not appear to be spreading yet. The Mediterranean species, *Stosatea italica*, has been established in Kent since at least the 1920s (Blower 1985) and may spread with a warmer climate.

Harvestmen: Arachnida: Opiliones

Of the 25 or so species of harvestmen (or harvest-spiders) known from Britain, one tropical species probably from southern Asia, *Boeorix manducus*, is recorded only from a hothouse at Kew. Most of the native species are either widespread, or have a southern distribution, so might be expected to survive or to expand in response to climate change.

Although with limited powers of natural dispersal, harvestmen may be assisted by man, probably through horticultural moving of soil containing their eggs. Three species thought to have been introduced to Britain in the twentieth century have now expanded over a large area. *Nelima sylvatica*, initially a south-western species, now occurs as far north as Aberdeen (Hillyard and Sankey 1989). The distinctive *Dicranopalpus ramosus*, the only British harvestman with conspicuously forked pedipalps, has a habit of holding its long, banded legs clustered together at right-angles to the body. It spread north across Europe in the twentieth century, and had arrived in Britain by 1957. The first record was from Bournemouth, and for some years it appeared to be confined to the south coast. By the mid-1980s it had spread about 100 km north, and it has since spread much further and become abundant over much of lowland England, and has been reported as far north as Edinburgh.

The most dramatic colonisation may be currently in progress. *Opilio canestrinii* was first found in Britain in 1999 (Hillyard 2000), following its spread across north-west Europe from its origins in Italy, Austria, Switzerland and Germany. As it spread across Europe, it was reported to have largely replaced the two common species, *Opilio parietinus* and *O. saxatilis* (Hillyard 2000). The same may be happening in Britain: the two common residents are now difficult to find in parts of Yorkshire where *O. canestrinii* has arrived (P. Richards, personal communication, 2008).

Finally, one rather poorly known taxon may decline in response to climate warming. *Mitopus ericaeus* was described as a species new to science (Jennings 1982), but has subsequently been treated as a sub-species (e.g. Hillyard and Sankey 1989). It is an upland taxon, not recorded below 250 m in Britain, and distinguished from the common and widespread *M. morio*, with which it occurs, by its larger body size, longer legs, details of its genitalia and its earlier maturation.

Pseudoscorpions: Arachnida: Pseudoscorpiones

These tiny arachnids, named because of their scorpion-like pincers, hold a fascination for almost everyone who has encountered them, even though the largest British species is a mere 4.5 mm long, and the smallest about 1.2 mm. Three of the 28 or so species are strictly coastal. Two of these have a wide intertidal range, so will probably track their habitat if sea levels rise and coasts erode: *Kewochthonius halberti* occurs at around the high tide mark and *Neobisium maritiumum* from splash zone to lower shore. The third coastal species, *Dactylochelifer latreillei*, lives among marram and

Sea Couch-Grass on coastal sand dunes, and will be vulnerable to losses of dunes from increased winter storms. A few species are associated with agricultural buildings: *Withius piger* is especially common in stored grain, *Allochernes powellii* in barn and stable refuse, and *Dinocheirus panzeri* among hay, straw and grain refuse, or in pigeon-lofts and chicken-sheds (Legg and Jones 1988). Each of these could decline due to better agricultural hygiene, and the conversion of barns to high quality dwellings. Two of our rarest species are associated with veteran trees within ancient parkland; both *Dendrochernes cyrneus* and the recently recognised *Larca lata* (Legg 2001) may have increased in response to the surfeit of dead wood resulting from Dutch Elm Disease, and may decline in future, especially if climate change does not favour long-lived trees of great girth.

Scorpions: Arachnida: Scorpiones

Although several species from around the world are occasionally imported in fruit and other produce, only a single species has become established here: there are colonies of *Euscorpius flavicauda* in a few sites, mainly in the London area, most famously Chipping Ongar railway station. This species may spread with climate warming, and others from southern Europe might eventually establish themselves if the temperature rise is sufficient.

Spiders: Arachnida: Araneae

With around 650 British species, the spiders are the most diverse terrestrial non-insect invertebrates for which there are good data. Almost half these species belong to a single family, Linyphiidae, mostly very small and unpatterned grey or black 'money-spiders'. Despite their apparent obscurity, even these have been sufficiently thoroughly recorded to provide meaningful distribution maps in the national atlas (Harvey *et al.* 2002). As with other arachnids, many species are imported with fruit and other foodstuffs from around the world, but do not become established. Several brought from mainland Europe with horticultural produce, especially house plants, and are now established here.

The distinctive *Uloborus plumipes*, with clumps of feathery hairs on the tibiae of its front legs, is now well established in heated greenhouses in garden centres and is spreading rapidly (Harvey *et al.* 2002). The large and conspicuous jumping spider, *Philaeus chrysops*, the male of which has a bright red abdomen with a black central stripe, has been recorded several times in England, but appears not yet to be breeding here, even within glasshouses, though it breeds in much of France (Roberts 1995). With warmer summers and frost-free winters, these species might eventually establish themselves outside in the mildest parts of Britain. A much longer-distance immigrant with a surprisingly restricted distribution is *Acaearanea verruculata*, which lives among trees and bushes on the Scilly Isles, having been introduced at the start of the twentieth century from New Zealand, where it is common.

Other species which probably arrived from Europe as natural colonists to the south coast of England are now spreading north and west. Most conspicuous of these is the Wasp Spider, *Argiope bruennichi* (see Figure 31.1), the female of which is very large (the black-yellow-white striped body over 15 mm long). First recorded in Sussex in 1922 (Locket and Millidge 1951), the species was for many years confined to the south coast from Kent to Dorset . Since the 1970s it has spread, with sites in Essex in 1997, Surrey by 1998 (Harvey *et al.* 2002), and by 2008 there was at least one substantial breeding colony in Cambridgeshire, with individual records as far north as Derbyshire. Another spider occasionally inspires fear in the populus: *Segestria florentina* is a large (up to 22 mm long) spider living in tube-webs in holes in brickwork, with conspicuously metallic-green fangs. It is well established in London Docklands and at other ports, but in recent years has been recorded at scattered sites across southern England. These and other recent colonists are likely to spread further north as climate warming continues.

Many southern species may expand their ranges, but some with specialised habitats, and perhaps a low reproductive output, may suffer. The attractive Ladybird Spider, *Eresus sandaliatus* (= *E. niger*), now occurs in very small numbers at a single sandy heathland in Dorset, although it was formerly slightly more widespread (Harvey *et al.* 2002). Its life cycle takes at least four years, and a single batch of 80–90 eggs is laid. Subtle changes in habitat, such as periodic loss of heather through Heather Beetle, *Lochmaea suturalis*, attack, or invasion by rhododendron, threaten the species' survival, and an increased frequency of heathland fires could eliminate it.

Many northern spiders will be under pressure through climate change, including several associated with Caledonian pine-woods, such as *Clubiona subsultans* and *Dipoena torva*, or found on Scottish high mountains, such as *Erigone tirolensis* and *Mecynargus paetulus*, which are usually found at above 850 m (Harvey *et al.* 2002).

Some eastern English wetland specialists are under threat as their habitats change due to summer drought, or damage from flash floods, e.g. *Clubiona rosserae* in reed-beds at Wood Walton Fen, Cambridgeshire, *Carorita paludosa* from *Sphagnum* in Norfolk and the large and handsome Great Raft-spider, *Dolomedes plantarius*, around fen pools at Redgrave and Lopham Fen, Norfolk/Suffolk and in ditches in the Lewes Levels, Sussex.

At least one rarity, the jumping spider, *Euophrys browningi*, which is associated with empty sea shells on shingle banks on the east coast, may be exceptionally vulnerable to the effects of sea-level rise.

Freshwater invertebrates

Water is heaviest at 4 °C and thereafter lighter till it freezes, with the result that ice forms at the top and rarely extends very far down. This may also lead to oxygen deficiency, but

Figure 31.1 Wasp Spider, *Argiope bruennichi*. First recorded in Sussex in 1922, this species has spread since the 1970s. By 2008 there was at least one substantial breeding colony in Cambridgeshire, with individual records as far north at Derbyshire (see colour plate). (Photograph by Philip Precey.)

the important consequence is that most freshwater animals never experience a temperature below freezing-point. Land animals do, and the amount of frost that different species can stand is an important factor governing the range of many.

The factors governing heat uptake of water are complex…It is, however, probably safe to make the generalisation that a piece of water does not get as warm as an adjoining piece of land.

So stated T.T. Macan in his seminal work *Freshwater Ecology* in 1963. These generalisations hold true in relation to prevailing air temperatures and insolation, but can be broadened to contend that fresh waters are relatively stable environments, at least when considering large-scale influences. Consequently, to be a 'common and widespread' species is not unusual in fresh waters, whereas the same does not hold true for terrestrial invertebrates. This property may provide an explanation for the relative ease with which alien species invade British and Irish fresh waters.

The factors which govern range contraction or expansion, occurrence or extinction of species tend to be secondary consequences of global pressures, such as disruption of river flows or destruction of wetland habitats due to increasing regularity or severity of drought or flood events. The most severe pressures are very much more at the local level and relate to human activity, such as development, with physical destruction of freshwater habitats, or pressures on water resources – both in terms of volume and quality – very much to the fore. Introduction and range expansion of alien species, either deliberately or unwittingly, completes the picture.

Thus, the 'minor orders' of freshwater invertebrates, including flatworms (Phylum: Platyhelminthes, Order: Tricladida), leeches (Phylum: Annelida, Sub-class: Hirudinea) and crustaceans across a range of classes and orders, respond slowly to subtle changes in the global environment, but rapidly to the more catastrophic and localised consequences of these, and to the intervention of human activity.

Freshwater flatworms: Platyhelminthes: Tricladida

A total of 12 flatworm species in the order comprising the larger ones – the triclads – inhabit British fresh waters. Several of these are alien species, which became established in Britain in the twentieth century. These primitive organisms are capable of reproduction sexually, but also asexually by fission and regeneration, and feed by means of a pharynx (their 'throat') which can be turned inside-out to engulf their prey.

A relatively recent introduction is *Phagocata woodworthi*, a species which is widespread in a range of freshwater habitats in eastern North America, but in Britain is found only in Loch Ness, where it was first discovered in the 1970s (Reynoldson *et al.* 1981). The species has a sexual reproductive strategy, so it is thought to have been introduced via egg cocoons attached to equipment brought from America by scientists searching for the Loch Ness monster. In the intervening decades, the species has been found at a number of sites in the loch, including some at depths down to over 200 m. Though currently restricted in its national distribution, its feeding biology (dietary overlap, rapid response to chemical cues produced by damaged prey items and relatively efficient ingestion using a branching pharynx) makes it a potential threat to native triclad species. When one considers the variety of habitats it colonises in its native range, the potential for this species to expand its range in Britain increases the potential for future damage to British ecosystems.

Another North American species, *Dugesia tigrina*, (see Figure 31.2) is much more widespread in Britain. It was introduced via the aquarium trade, and is thought to have appeared initially in London in the early twentieth century (Reynoldson 1956). It is spreading rapidly in both running- and still-water habitats, as a result of accidental introductions during fish stocking, plant introductions and biological surveys. The Environment Agency holds nearly 2600 records from 1982 to 2008, ranging from Kent through to Cumbria and Northumberland in the north, the far west and north of Wales and further westward as far as Cornwall. These records are predominantly from riverine environments. Addition of lake data from other sources leads to the conclusion that virtually all of England and Wales, and

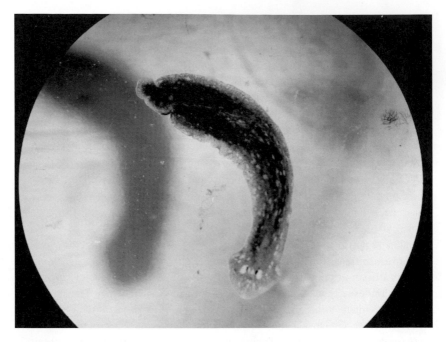

Figure 31.2 *Dugesia tigrina*. An immigrant flatworm from North America, widespread in lowland Britain and a threat to native flatworm species. (Photograph by Richard Chadd.)

probably much of Scotland, has been invaded by this species, at least in nutrient-rich lowland environments.

Dugesia tigrina is a potential threat to native triclads, particularly *Polycelis* spp., through inter-relationships between the native and immigrant species with regard to food resources (Young and Reynoldson 1999) and has been described as 'decimating' native species in productive environments supporting many triclad species (Reynoldson and Young 2000). It does, however, seem to co-exist with minimal impact in many examples of riverine triclad assemblages (Wright 1987). It usually reproduces asexually in Britain, but some sexually reproducing populations have been found in lake environments. Studies on these suggest a relatively high water temperature (14–16°C) to be critical in initiating and terminating reproductive behaviour. The species is absent from unproductive, cooler lakes, generally at higher altitudes, partially as a result of its dependence on higher temperatures. Rising temperatures resulting from climate change could increase its range and subsequent impact, especially in lakes.

The third non-native species, *Planaria torva*, is native to western Europe. It is thought to have crossed the sea in the early- to mid-twentieth century from

Scandinavia, via the timber trade, and was correspondingly associated mostly with ports and canals in East Anglia and the major cities in Scotland. It is spreading in Britain – of nearly 500 recorded occurrences since 1981, held by the Environment Agency, only 57 were taken in the 1980s (predominantly in the southern, eastern and midland counties). The remaining records were from the 1990s and 2000s, with many as far north as Cumbria and westwards to Devon and west Wales. Fish stocking is, again, thought to have assisted this spread. The species tends to be confined to calcium-rich, high-nutrient habitats, where its main prey items (gastropod molluscs) are abundant. This may limit its impact on the UK freshwater invertebrate fauna.

Some native species of triclad are under potential threat from rising water temperature associated with climate change, especially *Phagocata vitta*. This species is a stenotherm, which means that it cannot tolerate high summer temperatures, confining its distribution to streams and lakes at high altitudes, where the air and water are cool throughout the year – it is the commonest species in Snowdonia above 300 m.

It can also survive in lowland areas of Britain in cool spring waters, but never more than a few metres from the source, being the triclad species most typical of subterranean freshwater habitats. High flows will occasionally wash specimens to the surface.

Global changes in temperature may have little impact on the latter populations (apart from the secondary effects of drought limiting groundwater volumes), but are likely to drive the more common highland populations to progressively higher altitudes. Long-term data from the UK Environmental Change Network site on the River Cree in south-west Scotland show a run of records from 1995 to 2000, with a subsequent disappearance of the species from 2001 to 2007. This may be an early signal of the impact of raised water temperature, although the site is not very high above sea level and is atypical for the species. Records from the Environment Agency are inconclusive, with an even spread of around 100 records for each decade from 1981 to the present.

Leeches: Annelida: Hirudinea

Within the British leech fauna, comprising 16 species (all of which are associated with fresh waters), the only apparently immigrant ones are those which have been found in Britain in relatively recent times. All of them are native to Europe and may have recently spread to Britain (with or without the intervention of man), or been resident here for thousands of years and only recently found to be part of the British fauna. These include *Trocheta bykowskii*, *Dina lineata*, *Glossiphonia* (formerly *Batracobdella*) *paludosa* and *Glossiphonia* (formerly *Boreobdella*) *verrucata*. All of these, though uncommon in the British Isles, appear to be spreading.

Trocheta bykowskii (F: Erpobdellidae) is a large and slightly alarming (10–20 cm), dark brown predator of invertebrates, mostly living in rivers and streams. Originally found in Great Britain in the mid-twentieth century, Elliott and Tullett (1982) showed its occurrence in 24 10-km grid squares, throughout England and Wales and in Scotland in the Edinburgh area. Environment Agency data since then has added another seven sites in the 1980s, nearly 30 in the 1990s and just under 100 in the 2000s, from nearly 300 records.

Similarly, *Dina lineata*, a much smaller leech (2.5 cm) of the same family, was shown by Elliott and Tullett (1982) to have spread from a first record in the mid-twentieth century to 56 10-km grid squares in Britain. Forty-eight of these were located in Scotland, especially in the Glasgow/Edinburgh area, with many from Orkney and Shetland. It is the only erpobdellid leech resident in the far north of Scotland, as well as in the Scottish island fauna (Elliott and Mann 1979).

Only two squares were located in England in the 1982 record, both in the Reading area. Environment Agency data have changed the picture substantially, with around a dozen new grid squares added in the 1980s, just under 40 more in the 1990s and, thus far, ten more in the 2000s. All of the 60 or so new locations (from 90 records) are in England.

Dina lineata appears to favour swampy habitats which dry out in summer (especially beds of *Iris*), a habitat which does not seem to be favoured by other erpobdellids. The series of deep droughts which have characterised the last two decades may, therefore, have facilitated its range expansion, by drying out habitats which were more permanently wetted in preceding decades. In lowland east England, it is often found in streams in the urban environment, so the species may have benefited from expansion of housing and industry, and *Iris*-filled flood-relief reservoirs, in these areas. It is possible that an ability to exploit relatively harsh environments explains it exclusivity in northern Scotland.

The remaining two species, from family: Glossiphoniidae (*Glossiphonia paludosa* and *Glossiphonia verrucata*) were regarded as rare and very rare, respectively, by Elliott and Tullett (1982), who recorded 35 grid squares for the former and only two for the latter in Britain. Environment Agency records have added around 20 new grid squares (from 25 records) in England and Wales for *G. paludosa* (with all but one of these in the 1990s and 2000s), and approximately the same number for *G. verrucata* (from 35 records). Again, all but two of these latter records arose in the last two decades.

Interestingly, 17 of the *G.verrucata* records came from the catchments of the Rivers Nene and Welland in Northamptonshire and Rutland. Despite apparently clear evidence for expansion in range of all but one of the species mentioned above, it could be argued that the record set has expanded rapidly because more people are looking at leech species in the latter twentieth century and early twenty-first century. The *G. verrucata* recordset (and, to some degree, the *G. paludosa* one) counters this argument, in that the invertebrate species of the Nene and Welland (and neighbouring rivers in Lincolnshire) have been intensively studied for over 30 years. The recent rise in records of the two species seems, therefore, to be a genuine phenomenon, and may have resulted from improving riverine water quality.

By far the most spectacular British leech is the rare Medicinal Leech, *Hirudo medicinalis*. It is our only native species capable of sucking the blood of mammals, including man, and, as such, has been used in medicine for hundreds of years. A sharp decline in the species at the turn of the nineteenth and twentieth centuries may have been due to their use in the thousands in Victorian hospitals. Live leeches were transported in sacks filled with damp grass, and the mortality rates were high. On the other hand, many of the leeches were imported from Europe, so the release to British ponds of leeches, filled with a blood meal from unfortunate patients, may have actually facilitated their spread, but at the cost of continental populations. The more likely factor leading to a long-term decline in Britain and Ireland is a change in farming practices. The switch of water supplies for livestock, from old pasture ponds to drinking troughs and piped supplies, meant that many ponds were infilled, and those that remained (and supported populations of the leech) lost a regular food supply. Change in land use to arable cropping will also have led to infilling or separation of remaining ponds from their blood-bearing hosts. In salmonid-rearing areas, many ponds were deepened to provide cooler conditions, favouring the fish, but not the leech, which needs shallow, warm water to thrive.

By 1997, *Hirudo* occurred in only 20 known sites in England and Wales and has, sadly, long been extinct in Ireland. Recent work in Cumbria (Environment Agency 2006) has found a further 20 tarns supporting the leech, which is also known from sites in the south and east of England (including the New Forest, where a plentiful source of blood is provided by ponies and deer) and scattered sites in Wales and Scotland.

Its future is uncertain. A recent trend in the use in European medicine of an anticoagulant, hirudin, derived from leeches which are killed to extract it, could be a threat, but set against this is the possible increase in suitable shallow, warm waters as a result of rising average temperatures.

Freshwater crustaceans: Crustacea: Cladocera, Crustacea: Copepoda and Crustacea: Malacostraca

Freshwater crustaceans are extremely useful indicators of both long- and short-term environmental change. They are highly sensitive to a number of stressors, such as changes in water chemistry, temperature and current velocity and, unlike most insects, are ubiquitous in aquatic environments, from hypersaline lagoons, to sea water, to fresh water, both above ground and in the subterranean environment. There are some 200 species, sub-species and species varieties of so-called 'water fleas' – Cladocera and Copepoda – comprising the majority of the British zooplankton.

Long-term studies on the zooplankton fauna of Windermere have indicated changes in the phenology (life-cycle events) of certain water fleas, specifically the *Daphnia hyalina* species complex (Steve Thackeray, personal communication, 2008), with emergence of adult *Daphnia* from overwintering stages occurring progressively earlier in the year. The reasons for this are complex, but may relate directly to rising average water temperatures, or climate-mediated releases of nutrients from the lake and associated waters, influencing food availability. Similarly, fluctuations in zooplankton biomass in Windermere have been conclusively shown to be climatologically induced (George and Harris 1985; George and Taylor 1995). In this case, such fluctuations appeared to be influenced by the matching or mismatching of seasonal events in the zooplankton community with the availability of algal food.

The phylum also includes class: Malacostraca, which comprises around 40 of the larger taxa. This includes many invasive alien species, the most impressive of which is the Chinese Mitten Crab (*Eriocheir sinensis*), a large, vigorously burrowing and highly predatory native of China, accidentally introduced via ballast water from cargo ships.

The species first appeared in Europe in the River Weser, Germany, in 1912. It had spread to the Thames at Chelsea by 1935 and to Southfields Reservoir in Castleford, Yorkshire by 1949. British records were few until the 1970s, while on the continent, massive infestations were common; they may have been kept away from Britain by dynamic coastal currents, or by the highly polluted state of many British estuaries. Through the 1970s, they became more widespread in Britain, and then, in the early 1990s, a population explosion took place (Clark *et al*. 1998), possibly resulting from reaching optimal abundance for breeding, mediated by drought, where low river flow aids settlement of juveniles from the plankton. Such droughts have continued to aid the rise in numbers, and they are now known from the Thames, Medway, Darent, Great Ouse, Humber, Ancholme, Yorkshire Ouse, Wharfe, Tyne, Quaggy, Cray, Lee, Dee, Teign and Mersey. The Thames, Humber and Welsh sites are probably where initial introductions took place, with the rest resulting from larval drift along the coast (Josh Hellon, personal communication, 2008).

Mitten Crabs have no British competitor in the saline/freshwater transition zone that they inhabit, there are few predators in Britain big enough to eat the adults and the British climate and salinity match the native range. Although they can breed only in the sea, they prefer to moult in fresh water, and continental populations have been found over 700 km upriver. This covers the entire UK river system. In Germany alone, control measures to protect fisheries and flood defence structures undermined by burrowing has cost some €80 000 000, so the future, in ecological and economic terms, could be bleak.

Invasive crustaceans are superbly adapted omnivores, actively preying on much of their food. This is true of Mitten Crabs and also applies to the Bloody-red Shrimp, *Hemimysis anomala*, a member of the family: Mysidae, recently found in the River Trent and nearby canal systems in Nottinghamshire (Holdich *et al*. 2006). A native of the Black and Caspian Seas, this species can devastate native zooplankton and phytoplankton populations, and is thought to have been introduced by continental boats used at the rowing centre at Holme Pierrepoint.

An even more fearsome predator, dubbed the 'Natural Prawn Killer' by the *Daily Mail* in 2001, is *Dikerogammarus villosus*, an amphipod, also from the Ponto-Caspian region, which eliminates whole populations of native and non-native gammaridean amphipods (Dick and Platvoet 2000). It attacks virtually anything of its own size, or smaller, including fish fry, and is relatively large for an amphipod (up to 30 mm) with oversized and unusually powerful jaws. It frequently shreds up vast quantities of prey items without actually eating them. Not yet found in Britain, the species has colonised large parts of the continent through to the Netherlands and is likely to cross to British waters in coming years, probably via ballast water. Interestingly, the species is adapted to wait in ambush among beds of Zebra Mussels (*Dreissena polymorpha*), an invasive bivalve from the 'Killer' Shrimp's native range.

By far the most notorious of invading crustaceans are the many exotic species of crayfish, including the Signal (*Pacifastacus leniusculus*), Red Swamp (*Procambarus clarkii*), Spiny Cheek (*Orconectes limosus*) and Virile (*Orconectes virilis*) Crayfish from America. There are also invasive species from the Continent, most notably the Narrow-clawed Crayfish (*Astacus leptodactylus* species complex).

This notoriety arises because of the generally destructive behaviour they share with other exotic crustaceans, and because of the threat they pose to Britain's only native species, the White-clawed Crayfish, *Austropotamobius pallipes* species complex.

The threat arises partly through competition for food and shelter, and direct predation by the larger, more aggressive introduced species, but also, in the case of the American species, because of mass mortalities caused by 'crayfish plague'. The pathogen in this case is a fungus, *Aphanomyces astaci*, to which American crayfish are generally resistant – all of the American species can carry it, and the disease is only fatal when the carriers are stressed or under a high spore-load. It is, however, rapidly fatal to all European species. This means that, unlike the other primary invasives, the ecological threat of the Narrow-clawed Crayfish involves competition and predation/ grazing of native flora and fauna, not a status as a major disease vector.

The natural range of the Signal Crayfish, *Pacifastacus leniusculus*, is the temperate and sub-alpine region of north-western USA and south-western Canada. Released in Sweden in 1960 as an ecological and gastronomic analogue to replace diminishing stocks of native Noble Crayfish (*Astacus astacus*), it was first introduced into England in 1976. It has now spread throughout the country (every 10-km grid square in England has a confirmed presence), to all but the most upland parts of Wales and as far north as the Moray Firth, almost entirely via human introduction. Though confirmed in the Isle of Man, the species is not yet known in Ireland, where native crayfish are still widespread.

Of the remaining American species, all have the potential to spread and cause similar damage, although the Red Swamp Crayfish, as a native of the southern USA and Mexico, prefers generally warmer conditions than those encountered in Britain and may only become a major ecological threat with rising global temperatures. A novel threat (thankfully not yet in Britain, but present in Germany and the Netherlands) is the Marbled Crayfish (*Procambarus* spp.), which can reproduce parthenogenetically – without the need for sex – releasing, on average, 120 juveniles every 8–9 weeks. This is also a plague-carrier and gluttonous feeder, and is a favourite of aquarists, so that the excess are likely to end up dumped into fresh waters. British and EU legislation to limit trade in such species should be a priority.

Sadly, with the current mass infestation of the British countryside with exotic crayfish and the threat of a host of new ones (some from Australia) the future for many native British species, in addition to crayfish, looks grim. Certain rare mollusc species, for example, are under threat of extinction in Britain. It is to be hoped that viable controls can be found, but this looks unlikely at present.

Species at the 'frontier'

Extinction by 'global' factors might also be the fate of certain invertebrate species which, in Britain and Ireland, are at the limit of their distribution. Any climatic disruption could, therefore, become a threat to species which are already at their distributive 'frontier'. These include the Tadpole Shrimp. *Triops cancriformis* (Crustacea: Notostraca), and the Great Raft Spider. *Dolomedes plantarius* (Arachnida: Araneae).

The Tadpole Shrimp is a 'living fossil', substantially unchanged since the age of the dinosaurs, and resembles a tiny Horseshoe Crab. It is at the limit of its low-temperature tolerance in Britain, hence its extreme rarity. There are only two sites currently known – one in the New Forest (the stable population here inhabiting a single pool), with a second population, discovered in 2004 near the Solway Firth (it had been considered to be extinct in Scotland for 50 years, after a coastal pond in nearby Kirkcudbrightshire was lost to the sea). Tadpole Shrimps are restricted to ephemeral pools, possibly because of the need to avoid large predators, such as fish, in permanent water bodies (Bratton 1991).

The Great Raft Spider is the largest spider in the British Isles and inhabits grassy margins of old peat cuttings in ancient fenlands on the Norfolk/Suffolk border, the Pevensey Levels in Sussex and a disused section of the Tennant Canal near Swansea. It does not occur in Ireland. The lack of any reliable historical record for the species, and the disjunct nature of its distribution makes past and future trends difficult to assess, but its extreme rarity makes it very vulnerable to future changes in local or global conditions.

In both of these cases, warming climates could be beneficial. As large and impressive animals, both are suited to warm waters and are widespread on the continent. Temporary pools suitable for Tadpole Shrimps may become more widespread, and their dessication-resistant eggs could be spread by an increase in migration of continental birds, carrying the species to a warmer Britain. There is some contention, however, related to the taxonomy of *Triops*, so the British populations could be a distinct species. Spread of European populations might, therefore, dilute the endemic gene pool. For the Great Raft Spider, the threats relate more to disruption of the large wetland habitats in which they live: a warming Britain could see large-scale drying of such habitats, to the detriment of the species.

Fundamentally, with such rare species, their past is difficult to assess and their future is difficult to predict. We can only hope for good news in the future.

Conclusions

The diverse range of invertebrates in this chapter are of considerable ecological important, in fresh water and on land. Because of their heterogeneity, they are often neglected – even finding a clear title for the chapter proved difficult. But they include the most numerous animals in many microhabitats, vital to healthy soils and to river and pond ecosystems. Some native species are among the best indicators of 'habitat quality' and of environmental change. Recent experience shows that the introduction of alien species can have a major and rapid impact on our native fauna, with uncertain long-term consequences. Many of the species, native and alien, will respond to climate change: the detail of the response is difficult to predict, but may well have consequences for agricultural production, fisheries and ecological processes, as well as threatening species of great intrinsic interest.

References

Blower, J.G. (1985). *Millipedes. Synopses of the British Fauna (New Series)*, Vol. 35, London, The Linnaean Society of London, Academic Press.

Bratton, J.H. (ed.) (1991). *British Red Data Books: 3. Invertebrates other than insects,* Peterborough, JNCC.

Clark, P.F., Rainbow, P.S., Robbins, R.S. *et al.* (1998). The alien Chinese Mitten Crab, *Eriocheir sinensis* (Crustacea: Decapoda: Brachyura), in the Thames catchment. *Journal of the Marine Biological Association of the United Kingdom*, **78**, 1215–1221.

Cotton, D.C.F. (1992). *Dendrobaena altemsi* (Michaelson, 1902) and *Microscolex phosphoreus* (Dugès, 1837), two earthworms new to Ireland. *Irish Naturalists' Journal*, **24**, 74–75.

Dick, J.T.A. (2000). Invading predatory crustacean *Dikerogammarus villosus* eliminates both native and exotic species. *Proceedings of the Royal Society of London B*, **267**, 977–983.

Elliott, J.M. and Mann, K.H. (1979). *A Key to the British Freshwater Leeches. Freshwater Biological Association Scientific Publication No. 40*, Ambleside, Freshwater Biological Association.

Elliott, J.M. and Tullett, P.A. (1982). *Provisional Atlas of the Freshwater Leeches of the British Isles. Freshwater Biological Association Occasional Publication No. 14,* Ambleside, Freshwater Biological Association.

Environment Agency (2006). *Creating a Better Place for Wildlife: How Our Work Helps Biodiversity*, Bristol, Environment Agency.

Fryer, G. (1993). *The Freshwater Crustacea of Yorkshire: A Faunistic and Ecological Survey*, Huddersfield, Yorkshire Naturalists' Union and Leeds Philosophical and Literary Society.

George, D.G and Harris, G.P. (1985). The effect of climate on long-term changes in the crustacean zooplankton biomass of Lake Windermere, UK. *Nature*, **316**, 536–539.

George, D.G. and Taylor, A.H. (1995). UK lake plankton and the Gulf Stream. *Nature*, **378**, 139.

Gledhill, T., Sutcliffe, D.W. and Williams, W.D. (1993). *British Freshwater Crustacea Malacostraca: A Key with Ecological Notes. Freshwater Biological Association Scientific Publication No. 52,* Ambleside, Freshwater Biological Association.

Harvey, P.R., Nellist, D.R. and Telfer, M.G. (eds.) (2002). *Provisional Atlas of British Spiders (Arachnida, Araneae).* Volumes 1 and 2, Huntingdon, Biological Records Centre.

Hillyard, P.D. (1999). Spread of *Dicranopalpus ramosus. Ocularium,* **2**, 1.

Hillyard, P.D. (2000). *Opilio canestrinii* (Thorell, 1876) – new species record for Britain. *Ocularium,* **3**, 1–2.

Hillyard, P.D. and Sankey, J.H.P. (1989). *Harvestmen. Synopses of the British Fauna (New Series),* 2nd edn, Vol. 4, London, The Linnaean Society of London, Academic Press.

Holdich, D.M. (ed.) (2002). *Biology of Freshwater Crayfish,* Oxford, Blackwell Science Limited.

Holdich, D., Gallagher, S., Rippon, L., Harding, P. and Stubbington, R. (2006). The invasive Ponto-Caspian mysid, *Hemimysis anomala*, reaches the UK. *Aquatic Invasions*, **1**, 4–6.

Hopkin, S. (1991). A key to the woodlice of Britain and Ireland. *Field Studies*, **7**, 599–650. (Reprinted as an AIDGAP key, offprint No. 204.)

Hopkin, S. (2003). Woodlice, chiselbobs and sow-bugs. *British Wildlife*, **14** (6), 381–387.

Jennings, A.L . (1982). A new species of harvestman of the genus Mitopus in Britain. *Journal of Zoology, London*, **198**(1), 1–14.

Jones, H.D. (2005). Identification: British land flatworms. *British Wildlife*, **16**(3), 189–194.

Legg, G. (2001). Chelifer and Larca. *Galea,* **4**, 4.

Legg, G. and Jones, R.E. (1988). *Pseudoscorpions. Synopses of the British Fauna (New Series)*, Vol. 40, London, The Linnaean Society of London, Academic Press.

Locket, G.H. and Millidge, A.F. (1951). *British Spiders,* Vol. 1, London, Ray Society.

Macan, T.T. (1963). *Freshwater Ecology*, London, Longmans.

Moore, J, Gibson, R. and Jones, H.R. (2001). Terrestrial nemerteans thirty years on. *Hydrobiologia*, **456**, 1–6.

Oliver, P.G. and Meechan, C.J. (1993). *Woodlice. Synopses of the British Fauna (New Series)*, Vol. 49, London, The Linnaean Society of London, Academic Press.

Pantin, C.F.A. (1961). Geonemertes: a study in island life. *Proceedings of the Linnean Society of London*, **172**, 137–152.

Perring, F.H. and Walters, S.M. (eds.) (1962). *Atlas of the British Flora,* London, Thomas Nelson and Sons.

Roberts, M.J. (1995). *Spiders of Britain and Northern Europe*, London, HarperCollins.

Reynoldson, T.B. (1956). The occurrence in Britain of the American triclad *Dugesia tigrina* (Girard) and the status of *D. gonocephala* (Dugès). *Annual Magazine of Natural History*, **S.12**(9), 102–105.

Reynoldson, T.B. and Young, J.O. (2000). *A Key to the Freshwater Triclads of Britain and Ireland. Freshwater Biological Association Scientific Publication No. 58*, Ambleside, Freshwater Biological Association.

Reynoldson, T.B., Smith, B.D. and Maitland, P.S. (1981). A species of North American triclad new to Britain found in Loch Ness, Scotland. *Journal of the Zoological Society of London,* **193**, 531–538.

Sims, R.W. and Gerard, B.M. (1985). *Earthworms. Synopses of the British Fauna (New Series)*, Vol. 31, London, The Linnaean Society of London, Brill/Backhuys.

Souty-Grosset, C., Holdich, D.M., Noël, P.Y., Reynolds, J.D. and Haffner, P. (eds.) (2006). *Atlas of Crayfish in Europe*, Patrimoines Naturels, 64, Paris, Muséum National d'Histoire naturelle.

Sutton, S.L. and Harding, P.T. (1988). The spread of the terrestrial amphipod *Arcitalitrus dorrieni* in Britain and Ireland: watch this niche! *Isopoda*, **2**, 7–11.

Wright, J.F. (1987). Colonisation of rivers and canals in Great Britain by *Dugesia tigrina* (Girard) (Platyhelminthes: Tricladida). *Freshwater Biology*, **17**, 69–78.

Young, J.O. and Reynoldson, T.B. (1999). Continuing dispersal of freshwater triclads (Platyhelminthes; Turbellaria) in Britain, with particular reference to lakes. *Freshwater Biology*, **42**, 247–262.

32

Land and freshwater molluscs

Ian J. Killeen

Summary

Land and freshwater molluscs are a moderately large group of animals with just over 200 species known at present from Britain and Ireland. Many of the species are particularly sensitive to changes in land use and hydrology, and many are sensitive to pollution or disturbance. Therefore, they are one of the most useful groups of animals for assessing biodiversity and determining change in the quality of a particular habitat. There is a long history of their study, and detailed records extend back over 130 years. This not only allows change to be detected, but with repeated and ongoing recording, the changes may be accepted as real. This chapter gives an overview of the non-marine mollusc fauna of Britain and Ireland, the changes in the fauna over the last half century and gives examples of species whose range has reduced and the reasons why this decline has occurred. It is estimated that nearly 40% of the native species in Britain are in decline. Many freshwater snails have undergone major contractions in geographical range and the number of known sites. Large species of freshwater mussels have been affected both by pollution and the effects of invasive alien species. Very few native land or freshwater species are showing any signs of recovery and the prospects are generally poor. In contrast, the number of introduced species continues to increase and the majority of them are spreading rapidly.

Introduction

The general distribution of the land and freshwater mollusc fauna of Britain and Ireland is well known. The information arises principally from the recording schemes operated by the Conchological Society of Great Britain and Ireland since 1876. The results

Silent Summer: The State of Wildlife in Britain and Ireland, ed. Norman Maclean. Published by Cambridge University Press. © Cambridge University Press 2010.

of these recording efforts were published as 10-km square distribution Atlases (Kerney 1976, 1999). The 1976 Atlas showed records for pre- and post-1950 and the 1999 Atlas showed records as pre- and post-1965. Comparison of the data in both Atlases allowed threatened species to be identified for conservation priorities, but also revealed the general trends over time of declining and spreading species. These data from the 1976 Atlas were used by Bratton (1991) to compile accounts for threatened species in the *British Red Data Book*. A review of the changing mollusc fauna was carried out by Cameron and Killeen (2001), although this was restricted to land snails and slugs and only covered Britain.

In the years since 1965, which was the year selected to discriminate between modern and historical records in the 1999 Atlas, there has been a significant change in Britain and Ireland in terms of land use and agricultural practice. Thus the maps shown in Kerney (1999) may give a rather over-optimistic view of the present status of many species as a significant number of the records are 20–40 years old. Since 1999 there have been many targeted surveys carried out on EU Habitats Directive and UK Biodiversity Action Plan (BAP) priority species, but general countrywide mollusc recording has diminished considerably. This can be confirmed by viewing the maps in the National Biodiversity Network (NBN) gateway, which allows more refined discrimination of the records by date.

The present review continues on from Cameron and Killeen (2001), it provides an analysis of the present status of both the terrestrial and the freshwater fauna for Britain and Ireland, gives examples of declining and increasing species, and attempts to predict the future prospects.

The fauna

The number of species, and the composition of the known fauna of Britain and Ireland at the time of the 1976 and 1999 Atlases and the present day are shown in Table 32.1. This list excludes species known only as greenhouse aliens, and those that are restricted to semi-marine habitats such as brackish lagoons and saltmarshes.

Only six species were added to the fauna between 1976 and 1999, yet in the last 10 years, a further 12 species have been added, bringing the total to 204. Table 32.2 lists these species and the reasons for their addition.

Half of these new species come from taxonomic separations of species that were already present. This highlights the recent increased understanding of species taxonomy, particularly through the use of molecular techniques, and is likely to result in further expansions to the national lists in the near future. A recent checklist was produced by Anderson (2005), which updated the nomenclature of the British and Irish species in line with international usage. Some issues still remain, for example the number of slugs and freshwater snails (planorbiid and lymnaeid species) is still not fully resolved, and in mainland Europe some authors consider the pea mussels,

Table 32.1 *Composition of the mollusc fauna from 1976 to 2008*

	1976	1999	2008
Land snails	91	94	97
Land slugs	28	31	35
Freshwater snails	39	39	40
Freshwater bivalves	28	28	32
Total	**186**	**192**	**204**

Table 32.2 *Species added to the fauna since 1999*

	Species	Source
Land snails	*Balea heydeni*	Recently recognised segregate
	Cernuella aginnica	Recent discovery
	Papillifera papillaris	Recent discovery
Land slugs	*Arion occultus*	Newly described species
	Arion rufus	Recently recognised segregate
	Arion fuscus	Recently recognised segregate
	Lehmannia nyctelia	Formerly known only from greenhouses
Freshwater snails	*Stagnicola fuscus*	Recently recognised segregate
Freshwater bivalves	*Corbicula fluminea*	Recent introduction
	Sphaerium nucleus	Recently recognised segregate
	Pisidium globulare	Recently recognised segregate
	Mytilopsis leucophaeata	Recent discovery

Pisidium crassa and *P. ponderosa*, as distinct species, whereas here they are treated as ecophenotypic forms of *P. nitidum* and *P. casertanum*, respectively.

The additions include two invasive species, the Asiatic Clam (*Corbicula fluminea*) and the Dark False Mussel (*Mytilopsis leucophaeata*) and it is highly likely that other non-native species will arrive in Britain and Ireland, through continued passive dispersal of species that are suited to the climate.

Change in status of the fauna

Kerney (1999) provided data on the status of the fauna as to whether the species were native or introduced. This was based on evidence from post-glacial fossils, and

Table 32.3 *Species increasing and declining in Britain from 1999 to 2008*

		No. of species	Increasing	Decreasing	No change
Land snails	Native	87	8	38	41
	Introduced	10	7	0	3
Land slugs	Native	27	2	6	19
	Introduced	8	8	0	0
Freshwater	Native	35	0	11	24
snails	Introduced	5	4	0	1
Freshwater	Native	28	0	10	18
bivalves	Introduced	4	3	1	0

thus he regarded species which were not present before *c.* 2000 years ago as introduced. However, the Roman Snail (*Helix pomatia*) – a species that was introduced by the Romans – has recently been afforded protected status under the Wildlife and Countryside Act. Therefore, for the purposes of the following analysis, all species introduced around 2000 years ago (i.e. long-term introductions) are considered to be native, and recent introductions are those species which were unknown before the industrial revolution.

Interpretation of change is complex because of a range of factors. Difficulties arise in identifying declines where, as is the case with molluscs, there has been an overall decrease in general recording effort. The exception to this is the detailed surveys that have been carried out on species listed under the EU Habitats Directive and UK BAP. Taking a simplistic view based upon older records and assuming the situation remains the same can lead to failure to recognise species which are in trouble until it is too late. Therefore, in the following sections, change (decline and increase) has been determined from a wide range of published sources, grey literature, Conchological Society data and data from the Republic of Ireland Molluscan Database. Table 32.3 shows a summary of species change shown in Kerney (1999) and those for which there is good evidence of decline or increase in the ensuing 10 years based upon general Conchological Society recording efforts or from surveys targeted towards particular species.

Of the 87 native species of land snails in Britain, 38 (44%) are in decline, whereas only 8 (9%) are increasing – and most of these are longer-term introductions. Change in the status of the native slug species is more difficult to assess, but of the 27 species, six (22%) are declining and two (7%) are probably increasing. For the freshwater species, of the 63 native snails and bivalves, at least 21 (33%) are declining and none are believed to be increasing. Thus, for the overall native mollusc fauna, at least 37% of the species are in decline, and this may be a conservative estimate. A very similar pattern of decline has been recorded in Ireland (Moorkens 2006).

Table 32.4 *Declining native terrestrial species by habitat (adapted from Cameron and Killeen 2001).*

Wetland	Open, exposed	Woodland	Other habitats
Quickella arenaria	*Truncatellina cylindrica*	*Acicula fusca*	*Vertigo pusilla* (walls and rocks)
Succinella oblonga	*Pomatias elegans*	*Leiostyla anglica*	*Vertigo alpestris* (walls and rocks)
Oxyloma sarsii	*Abida secale*	*Spermodea lamellata*	*Balea heydeni* (rocks, walls, tree trunks)
Vertigo antivertigo	*Pupilla muscorum*	*Ena montana*	*Balea perversa* (rocks, walls, tree trunks)
Vertigo substriata	*Helicella itala*	*Limax cinereoniger*	*Helicigona lapicida* (rocks and woods)
Vertigo moulinsiana	*Monacha cartusiana*	*Malacolimax tenellus*	
Vertigo geyeri		*Zenobiella subrufescens*	
Vertigo angustior		*Helicodonta obvoluta*	
Vertigo lilljeborgii			

Native species: terrestrial

The species that have undergone the greatest declines are those which live in wetlands, old woodland and open grassland. These species tend to be much more sensitive to loss of habitat, changes in land use and hydrology, changes in management (e.g. relaxation or increase in grazing) and atmospheric pollution. A table of terrestrial species by habitat for which there is clear evidence of decline was published by Cameron and Killeen (2001) and is reproduced here with some amendments (Table 32.4). There are a further 14 species which were included in the analysis for Table 32.3 which have not shown significant declines over the last 50 years, but whose habitat is especially vulnerable and therefore the species' overall status is in decline.

Three of the species of whorl snails included in Table 32.4 (*Vertigo moulinsiana, V. geyeri* and *V. angustior*) are Habitats Directive species which have been the target of many surveys in Britain and Ireland and all show several more 10-km records than were known at the time of the 1999 Atlas. Thus, if 2008 dot distribution maps were produced there would be a clear inference that these species were expanding and not decreasing. But 10-km maps alone do not reveal the species' true status. Tattersfield and Killeen (2006) reported several localised extinctions in SAC sites for Desmoulin's

Whorl Snail (*Vertigo moulinsiana*) in southern England. If habitat pressures continue such that fragmentation of habitat and impacts of water abstraction become more evident, then decline is inevitable. This rationale was accepted by the Irish Government in the recent assessment of Habitats Directive species and habitats where the condition of all three of these whorl snails was assessed as either poor or bad (National Parks and Wildlife 2008).

Not all declines are explained merely through obvious habitat loss or change. The Cylindrical Whorl Snail (*Truncatellina cylindrica*) is a species characteristic of exposed calcareous grassland with bare patches and plants such as *Sedum, Helianthemum* and *Thymus*. Although the species was never common in Britain, it was known from sites ranging from Somerset to Fife. In the last 10 years there are records of living animals only from three sites, and from where numbers of individuals found have been extremely low, evidence which has prompted the addition of the species as a UK BAP priority. At a site in Bedfordshire where it was formerly abundant, it is on the verge of extinction for reasons that are not fully understood. Wall maintenance was carried out in 2003, suggesting that the snail is highly vulnerable to disturbance and habitat destruction (even on a minor scale or for a relatively short period of time).

Native species: fresh water

Whilst the percentage of the freshwater species in decline appears to be less than that for terrestrial species (Table 32.4), the decline in some species in the latter part of the twentieth century in terms of geographical range, number of sites and population size has been catastrophic.

The Freshwater Pearl Mussel (*Margaritifera margaritifera*) (Figure 32.1) is one of the most endangered animals in Britain and Ireland, but is another example of a species where distribution mapping alone gives a misleading impression of the species' status. The 1999 Atlas shows records from nearly 400 10-km squares with a 31% decline from 1965 onwards. A 2008 distribution map would probably show nearer 500 records, resulting from recent detailed surveying, but this does not indicate the status of the populations, only their distribution. The Freshwater Pearl Mussel is a long-lived animal with a lifespan in excess of 100 years and a river can retain large numbers of adult mussels over an extended time period without any effective reproduction or recruitment. This situation is now the case for a large majority of Pearl Mussel rivers in Britain and Ireland.

The Freshwater Pearl Mussel lives principally in oligotrophic streams and rivers with a pH of 5.5 to 7, with low calcium and low conductivity. It prefers stable stream beds of sand, gravel and cobbles into which it buries or where it can become lodged between larger stones. There are a number of factors leading to the decline and loss of Pearl Mussel populations, but the over-riding factor is continuous failure to produce new generations of mussels because of the loss of clean gravel beds, which have

Figure 32.1 Freshwater Pearl Mussel (*Margaritifera margaritifera*) (see colour plate).
(Photograph by Pete McCullough.)

become infiltrated by fine sediment and/or overgrown by algae or macrophytes. These
block the required levels of oxygen from reaching young mussels, which spend their
first five to ten years buried within the river-bed substrate. Other ways in which mussel populations can decline and be lost is through adult mussel kills, or loss of host
fish which are essential to the life cycle of Pearl Mussels. As river quality becomes
depressed, breeding stops and populations become 'functionally extinct', i.e. older
adults persist, but are not replaced by a new generation. The mussel population eventually dies out when the older individuals die of old age. Once breeding stops, it becomes
very difficult to save a population.

It has been estimated that there was been a decline of more than 90% of individuals
in European populations during the twentieth century (Bauer 1988) – in most countries
the mussel has declined dramatically or has become extinct. In Britain, the stronghold
of the species is in Scotland where it is estimated that there are 10 rivers which may
support populations with over 100 000 individuals, some of which are recruiting. A
similar number of large populations are known from Ireland, but few are recruiting.
In both countries there have been a significant number of declines and extinctions.
With the exception of one river in Cumbria, the situation in England and Wales is very
serious.

The Freshwater Pearl Mussel was formerly widespread in Wales, and in a number of rivers from Cornwall and Devon to Cumbria and Northumberland, with several rivers supporting large populations. However, there has been a dramatic decline over the last 30 years such that most of the rivers it formerly inhabited now only support a few aged individuals, and the few with sizable populations cannot be sustained after the current generation unless conditions that have led to the decline in juvenile survival are quickly reversed.

The five species of large mussels that live in lowland rivers are also declining, although not at the rate of the Pearl Mussel. The rarest of these is the Depressed River Mussel (*Pseudanodonta complanata*) which was shown by Müller (1999) to be absent from as many as 30% of the waterways for which old records exists. Although there is less detailed survey, there are indications that the Swollen River Mussel (*Unio tumidus*) and the Painter's Mussel (*Unio pictorum*), and to a lesser extent, the Duck and Swan Mussels (*Anodonta anatina* and *A. cygnea*) have all declined over the last 25 years. Much of this is attributed to deterioration of habitat and water quality, watercourse management, and especially in the last 10 years, the impact from the invasive Zebra Mussel (see below). Repeated surveys in the River Thames, River Great Ouse and elsewhere by Aldridge *et al.* (2004) showed that the proportion of river mussels infested by Zebra Mussels had increased significantly in all sites studied during a five-year period, and that the ecology of recently invaded sites has been deleteriously affected.

Two freshwater gastropod species, the Shining Ram's Horn (*Segmentina nitida*) and the Glutinous Snail (*Myxas glutinosa*), have experienced extreme declines in geographical range and numbers of populations – both having disappeared principally as a result of changes in agricultural practice and eutrophication. In the early twentieth century, the Shining Ram's Horn was recorded in 100 10-km squares as far north as Yorkshire and Lancashire, throughout the Midlands, East Anglia, around London and in south-east England. By 1965, the range had contracted to 14 10-km squares in East Anglia, Kent, Sussex and a single site in Somerset. Contemporary data resulting from studies arising from the species inclusion as a BAP priority species have shown that most existing populations have been maintained (Killeen and Willing 1997), and it has been recently rediscovered at a site in Yorkshire (Norris and Lindley 2007). The decline of Shining Ram's Horn populations is assumed to be a consequence of over-frequent dredging of ditches, eutrophication and drainage – resulting in surviving populations being restricted to areas of grazing marsh with limited nutrient inputs (Kerney 1999). The species requires ditches with a high diversity of aquatic plants and which are at a very late stage of the hydrosere (Watson and Ormerod 2004). This can lead to a conflict of interest, whereby rotational management and ditch clearance, often targeted towards maintaining all botanical and entomological diversity, or indeed specific measures focused towards other single species (e.g. the Norfolk Hawker, *Aeshna isosceles*), means that many ditches never achieve the successional stage required by the Shining Ram's Horn.

The decline of the Glutinous Snail has been similarly dramatic. In the early twentieth century, there were records from 40 10-km squares ranging from Windermere to

Dorset. The Glutinous Snail requires very clear (usually calcareous) water, with low levels of suspended solids, nitrate and phosphate, and a firm substratum on which the snail can crawl. By 1999 the species had declined to two known sites and is now known only from one site in north Wales (UK BAP). The species is faring better in Ireland than in Britain, but again there has been decline, with many extinctions over the last 30 years. It is now known only from small parts of two canals in the east and two lakes in the west (Moorkens 2006).

Many other species of freshwater snails are also showing evidence of decline. The Little Whirlpool Ram's Horn (*Anisus vorticulus*) has a very restricted range in Britain and is known only from a few ditches in Sussex and East Anglia. Although the species' range has not contracted, the number of known ditches has decreased significantly over the last 20 years. The decline has also been noted elsewhere in its European range, such that it has recently been added to Annex IV of the European Habitats Directive (see Terrier *et al.* 2006). The Mud Snail (*Omphiscola glabra*) was formerly widespread throughout acidic lowland areas of Britain and in southern Ireland. However, it has undergone a marked decline and is now scarce. It is thought to have become extinct in Ireland, and the 25-year decline in the British population is 25–49%. The Mud Snail is found in soft, nutrient-poor waters such as freshwater marshes, small ditches, temporary pools or seepages that dry up or significantly diminish in summer. Most populations are found on uncultivated land with acidic, sandy or gravely soils, such as heaths and commons, or other unimproved grasslands – the types of habitat that until the last 20 years may not have been considered to have any conservation value. The 1999 Atlas also shows marked declines in other snails, e.g. the Moss Bladder Snail (*Aplexa hypnorum*) and the Smooth Ram's Horn (*Gyraulus laevis*); species which occur in small, vulnerable habitats.

Introduced species

A very different picture can be seen when examining the changes in the recently introduced fauna. Of the 18 terrestrial species (10 snails and eight slugs), 15 are increasing and none are believed to be declining. Many of these species have great powers of dispersal and some of the slugs in particular have become widespread across Britain and Ireland in a relatively short time, such as Caruana's Slug (*Deroceras panormitanum*) since the 1930s and the Worm Slug (*Boettgerilla pallens*) since 1972. The introduced snail that has undergone the most spectacular increase in the last 20 years is the Girdled Snail (*Hygromia cinctella*). Figure 32.2 shows the distribution of the species according to three date classes. Prior to 1976, the Girdled Snail was known only from south Devon, where its distribution had remained more or less unchanged for over 25 years. By 1999, it had spread over much of south-west England, most likely by passive dispersal of garden plants, as far north as Worcester and as far east as London, and in the last 10 years it has spread over much of south Wales, into East Anglia, north to Yorkshire and into Ireland. This snail, which is native to southern France, will no

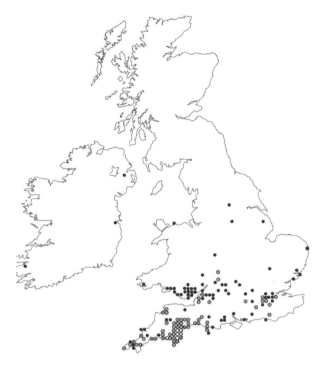

Figure 32.2 Distribution of the Girdled Snail (*Hygromia cinctella*). Open circles = pre-1976, grey dots = 1976–99, black dots = post-1999.

doubt continue its spread in Britain and Ireland and continued climatic trends towards fewer frost days will benefit its survival. This is also likely to favour other southern European species which are already increasing, such as *Theba pisana, Paralaoma servilis* and *Cochlicella barbara*.

With the nine introduced freshwater species, eight are increasing and only one is showing clear evidence of decline. Of these, the most spectacular spread has been that of Jenkin's Spire Snail (*Potamopyrgus antipodarum*). A native of New Zealand, the species was first recorded in the London area in the early- to mid-nineteenth century. Yet in a little over 150 years it has expanded to become one of the most widespread and abundant freshwater snails in Britain and Ireland. Whether this has had any effect on the native fauna is unclear, but in the case of two other particularly pernicious invasive species, the effect on the native fauna is potentially severely adverse. A relatively long-established alien is the Zebra Mussel (*Dreissena polymorpha*). Known in Britain for around 200 years, the Zebra Mussel quickly spread around the canal system of lowland England, Wales and Scotland. The distribution then remained fairly static; indeed, it disappeared from many sites in the north of its range, until the last 10 years, when the species began a new spread and in places became a locally abundant biofouling pest. The most notable increases have been in southern, central and eastern England, e.g. a newly recorded population of Zebra Mussels in the River Darent, Kent contained Zebra Mussels in dense mats of up to 11 000 individuals per m^2 and up to 20 cm in depth (Aldridge *et al.* 2004). This re-invasion is believed to be a result of the arrival of new genetic stock, but also of the increased movement of leisure craft. This latter factor is considered to have been responsible for the introduction of the Zebra Mussel to Ireland in 1994. It has since spread at a rapid rate through the Shannon–Boyle river catchment, into the Grand and Royal Canals, and many isolated loughs where it is having a significant negative effect on native mussel species (Minchin *et al.* 2002, 2005; Moorkens and Killeen 2005).

The Asiatic Clam (*Corbicula fluminea*) is also spreading rapidly since its discovery in the River Chet, Norfolk in 1998 (Aldridge and Müller 2001). It has since spread throughout the Broads drainage system, and was recorded in the Great Ouse and the Thames, both in 2004. At present, the species is restricted to a relatively short section of the Thames between Brentford and Richmond, it is known to be reproducing and its further spread into the rest of the river and its tributaries seems inevitable. If it is introduced to Ireland, it is likely to spread at a similar rate to the Zebra Mussel. The Asiatic Clam can alter the substrate of a river by siltation derived from deposition of pseudofaeces, and thus make the substrate unsuitable for other species of bivalves. Both Asiatic Clams and Zebra Mussels have great fecundity, rapid growth rate and exceptional powers of dispersal.

Whilst some freshwater alien species are continuing to successfully invade our waterways, there are examples of long-established species whose status is changing. The Trumpet Ram's Horn (*Menetus dilatatus*) was first found near Manchester in 1869 and was then found in another 9 10-km squares in the Lancashire area. However, it has rarely been found alive in this region for over 20 years. Subsequently the species was found in north Wales (1969), Gloucester, London (1974) and Essex (1986). It is now living in three lakes in north Wales, but its status at the other sites is unknown. However, there have been recent records from Gloucestershire, Oxfordshire and Hampshire suggesting the species is still spreading. The Oblong Orb Mussel (*Musculium transversum*), on the other hand, was formerly known from over 50 10-km squares ranging from Lancashire and Yorkshire to London and Somerset. In the 1999 Atlas, Kerney showed that only 14 of those squares had records since 1965. The decline has continued for reasons unknown, but the only published record of living animals since 2000 is from a canal in north Yorkshire (Lindley 2006).

What are the prospects?

Molluscan populations, like all other faunal groups, are not static, but are subject to pressures that encourage spread in some cases and decline in others. The climatic influences on Britain and Ireland are very different today from the period when most of the current native mollusc species reached their local habitats over land when those land bridges still existed. Our climate is continuing to change, and the concept of 'climate space', i.e. the envelope within Britain and Ireland where the preferred temperature ranges of each species exists is likely to change significantly within the next 50 years. The MONARCH project (Berry *et al.* 2007) has provided a bleak projection for our rare relict colder species into the future, and the spread of species from warmer regions is inevitable. If it was a case that species merely moved with climate space, then globally there would be no loss of biodiversity apart from high mountains and cold places, but the most vulnerable molluscs are already isolated in small habitat patches with no hope of natural dispersal, so some emphasis should be given to species that are relict or very rare, to ensure they have the conservation aid required to expand into suitable regions for them in the future. Keeping 'space for change', i.e. land masses for biodiversity maintenance, requires an eye on the future as well as the present. The most protected biodiversity sites at a European level are those in the Natura 2000 network (Special Areas of Conservation). Their boundaries are based on current habitat limits, as defined by Annex I (and Annex II for species) of the EU Habitats and Species Directive. However, the prediction of sea-level rise and coastal erosion is likely to shift, for example, coastal dune systems inland. If the inland area has been intensively developed, the economic loss from such dune movement would be significant and measures to prevent coastal erosion will become more intensive. The Narrow-mouthed Whorl Snail (*Vertigo angustior*) is one species that is likely to lose in this scenario.

Responding to climate change into the future will require international co-operation in both policy and active conservation projects. If we look at other pressures and threats that are acting on our species at present, the conservation effort needs to be local, and well integrated into all aspects of political and administrative decision-making. Much of the future of our molluscan biodiversity rests with appropriate management of agriculture, forestry, industry and housing planning.

The benefits of increased biodiversity protection are not immediately obvious, but over time it should become evident that species that might otherwise be in decline are stable and healthy. This is particularly true of habitats that are not groundwater dependent, where conservation and appropriate management within the habitat boundaries is enough to protect the species and its habitat. Well-managed woodlands and dry grasslands and heaths are examples of these.

In acknowledgement of the severe decline of many of the native British molluscs, the number of priority species on the UK BAP has been increased from 11 to 19 in the 2006 Joint Nature Conservation Committee (JNCC) review (http://www.jncc.gov.uk). A recent review of the status of the Irish fauna (Moorkens 2006) assessed 25 of the 162 species as being under threat at present. The habitats of species that are considered to be under the most severe threat are those that cannot be protected within the boundaries of their immediate living space, but can be impacted from a wider area. Of particular importance is the protection of ephemeral ponds, where species may require the occurrence of a meta-population, so that when one pond dries up, the species that it has lost will be reintroduced over time from another pond nearby. Protecting one isolated pond will not be as useful as protecting a necklace of local ponds.

Protecting wetland molluscs requires an understanding of the wider groundwater regime that influences the important protected habitats, which can be quite localised. The movement of water into groundwater seepages of our highest quality fens is often very poorly understood. Without this understanding the impacts of potential development cannot be properly assessed. Of particular concern are the groundwater-dependent whorl snails such as Desmoulin's Whorl Snail and Geyer's Whorl Snail (*Vertigo geyeri*). Both species require the presence of groundwater at a level that is narrow in range and stable over the short and long term. Thus many of the populations of these species have become isolated or fragmented and ultimately dependent on conservation management. Indeed, all the protected whorl snails are considered to be conservation dependent.

Of all the habitats that are difficult to manage, the river habitats are the most difficult and have the widest range of threats and capacity for cumulative effects. This is seen in its extreme in the collapse of our Pearl Mussel populations, and highlights how small individual inputs from erosion, field fertilisation and sewage outfalls have led to the shift of the natural oligotrophic riverine habitats to eutrophic in condition. The Water Framework Directive has been frequently cited as the mechanism by which our water quality will be brought up to a sufficiently high level by 2015, but it is clear that a return to oligotrophic water will require protection measures throughout the entire catchment of the most sensitive rivers. In the meantime, there has been effort in at least 10 sites throughout Britain and Ireland to rescue populations of very stressed pearl mussels into 'arks' and to captive breed them in an effort to maintain adequate numbers until their rivers are restored. This requires optimism for the future, but then again, so does all wildlife conservation effort.

Acknowledgements

I am grateful to Dr Evelyn Moorkens for providing records and information on the status of Irish molluscs. I thank Adrian Norris, non-marine mollusc recorder for the Conchological Society for provision and use of records. The National Museum Wales kindly permitted use of their Girdled Snail records collected by schools and families on behalf of the museum's Snail Search outreach programme, http://www.museumwales.ac.uk/scan/snails. Evelyn Moorkens and Dr Peter Tattersfield also reviewed the manuscript and provided helpful advice.

References

Aldridge, D.C. and Müller, S.J. (2001). The Asiatic clam, *Corbicula fluminea*, in Britain: current status and potential impacts. *Journal of Conchology,* **37**, 177–184.

Aldridge, D.C., Elliott, P. and Moggridge, G. (2004). The recent and rapid spread of the zebra mussel (*Dreissena polymorpha*) in Great Britain. *Biological Conservation*, **119**, 253–261.

Anderson, R. (2005). An annotated list of the non-marine Mollusca of Britain and Ireland *Journal of Conchology*, **38**, 607–637.

Bauer, G. (1988). Threats to the freshwater pearl mussel *Margaritifera margaritifera* L. in central Europe. *Biological Conservation*, **45**, 239–253.

Berry, P.M., O' Hanley, J.R., Thomson, C.L. *et al.* (eds.) (2007). Modelling natural resource responses to climate change (MONARCH): MONARCH 3 Contract report, Oxford, UKCIP Technical Report.

Bratton, J.H. (ed.) (1991). *British Red Data Books: 3. Invertebrates Other Than Insects*, Peterborough, JNCC.

Cameron, R.A.D. and Killeen, I.J. (2001). Land slugs and snails. In Hawksworth, D.L., ed., *The Changing Wildlife of Great Britain*, London, Taylor & Francis, pp. 353–366.

Kerney, M.P. (1976). *Atlas of Non-marine Mollusca of the British Isles*, Cambridge, Institute of Terrestrial Ecology.

Kerney, M.P. (1999). *Atlas of the Land and Freshwater Molluscs of Britain and Ireland*, Colchester, Harley Books.

Killeen I.J. and Willing, M.J. (1997). EN Species Recovery Programme: survey of ditches in East Anglia and south-east England for the freshwater snails *Segmentina nitida* and *Anisus vorticulus*, English Nature Research Reports No. 229, Peterborough, English Nature.

Lindley, D. (2006). Yorkshire notes. *Mollusc World*, **10**, 16–17.

Minchin, D., Lucy, F. and Sullivan, M. (2002). Monitoring of Zebra Mussels in the Shannon–Boyle Navigation, other navigable regions and principal Irish lakes, 2000 and 2001, *Marine Environment and Health Series, Vol. 5.*

Minchin, D., Lucy, F. and Sullivan, M. (2005). Ireland: a new frontier for the zebra mussel *Dreissena polymorpha* Pallas. *Oceanological and Hydrobiological Studies*, **34**, 19–30.

Moorkens, E.A. (2006). Irish non-marine molluscs – an evaluation of species threat status. *Bulletin of the Irish Biogeographiocal* Society, **30**, 348–371.

Moorkens, E.A. and Killeen, I.J. (2005). The aquatic mollusc fauna of the Grand and Royal Canals, Ireland. *Bulletin of the Irish Biogeographiocal Society*, **29**, 143–193.

Müller, S. (1999). Population genetics, ecology, and waterway management in the conservation of the depressed River Mussel (*Pseudanodonta complanata*), MPhil Thesis, University of Cambridge.

National Parks and Wildlife (2008). *The Status of EU Protected Habitats and Species in Ireland*, Dublin.

Norris, A. and Lindley, D. (2007). The rediscovery of *Segmentina nitida* (O.F. Müller, 1774) in Hornsea Mere, Yorkshire. *Mollusc World*, **15**, 19.

Tattersfield, P. and Killeen, I.J. (2006). Major declines in populations of the wetland snail *Vertigo moulinsiana* in a UK protected wetland site. *Tentacle*, **14**, 17–18.

Terrier, A., Castella, E., Falkner, G. and Killeen, I.J. (2006). Species account for *Anisus vorticulus* (Troschel, 1834) (Gastropoda: Planorbidae), a species listed in Annexes II and IV of the Habitats Directive. *Journal of Conchology*, **39**, 193–206.

Watson, A.M. and Ormerod, S.J. (2004). The distribution of 3 uncommon gastropods in the drainage ditches of British grazing marshes. *Biological Conservation*, **188**, 455–466.

33

The seashore

S.J. Hawkins, H.E. Sugden, P.S. Moschella, N. Mieszkowska,
R.C. Thompson and M.T. Burrows

Summary

Great Britain and Ireland have extensive and varied seashores. They range from exposed rocky headlands, to coarse shingle, broad sandy beaches, estuaries and saltmarshes. The seashores of Great Britain and Ireland provide a wealth of biodiversity, which not only contributes to the functioning of these ecosystems, but also provides an aesthetic value enjoyed by the general public. These shores are, however, subject to a variety of impacts which range from eutrophication, pollution by sewage, heavy metals and chemicals, littering, the establishment of non-native species, as well as the over-arching direct and indirect effects of global climate change. These impacts all have implications for biodiversity on the seashore and range from sub-lethal effects on individuals, through populations, to community-level responses. Despite this, the outlook for seashores is an optimistic one; as the very nature of these shores means they are highly resilient and pollution control in recent years has led to real improvement. It is important, however, to emphasise that these impacts will not act in isolation but will interact with one another. Caution is emphasised, as current information on many of these interactions is lacking. The current state of seashores is considered before discussing the future, focusing on the interactions of global change with regional- and local- scale impacts.

Introduction

Seashores and coastal ecosystems contain a huge variety of habitats and species and these areas often provide the first and only experience of marine biodiversity for many people. As an interface between the land and the sea, seashores are particularly

Silent Summer: The State of Wildlife in Britain and Ireland, ed. Norman Maclean. Published by Cambridge University Press. © Cambridge University Press 2010.

accessible, but as a direct result of this they are subject to both marine and terrestrial impacts.

In this chapter we consider the current state of the seashores of Britain and Ireland and likely future trends (see Tables 33.1 and 33.2). After briefly summarising the value of seashore biodiversity and its role in ecosystem functioning, we consider the consequences of global environmental change and regional- and local-scale impacts. These impacts often change the goods and services provided to society by seashore biodiversity and coastal ecosystems, especially reducing the simple pleasures of beachcombing and rock-pooling – a quintessential component of traditional seaside holidays in Britain and Ireland.

More technical considerations of global-scale impacts on the seashore are outlined in several recent reviews (Thompson *et al.* 2002), and for the interested reader more detailed accounts of seashore ecology (Raffaelli and Hawkins 1999; Little 2000; Little *et al.* 2009) and general natural history are available. Although depositing shores are considered in this chapter, the focus is on rocky shores reflecting our interests and experience.

Seashore biodiversity and functioning of coastal ecosystems

Natural heritage value

Great Britain and Ireland have extensive and varied seashores. Rocky shores range from wave-cut platforms at the base of cliffs on exposed headlines, through to sheltered bedrock and boulders in rias (flooded river mouths) and fjordic sea lochs (in Ireland loughs). Coarse shingle and sandy shores occur in wave-exposed areas, with broad sandy beaches often being interspersed between rocky headlands. In more sheltered conditions, muddy shores predominate, especially in the upper reaches of estuaries. Saltmarsh vegetation colonises in more sheltered conditions. Rocky coasts are most prevalent on western coasts of Great Britain and Ireland, and into the North Sea southwards to Flamborough Head and eastwards up the English Channel to the Isle of Wight. Between the Isle of Wight and the Humber, the coast is predominantly soft, with limited areas of rocky shore (i.e. limestone at Beachy Head), along with softer rocks such as chalks together with clays, shingle and sandy beaches.

Great Britain and Ireland also have a variety of estuaries from large systems, such as the Tamar complex, Severn, Shannon, Dee, Mersey, Solway, Clyde, Forth, Tyne, Tees, Humber, Thames, and Southampton Water, to many smaller estuaries of limited extent. Few are untouched by human activities with extensive modification by ports, reclamation and straightening via levees and channelisation to improve navigation in the upper reaches.

Most of the sessile and sedentary organisms found on the seashore are marine in evolutionary affinity and encompass all the major invertebrate phyla and the three main

Table 33.1 *Past perspectives and evidence of impacts on rocky shores from the 1960s, 1980s and 2000s, predictions for trends in severity by the 2020s, along with an estimate of our ability to make predictions based on existing evidence*

	1960s	1980s	2000s	2020s	
Pollution					
Endocrine disrupters	–	*	***	↑	••
Oil spills	***	**	***	↓	•••
Eutrophication	–	*	***	–	••
Harmful algal blooms	–	**	***	↑	••
Living resources and recreation					
Gathering food and bait	*	**	***	↑	•••
Recreation, research and education	–	–	*	↑	••
Non-native species	*	**	***	↑	•
Genetically modified organisms	n/a	n/a	?	↑	•
Global Change					
Warming	–	*	**	↑	••
UV radiation	–	–	*	↑	•
Sea-level rise	–	–	*	↑	••
Stormier weather	–	*	**	↑	••
Modification of coastal processes					
Sea defences	–	*	**	↑	••
Sedimentation	*	**	**	↑	•
Renewable energy	*	*	**	↑	•

Note: Evidence of impacts: negligible evidence (–), evidence of isolated incidents/occurrences (*), concerns and some evidence of impacts (**), evidence of major impacts (***), not applicable (n/a), unclear evidence (?). Expected trends in severity: little overall change (–), increasing severity (↑), decreasing severity (↓). Ability to predict impacts based on current evidence: low (•), moderate (••), high (•••).
Source: Based on Thompson *et al.* (2002).

groups of seaweeds. Micro-organisms, although inconspicuous, play an important role in coastal ecosystems, as do meiofauna (small benthic organisms <1 mm >0.45 mm in size) that live in and amongst sand grains and algal filaments. A uni-directional stress gradient occurs from fully marine conditions below low water to the furthest extent of the splash and spray zone above the high-tide mark. There are a few organisms of

Table 33.2 *Changes in the abundance of selected key intertidal species, their drivers and predicted future states*

Driver	Species	Observed changes
Warming climates	Limpets	There have been eastward range extensions of both *Patella ulyssiponensis* and *Patella depressa* due to warming climates.
		Conversely *Testudinalia (Tectura) testudinalis* have shown reductions in abundance at their southern distributional limits, a trend which is also being observed in the common limpet, *Patella vulgata*.
	Topshells	Range extensions of *Osilinus lineatus* and *Gibbula umbilicalis* both northwards due to warming climates leading to increased reproductive effort and juvenile success, and eastwards due to the proliferation of sea defences. It is likely that these extensions and increases in abundance will continue to accelerate.
	Barnacles	Range extensions and increases in abundance have been observed in the southern species, *Chthamalus montagui, Chthamalus stellatus* and *Perforatus (Balanus) perforatus,* past previous biogeographic boundaries due to warming climates.
		Negative effects of warm springs on the survival of the northern species, *Semibalanus balanoides*, are leading to decreases in its abundance and southern limit. This allows the southern *Chthamalus* spp. to proliferate further due to reduced competition. This trend is set to continue as conditions become more extreme.
Endocrine disrupters	Imposex	Populations of *Nucella lapillus* dramatically crashed in the mid-1980s with the impact of TBT pollution. Since its ban from use in anti-fouling paints in 1987, populations have been steadily recovering. Populations will continue to recover with increasing use of less toxic anti-fouling paints.
	Intersex	More recently the phenomenon of intersex has been documented in many species of fish, as well as more rarely in some invertebrate species, the best documented being *Scrobicularia plana*. It is caused by the presence of (xeno)oestrogens in the water, and populations may be vulnerable through reductions in recruitment.

Table 33.2 (cont.)

Driver	Species	Observed changes
Alien species	Introduced species	The native British oyster, *Ostrea edulis*, has been declining in abundance since the late 1800s due primarily to over-exploitation. The deliberate commercial introduction of the American oyster, Crassostrea virginia, along with the introduction of *Bonamia ostreae*, a parasite, has devastated native oyster stocks further. It is now considered severely depleted. The introduced Pacific Oyster, *Crassostrea gigas*, has also proliferated due to recent milder winters.
	Invasive species	*Elminius modestus* was accidentally introduced to the UK in the 1940s through the shipping industry (ships' hulls and ballast water) and since then has been very successful in becoming an established non-native species due to its tolerance for both cold and warm sea temperatures, as well as rapid reproduction and quick growth. It is likely that it will quickly adapt to changing future conditions and remain a common species on UK shores. *Sangassum muticum* introduced in the 1970s has rapidly spread in recent years and now occurs widely throughout Britain and Ireland.

terrestrial origin between the tides, perhaps the most conspicuous being angiosperm seagrasses (Zostera), which can occur inter tidally and sub-tidally, and saltmarsh plants (Raffaelli and Hawkins 1999).

The seashore is also used for feeding by mobile animals: from the land (birds and mammals) when the tide is out; and from the sea (fish and crustaceans) when the tide is in. They also provide hauling-out grounds for seals and feeding areas for otters.

Biodiversity: patterns and processes

Patterns of biodiversity on the seashore often follow the vertical upshore abiotic unidirectional stress gradient, with diversity decreasing higher up the shore as conditions for marine life become much harsher. As a result of this, distinct zones are often observed, with upper limits set by intolerance to the environment and lower limits usually set by biological interactions. There is also growing evidence that upper limits can sometimes be set by biological interactions, especially on the mid and low shore.

Some habitats with reduced stress, such as rock-pools and the underside of boulders, are particularly species-rich, providing important areas of refuge from the harsh tide-out environment. Physical disturbance from wave impact and scouring by wave-borne sand, gravel, pebbles and even small boulders are important on rocky shores, influencing the diversity of species in a given area at a given time. It is thought that low diversity is associated with areas which are either frequently (e.g. subject to heavy sand scouring) or rarely disturbed (e.g. algal canopies in sheltered areas). In contrast, diversity is generally higher in areas of intermediate frequencies and intensities of disturbance, for example on open rock, in pools and in boulder fields. This is not, however, always the case and caution must be exercised when investigating disturbance regimes. Some of the anthropogenic impacts discussed act by modifying natural disturbance regimes.

More sheltered rocky shores are dominated by large seaweeds (fucoids), as is the region either side of low water (kelps). Seaweed dominance on the midshore decreases on more exposed shores, which become dominated by filter-feeding barnacles and mussels. Grazing by limpets (which can be considered a biological disturbance) limits algal establishment and growth on more exposed shores, becoming increasingly uncommon on exposed and steeply sloping shores. Mussels can, however, provide a refuge from grazing, and a small stunted fucoid, *Fucus vesiculosus* evesiculosus, occurs on exposed shores. Low on the shore, *Fucus serratus* canopies give way to *Himanthalia elongata*, before being replaced by algal turfs at very exposed sites. The kelp, *Laminaria digitata*, gives way to opportunist *Alaria esculenta* at more exposed sites, which grows in gaps created in the *Laminaria* canopy by wave disturbance. Alaria is the only kelp able to survive low on the shore in extreme exposure.

On depositing shores cobbles and shingle are virtually devoid of life, except above the tide marks, where some rare and interesting higher plants grow (e.g. Sea Rocket, *Cakile maritima*; Sea Sandwort, *Honckenya peploides*; Sea Couch, *Elytrigia atherica*; and Sand Couch, *Elytrigia juncea*). There is an impoverished fauna of a few species of amphipods and isopods in coarse sand on wave-exposed beaches. Interstitial meiofauna can be an important component of such beaches, along with unicellular diatoms. In more sheltered conditions, worms become common as sand becomes finer. In muddy sands and sheltered muddy environments, bivalves are found along with marine worms such as the Lugworm, *Arenicola marina*, which creates semi-permanent burrows, thus oxygenating the sediment. Stable sands and muds can develop a rich film of diatoms which have the ability to migrate in the sediment during certain stages of the tidal cycle. These microphytobenthos are the main primary producers on sedimentary shores (Raffaelli and Hawkins 1999).

Role in coastal ecosystems

Very little rocky shore primary production is consumed *in situ*. Much is exported as detritus, fuelling coastal food webs, including strand lines supporting invertebrate communities (larval dipterans, amphipods, worms) that in turn are important for birds. Filter-feeding barnacles and mussels import phytoplankton and other seston (fine particulate organic matter suspended in the water column) including fine detrital material.

Grazers feed on macroalgae, drift seaweeds and microbial films which are maintained in an early successional state by limpet grazing. On the interface of sand and rock, colonial tube-building worms, *Sabellaria alveolata*, form reefs. These can support a wide variety of other species, and have been designated as both Biodiversity Action Plan (BAP) species and habitats.

In very sheltered areas, particularly in estuaries, vegetation of terrestrial origin colonises sediment to form saltmarshes at higher tidal levels. Salt and disturbance-tolerant plants can extend furthest down the shore, whilst more competitive species dominate at higher shore levels. Thus, physical factors set seaward limits and biological factors set landward limits in a mirror image of the processes operating on rocky shores (Adam 2000). Exported saltmarsh detritus can make an important contribution to food webs in coastal ecosystems. Saltmarshes also provide important nursery grounds for fish and mobile invertebrates such as crabs, as well as being extensively grazed by wildlife (mammals and birds) and domestic livestock (Adam *et al.* 2008).

Importance of UK shores and mudflats for overwintering and migrant birds

Birds extensively feed on the rich resources of both rocky (e.g. Oystercatchers, *Haematopus ostralegus*, and Dunlin, *Calidris alpina*) and depositing shores (e.g. various waterfowl, Oystercatchers, *Haematopus ostralegus*, and Godwits, *Limosa* spp.). Mudflats in estuaries are heavily used by both resident and migratory birds which either make short stop-overs or more extended overwintering stays. In the past these populations were heavily exploited by wildfowlers. Some of the estuaries inhabited by these large bird populations are far from pristine (i.e. the Mersey and Tees). In the 1980s massive bird mortalities occurred in the Mersey. As the estuary recovered from the excesses of pollution in the first part of the twentieth century, birds took advantage of the abundant food (clams, *Macoma balthica* and other invertebrates) prospering in a highly productive eutrophic estuary. Unfortunately, these invertebrates were accumulating organic lead compounds associated with a petrol-additives plant, which in turn bioaccumulated up the food chain leading to the extensive death of waders, wildfowl and gulls (Bull *et al.* 1983). Lead is no longer added to petrol: therefore this is a problem which is unlikely to recur. Today the Mersey, Thames, Tees and other industrialised estuaries are much cleaner than they were before and support diverse and productive assemblages. The recent discovery of endocrine disrupters affecting clams by causing intersex (feminisation of males – Chesman and Langston 2006) was a nasty surprise, however, and other such surprises may be in store in the future (Thompson *et al.* 2002).

The Mersey is one of a network of Special Protected Areas (SPAs) established under the EU Habitats Directive to protect the habitat of birds, their food supply and hence their populations. These SPAs all include extensive intertidal areas in the Exe, Severn, Dee, Mersey, Morecombe Bay, Solway Bay, Dyfi, Firth of Forth and Humber estuaries. Perhaps the best studied in terms of bird feeding is the Ythan Estuary in Scotland

(Hall and Raffaelli 1991). The central role of birds in estuarine food webs has been demonstrated, as well as the dependence of birds on the rich algae and invertebrate foods of estuaries and mudflats.

Global environmental change

In addition to climate change, there are other global-scale phenomena which need to be considered. The introduction of non-native species and the huge amounts of plastic debris that despoil our shores and strandlines worldwide are important impacts which interact to facilitate change and warrant discussion in the context of climate and global environmental change.

Climate-change responses and impacts

As discussed in Chapter 2, our global climate is changing. In the words of the IPCC 2007, 'continued emissions of greenhouse gases at or above current rates will induce many changes in the global climate system during the 21st century that are likely to be larger than those observed during the 20th century' leading to warmer temperatures, rising and stormier seas and more frequent extreme events over larger geographical areas. Winters will in general be milder, wetter and windier – although cold winters such as 2008/9/10 will still occur. Summers are likely to be hotter and drier throughout the British Isles and Ireland. There will be some regional variations, but these changes will affect all British estuaries, shores and coasts. The shores of Britain and Ireland straddle a marine biogeographic boundary and thus intertidal species are likely to be particularly sensitive to climate change (Forbes 1858; Southward *et al*. 1995).

Most attention has been given to the consequences of global warming. It has long been known that the marine life around the coasts of Britain and Ireland has fluctuated in response to natural climate cycles. The English Channel was late to open after the last Ice Age. Species on the seashore recolonised the coasts of Britain and Ireland from the south and west, up the Channel and up around Ireland and Scotland into the North Sea. Palaeo-ecological, archaeological and historical evidence shows fluctuations in offshore and onshore species during both warmer periods (e.g. fourteenth century, nineteenth to twenty-first centuries; with recent warm periods occurring in the 1870–80s, 1900s, 1930–50s and the 1980s onwards) and little ice ages (e.g. the fifteenth to eighteenth centuries; with recent cold periods occurring more specifically in the 1860s, 1910–20s, 1960–80s). Driven by climate, fluctuations of warm-water Pilchards (also called Sardines – *Sardina pilchardus*) and cold-water Herring (*Clupea harengus*) have been recorded since the middle ages in south-west England (Southward *et al*. 2005). In recent years, southern species of fish have become more common in south-west Britain (Genner *et al*. 2004). In parallel to changes offshore, seashore species have responded to climate change. Rocky-shore species are particularly sensitive indicators of climate change, being influenced both by marine conditions and the ambient terrestrial environment when the tide retreats (Helmuth *et al.* 2006).

The best quantitative data have come from broad-scale and long-term surveys initiated by Crisp and Southward in the 1950s – in the case of barnacles, maintained by Southward and co-workers (including some of the current authors) for well over 40 years. These show that the dominant barnacle in south-west England in the 1930s – the boreal cold-water *Semibalanus balanoides* – became rarer in the warmer 1950s, and then much more common again following the extremely cold winter of 1962/3. In the 1950s it was largely replaced by southern warm-water barnacles of the genus *Chthamalus*, which in turn became much rarer in the 1960s. This phase lasted until the mid-1980s, when conditions became much warmer again after 1988. Similar changes have occurred in many intertidal species. However, responses tend to be species specific: whilst many, such as intertidal limpets (the northern *Patella vulgata* and southern *Patella depressa*) and topshells (the southern *Gibbula umbilicalis* and *Osilinus lineatus*), have waxed and waned broadly in synchrony with the barnacles (Herbert *et al.* 2007, Mieszkowska *et al.* 2007), some idiosyncratic responses have occurred. For example, the cold-water kelp, *Alaria esculenta*, disappeared from most shores in the English Channel in the warm 1950s, being confined to the tip of Cornwall and occasional deep-water refuges, such as on the pinnacle of the Eddystone Rock. In the 1960s it failed to recover, and during the current warmer spell seems to have retreated further in both south-west Britain and Ireland. In contrast the warm-water hermit crab, *Clibanarius erythropus*, appeared at the end of the warm spell in the 1950s and early 1960s and then disappeared in the 1970s and 1980s (Southward and Southward 1988). It has not recovered since – perhaps due to a shortage of dog whelk *Nucella lapillus* shells, as a consequence of Tributyltin (TBT) pollution (see below).

In recent years, many southern species have extended their range northwards and eastwards around Scotland and into the colder waters of the eastern English Channel and North Sea (Figure 33.1). Paradoxically northern species seem to be extending southwards into the North Sea; this is because it has colder winter temperatures in the land-locked southern basin. Fewer retreats in the range of northern species have been recorded – although the boreal-arctic Tortoiseshell Limpet, *Testudinalia* (Tectura) *testudinalis*, has not been seen in recent years on the Isle of Man, where it was once common. Relative abundance of some northern species (e.g. *Patella vulgata*, *Alaria esculenta*) does, however, seem to be decreasing (Hiscock *et al.* 2004).

Modelling exercises have been used to predict what British and Irish shores will look like in the future (Mieszkowska *et al.* 2006) using various future climate scenarios produced by the United Kingdom Climate Impact Programme (UKCIP). It is possible that some species may jump across distributional gaps (i.e. the limpet, *Patella depressa*, and the barnacle, *Perforatus (Balanus) perforatus*, may at last colonise Ireland; *Osilinus lineatus* could colonise Scotland from Ireland, and the Isle of Man from Wales and/or Ireland; *Gibbula pennanti* could reach Britain from the French coast and Channel Islands). Furthermore some hydrographic barriers at headlands due

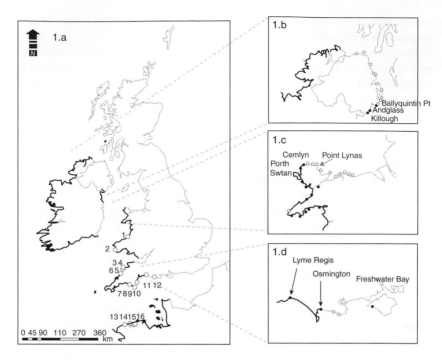

Figure 33.1 Range expansion of the intertidal snail *Osilinus (Monodonta) lineatus* in response to recent warming. (a) Previous northern and eastern distribution range limits (black line) of the intertidal snail *Osilinus lineatus*. Quantitative sampling sites from Kendall (1987) and 2002 resurveys in Britain and France (open circles): 1, Aberaeron; 2, West Angle Bay; 3, Hartland Quay; 4, Welcombe; 5, Widemouth; 6, Crackington Haven; 7, Wembury; 8, Noss Mayo; 9, Prawle; 10, Churston; 11, Lyme Regis; 12, Osmington Mills; 13, Locquirec; 14, Le Guersit; 15, Ille Calot; 16, Roscoff; 17, Brignogan. Observed range extensions in (b) Northern Ireland; (c) north Wales and (d) the English Channel. Black line, current range; closed circles, *O. lineatus* present; open circles, sites where *O. lineatus* not found in 2002. (Reproduced with the author's permission. First published in *Journal of the Marine Biological Association of the United Kingdom* in 2007 (Mieszkowska *et al.* 2007, *JMBA*, **87**, 537–545).

to offshore dispersal have been breached by some species (i.e. *Melarhaphe neritoides, Patella ulyssiponensis, Gibbula umbilicalis, Perforatus (Balanus) perforatus*), whose ranges have extended beyond the Isle of Wight into the eastern basin of the English Channel. Thus increasing diversity is likely on northern and eastern seashores in the British Isles and Ireland. Some retreats of northern species may occur. Further south in Europe many northern species inhabit estuarine refuges, which could also enable persistence in the future in the UK.

Although the physical environment in general and temperature in particular drive responses to climate change, modulation can occur through changes in the sign (positive/negative) and intensity of biological interactions. A good example is recent work modelling responses of southern (*Chthamalus montagui* and *Chthamalus stellatus*) and northern (*Semibalanus balanoides*) barnacles to climate change (Poloczanska *et al.* 2008). Warm springs appear to have direct negative effects on cold-water *S. balanoides*. There was no evidence of direct responses of warm-water *Chthamalus* to higher temperatures. Release from competition from the competitively superior S. balanoides does, however, lead to increases in *Chthamalus* spp. Models only worked well when competition was incorporated into them, allowing prediction of future abundance under different emission scenarios.

There will also be changes in overall community structure and ecosystem functioning on rocky shores. There is evidence that the north-east Atlantic has become rougher in recent years, perhaps in response to a greater preponderance of North Atlantic Oscillation Index positive years, with their wetter and windier winter weather. This may well shift the balance along the wave-action gradient between fucoid dominated sheltered shores and more suspension-feeder (mussels and barnacles)-dominated exposed shores. Large fucoid seaweeds and kelps are much more common in northern Europe and on more sheltered shores. Many species reach their southern limit in the Iberian Peninsula. This balance is mediated by physical factors causing stress, but also grazing pressure, which is thought to increase further south in Europe. The expectation would be that the likelihood of *Fucus* escapes on the midshore will decrease as Britain and Ireland warm and seas get stormier. Increases in grazer diversity will reduce the likelihood of such escapes, as will warmer conditions slowing early growth of fucoids. There is some evidence of increases in limpet grazing impacting *Ascophyllum* beds in both France and Northern Ireland (Davies *et al.* 2007). Climate-driven changes in wave action were implicated along with warmer winters boosting limpet survival in driving this shift in relative abundance. This trend would be expected to continue leading to less production of macroalgae and subsequent detrital export to inshore ecosystems (Hawkins *et al.* 2009a).

Rising sea levels and rougher seas will also lead to the proliferation of sea defences and the strengthening and extension of existing ones. Thus, many soft shores will be artificially hardened by sea walls, groynes and shore-parallel low-crested structures (see Figure 33.2). This will particularly be the case in low-lying areas prone to flooding in southern and eastern England from the Humber to the Solent, and also in north Wales and north-west England. Coastal fringe habitats such as sandy beaches, mudflats and saltmarshes will be squeezed between rising waters and coastal defences. Difficult decisions will have to be made. Some areas of coast will not be defended, leading to the loss of homes and agricultural land. Managed realignment will need to be implemented in some areas to ensure coastal squeeze does not occur; reclaimed pasture will revert to saltmarshes and creeks (see below). Where human populations are dense or where major infrastructure such as railways, roads and port installations occur, there

Figure 33.2 The Elmer sea defence system near Bognor Regis on the south coast of England. These defences have modified sedimentary habitats (Martin *et al.* 2005) and provided new habitat for rocky shore species (Moschella *et al.* 2005) – as well as preventing flooding to nearby homes (see colour plate).

will be a need to build new defences. Such defences must, however, be built in an environmentally sensitive manner. Care must be taken so that local solutions do not export problems elsewhere in the coastal system – nor that a whole series of local solutions scale up to a regional-scale impact as has occurred in the Adriatic.

Sea defences will have impacts on soft-sediment communities by modifying sedimentary regimes. Seawalls and dykes tend to lead to coarsening sediments in front of them. Shore-parallel low-crested structures (offshore artificial structures providing protection from erosion on the shore) and fish-tailed groynes (Y- or T-shaped coastal-defence structures perpendicular to the shore helping to prevent littoral drift) will lead to reduced hydrodynamics and hence the accumulation of finer, muddier sediments on the landward sides. Such changes will alter community composition. The defences themselves provide new hard substrata which can support rocky-shore assemblages. These artificial shores tend to be somewhat impoverished compared to natural rocky shores because of their smaller extent, reduced micro habitat variation, and scouring at the interface of rock and sand. Small modifications in design features can, however, increase biodiversity and the amenity value of sea defences. Rock-pools and complex surfaces can be incorporated into the design to increase microhabitat complexity; aprons at the front of defences can minimise scouring; larger rock units can make the structures more porous, allowing greater water exchange between the landward and seaward sides. Environmentally sensitive design can enable a greater variety of species to colonise structures, thereby enhancing biodiversity (Moschella *et al.* 2005; Burcharth *et al.* 2007). These sea defences can also provide stepping stones, enabling range extensions of species. This appears to be happening on the south coast of England and may partly explain range extensions beyond the Isle of Wight in some species.

Plastic debris

An increasingly common and unattractive feature of the strandline on shores worldwide is the mass of plastic debris derived from litter and non-degradable fragments (see Figure 33.3). These come from both terrestrial sources and marine jetsam discarded

Figure 33.3 Plastic debris littering the strandline providing an unsightly environment and a hazard to marine and terrestrial wildlife, as well as a danger to the public (Thompson *et al.* 2004) (see colour plate). (Picture courtesy of Prof. R.C. Thompson.)

from vessels. Plastic fragments, some smaller than the diameter of a human hair, have been found in the pelagic realm via the Continuous Plankton Recorder and are now a ubiquitous feature of all coastal waters (Thompson *et al.* 2004). Large items of plastic debris are known to present a hazard to a wide range of marine life (Derraik 2002). Recent work has also shown that microscopic pieces of plastic that appear to form through the fragmentation of larger items could present toxicological hazards to wildlife (Thomson *et al.* 2009).

These more subtle effects of toxicity aside, plastic rubbish has also been shown to act as floats, aiding larval dispersal. With an increase in the availability of these vectors for transport in the water column, the potential for invasive species to be carried into previously uncolonised areas is much greater.

Non-native species

Human beings have acted as deliberate introducers and accidental vectors of many non-native or alien marine species from outside the north-east Atlantic biogeographic region (Minchin and Eno 2002). Many so-called cosmopolitan species of hydroid, bryozoan and tunicate are probably early introductions via sailing ships. Recent advances in molecular genetics have shown that many of these species may have been accidentally introduced. The so-called Portuguese Oyster (*Crassostrea angulata*) was probably brought back to Europe from the Far East by early Portuguese navigators in the fifteenth and sixteenth centuries, and may be the same species as or very closely related to *Crassostrea gigas* (the Pacific/Japanese Oyster). American Oysters (*Crassostrea virginica*) were introduced to Britain in the late nineteenth century.

International introductions for aquaculture continue to this day, with widespread introductions of the Pacific Oyster (*Crassostrea gigas*) occurring worldwide as native oyster stocks have declined due to disease or over-fishing. In Britain these species were introduced from British Columbia in the 1960s and 1970s, using stock that was itself non-native in Canada. Other introductions have occurred throughout Europe. In the UK *Crassostrea gigas* was deliberately introduced through hatchery culture by a government department (Ministry of Agriculture Fisheries and Food – MAFF). At the time in the 1960s and 1970s it was felt that it would be too cold for it to breed in the wild. A succession of warm summers post-1988 has, however, allowed it to naturalise and spread into the wild.

Other species come with these introductions, including pathogenic organisms that can wreak havoc on native species, for example the disease *Bonomiosis*, which attacks the Native Oyster, *Ostrea edulis*, and has severely impacted populations in the UK. It is caused by the parasitic protozoan, *Bonamia ostreae*, which arrived in the UK through the accidental introduction of the American Oyster (*Crassostrea virginica*). The Slipper Limpet (*Crepidula fornicata*) and a predatory whelk (the Oyster Drill, *Urosalpinx cinerea*) also arrived with American Oysters in the late nineteenth century. The fast-growing seaweed, *Sargassum muticum*, arrived with

Pacific Oysters in Europe, but has since become very widely spread on British and Irish shores.

Non-deliberate introductions have occurred on ship hulls and ballast water. The barnacle, *Elminius modestus*, probably arrived from Australasia via convoys in World War II. It has since spread to occupy an extensive niche in estuaries and on more sheltered shores, where it is now more abundant than the native *Semibalanus balanoides*. Its success can be attributed to its ability to release multiple broods each year and tolerate reduced salinity. Many hydroid and tunicate species have hitched a ride in recent years and are common fouling species in marinas, but also occur on rocky shores (e.g. the solitary ascidian, *Styela clava*, and the colonial ascidian, *Didemnum* spp. and the brackish water hydroid *Cordylophora caspia* – which arrived on imported timber).

Many species seem to have become assimilated into the native fauna and flora – in many cases with no discernable major impacts on native species and assemblages. This does not, however, excuse negligent and deliberate introductions of non-native biodiversity. Global homogenisation is occurring: Figure 33.4 shows *Mytilus/Elminius* assemblages in New Zealand and Merseyside. Thus in some areas there is domination by species which are becoming the equivalent of worldwide consumer brands: widespread and successful. Perhaps *Mytilus galloprovinciallus* is becoming the Big Mac of the mussel world, having successfully invaded South Africa! Whether it is a native of Australasia – or more likely not – is currently being resolved using molecular phylogeography.

Climate change increases the risk of accidental non-native introductions (Stachowicz *et al.* 2002). Many introduced species in the UK come from eastern continental seaboards (i.e. Atlantic coast of America, East Pacific coasts of China, Japan and Korea). This may just reflect trade routes, but may also stem from the more continental climate on such seaboards which enables these species to survive extremes – which will become more likely in future years in a warmer, but more extreme world.

Regional- and local-scale impacts

Most impacts on the seashore are local, although they can scale up to affect whole regions. Eutrophication (increase in nutrients in the water leading to increased primary productivity with possible declines in oxygen, water quality and species diversity) is one example of a regional-scale influence, particularly in enclosed seas, such as the Baltic and Adriatic. Fortunately there is little evidence of regional-scale impacts in British and Irish waters. However, local point-source pollution into enclosed bays can lead to localised eutrophication (e.g. Dublin Bay on the east coast of Ireland and Morecombe Bay in north-west England) which can influence the shoreline. In Dublin in the 1980s and early 1990s, unsightly brown algal tides (*Ectocarpus siliculosus*) were common, due to localised eutrophication caused by sewage pollution.

In the 1980s TBT (Tributyltin) pollution caused imposex in dogwhelks (females became masculinised and in extreme cases sterilised) by leaching from anti-fouling

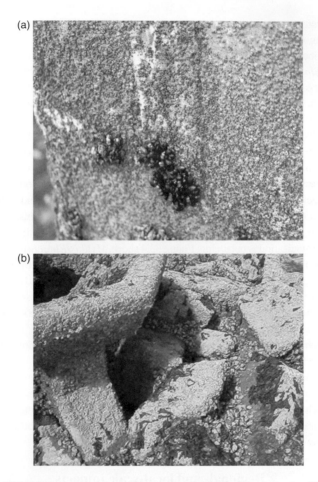

Figure 33.4 Homogenisation of assemblages on artificial structures: barnacles (*Elminius modestus*) and mussels (*Mytilus* spp.) (a) Quay wall in Nelson Harbour, New Zealand and (b) sea defences on the Wirral, Merseyside, UK. *Elminius* was introduced to Britain from Australasia in the mid-1940s and *Mytilus* is currently thought to have been introduced to Australasia. Both species are successful invaders and are now common sights on artificial structures (see colour plate).

paints, mainly from local sources such as ports and marinas (Bryan *et al.* 1986). This effect scaled up to affect most of the UK coast. Once control measures were put in place on small boats (< 25 m) in the late 1980s recovery began to occur, but was slow (Hawkins *et al.* 2002). Residual pollution still occurs in areas of major commercial shipping activity (e.g. Southampton Water) where large boats still dock, or is liberated following the disturbance of organo-tins in sediments through dredging operations.

More recently, intersex through endocrine disruption by discharged steroidal hormones or their man-made mimics has been detected in soft-sediment clams – *Scrobicularia plana* (Chesman and Langston 2006; Langston *et al.* 2007). This is surprisingly widespread in the UK, with populations in areas with limited levels of discharge showing significantly high levels of intersex. Although the causes and consequences of this condition are still highly debatable, the problem is clearly a regional-scale impact which requires further consideration in order for future remediation policy to be developed. Current thinking is that catchments influenced by intensive dairy farming are the cause because of the high levels of oestrogen-like compounds in lactating cows. In industrialised catchments such as the Mersey, surfactants (i.e. alkylphenol polyethoxylate, APE) and possibly plasticisers which mimic oestrodials may also be a cause (Blackburn *et al.* 1999).

Sewage pollution via long and short outfalls caused many problems on British seashores up to the 1990s. In addition to public-health risks, unsightly sewage-derived solids were a major aesthetic impact. Any ecological effects on community structure were very limited. Successive EU directives (EC Shellfish Waters Directive, Bathing Waters Directive, the Water Framework Directive) have led to improvements and other than after severe storm events, most beaches are now much cleaner and safer than they once were.

The most dramatic impacts on the seashore are those caused by oil spills. Fortunately, chronic pollution from tankers cleaning tanks at sea has now largely stopped due to tighter regulation, except for occasional rogue incidents. Oil spills have repeatedly hit UK shores since the *Torrey Canyon* captured headlines in the late 1960s. Since then there have been major incidents in Shetland (*MV Braer*, 1993) and south-west Wales (*Sea Empress*, 1996). Over the years treatment has improved. Recovery from the *Torrey Canyon* was very slow due to the toxic dispersants used – up to 15 years in some cases, because of the large mortality of *Patella* spp., the major grazer on rocky shores in England (Southward and Southward 1978). On shores where dispersants were not applied, such as Godrevy, recovery was much quicker (1–2 years). Subsequently, dispersants have become less toxic and their use has been targeted, usually at sea, with limited use on the shore. This speeds recovery and usually 2–3 years is required for conditions to get back to normal, but in heavily oiled areas, such as after the *Sea Empress*, this can take five years (Crump *et al.* 1999). Oil spills will continue to happen in areas en route to and around major terminals. Better design of vessels and navigation systems will reduce these risks and eventually, as dependence on hydrocarbons wanes, such incidents will hopefully become an unpleasant folk memory, along with London smogs.

Recovery and restoration

Coastal waters are subject to a large variety of impacts due to high levels of human activity, the ease of accessibility to the shore and the open nature of most coastal habitats (Hawkins *et al.* 2002). This not only leads to the exploitation of many species (see next section), but also to the degradation and modification of many habitats (Airoldi and Beck 2007) due to localised pollution, extraction of materials from beaches (Kenny and Rees 1994), coastal-defence schemes, dumping of materials, land reclamation (McKlusky *et al.* 1992), heavy recreational use and introduced species.

Rocky shores are one of the most open coastal habitats, with large imports and exports of both material and propagules. This openness provides considerable potential for natural recovery within a shore as widely dispersed propagules from unimpacted systems can recruit into degraded areas and subsequent rapid succession follows. In this way an impacted shore can return to its previous state in a relatively short period of time compared to a number of other coastal ecosystems such as saltmarshes or seagrass beds (Hawkins *et al.* 2002). Active restoration of these areas is extremely difficult because improvements in, for example, water quality cannot be achieved on a local scale, but must be initiated on a regional and even a global level with international conventions and directives put in place. Despite this, there are many examples of recovery in key rocky-shore species such as kelp beds (Kain 1975) and grazers, as well as from the impacts of pollution (Prince 1997) and habitat modification (Jackson *et al.* 2008).

In the UK there also is increasing pressure to restore mudflat and sediment shores as they provide important feeding grounds for many species of birds. A common disruption on sediment shores is the dumping of often contaminated material (e.g. muds with persistent organics and heavy metals), as part of dredging maintenance of ports and marinas. Natural recovery can be slow. Restoration in these areas is also very limited and has not been attempted to any major degree (Hawkins *et al.* 2002). The Humber Estuary is a Special Area of Conservation, Special Protection Area and a Ramsar Site due to its high diversity of habitats and the importance of the mudflats, marshes and coast for many species of birds, mammals and fish. Historically it is an area with heavy industry and mining, as well as providing important trade and communication routes. This legacy of heavy industry had led to contamination of sediments with trace metals that are far above 'background levels'. With the introduction of the EU Water Framework Directive, along with managed realignment schemes (see below) it is hoped that contamination in the sediments of UK estuaries can be reduced, but this is a process which is still being developed (Andrews *et al.* 2006).

Saltmarshes provide important habitats for birds as well as coastal protection, but they are becoming increasingly squeezed between artificial hard defences and the land as sea levels rise (see above). Managed realignment is seen as a good method of restoring, conserving and mitigating the loss of these key coastal habitats (Zedler and Adam 2002). Managed realignment allows an area that was previously not exposed to the sea, usually an area that has previously been claimed from the sea and protected by artificial defences in low-lying sediment areas, to be exposed to flooding. Although these schemes result in the loss of coastal land, the trade-off allows areas of greater importance (towns, industry and infrastructure) further inland to be protected, as well as improvements in coastal stability as artificial hard defences are replaced with natural soft defences (Zedler and Adam 2002). The first large-scale area of managed realignment was in Tollesbury in Essex, where sea defences were breached in 1995 (Garbutt *et al.* 2006). Although there is still debate as to the success of this and other managed realignment schemes in terms of their functionality and the natural saltmarsh species they contain (Hughes and Paramor 2004), it is clear that they continue to provide coastal defences through the dissipation of energy, as well as the provision of habitat for birds.

Horizon scanning: future impacts

Collection of food and bait

The archaeological record shows that the seashore was extremely heavily exploited by our ancestors. This tradition of collecting seafood continues in much of the rest of the world, including further south in Europe (France, Spain and Portugal) and on the Atlantic islands of Macaronesia. In the British Isles it is likely that collection of seafood will increase. This is partly due to British people becoming more adventurous, perhaps because of holidays abroad and trendy TV cooking programmes advocating collecting wild food. It is also due to human migration, both within the European Union and beyond. On recent sampling trips on the south coast, in addition to traditional collecting of winkles (*Littorina littorea*), there was considerable collection of prawns (*Palaemon serratus*) by the local ethnic Chinese population. The winkles are now being collected by eastern Europeans. This availability of cheap labour makes collection profitable, thereby increasing pressure – unfortunately sometimes with tragic consequences (i.e. the drowned Chinese cockle collectors in Morecambe Bay). Early one morning, whilst surveying limpets on the south coast, one of us (SJH), observed a Portuguese man collecting vast numbers of limpets (*Lapas*), which are highly prized on the Iberian Peninsula. Such activities are likely to increase with greater social mobility, with changes in fashion (e.g. razor shells from Scotland on sale in much of Devon and Cornwall for the gourmet market) and ultimately increased food prices. A dramatic example of exhaustive use of the shore comes from the Channel Islands during the latter part of the German occupation post-D-day: under siege, food was limited and the shores were used extensively for food collection (A.J. Southward, personal communication). Ironically, cleaner, less-polluted seashores encourage people to collect more food from them, which was not the case when short sewage outfalls were a feature of much of our coastline.

Currently, there are hotspots of collection of bait, both on soft shores through digging for worms and on hard shores through turning rocks for crabs. Both activities cause considerable damage. Bait digging is less prevalent now that worms are reared and sold via commercial bait farms. Arrays of tiles or half drainpipes are a common site in many estuaries; these are deployed to provide shelters for moulting crabs and enable collectors to easily find soft and peeler crabs for sale as bait. Such arrays modify soft-sediment habitats, providing settlement sub-strata for rocky-shore species such as barnacles and seaweeds.

Climate change: mitigation

Adaptational responses to rising and stormier seas have already been discussed. Mitigational measures to reduce greenhouse-gas emissions, such as offshore wind and wave farms, tidal turbines and estuarine barrages, whilst providing much needed long-term environmental gains are likely to have localised and shorter-term impacts. There is likely to be renewed interest in nuclear power, with inevitable localised impacts due to vast amount of cooling water and the mortality to fish and mobile crustaceans caused by abstraction and capture on intake screens. Renewable energies, such as wind farms are already proliferating in shallow waters and it is anticipated that several thousand more turbines will be added around our coasts. In essence, these are offshore pillar-like rocky shores in areas without hard sub-strata. These devices will increase connectivity between patches of habitat, enabling colonisation by species previously absent. Offshore wave-energy devices will modify hydrodynamic regimes and, if extensive, could modify distribution patterns of both soft and hard shores. Tidal turbines in suitable high-energy locations, such as straits, will have localised impacts. Major barrage schemes have generated renewed interest and the Severn and Mersey estuaries are candidates for which previous investigations have already been made. The only major working tidal barrage in Europe is the La Rance scheme in northern France. This scheme has had considerable impact on intertidal systems by reducing water flow and changing the extent of the tidal excursion (Retiere 1994). Clearly, major barrage schemes will impact the shore. Feeding grounds will be lost for fish; migration routes will be blocked for fish such as salmonids, shads and eels. Thus there will be considerable consequences for biodiversity and ecosystem functioning to set against the mitigation gains for reducing reliance on carbon-based energy. This will present a real ethical dilemma in how to trade off long-term and broad-scale gains in combating climate change against localised and shorter-term impacts.

Concluding comments: prognosis for the future?

The seashores of Britain and Ireland provide a wealth of biodiversity, which not only contributes to the functioning of these ecosystems, but also provides an aesthetic value enjoyed by the general public (Dayton *et al.* 2005). Shores are subject to a variety of impacts which will range from sub-lethal effects on individuals, through populations to community-level responses (Thompson *et al.* 2002).

Global climate change will have both direct and indirect impacts, with long-lasting effects. Primarily, this will lead to changes in species ranges and shifts along a number of environmental gradients will occur: towards the poles on a biogeographic axis, as well as localised shifts up and down the shore in response to changes in desiccation stress and increased disturbance due to greater wave action (Thompson *et al.* 2002). Extinctions of boreal species may occur as range shifts change and they are increasingly squeezed with nowhere to go.

Indirect effects of changing climates include the proliferation of coastal defences and renewable-energy devices modifying both sediment and rocky shores, changing hydrodynamic regimes and impacting the whole of the coastline. These structures provide new habitat for colonisation – not only aiding the migration of range-shifting species, but also allowing colonisation by invasive/non-native species, potentially excluding native biodiversity from an area and leading to permanent changes in community composition and structure.

The impact of pollution on coastal habitats is now being ameliorated, as a number of initiatives, global and European, such as the Bathing Water Directive, Urban Waste Water Directive and the comprehensive Water Framework Directive, have been put in place. The exploitation of intertidal species, however, is set to increase as the migration of human populations with distinct culinary traditions changes. This in itself could pose a major threat to rocky-shore ecosystems if large grazers, such as limpets, are removed from the shore, changing the community structure of an area leading to dominance by ephemeral green algae and fucoids.

Though the impacts on both rocky and sediment shores are severe and potentially long-lasting, the very nature of these shores means they are highly resilient to the expected effects and are able to naturally recover in relatively short periods of time. This ability to recover, coupled with active restoration programmes, enable us to paint a much more optimistic picture than some other chapters in this book. It is also important to emphasise that these impacts will not act in isolation, but will interact with one another, producing both positive and negative effects of these synergies. Thus caution is needed, as current information, particularly on multiple impacts, is lacking. Only through the collection of data from long-term observations coupled with the forecasting capabilities of environmental modelling will we be better informed to predict and negate impacts on coastal ecosystems (Table 33.1).

References

Adam, P. (2000). Morecambe Bay saltmarshes: 25 years of change. In Sherwood, B.R., Gardiner, B.G. and Harris, T., eds., *British Saltmarshes*, Tresaith, UK, Forrest Text, pp. 81–107.

Adam, P., Bertness, M.D., Davy, A.J. and Zedler, J.B. (2008). Saltmarsh. In Polunin, N., ed., *Aquatic Ecosystems: Trends and Global Prospects*, Cambridge, Cambridge University Press.

Airoldi, L. and Beck, M.W. (2007). Loss, status and trends for coastal marine habitats of Europe. *Oceanography and Marine Biology*, **45**, 345–405.

Andrews, J.E., Burgess, D., Cave, R.R. *et al.* (2006). Biogeochemical value of managed re-alignment, Humber estuary, UK. *Science of the Total Environmentl,* **371**, 19–30.

Blackburn, M.A., Kirby, S.J. and Waldock, M.J. (1999). Concentrations of alkyphenol polyethoxylates entering UK estuaries. *Marine Pollution Bulletin,* **38**, 109–118.

Bryan, G.W., Gibbs, P.E., Hummerstone, L.G. and Burt, G.R. (1986). The decline of the gastropod *Nucella lapillus* around southwest England – evidence for the effect of tri-butyltin from antifouling paints. *Journal of the Marine Biological Association of the UK,* **66**, 611–640.

Bull, K.R., Every, W.J., Freestone, P. *et al.* (1983). Alkyl lead pollution and bird mortalities on the Mersey Estuary, UK, 1979–1981. *Environmental Pollution (Series A),* **31**, 239–259.

Burcharth, H.F., Hawkins, S.J., Zanuttigh, B. and Lamberti, A. (2007). *Environmental Design Guidelines for Low Crested Coastal Structures*, Amsterdam, Elsevier.

Chesman, B.S., and Langston, W.J. (2006). Intersex in the clam *Scrobicularia plana*: a sign of endocrine disruption in estuaries? *Biology Letters,* **2**, 420–422.

Crump, R.G., Morley, H.S. and Williams, A.D. (1999). West Angle Bay, a case study. Littoral monitoring of permanent quadrats before and after the Sea Empress oil spill. *Field Studies,* **9**, 497–511.

Davies, A.J., Johnson, M.P. and Maggs, C.A. (2007). Limpet grazing and loss of *Ascophyllum nodosum* on decadal time scales. *Marine Ecology-Progress Series,* **339**, 131–141.

Dayton, P., Curran, S., Kitchingman, A. *et al.* (2005). Coastal Systems. In Baker, J., Casasola, P.M., Lugo, A., Rodríguez, A.S.r., Dan, L. and Tang, L., eds., *Ecosystems and Human Well Being: A Framework for Assessment*, Geneva, Intergovernmental Panel on Climate Change.

Derraik, J.G.B. (2002). The pollution of the marine environment by plastic debris: A review. *Marine Pollution Bulletin,* **44**, 842–852.

Forbes, E. (1858). The distribution of marine life, illustrated chiefly by fishes and molluscs and radiata. In Johnston, A.K., ed., *A.K.Johnston's Physical Atlas*, Edinburgh, W. & A.K. Johnston, pp. 99–101.

Garbutt, R.A., Reading, C.J., Wolters, M., Gray, A.J. and Rothery, P. (2006). Monitoring the development of intertidal habitats on former agricultural land after the managed re-alignment of coastal defences at Tollesbury, Essex, UK. *Marine Pollution Bulletin,* **53**, 155–164.

Genner, M.J., Sims, D.W., Wearmouth, V.J. *et al.* (2004). Regional climatic warming drives long-term community changes of British marine fish. *Proceedings of the Royal Society of London Series B: Biological Sciences,* **271**, 655–661.

Hall, S.J. and Raffaelli, D. (1991). Food-web patterns: lessons from a species-rich web. *Journal of Animal Ecology,* **60**, 823–841.

Hawkins, S.J., Allen, J.R., Ross, P.M. and Genner, M.J. (2002). Marine and coastal ecosystems. In Perrow, M.R. and Davy, A.J., eds., *Handbook of Ecological Restoration: Restoration in Practice*, Cambridge, Cambridge University Press, pp. 121–148.

Hawkins, S.J., Sugden, H.E., Mieszkowska, N. *et al.* (2009). Consequences of climate-driven biodiversity changes for ecosystem functioning. *Marine Ecology Progress Series*, in press.

Helmuth, B., Mieszkowska, N., Moore, P. and Hawkins, S.J. (2006). Living on the edge of two changing worlds: forecasting responses of rocky intertidal ecosystems to climate change. *Annual Review of Ecology, Evolution and Systematics*, **37**, 373–404.

Herbert, R.J.H., Southward, A.J., Sheader, M. and Hawkins, S.J. (2007). Influence of recruitment and temperature on distribution of intertidal barnacles in the English Channel. *Journal of the Marine Biological Association of the United Kingdom*, **87**, 487–499.

Hiscock, K., Southward, A.J., Tittley, I. and Hawkins, S.J. (2004). Effects of changing temperature on benthic marine life in Britain and Ireland. *Aquatic Conservation, Marine and Freshwater Ecosystems*, **14**, 333–362.

Hughes, R.G. and Paramor, O.A.L. (2004). On the loss of saltmarshes in south-east England and methods for their restoration. *Journal of Applied Ecology*, **41**, 440–448.

Jackson, A.C., Chapman, M.G. and Underwood, A.J. (2008). Ecological interactions in the provision of habitat by urban development: whelks and engineering by oysters on artificial seawalls. *Austral Ecology*, **33**, 307–316.

Kain, J.M. (1975). Algal recolonization of some cleared subtidal areas. *Journal of Ecology*, **63**, 739–765.

Kenny, A.J. and Rees, H.L. (1994). The effects of marine gravel extractions on the macrobenthos: early post-dredging recolonization. *Marine Pollution Bulletin*, **28**, 442–447.

Langston, W.J., Burt, G.R. and Chesman, B.S. (2007). Feminisation of male clams *Scrobicularia plana* from estuaries in Southwest UK and its induction by endocrine-disrupting chemicals. *Marine Ecology Progress Series*, **333**, 173–184.

Little, C. (2000). *The Biology of Soft Shores and Estuaries*, Oxford, Oxford University Press.

Little, C., Williams, G.A. and Trowbridge, C. (2009). *The Biology of Rocky Shores*, New York, Oxford University Press.

Martin, D., Bertasi, F., Colangelo, M.A. *et al.* (2005). Ecological impacts of coastal defence structures on sediment and mobile fauna: evaluating and forecasting consequences of unavoidable modifications of native habitats. *Coastal Engineering*, **52**, 1027–1051.

McKlusky, D.S., Bryant, D.M. and Elliott, M. (1992). Impact of land claim on macrobenthos, fish and shorebirds on the Forth Estuary, eastern Scotland. *Aquatic Conservation, Marine and Freshwater Ecosystems*, **2**, 211–222.

Mieszkowska, N., Hawkins, S.J., Burrows, M.T. and Kendall, M.A. (2007). Long-term changes in the geographic distribution and population structures of *Osilinus lineatus* (Gastropoda: Trochidae) in Britain and Ireland. *Journal of the Marine Biological Association of the UK*, **87**, 537–545.

Mieszkowska, N., Leaper, R., Moore, P. *et al.* (2006). Marine Biodiversity and Climate Change: Assessing and Predicting the Influence of Climatic Change using

Intertidal Rocky Shore Biota. Scottish Natural Heritage Commissioned Report No. 202 (ROAME No. F01AA402).

Minchin, D., and Eno, C. (2002). Exotics of coastal and inland waters of Ireland and Britain. In Leppakoski, E., Gollasch, S. and Olenin, S., eds., *Invasive Aquatic Species in Europe. Distribution, Impacts and Management*, Dordrecht, Kluwer Academic Publishers, pp. 267–275.

Moschella, P.S., Abbiati, M. Aberg, P. *et al.* (2005). Low-crested coastal defence structures as artificial habitats for marine life: using ecological criteria in design. *Coastal Engineering, 52*, 1053–1071.

Poloczanska, E., Hawkins, S.J., Southward, A.J. and Burrows, M.T. (2008). Modelling the response of populations of competing species to climate change. *Ecology, 89*, 3138–3149.

Prince, R.C. (1997). Bioremediation of marine oil spills. *Trends in Biotechnology, 15*, 158–160.

Raffaelli, D. and Hawkins, S.J. (1999). *Intertidal Ecology*, 2nd edn., London, Kluwer Academic Publishers.

Retiere, C. (1994). Tidal power and the aquatic environment of La Rance. *Biological Journal of the Linnean Society, 51*, 25–36.

Southward, A.J., and Southward, E.C. (1978). Recolonisation of rocky shores in Cornwall after the use of toxic dispersants to clean up the Torrey Canyon oil spill. *Journal of the Fish Research Board of Canada, 35*, 682–706.

Southward, A.J., and Southward, E.C. (1988). Disappearance of the warm-water hermit crab *Clibanarius erythropus* from southwest Britain. *Journal of the Marine Biological Association of the UK, 68*, 409–412.

Southward, A.J., Hawkins, S.J. and Burrows, M.T. (1995). 70 years observations of changes in distribution and abundance of zooplankton and intertidal organisms in the western English-Channel in relation to rising sea temperature. *Journal of Thermal Biology, 20*, 127–155.

Southward, A.J., Langmead, O., Hardman-Mountford, N.J. *et al.* (2005). Long-term oceanographic and ecological research in the western English Channel. *Advances in Marine Biology, 47*, 1–105.

Stachowicz, J., Whitlach, R. and Osman, R. (2002). Species diversity and invasion resistance in a marine ecosystem. *Science, 286*, 1577–1579.

Thompson, R.C., Crowe, T.P. and Hawkins, S.J. (2002). Rocky intertidal communities: past environmental changes, present status and predictions for the next 25 years. *Environmental Conservation, 29*, 168–191.

Thompson, R.C., Moore, C., vom Saal, F.S. and Swan, S.H. (2009). Plastics, the environment and human health. *Philosophical Transactions of the Royal Society B, 364*, 1969–2166.

Thompson, R.C., Olsen, Y., Mitchell, R.P. *et al.* (2004). Lost at sea: where is all the plastic? *Science, 304*, 838–838.

Zedler, J.B. and Adam, P. (2002). Saltmarshes. In Perrow, M.R. and Davy, A.J., eds., *Handbook of Ecological Restoration*, Cambridge, Cambridge University Press, pp. 238–266.

34

The offshore waters

John M. Baxter

Summary

The continental shelf waters around the UK and Ireland cover an area of over 1 500 000 km^2, nearly five times that of the land area. Much of this remains unexplored, but with recent advances in technology we are beginning to get a picture of a complex area with vast sedimentary plains and dramatic underwater mountain ranges and canyons. For too long the seas have been regarded as an indestructible and inexhaustible resource, but it is now becoming increasingly apparent that we have been systematically damaging it and we are rapidly reaching the point where irreversible damage may have been done.

In the last 20 years, significant measures have been taken to address some of these abuses, and the UK Marine and Coastal Access Act, together with the Marine (Scotland) Bill promise even greater powers to manage activities in the marine environment and protect the most fragile and special habitat and communities with Marine Protected Areas. There is, however, still further work required, as to how broad-scale conservation and protection can be achieved. This progress is not before time, but it occurs in the face of the even greater challenges of climate change and ocean acidification. It is important, having recognised these threats and their implications for the basis of marine ecosystems, that action is taken now to minimise the inevitable impact.

Introduction

Standing on the shore, looking out to sea with an uninterrupted view, a person of average height can see to the horizon about 5 km away. If you were lucky enough to be standing on the top of Conachair, on the north coast of Hirta, the main island in the St

Silent Summer: The State of Wildlife in Britain and Ireland, ed. Norman Maclean. Published by Cambridge University Press. © Cambridge University Press 2010.

Kilda archipelago, at 430 m above sea level the highest cliffline in GB, the horizon in all directions would be some 74 km distant. This view would only begin to reveal the vastness of the offshore waters that surround us and would only tell a very small part of the story because so much more lies below the surface, both in the water column and on and beneath the seabed.

Whilst the seashore (Chapter 33) is somewhere we all know and love, to many of us what lies offshore beneath the waves remains a largely inaccessible and mysterious place, the realm of largely unfamiliar and strange-looking animals and plants. In the Introduction to *The Open Sea Its Natural History* by Sir Alister Hardy, first published in 1956 he said '...the picture of life in the sea is continually growing: the chapters which follow will endeavour to sketch an outline of what has been achieved ... there are so many gaps in the story yet to be filled in. There are still many original discoveries to be made.' This is as true now as it was then, 50 years ago. We are still just at the beginning of our exploration of the marine realm even though great advances have been made in the technologies that enable us to explore this world, and in our understanding and appreciation of the chemistry, physics and biology. We know so little of its riches and perhaps even less of the damage we have already wrought.

For too long the sea was regarded as the dustbin of the planet, so large that it could cope with whatever we chose to dump in it. No longer. Its natural resources, fish, marine mammals etc. are not inexhaustible and need to be used and exploited with care. Nor is the sea immune from the growing threat of global climate change, with rising temperatures, changing salinities, disrupted food webs and acidification just some of the stresses to be considered.

In this chapter I consider the advances that have been made, that mean we are wiser and better able to take informed decisions that will ensure the future of the diversity of life in the seas. There are significant changes planned through new legislation that, amongst other things, will see greater protection for our rare and vulnerable marine wildlife. It is often said that we need more powers to 'manage the marine environment'. If we believe this it puts us in the same bracket as the much misquoted King Canute the Great, who is reputed to have tried to prevent the tide from coming in. In fact he was much wiser than he is often given credit for and only performed this act to show his court that there were some things no mortal man could do. We would be wise to listen to his words: 'Let all men know how empty and worthless is the power of kings. For there is none worthy of the name but God, whom heaven, earth and sea obey.' What we can simply aspire to do is to manage much better our own activities and how they impact on the marine environment. If we can do this, then there is a chance that recovery can start.

The physical environment

The UK Continental Shelf Area, as defined in the Continental Shelf Act 1964, covers over 875 000 km^2 compared to the UK land area of around 245 000 km^2.

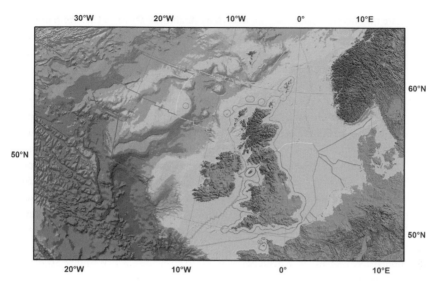

Figure 34.1 Continental Shelf Area boundaries (red line Territorial sea limit, yellow line UK CSA, pink line Ireland CSA) (see colour plate).

The Continental Shelf Area of Ireland covers some 652 000 km², around nine times larger than the land area of Ireland at 70 280 km². Thus, in total, the offshore waters of the UK and Ireland cover an area of over 1 500 000 km² (Figure 34.1), a vast area, much of which remains largely unexplored. The exact extent and boundaries of these Continental Shelf Areas are subject to ongoing claims to the UN Commission on the Limits of the Continental Shelf, with the UK, Ireland, Faroe Islands/Denmark and Iceland disputing boundaries in the Hatton–Rockall area, and the UK, Ireland, France and Spain seeking resolution of boundaries in the Celtic Sea and the Bay of Biscay.

A range of conditions prevail in this offshore area. In the north-east Atlantic waters off the west coast, the major residual current flow is dominated by the north-east Atlantic Drift (often referred to as the Gulf Stream) that brings warm waters up from the Gulf of Mexico. The Irish Sea and North Sea are less affected by this warm water current, and because of their more enclosed nature there is less overall water movement. At the very local scale, the waters of many of the coastal bays and sea lochs/loughs, particularly along the west coast of Scotland and Ireland, and the voes in Shetland, create very localised conditions in which unusual and particular communities of animals and plants survive.

The waters around the UK and Ireland vary greatly in depth with the continental shelf (maximum depth 200 m) covering most of the North Sea and Irish Sea basins. The North Sea has an average depth of around 95 m (maximum depth 700 m) and the Irish Sea ranges from 20–100 m over much of the basin, with a deep sea trench which reaches a maximum depth of 302 m, known as Beaufort's Dyke, in the North Channel between Scotland and Northern Ireland. To the west, the continental shelf extends between 20 and 80 km offshore before the continental shelf break, where the seabed falls away rapidly to depths in excess of 2000 m and in places, such as the abyssal plain of the Porcupine Bank, to depths in excess of 4850 m.

The seabed does not have the monotonous, uniform topography it was once thought to possess, but is highly varied, with large sedimentary plains in places and elsewhere has dramatic underwater mountain ranges, such as the Wyville Thomson Ridge. This is a 200-km long rock spine that rises from the seabed at over 1000 m depth to within 400 m of the surface. Even more dramatic are seamounts, that have been described as oceanic oases, which are undersea mountains (usually of volcanic origin) rising from the seafloor. The Anton Dohrn Seamount rises from the seabed of the Rockall Trough at around 2100 m depth to a height of 1500 m (Ben Nevis, the highest mountain in the UK, is 1344 m high), whilst the Rosemary Bank is around 70 km in diameter and around 2000 m high, rising from the seabed at a depth of 2300 m.

The offshore waters are a demanding place to live, the surface waters experience fluctuating temperatures throughout the year and storms and wave action can restrict what can live where in the shallower coastal waters. With depth. the challenges alter, temperature is much more constant and in the abyss remains throughout the year at between 2 and 4 °C, wave action stops having an effect at around 70 m depth, but here darkness prevails and the pressure increases by one atmosphere for every 10 m depth.

Pollution

Many of us have grown up and lived believing that the ocean has a somehow limitless capacity and power to absorb and 'neutralise' anything that we choose to throw at it. We have convinced ourselves that it is beyond our capability to pollute or change. As ever, we were wrong and we have been slowly poisoning this world.

Human debris is a considerable problem in the seas around the UK and Ireland. This can originate from land-based activities such as refuse (in its widest sense) disposal and sewage discharges. Industrial activities also have an impact both through their 'normal' operations and also as a result of accidents such as oil spills.

Some areas, such as the deep water of Beaufort's Dyke, have been used to dump waste munitions and chemical weapons. Around one million tons of munitions were dumped here at the end of the Second World War. Over time these munitions have spread over a wide area and although at present there is no indication of any leaching of the material, it remains a realistic threat.

Progress has, however, been made on many fronts, although dumping of dredge material still takes place, and this spoil is often from port or harbour channels and heavily contaminated. There is now legislation in place that prevents the marine disposal of most types of waste. Radioactive waste dumping at sea was stopped in 1982, burning of waste at sea has been forbidden since 1990, dumping of industrial waste stopped at the end of 1992 and dumping of sewage sludge stopped at the end of 1998.

It is not, however, all good news, and plastics of all sorts are the new major problem. Plastic is very slow to degrade and floating plastic debris is now the most common man-made item found in the sea. It can act as platforms for colonisation, increasing the risk of the introduction and eventual establishment of non-native species. Seabirds are known to ingest small bits of plastic litter and then to pass this on to their chicks by regurgitation. Sea turtles ingest plastic litter, mistaking it for jellyfish, causing gut blockages and eventual death through starvation. Lost or discarded fishing net is also a hazard to many larger animals, including fish, whales and dolphins, seals and seabirds, which get entangled and drown.

Exploration and interpretation

Expeditions by Wyville-Thomson on the naval vessels *HMS Lighting* (1868) and *HMS Porcupine* (1869) in the north-east Atlantic are regarded by many as the start of the scientific investigation of the ocean. Since then there have been other surveys in the region such as that conducted on *HMS Rosemary* in 1929/30 which identified the seamount area that now bears its name, the Rosemary Bank. Similarly in 1955 the German *FRV Anton Dohrn*, named after the nineteenth-century German scientist of the same name who founded the Stazione Zoologica in Naples in 1872, discovered the Anton Dohrn a large seamount that rises from the seabed in the Rockall Trough to the west of the Outer Hebrides.

This pioneering work gave us the first tantalising glimpses of the biodiversity in the seas around the UK and Ireland through what was brought on board from grabs and trawls. Invaluable as this was, it was difficult, if not impossible, to appreciate the structure and organisation of the ecosystems on the seabed. Our understanding of the pelagic realm was informed by the many fisheries surveys that have been undertaken and the long-term records collected by the Sir Alister Hardy Foundation for Ocean Science (SAHFOS) since its establishment in 1931. The Continuous Plankton Recorder (CPR) surveys in the North Sea that started in 1946 are generally regarded as the longest complete series of plankton samples anywhere in the world.

With the development of scuba diving in the 1960s, the opportunity to make direct observations of the shallow sub-littoral habitats and communities provided the first real insights into the complexity and organisation of the communities found around our coasts down to depths of around 40–50 m. It was the expansion of the offshore oil industry in the 1960s and 1970s that stimulated even further technological developments that eventually made the deep-water areas accessible, providing direct observations to supplement the grab and dredge samples through the use of Remotely Operated Vehicles (ROVs) equipped with both video and still cameras.

Even with all this new technology it was still only possible to capture snapshots of the seabed and at great expense. The final challenge is to map, not only the topography of the seabed (Figure 34.2), but also the distribution of habitats and communities found in places we can never expect to visit (Figure 34.3), but all too frequently we damage through fishing and other activities. Remote sensing techniques using multibeam sonar, sidescan sonar, Acoustic Ground Discrimination Systems (AGDS) and 3D seismics and sub-bottom profiling provide details that would have been unimaginable even 10 years ago. The next challenge is making this available and understandable to decision-makers. Since many of the animals in the sea are unfamiliar to most

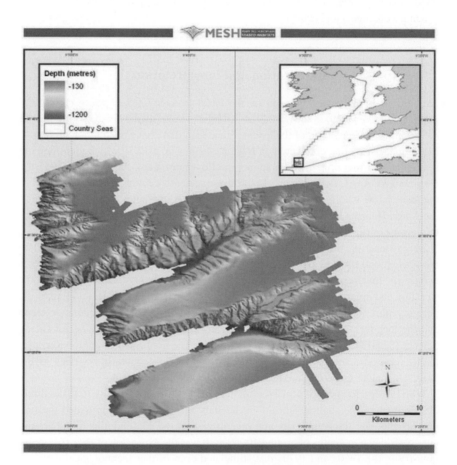

Figure 34.2 High-resolution topographic image of the seabed in the south-west approaches showing a series of canyons that varied in depth from 138 m to 1165 m with a complex network of tributary valleys (see colour plate).

Figure 34.3 Mixed sediment seabed on the steep slopes of the tributaries at around 140 m depth with dense aggregations of the crinoid, *Leptometra celtica*, and the squat lobster, *Munida* spp. (see colour plate).

people, it is essential that the best possible advice and information is provided. To this end the MarLIN (Marine Life Information Network for Britain and Ireland; http://www.marlin.ac.uk/) programme was established in 1998 at the Marine Biological Association in Plymouth, in collaboration with the main nature-conservation agencies in Britain and Ireland, together with key academic institutions. It provides independent, peer-reviewed information to help with decisions on marine environmental management, thus supporting good stewardship of the marine environment. Knowing what is there is key, and the Census of Marine Life (http://www.coml.org/) is another project that started in 2000 and is due to report in 2010, when it aims to present the first comprehensive census of marine life explaining the diversity, distribution and abundance of the 230 000+ known species of animals found in the seas.

Trends

Part of the challenge in the marine environment is having the historical data that allow realistic comparisons with the present to be made. There is all too little of this for much of the biology, but some does exist.

Cetaceans

The waters around Great Britain and Ireland are home to 28 species of cetacean. Some of these have a worldwide distribution, and others are migratory, moving through our waters between their high latitude feeding areas and the warmer-water southern breeding grounds.

In 1994, the Small Cetaceans in the European Atlantic and North Sea (SCANS1) Survey was undertaken, covering the North Sea, Skaggerat and Kattegat and the Celtic Sea (Hammond *et al.* 1995). A second SCANS survey (SCANSII) was carried out in 2005 that covered an even greater area, including the continental shelf waters west of GB and Ireland. In addition, in 2007, a further survey, the Cetacean Offshore Distribution and Abundance in the European Atlantic (CODA), covered the offshore waters of the eastern Atlantic.

For those species most regularly seen in these waters, the estimated abundances show very little change over the last 10 years. The estimated population size in European continental shelf waters for Minke Whale (*Balaenoptera acutorostrata*) is 18 600 (95% confidence limits: 10 500–33 200) (SCANSII 2008), for Common Bottlenose Dolphin (*Tursiops truncatus*) it is 12 600 (95% CL: 7500–21 300), with the greatest numbers seen in the Celtic Sea Area; the estimated offshore abundance is 19 300 (95% CL: 11 800–31 400). White-beaked Dolphins (*Lagenorhynchus acutus*) are estimated to number 22 700 (95% CL: 10 300–49 700) in European continental-shelf waters, and the Harbour Porpoise (*Phocoena phocoena*), the most abundant of our cetaceans, has an estimated continental-shelf population of 385 600 (95% CL: 261 300–569 200).

Other species, such as Killer Whales (*Orcinus orca*), that are largely confined to the more northern latitudes, have no accurate population estimate, although anecdotally there have been more reported sightings in recent years. Many species of large cetacean suffered badly from whaling in the nineteenth and early twentieth centuries and some have not fully recovered, especially the Northern Right Whale (*Eubalaena glacialis*), which is the most endangered species of cetacean, with the North Atlantic population thought to be approximately 400. Any sighted in the eastern Atlantic are likely to be wanderers from the western North Atlantic.

Fish stocks

Over 1000 fish species have been recorded in the north-eastern Atlantic and North Sea region, of which about 5% are commercially exploited. In 2005, 65% of the 26 fish stocks around the UK that were assessed were considered to have stock-spawning levels insufficient to guarantee stock replenishment. In recent times, many traditionally fished stocks have been severely depleted and exploited to the brink of collapse. As a result, other species, such as Orange Roughy (*Haplostethus atlanticus*), Black Scabbardfish (*Aphanopus carbo)* and Roundnose Grenadier (*Coryphaenoides rupestris*), previously largely unexploited and mainly from deeper offshore waters, have been targeted in a largely uncontrolled way.

The International Council for the Exploration of the Sea (ICES) (http://www.ices. dk/) provides advice on a range of human activities affecting, and affected by, marine ecosystems, including stock assessments and the impacts of fisheries on the ecosystem. Increasingly the advice given has provided for a precautionary approach to fisheries management, in which key reference points, namely precautionary and limit, are identified. The principle is that a fishery should be managed so as to avoid reaching the precautionary reference point so that the limit reference point (at which it is deemed there is a serious risk of stock collapse) is never reached. The Cod (*Gadus morhua*) fishery in the North Sea is one such stock to which these principles have been applied in recent years. Spawning stock biomass of North Sea Cod fell from 157 000 T in 1963 to a low of 38 000 T in 2001 (a 76% decrease), although it has since shown a slight increase.

Since 2003, ICES have advised that there should be a zero catch of Cod, based on the spawning stock biomass (SSB) being below the limit reference point, although the stock has shown a modest increase since 2006. An EU recovery plan has been implemented, aimed at reversing the declining trend in SSB and increasing the spawning stock above the limit reference point. In particular it is necessary to reduce fishery-related mortality in the youngest age classes, thus allowing more fish to reach maturity. This is a difficult outcome to achieve whilst the considerable fishery pressure continues. Over the last five years, an average of 82% of landings of North Sea Cod have consisted of juveniles (ages 1–3 years) that have consequently made no contribution to future recruitment. The recruitment of the relatively abundant (274 458 individuals) 2005 year class to the fishery was an opportunity to start rebuilding the stock on a better foundation, but in 2006, the 2005 year class comprised 62% of the total catch by number and then again in 2007 it was 58%. The 1996 year class was the last really substantial one (837 455 individuals) to enter the fishery, but it was heavily exploited (and discarded) by the fishery in its first five years and effectively disappeared, leaving no long-term benefit to the SSB. The key to the long-term future of the Cod fishery is to greatly improve the survival of young Cod so that the age-class structure can readjust and a complete collapse, as was witnessed in the Grand Banks Cod fishery off North America, can be avoided. It is also important to remember that other pressures, such as climate change, have an impact on Cod numbers and a 'simple' application of the ICES formula may not in itself be enough to ensure the economic survival of the population.

North Sea Herring (*Clupea harengus*) is another species that has suffered major fluctuations in its fortunes over the last 60 years, from a high in the years just after the Second World War, following a period of much reduced exploitation. Landings peaked in 1965 at over 1 million tonnes, of which 80% were juvenile fish. There then followed a very rapid decline in both SSB and landings. By 1975, whilst the SSB had fallen to just 83 000 T, the landings were still over 300 000 T. A moratorium on targeted Herring fishing in the North Sea was declared from 1977–80. By 1981 the SSB had, however, increased to over 200 000 T, and a managed fishery was reopened with an annual Total Allowable Catch (TAC) being set. Despite this control, by 1996 the SSB had again declined alarmingly low, but the lessons learned in the 1970s meant that decisions were taken quickly to try to halt this decline, resulting in a drastic cut in the TAC.

Thus there is evidence that with careful and strong management, based on good information about stock levels and catches, it is possible for formerly over-exploited fish stocks to recover. At the same time, however, it is important to recognise that such recoveries take time and it is not only necessary for the stock levels to increase, but that the overall population structure needs to be re-established. Furthermore, it is important to take account of external factors such as climate change and the effects this has on the wider ecosystem and food webs.

Aquaculture is an increasingly important industry that depends on clean water in which to rear its fish. The mainstay of the marine fin fish industry for the last 40+ years has been the Atlantic Salmon (*Salmo salar*), with the major concentrations of fish farms in the Northern Isles, the west-coast sea lochs of Scotland and in the west of Ireland. In 2007, the total production for Scotland was 129 930 T (FRS 2008), and around 10 000T in Ireland. In response to the continuing decline in stocks of various wild fish, there has been recently considerable effort put in to developing aquaculture techniques for Cod, Haddock (*Melanogrammus aeglefinus*) and Atlantic Halibut (*Hippoglossus hippoglossus*). These are still very much fledgling industries with around 1110 T of Cod and 147 T of Atlantic Halibut produced in Scotland in 2007 (FRS 2008).

As with any new development that would appear to 'solve' a problem, in this case declining wild fish stocks, the rise in aquaculture comes at a price. It resulted in the development of the industrial fishery for a number of species, including Sandeels (*Ammodytes* spp.) and Capelin (*Mallotus villosus*), that were previously unexploited, to supply the fishmeal industry that grew up with the aquaculture industry.

The Sandeel fishery started in the 1970s and peaked in 1998 with landings of more than 1 million tonnes, which then declined rapidly to a historic low in 2005. The almost exponential growth and then equally dramatic crash (which had remarkable similarities to the Herring fishery a few years earlier) as a result of declining stocks is yet another example of the reckless management of an uncontrolled and poorly under-stood fishery. The Sandeel stocks are driven by highly variable recruitment and high natural mortality, in addition to the fishery burden, but also to environmental factors. The rise in sea temperature in the southern North Sea has been linked to poor Sandeel recruitment and a movement of stocks further north. It is not just the direct effect of temperature on the population, however, but the changes that are occurring in their main prey species, such as the decline and redistribution of the copepod, *Calanus finmarchicus*, as a result of sea temperature rise (see 'Climate Change' section). The decline in Sandeel numbers has also been implicated in the reduction in the breeding success of a number of surface-feeding seabirds, not least the Black-legged Kittiwake (*Rissa tridactyla*) and terns (*Sterna* spp.). The complexity of the linkages between planktonic prey, Sandeels, top predators and fisheries, combined with the stresses of climate change, illustrates the need for very careful and balanced management, especially the need to avoid the temptation of over-exploitation in the good times.

Habitats

Despite the improvements over recent years in technology that has allowed exploration of deep-water areas, our knowledge is still very incomplete and there are no extensive, good historical data from which to construct any sort of trends.

From current observations, however, there is cause for concern, as many habitats are being altered by fishing activities in particular. Although in recent years the overall level of fishing activities has declined and some fish stocks may have benefited, it will take much longer before marine habitats and their associated communities recover. Even as this potential for recovery has materialised, some areas that were previously avoided by fishermen have become vulnerable as improved navigational accuracy with GPS has given them the ability and confidence to fish grounds they might previously have avoided. The growing development pressures from the offshore renewable-energy sector, both wind and tidal power, are new concerns. In particular, the high-energy areas where tidal power installations might be sited and which support specialist and unusual communities of animals adapted to living there may be altered beyond repair.

In some instances, however, even where change and loss is high, such as with *Sabellaria* reefs, the potential for recovery is great, as the animals are able to re-colonise areas rapidly and are fast growing. In other cases, the consequences are much more long term, such as with the cold-water corals that have only quite recently been found off the west coasts of Scotland and Ireland. The main reef-forming species is *Lophelia pertusa*, but often other species occur in association, such as *Madrepora oculata* and *Solenosimilia variabilis*. *L. pertusa* appears to favour oceanic waters with a temperature range of 4–12 °C. The initial review of their distribution off the north and west of Britain and Ireland was carried out by Wilson (1979) and since then it has been updated by Long *et al.* (1999) and Rogers (1999). There are a number of areas where *Lophelia* has been found so far, including the Rockall Bank and around the shelf break north and west of Scotland, in water depths ranging from 200 –>1000 m. The Darwin Mounds (named after the survey vessel *Charles Darwin*), which cover an area of ~100 km^2, have extensive patches of coral. Towards the southern end of the Rockall Bank off the north-west of Donegal and further south on the Porcupine Seabight there are more extensive reefs lying in 400–1000 m. More recently, further extensive reefs have been found in more inshore waters to the east of the island of Mingulay, in water depths of around 100 m+, at the southern end of the Outer Hebrides (Roberts *et al.* 2004). Whilst these reefs appear undamaged by trawling, there have been a number of documented examples of damage to *Lophelia* reefs in the north-west Atlantic. The

Darwin Mounds' reefs which were only discovered in 1998 during an oil-industry-funded survey, showed signs of considerable damage when they were revisited in 2000, with broken coral spread over the seabed and evidence of parallel scar marks from bottom trawling (ICES 2002).

The speed with which the damage occurred after the discovery of the reefs is alarming. It is a timely reminder of the vulnerability of so much of the marine ecosystem to damage and even loss. There is a real danger that there remain many features undiscovered that could very easily be destroyed before they are even found.

As our knowledge grows it is increasingly apparent that the seas around the UK and Ireland support a remarkable diversity of life. New species/records continue to be found, but Davison and Baxter (1997) estimated a total of around 11 500 species (excluding Protista, bacteria and viruses) from UK waters. The Marine Habitat Classification for Britain and Ireland v04.05 lists 370 different biotopes/sub-biotopes, (a biotope is defined as the combination of an abiotic habitat and its associated community of species) (Connor *et al.* 2004). Some of the most notable and at-risk habitats are listed in Annex I of the Habitats Directive and on the OSPAR list of Threatened and/or Declining Species and Habitats (OSPAR 2008) (Table 34.1).

Protecting the marine environment

The resources of the marine environment have been exploited for many years and historically this has been controlled and managed on a sector-by-sector basis, with little consideration of the cumulative impact on the environment and its flora and fauna.

There is now, however, a growing realisation and appreciation that marine habitats and species need to be protected and there is an increasing number of drivers and legislative measures that have been or are being developed. These include the Ramsar Convention on Wetlands, the UN Convention on Biological Diversity (CBD) that was signed by the UK and Ireland at the Earth Summit in Rio de Janiero in 1992, aimed at halting the worldwide loss of animal and plant species; the International Convention for the Control and Management of Ships Ballast Water and Sediments, which has led to the development of the Global Ballast Water Management Programme to try to reduce the risk of the introduction of non-native species; the EC Water Framework Directive (00/60/EC), which includes coastal waters out to 1 NM for England, Wales, Northern Ireland and the Republic of Ireland and 3 NM for Scotland, and aims to protect and improve the water environment, through preventing deterioration and where possible restoring polluted waters to good ecological status by 2015.

Other relevant legislation includes the EC Marine Strategy Framework Directive (08/56/EC), the Shellfish Waters Directive (2006/113/EC), the Environment Liability Directive (2004/35/EC) and the Strategic Environmental Assessment Directive (2001/42/EC).

Table 34.1 *Most notable and at-risk habitats as listed in Annex I of the Habitats Directive and on the OSPAR list of Threatened and/or Declining Species and Habitats*

OSPAR Threatened and/ or Declining Habitats

Carbonate mounds
Coral gardens
Deep-sea sponge aggregations
Intertidal *Mytilus edulis* beds on mixed and sandy sediments
Intertidal mudflats
Littoral chalk communities
Lophelia pertusa reefs
Maerl beds
Modiolus modiolus beds
Oceanic ridges with hydrothermal vents/fields
Ostrea edulis beds
Sabellaria spinulosa reefs
Seamounts
Sea-pen and burrowing megafauna communties
Zostera beds

Habitats Directive Annex I Habitats

Sandbanks which are slightly covered by sea water all the time
Estuaries
Mudflats and sandflats not covered by sea water at low tide
Coastal lagoons
Large shallow inlets and bays
Reefs
Submerged structures made by leaking gases
Submerged or partially submerged sea caves

A number of international and national instruments have very specific marine management and nature conservation objectives. The Convention for the Protection of the Marine Environment of the North-east Atlantic (OSPAR), as part of its function, has developed a Joint Assessment and Monitoring Programme (JAMP) which aims to assess the status of the marine environment. OSPAR periodically publishes Quality Status Reports, the next one is due in 2010. It will contain assessments of all anthropogenic impacts, including both long-standing operations, such as fisheries, oil and gas industry, and contaminants, but also new activities, such as offshore renewable-energy developments. It has developed a system of Ecological Quality Objectives (EcoQOs) to describe the desired state of components of the marine ecosystems. As part of its Ecosystems and Biological Diversity Strategy it aims to establish an ecologically coherent network of well-managed marine protected areas (MPAs) by 2010.

The European Directives on the Conservation of Natural Habitats and of Wild Fauna and Flora (92/43/EEC), otherwise known as the Habitats Directive, and on the Conservation of Wild Birds (79/409/EEC), the Birds Directive, regulate for the protection of certain habitats and species of European importance, in particular through the designation of Special Areas of Conservation (SAC) and Special Protection Areas (SPA), respectively. These sites together form the basis of the EU-wide network of protected areas, known as the Natura 2000 Network. Under the Wildlife and Countryside Act 1981 for Great Britain and the Nature Conservation and Amenity Lands (NI) Order 1985 for Northern Ireland, there is the opportunity to designate Marine Nature Reserves (MNR) in waters out to 12 NM, but this power has been seldom used.

The UK Marine and Coastal Access Act, 2009, which covers all UK waters except the territorial waters of Scotland and Northern Ireland, contains a series of measures to improve the decision-making process on activities affecting marine waters and as part of this there is the proposal to establish a new type of MPA called a Marine Conservation Zone to promote the conservation and recovery of marine flora and fauna, habitats and features of geological and geomorphological interest. The Marine (Scotland) Bill going through the Scottish Parliament is intended to improve management of the seas around Scotland and includes new powers for the designation of Marine Protected Areas in Scottish waters and is expected to be given Royal Assent in early 2010.

What is common to these is the central aim of recreating in the marine environment something similar to what exists on land, through a series of designated sites designed to afford protection to particular features of 'interest'. These features are defined on the basis of a number of criteria such as rarity, representativeness, and declining and /or threatened habitats and species. As individual sites, with the appropriate level of protection from damaging activities, there is the potential for them to afford a degree of protection at the site-specific level. The aspiration of an ecologically coherent network, however, is a much larger challenge, as this implies at least some form of mutually supportive mechanism and connectivity between the sites through the exchange of larvae and other ecosystem services. There is a need to critically review how marine conservation and protection can be delivered and the concept of a collection of discrete, disconnected, typically small protected areas to be challenged. As stated earlier, it is not the marine environment that can be managed, but the human activities that impact on it. Constraining these within a very limited space is unlikely to be sufficient to restore the seas to health and a wholesale review and revision of the way that all activities are managed is urgently required.

Climate change

The greatest challenge facing the marine environment and the animals and plants living there is climate change. The impacts on the marine environment will be numerous and are summarised in the Marine Climate Change Impacts Partnership (MCCIP) Annual Report Cards (http://www.mccip.org.uk/arc).

In addition to rising sea temperatures and rising sea levels, it is projected that there will be a greater frequency of severe storms that not only have implications for the shallow benthic communities that may be affected around the coast, but it also increases the risk of shipping accidents and damage to a range of structures with the resulting pollution. There is already good evidence that changes in the distribution of species is taking place. The long-term records from the CPR show changes in the composition and distribution of key zooplankton species (Edwards *et al.* 2008). *Calanus finmarchicus* is a northern species that has shown a dramatic decline in abundance in the North Sea over recent years and a marked retreat northwards. It has been replaced by another more southern species of copepod, *C. helgolandicus*, but in much smaller numbers. These zooplankton are a key component of the marine food chain, and essential prey to the larvae of many commercial fish species. Any additional stress on the recruitment to the fish stocks further exacerbates the decline in stock caused by excessive fishing. The impact on one element has many consequences, as described in the MCCIP 2009 ARC (MCCIP 2009).

Sea temperature rise has also resulted in the introduction and establishment of many new species that are now not only able to survive in these waters, but to successfully breed. This has meant that many non-native species that historically may have been accidentally introduced by one means or another and only just survived are now able to reproduce and spread. This risk is compounded by the reduction in extent of Arctic sea ice and the opening of the passage between the Pacific and the Atlantic, enabling more non-native species to invade and become established, such as the Pacific diatom, *Neodenticula seminae*, that arrived in North Atlantic waters in 1999 after becoming locally extinct 800 000 years ago.

As the environmental conditions change, so many species naturally expand their range. There is no better illustration of this than the change in fish species richness over a 22-year period in the North Sea (Hiddink and ter Hofstede 2008). There is a very clear correlation between species richness and average winter bottom temperature, with many of the incoming species being small sized and of little commercial value. The five species whose ranges have increased most are: Anchovy (*Engraulis encrasicolus*), Red Mullet (*Mullus surmuletus*), Scaldfish (*Arnoglossus laterna*), Solenette (*Buglossidium luteum*) and Lesser Weever (*Echiichthys vipera*). As some fish advance, a few have retreated, in particular Wolfish (*Anarhichas lupus*), Spurdog (*Squalus acanthius*) and Ling (*Molva molva*). Similarly new models predict that the warming North Sea may see a northward shift of Cod and its abundance reduce by more than 20% from an already very low base (Cheung *et al.* 2009).

The potential for a breakdown in food webs and ecosystem structures, that are already under stress from a range of factors, as a result of climate change, is great, but perhaps the most important factor that needs to be taken into account in looking to the future health of the oceans is ocean acidification. This is the result of the elevated levels of carbon dioxide in the atmosphere being absorbed by the surface waters of the oceans and forming carbonic acid. Since the beginning of the industrialised age in the eighteenth century, the surface ocean acidity has increased by 30%, with over half of this increase occurring in the last 30 years, and the current rate of increase in acidity is the most rapid in over 55 million years. Some coastal areas are now season-ally bathed in water that is corrosive to some bottom-dwelling organisms. There is evidence that a previous natural ocean acidification event some 55.5 million years ago is linked to a mass extinction of many calcareous organisms and that it took hundreds of thousands of years for widespread recovery of coral reefs. The implications of ocean acidification are considerable: as well as affecting the ability of many organisms to build their calcareous shells, it can affect their metabolism, physical activity and repro-ductive capability. In particular, there is evidence of various phytoplankton, in par-ticular coccolithophores, which, as well as absorbing large amounts of carbon dioxide are also an important food source for fish larvae, being affected. Furthermore, it is projected that many of the cold-water corals that have been found off the north-west of Scotland and Ireland could be exposed to corrosive waters by 2100 and it is unlikely that they would be able to calcify under such conditions (Turley *et al.* 2007).

Past lessons; future challenges

The expanse of ocean that surrounds these islands knows no boundaries and is influ-enced by events far away through the far-reaching oceanic currents and now from new directions, with the reduction in the extent of Arctic sea ice.

We have lived off its bounty for as long as humans have inhabited these islands, but in recent years we have sorely abused it and inflicted serious damage. Many of the wrongs can be put right with time; we have started this with better controls on what we dump in the seas. We know we have a challenge to better manage our fisheries, so that stocks recover to robust and sustainable levels and we reduce the damage that fishing activities have on the marine benthos. We have still, however, to accept that this will involve some considerable pain and is not going to be solved in a year or even a decade of doing the right thing.

Our arrogance, or perhaps it is naivety, of mind-set, that we 'can manage the sea' must be dispelled and we must accept that nature will take its course and we must work with it.

Comparisons have already been drawn with the warnings of possible catastrophic effects of widespread damage to the world's ecosystems by Rachel Carson in her 1962 book *Silent Spring*. But in the preface to the 1961 edition of her earlier book entitled *The Sea Around Us*, first published in 1951, she wrote:

> The mistakes that are made now are made for all time. It is a curious situation that the sea from which life first arose, should now be threatened by activities of one form of that life.

But the sea, though changed in a sinister way will continue to exist; the threat is rather to life itself.

Fifty years on, the sea does indeed continue to exist, the threats, though different, are perhaps greater than ever. A sad indictment of us all.

References

Carson, R. (1989). *The Sea Around Us*, Oxford, Oxford University Press.

Cheung, W.W.L., Lam, V.W.Y., Sarmiento, J.L., Kearney, K., Watson, R. and Pauly, D. (2009). Projecting global marine biodiversity impacts under climate change scenarios. *Fish and Fisheries*, doi 10.1111/j.1467–2979.2008.00315x.

Connor, D.W., Allen, J.H., Golding, N. *et al.* (2004). The Marine Habitat Classification for Britain and Reland version 04.05, Peterborough, JNCC. Internet version http://www.jncc.gov.uk/Marine HabitatClassification.

Davison, A. and Baxter, J.M. (1997). The number of marine species that occur in Scottish coastal waters. In Fleming, L.V., Newton, A.C., Vickery, J.A. and Usher, M.B., eds., *Biodiversity in Scotland: Status, Trends and Initiaitves,* Edinburgh, The Stationery Office, pp. 57–62.

Edwards, M., Johns, D.G., Beaugrand, G., Licaidro, P., John, A.W.G. and Stevens, D.P . (2008). Ecological Status Report: results from the CPR survey 2006/2007. *SAHFOS Technical Report,* **5**, 1–8.

FRS (2008). *Scottish Fish Farms Annual Production Survey 2007*, Aberdeen, FRS.

Hammond, P., Benke, H., Berggren, P. *et al.* (1995). Distribution and abundance of the harbour porpoise and other small cetaceans in the North Sea and adjacent waters. LIFE92–2/UK/027 Final Report, October 1995.

Hardy, A. (1956). *The Open Sea I: The World of Plankton*, New Naturalist Series No. 34, London, Collins.

Hiddink, J.G. and ter Hofstede, R. (2008). Climate induced increases in species richness of marine fishes. *Global Change Biology,* **14**, 453–460.

ICES. (2002). Distribution of cold-water corals in the Northeast Atlantic in relation to fisheries. ACE Report, Chapter 3, Copenhagen, ICES.

Long, D., Roberts, J.M. and Gillespie, E.J. (1999). Occurrence of *Lophelia pertusa* on the Atlantic Margin. British Geological Survey Technical Report WB/99/24, Edinburgh, BGS.

MCCIP. (2009). Marine Climate Change Ecosystem Linkages Report Card 2009, Summary Report, Baxter, J.M., Buckley, P.J. and Frost, M.T., eds., Lowestoft, MCCIP.

OSPAR. (2008). OSPAR List of Threatened and/or Declining Species and Habitats, Ref. no. 2008–6.

Roberts, J.M., Brown, C.J., Long, D. *et al.* (2004). Final Report of Mapping Inshore Coral Habitats: The MINCH Project, Oban, SAMS.

Rogers, A.D. (1999). The biology of *Lophelia pertusa* (Linnaeus 1755) and other deep-water reef-forming coral and impacts from human activities. *International Review of Hydrology,* **84**, 315–406.

SCANS II (2008). Small Ceatceans in the European Atlantic and North Sea. Final
    Report submitted to the European Commission under project LIFE04NAT/
    GB/000245. Available from SMRU, Gatty Marine Lab, University of St Andrews,
    St Andrews, Fife KY16 8LB.
Turley, C.M., Roberts, J.M. and Guinotte, J.M. (2007). Corals in deep water: will the
    unseen hand of ocean acidification destroy cold-water ecosystems? *Coral Reefs,*
    26, 445–448.
Wilson, J.B. (1979). The distribution of the coral *Lophelia pertusa* (L.) [*L. prolifera*
    (Pallas)] in the north-east Atlantic. *Journal of the Marine Biological Association
    of the UK,* **59,** 149–164.

35

Plants

Andrew Lack

Summary

The flora of the British Isles consists of about 1300 native species and 150 'archaeophytes' introduced by people before 1500 AD, considered here, plus 'neophytes', introduced after 1500, considered in Chapter 5. General trends in our flora since 1945 have included a gradual retreat of northern plants from their southernmost localities and an advance of southern plants. This is likely to be a result of habitat change, especially eutrophication (nutrient enrichment), rather than climate change, though mild Januaries and summer drought may have contributed.

The habitats that have changed most are agricultural, the predominant habitats of the lowlands. Mechanisation and high inputs of fertiliser and pesticide have led to declines in species diversity, including much local extinction. Arable weeds and species-rich hay meadows have suffered the most. Much calcareous grassland, lowland heath and acid grassland has disappeared to agriculture, housing, industry or forestry. Some of the rest has seen species diversity decline through a decline in, or complete cessation of, grazing, along with some eutrophication. A similar story is seen in freshwater habitats. Some woodlands have been destroyed, but extant woods, though seeing great changes in use and an increase in shade and grazing, appear to have kept most of their flora, albeit sometimes in reduced quantity. In the uplands, heather moorland and our internationally important boglands have declined with over-grazing, frequent fires or plantation forestry. Upland grassland has increased. The coasts have remained largely unchanged, with a few losses around the edges, often, again, because of inappropriate grazing. Plants associated with habitation, industry and ruderal areas, such as wasteland and rubbish tips, have mainly increased.

Many of the losses of the post-war years were stopped during the 1980s when conservation took a far higher profile. We have seen a reversal of

Silent Summer: The State of Wildlife in Britain and Ireland, ed. Norman Maclean. Published by Cambridge University Press. © Cambridge University Press 2010.

fortune in certain restricted areas, especially with environmental schemes within agriculture and forestry, and nature-reserve management restoring habitats. Problems remain, many associated with grazing, even within nature reserves.

A few plants are endemic to the British Isles, but these are recently formed, mostly very restricted in range, and are of minor importance in our flora. The British orchids are a well-known family that can provide a monitor, reflecting on the flora as a whole.

Historical background

The native flora of the British Isles, numbering some 1300 vascular plant species,[1] is made up of those plants that have managed to colonise effectively, mainly from southern Europe, in the last 10 000 or so years since the glaciers finally retreated. During glacial times there were no oak or beech woods in Britain; grassland areas had a quite different species composition and were only in the south; we were attached to continental Europe and the Thames was a tributary of the Rhine. The only plant species that are still present from those days are those with a very wide tolerance or those that have now retreated to the north of the country and up mountains.

The introduction of Neolithic agriculture brought crops and domestic animals to this country, some 6000 years ago, at around the time of our isolation as an island. Woods were cleared for arable land and pasture, and the balance of the flora changed profoundly. Successive waves of colonists after this brought with them a number of plant species, either deliberately for their uses or inadvertently as weeds. About 150 of these are still present and known as 'archaeophytes'.

Since 1500, the world has opened up. The result has been enormous changes in the fate of particular habitats and their constituent species, something that has only increased over the last 50 years or so. It is these changes in the native and archaeophyte flora, mainly since 1945, that I am considering here. Many plants have been introduced from around the world since 1500. These are known as 'neophytes' and are considered in Chapter 5.

Two major recent publications give details of changes in our flora: the *New Atlas* of Preston *et al.* (2002a) and *Change in the British Flora 1987–2004* by Braithwaite *et al.* (2006). Much of the information here is contained in these indispensable publications, along with the briefer Preston *et al.* (2002b) that summarises some

---

[1] I will only consider the vascular flora here, consisting of flowering plants, conifers, ferns, horsetails and clubmosses. The 900+ species of mosses and liverworts will not be included.

of the Atlas information. Here I point out the major changes that have happened over the last 60 years or so, with representative examples. There have been numerous small changes in our flora and each species has reacted differently in different places. Our tradition of county flora writing continues and the latest county floras detail the changes that occur at that scale.

Some general trends

Our flora has been divided into eight or nine categories, known as 'elements', based on their wider distribution, ranging from 'Mediterranean' to 'Arctic-montane' (Preston and Hill 1997). Some of our commonest plants are those that are most widely distributed across much of Europe. It is those plants with a wide tolerance that have survived the glaciations of the last two million years. They are clearly adaptable to many different climatic regions and different habitats and have, in general, fared quite well over the last 50 years. Some have increased. Other plants that have done well are those whose main distribution is to the south of the British Isles. This includes the small group of about 90 species that are centred on Mediterranean Europe and reach their northern limits with us. By contrast, many of those whose main distribution is in northern Europe and in uplands have decreased in the southern parts of the British Isles.

The brief description above would immediately suggest that we are seeing the effects of global warming in our flora. Although this cannot be ruled out, several other factors are probably much more important. Many of our most widespread plants and those with a generally southern distribution are short-lived and adaptable, often grow on fertile soils and can take advantage of 'ruderal' habitats, such as building sites, waste ground, gardens etc. Ruderal habitats have increased, especially in the south. Most of those plants with a northern distribution are typical of acidic nutrient-poor soils of such habitats as heathland, moor and bog that abound in northern Europe. It is just these habitats that have decreased in southern Britain as a result of agricultural 'improvement', urbanisation and forestry. Two aspects of recent climate developments may be important: a run of mild winters, especially noticeable in high January temperatures, and a number of serious droughts in summer that have caused vegetation gaps suitable for colonisation, especially by plants of ruderal habitats.

The increased level of soil fertility appears to be a general feature across the country. This eutrophication is mainly associated with agricultural 'improvement', but it has permeated through to many other habitats, especially marginal lands, roadsides and in run-off into fresh water. It even affects our woodlands and 'unimproved' grasslands. It is felt almost throughout the British Isles, but is most prominent in the southeast. What has resulted is that many of those plants that thrive on the richer soils with high nutrient content have done well, whereas those of poor soils have declined. The numerous features of habitat change are superimposed on this.

At national level, extinctions since 1800 have been minor.[2] At regional and county level it has been much more serious. Rate of loss, which stood at an average of about two species per county per decade during the nineteenth century rose to four per decade by 1950 and may now be higher still. But in the most populated counties, like Cambridgeshire, losses were more than twice that in some decades, especially around 1950 (Walker 2007). Taking the counties of England east of a line from Poole (east Dorset) to Goole (south-east Yorkshire) together, Walker (2007) recorded 23 species extinctions and 23 further large declines since 1800. Loss of habitat, especially of nutrient-poor wetland and heathland is the main cause. Rich (2001) showed that the combined distributions, even on the extremely coarse 10-km square basis, of grassland, arable, heathland and wetland native plants declined by 13% between 1973 and 1998. The equally striking increase of introduced plants, mainly in ruderal habitats, is considered in Chapter 5.

The habitats

Agricultural land

Agricultural land is the predominant landscape of lowland Britain, and as such, outside the urban environment, is not only the most familiar, but the most important of habitats in our islands. Something near 70% of the land of the British Isles is under some form of agriculture. Our culture is shaped by it, and the plants of agricultural land were part of our lives for hundreds of years. They are the ones that are entrenched most deeply in our folk memories. They are also the ones that have seen the most radical changes over the centuries.

Since this is, fundamentally, land that is being used to produce food for us, human intervention is of the essence. We have always battled against unwanted plants, the weeds, but this took on a greater intensity with the mechanisation of agriculture coupled with the Enclosure Acts, most of which were passed between about 1770 and 1830. This led to the early decline of some weeds. At the same time, industry started taking over some of the land and the human population started to rise, but became increasingly displaced from the land itself.

During the twentieth century there was an even bigger change. Arable land increased in area during both the First and Second World Wars, as a consequence of the food shortages created by lack of imports from Europe. The idea that we should remain self-sufficient in food persisted for at least 30 years after 1945. At the same time, increased mechanisation, improved seed sorting and the widespread introduction of inorganic

---

[2] Walker (2007) recorded nine extinctions from the UK since 1800. Four have been reintroduced, two are still in Ireland, one is a recent neophyte derivative; there are unconfirmed reports of another. Rich (2001) suggested that there have been a total of 21 extinctions in Britain and 11 in Ireland since records began.

fertilisers and pesticides (themselves imported) made for further losses of wild plants. It also led to much increased food output, though at a high cost in terms of inputs. Grants were given for increasing food production by whatever means were available. This meant that the flora, except for the desired crops, suffered on all fronts – mixed farming declined as arable became more concentrated in the south-east; herbicides killed the wild plants directly; insecticides and fungicides killed many of their associates; fertilisers encouraged the fast-growing, but greedy crops to outcompete the 'weeds'. In addition, hedges were removed to allow heavy machinery to manoeuvre, leading to many fewer marginal areas, and seed sorting became more efficient still, so any weed seeds were sifted out.

By 1980, the disappearance of our traditional countryside was becoming more widely recognised and it was in that year that awareness was much enhanced by the publication of two seminal books: Marion Shoard's *The Theft of the Countryside* and Richard Mabey's *The Common Ground*. Their powerful language ('the English landscape is under sentence of death' – Shoard, 1980; 'insidious...changes in the internal workings of the countryside.' – Mabey, 1980) contributed immensely to the debate. There also came the awareness that true self-sufficiency, i.e. including imports of oil, pesticide and fertiliser, was an impossible pipe-dream for this country. The result has been that some, though by no means all, of the reforms of the post-war years have been put into reverse since about 1985. The 'Set-Aside' scheme was first introduced in 1989 and became obligatory for large farms in 1992. Various 'agri-environment' schemes have appeared and there has been a groundswell of interest in organic farming. Despite this, many areas have remained committed to intensive farming. The impact of these changes on our most familiar flora is immeasurable.

In the more marginal places for agriculture, in the north and west and in uplands, there has been less possibility for 'improvement', and traditional farming has maintained its position. This has meant that more of the wildlife value has been saved. It has also put these farmers at a serious disadvantage. Farming subsidies went first to intensify and therefore damage the wildlife value, and then to de-intensify and restore some of the wildlife. These farmers have had neither, and some have abandoned their farms as impossible to keep up.

There is one other change to our farmland flora that has not, as far as we can tell, been at the hands of the agricultural 'revolution' of the post-war years. It occurred quite independently and unexpectedly. The English Elm, *Ulmus procera*, the most common and characteristic of all farmland trees through much of England and Wales, has disappeared. Dutch Elm Disease, the fungus *Ophiostoma (Ceratocystis) novi-elmi*, that appears to be a much more virulent form of a disease that was already well known, was imported with American timber in about 1965. It is spread by the Elm Bark Beetle, and by 1980 all the elms were gone. The disease hits the other elm species too, including the mainly East Anglian, *Ulmus minor*, and the Wych Elm, *U. glabra*. This last is the only elm to occur regularly in woodland and is somewhat more resistant. A few survive. Some elm plants remain, as hedgerow shrubs, spreading by suckering, but are killed as soon as they reach about 5 m in height. They are still common in places, so are not lost to our flora; just lost as trees.

Arable land

Approximately 25% of the land area of the British Isles is under arable agriculture, concentrated in the lowlands and in southern and eastern England in particular. Apart from land that is used for houses or roads etc., arable land is used more intensively than any other habitat. Any plant other than the intended crop will be seen as a weed. It is also the classic habitat in which our archaeophytes occur. Indeed, most of our agricultural weeds are archaeophytes, including such well-known plants as the Corn Poppy, *Papaver rhoeas*, and Charlock, *Sinapis arvensis*. A number of native plants occur here too, such as the Corn Mint, *Mentha arvensis*, and Field Madder, *Sherardia arvensis*. These plants will have been among the most familiar of plants to the general populace prior to 1800, and even until 1945 remained familiar to many country people. The result is that many of these plants have evocative English names, and there are numerous other folk names for them from across the country. These now represent for us a deep nostalgia for a slower, forgotten way of life – Corn Marigold and Shepherd's Needle, Venus's Looking-glass, Corn Buttercup and Cornflower, Pheasant's Eye and Corn Spurrey; with folk names for these plants including 'Hedgehogs' and 'Lady's Comb', 'Devil's Claws' and 'Hard-iron', 'Bluebottle', 'Witch Bells', 'Jack-in-the-Green', 'Pickpocket', 'Beggarweed' and many others (Grigson 1958).

Efficient seed sorting led to some early declines, e.g. the Corn Cockle, *Agrostemma githago*, an attractive flower (Figure 35.1), with an attractive seed (like a miniature cockle), but those seeds made grey, bitter bread. Corn Cockles declined slowly and could still be locally plentiful by 1950. Many others declined through the nineteenth century, some, such as Thorow-wax, *Bupleurum rotundifolium*, declining markedly.

With the post-1945 onslaught, it is not surprising that many of our arable weeds declined so rapidly that a few, such as Swine's Succory, *Arnoseris minima*, Thorow-wax, Downy Hemp-nettle, *Galeopsis segetum*, and possibly even the Corn Cockle became totally extinct here by the mid-1980s.[3] What is almost more surprising is that most managed to hang on in certain field margins, where perhaps there was gentler treatment or where more hedges survived. A few even managed to thrive, most notably the Corn Poppy. Though it declined in certain places, it has remained a remarkably common sight, mainly owing to a long-lived seed bank of small seeds and fast growth. Another is the pernicious Black Grass, *Alopecurus myosuroides*, resistant to many herbicides as it is itself a grass like the crops, and a plant that thrives in the autumn sowings that have become the norm.

---

[3] The Corn Cockle has long-lived seeds and it is probable that in at least one abandoned quarry it returned of its own accord (Mabey 1980). Swine's Succory, Thorow-wax and Corn Cockles have been reintroduced in a few places in recent years.

Figure 35.1 Corn Cockles at a reintroduction site (see colour plate).

The change of heart since the mid-1980s has led to less subsidy for high-input high-output farming and grants have been provided for reversing some of the ravages of the post-war years. The result has been that some of our arable weeds have increased again. Field margins can have quite a variety of weeds, like Field Pansies, *Viola arvensis*, Small Bugloss, *Lycopsis arvensis*, cranesbills, *Geranium* spp., and, of course, poppies, and colour has returned in places. Unfortunately others, such as the Pheasant's Eye, *Adonis annua*, Corn Marigold, *Chrysanthemum segetum*, Large Hemp-nettle, *Galeopsis speciosa*, and Night-scented Catchfly, *Silene noctiflora*, have continued to decline, and the Corn Cleavers, *Galium tricornutum*, may now be confined to a single small field at Rothamsted, Hertfordshire. It appears that those associated with root crops may be the most vulnerable. The great majority remain rare on a national scale compared with what they were in 1945.

Sterling work is now being done by conservation agencies, e.g. Plantlife has its flagship farm at Ranscombe in Kent; RSPB and others have farmland Nature Reserves that encourage less intensive farming; the Game Conservancy Trust pioneered the idea of 'conservation headlands' in fields, since these have great benefits for game birds; and initiatives like Set-Aside and Environmentally Sensitive Area schemes were or are helping in places.

A few plants, such as the lovely Cornflower, *Centaurea cyanus*, and the two may-weeds, *Matricaria recutita* and *Tripleurospermum inodorum*, seem now to be occupying roadsides or farm tracks and gateways, rather than the crops themselves. It is likely that in some places they managed this themselves, but these and some others are sometimes included in seed mixes for spreading on new roadsides.

The disappearance from our lives of arable weeds has been the single most obvious change in our flora as a whole during my lifetime. The swathes of yellow of the Corn Marigold and, just once, the blue of Cornflower that I can remember vividly from my 1960s childhood have gone altogether, along with numerous smaller plants.

Some of our arable weeds seem now to be forced to survive as museum pieces, in fields and places deliberately left for them. Although this is unquestionably better than their total disappearance, they have lost their appeal as part of the rich working landscape. It somehow mirrors the disconnection of people from that landscape too, in our increasingly rootless urban and industrial society. Reconnection has to be a deliberate act at weekends. It is indeed in the more rural parts of the country, such as the south-west, that the plants, and the people, survive better as part of the agricultural scene.

Meadows

Meadows have, if anything, suffered even more destruction than arable land. The grassy, flower-rich meadows have gone, especially those to be cut for hay in mid-summer, many on river floodplains. They were a part of life in the country for many centuries. As with our arable weeds, they are deeply imprinted in folk memory. The massive losses between 1945 and 1985 have been well documented – something over 95% either lost altogether, usually by drainage and ploughing, or sometimes sand or gravel extraction, or irreparably altered by addition of fertiliser. Most have been converted to arable or to species-poor grass leys for silage. The traditions of lot allocation have died with them. In addition to the fields given over solely for hay, in a mixed farming system the edges of arable fields were used as 'grass walks' (Mabey 1980). These were used for access and often cut for hay too. In an intensive system these are simply wasted space.

Most of the plants of traditional hay meadows occur in other habitats, and remain frequent in grassy places. The ones that are more nearly confined to hay meadows have largely gone, such as the Greater Burnet, *Sanguisorba officinalis*, Pepper Saxifrage, *Silaum silaus*, and Green-winged Orchid, *Anacamptis* (*Orchis*) *morio*. Apart from these, what has gone is the riot of colour, often starting with huge numbers of Cowslips, *Primula veris* (Figure 35.2), the source of cowslip wine, now a forbidden drink, followed by buttercups, *Ranunculus* species and Green-winged or Marsh Orchids, *Dactylorhiza incarnata* and *D. praetermissa* or *purpurella*. These are followed in their turn by the great flowering in June (Figure 35.3) with Knapweed, *Centaurea nigra*, Meadowsweet, *Filipendula ulmaria*, various 'dandelion'-type composites, e.g. *Leontodon hispidus*,

Figure 35.2 Cowslips in one of the few remaining 'unimproved' hay meadows of southern England, Yarnton, Oxfordshire (see colour plate).

Figure 35.3 A flower-rich hay meadow in June with Greater Burnet, Red Clover, Knapweed, Rough Hawkbit, Ox-eye Daisy and other plants, Oxfordshire (see colour plate).

Meadow-rue, *Thalictrum flavum*, Yellow Rattle, *Rhinanthus minor*, Devilsbit Scabious, *Succisa pratensis*, and numerous others, the composition varying greatly from place to place. Usually they are full of insects and other invertebrate life as well.

When it was first realised that these meadows had largely disappeared by the late 1970s, a survey was sent out to find out where any still existed. Richard Mabey (1980) quotes one of the most poignant responses from a Sussex farmer: 'You may be interested to know that we have one meadow fitting the description given. An admission to bad farming but a field full of flowers and butterflies.'

The very few traditional meadows that have survived are probably all now conserved, but there is a ray of hope for some others. The hay crop is low by comparison with the fertiliser-addicted leys, but it seems that there is a premium price to be paid by owners of thoroughbred racehorses. This hay is nutritious and is particularly valuable for them. Hay-meadow seed mixes are being sown, both for racehorses and for straight conservation reasons, but the number is still minuscule compared with what there was before the war.

Grazing meadows, which have some of the same species as hay meadows, have been 'improved' in similar ways, though they have never had the range of plants or the obvious attractions of hay meadows. Continuing losses from this habitat include the Meadow Saxifrage, *Saxifraga granulata*, increasingly confined to edges, and Yellow Rattle, both plants of less-fertile soils. There have been increases in plants of disturbed places that thrive on eutrophic soils, e.g. Hairy Sedge, *Carex hirta*, and Lesser Trefoil, *Trifolium dubium*. In the BBC Natural World series on 20 February 2009, film-maker Rebecca Hosking showed a grazing meadow on which a diversity of species was grown, giving a tougher sward than the leys of one to three species. Here cattle were kept on the meadow all winter, so plant diversity may even be economically more effective.

Since the mid-1980s, losses of these grasslands have almost ceased, though some eutrophication has continued, mainly through leaching from adjacent arable land or winter flooding by eutrophicated rivers.

Calcareous grassland

Chalk and limestone grassland has a famously rich and diverse flora and butterfly fauna, full of colour and fragrant with herbs such as thyme, marjoram and salad burnet. It is formed by grazing animals, especially sheep, and its fortunes have fluctuated considerably over the centuries with the price of wool and mutton. The greatest extent of chalk downland was formed during the wool era of the eighteenth century. Many parts have been ploughed up at different times and then allowed to return to grassland and part of the great floral richness comes from the variety of management history (Wells *et al.* 1976). Some of the places with the oldest of grassland are the numerous hill forts that dot the chalk country of southern England, with earth ramparts too steep for ploughing.

This is another much-loved habitat that has seen the same depressing losses to agriculture that other lowland habitats have seen since 1945 – both to arable and fertilised grass

Figure 35.4 The 'Cerne giant', a seventeenth-century cartoon of Oliver Cromwell as Hercules, on the Dorset chalk in late summer. The only remaining unfertilised chalk grassland shows pale immediately around the figure.

leys (Figure 35.4). The agriculture that has replaced it is only viable in many places in a high input system reliant on subsidy. There have been two other notable changes:

1. Grazing has reduced, in places considerably. Sheep grazing declined steeply in the nineteenth century with imports of cotton. But rabbits[4] stepped in, and their population increased, so grazing continued without a break until myxomatosis hit the rabbits in 1954. After myxomatosis, for the first time, there was nothing to graze the grass and it became long and rank, affecting all the small plants and many insects. This led to scrub invasion in many places and total loss of the habitat.

2. Many quarries were opened, leading to initial annihilation of the habitat, though now, since many quarries have been subsequently abandoned, plant colonisers of bare chalk have been increasing again.

Like other lowland habitats, the destruction largely stopped in the mid-1980s. Now nearly all remaining chalk and southern limestone grassland has some form of protected status, including much military land on Salisbury Plain. There have been efforts to restore degraded calcareous grassland to its former state. Parts of the limestone grasslands of the north and west are similarly protected and nearly all floristically diverse areas are designated SSSIs. Some upland areas are less vulnerable anyway.

[4] Rabbits had been introduced in the eleventh to twelfth centuries by the Normans and were warrened for centuries. Although often escaping, increases were local until the nineteenth century, when superior firearms considerably reduced their predators, and the disappearance of the sheep meant that much more grazing land was available.

The many conservation bodies have been battling to work out the best way to maintain the richness of their sites. The biggest problem is grazing. In most places, it is very hard to introduce adequate grazing animals, and the sites are under-grazed. The ideal intensity and timing of grazing will differ in different sites and for different purposes, and some variation in grazing intensity within a site will increase diversity. In some places, the rabbits have returned in numbers, but this has not happened, nor is it desirable, within a mainly arable landscape. Here grazing is normally impossible. In certain special places some ingenious and at least partially successful substitutes have been tried, such as mowing and even fire or grass skiing (Smith 1980), but these are labour-intensive. It will always be difficult to maintain the variety of habitat in a small site. Many places have suffered from these problems, and small sites in particular have slowly lost some of their special species.

Two other factors increase the problems: (1) the species-richness can only return to any kind of stability over a long time period; (2) eutrophication is increasing as a result of previous agricultural 'improvement' and from drift from the neighbouring fields.

The plants of calcareous grassland have shown a general and continuing decline, though this has slowed considerably since the mid-1980s. This is particularly true of low-growing plants and those of the most infertile sites. These require fairly intense grazing pressure and no eutrophication. Examples are the Stemless Thistle, *Cirsium acaule*, Common Milkwort, *Polygala vulgaris*, Burnet Saxifrage, *Pimpinella saxifraga*, Harebell, *Campanula rotundifolia*, Small Scabious, *Scabiosa columbaria*, Squinancywort, *Asperula cynanchica*, Burnt Orchid, *Neotinea* (*Orchis*) *ustulata*, and Basil Thyme, *Clinopodium acinos*, these last two seeing particularly serious declines (Figure 35.5). It seems that some, at least, of the rather taller and coarser species have fared better, such as Marjoram, *Origanum vulgare*, Hawkweed Oxtongue, *Picris hieracioides*, and Musk Thistle, *Carduus nutans*. But there is much variation and trends are hard to discern. For instance, Greater Knapweed, *Centaurea scabiosa*, and Wild Parsnip, *Pastinaca sativa*, both common tall-growing plants of rough chalk grassland appear to be declining as are the grasses, Upright Brome, *Bromopsis erecta*, and Quaking Grass, *Briza media*, probably all victims of eutrophication.

One small group of calcareous grassland plants has been increasing – colonisers of bare chalk and newly formed grassland, including roadsides. Two of the most striking of these are the Pyramidal and Bee Orchids, *Anacamptis pyramidalis* and *Ophrys apifera*. Wild Onion (or Crow Garlic), *Allium vineale*, Field Madder, *Sherardia arvensis*, and Fern-Grass, *Catapodium rigidum*, appear also to be taking advantage of these ruderal sites.

Ponds

Until the end of the nineteenth century, ponds were a feature of farms and commons across the country. They were used as watering places for livestock, especially cattle,

(a)   (b)
Orchis ustulata Burnt Orchid   **Orchis ustulata** Burnt Orchid

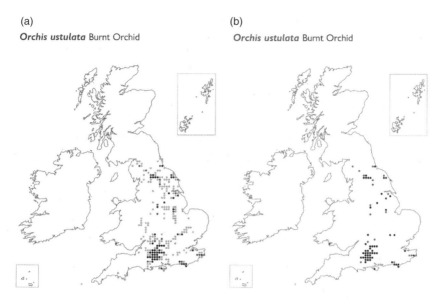

Figure 35.5 The distribution of the Burnt Orchid: (a) all records; (b) records since 1970, dark dots depicting extant sites, pale dots sites that have disappeared since 1987. (From Preston *et al*. 2002.)

and were often situated by drovers' roads. This meant that there was constant trampling, grazing and exposure of the mud. If the pond filled in, as a pond will if neglected, it would be dredged out again. Ponds now have no practical use, so most have been deliberately filled in as occupying space that could be more profitably used, and the remainder have filled in of their own accord.

Not surprisingly, there is a flora associated with the type of pond that used to be so common, and, also inevitably, that flora is in serious trouble. This is a flora that thrives on disturbance, and the only way to keep it is to do something that appears to be destructive. Plants concerned include the Starfruit, *Damasonium alisma*, Strapwort, *Corrigiola litoralis*, Pennyroyal, *Mentha pulegium*, Grass Poly, *Lythrum hyssopifolia*, Mudwort, *Limosella aquatica*, and Adderstongue Spearwort, *Ranunculus ophioglossifolius*. Some of these were always restricted in distribution, but all declined to critical levels and have only been saved by serious conservation efforts. A few, such as the Celery-leaved Buttercup, *Ranunculus sceleratus*, always commoner than those mentioned above, have suffered some losses, but have proved themselves more resilient. Most or all of these have a potentially long-lived seed bank, so can re-establish given the right conditions. One of Plantlife's first successes in their 'Back from the Brink' campaign was to clear vegetation from a pond known to have had Starfruit growing and finding the plant turning up again on its own after 27 years (Marren 1999).

Lakes, canals, riversides, marshes

Many of our larger lowland wetlands have suffered from a combination of eutrophication and lack of grazing that has led to increased density of vegetation. Tall plants of water margins, tolerant of this, have done well, such as Branched Bur-reed, *Sparganium erectum*, Bulrush (Reedmace), *Typha latifolia*, Yellow Flag, *Iris pseudacorus*, and Common Reed, *Phragmites australis*. It is, as ever, those vulnerable to competition that have declined. This includes common and widespread species like the Marsh Marigold or Kingcup, *Caltha palustris*, Wild Angelica, *Angelica sylvestris*, and Water Forget-me-not, *Myosotis scorpioides*, along with the more restricted Water Dropworts, *Oenanthe aquatica* and *O. fistulosa*, and Lesser Marshwort, *Apium inundatum*.

Of the truly aquatic plants, the picture is somewhat confused. There has been a big increase in the number of garden ponds in the last 30 years. Many natives have been planted as ornamentals or submerged oxygenating plants, as well as introduced plants. Sometimes these have been thrown out again into our waterways. Several neophytes have spread rapidly (Chapter 5). It appears that the floral composition of our waterways is quite dynamic, with species often being found in different places in subsequent years. That, coupled with poor recording of this difficult habitat, means that trends are hard to see. There have been some declines, such as the Frogbit, *Hydrocharis morsus-ranae*, and a few pondweeds, e.g. *Potamogeton praelongus*, *P. obtusifolius* and *P. acutifolius*. Eutrophication is the likely cause.

Woodlands

Broad-leaved lowland woods

We have utilised trees for so long, and encouraged some species at the expense of others, that their distributions have been gradually and irrevocably changed by human activity. For some species we cannot now distinguish where it is native and where planted or encouraged. Timber for construction and coppice for firewood are the main uses and these practices have led to a most distinctive habitat. Frequently woods are dominated by a single canopy tree species, often Oak, *Quercus robur*, or Beech, *Fagus sylvatica*, that is periodically felled. Coppice is often dominated by Hazel, *Corylus avellana*, Maple, *Acer campestre*, or other species which sprout vigorously from cut stools. Many woods have remained under woodland cover of some kind since 1600, most since long before that. They have been called 'ancient woods' by Oliver Rackham, who has made a comprehensive study of them over several decades (e.g. Rackham 2006).

Ancient woods may have a distinctive flora of 'indicator' plant species, though these indicators vary in different parts of the country. Some, such as Wood Melick, *Melica uniflora*, Woodruff, *Galium odoratum*, Wood Anemone, *Anemone nemorosa*, and Herb Paris, *Paris quadrifolia*, are widespread indicator species. The majority of these species are confined to ancient woods because they have very poor means of dispersal, mainly spreading through clonal growth. They can spread to any attached piece of recent woodland, but cannot cross a different habitat. Most of them thrive in coppice. It is also in coppice woods that some other characteristic and well-loved woodland plants such as the violets grow, especially Sweet Violet, *Viola odorata*, and Dog Violet, *V. riviniana*, Primroses, *Primula vulgaris*, and, most spectacularly, Bluebells, *Hyacinthoides non-scripta* (an ancient woodland indicator in some parts of the country). There are numerous others.

Ancient woods suffered some serious losses to agriculture in the early nineteenth century, but by 1945 the majority of the woods present in 1350, and many since the Domesday survey of 1086, were still extant. But between 1945 and 1975 about one-third of all remaining ancient woods were destroyed, more in some counties, for agriculture, housing, roads or, ironically, forestry (Rackham 1986). The woodland flora has completely disappeared from most of these places except in the odd corner.

Since about 1900, our woodlands have lost their traditional function. As a source of material for building houses, ships and other structures, trees have become largely irrelevant, and, equally, coppicing declined with the rise in fossil fuels and other materials for fencing etc. Remaining woods have not been used and have been neglected, so coppice has mostly grown out leading to a more continuous denser shade and a much less dense layer of low shrubs. In parallel, there has been huge increase in demand for pulp wood, and plantations are considered below.

Since 1980 many of the trends have been reversed. The ecological and amenity value of woodland in general, and ancient woodland in particular, has increasingly been appreciated, through the efforts of Oliver Rackham and others. Much is now protected in some form and in some places coppicing has been reintroduced, usually for conservation and amenity. Successive governments have encouraged forestry to adopt a stance with amenity and conservation in mind as well as a commercial crop. Some of the conifer plantings in ancient woods have been removed again, and these woods have a chance to recover at least some of their former flora. A greater variety of trees has been planted in new forests, including native species, especially Beech. Even Birch has been planted in places, though traditionally regarded with disdain by foresters as a weed. More notice is taken of the landscape value and rigid lines have been avoided.

Coinciding with all these changes has been a great increase in deer populations, spearheaded by the Muntjac in southern England, with Red or Fallow in some parts and increasingly including Roe almost everywhere. This has meant that grazing pressure has increased enormously in many woods. Grazing has always been a part of the woodland habitat, but these increases have resulted in much greater intensity than ever before. As a short-term measure Rackham (1986) has suggested that the best conservation measure for most woods is the simplest: three strands of barbed wire (Figure 35.6).

So what, with all these changes, has happened to the flora of our extant woods over this time? The answer is rather surprising: remarkably little. The great majority of species have survived, sometimes in rather reduced numbers or ground cover. But where some species do appear to have declined, such as the Early Purple Orchid, *Orchis*

Figure 35.6 The impact of grazing in an upland wood: a fence erected in 1965 excludes sheep from part of Wistman's wood on Dartmoor. Photograph taken in 2007.

mascula, Wood Spurge, *Euphorbia amygdaloides*, Goldilocks Buttercup, *Ranunculus auricomus*, and Great Bellflower, *Campanula latifolia*, Common Cow-wheat, *Melampyrum pratense*, and Wood Vetch, *Vicia sylvatica*, others have increased, such as the Tutsan, *Hypericum androsaemum*, Pendulous Sedge, *Carex pendula*, Stinking Iris, *Iris foetidissima*, probably all enhanced by garden escapes, and, more surprisingly, the parasitic Toothwort, *Lathraea squamaria*.

Many of the increases are of southern plants that appear to be spreading northwards. By contrast, several of those with a mainly northern distribution are not doing so well. The spectre of climate change again presents itself as a cause, but, actually, the main reasons appear to be those already mentioned – increase in shade, increased grazing pressure and perhaps eutrophication. If climate is important, the most likely determinant has been the succession of warm Januaries since the mid-1980s.

Caledonian pine forest

The native pinewoods of Scotland form one of our most distinctive habitats. Their flora, consisting of an outlying remnant of the great boreal forest flora, includes specialists such as the Twinflower, *Linnaea borealis*, Creeping Lady's Tresses, *Goodyera repens*, Chickweed Wintergreen, *Trientalis europaea*, and some true wintergreens, *Pyrola media* and *Moneses uniflora*, but otherwise is mainly similar to that of moorland. This genuine native Caledonian forest was slowly, but inexorably cleared throughout medieval times and up until about 1700, for timber, and then left to form open grazing land, usually heath. Clearance has been sporadic since 1700, and in places the forest has increased. Native pine forest now covers around 25 000 ha in total, much of it protected (Averis *et al.* 2004).

The pine is, in essence, a pioneer tree of rocky soils. Its specialist flora has shifted with it to an extent, but many of these plants are long-lived and can persist even long after the trees have been removed. There has been no significant change in the extent of the forest in the last 50 years (Rackham 2006), but regeneration is a problem in many places. The population of Red Deer is now much greater than it has probably ever been, and can prevent natural regeneration. Fenced areas in some nature reserves, as at the RSPB's Abernethy Forest, demonstrate this clearly. Goats and cattle, which have gone from the pinewoods, were the traditional browsers of Scotland, but at low intensity (Rackham 2006). The future for this habitat looks fairly secure at present.

Plantations

Dense plantations, almost entirely of introduced conifers, have become a prominent feature of much of the upland regions, including the National Parks. They are more limited in lowland areas, mainly to acid substrates, replacing lowland heath or acid grassland, but replacing some broad-leaved woods, including ancient woods.

These are generally considered to have a very poor flora and this is certainly true of a mature plantation, but in the early stages and by tracks and in clearings some plants do well. Most of these are widespread pioneer plants of many habitats, but there have been some more unusual plants that appear to have increased. Lesser Twayblade, *Listera cordata*, found most commonly on moorland, and Climbing Corydalis, *Ceratocapnos claviculata* (Figure 35.7), both appear to be colonising plantations in the north and west. Lesser Twayblade, in particular, is inconspicuous and this may simply be better recording. Stagshorn Clubmoss, *Lycopodium clavatum*, and Sand Spurrey, *Spergularia rubra*, seem to have become almost specialist at colonising forestry tracks, and the sedge, *Carex binervis*, also colonises these well. Some pinewood specialists have, rarely, colonised conifer plantations, e.g. Creeping Lady's Tresses in Norfolk.

Since the 1980s there has been a greater awareness of the role that forestry has in conservation and as an amenity (see 'Moorland, bog and montane habitats'). This has led to a greater variety of species being planted, including broad-leaved and native species, more spaces and a sensitivity to the landscape value. The result has been that these plantations have a richer flora than the earlier dense squares of Sitka Spruce or Douglas Fir.

Lowland heathland, acid grassland and related habitat

The decline of lowland heath since 1800 is well known (Moore 1962). That decline and its associated acid grassland continued right up until 1985, with many losses to

Figure 35.7 Climbing Corydalis, a plant that is increasing with the increase in forestry.

agriculture and some to forestry, roads and housing. Most lowland heaths were once common land, used, especially in winter, for grazing of cattle and other livestock. This traditional use has mainly vanished and some of the remaining heath has lost much of its variety and species richness, owing to a reduced level or cessation of grazing. Scrub or trees have regenerated. Some of the wetter areas have been drained. Eutrophication, including run-off from nearby sites and perhaps from nitrogen-rich rain, is likely to be a particular problem in these habitats. They are fundamentally nutrient poor. Losses of heath to Bracken, *Pteridium aquilinum*, so serious in the early twentieth century, were probably associated with lower numbers of cattle. They can trample emerging fronds and bracken can be collected as bedding. Bracken appears now to be stable.

The picture for the plants is one of almost universal decline. Most of the character-istic species are becoming much rarer. Our three common heathers themselves: Ling, *Calluna vulgaris*, Bell, *Erica cinerea*, and Cross-leaved, *E. tetralix*, all show losses, but some of their once common associates are doing even less well. Lousewort, *Pedicularis sylvatica*, Golden Rod, *Solidago virgaurea*, Heath Bedstraw, *Galium saxatile*, Tormentil, *Potentilla erecta*, and several others all are victims, especially in the south where the habitat has become more and more fragmented. Even the abun-dant Sheep's Sorrel, *Rumex acetosella*, has declined steeply. There has been a similar decline of some rarities, such as the spectacular Marsh Gentian, *Gentiana pneumonan-the*, again throughout its range. This plant suffers particularly from a lack of grazing. It has disappeared completely from many of its northern and eastern sites. The New

Forest, happily, now has full protected status and forms probably the most important and extensive area of lowland heathland in Europe (around 13 500 ha of heath plus 1500 ha of valley mire).

The dry Breckland grass-heaths of inland East Anglia have a unique flora within Britain with affinities to eastern Europe. The great losses to housing, agriculture and forestry that occurred in the early twentieth century have now mainly ceased. The remaining few sites with a rich flora all have some form of protection though there still may be some changes, e.g. the return of intensive rabbit grazing appears to have led to a decline in Spanish Catchfly, *Silene otites*, and Field Wormwood, *Artemisia campestris*, but an increase in Breckland Thyme, *Thymus serpyllum*, and Spring Speedwell, *Veronica verna*.

Moorland, bog and montane habitats

It is easy to forget that around 30% of the land area of the British Isles is upland, as it houses less than 1% of the human population. The majority of this is moorland, dominated by heather or grasses, or bog habitats, both of which are particularly well represented in these islands. The most characteristic of all is heather moorland, described aptly by A.S. Watt as 'at once the glory and the tragedy of the Scottish Highlands' (Gimingham 1972). It occurs thoughout the uplands and is managed by grazing and/or periodic burning for Grouse. Without this, the great majority would eventually become some form of woodland, though this would probably take centuries in many areas. Botanically it is poor; besides the Ling (and sometimes other heaths) the only common vascular plants are Bilberry, *Vaccinium myrtillus*, Cowberry, *V. vitis-idaea*, Crowberry, *Empetrum nigrum*, and one or two grasses such as Wavy Hair-grass, *Deschampsia flexuosa*. A number of bryophytes and lichens can form a thick ground cover. Its glory is the purple carpet of flowering heather in late summer. With intensive grazing, or burning that is either too frequent or too hot, it becomes a heather/grass mixture and eventually grassland, and loses its bryophytes. This is what has happened over large areas of Wales and the Pennines within the last 50 years (Averis *et al.* 2004). Many grouse moors would be botanically richer if they were burned less frequently.

Upland grassland has expanded. This may be dominated by Wavy Hair-grass or, in the richer spots, Sheep's Fescue, *Festuca ovina*, and Common Bent, *Agrostis capillaris*, much liked by hill sheep farmers. In the most heavily grazed places, the unpalatable Mat Grass, *Nardus stricta*, takes over. Recent years have seen a marked increase in these habitats (Averis *et al.* 2004). Their associated flora is normally very limited, often with only Tormentil, *Potentilla erecta*, Heath Bedstraw, *Galium saxatile*, and, in places, Bilberry, being common, except in the wet flushes or other places with a rich soil.

Bogs are a special feature of the British Isles, and probably represent a climax or at least very long-lasting vegetation type. Averis *et al.* (2004) estimated that around 13% of the blanket bog of the world occurs in the British Isles. Here bryophytes, especially *Sphagnum* species, dominate, and many other bryophytes occur. Loss of bogs means that these plants, in particular, suffer, along with breeding Dunlin and Greenshank (Chapter 17). A few vascular plants are closely associated with bogs too, such as Bog Rosemary, *Andromeda polifolia*, Dwarf Birch, *Betula nana*, Cloudberry, *Rubus chamaemorus*, and Dwarf Cornel, *Cornus suecica*, as well as the common heathers and grasses of the uplands. We have lost 21% of our bogs since the 1940s (Averis *et al.* 2004), through drainage, sometimes for commercial peat cutting or through drainage of adjacent land and forestry. Some of the rest has degraded through over-grazing or burning, becoming dominated often by cotton-grasses, *Eriophorum angustifolium* and *E. vaginatum*, or Purple Moor-grass, *Molinia caerulea*, but with few other species. Bogs occur in places with a cool climate and are nutrient-poor. Growth will be slow. Industrial pollution affected the southern Pennines, killing large areas of *Sphagnum* bog in the nineteenth century and these have never fully recovered. All of these changes have reduced the plant diversity. The southern parts of the habitats' range have been worst hit.

Plantation forestry has been responsible for half the losses of bog. This reached a head in the 1980s with the planting up of parts of the boggy 'Flow' country in northernmost mainland Scotland, as a tax-dodge by the rich. These plantations were both damaging and singularly inappropriate. Many have been removed again. Bogs and moorland are recolonising slowly. The furore led directly to the break-up of the Nature Conservancy Council, but, more positively, to the realisation that forestry needed to be more sensitively managed with wildlife in mind.

Some characteristic species have retreated northwards, such as the Butterwort, *Pinguicula vulgaris*, Deer-sedge, *Trichophorum cespitosum*, and Cotton-grass, *Eriophorum angustifolium*, though the last two of these have thrived on the overgrazed parts of Scotland. Oblong-leaved Sundew, *Drosera intermedia*, Lesser Spearwort, *Ranunculus flammula*, and Marsh Violet, *Viola palustris*, have declined throughout, and these last, in particular, suggest that there has been a general rise in nutrient levels throughout the country. This stems from adjacent land use to these sites, such as forestry, but some probably coming in the rain.

The celebrated 'arctic-alpines'[5] in the highest montane areas appear to have seen little change except around the edges, mainly at their southern extremes in the Pennines and parts of Wales. A few declines are apparent, such as Purple Saxifrage, *Saxifraga oppositifolia*, and Bladder Fern, *Cystopteris fragilis*, but the reason is not clear. Perhaps these really are ascribable to climatic warming. But grazing levels, by sheep and, in places, deer have increased and some plants may be becoming more confined to inaccessible rocks and cliffs. This especially applies to upland willow scrub dominated by the Downy or Mountain Willows, *Salix lapponum* and *S. arbuscula* (occasionally other species). These can be rich in plant species and form extensive stands in Scandinavia. They could do in this country in favoured localities such as Ben Lawers and Caenlochan in the Grampians. These Nature Reserves have some exclosures where this rare habitat is increasing in the absence of grazing (Averis *et al.* 2004).

---

[5] The 'arctic-montane element' of Preston and Hill (1997), comprising about 60 species.

In general, our uplands have the opposite problem from the lowlands – they are over-grazed. This is now almost entirely by sheep and, in places, deer. Formerly it was more varied, including cattle and goats too and the loss of these has contributed to the more uniform over-grazing. Our upland habitats are maintained by light grazing, and the occasional fire, so there is a real management problem here. If there is no grazing, the smaller plants and bryophytes disappear, as they do in the lowlands.

Coasts

Our coasts are the most obvious habitats to be threatened by rising sea levels. Erosion on the east coast of England has been widely documented and some areas in Essex and elsewhere have been left to the rising sea. We will see more of this. But our salt-marshes and sand dunes remain as sea barriers. By their very nature they are dynamic habitats, either advancing or eroding all the time. They may be able to keep pace with the changes. Sand-dune erosion is still a problem at popular beaches and pressure from large numbers of people can stop any further seawards expansion of dune systems and erode existing dunes. Measures are in place on many dunes to limit erosion. The biggest problem on sand dunes is, yet again, grazing. Dunes are the classic localities for rabbits and many names indicate this, such as Braunton Burrows in Devon or Newborough Warren on Anglesey. Some dune systems have a large rabbit population; on some it is small or non-existent. Where there is no grazing, vegetation often becomes dense with tall coarse grasses, shrubs or trees shading out the smaller vegetation. In places, including some Nature Reserves, domestic grazing animals, often goats, are introduced to dune systems especially where scrub such as brambles, *Rubus* spp., bushy willows, *Salix* spp., Sea Buckthorn, *Hippophae rhamnoides*, or other species, are spreading, to the detriment of the smaller plants.

Some characteristic plants of sand dunes and, especially, dune slacks are low growing, such as the Knotted Pearlwort, *Sagina nodosa*, and Seaside Centaury, *Centaurium littorale*, both distributed quite widely on northern dune systems, but declining with the decline in grazing. In south Wales, two rare dune plants, the Fen Orchid, *Liparis loeselii*, and the Dune Gentian, *Gentianella uliginosa*, can only persist where the dune slacks are grazed.

Cliffs and salt marshes are generally not under any particular pressure, though prior to 1930, some salt marshes were claimed for agriculture. Most saltmarshes are not grazed to any significant extent, but a few, such as the huge saltmarsh that lines the north coast of Gower in south Wales, and some other western saltmarshes, are grazed heavily. There has been little change in plant distribution. Some cliff edges have become overgrown with brambles with the decline of grazing, where arable land extends to near the cliff edge.

Many of our coastal plants are pioneers, and all our coastal habitats are prone to erosion or accretion or both. This newly created habitat gives them an opportunity to colonise. In overall distribution there appears to be little change in most of our coastal plants, except for the inland colonisation along roadsides (see 'Salt-tolerant plants by roads').

Gardens, built-up areas and ruderal sites

The extent of these habitats has, clearly, increased hugely over the last 50 years and continues to expand. In addition to simple expansion, there have been some changes in fashion in gardening and parkland that have had an effect on our plants:

1. Large areas of re-development have imported topsoil or seed mixes, allowing transfer of seeds, sometimes over long distances.
2. There has become increasing emphasis on natural-looking ornamental parks and gardens with low maintenance.
3. There has been a decline in intensive gardening, especially for vegetables.
4. The burgeoning success of garden centres has further allowed weeds to spread.
5. Towns have become warmer, larger and with more sheltered places for tender plants to survive.
6. Many new plants have been introduced and have spread. These are not considered here, but see Chapter 5.

As expected, many plants characteristic of this habitat have shown a marked increase, and the habitat has shown distinct increases in a number of archaeophytes, including Caper and Sun Spurges, *Euphorbia lathyris* and *E. helioscopia*, Feverfew, *Tanacetum parthenium*, Wall Barley, *Hordeum murinum* and Annual Mercury, *Mercurialis annua*, in contrast to the decline of many archaeophytes in agricultural land. Some smaller weeds have also increased, e.g. Slender Trefoil, *Trifolium micranthum*, two cranesbills, *Geranium rotundifolium* and *G. lucidum*, Annual Pearlwort, *Sagina apetala*, and Ivy-leaved Speedwell, *Veronica hederifolia* (another archaeophyte), and a whole collection of neophytes (see Chapter 5). Some of these are mainly southern and have undoubtedly been favoured by a run of mild winters and perhaps by some summer droughts, as well as the expansion of their habitat.

By roads, railways and other ruderal habitats, many of the same plants have increased, with some additional species, again including some archaeophytes: Mugwort, *Artemisia vulgaris*, Common and Dwarf Mallows, *Malva sylvestris* and *M. neglecta*, Prickly Lettuce, *Lactuca serriola*, with its native congener Great Lettuce, *L. virosa*, and Perennial Wall-rocket, *Diplotaxis tenuifolia*. Spread of several species on roadsides has been enhanced by the fashion for planting seed mixes (Chapter 5).

The importance of roadsides for wildlife has been recognised increasingly, and some have a range of plants that do not occur in the country around them. The abundant Meadow Cranesbill, *Geranium pratense*, on limestone roadsides in the Cotswolds and the Derbyshire dales is just one spectacularly beautiful example. When the final stretch of the M40, between Wheatley and Bicester in Oxfordshire, was being proposed in the mid-1980s, the nature conservation organisations stated that it would lead to improved habitat for wildlife on the verges compared with the existing agricultural land. There are now some roadside nature reserves.

Salt-tolerant plants by roads

One addition to our roadside flora has been the extraordinary spread of a few salt-tolerant plants, taking advantage of the widespread salting of our major roads that began in the mid-1960s. This has happened throughout, except in southern Ireland where salt is not used. It is most prominent on dual carriageways, but occurs on some single-track main roads too. The plants usually form a narrow belt, up to 3 m wide, immediately adjacent to the carriageway. In the vanguard was the Reflexed Saltmarsh-grass, *Puccinellia distans*, first reported in around 1970. It is now common by roads in eastern England (Scott and Davison 1982). This has been followed by the most obvious colonist, the Danish Scurvy-grass, *Cochlearia danica*. Until 1980, this annual plant was strictly coastal, growing commonly in bare places on cliff tops, rocks and sand dunes, and in coastal towns. Its slightly pinkish white flowers can now be seen in abundance in early spring along many roads, mainly in England, in places as mono-specific stands (Figure 35.8). In northern England and Scotland, Lesser Sea Spurrey, *Spergularia marina*, has colonised similarly and in eastern England the Grass-leaved Orache, *Atriplex littoralis*. Several other species have been recorded more rarely, such as two other *Puccinellia* species, Sea and Buckshorn Plantains, *Plantago maritima* and *P. coronopus*, Common Scurvy-grass, *Cochlearia officinalis*, Greater Sea spurrey, *Spergularia media*, and Sea Pearlwort, *Sagina maritima*. Yet others seem to have appeared briefly but gone again (Scott and Davison 1982). It is likely that a number

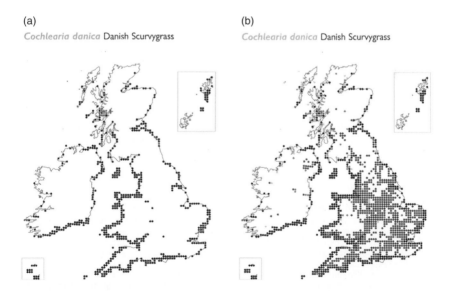

(a)
Cochlearia danica Danish Scurvygrass

(b)
Cochlearia danica Danish Scurvygrass

Figure 35.8 The distribution of Danish Scurvy-grass: (a) before 1980; (b) by 2002. (From Preston *et al.* 2002.)

of other, partially salt-tolerant, but widespread, species have taken advantage too, e.g. other oraches, *Atriplex* spp., Scentless Mayweed, *Tripleurospermum inodorum*, and Groundsel, *Senecio vulgaris*. It will be fascinating to see what happens to this changeable situation in the next few years.

Archaeophyte herbs

A major group of archaeophytes is pot herbs introduced for culinary or medicinal use. These have fared much better than the arable weeds, as they were mainly grown near habitation and spread from there. Many of these have held their ground, such as Horseradish, *Armoracia rusticana*, Greater Celandine, *Chelidonium majus*, and Hemlock, *Conium maculatum*. A few have been gradually declining, such as Good King Henry,[6] *Chenopodium bonus-henricus*, Chicory, *Cichorium intybus,* Elecampane, *Inula helenium*, and Henbane, *Hyoscyamus niger*, but equally some have increased, e.g. those on roadsides (see 'Gardens, built-up areas and ruderal sites') and Alexanders, *Smyrnium olusatrum*, appears to be spreading from its largely coastal distribution (not just on roadsides, so probably not associated with salt tolerance). The abundance and persistence of Ground Elder, *Aegopodium podagraria*, will be well known to many a gardener.

A word about endemics

There are some species endemic to the British Isles. These are, without exception, either apomictic 'microspecies' or are derived by some form of rapid evolution, most either by hybridisation or persistent self-fertilisation, from more widespread species. Nearly all are normally self-fertilising or apomictic and are likely to have formed within the last 5000 years, perhaps considerably less. The apomicts all belong to the genera *Hieracium* (Hawkweed), *Taraxacum* (Dandelion), *Rubus* (Bramble), *Sorbus* (Whitebeam), *Alchemilla* (Lady's Mantle) or *Limonium* (Sea-lavender).[7] Among the others are a few celebrated species: the Scottish Primrose, *Primula scotica*, Early Gentian, *Gentianella anglica*, and the Isle of Man and Lundy Cabbages, *Coincya monensis* ssp. *monensis* and *C. wrightii*.[8] There are also two helleborines, *Epipactis*

---

[6] This curious name derives from the German 'Good-Henry', their equivalent of our mischievous sprite, Robin Goodfellow. The 'King' is an English addition, presumably sycophantic.

[7] The apomictic species are normally formed from hybridisation between two (or sometimes more) sexual species. These hybrids are infertile, often because of differences in ploidy level, but can produce seeds without fertilisation. Each is then a clone with no genetic variation and has defining characters, though the differences are often tiny. Numbers of micro-species described from the British Isles are: *Hieracium* 262, *Taraxacum* 229, *Rubus* 320, *Sorbus* 18, but more being added (Rich and Proctor 2009), *Alchemilla* 12, *Limonium c.* 12. The majority are endemic except in *Alchemilla* (one endemic only). There are other apomictic groups that have not been fully studied, e.g. Goldilocks Buttercup, *Ranunculus auricomus*, meadow-grasses, *Poa* spp., perhaps the elms, *Ulmus* spp. that spread vegetatively, and others.

[8] Recent molecular work by Dr S. Compton at Leeds (personal communication) has suggested that populations of these two 'species' in south Wales and Lundy are very closely related, but that *Coincya m. monensis* populations in north-west England may be more distant. What is now called *C. monensis* ssp. *cheiranthos*, an established alien in Britain, seems to be entirely separate. Taxonomic revision is clearly needed.

dunensis and *E. sancta*, three marsh orchids, *Dactylorhiza traunsteinerioides*, *D. ebudensis* and *D. occidentalis*, Shetland Mouse-ear, *Cerastium nigrescens*, Mountain Scurvy-grass, *Cochlearia micacea*, two grasses, Interrupted Brome, *Bromus interruptus*, and Scottish Small-reed, *Calamagrostis scotica*, nine eyebright species, *Euphrasia*, Western Fumitory, *Fumaria occidentalis*, and perhaps the 'wild' Cotoneaster, *Cotoneaster cambricus* (*integerrimus*), though that may well be of garden origin. Almost all are restricted in range, most to coasts or hills, and several have only a handful of plants.

There have been some serious conservation efforts on behalf of, for example, the Bristol Whitebeam, *Sorbus bristoliensis*, and the Lundy Cabbage (clearance of invading shrubs such as rhododendron), but most are regarded as stable in distribution. A few new endemics have derived from introductions, considered in Chapter 5. As species, the great majority at least must be considered of marginal importance.

The British orchids

As an overall monitor on the situation with our flora let us take a look at all members of one family, the Orchidaceae (Table 35.1). Orchids have always been the most glamorous members of our flora, with their exotic flowers, peculiar pollination mechanism, their rather exacting requirements and perceived rarity. The Military Orchid even has the extraordinary distinction of appearing as a pin-up – a large photograph on Page 3 of the *Daily Mirror* on 11 June 1975 with the headline 'The Beauty that Must Blossom in Secret'. The Orchidaceae is the world's most species-rich family, the great majority of them being tropical. They have a special status in peoples' imaginations. Several books have been written about British orchids, e.g. Foley and Clarke (2005) from which much of the information here is taken.

It is an appropriate family to illustrate all the losses, gains and problems that are happening in our flora as a whole, because:

1. For the reasons outlined above, they are among our best-known plants.
2. It is a large family in Britain, with about 55 species and, although many are famously rare, some are common. Members of the family occur throughout the British Isles in almost all habitats.
3. One speciality of orchids, not shared with many families, is their tiny wind-blown seeds that can disperse widely. These allow many of them to colonise sites readily if conditions are suitable. This, and the fussy requirements of some, means that they can act as early warning for habitat change – the 'miners' canaries' of the flora.

The popularity of orchids has resulted in some fairly extreme conservation measures for the rarities, such as covering each plant with wire netting (Figure 35.9) and having a volunteer warden in a caravan guarding them round the clock. The best-known example is the spectacular Lady's Slipper, *Cypripedium calceolus*. This did once occur in a

Table 35.1 *The wild British orchids and their status. (Summarised mainly from Preston et al. (2002), Foley and Clarke (2005) and Braithwaite et al. (2006).)*

Species	Distribution	Habitat	1700–1945	Status, 1945–present
Lady's Slipper, *Cypripedium calceolus*	Northern England, one site	Semi-shaded limestone woods and scree	Massive losses to collecting and habitat loss	Declined to one individual. Propagation *in vitro* (see text)
Red Helleborine, *Cephalanthera rubra*	Southern England, three sites	Beechwoods with sparse ground flora on calcareous soils	Unknown	Few individuals. Protected, stable
Narrow-leaved Helleborine, *C. longifolia*	Widespread, but very local	Open woods on calcareous soils	Big losses with wood disturbance, especially in north	Stable or decreasing; declines with too much or too little shade
White Helleborine, *C. damasonium*	Southern England, locally common	Lightly shaded Beechwoods on calcareous soils	Unknown	Decline with wood clearance. Now stable and colonising new Beech
Lesser Twayblade, *Neottia (Listera) cordata*	Scotland, northern England, northern Wales	Heavy shade under heather or woods; acid soils	Decline in lowlands with habitat loss	Stable or increasing, e.g. in conifer plantations
Common Twayblade, *N. (L.) ovata*	Widespread, common	Mainly woodland, plus pasture, dune slacks and pioneer sites	Apparently stable	Stable, may colonise new sites
Birdnest Orchid, *N. nidus-avis*	Widespread, very scattered	Woods, mainly beech on calcareous soils. Often in deep shade	Big decline with woodland disruption	Decline with coniferisation. Now erratic, but generally stable
Marsh Helleborine, *Epipactis palustris*	Widespread except in Scotland	Marshes and dune slacks, mainly calcareous	Large losses to drainage, especially inland	Stable
Dark Red Helleborine, *E. atrorubens*	Northern and western, limestone	Confined to exposed limestone, especially pavement	Unknown	Mainly stable. Small declines with quarrying
Broad-leaved Helleborine, *E. helleborine*	Widespread, frequent	Mainly calcareous woodland, but colonises gardens, quarries etc.	Some losses with wood clearance	Stable
Violet Helleborine, *E. purpurata*	Southern England, local	Deep shade, mainly in calcareous Beechwoods	Some losses with wood clearance	Stable

Species	Distribution	Habitat	Losses/Reason	Status
Narrow-lipped Helleborine, *E. leptochila*	Southern England; isolated north to central Scotland	Shady Beechwoods on calcareous soils; metal spoil	Some losses with wood clearance	Stable
Green-flowered Helleborine, *E. phyllanthes*	England, local, mainly southern	Shady woods and scrub, acid and calcareous	Unknown	Decline in south with wood clearance; increase in north
Dune Helleborine, *E. dunensis*	Endemic; dunes in north-west England and by River Tyne	Dune slacks and river gravel with birch	Unknown	Stable, though vulnerable. Recent segregant species
Lindisfarne Helleborine, *E. sancta*	Endemic to Lindisfarne	Dune slacks	Unknown	Stable. Recent segregant species
Ghost Orchid, *Epipogium aphyllum*	Chilterns; formerly Herefordshire, Shropshire	Deep shade in Beechwoods	Lost from western sites. Reason?	Rarely seen and ?extinct (see text)
Fen Orchid, *Liparis loeselii*	Norfolk, south Wales, rare	Fens and dune slacks	Big losses, especially East Anglia, to drainage	Mainly stable, but some losses (see text)
Bog Orchid, *Hammarbya paludosa*	Widespread, but very local	Acid *Sphagnum* bogs and peat	Big losses from drainage, especially eastern England	Most now stable
Coralroot Orchid, *Corallorhiza trifida*	Eastern Scotland, northern England	Wet, mossy woods and dune slacks	Unknown	Stable
Creeping Lady's Tresses, *Goodyera repens*	Scotland, northern England, Norfolk	Mature Pinewoods	Stable or small decline	Largely stable, but Norfolk sites are new colonies, ?natural dispersal
Irish Lady's Tresses, *Spiranthes romanzoffiana*	Western Ireland, western Scotland, very local	Wet grassland and bog	Unknown	Erratic, probably stable, though a few sites lost to drainage
Autumn Lady's Tresses, *S. spiralis*	England and Wales, mainly southern, locally common	Short turf, mainly calcareous and coastal	Big losses to arable and eutrophication	Still decreasing inland from under-grazing

Table 35.1 (cont.)

Species	Distribution	Habitat	1700–1945	Status, 1945–present
Summer Lady's Tresses, *S. aestivalis*	Formerly New Forest and Channel Isles	*Sphagnum* bog and wet turf	Large losses to collecting and drainage	Last seen in 1959 (see text)
Musk Orchid, *Herminium monorchis*	Southern England, mainly eastern, very local	Short calcareous grassland	Big losses, especially Norfolk, to arable and grazing changes	Small declines with under-grazing. Some colonisation
Man Orchid, *Orchis (Aceras) anthropophora*	South-east England, mainly Kent	Calcareous grassland, disturbed land and semi-shade	Losses to arable and eutrophication; erratic	Decline with excessive or too little grazing, landfill in quarries etc.
Monkey Orchid, *Orchis simia*	Three sites, Kent and Oxon; occasional elsewhere	Warm calcareous grassland	Large decline to arable and grazing changes	Increasing with management (see text)
Military Orchid, *O. militaris*	Two/three sites, Buckinghamshire and Suffolk	Dry calcareous grassland and light scrub	Large decline to grazing changes and collecting	Increasing with management (see text).
Lady Orchid, *O. purpurea*	Kent; occasional elsewhere	Dry calcareous open woodland	Some losses	Stable
Early Purple Orchid, *O. mascula*	Widespread, common	Woodland, grassland etc., especially on calcareous soils	Stable	Declines with increased shade, grazing and eutrophication
Small White Orchid, *Pseudorchis albida*	Northern and western, local	Upland acidic pastures	Large declines: habitat loss and under-grazing	Continuing loss from 'improvement', especially Ireland, northern England
Lesser Butterfly Orchid, *Platanthera bifolia*	Widespread, mainly western	Damp upland pasture and flushes. Beech woodland in southern England	Many losses to drainage, woodland disturbance etc.	Declining: uniform moor management and eutrophication

Species	Distribution	Habitat	Losses	Status
Greater Butterfly Orchid, *P. chlorantha*	Widespread, especially southern England, western Scotland	Damp mainly calcareous woods; pastures	Losses to conifers and other woodland disturbance	Declining: excess shade and eutrophication
Fragrant Orchid, *Gymnadenia conopsea s.l.*	Widespread, common in places	Calcareous grassland, mires and upland pasture	Losses to arable and eutrophication	Stable
Early Marsh Orchid, *Dactylorhiza incarnata*	Widespread, frequent; occurs in many forms	Calcareous fens, upland flushes, dune slacks	Losses from drainage	Continuing losses from drainage
Frog Orchid, *D. (Coeloglossum) viride*	Widespread, local	Short grassland, especially calcareous, dunes, upland flushes	Big losses, especially central England to arable and eutrophication	Mainly stable; small declines
Common Spotted Orchid, *D. fuchsii*	Widespread, common	Base-rich to neutral grassland, wood edge, marshes etc.	Stable	Stable, perhaps increasing as often colonises new sites
Heath Spotted Orchid, *D. maculata*	Widespread, common in north and west	Acid marshes and peat	Losses in lowlands to drainage	Mainly stable; a few continuing drainage losses
Southern Marsh Orchid, *D. praetermissa*	Southern England and Wales, locally common	Calcareous fens, wet grassland, dune slacks	?possible losses through drainage	Stable or increasing as colonises well
Narrow-leaved Marsh Orchid, *D. traunsteinerioides*	Endemic. Widespread, but very local	Calcareous flushes and fens	Losses through reduced water table	Stable
Hebridean Marsh Orchid, *D. ebudensis*	Endemic. North Uist only, c. 2000 plants	Machair (dune grassland)	Unknown	Stable
Northern Marsh Orchid, *D. purpurella*	Scotland, Wales, northern England, Northern Ireland	Base-rich or neutral wet grassland and flushes	Unknown	Stable, perhaps increasing as often colonises new sites
Irish Marsh Orchid, *D. occidentalis*	Endemic to Ireland; scattered throughout	Marshes, damp grassland	Unknown	Stable
Dense-flowered Orchid, *Neotinea maculata*	Western Ireland, formerly Isle of Man	Short calcareous grassland	Unknown	Stable in Ireland. Isle of Man found 1966, extinct 1986

Table 35.1 (cont.)

Species	Distribution	Habitat	1700–1945	Status, 1945–present
Burnt Orchid, N. (Orchis) ustulata	England north to Scottish border, very local	Short calcareous grassland, mainly south-facing	Large declines with habitat loss	Seriously declining; ploughing and cessation of grazing
Lizard Orchid, Himantoglossum hircinum	South-east England, scattered and erratic	Tall calcareous grassland and light scrub	Increase to 1930 then decline	Erratic appearance; slight increase since 1980
Loose-flowered Orchid, Anacamptis (Orchis) laxiflora	Jersey and Guernsey only	Wet meadows	Decline to drainage, housing, eutrophication	Continuing decline to 1970. Now stable in nature reserves
Pyramidal Orchid, A. pyramidalis	Widespread, mainly southern, common in places	Calcareous grassland and ruderal habitats	?possible losses to agriculture	Increasing especially in ruderal sites
Green-winged Orchid, A. (Orchis) morio	Widespread in England and Wales, local Ireland	Calcareous grassland; 'unimproved' meadows	Some losses to agriculture	Large losses to agricultural 'improvement'; stable since c. 1985
Tongue Orchids, Serapias spp.	Recent colonists, Cornwall, Devon, Kent, Guernsey	Grassland	Not applicable	New colonies (see text)
Fly Orchid, Ophrys insectifera	England, mainly south-east, local	Calcareous woods, scrub and occasionally pasture or fen	Big losses, especially East Anglia, to shade and disturbance	Decline with tree felling, disturbance and eutrophication, but erratic
Bee Orchid, O. apifera	Widespread in England; local Wales, Ireland	Dry calcareous grassland and ruderal habitats; light woodland	Some declines, mainly to arable	Increasing especially in north and west and on roadsides, quarries etc.
Late Spider Orchid, O. fuciflora	South-east Kent only, five sites	Short, dry chalk grassland	Declines with ploughing and grazing changes	Stable or slow increase; all sites are managed for it
Early Spider Orchid, O. sphegodes	South and south-east England, rare	Short calcareous grassland, often coastal	Huge declines, many inland sites to extinction	Stable; most sites protected and managed

Figure 35.9 A wild Military Orchid in a numbered cage, Buckinghamshire. Such intensive conservation measures may have saved some of our rarest plants.

number of places on the limestones of northern England. Over-collecting in the nineteenth century extinguished it from all but one colony, and this went down to a single individual. Since 1992 there have been some attempts at laboratory propagation of the last remaining British material. From this, plants have been reintroduced to the extant site and other suitable sites. It is a long-lived species that can take 10 years to flower, so it is early days yet. Some gardens may still have remnants of native stock.

The Military Orchid, *Orchis militaris*, and the Monkey Orchid, *Orchis simia*, have had similar, but more successful, conservation measures. The Military was considered extinct in Britain until re-found in 1947. The Monkey was reduced to a single Oxfordshire site but then was re-found in Kent in 1955. These populations consisted of just a few individuals in two or three sites. Since then both have increased considerably of their own accord as better conditions are now provided for them, mainly to do with more appropriate grazing regimes. One of the Military's sites is an abandoned quarry in Suffolk, where it was first found in 1954. This has affinities with continental Military Orchids and must be the result of long-distance colonisation.

One of our tallest and most dramatic orchids, the Lizard, *Himantoglossum hircinum*, has a habit of colonising odd places. It is rare, but can turn up, sometimes in numbers, as it did in the 1990s at Sandwich in Kent. It can disappear again equally quickly.

The diminutive and endangered Fen Orchid, *Liparis loeselii*, can, frustratingly, do a similar thing: it colonises new dune slacks, but disappears again when the vegetation gets thicker. It was found outside its present range at Braunton Burrows in Devon in 1966, but had gone 20 years later (Foley and Clarke 2005). A similar brief visit was made to Crymlyn Burrows near Swansea in the late 1970s and early 1980s. Grazing of the slacks can prolong its stay.

One orchid species has disappeared from our flora in the last 50 years. The Summer Lady's Tresses, *Spiranthes aestivalis*, had sites in the New Forest and in the Channel Islands. Drainage and collecting had diminished the populations and the last record was in 1959 from a New Forest bog that was being drained. Another possibly extinct species, the Ghost Orchid, *Epipogium aphyllum*, was last definitely seen in 1986, but reports from the 1990s suggest that it is still around. It has no green parts, being entirely dependent on its mycorrhizal fungi, and has always been rare and a sporadic flowerer. It occurs under Beech or occasionally Oak, mainly in the Chilterns. It only appears above ground when in flower, so it is possible that it will be found again.

Happily, one orchid, of a genus not previously occurring in the British flora, appears to have colonised Britain. It almost certainly came through natural wind-blown seed, though deliberate or accidental introduction remains a possibility. The Small-flowered or Lesser Tongue Orchid, *Serapias parviflora*, turned up by the south Cornish coast in 1989, since when a few individuals have flowered there intermittently. Some seed has been collected from the site and the population augmented. Astonishingly, there has followed a short spate of other tongue orchid records: a single plant of its close relative, *Serapias lingua*, was found in Guernsey in 1992 and then another single *S. lingua* in Devon in 1998, and in 1996, two individuals of yet another species, *Serapias cordigera*, turned up in Kent (Marren 1999). These two species have disappeared again. Though doubts are expressed as to their 'natural' status, all three species occur only just over the channel and orchid seeds are very light. These and other orchids could well colonise these islands if the heat really is turned up, as is so constantly threatened.

Conclusion and the future

Great changes are likely to continue, and what will happen with increased climate change remains almost impossible to predict. Even assuming that this effect will be quite small, we can be sure that there are habitats and species that are unlikely ever to return to what they were like in 1945. This is partly from the increasing pressure for living space and food from a burgeoning and more demanding population. We will have to accept that much of the remaining rich habitat, especially in the lowlands, is under some form of preservation order, maintaining it as an exhibit rather than as a working landscape. Many conserved areas are small, and sensitive management may be difficult or impossible for all species. Particular requirements are often not known adequately. Ideally we should conserve enough of our remaining flora for evolution to happen. Plants hybridise frequently and these can give rise to new species; the flora of these islands, as of everywhere, is never static and can never be a museum piece.

Grazing, either too much or too little, is the biggest single issue facing so many of our habitats, and problems connected with grazing are likely to continue as the main cause of decline in many plants. Under-grazing remains a most difficult problem in almost all lowland grassland, coastal and heathland sites. Grazing by domestic animals away from arable land and fertilised pasture has disappeared over most of the lowlands. Rabbits that had taken their place have only re-colonised locally after myxomatosis. Grazing has been reintroduced in a controlled way on some grasslands, often with ancient breeds, but there remains a particular problem with numerous sites, especially the small sites. By contrast, in woods and throughout upland habitats over-grazing is frequently a problem, either by sheep or by the increasing deer population.

On the plus side, it does seem that conservation measures that have now been in place for 20–25 years have borne fruit. There are several encouraging changes for our flora. The destruction of woods and hedgerows and the huge losses in species diversity in almost all our lowland habitats have ceased since about 1985. With the gradual decline in subsidy for agriculture, marginal land is going back out of production. Some is uneconomic without subsidised inputs and more has been 'Set-Aside'. There have been some encouraging noises about sustainable agricultural systems, and sustainability nearly always means a greater variety of wildlife too. Some of our arable fields are beginning to look colourful again on the margins, sometimes enhanced by seed mixes. Nature-reserve managers are introducing measures to restore habitat, notably lowland heath and seasonally flooded meadows. The greater awareness of habitat destruction and increase in leisure activities has led to some serious conservation, sometimes over a wide area, especially in the uplands. The rapid rise in influence of the plant-conservation charity, Plantlife, and a greater awareness by all conservation organisations has enhanced the prospects for our flora.

Acknowledgements

I am most grateful to Drs Chris Preston, Mike Pienkowski, Colin Galbraith and Des Thompson for comments and suggestions on this chapter.

References

Averis, A.M., Averis, A.B.G., Birks, H.J.B. *et al.* (2004). *An Illustrated Guide to British Upland Vegetation*, Peterborough, Joint Nature Conservation Committee.

Braithwaite, M.E., Ellis, R.W. and Preston, C.D. (2006). *Change in the British Flora 1987–2004*, London, Botanical Society of the British Isles.

Foley, M. and Clarke, S. (2005). *Orchids of the British Isles*, Cheltenham, Griffin Press.

Gimingham, C.H. (1972). *Ecology of Heathlands*, London, Chapman and Hall.

Grigson, G. (1958). *The Englishman's Flora*, London, Phoenix House Ltd.

Mabey, R. (1980). *The Common Ground*, Londond, Hutchinson.

Marren, P. (1999). *Britain's Rare Flowers*, London, T. and A.D. Poyser.

Moore, N.W. (1962). The heaths of Dorset and their conservation. *Journal of Ecology*, **60**, 369–391.

Preston, C.D. and Hill, M.O. (1997). The geographical relationships of British and Irish vascular plants. *Botanical Journal of the Linnean Society*, **124**, 1–120.

Preston, C.D., Pearman, D.A. and Dines, T.D. (2002a). *New Atlas of the British and Irish Flora*, Oxford, Oxford University Press.

Preston, C.D., Telfer, M.G., Arnold, H.R. *et al.* (2002b). *The Changing Flora of the UK*, London, DEFRA.

Rackham, O. (1986). *The History of the Countryside*, Londond, J.M. Dent & Sons.

Rackham, O. (2006). *Woodlands*, London, Collins.

Rich, T.C.G. (2001). Flowering plants. In Hawksworth, D.L., ed., *The Changing Wildlife of Great Britain and Ireland*, London, Taylor & Francis.

Rich, T.C.G. and Proctor, M.C.F. (2009). Some new British and Irish *Sorbus* L. taxa (Rosaceae). *Watsonia*, **27**, 207–216.

Scott, N.E. and Davison, A.W. (1982). De-icing salt and the invasion of road verges by maritime plants. *Watsonia*, **14**, 41–52.

Shoard, M. (1980). *The Theft of the Countryside*, London, Temple Smith.

Smith, C.J. (1980). *Ecology of the English Chalk*, London, Academic Press.

Walker, K.J. (2007). The last thirty five years: recent changes in the flora of the British Isles. *Watsonia*, **26**, 291–302.

Wells, T.C.E., Sheail, J., Ball, D.F. and Ward, L.K. (1976). Ecological studies on the Porton Ranges: relationships between vegetation, soils and land-use history. *Journal of Ecology*, **64**, 589–626.

36

Conclusion: what is the likely future for the wildlife in Britain and Ireland?

Norman Maclean

The introductory chapter of this book spoke of wildlife in Britain and Ireland in the context of a possible Great Extinction. In terms of wildlife worldwide, I have no doubt whatsoever that this prognosis is accurate, but I am pleased to say that the prediction seems to me to be somewhat less applicable to the future of wildlife in Britain and Ireland. As I will emphasise in more detail later in this chapter, there have certainly been some very serious declines, especially of insects such as dragonflies, riverflies and Lepidoptera (butterflies and moths), but the prediction is presently much less applicable to vertebrates. Why should this be? Perhaps many vertebrates such as mammals and birds are, because of their behavioural sophistication, more able to ride storms of change in terms of food availability and habitat loss, or perhaps the widespread use of insecticides has simply hit insects selectively. Some bats, and some non-flying mammals such as Red Squirrel and Water Vole are in steep decline, and some birds such as Willow Tit and Corn Bunting are perhaps species with somewhat specialised niches which cannot readily adapt in the short term, but for most vertebrates, although there remains cause for anxiety and a need for rapid action, the immediate outlook is not catastrophic.

However, this optimistic prognosis for vertebrates could easily have a false basis in the longer term. If, as is clear, the steepest declines are in the invertebrates, especially insects, it may well be that these dramatic declines in species low down in the food chain will inevitably be followed by subsequent serious declines in vertebrates and flowering plants which depend on insects for food or pollination. So we in Britain and Ireland may yet come to share the dramatic declines and ecological catastrophes which already threaten so many habitats in the rest of the world. But maybe not. Perhaps, being a democratic, sophisticated and wealthy society, our successful efforts with species such as Otter, Red Kite, Osprey, White-tailed Eagle, Marsh Harrier and Avocet can be followed by more widespread ecological recoveries. There is already in place a British commitment to reverse the decline in farmland birds by 2020 (Public Service Agreement Target). Such ambitions will certainly require major changes in how we use

Silent Summer: The State of Wildlife in Britain and Ireland, ed. Norman Maclean. Published by Cambridge University Press. © Cambridge University Press 2010.

water and energy, how we farm, how much we can rein in urban spread and water pollution, and most of all, how stringently we can control and even reduce our human population and its dark ecological footprint. Of course, in some ways Britain and Ireland have already experienced the forest clearance and intensification of agriculture that currently threatens habitats such as tropical rainforest, and our present fauna and flora, the survivors from this trauma of the last few thousand years, are now experiencing a further series of difficulties.

What seems to me certain, however, is that we must all modify our expectations of wildlife richness in the future. We will have to learn to live without the insect abundance which characterised our countryside before the 1960s, and simply concentrate our conservation efforts on what is left. Better to make a good job of conserving what remains rather than waste our energies in bemoaning what has already gone.

The data provided in Chapter 30 on aerial insects taken in the Rothamsted suction traps deserve special comment. Why are populations of aphids stable whilst other insects are declining? Presumably the chief explanation is that agricultural intensification has not reduced common crop aphids such as cereal aphids. Indeed in some cases they may have increased. Good news for Common Swifts, perhaps.

We must, however, guard against a dangerous and invidious tendency. It is a common human trait to regard whatever was the norm in early life as 'standard' and any increase or decline since then as significant. This perception totally fails to take account of earlier norms which were evident before we ourselves came on the scene. So those of us over 60 have a very different perception of what was normal for numbers of particular butterfly species, say Meadow Browns or Small Coppers, than for those aged 30 or 40. These latter folk never knew the previous abundances of these species and think that much lower abundances are the acceptable base level. American marine biologists have recently coined a name for this false perception. They call it the 'shifting-baseline syndrome' (see an excellent account of this in McCarthy's book of 2008). The world pre-Rachel Carson was not a wildlife paradise, but it was strikingly different from the present and we should all endeavour to appreciate that.

I will now discuss and summarise in more detail the most serious wildlife-conservation problems highlighted in previous chapters, and also emphasise the particular success stories on which future optimism can be based.

As we have stressed elsewhere in this book, taking a current snapshot of our wildlife is not absolutely straightforward. Some bird species, such as Wryneck and Red-backed Shrike have diminished or disappeared through range reduction, while Cetti's Warbler, Little Egret and maybe Cattle Egret have arrived through range expansion. The reasons for these range changes are not completely understood and may have little or nothing to do with the parameters listed as drivers of change. The other more major problem is determining actual numbers and biomass. It is easy to say if a species is present or absent, but decline or increase is mainly about calculating population and estimating numbers of individual species. A huge national effort goes into determining biomass figures for birds (see Table 17.1), although even here the figures for 50 years ago may not be very accurate. But for most insects there are neither good figures for the 1960s nor the present, purely because of the difficulty of doing the assessment. Often, if the numbers of a species were very abundant, like the Meadow Brown Butterfly, the Magpie Moth or the House Cricket, there seemed no reason to count them. This is where the data provided in Chapter 27 are so precious, since it is almost unique.

Present and future problems

Human population increase

As we have emphasised in Chapter 6 and elsewhere, the problem which underlies so many aspects of the declines in some of our wildlife, and threatens to impact increasingly, is our ever-growing human population. Human numbers have risen by more than 15% over the last 50 years to just over 60 million in Britain and Northern Ireland, and present political and economic forecasts, rather than promising a slowing population growth, do the very reverse and predict figures like 75 million by 2030 (see Figure 6.1a). In terms of wildlife conservation, that is pretty frightening, especially for southern and eastern parts of England. Even if we learn to economise on travel, to run less-thirsty cars and to reduce the carbon footprint of our lifestyles, it is hard to see the future in rosy terms. We in the UK pride ourselves on our enlightened and liberal attitudes, so talk of reining in population growth either by limiting immigration or by reducing birth rate, or both, is rather muted. It should not be so. Population growth and associated urbanisation is probably our number one problem both nationally and globally.

Water abstraction

Not only is the demand for water per person increasing in Britain and Ireland through the increasing use of water for agricultural irrigation, for washing machines, car washes and the like, but the predicted population increases promise even greater demand. As a result, many rivers which previously provided havens for wildlife have shrunk through over-abstraction. It is also important to stress that reduced flows in rivers serve to magnify the effects of water pollution and water temperature increases from climate change. There are some long-term factors that could help balance the serious problems of water abstraction, such as increasing return of cleaned sewage water to rivers, increasing use of domestic water meters, new reservoir construction, and even major water redistribution between Scotland, Wales and England. But, for the present, industrial, agricultural and domestic demand for water threatens the welfare of much wildlife that is entirely or partially dependent on fresh water. Such species include Water Voles and Otters of course, and birds that nest in freshwater marshes such as Redshank, Snipe, Reed Bunting, Yellow Wagtail, and many species of riverflies and dragonflies.

Downstream there will be effects on estuaries with greater saline penetration upstream and less flow for migratory fish moving both downstream (eels) and upstream (salmonids, lampreys and chads). Some molluscs, notably the Whorl Snails (*Vertigo geyeri* and *V. moulinsiana*) and the Freshwater Pearl Mussel (Margaritifera *margaritifera*) have been seriously affected by water abstraction and reduced river flows.

Flooding

It may seem bizarre that both water abstraction and flooding should be cited as problems for wildlife conservation, but such is indeed the case. As emphasised in Chapter 2, climate change, in addition to drought, has resulted in an increased frequency of storms and the sudden torrential rainfall and flooding that accompanies them. This aspect of our climate may well be an increasing future threat also, leading to changing concepts of where houses may be built. Flooding is also exacerbated by the widespread covering of surfaces with concrete and tarmacadam. Another knock-on effect of flooding which seems to be rarely emphasised is that in times of flood, all manner of contaminated material from flooded properties, such as oils, paints and cans of insecticides, may end up on the land and in the rivers as the floods recede. Flooding unfortunately ensures that no matter how careful we are with toxic materials when the wind blows gently, in sudden flood emergencies all manner of polluting material may inadvertently escape into our rivers and countryside. It is surely clear that totally new legislation is needed to apply to buildings, farms and houses which are in reasonable danger of being flooded, in order to help prevent the catastrophic pollution that may accidentally result. Floods are an important factor in wetland ecology, and greater flood defences for property and homes may lead to less flooding of adjacent habitats with consequences for wetland habitats and their species.

Noise and light pollution

Human activity inevitably also brings increased noise to the countryside, whether it be traffic noise, aircraft noise or sometimes the din of heavy industry. Why noise pollution may be even more serious for non-human animals than for ourselves is that many of them communicate by calling to one another, either through the songs and calls of birds, the barking of deer or the croaking of frogs. Probably birds suffer most, and there are reports (Slabbekoorn *et al.* 2008) of diminishing populations of songbirds in fields and woodland adjacent to major highways. It seems likely that this results from such birds being unable to set up vocal territories or attract mates through song.

Another aspect of noise pollution is the sub-surface noise in the sea emitted by ships' engines and naval activity involving sonar. There is increasing evidence that the disorientation or even beaching of whales and dolphins is frequently a result of noise pollution.

Light pollution is also problematic. It seems both actual and metaphorical that city lights prevent us from seeing the stars. The effects of constant light lead to altered growth of some trees and even to unseasonal flowering. It may also cause huge losses of moths and other flying insects, which are often attracted to an early death by bright lights. However, sometimes city lights seem to be positively beneficial to some bird species, in that birds such as gulls may extend their feeding times when light is available at night, and the attraction of insects to lights is often fortuitously utilised by bats as a good feeding location.

Litter

Litter is of course unsightly, and it is very encouraging to see the activity of people like Bill Bryson and the Campaign to Protect Rural England in both highlighting the problem and doing something to reduce the effects. Some litter can be pressed into service as nesting material by birds, but there are many more examples of animals becoming fatally entangled in discarded fishing nets and lines, both in fresh and sea water (see Figure 36.1), and of small mammals becoming fatally trapped in bottles or

Figure 36.1 Young Gannet entangled in nylon ropes from discarded fishing tackle (see colour plate). (Reproduced by kind permission of James Fair.)

cans. Certainly some litter can be beneficial, such as disused sheets of corrugated iron providing a favourite cover for snakes, but by and large, litter not only despoils the beauty of the countryside, but can also bring premature death to some of its occupants (see Chapter 33). Litter also greatly reduces the enjoyment which many people actually derive from the countryside, and maybe this is its greatest downside, since without enjoyment, humans will stop going there and the cause of wildlife conservation will be even more remote from the lives and interests of many ordinary people. Also, litter is not restricted to the land: plastic debris disfigures our coasts and seas with implications for the species present (see below).

Marine pollution and shoreline degradation

Chapter 33 emphasises how marine pollution from oil, plastic, endocrine disrupters such as TBT and other toxic compounds have posed and do pose problems and threats to wildlife, although there are grounds for some optimism on these fronts for the future. However, it is less easy to be optimistic about the threats from future building and attempts to derive energy from tidal estuary flows. Many millions of wading birds, ducks and geese feed on the mudflats and salt marshes of Britain and Ireland during passage or overwinter. We currently provide food and security to large proportions of the world populations of birds such as Brent, Barnacle, Pink-footed and White-fronted Geese, and innumerable waders such as Godwits, Curlew, Redshank, Dunlin and Sanderling. The coastal mudflats may often look somewhat unattractive to us, but they are precious havens and food sources for these birds and we clearly have an important national and international responsibility to conserve them. This is also an area where wildlife conservation and field sports can and do work together for the common good. More worrying is the possible return of serious human viruses such as the H5N1 strain of influenza virus. If public panic in the face of such threats became the norm, then there might be calls for widespread culling of estuarine and sea shore migrant birds. Let us hope that we can hold our nerve in the face of such future fears.

Also, rising sea levels will lead to hardening of our coastline in areas of urban development and major infrastructure such as roads and railways. This will squeeze fringing habitats. In rural areas there will be pressure for managed retreat – but in a world in which food shortage is growing, defending agricultural land may well come back into fashion.

There is also increasing concern for the welfare of whales and dolphins, many species of which have been decimated by many years of destructive whaling. These wonderful animals seem to be hit both by whaling activity, noise pollution in the sea, and reduction in their food supply as a result of warming of the ocean, especially the polar ocean, and over-fishing. The next 10 or 20 years will reveal in greater detail whether our efforts to conserve whales and dolphins are sufficient to counter the negative factors.

Use of insecticides, herbicides and fungicides in farms, smallholdings and gardens

Rachel Carson was most concerned about the widespread use of insecticides and her anxieties have proved to be well founded. There is absolutely no question but that over-use of insecticides and their sloppy disposal has made very serious inroads on our wildlife. Most recently-produced insecticides are believed to have fairly short half-lives in the environment (days or weeks rather than months or years as in the past with DDT and others), but there is no doubt but that insecticides continue to pose serious threats. There is also a recent worrying report of continuing DDT release from the North Atlantic waters (Stemmler and Lammel, 2009; Lovell, 2010). The declines in butterflies and moths must surely be partly related to the widespread use of insecticidal sprays in gardens and farms. Synthetic pyrethroids such as permethrin continue to be widely used in wood treatment, sheep dip and impregnated cattle tags, and no doubt some of these compounds enter our rivers and contaminate our countryside. One aspect of permethrin use is that cows with milking calves are often provided with permethrin-impregnated ear tags to help reduce the fly-borne summer mastitis which leads to localised udder inflammation. When such cattle are kept in fields adjacent to rivers, and especially when the cattle wade in these rivers, the powerful insecticides must enter the river water and help kill off the riverfly nymphs and larvae of insects that depend on this habitat.

Fungicides continue to be an essential component in farm and garden management, especially to combat potato blight, mildews and rusts in cereal crops, and mildews and black spot in garden roses. It is assumed that fungicides have little impact on most wildlife other than fungi themselves. Let us hope that this is indeed the case. One curious twist to the story of fungicide use in potato fields is that every potato field receives multiple treatments per year to combat blight disease, so a GM potato with blight resistance might prove very efficacious in this situation. The problem is that many different potato varieties are grown, so a whole range of blight resistant varieties would be needed.

Herbicides continue to be widely used in farms, smallholdings and gardens, and, as is stressed in Chapter 34, they have caused a decline in many previously common cornfield weeds such as Corn Cockle and Cornflower. However, the increased use of wide field margins (which remain unsprayed) to encourage beneficial insects and birds may allow the slow return of some of these once common countryside flowers.

Insect decline

The steep declines recorded over the last 50 years in populations of butterflies, moths, bumblebees, dragonflies and riverflies are very worrying. It seems likely that they are accompanied by serious declines in other insects such as beetles, land and water bugs, grasshoppers and crickets, and others. Our summers are now much more silent because of the conspicuous reductions in grasshoppers and crickets, and even once common species of beetles such as Violet Ground Beetles and Cockchafers seem to be much more difficult to find. These insect declines are likely to have unfortunate implications for other wildlife, since insects are near to the bottom of many crucial food chains. Already declines in insectivorous birds such as Spotted Flycatchers, House Sparrows (whose juveniles are insectivorous) and of many bats are perhaps only the beginning of longer-term repercussions from declines in insect populations.

Climate change

As discussed in more depth in Chapter 2, our climate has slowly warmed over the last decade or so, more as a result of less severe winter weather than of hotter summers. The most conspicuous change is in warmer weather in the late winter and early spring, which has led to many recorded changes in the times of nesting and egg-laying in birds, and bud burst and flowering in many plants. The 'green wave' which is visible from space as the tree bud-burst moves northwards across Europe, is now advanced by some 10 days compared with 10 or more years ago. There is also little doubt but that the main driver of this warming is anthropogenic (man-made). The immediate effects on our wildlife are quite mixed, as discussed in Chapter 2 of this book. So some southern butterflies and dragonflies have extended their range northwards, and birds at the northern edge of their ranges in Britain such as Dartford Warbler, Cetti's Warbler and, very recently, Little Egret, are doing well. The loss of northern species of plants and animals will be slower to show, and is likely to include some of our alpine flowers, such as Purple Saxifrage, which seems to be already retreating at the southern edges of its range, and maybe nesting Snow Bunting, Ptarmigan and Black-throated Diver. To a great extent we just have to wait and see, and meanwhile do all we can to reduce the factors which drive global warming. Climate change is also driving shifts in abundance in marine species with major range extensions of southern species and decreases in abundance of northern species, some of which are also retreating. Rocky shores in the UK are likely to become less dominated by primary producing and habitat-forming seaweeds, that are likely to retreat more into shelter, as occurs in southern Europe.

Intensive farming

We in Britain and Ireland have seen our agriculture go through a period of progressive intensification (although less so in Ireland) involving the widespread use of pesticides, fungicides and herbicides, and the minimal retention of hedgerows. This has resulted in the familiar sight of completely uniform crop fields and minimal waste ground. True there have been some moves to develop set-aside land (actually to reduce yield rather than to conserve wildlife) and to encourage game birds by the retention of coverts and the planting of specific game-related crops. But very recently there has been a renewed drive for extra yield in food crops driven by increased world demand. Certainly large numbers of us have long since concluded that we would be glad to opt for less intensive and more eco-friendly farming, even at the expense of higher food prices. The EC

'Common Agricultural Policy' has much to answer for in terms of the degradation of our countryside and the demise of our wildlife. The growth of the demand for so-called organic foods help to underline this. However, it is hard to predict the future. If we in Britain and Ireland are more concerned about food prices than we are about the welfare of our countryside and the wild plants and animals with which we share it, then the future will reveal this at an accelerating rate. The intensification of farming must be seen for what it is, namely a major threat to much of our wildlife.

Reduced interest in wildlife

One of the striking changes which has occurred over the last 50 years is a decline in interest in wildlife, especially by those under 30. We have become increasingly urbanised and home based through the advent of television and the home computer. There has also been an unintentional reduction in interest through the pressure not to pick wild flowers or collect birds' eggs or insects. More than 50 years ago, when I was a boy, many country boys collected birds' eggs, and some of us collected and pinned out our collections of insects. Now it would be a backward step to return to the collecting days of yore, but unfortunately it is by far the easiest way for children to relate to wildlife. In my view we should encourage our children to collect common plants and insects as a guide to identification, and maybe also items such as bird feathers or disused birds' nests. Of course the ease of use of the even cheaper digital camera provides a partial return to collecting, and maybe we should encourage even young children to collect their own photographic images of butterflies, dragonflies, rock-pool animals and flowers. Certainly, with tricky identification species such as dragonflies, a photographic record presents much the easiest way to be positive about the identification. Bird photography is far from easy, but the new trend for 'digiscoping', involving the use of a telescope on a tripod linked to a digital camera via a simple mount, has made photography an invaluable aid in bird identification also. So perhaps we should encourage our youngsters to use their mobile phones to exchange photographic images of interesting wildlife. Of course, bird identification still attracts good numbers of young males, but it remains a minority interest.

Animal and plant introductions

As discussed in depth in Chapters 4 and 5, and in passing in many other chapters, a large number of non-native fauna and flora have been introduced to our islands by intention or accident. Some, such as the Little Owl and the Snakes-head Fritillary, have turned out to be welcome additions, but most have proved to be more problematic. Arguably, the most worrisome additions to our flora are the aquatic plants Nuttall's Waterweed and New Zealand Pigmyweed and also Japanese Knotweed and Wild Rhododendron.

Amongst the animals there are also some serious problems. Grey Squirrels and American Mink have proved to be mammals that we could well do without. Muntjac Deer, Ring-necked Parakeet and Canada Geese are problematic in some areas. There are no really serious invaders amongst other vertebrates, but the invertebrates include some troublesome additions such as Mitten Crab, Signal Crayfish, Zebra Mussel (*Dreissena polymorpha*) and perhaps, very recently, Harlequin Ladybird.

Large seaweeds such as Japweed and Wire-Weed, and the kelp, *Undaria pinnatifida*, have hitched a ride via aquaculture or yachts and are proliferating on our shores and changing their ecologies. The Pacific Oyster was deliberately introduced via hatchery culture in the 1960s and 1970s. At the time it was firmly stated that it would not breed in the wild – recent warming has ensured that it has and it is now spreading and dominating parts of estuaries such as the Yealm in Devon.

However, it is perhaps amongst small organisms or micro-organisms that the most serious threats to our wildlife appear. Thus we have almost lost that flagship tree the English Elm as a result of the dual devastation wrought by Dutch Elm Disease – a fungus transmitted by a beetle. Sudden Oak Death, also fungal, is new and worrisome, as is the new small moth *Cameraria ohridella*, whose larvae cause premature browning of the leaves of Horse Chestnut, admittedly not an original British native, but now an important part of our parks and mixed woodland.

It will be ever more difficult to keep out such unwelcome guests due to increasing human mobility, and perhaps a century from now the diverse fauna and flora of the world will become even more homogenised as a result of such accidental mixing. This will be yet another situation where the rate of evolution of species will be insufficient to prevent serious losses and management difficulties in conservation.

The multiple perils of songbird migration

Much of the delight of the North European spring is welcoming back the summer songbird migrants from Africa. Who does not experience a moment of ecstasy on seeing the first swifts and swallows or hearing the first cuckoo or nightingale? Such moments are enshrined in our culture, our language and our poetry. But for how much longer will they continue? The multiple factors of climate change, agricultural intensification, insect decline, urbanisation and African desertification make what has always been a hazardous lifestyle adaptation by songbirds into a catastrophic one. Michael McCarthy has written a very special book on this – *Say Goodbye to the Cuckoo*–and here I quote from the last page in his book. 'But what if they don't make it? By 2007, forty-one percent of Britain's swifts had failed to return since 1994. Thirty-seven per cent of the cuckoos. Forty-seven per cent of the yellow wagtails. Fifty-four per cent of the pied flycatchers. Fifty-nine per cent of the spotted flycatchers. Sixty per cent of the nightingales. Sixty-six per cent of the turtle doves. Sixty-seven per cent of the wood warblers. All gone already in thirteen years, with the remainder on slopes of decline which stretch sharply down towards the zero at the bottom of the graph. Is the globe (planet earth) still working when this is happening?'

Summary of future problems

In the light of these 12 summarised topics, our wildlife is clearly in for a bumpy ride. However, as I will discuss in the next concluding section, there are also some solid grounds for optimism.

Optimism and future remedial action

Conservation successes in Britain and Ireland

There are many solid successes resulting from public investment in conservation measures. All of these are relative, but some conspicuous successes spring to mind. Amongst mammals, the return of the Otter is an outstanding achievement, resulting partly from deliberate introduction, but also the cessation of Otter hunting, and good riverine management. Both Badgers and Foxes have very successfully adapted to countryside changes, and all our native and introduced deer are doing almost too well. The Pine Marten has capitalised on the extension of coniferous woodland. The Grey Seal has prospered around our coastline, although the Common Seal is showing signs of decline. The remaining targets for future conservation improvements are Wild Cat, Harvest Mouse, Red Squirrel, Hazel Dormouse and many bat species.

Birds attract greater public support than any other class of vertebrates, largely because most are diurnal, easily seen, and have some striking plumage and behaviour. So it is no surprise that we have been prepared to invest heavily and very successfully in recovery programmes for Red Kite, White-tailed Eagle, Peregrine Falcon, Marsh Harrier and Avocet. Other obvious successes include Stone Curlew, Cirl Bunting and perhaps Bittern and Corncrake. Of course, plenty of failures spring to mind, birds such as Corn Bunting, Willow Tit, Lesser-spotted Woodpecker, Spotted Flycatcher, Yellow Wagtail and Turtle Dove, all of which show signs of substantial decline, and there are urgent concerns about many of our sea bird colonies and their recent poor reproductive success. However, we continue to provide food and shelter for thousands of both overwintering geese and ducks and huge numbers of wading birds on passage. Many of these, especially the geese and ducks, bear testament to the effective rapport that exists between wildfowlers and conservationists.

Our reptiles and amphibians hold on, but not in the numbers that we once enjoyed. There is certainly much less wanton killing of snakes, but Smooth Snake, Sand Lizard, Natterjack Toad and Great-crested Newt still require careful management of the remaining suitable habitat. There is also a worrying chytrid fungal disease of frogs moving around the world, and there is some evidence for concern regarding our own Common Frog population.

In general, fish species have benefited by the reduction of river pollution over the last 50 years, although acidification of lochs and lakes led to some threats to fish such as Arctic Charr. The acid-rain problem seems to have reduced in recent years as industrial air pollution has been reined in. The Burbot appears to have disappeared entirely and there is cause for concern regarding populations in particular river systems of Atlantic Salmon, Common Eel, and both Brook and River Lampreys (see Chapter 21).

Conservation efforts for invertebrates are generally more low key than those for vertebrates. However, the Large Blue Butterfly has been successfully reintroduced thanks to a better understanding of its requirements, and Swallowtail Butterflies still breed in East Anglia. Some butterflies have done well, perhaps because they are generalists, and these include Comma, Holly Blue and Brimstone, and, with the assistance of some climate change, we are visited more often by Clouded Yellows. So although most Lepidoptera, and indeed most insects, have not done well in Britain and Ireland over the last half century, there are a few that have bucked the trend. The Common Mayfly has also defied the declines that have come to characterise other riverflies, and a newish dragonfly, the Small Red-eyed Damsel Fly has recently expanded its range to join us from the continent.

Gardens as wildlife havens

One outstanding success story over the last decade or two has become apparent, namely so many people seeing their garden as a wildlife haven, rather than perceiving wildlife simply as pests and problems for horticulture. It is now commonplace for gardeners to adopt a more eco-friendly approach, leaving piles of dead logs and even nettle patches to act as shelter for wildlife species. This has clearly fostered the success of mammals like Foxes and Hedgehogs, although not everyone is happy with the parallel increase in Grey Squirrels. Feeding garden birds on peanuts, sunflower seed and niger seed has undoubtedly been a major factor in the increases seen in populations of Great Spotted Woodpecker, Nuthatch, Goldfinch and Siskin. Even Reed Buntings have become frequent visitors to some winter bird-table food, and the spread of the Rose-ringed Parakeet is at least in part attributable to the availability of peanuts in London gardens.

A wider understanding of how to manage wild-flower meadows and remaining pockets of chalk downland by ensuring that they remain or become nutrient-poor has led to many more areas of flower-rich meadow, although sometimes after cultivation and enrichment, the return to a state that favours non-grass species is very slow. But these areas have become marvellous islands for less common plants such as Yellow Rattle, Wild Thyme, Rockrose, Fragrant and Pyramidal Orchids, while the insects attracted to these flowers include many bumblebee species, Burnet Moths, and butterflies such as Skippers, Marbled White, Gatekeeper and Dark Green Fritillary. True, many of these areas are not actually enclosed gardens, but even small areas of flower meadow within gardens can be remarkably productive and attract many insect species that would not otherwise visit.

So too with the popularity of garden ponds, which rapidly attract dragonfly and damselfly species, as well as breeding frogs and newts. However, it is often necessary to abandon ideas of keeping ornamental fish, if populations of amphibians are to thrive. Before I got rid of my Goldfish, the visiting frogs and newts provided an annual tadpole bonanza for the fish, but not much more.

Thus, a garden planted with shrubs and a few trees, with semi-wild areas of dead wood, ivy, and even nettles (food for various butterfly larvae), a pond, a bird-feeding station, and bird-bath in the absence of a pond, and a very stringent attitude to the use of garden insecticides, goes some way to help mitigate the loss of habitat that has become the norm through urban spread and motorway development.

However, I cannot retain my honesty without emphasising the downside that many of us innocently introduce to our gardens, namely a domestic cat. Sadly our beloved moggies are ruthless hunters. There are reckoned to be about 9 million domestic cats in the UK, and in the now famous study of 986 cats carried out by Woods *et al.* (2003) in the spring and summer of 1997 through a detailed questionnaire, a total of over 14 000 prey items were recorded. When these are rounded up to the UK annual toll from 9 million cats, the answers are 139 million mammals, 65 million birds, and 12 million amphibians and reptiles. (These totals are based on an extrapolation of five months to 12 months, assuming that the five months of the study would reflect 12 months of a year.) The annual totals might be slightly less if winter yields of cat prey items are less. The placing of bells on cats and keeping them indoors at night significantly reduced the toll of mammalian prey, but, on the other hand, the provision of a bird-feeding station significantly increases the toll of birds taken. So we should perhaps try to switch from hunting cats to cats which are kept indoors, or maybe switching to a small dog instead. So there it is. A tricky decision for the average British family.

Development of hedges and corridors between wildlife sanctuaries

We have all become familiar with the importance of providing corridors of appropriate habitat to link together areas of tropical rainforest containing endangered bird or mammalian species. It seems to be less widely appreciated that the same holds true for our own islands of eco-friendly habitat within urban or rural landscapes. Indeed as the relentless encroachment of roads and towns increases, what were once large areas of heath, forest or marsh are now often reduced to isolated islands of habitat in which the remaining wildlife is concentrated and isolated. These areas may be small gardens or substantial Nature Reserves, but the principles continue to apply.

A partial answer to this isolation of pockets of habitat is the preservation or construction of communicating corridors. In some very commendable initiatives by local groups of gardeners and others, attempts are underway to plan linking series of gardens, 'waste ground' and natural hedgerow or coppice, to try to ensure that both fauna and flora are able to move freely between large important island habitats. Thus a series of wildlife-friendly gardens can be effective links in a chain of natural movement and spread for both fauna and flora between, say, an important mixed woodland and large local cemetery which, through partial neglect had become itself a wildlife haven. These principles apply both on a small scale and also on a large scale. So it is increasingly important to try to preserve or develop such corridors between areas of, say, chalk downland or relatively wildlife-friendly farms. This is an area where game enthusiasts can show conservationists the way, since the devotees of pheasant shooting arc often skilled at persuading local farmers to foster wildlife-friendly crops such as fields of brassica vegetables, or to preserve copses and coverts within their farms rather than press them into active food production.

Species using corridors are familiar to most of us. Garden mammals such as Hedgehogs, Woodmice and Bats, garden birds such as Long-tailed Tits, Song Thrushes and House Sparrows, readily move along corridors, as do insect species such as Stag Beetle, Common Blue and Large Skipper Butterflies, and amphibians such as newts and toads. In the broader picture, many comparatively sedentary species such as Corn Bunting, and insects such as Adonis, Chalk Hill Blue and Duke of Burgundy Butterflies are in danger of serious island isolation of sub-populations which rapidly lose their genetic fitness via diversity and become gradually enfeebled and extinct. Many wildlife species have a critical mass of minimal interbreeding population size, and when this is threatened, local extinctions occur.

What has been said above about interconnecting corridors applies substantially to hedgerows. The bigger and wider the hedge and adjacent uncultivated land, the better. Farmers have also begun to develop uncropped areas in fields referred to as 'beetle banks' (see Glossary). Not only small birds like Wrens and Whitethroats move along hedgerows. So too do Kestrels and Grey Partridges. And the movement of insect species such as Glow-worms and Gatekeeper Butterflies is evident for all who keep their eyes open. All who visit the North Norfolk coast in spring or summer cannot help but notice the spread along many miles of road via the hedgerows, of the bright green Umbellifer, Alexanders (*Smyrnium olusatrum*), said to have originally been introduced by the Romans. Many other plants such as Oxford Ragwort have spread in a similar way.

Mutual benefits between field sports and wildlife conservation

We emphasise in Chapters 7 and 8 that field sports are, in general, a major asset to wildlife conservation. This is much less widely appreciated than it should be and it will be important in the future to have this close coupling realised. It is, of course, obvious that wildlife conservation benefits those who shoot wildfowl or gamebirds, and there are good secondary benefits for fishermen and deer hunters also. It is the reverse that is so much less well understood, namely the huge benefit that wildlife conservation gains from field sports. This is partly because the considerable money and effort which go into the preservation of countryside suitable for field-sport activity also facilitates the welfare of the other wildlife present. In future, this commonality of interest will be ever more valuable for the welfare of both the field sports and the wildlife that benefits from it. Much of the wild open spaces of Britain and Ireland are only sustainable if the money drawn from field-sport activity continues to flow in, and the interest of many farmers in shooting proves a strong incentive for the development and preservation of on-farm habitat that favours wildlife, whether they be Pheasants or Yellow Hammers.

The role of television and media

There is no question but that knowledge and armchair watching of wildlife has increased enormously in Britain and Ireland as a result of excellent television programmes made at considerable cost in some very remote areas. It is not uncommon for people to meet up in airports around the world and suddenly find common interest in having watched compelling footage on the life of the Snow Leopard or the displays of lekking Birds of Paradise. Wildlife has been 'captured' by the camera and made visually accessible in our kitchens and living rooms as never before. So too series compèred by people such as Bill Oddie, Chris Packham and Simon King have stimulated the national interest in our countryside and its wildlife. Wildlife photography has reached new peaks of perfection, sometimes by some skilful behind-the-scenes fabrication, but more often from long hours spent in uncomfortable hides by the dedicated photographers. The presenters of such programmes can hardly be blamed for having provided a somewhat rose-tinted view of what is currently going on in the world's deserts, mountains and rainforests. However, there is also no doubt that David Attenborough has shown admirable courage and honesty in alerting us to the urgency of many wildlife-related problems.

Since media impact is so powerful, it is to be hoped that an honest balance between optimism and doom and gloom will be struck in future presentation of the state of our wildlife. Doom and gloom does not generally sell books nor capture television audiences, yet if we want to continue to enjoy and share our rich wildlife inheritance, we must face some unattractive prospects. As the inheritors of a national and traditional concern for animals and plants through our worthy forebears, Gilbert White, Charles Darwin, Peter Scott and many others, we must honour our responsibilities to our country and our planet and seek to foster the health of our countryside and all the fauna and flora with which we share it.

It is an ever-present ambition of those with a wildlife interest in birds, plants, butterflies or whatever, to persuade the wider public that our wildlife does need cherishing and conserving, so maybe we can increasingly co-opt the media to our side and stimulate increasing interest amongst the young and the old and all those in between. The success of the Wildlife Trusts, the Woodland Trust, RSPB, Butterfly Conservation, the Campaign to Protect Rural England, and other organisations and charities is heartening, and perhaps a new concern for the other species with which we share these islands is now growing.

Table 36.1 *A table of some species gains and losses over the last 50 years. (Some but not all of these gains are the result, at least in part, of conservation programmes.)*

Gains		Losses/Declines
Mammals		
Otter		Water Vole
Badger		Wild Cat
Polecat		Dormouse
Pine Marten		Red Squirrel
Grey Seal		Brown Hare
Roe Deer		Greater Mouse-eared Bat (no longer a
Red Deer		breeding species)
Fallow Deer		Common Seal (Harbour or Harbor Seal)
Sika Deer		
Muntjac Deer		
Chinese Water Deer		
Wild Boar (now breeding widely following escape)		
Lesser Horseshoe Bat (recent gain after earlier substantial loss)		
Nathusius's Pipistrelle (now known to breed)		
Soprano Pipistrelle (recently recognised as a distinct species)		
Supporting data for Gains and Losses		
Gains from 1977 to 2002	Otter	Up from 6 to 36% hectads[a] in England and 21 to 74% in Wales
	Badger	Estimated 193 000 adults in late 1980s to 309 000 in 1990s
	Polecat	93 hectads in 1962 compared to 802 hectads in 2002
	Pine Marten	24 tetrahectads (20 km^2) in 1929 to 156 in 1982
	Grey Seal	*c.* 500 in 1914 to 128 000 in 2007
	Roe Deer	*c.* 15 000 in 1977 to *c.* 58 000 in 2007
Losses/declines from 1977 to 2002	Water Vole	Signs of presence at 48% of sites in 1990 to 38% of sites in 1998
	Wild Cat	Hard to quantify, but strong evidence for gene introgression from feral domestic cats
	Dormouse	51 counties in 1900 to only 38 in 1990s
	Red Squirrel	Down from 741 hectads in 1959 to 386 in 1993
	Brown Hare	Game bags suggest decline from 12 to 2 per km^2 from 1960 to 1989 on hunting estates

Table 36.1 (cont.)

Gains	Losses/Declines
Birds[b]	
Great-crested Grebe[c]	White-fronted Goose
Cormorant	Mallard
Little Egret	Pochard
Mute Swan	Scaup
Pink-footed Goose	Kestrel (BTO results suggest fluctuation)
Brent Goose	Grey Partridge
Gadwall	Lapwing (recent decline)
Wigeon	Redshank (moderate decline)
Goosander (recent localised increase in breeding sites)	Snipe (moderate decline)
White-tailed Eagle[c]	Roseate Tern
Osprey[c]	Turtle Dove
Red Kite[c]	Lesser-spotted Woodpecker (recent decline)
Marsh Harrier[c]	Wryneck
Common Buzzard	Skylark (moderate decline)
Sparrowhawk	Nightingale
Goshawk	Whinchat
Hobby	Marsh Warbler
Peregrine Falcon[c]	Spotted Flycatcher
Avocet[c]	Willow Tit
Little Ringed Plover[c]	Red-backed Shrike
Great Skua	Starling
Guillemot	House Sparrow
	Tree Sparrow
Stock Dove	Lesser Redpoll
Wood Pigeon	Bullfinch (decline recent and moderate)
Collared Dove	Corn Bunting
Rose-ringed Parakeet	Cirl Bunting (long–term decline but recent modest recovery)
Green Woodpecker	
Great-spotted Woodpecker	
Woodlark[c]	Other bird species, especially Summer
Blackcap	migrants such as Cuckoo, Yellow Wagtail,
Cetti's Warbler	Tree Pipit and Wood Warbler, also show
Nuthatch	recent signs of decline
Magpie	

Table 36.1 (cont.)

Gains	Losses/Declines
Carrion Crow	
Goldfinch (BTO results suggest fluctuation)	
Siskin	
Reptiles	
Sand Lizard, possible increase from 7000 in 1970s to 50 000 today. (Almost certainly the earlier figure was a serious underestimate)	Adder, Grass Snake, Slow Worm, Common Lizard all probably in decline
Amphibians	
	Natterjack Toad
	Great Crested Newt
	Common Toad
Fish	
Grayling	European Eel
Pike	Vendace
Bream	Arctic Charr
Minnow	Sea Lamprey
Dace	Allis Shad
Sunbleak (*Leucaspius delineatus*) and Topmouth Gudgeon (*Pseudorasbora parva*) are two introduced alien fish species which the Environment Agency is currently trying to eradicate	
Insects: Butterflies[d]	
Holly-blue	Wood White
Speckled-wood	High Brown Fritillary
Comma	Pearl-bordered Fritillary
White Admiral	White-letter Hairstreak
Large Blue (small recovery following better management and reintroduction programme)	Duke of Burgundy
	Chequered Skipper
	Grizzled Skipper
	Dingy Skipper
	Marsh Fritillary
	Grayling
	Large Heath
	Brown Hairstreak
	Silver-studded Blue
	Small Tortoiseshell?[e]

Table 36.1 (cont.)

Gains	Losses/Declines
Insects: Crickets	
	Field Cricket
	Mole Cricket
Insects: Riverflies	
	Mayfly spp. (*Ameletus inopinatus*)
Large Mayfly (*Ephemera danica*)	Iron Blue (*Alainitis muticus*)
Yellow May Dun (*Heptagenia sulphurea*) moving northwards	Southern Iron Blue (*Nigrobaetis niger*)
Yellow Evening Dun (*Ephemeretha notata*)	Scarce Iron Blue (*Nigrobaetis digitatus*)
	Blue-winged Olive (*Ephemerella ignita*)
	Most Caddis Flies (*Trichoptera*), except Welshman's Button (*Sericostoma personatum*)
Insects: Bumblebees	
	Bumblebees extinct in UK:
Tree Bumblebee (*Bombus hypnorum*)	Cullum's bumblebee (*Bombus cullumunus*)
	Short-haired bumblebee (*B. subterraneus*)
	Apple bumblebee (*B. pomorum*)
	Bumblebees now rare in UK:
	Great Yellow Bumblebee (*B. distinguendus*)
	Shrill Carder Bee (*B. sylvarum*)
	Moss Carder Bee (*B. muscorum*)
	Red-shanked Carder Bee (*B. ruderarius*)
	Ruderal Bumblebee (*B. ruderatus*)
	Brown-banded Carder Bee (*B. humilis*)
Insects: Bugs	
Water stick insect (*Ranatra linearis*)	
Insects: Beetles	
Lily Beetle	
Harlequin Ladybird	
Vine Weevil	

Table 36.1 (cont.)

Gains	Losses/Declines
Insects: Dragonflies	
Banded Demoiselle	Norfolk Damselfly[f]
Small Red-eyed Damselfly	Dainty Damselfly[f]
Migrant Hawker	Variable Damselfly[f]
Southern Hawker	Orange-spotted Emerald[f]
Emperor Dragonfly	Southern Damselfly
Lesser Emperor Dragonfly	Scarce Blue-tailed Damselfly
Red-veined Darter	Scarce Emerald Damselfly
Broad-bodied Chaser	Small Red Damselfly
Scarce Chaser	White-faced Darter
Black-tailed Skimmer	
Ruddy Darter	
Details	
Banded Demoiselle	Since 1996 has increased considerably in northern England recorded from 3 hectads in Scotland between 1997 and 2006
Small Red-eyed Damselfly	First British (English) record 1999. Now locally common breeder in south-east England. 81 new hectads between 2003 and 2006
Migrant Hawker	Since 1996 considerable increase in northern England, some expansion in south-west England. Has now reached Scotland and Ireland with records from 5 hectads in the former between 1997 and 2006
Southern Hawker	Recorded from 33 new hectads in Scotland between 1997 and 2006 compared with only 13 before that date
Emperor Dragonfly	Marked northerly and westerly range expansion. Now reached Scotland and Ireland with records from 10 new hectads in the former between 1997 and 2006 compared with only two before that date
Lesser Emperor Dragonfly	First British (English) record 1996. Immigrants now annual. Has bred and is a potential colonist

Table 36.1 (cont.)

Gains	Losses/Declines
Red-veined Darter	Once a sporadic vagrant, now a regular immigrant. Breeds in most years, with one or two semi-permanent colonies established. Between 1997 and 2006 recorded from 17 new hectads north of the Humber compared to seven before that date
Broad-bodied Chaser	A marked increase in northern England and recorded from 2 hectads in Scotland between 1997 and 2006
Scarce Chaser	Since 1996 recorded in 28 new hectads with some indication of a northwest spread
Black-tailed Skimmer	A clear increase in the north, especially north-westwards and recorded in 3 hectads in Scotland between 1997 and 2006
Ruddy Darter	A clear northwards spread with recordings from 42 new hectads north of the Humber between 1997 and 2006 compared with only 19 before that date
Norfolk Damselfly	Last seen in Britain in 1958
Dainty Damselfly	Last seen in Britain in 1952
Variable Damselfly	Still doing fairly well in some strongholds, but of 281 hectads from which it has been reported only 101 have post-1995 records
Orange-spotted Emerald	Last seen in Britain in 1963
Southern Damselfly	Lost from 16 hectads when comparing 1997 – 2006 with before 1997. 29% reduction
Scarce Blue-tailed Damselfly	A severe decline (64%) in the number of hectads from which it has been recorded when comparing 1997–2006 with before 1997
Scarce Emerald Damselfly	In 1997–2006 it has been lost from the western part of its range and become very much restricted to Norfolk and Essex. However, there have recently been signs of some recovery
Small Red Damselfly	Lost from about half of its hectads when comparing 1997–2006 with before 1997

Table 36.1 (cont.)

Gains	Losses/Declines
White-faced Darter	Now extinct in southern England. Since 1996 lost from 42 hectads and only recorded from 12 new ones
Insects: Moths	
L-album Wainscot	Essex Emerald
Varied Coronet	Lesser Belle
Cypress Pug	Cudweed
Light-brown Apple Moth	Lewes Wave
Cypress Carpet	Small Lappet
Horsechestnut Leaf-miner (*Cameraria ohridella*)	Viper's Bugloss
Crustaceans	
American Signal Crayfish	White-clawed Crayfish
Molluscs	
Zebra Mussel (*Dreissena polymorpha*) recent invader	Freshwater Pearl Mussel
	Shining Ram's horn Snail
	Little whirlpool Ram's horn Snail
	Mud Snail
	Glutinous Snail
	Whorl Snails (*Vertigo geyeri* and *V. moulinsiana*)
Seashore	
Major recovery by Dog Whelk populations following decline caused by use of anti-fouling agent tributyl tin (TBT)	Range reduction of Kelp (*Alaria esculenta*) due to warming seas in south-west Britain
Stalked barnacle (*Pollicipes pollicipes*) now extended its range into south-west coasts of Britain	
Introduction of several non-native species such as Pacific Oyster (*Crassostrea gigas*), Slipper Limpet (*Crepidula fornicata*), Sargassum Seaweed (*Sargassum muticum*) and the Kelp (*Undaria pinnatifida*)	

Table 36.1 (cont.)

Gains	Losses/Declines
Plants	
Mugwort	Corn Buttercup
Wall Barley	Shepherd's Needle
Round-leaved Cranesbill	Lousewort
Bee Orchid	Pepper Saxifrage
Stinking Iris	Burnt Orchid
Climbing Corydalis	Common Cow-wheat
Danish Scurvy-grass	Frogbit
	Golden Rod

Notes:

[a] Hectad – 10-km square.

[b] A detailed account of status of British birds will be found in Eaton *et al.* (2009); with Snipe and Mallard it is the breeding birds that are in decline. Like most overwintering wildfowl, both of these species continue to do well as winter migrants. (See actual figures provided in Appendix table of Chapter 17.)

[c] Population increases that can be attributed, at least in part, to conservation management.

[d] There is detailed information on gains and declines in British Butterflies in *The State of Britains Butterflies* (Fox *et al.* 2006).

[e] This species has shown many temporary declines and increases since detailed monitoring began in 1976. Recently there was a high in 2003 followed by a sharp decline to 2006/7. The present scarcity may just be one of these blips.

[f] Extinct in Britain and Ireland.

Please note that the above list is exclusive of the UK Overseas Territories.

Table 36.2 *Additional minor losses and gains. These involve significant populations with lesser numbers, and reintroductions where permanent establishment remains to be demonstrated*

Gains	Losses
Mammals	
Red-necked Wallaby (Peak District and Isle of Man)	
Parma Wallaby (Isle of Man)	
Eurasian Beaver (recent reintroduction in Knapdale, Scotland)	
Mink (widespread increase following deliberate release but more recent reduction by trapping)	
Birds	
Snow Goose (breeding feral colonies in Mull and Coll)	Golden Pheasant (declining population of feral birds)
Greater Canada Goose (widespread increase of feral populations)	Lady Amherst's Pheasant (as above)
Egyptian Goose (increase in numbers and distribution of feral colonies)	Muscovy Duck (feral population now confined to Ely)
Greylag Goose (increasing breeding by feral birds)	Ruddy Duck (deliberate eradication of quite widespread feral population in southern England to avoid hybridisation with European populations of White-headed Duck)
Great Bustard (recent breeding of reintroduced birds on Salisbury Plain)	
Eurasian Eagle Owl (recent breeding of escaped birds in several localities)	
Common Crane (small increasing population in Cambridgeshire)	
Fish	
Increases of both introduced Wels and Zander	
Reptiles	
Aesculapian Snake (small populations in N. Wales and Regents Park, London)	

References

Eaton, M.A., Brown, A.F., Noble, D.G *et al.* (2009). The population status of birds in the United Kingdom, Channel Islands and Isle of Man. *British Birds,* **102**, 296–341.

Lovett, R. *Nature* doi: 10 1038/news. 2010.4 (2010).

McCarthy, M. (2008). *Say Goodbye to the Cuckoo*, London, John Murray.

Slabbekoorn, H. and Ripmeester, E.A. (2008). Birdsong and anthropogenic noise; implications and applications for conservation. *Molecular Ecology,* **17**, 72–83.

Stemmler, I. and Lammel, G. Biogeochemistry; DDT in the ocean. *Geophys. Res. Lett.* 36, L24602 (2009).

Woods, M., Mcdonald, R.A. and Harris, S. (2003). Predation of wildlife by domestic cats Felis catus in Great Britain. *Mammal Review,* **33**, 174–188.

Glossary

aculeate	of Hymenoptera, having a pointed ovipositor modified to include a sting. The Aculeata includes all social wasps, bees and ants, but not sawflies or parasitoid wasps
adventive	an introduced species that has yet to become naturalised
Aleutian disease	a viral disease of mink caused by parvovirus
anadromous	ascending into fresh water from the sea for breeding
androgenic	male-like or making more male
Anisoptera	sub-order of the Odonata containing dragonflies, as distinct from damselflies
anthropogenic	caused by humans
Anton Dohrn	a seamount in the Rockall Trough
archaeophyte	a plant species introduced by humans prior to 1500 and often in Roman times or earlier
atrazine	widely used herbicide
Auchenorrhyncha	the group of Hemiptera bugs that encompasses leafhoppers, planthoppers, treehoppers, froghoppers and cicadas
avifauna	birds
Beaufort Dyke	a deep sea trench between Scotland and Northern Ireland
beetle bank	an area in a field crop left aside to encourage beetle production
benthic	living on the sea bottom
berm	the strip of flat ground between a ditch and a mound
biomass	the mass of numerous individuals of a species or group of species
biodiversity	biological species richness or variation at genetic, species, ecosystem and other levels
bryophytes	mosses and liverworts
calcareous	rich in or overlying chalk or limestone (calcium carbonate)
carnivore	an animal feeding on other animals for food
chytridiomycosis	a fungal disease of amphibians that appears to grow in the skin cells, causing an increase in dermal sloughing

	and ulceration and hyperaemia of the ventral and dermal skin; this may affect respiration and osmoregulation
Coleoptera	beetles
Conservation Headland	land at the edges of field crops, set aside for wildlife conservation
coppice stool	remnant of a tree that has been cut to, or near, ground level, and from which coppice growth develops
Crown Dependencies	the geographical areas of Isle of Man, Jersey, Guernsey, Alderney and Sark, which have their own legislatures and administrations and are not represented in UK Parliament, but the UK has responsibility for foreign relations and defence
cryptic	hard to see because of camouflage
defoliation	removal of leaves from a plant
demography	study of populations structure, especially of humans
diadromous	of fish which travel between fresh and salt water
Dictyoptera	cockroaches and mantids
Diptera	true flies
endemic	confined to a particular geographical area
eudicot	of flowering plant families that are true dicotyledons i.e. excluding Magnolias
eutrophic	rich in mineral and organic nutrients
eutrophication	enrichment with nutrients
exuvia	shed or cast-off skin of, for example, dragonfly
Fish Stat	Universal Software for Fisheries Statistics
genetic	of or relating to genes or heredity
grilse	Salmon returning to fresh water after one year at sea
headland	(as in Conservation Headland) land maintained to encourage biodiversity at the edges of field crops
Hemiptera	an insect order of the true bugs including Homoptera and Heteroptera (aphids, shield bugs, froghoppers etc.)
herbivore	an animal feeding on plants
Holocene	the current geological epoch post 11 000 years ago, since the last major glaciation
Hymenoptera	bees, ants and wasps and allied insects
hypolimnion	dense bottom layer of water in a thermally stratified lake
icthyofauna	fish
immunosuppression	an effect of some drugs which depresses the immune response
invasive	an alien species that has entered ('invaded') another country (not necessarily a species that has caused harm)
kleptoparasite	a species which steals food or nesting material from individuals of another species

Lepidoptera	butterflies and moths
machair	coastal ecosystem of sandy soil resulting from wind-blown shell-sand and particularly well developed on the western seaboard of the Outer Hebrides
macrophyte	large aquatic plant
metamorphosis	sudden change from one life form to another, as in a caterpillar to a pupa or a pupa to a butterfly
methylanthranilite	chemical biodegradable repellent of birds and mammals
microphyte	small aquatic plant
monocot	an abbreviated term for monocotyledons, which are plants such as grasses and lilies which have a single cotyledon
montane	of mountains
myrmecophiles	species living in association with ants
myxomatosis	a fibromatic viral disease of rabbits spread by fleas
naturalised	of a plant or animal originally introduced by humans that has formed a self-sustaining population
neophyte	a plant species, introduced by humans since 1500 AD
Odonata	dragonflies (Anisoptera) and damselflies (Zygoptera)
oestrogenic	female-like or making more female
oligotrophic	with low levels of organic and mineral nutrient
omnivore	an animal utilising both plant and animal material as food
Orthoptera	grasshoppers and crickets
Palaearctic	area of the world recognised as a Biological Distribution Zone. the western Palaearctic, in which Britain and Ireland reside, includes Greenland, Europe, the Middle East and North Africa
parapox virus	a viral disease of squirrels, affecting especially Red Squirrel
passerine	the sub-division of birds (formally Passeriformes) that comprises the perching birds
pathogen	any micro-organism capable of causing disease
pathogenicity	ability to cause disease
pelagic	living and free swimming on the surface or at middle depths of the sea
permethrin	a commonly used synthetic insecticide
Permian period	the most recent of the Palaeozoic periods, about 250 to 290 million years ago
pH	a measure of acidity and alkalinity (low pH is acidic; high pH is alkaline. The median is 7)

phenology	life-cycle timing: seasonality and timing of biological phenomena
phenotypic	characteristics of an individual caused by the interaction of its genotype with the environment
phytophagous	plant-eating
piscicides	fish poisons
pizzle	penis
Pollard Walk	transect counts of insects, structured to follow physical features and made under standardised conditions
Ramsar Convention	the International Convention on Wetlands of International Importance (signed in Ramsar, Iran)
Red Data Book	an analysis of threatened species based on the IUCN Red List criteria
Red List	a list of threatened species listed by IUCN
refugia	small isolated areas used by animals (and plants) to escape unfavourable conditions
rhizome	horizontally creeping underground stem that bears roots and leaves and persists from season to season
ria	rivermouth flooded by the sea, usually forming an inlet of complex shape
roding	crepuscular (dawn and dusk) territorial flights of male Woodcock
ruderal	growing in wasteland
seamount	a mountain rising from the ocean floor that does not reach the surface
seral	of stages in an ecological succession
strongylosis	infection with nematode roundworms, especially of Red Grouse
super-species	a complex of related species sharing adjacent territory and sometimes hybridising
sympatric	species that occupy similar habitats or whose habitats overlap
synanthropic	ecologically associated with humams
taxon	a taxonomic group, e.g. species, genus. pl. taxa
topography	surface shape and landscape composition
understorey	trees of lower canopy levels, as distinct from crown or upper-storey species
usufruct rights	the right to use and profit from another's property on the condition that the property remains uninjured
vascular flora	higher plants with a conducting system such as xylem and phloem, i.e. all plants except bryophytes. Includes

	clubmosses, ferns and all seed plants, often referred to
	as higher plants
Wallace's Line	the deep water running between Bali and Lambok
	in the chain of islands east of Java that separates the
	biogeographic regions of Asia and Wallacea
warfarin	a synthetic rat poison which inhibits blood clotting
Zygoptera	sub-order of the Odonata containing damselflies, but
	not dragonflies (Amisoptera)

Name index

Subject index